For Carole, *más que nunca*

Era la misma
Pena cantando
detrás de una sonrisa.

Federico García Lorca, 'Juan Breva'

Algo que también es primordial es respetar los propios instintos. El día en que deja uno de luchar contra sus instintos, ese día se ha aprendido a vivir.

Federico García Lorca,
interviewed by Pablo Suero, *Noticias Gráficas*, Buenos Aires,
14 October 1933

Je me demande comment les gens peuvent écrire la vie des poètes, puisque les poètes eux-mêmes ne pourraient écrire leur propre vie. Il y a trop de mystères, trop de vrais mensonges, trop d'enchevêtrement.

Jean Cocteau, *Opium*

Contents

CONTENTS

List of Illustrations

FEDERICO GARCÍA LORCA
A Life

IAN GIBSON

PANTHEON BOOKS NEW YORK

Drawings and Spanish texts of poetry, plays, letters, lectures, and
other material by Federico García Lorca copyright © 1989 by
Herederos de Federico García Lorca

English translations of the Spanish texts of poetry, plays, letters,
lectures, and other material by Federico García Lorca copyright ©
1989 by Herederos de Federico García Lorca and Ian Gibson

Permission acknowledgments can be found on page 552.

Library of Congress Cataloging-in-Publication Data
Gibson, Ian.
    [Federico García Lorca. English]
    Federico García Lorca: a life/Ian Gibson.
      p.   cm.
    Rev. translation of: Federico García Lorca.
    Bibliography: p.
    Includes index.
    ISBN 0-394-50964-1
    1. García Lorca, Federico, 1898–1939—Biography.
    2. Authors, Spanish—20th century—Biography.   I. Title.
PQ6613.A763Z647713   1989
868'.6209—dc19
[B]   88-28871

Acknowledgements

In February 1978, while living in the south of France, I felt an irresistible urge to return to Spain after an absence of eight years and embark on a biography of Federico García Lorca. General Franco had died three years earlier, the new democratic Spain was changing at a vertiginous pace, my book on the poet's death had just been successfully published in Barcelona (it had first appeared in Paris in 1971) and the time seemed ripe for settling in Madrid and picking up from where I had left off. I put the idea of the biography to Doña Isabel García Lorca, Lorca's sister, and in March she wrote promising to allow me to consult the poet's papers, which included many unpublished manuscripts, his letters to his family, and a wide range of correspondence received. Thus encouraged, I decided to go ahead.

A few months later my family and I were in Madrid. Isabel García Lorca kept her word, and over the following years allowed me to consult whatever papers I asked to see, as well as providing much useful information about her brother. To her, therefore, I must express my sincere gratitude. Her nephew Manuel Fernández-Montesinos, secretary of the Fundación Federico García Lorca (set up in Madrid six years after my arrival) also proved willing to make documents available when these had not already been exclusively apportioned to some other researcher. During my work on Lorca I have learnt to be grateful for small mercies.

But this is to talk of the time since the summer of 1978. Thirteen years earlier, I had gone to Granada in search of the poet, inspired by the example of the late Gerald Brenan, to whom I owe so much. In Granada and Madrid I met many people who contributed to my investigation into the poet's assassination and who were forthcoming, too, with vital information on the background to Lorca's life and art. As I was writing this biography their names (and faces) often came back to me, particularly of the friends and acquaintances who had died in the intervening years – Miguel Cerón Rubio, Antonio Mendoza Lafuente, Antonio Pérez Funes, José Rodríguez

Contreras, Rafael Jofré, Gerardo, Miguel and José Rosales Camacho, Manuel Angeles Ortiz, Angelina Cordobilla González, Carmen Ramos, Eduardo Molina Fajardo, Marcelle Auclair (then working on her biography of Lorca) and María del Reposo Urquía.

As for my research since moving to Spain, I am much in debt to what I like to call the Lorca International; first and foremost to my friend Eutimio Martín, who has always been eager to put his Lorca knowledge and, wherever possible, documentation, at my disposal. Such generosity is rare indeed. I am grateful to the following scholars and writers, both for their published work on the poet and related topics, and their comments and observations made to me personally: Andrew Anderson, María Teresa Babín, André Belamich, Fina de Calderón, Antonio Campoamor, José Luis Cano, Claude Couffon, Daniel Eisenberg, José Luis Franco Grande, Miguel García-Posada, Ernesto Guerra da Cal, Mario Hernández, Arturo del Hoyo, Allen Josephs, Marie Laffranque, José Landeira Yrago, Rafael Martínez Nadal, Christopher Maurer, Piero Menarini, Helen Oppenheimer, Antonina Rodrigo, Luis Sáenz de la Calzada, Angel Sahuquillo, Agustín Sánchez Vidal, Rafael Santos Torroella, Leslie Stainton and Margarita Ucelay. Without their labours my task would have been very much more difficult.

It is my obligation to express very special thanks to the following institutions which answered my, at times, desperate calls for financial assistance. The Instituto de Cooperación Iberoamericana in Madrid gave me a subsidy in 1980, and another in 1986 to visit Buenos Aires; a travel grant from the US–Spanish Joint Committee for Cultural and Educational Cooperation got me to the USA and back and helped to defray the costs of following Lorca's footsteps in New York and Vermont; the Ministry of Culture of the Andalusian Regional Community awarded me a generous and much appreciated subvention; through the good offices of the Irish National Commission, in the person of Mary McCarthy, support was given by the UNESCO Participation Programme 1984–5; the Cuban Writers and Artists Association (UNEAC) kindly invited me to Havana to research Lorca's stay there; the Spanish Ministry of Foreign Affairs paid my air fares from Cuba to Buenos Aires and back to Madrid; and in the Argentinian capital the hotel bill was footed by my Spanish publisher, Editorial Grijalbo.

Then, I owe a huge debt of gratitude to Siemens, SA, Madrid, who on the initiative of the company's managing director, Baldur Oberhauser, a friend indeed, made me the incredible gift of a computer on which to complete my work. I feel certain that it saved me from despair.

My research has taken me to many libraries and archives, where I have met with unfailing courtesy. It is a pleasant duty to thank the staffs of the Arxiu Històric de la Ciutat, Manresa (Catalonia); the British Library; the

British Newspaper Library, Colindale, London; the London Library; the Fine Arts Faculty, Universidad Complutense, Madrid; the National Library, Madrid; the Central Library of Granada University; the Hemeroteca Municipal, Madrid; the Hemeroteca Nacional, Madrid; the Casa de los Tiros, Granada; the Casa de l'Ardiaca, Barcelona; and the Institut Municipal d'Història (Barcelona).

Hundreds of people, as well as those already mentioned, have in one way or another made their contribution to this book, in Europe and both Americas. It is not feasible to quantify here what I owe to each, and I hope that I will be forgiven for this and for the many, many names which, unintentionally, I have overlooked:

Rafael Abella, Sam Abrams, Bernard Adams, Manuel del Aguila Ortega, Francisca Aguirre, Rafael Alberti, Antonio and María Alcaraz, José María Alfaro, Vicente Aleixandre (+)*, Javier Alfaya, Dámaso Alonso, José María Alvarez Romero, Frederic Amat, José Amorós, Alberto Anabitarte, Cayetano and María del Mar Anibal, José Arco Arroyo, Adoración Arroyo Cobos, Antón Arrufat, Peter G. Ashton, Enrique Azcoaga (+), Jesús Bal y Gay, Pío Ballesteros, Miguel Barnet, Angela Barrios, Antonio Barrios, Manuel Barrios, José Bello, Juan Benito Argüelles, José Bergamín (+), Ciro Bianchi Ross, Enrique Blanco, Eduardo Blanco-Amor (+), Norah Borges, Carlos Bousoño, José and María Fernanda Caballero, Lydia Cabrera, Francisco Caracuel, Angel Carrasco, Eduardo Carretero, Antonio Carrizo, Emilio Casares Rodicio, Jim and Maisie Casey, Manuel Castilla Blanco, José Castilla Gonzalo, José Miguel Castillo Higueras, Josefina Cedillo, Jacques Comincioli, Miguel and Carola Condé, Pádraic Collins, Evaristo and María Correal, Maribel Falla, Natalia Jiménez de Cossío (+), Falina Cristóbal, Arturo Cuadrado Moure, Bernardo Cuadrado Moure, Aurora de la Cuesta de Garrido, Philip Cummings, Dardo Cunio, Alvaro Custodio, Ana María Dalí, Salvador Dalí (+), José Delgado, Nigel Dennis, Ernesto Dethorey, James Dickie, Gerardo Diego (+), María Luisa Díez-Canedo de Giner, Fulgencio Díez Pastor (+), Francisco Javier Díez de Revenga, Elizabeth Disney, Luis Domínguez Guilarte, Ernesto Durán (+), Fernando de Elizalde, Gervasio Elorza, Lidia Espasande, José Angel Ezcurra, José Luis Fajardo, Jorge Feinsilber (+), Carlos Fernández, José Fernández Berchi, José Fernández Castro, Angel Flores, J. V. Foix, Miguel Angel Furones, David Galadí Enriquez, Antonio, Nieves and María Galindo Monge, Patrick Gallagher, José Carlos Gallardo, Rosa García Ascot, María del Carmen

* (+) after the name indicates that the person is deceased.

García Lasgoity, José García Ladrón de Guevara, Francisco García Lorca (+), Isabel García Palacios (+), Federico García Ríos (+), Clotilde García Picossi (+), Paulino García Toraño, Alfonso García Valdecasas, Emilio Garrigues, Juan Gil-Albert, Ernesto Giménez Caballero (+), Francisco Giner de los Ríos, Nigel Glendinning, Julia Gómez Arboleya, José Antonio Gómez Marín, Emilio Gómez Orbaneja, María Luisa González, Alejandro González Acosta, Luis González Arboleya, Rafael Hernández, Antonio González Herranz, Pedro Miguel González Quijano, Jaime Gorospe, Félix Grande, Helen Grant, Caritat Grau Sala, Günter and Susanna Grossbach, José Gudiol (+), José Luis Guerrero, Jorge Guillen (+), Campbell Hackforth-Jones, Cristóbal Halffter, Ernesto Halffter, David Henn, Francisco Hernández, Eulalia-Dolores de la Higuera Rojas, Modesto Higueras (+), James Hourihan, Gloria Ibáñez, Rafael Inglada, Antonio Jiménez Blanco, Paz Jiménez Encina, Aurelia Jiménez González, Luis Jiménez Pérez, José Jiménez Rosado, José Jover Tripaldi (+), Richard Kidwell, Ute Körner de Moya, Ignacio Lassaletta, William Layton, Manuel and Mercedes López Banús, Miguel López Escribano, Pilar López Júlvez, José López Rubio, Juan de Loxa, Dulce María Loynaz, William Lyon, Cristino Mallo (+), Maruja Mallo, Antonio Manjón, Manuel Marín Forero, Robert Marrast, Agenor Martí, Francisco Martín, Jacinto Martín, José Martín Jiménez, Carlos Martínez Barbeito, Luis Martínez Cuitiño, Pedro Massa (+), Blas Matamoros, Angel Mateos, Gonzalo Menéndez Pidal, José Mercado Ureña, Thomas Middleton, César Antonio Molina, Miguel Molina Campuzano, Ricardo Molinari, Charles Montagu-Evans, Maricarmen Montero, Francisco Montes Valero, José María Moreiro, Francisco Moreno Gómez, Roger Mortimore, Rosemary and Seán Mulcahy, Mary Carmen Muñoz, Ricardo Muñoz Suay, William Ober, Carlos Olmos, Santiago Ontañón, Manuel Orozco, Roberto Otero, Mariano de Paco, Fernando Pajares, Matilde Palacios García, Josep Palau i Fabre, Carmen Perea (+), Moisés Pérez Coterillo, Juan Antonio Pérez Millán, Lluís Permanyer, Antoni Pixtot, Ana María Prados, Jesús Prados Arrarte (+), Orlando Quiroga, Antonio Ramos Espejo, Manuel Ravina Martín, Juan Reforzo Membrives, Alvaro Restrepo, Laura de los Ríos de García Lorca (+), Enrique de Rivas, Manuel Rivera, Pablo Robredo, Ana Rodríguez Cortezo, Ricardo Rodríguez Jiménez, Alfredo Rodríguez Orgaz, Tomás Rodríguez Rapún, Isabel Roldán García de Carretero (+), Antonio Rodríguez Valdivieso, Eduardo Rodríguez Valdivieso, Alfredo Rollano, Esperanza Rosales Camacho, Luis Rosales Camacho, José Antonio Rubio Sacristán, Ramón Ruiz Alonso (+), Arturo Ruiz-Castillo, José Ruiz-Castillo, Enrique Ruiz Roldán, Luis Ruiz-Salinas, Carlos Ruiz Silva, Arturo Sáenz de la Calzada, Regino Sainz de la Maza (+), Pedro Sainz Rodríguez (+), Luis Saiz, Melchor Saiz Pardo, Horacio Salas, Clara

Sancha, Alcaín Sánchez, Juan Pedro Sánchez, Rafael Sánchez Ventura (+), Sanford and Helen Shepard, Emilio Santiago Simón, Andrés Segovia (+), Antonio de Senillosa, Leslie Sheil, Francisco Sierra, Philip Silver, Jaume Sobrequés, Andrés Soria Ortega, Herbert Southworth, Coen Stork, Daniel Sueiro (+), Hugh Thomas, Mauricio Torra-Balari, Amelia de la Torre (+), César Torres Martínez (+), Javier Torres Vela, Margarita Ucelay, Rafael Utrera, Agustín Valdivieso, Felipe Vallejo, Benigno Vaquero Cid, Pilar Varela, Roberto Villayandre, Roger Walker, Anthony Watson, Jane Wellesley, His Grace the Duke of Wellington, John Wolfers, Hector Yanover, Alberto Zalamea, Julio Oscar Zolezzi and Ofelia Zuccoli Fidanza.

When this book was signed up with Pantheon and Faber and Faber in 1979, I naïvely hoped that it would be possible to finish it by 1984. I (and the publishers) also assumed, naturally, that it would be written in English. But in the event the book took shape irremediably in Spanish, appearing in Barcelona between 1985 (Volume I), and 1987 (Volume II). My American and English publishers, André Schiffrin and Robert McCrum, were, not surprisingly, dismayed. I have to say, however, that they both behaved in a gentlemanly fashion towards the wayward author. To Robert McCrum I am indebted for his support over years whose difficulty he fully appreciated (not least the trauma of having to produce a biography in two languages). Once the English manuscript was finally handed over, Helena Franklin at Pantheon gave magnificent editorial advice, while Faber and Faber's copy-editing unit was efficient and courteous, as were Fiona McCrae, Jane Robertson, Mary Hill and Joanna Labon. It is indeed a privilege to have such publishers.

I am extremely grateful to John Pisano, who read the galley proofs with an eagle eye and suggested numerous improvements.

Finally, a word about my family. Despite the upheavals (first France, then Spain) to which they have been subjected since 1975, as a result of my stubborn determination to escape from Academe and write full-time, they have never complained. Now that this book is at last about to appear in English I realize fully to what an extent the lives of my children Tracey and Dominic (no longer children) have been conditioned by my obsession with the poet. I hope they will forgive me, and him. Above all, without the encouragement, abnegation, intelligence and sheer guts of my wife, Carole Elliott, the biography could never have been finished – either in Spanish or English. She richly deserves the proverbial medal.

Ian Gibson
Madrid, February 1989

Introduction

Federico García Lorca was thirty-eight when anti-Republican rebels in Granada assassinated him at the beginning of the Spanish Civil War in 1936. For almost twenty years after his death the poet's name was taboo in Franco's Spain and his work banned. Although the thaw began in 1953 when the Caudillo personally authorized an expensive censored volume of the *Obras completas* (in reality far from complete), it was not until the dictator's demise in 1975 that the facts of Lorca's tragic disappearance could be openly discussed in the country.

Thirteen years later Spain has undergone a profound transformation, and, at last, after so many centuries, is enjoying stable democracy. A new generation of historians is able to view the events of the Civil War with objectivity, and much research material inaccessible under the previous regime has become available. It is all something of a miracle.

Where the circumstances surrounding Lorca's death are concerned, the broad picture is now clear. The same cannot be said, however, about his private life. Among the poet's friends (and family) there has been a deep unwillingness to discuss or even acknowledge his homosexuality, and a shortcoming of this biography, as compared, say, to P. N. Furbank's life of Forster, is that it has simply not been possible to gain more than a rudimentary insight, by European or American standards, into this fundamental aspect of Lorca's life. Only one or two of his many letters to the adored Salvador Dalí have come to light (luckily we have the painter's to him); hardly anything is known of his passionate relationship with the sculptor Emilio Aladrén, who died in 1944 – except that it was passionate; and little can now be gleaned about his deep involvement with Rafael Rodríguez Rapún, who was killed during the war. Many other acquaintances who could have told us more disappeared in the same conflagration, were executed afterwards, or ended their days in exile (France, Russia, Mexico, Argentina, Venezuela, the United States . . .); and there are persons still alive who stubbornly refuse to share what they know.

To make matters worse, Lorca seems never to have kept a diary, and in his letters was usually discretion itself, at least in those that can be consulted today. The first-hand information the biographer craves for is often simply not available in a country where, as Gerald Brenan has pointed out, biography as a genre is still in its infancy. In Lorca's case we know a great deal about the public man (the poet was famous in his own lifetime and his activities were widely covered in the prolific Spanish press of those years), but much, much less about the inner one. Thus the present biographer's desire to explore the hidden, and often tormented side to Lorca's character met with constant difficulties.

Many people who knew Lorca reasonably well are still unable to accept that he was either homosexual or anything other than a brilliantly-endowed child of the muses, who lived his brief life without a care, in a constant whirl of success and adulation. Perhaps such incredulity is hardly surprising, for not only was Federico – as he is almost universally known in Spain – extremely jealous of his intimacy but his dazzling range of gifts and huge charm so seduced most (not all) of those who came within his orbit that they had eyes – and ears – only for the staggering one-man show. Pianist, poet, dramatist, lecturer, conversationalist, raconteur, actor, theatre director, mimic, Lorca could also sing folksongs feelingly and draw well enough to merit the praise of a critic as severe as Dalí. If ever anyone was the charismatic life and soul of a party it was Federico.

Complementing his seemingly endless gifts the poet had a big, striking and lively head set on a clumsy, flat-footed body (height: 1.702 metres or 5′ 6″) and, while not good-looking in a conventional sense – indeed some people thought him positively ugly – his features at times took on a strange beauty, as several of the photographs show. Lorca's sense of humour was contagious, his bursts of laughter proverbial; and he spread around him an aura of happiness. Thanks to his flair for impromptu sessions at the keyboard (he could also perform competently on the guitar), linguistic and cultural barriers were irrelevant: it was all the same whether the venue was New York, Barcelona or Havana. His fellow countrymen recognized in the man and his work an extraordinary synthesis of the traditional and the avant-garde, while foreigners who crossed his path always thought of Spain thereafter in terms of the amazing, ebullient Andalusian. The nostalgia of the American critic Herschel Brickell, who entertained Lorca at his Manhattan home in 1929, is typical. 'In a fairly long lifetime spent with artists of various sorts,' Brickell wrote nine years after the poet's assassination, 'García Lorca was the nearest thing to a pure genius I have ever known'.[1]

It was hardly surprising, then, that few people suspected the anguished side to him. A side every bit as real as the other, as might perhaps be deduced from a work in which death and frustrated love are obsessively recurrent themes. It was difficult enough to be homosexual in that society, but Lorca's dilemma was aggravated by deep emotional conflicts which threatened at times to overwhelm him (as can be seen from the letters to his Colombian friend Jorge Zalamea). Several companions of the poet have recorded his disconcerting tendency suddenly to switch off in the middle of a lively conversation and to go deep within himself, his lips pursed and the light of his dark eyes temporarily extinguished. Soon afterwards he would 'return' and carry on from where he had left off, as if emerging from an hypnotic trance. Lorca called these moments his 'dramones' ('big dramas'), but if he ever told anyone what he lived through on such occasions the information has not been passed on to us.

The Uruguayan poetess Juana de Ibarbourou, who met Lorca during his visit to Montevideo in 1933, wrote that Federico's large eyes were 'oddly melancholy despite the euphoria of his personality'.² Several other friends have confirmed this observation, and no one more tellingly than Vicente Aleixandre, whose beautiful evocation of the poet, written in 1937, is the finest tribute of them all (and there have been literally hundreds). 'Lorca was capable of the greatest happiness in the Universe', Aleixandre recalled in his vignette of the mysterious, nocturnal, *lunar* Federico, 'but his deepest self, as in the case of all great poets, was not happy. Those who thought of him as a gaily-coloured bird passing blithely through life never really knew their man.'³

The French writer Marcelle Auclair did know her man, and, in her book *Enfances et mort de Garcia Lorca*, published in 1968, analysed the homosexual aspect of the poet with sensitivity, reaching the conclusion that Federico's 'greatest fear was, undoubtedly, that his parents would discover that he was an "invert" '.⁴ The writer does not tell us if Lorca himself confided this fear to her, but at any rate we may be fairly sure that the necessity of having to lead a double life in a society where homosexuality was considered abhorrent played a large part in the poet's underlying sadness and, at times, despair.

More has now been written about Lorca, in many languages, than about any other Spanish writer with the exception of Cervantes (who has the advantage of having been born three hundred years earlier); and he is the most-translated Spanish writer of all time, the author of *Don Quixote* included. The immense bibliography continues to grow apace, the translations multiply and the international appeal of his plays fills theatres all over the world, season after season, and has recently been ratified by the success of the London productions of *The House of Bernarda Alba* and *The*

Public. Clearly the Andalusian poet has something valuable to convey to the world.

But what? My own feeling is that Lorca's best work, both the plays and the poetry, puts us in touch with our emotions and reminds us forcefully, in a world ever more computerized and machine-controlled, that we are an integral part of Nature – a Nature that all too often we tend to forget. 'Only mystery enables us to live, only mystery', the poet wrote beneath one of his enigmatic drawings. His work, due largely to the power of its earthy imagery, makes us experience that mystery more acutely than perhaps any other poet of the century. If it is true that poets are the last animists in our industrial society, then Lorca is surely one of the greatest. Reading him, or seeing his plays, we enter a pre-logical world, presided over by the moon, where man is one more strand in the intricate fabric of life. Lorca himself liked the word 'telluric', and was perfectly aware that his was a primitive, mythical vision with roots deep in the ancient cultures and religions of the Mediterranean.

To have been able to spend so many years researching the life, work and death of such a genius has been a privilege indeed. I hope that this book repays a small part of the debt.

I should point out that all the translations of Lorca are my own. I have aimed at straightforward literal renderings that will help the reader to appreciate the Spanish originals.

BOOK ONE

From Fuente Vaqueros to New York
1898–1929

I

Childhood

The Vega of Granada

Of all the *vegas* of Spain – the word, pre-Roman in origin, denotes a fertile plain between hills – that of Granada, which forms the Andalusian backdrop to the life and work of Federico García Lorca, is arguably the most beautiful. Separated from the Mediterranean, only 30 miles away as the crow flies, by the imposing barrier of the Sierra Nevada, the highest mountain range in the peninsula, and traversed by the river Genil and its tributaries, the Vega, with Granada at its eastern edge, was for many centuries a world unto itself. An enclosed world, some 700 square miles in area, where life flowed quietly along traditional channels and man lived in intimate contact with the earth.

The Arabs of Granada were expert horticulturalists, as well as engineers, and in the Vega they created an intricate irrigation system, today still largely extant, which improved notably on that left by the Romans. For hundreds of years the plain was a paradise.[1] But with the fall of Granada, the last bastion of Islam in Spain, to Ferdinand and Isabella in 1492, the Vega entered on a period of prolonged decline. The Christians were accustomed to cruder methods of husbandry and proved themselves unable, or unwilling, to adapt to the techniques elaborated and perfected during the eight centuries of Arab rule. Little by little the prosperity of the region dwindled. The process culminated in 1609 with the expulsion of the *moriscos* (converted Moors), who carried away with them into exile the last secrets of a system as sophisticated as it was practical.

In the centre of the Vega, 10 miles from Granada, there lay an extensive estate which, stretching along both banks of the river Genil and known as the Soto de Roma, had belonged to the Moorish kings. The experts disagree about the origins of the word *Roma* (there appears to be no connection with the Italian homonym), although it seems probable that the word derives from an Arabic root meaning 'Christian'.[2] This etymology is perhaps

3

supported by the fact that, not far from the Soto, on the left bank of the Genil, stands a small village called Romilla where, according to tradition, lived Florinda, the alluring daughter of Count Julian, the traitor blamed for opening the gates of Spain, in AD 711, to the Muslims.[3] As for *soto*, it poses no problems to the etymologists: it is from the Latin *saltus* and means 'meadow' or 'estate'. It seems, then, that Soto de Roma may have the sense of 'The Estate of the Christian Girl'.

The inhabitants of Romilla are known as *romerillos* or *romanos*, a designation that enables us to identify the geographical origins of Pepe *el romano* in Lorca's *The House of Bernarda Alba*. It may be added that between Romilla and the Genil are still to be seen the ruins of an Arab watchtower known locally as the Torre de Roma and originally taken to mark the southern limit of the Soto.[4] An eerie place it seemed to Lorca as a child – there were toads and creepy-crawlies, too – and he used to visit the tower with some trepidation.[5]

Ferdinand and Isabella distributed the fertile lands of the Vega among their nobles. But they took good care to reserve the Soto de Roma for the sole use of themselves and their descendants, and to the estate's name was added from this moment the title of Royal Demesne (*Real Sitio*).

In the sixteenth century the Soto was thickly wooded, and teemed with game.[6] Ginés Pérez de Hita, author of *Guerras Civiles de Granada* ('The Civil Wars of Granada'), published in 1595, refers in the first part of his monumental work to the density of the place's vegetation. 'Unless you know the paths well you can easily get lost,' he writes.[7] Four hundred years later, although the vegetation has changed, it is still possible to go astray in the woods of the Soto, now luxuriantly green poplar groves.

For three centuries the Soto remained in the hands of the Crown, undergoing only minimal agricultural exploitation and serving almost exclusively to satisfy the hunting proclivities of the royal family who, during their infrequent visits, lodged at the Casa Real, or Royal House, erected beside the river Cubillas near where it meets the Genil and about half a mile from Fuente Vaqueros.

In 1765 Charles III granted the estate to Richard Wall, the son of Irish immigrants, who had been Spanish Ambassador to the Court of Saint James and Secretary of State for the years 1754–64.[8] In the tiny village of Fuente Vaqueros, Wall began the construction of the parish church of Our Lady of the Annunciation, but died, in 1777, before he could see the work completed.[9] The estate then reverted to the Crown, being granted not long afterwards to Manuel Godoy, Charles IV's minister between 1792 and 1797 and lover of María Luisa, the king's plump wife, immortalized in Goya's painting of the royal family.[10] It seems that Godoy never visited the Soto de Roma, and when he fell from favour after Nelson's victory at Trafalgar the estate returned once again to the Crown.

Four years later the fortunes of the Soto de Roma took a strange turn. In 1812 Arthur Wellesley, the first Duke of Wellington, conqueror of Napoleon at Salamanca, became the idol of Spain. As an expression of gratitude for his contribution to the freeing of the country, the Liberal Parliament of Cadiz conferred on Wellesley, in 1813, the title of Duke of Ciudad Rodrigo, and granted to him and his successors, in perpetuity, not only the Soto de Roma but another estate, situated on the rising terrain to the north-west, called Molino de Rey ('King's Mill').[11] For more than a hundred years the Soto, once hunted over by the Moors, was to belong, lock, stock and barrel, to the Wellesley family.

In 1813 the Soto de Roma boasted some 700 inhabitants living in several villages, the largest of which was Fuente Vaqueros.[12] Sir Arthur never deigned to visit his estates in Granada, which during the nineteenth century were run by a series of agents, usually incompetent, normally absent and almost always corrupt. One exception was the first administrator, General O'Lawlor, a Spaniard, like Richard Wall, of Irish extraction. O'Lawlor had been Wellington's aide-de-camp during the Peninsular campaign, and had served him loyally. Now he combined his post as the Duke's agent with that of Captain General of Granada. In 1831, Richard Ford, author of the greatest guidebook to Spain ever written, spent a few days in Fuente Vaqueros with O'Lawlor, leaving for posterity three or four sensitive pencil drawings of the Casa Real.[13] In his guide, published in 1845 by John Murray, Ford included some carefully documented pages on Fuente Vaqueros, and made the point, commenting on the labours of Wall and O'Lawlor, that the Soto twice owed its restoration 'to Irish care'.[14]

Until the end of the nineteenth century, when the Genil was contained within embankments, the Soto was subject to frequent flooding. Each autumn, when the rains began, both the river and its tributary the Cubillas – which today meet not far from Fuente Vaqueros, near the Casa Real – overflowed, as did the irrigation channels of the estate. The fragile wooden bridges spanning the rivers used invariably to be carried away in the deluge and, the rivers themselves being unfordable, communication between the tenants and the outside world, as well as between them and the land they worked, would be severed.

The Genil ran formerly to the north of Fuente Vaqueros.[15] But in 1827, after particularly torrential rains, the river burst its banks near Santa Fe and changed course, moving to the south of the village, where we find it today.[16] As a result of the humidity of the area, La Fuente, as Fuente Vaqueros is universally known in the Vega, was considered unhealthy until the beginning of the twentieth century.[17]

Horacio Hammick, friend and subsequently agent of the second Duke of Wellington, attempted to visit Fuente Vaqueros in the autumn of 1854. The rains prevented him from doing so.[18] In the autumn of 1858 he had better luck and, after numerous difficulties, managed to reach the village. He found it and the Soto in a state of the utmost dilapidation. Many of the inhabitants were undergoing desperate hardship; half-naked beggars pullulated; work on the land was at a standstill; there was a dire shortage of bread, and many people were dying of fever. 'And they earnestly entreated us', records Hammick, 'to acquaint their lord, the Duke of Ciudad Rodrigo, with their miserable condition.' The Casa Real was practically in ruins; there were no doors or windows; the walls were cracked and the upper floor was occupied by Gypsies.[19]

But if the floods brought hunger and misery each year to the Soto de Roma, it was also true that the soil of the estate owed its fertility to the carpets of loam spread over the area down the centuries by the Genil and the Cubillas. The earth of Fuente Vaqueros, due to the proximity of the village to both rivers, was – and remains – particularly rich.

The population of the Soto was on the increase and, by 1868, the 700 inhabitants registered in 1813 had grown to some 3,000.[20] Such rapid expansion was due in part to the agricultural innovations introduced by the English agents, which, if not spectacular, were an improvement on previous methods. Another stimulus was a strong industrial demand for hemp and flax, both of which flourished well in the Vega.[21] Hammick was of the opinion that the system whereby the tenants of the Soto could let and sublet their holdings almost *ad infinitum* also assisted this population explosion.[22]

Towards 1880 another, much more decisive, factor came to bear on the situation, promoting the development and enrichment not only of the Soto de Roma but of the Vega in general: the discovery that sugar-beet could be grown there very successfully.[23] Soon the Vega was a hive of activity. Tall-chimneyed factories for the processing of the beet sprang up and many landowners made rapid fortunes, among them Federico García Rodríguez, the future poet's father. The loss of Cuba to the United States in 1898 came as a further fillip to the Vega's economy, for it meant that the importation of cheap sugar from the island had come to an end. The plain was booming, and by the time Lorca* was born in Fuente Vaqueros in the summer of 1898, his father had become one of the wealthiest men in the village.

---

* According to Spanish custom, the father's surname is followed by that of the mother. Often the mother's is dropped, but when hers is the more unusual of the two, as in the case of García Lorca, the tendency is to use the latter.

Lorca's paternal great-grandfather, Antonio García Vargas, had been born and bred in Fuente Vaqueros where, in 1831, he married a local girl, Josefa Paula Rodríguez Cantos.[24] Unlike most of the inhabitants of the Soto de Roma he could read and write, and for many years held the post of secretary to the town hall.[25] Antonio García's wife was celebrated for her beauty[26] and, according to family tradition, may have been of Gypsy extraction.[27] More likely, perhaps, is that his mother was from such a background, given the frequency of the surname Vargas among the Gypsies of Andalusia. It is hard to imagine, at all events, that the suspicion of having Romany blood in his veins, from whatever source and no matter how diluted, would have been a matter of indifference to the author of *Gypsy Ballads*.

The Garcías of Fuente Vaqueros possessed uncommon musical ability, which was inherited by the poet. Great-grandfather Antonio had a fine singing voice, and played the guitar well, while his brother Juan de Dios was a competent violinist.[28] And Antonio's four children all turned out to be similarly endowed.

Of these, Enrique (1834–1872), the poet's grandfather, was the most serious. Both fervently Catholic and a liberal in politics[29] – a combination rare in Spain – Enrique García Rodríguez was widely respected for his common sense and flair for giving sound advice. From his father he inherited the post of secretary to the town hall.

Enrique's brother Federico, the eldest, an outstanding performer on the type of lute known as the *bandurria*, achieved celebrity in Malaga, where he played at the Café de Chinitas,[30] one of the most famous *cafés chantants* in Andalusia. Francisco García Lorca, the poet's brother, has suggested that his family's love of Malaga was perhaps not unrelated to the fact of their musical forebear's protracted residence there.[31] Enrique called his first son (the poet's father) Federico after his brother, for whom he had the deepest admiration.[32]

Baldomero García Rodríguez was the most eccentric, Bohemian and original of the four brothers (the other, Narciso, was a teacher, with a talent for drawing),[33] and played with consummate skill his role as the black sheep of the family.[34] Lame from a congenital defect in both feet, notorious tippler, improviser of malicious ditties, expert on both guitar and *bandurria*, occasional teacher and, in 1892, secretary to the town hall of the village of Belicena,[35] not far from Fuente Vaqueros, Baldomero was well known in the Vega. 'He sang like an angel,' Lorca's mother recalled.[36] Among his repertory of folk songs, the *jabera*, a nowadays little-heard variety of flamenco, was a speciality.[37] Baldomero was a latterday *juglar* or minstrel, and in the villages of the Vega his witty verses, often painfully to the point, were widely repeated and much celebrated. He excelled at weddings and

7

festive occasions, and could always be relied upon to come up with appropriate lines. But he was more than simply a village minstrel. In 1892 he published in Granada a slim volume of verse, *Siemprevivas* ('Forget-me-nots'), subtitled *A Small Collection of Religious and Moral Poems*. The tone of these compositions is indeed religious and moral, but not stiflingly so. Baldomero sings the goodness of God and the folly of those who fail to appreciate it; praises Nature, in whose loveliness he sees the ever-present hand of the Creator, and exhorts the reader to abjure the futile struggle for worldly success.[38]

Baldomero breathed his last in the hospital of St John of God, in Granada, on 4 November 1911, at the age of seventy-one.[39] There is no doubt that Lorca both met and revered his wayward great-uncle, many of whose verses he appears to have known by heart, and he must surely have been acquainted with *Siemprevivas*. Family tradition records an occasion on which the poet's mother, after Federico had expressed himself in some particularly colourful fashion, exclaimed, 'He's another Baldomero!' 'I'd consider it an honour to be like him!' her son is said to have rejoined.[40] In 1931, already famous, Lorca remembered Baldomero in the course of an open-air talk given in Fuente Vaqueros. 'My forebears served this village generously,' he said proudly, 'and even many of the tunes and songs you sing were composed by an old poet of my family.'[41]

If the García menfolk were of a musical bent, their women were also talented and often unusual. The wife of grandfather Enrique, Isabel Rodríguez Mazuecos (1834–98),[42] for example, was a considerable personality in her own right. Like her husband a liberal in politics, but unlike him somewhat anticlerical; highly sociable, with a kind word for everyone; extraordinarily lively – grandmother Isabel was adored by all the large family. One of the results was that the name Isabel proliferated among her children's offspring, causing constant problems of identification.[43]

Grandmother Isabel shared her husband Enrique's love of literature, making frequent trips to Granada to buy books, and took extreme pleasure in reading not only to her own children but to her neighbours and friends, many of whom were illiterate. Her favourite poets were Zorrilla, Espronceda, Becquer and Lamartine; her novelists, Dumas *père* and, especially, Victor Hugo. The latter she worshipped, and on a sideboard, prominently displayed, there stood a lifesize plaster head of the great man.[44] This love of Hugo, in which she was joined by great-uncle Baldomero, she transmitted to her children and grandchildren, and Francisco García Lorca has recalled that not only did his family possess the complete works of Hugo in a handsome, leather-bound edition but that these volumes constituted his brother's first reading matter. There are numerous allusions to Hugo in

Lorca's early work, and recent criticism has assigned to him a seminal influence on the poet's development.[45]

In her passion for reading, Isabel Rodríguez was by no means unique in Fuente Vaqueros, and the villagers had a reputation in the Vega for their love of books.[46] How can such a phenomenon be accounted for? It is possible that it had something to do with the fact that La Fuente belonged to the Duke of Wellington, a circumstance that set these people apart from the rest of the inhabitants of the plain and gave them, perhaps, through their contact with the Protestant English, a broader view of life and the world. On the other hand the locals resented the latter to a greater or lesser extent, for despite having to make only minimal payments – always in kind – to the landowner, it rankled to be tenants of a foreign nobleman, no matter how distinguished might have been the contribution of his great forebear to the well-being of the nation. All this probably served to sharpen the villagers' sense of irony.[47]

As for the English, they had a pretty poor opinion of their tenants. They did not trust them. They spoke of the 'doubtful reputation' of the village; of left-wing agitators who operated there to stir up trouble.[48] The Wellesleys believed, it appears, that in the eighteenth century Charles III had settled the area with convicts, and that this accounted for a 'mutinous streak' in the population, always liable to break out.[49] There is no hard evidence for the claim, however, and the rebelliousness of La Fuente needed no such atavistic explanation. It was simply that the villagers felt humiliated by their thraldom to the foreigner.

But whatever explanations may be offered, the fact remains that Fuente Vaqueros was different from the other villages of the Vega. Liberal, 'a bolshie lot, always against authority' (as one disgruntled English agent termed it in 1980),[50] and unconcerned about religious matters, these people were surprisingly open and progressive.

Enrique García and Isabel Rodríguez produced four sons and five daughters. All of them inherited the musical ability for which the family was now celebrated. Luis was an excellent pianist with a faultless ear, and also played the guitar, the flute and the *bandurria*.[51] Later, in Granada, he became a friend of Manuel de Falla, who greatly admired his skill at the keyboard.[52] Isabel sang exquisitely, accompanying herself at the guitar,[53] and was, according to Lorca, one of the 'dominant artistic influences' of his childhood.[54] The other brothers and sisters were similarly talented.

Federico García Rodríguez, the poet's father, was born in Fuente Vaqueros in 1859, the eldest of the nine. A photograph taken when he was twenty suggests a personality in which seriousness, sensitivity and determination blend smoothly. Lorca inherited his father's eyes, thick eyebrows, wide forehead and delicately modelled lips. Also, according to the poet, his deep feeling. Tolerant, sensible, measured in his judgements, a fine horseman, always willing to lend a hand to others, with an innate dignity, a good sense of humour and a complete lack of pretentiousness, García Rodríguez was respected by all who knew him. Moreover, he played the guitar well, performing with gusto at the reunions in which the large family revelled.[55]

In 1880, when only twenty, Federico had married a local girl, Matilde Palacios, the same age as himself. Matilde's father, Manuel Palacios Caballero, was a well-off farmer with land of his own outside the Soto de Roma, so the match, from a material point of view, was undoubtedly an advantageous one for the groom. Manuel Palacios built a spacious house for the young couple, at 4 Calle de la Trinidad ('Trinity Street'), and it is likely that, during the early years of his marriage, Federico worked for his father-in-law.[56]

All seemed set fair for the young couple, and the discovery that Matilde was unable to have children must have come as a terrible blow. Federico, meanwhile, inherited from his father the post of secretary to Fuente Vaqueros town hall and, in 1891, the year of his father's death, we find him acting in a temporary capacity as municipal judge. By the age of thirty Federico García Rodríguez was a man of standing, if not yet of great substance, in the village.[57]

On 4 October 1894, fourteen years after her marriage, Matilde Palacios died suddenly from 'intestinal obstruction'. The house the couple had occupied passed for life to her husband, as well as a considerable sum of money.[58] Years later, as he was writing *Yerma* and mulling over the terrible frustration of a village woman unable to have a child, Lorca may well have had the unfortunate Matilde in mind. And once he went on record as saying that during his childhood he was obsessed by the photographs of 'that other woman who could have been my mother'.[59]

Federico García Rodríguez was a man of business acumen, with a good head for figures. On the death of his wife he decided, with ready money to hand, that the moment had come to invest in land, and in 1895 acquired a series of excellent properties in the vicinity of Fuente Vaqueros, just outside the Soto de Roma.[60] Among these was a large estate, Daimuz, situated close to the meeting of the Genil and Cubillas, that was to form the basis of his wealth. Daimuz – the name is Arabic, meaning 'Cave Farm' – had belonged, after the fall of Granada, to one of Ferdinand's and Isabella's admirals, and then, for centuries, to an aristocratic family in the provincial capital.[61] It comprised many acres of irrigated land, a drier, arable area and, along the right bank of the Cubillas, thick poplar groves.

García Rodríguez bought Daimuz thinking, typically, not only of the advantages to himself but with a view to bettering the lot of his eight brothers and sisters, among whom he distributed portions of the extensive estate.[62]

These were the days of the sugar boom. Federico seized his opportunity, planted his lands with beet and, before long, became one of the richest men in the community.

It is likely that, before the death of Matilde Palacios, García Rodríguez had met Vicenta Lorca Romero, from Granada, who began to teach at the Fuente Vaqueros primary school for girls in 1892 or 1893.[63] About the pair's courtship we know little, but tradition has transmitted the indignation of Federico's brothers at the idea that he, head of the family and now a rich man, should stoop to marrying a poor schoolmistress who would bring nothing but herself to the union.[64] Such fraternal resistance proved useless, however, and the marriage took place in Fuente Vaqueros parish church on 27 August 1897.[65] Federico was then thirty-seven, his bride twenty-six.[66]

Vicenta Lorca's family was neither as numerous nor as original as her husband's. She was an only child, daughter of Vicente Lorca González, of Granada, and María de la Concepción Romero Lucena, of Santa Fe.[67]

Vicenta's paternal grandfather, Bernardo Lorca Alcón (1802–1883), hailed from Totana, in Murcia,[68] and it is not known why or when he moved to Granada, where he married a local girl, Antonia Josefa González.[69] In a document of 1840 Bernardo Lorca is described as an 'agricultural worker'.[70]

The grandfather's surname may indicate that the family was of Jewish origin. Lorca, an important town in Murcia close to Totana, had a flourishing Jewish community in the Middle Ages, and, as is well known, it was common practice, once the Inquisition got under way, for converted Jews to change their names to that of the town of their origin, hoping thus to disguise their Semitic provenance. Certainly, the poet not only believed that he had inherited Jewish blood from his mother, albeit pretty watered down, but expressed his satisfaction at the fact that his second surname linked him to a town in Murcia with significant Jewish antecedents.[71]

Vicenta Lorca never knew her father, who died in 1870, at the age of twenty-seven, a month and a half before her birth.[72] The widow, the same age as her husband, was, like him, of humble origins, her father being classified in contemporary legal documents as an 'agricultural worker', the same category as grandfather Bernardo Lorca Alcón.[73]

Vicenta Lorca's early years were hard. The records show that the family moved house frequently, presumably under the pressure of financial difficulties. In 1883, after the death of Bernardo Lorca, we find Vicenta boarding at a charity school run by nuns, the Colegio de Calderón, founded a few years earlier for the education of poor girls.[74]

The years passed in this establishment left their mark on Vicenta, and produced in her a strong reaction against the conventual life. She was a delicate child, and would never forget how the nuns (mainly French) forced her on one occasion to eat lentils, a dish she detested. As a result of such experiences she was to prove indulgent about the eating whims of her own children.[75]

Vicenta told the latter about the disagreeable things that happened to her at the college, where bickering, envy and malice were ubiquitous.[76] Years later her daughter Concha attended the same establishment (by that date no longer reserved for indigent children) and underwent similar trials and tribulations. Lorca alludes to the school experiences of both his mother and sister in his last, unfinished play, *The Dreams of My Cousin Aurelia*, in which the protagonist recalls the terrors of the Colegio de Calderón.[77]

Vicenta decided that she wanted to be a primary school teacher, and in 1888 entered the Women Teachers' Training College at Granada, where she proved a hard-working, diligent student, taking her degree in 1892 and getting her first appointment, to Fuente Vaqueros girls' primary school, shortly afterwards.[78] Her mother went to live with her in the village, but Concepción Romero died in 1893 just after they had set up house.[79] It was a heavy blow for the daughter. 'After such a struggle to become a teacher I finally succeeded,' she told one of her nieces, 'and then what happened? My mother died on me.'[80]

But soon afterwards the tide turned in Vicenta's favour, when she caught the eye of the widowed Federico García Rodríguez. Almost exactly nine months after their marriage, while the newspapers were full of news of the Cuban war, Vicenta gave birth to the future poet, on 5 June 1898.[81] He was baptized, on 11 June, Federico del Sagrado Corazón de Jesús ('Frederick of the Sacred Heart of Jesus').[82]

Vicenta Lorca was in poor health at the time, and unable to breastfeed her baby. Federico was confided during these early months of his life to a wetnurse, the wife of José Ramos, Don Federico's foreman, who lived in the house opposite.[83] One of the woman's daughters, Carmen, six years older than the child, was to be a close companion during the Fuente Vaqueros years, and a perceptive witness to the development of Federico's personality.[84]

It has been said that, a few months after his birth, Federico underwent a serious illness which prevented him from walking until he was four.[85] This story probably derived from the poet himself, who was in the habit of saying that his inability to run was the result of an injury to his legs sustained when young.[86] But in the poet's family no account of such an illness was transmitted, an unlikely lapse if this had really existed.[87] Carmen Ramos for her part always denied that the child had had any such problem and used to insist that, on the contrary, he walked normally at fifteen months.[88] It is a fact, however, that the poet had extremely flat feet[89] and that his left leg was marginally shorter than the other, defects no doubt congenital and which lent to his gait a characteristic swaying motion.[90] In an early poem Lorca complains of his 'clumsy walk', almost certainly an allusion to this handicap, considering that it could be a reason for being rejected in love; and numerous friends later recalled his fear of crossing the street where, given his lack of agility, he felt he might easily be run over. There is no record of anyone ever having seen Lorca run.[91]

As for the legend concerning Lorca's childhood speech difficulties, according to which he could not talk until he was three, there is no evidence for such a claim.[92] The poet's brother Francisco, who received trustworthy information on the point from his mother, declared that, on the contrary, Federico was a precocious talker.[93]

Even more precocious was the appearance of the García musical ability. 'Before Federico could talk he was already humming folk songs and loved to listen to the guitar,' his mother recalled.[94] Vicenta, who was musical herself although she played no instrument, encouraged in her child the development of what was quite clearly an innate disposition.[95]

Federico's lack of physical agility made it impossible for him to participate fully in games requiring speed and dexterity.[96] But he was no recluse, and it would be an error to imagine him as a lonely child without friends. He was extremely popular in the village and so often invited to eat in other children's houses that at times his mother had to complain.[97] In 'My Village', one of his earliest efforts in prose (not published in his lifetime), Lorca evokes nostalgically the games he used to organize in the attic of the large house to which the family moved in 1902, situated in Calle de la Iglesia ('Church Street') and no longer extant. One gets the impression from his account that, by himself orchestrating these activities and giving all the orders, he was compensating for his lack of physical nimbleness.[98] Be this as it may, the poet never forgot the games and songs of his childhood in Fuente Vaqueros, and many of them reappear (sometimes transformed, sometimes merely hinted at) in his poetry and theatre.

It is likely, moreover, that the child's less than normal agility of body had the effect of sharpening both his imagination and his powers of observation. From the earliest years he showed himself extraordinarily alert to the world around him, and quickly developed a passionate love of nature.[99]

The nine children of Enrique García and Isabel Rodríguez all married, all produced offspring and, with the exception of Isabel, all lived simultaneously with their families in Fuente Vaqueros. As a result, Federico had more than forty cousins in the village – a circumstance that would later cause much amusement to his friends in Granada. Among the females he had several favourites, some of whom appear under thin disguises in his work. Aurelia González García, the daughter of Aunt Francisca, for example, is the protagonist of Lorca's last (unfinished) play, *The Dreams of My Cousin Aurelia*. Born about 1885, she was some thirteen years older than Federico and, as the play confirms, the child adored her.[100] Both Aurelia and her mother were terrified of thunderstorms, and Federico enjoyed visiting them on such occasions, which are quite common in the Vega during the hot summer months. 'Federico told me', writes Francisco García Lorca, 'that our cousin Aurelia, in a state of semi-collapse during a storm, and not without a certain theatricality, would exclaim, lying back in her rocking chair: "Look! I'm dying!" '[101] On some occasions, she would even fall to the ground in a fit, her teeth locked tight. Aurelia, like so many other members of the family, accompanied herself marvellously on the guitar and spoke an earthy, metaphorical Spanish. 'Put the eggs in when the water begins to laugh,' she was once heard to instruct, without any notion that she was employing a poetic image.[102]

Another favourite older cousin was Clotilde García Picossi, the daughter of Uncle Francisco. The green dress worn by the protagonist of *The Shoemaker's Prodigious Wife*, and that of the same colour put on by Adela, as a gesture of rebellion, in *The House of Bernarda Alba*, are allusions to one owned by Clotilde, which she was not allowed to wear during a period of mourning.[103] Then there was Matilde Delgado García, the daughter of Aunt Matilde. She was eight or ten years older than Federico, and, since she lived just across the street, was always at hand to play with him. Years later she recalled the child's timidity:

He was very shy, certainly, and when he came to my house – he had only to cross the street – would stand in front of the door without entering. 'Come in Federico, come in, dear,' we'd say to him, and he'd reply without moving an inch: 'No, no, I can't, *because I'm frightened of the danger*.' We'd kill ourselves laughing at his ideas. The 'danger' in question was the little doorstep you find at the entrance to all village houses![104]

Lorca wrote to a friend in 1932 that his mother, although she gave up teaching on marrying, never lost her vocation and taught 'hundreds of peasants' in Fuente Vaqueros to read. Vicenta got along well with the numerous García relatives she acquired as a result of her marriage, and, like them, deeply admired Victor Hugo, whose works, following the example of Grandmother Isabel Rodríguez, she used to read aloud to the servants and anyone else who cared to listen. 'One of my most moving childhood memories', wrote Federico:

is of her reading Victor Hugo's *Hernani* in our huge kitchen at Daimuz to the farm labourers, servants and administrator's family. My mother read admirably, and I observed with amazement that the servants were weeping although, naturally, I understood nothing of what was going on . . . Nothing? Well, I did grasp the poetic atmosphere but not at all the human passions of the drama. Although that cry 'Doña Sol, Doña Sol', in the last act, has exercised a considerable influence over my current practice as a dramatist.*

Not surprisingly, Federico felt that his mother, more than anyone else, had moulded his artistic temperament. 'I owe her everything I am and everything I will be,' he declared emphatically in the same letter. A few years earlier he had said that, if his deep feelings came from his father, he inherited his intelligence from his mother.[105]

The debt included, no doubt, the religious fervour of those early days. Vicenta Lorca was a practising Catholic, and Federico accompanied her often to the chapel, whose liturgy, processions and festivities impressed him deeply. In 'My Village' he remembers with affection the tower of the church, 'so low that it hardly stands out from the rest of the houses, so that when the bells peal they seem to emanate from the depths of the earth'. Crowning the façade – both it and the church, with the exception of the tower, are today much altered – was a statue of the Virgin, babe in arms, whom the villagers, despite their general lack of interest in religion, held in high esteem. Behind the altar stood a smiling image of the Virgin of Good Love (*La Virgen del Buen Amor*). 'When the organ started up,' continues the adolescent Lorca in 'My Village',

my soul was in ecstasy and I fixed my eyes tenderly on the child Jesus and the Virgin of Good Love, always laughing and a little silly with her tin crown, stars and spangles. When the organ started up, the smoke of the incense and the tinkling of the little bells excited me, and I would become terrified of sins which today no longer concern me.[106]

The poet always remembered with deep affection the Virgin of Good Love – so sweet, so human – who stood by the altar of the little parish church of La Fuente in which he had spent so many hours of his childhood.

Fascinated by the rituals of the Church, Federico soon began to imitate them in his own way. One of his favourite games was 'saying Mass', as Carmen Ramos delighted in recalling. In the back yard of the house there was a low wall on which the child placed a statue of the Virgin and some roses cut from the garden. Servants, family, friends – they were all made to sit down in front of the wall while Federico, wrapped in an odd assortment of garments culled from the attic, would 'say Mass' with enormous conviction.

---

* It is hard to know what Lorca meant by this comment since in point of fact there is no such exclamation in the harrowing last act of *Hernani*, which culminates in the death by poison of the two lovers and the suicide of the jealous Don Ruy Gómez.

Before he began he imposed a sole condition: that it was the obligation of the congregation to weep during the sermon. Carmen Ramos's mother never failed to produce real tears.[107]

It was almost certainly on the Daimuz estate that occurred an incident which, according to the poet, contributed decisively to the unfolding of his artistic sensibility. In an interview given in 1934 he recalled:

It happened round about 1906. Our land, agricultural land, had always been ploughed by old wooden ploughs, which hardly scratched the surface. But in that year some of the farmers acquired the new Bravant ploughs (I've never forgotten the name), which had been awarded a prize at the Paris Exhibition of 1900 for their efficiency. I, inquisitive child that I was, used to follow our new, vigorous plough everywhere. I enjoyed watching how the huge steel blade opened a slit in the earth, a slit from which roots, not blood, emerged. Once the plough stopped. It had hit against something hard. A second later the shining steel blade turned out of the earth a Roman mosaic. It bore an inscription which I don't recall, although for some reason, I don't know why, the names of the shepherds Daphnis and Chloë come into my mind.

This, my very first experience of artistic wonder, is related to the earth. The names of Daphnis and Chloë also taste of earth and love.[108]

Did this scene really take place as the poet described it? Francisco García Lorca, four years younger than Federico, doubted it, alleging that, if on the nearby estate of Daragoleja Roman remains had been found by this date, such was not the case with Daimuz. Nevertheless the poet's memory seems not to have played him false. A few years ago, after Francisco's death, the remains of a Roman farmhouse came to light under the fertile soil of Daimuz. Numerous Roman coins have been found on the site, almost all from the period of Constantine, and a large quantity of mosaics.[109] It is almost certain, then, that in evoking his first experience of 'artistic wonder', the poet was remembering a true event and that, in a thrilling, unexpected way the ancient history of Andalusia had suddenly been made palpable to him. The Romans had lived on this very estate, now belonging to his father, years before the arrival of the Arabs who, in turn, had named it Daimuz! It is difficult not to relate the experience, recalled by the poet so vividly, to the Andalusia he lovingly assembled later in his ballads, a mythical Andalusia whose personality is composed of elements as diverse as the Tartessian,* the Roman, the Christian, the Jewish, the Moorish and the Gypsy.

The first of Lorca's brothers and sisters, Luis, had been born on 29 July 1900, shortly after Federico's second birthday.[110] The child lived for only two years, dying, a victim of pneumonia (an illness common in Fuente Vaqueros), on 30 May 1902.[111] A reference in an early poem suggests that

---

* The biblical Tartessos is reputed to lie somewhere under the vast marshes at the mouth of the river Guadalquivir, near Seville.

the loss of this brother was deeply felt.[112] Francisco was born on 21 June 1902,[113] and followed by María de la Concepción ('Concha') on 14 April 1903.[114] Then came a considerable gap, the last child, Isabel, arriving – in Granada – on 24 October 1909.[115]

It seems that Don Federico's obsession with the health of his children derived in large measure from the death of Luis in 1902. Francisco recalled that the doctor would be there for the slightest thing,[116] while Isabel has spoken of her father's almost pathological fear of illness and death. When the family went on a trip into the countryside, for example, Don Federico, his mind haunted by thoughts of venomous snakes, always took with him a more than ample supply of serum. And if some relative fell ill, he was never off the telephone.[117] Similar preoccupations are well documented in the case of the poet, and can hardly have been unrelated to paternal attitudes in such matters. For Lorca the merest hint of illness was always enough to convince him that his immediate demise was at hand.

Recollections of Village Life

The Fuente Vaqueros annual fair is held traditionally on the first three days of September. During the festivities the village patron, the Christ of Victory, is taken from the church and carried in procession through the streets to the accompaniment of noisy fireworks. Federico loved the fair and in later years often made an effort to visit the village on these dates.[118] One anecdote, referring back to his childhood, is perhaps worth recording. Don Federico García was a leading shareholder in the sugar factory, La Nueva Rosario, in the nearby town of Pinos Puente, and a close friend of the Torres and López families who, between them, controlled the board of the thriving concern. During the Fuente Vaqueros fair of 1905 or 1906, Don Rafael López, manager of the factory, visited the García Lorcas with his wife and children. Shortly after their arrival Federico appeared, and without a moment's hesitation asked for permission to inspect the girls' feet. This was granted. Having completed his investigation the child exclaimed, addressing himself solemnly to the girls:

I thought as much! You must be half dead! They've made you wear new shoes just like they have me, because it's the fair! And you can hardly walk in them! I've had to put on this new suit as well and they won't let me eat doughnuts or anything! I'm fed up![119]

The *cosas de Federico*, 'Federico's things', were already attracting attention . . . and would never fail to do so in the future.

At about the same time a travelling puppet theatre arrived in La Fuente. Federico had never before attended such a function – puppet shows were a rarity in the village – and his excitement was intense. 'Federico was returning from the chapel when he saw the actors putting up the little theatre in the square,' Carmen Ramos recalled. 'He refused to leave the square or to eat supper. After the show he returned home tremendously worked up. And next day a puppet theatre took the place of the "altar" on the garden wall.'[120] Carmen's mother was enlisted to make the rag and cardboard puppets. In the attic of the García Lorcas' spacious house there were trunks full of old clothes. Federico chose the garments that most caught his fancy, and his former wetnurse spent hours adapting these to the requirements of the fledgling puppeteer. Carmen Ramos used to add that shortly afterwards Vicenta Lorca returned from a day in Granada with a very special present for Federico, bought at the best toy shop in town: a real puppet theatre.[121]

In this first contact with the tradition of Andalusian puppetry we may be permitted to see the origins, not only of Lorca's love of the genre – he himself would write several puppet plays – but of his later enthusiasm for the work of the Barraca, the itinerant university theatre founded by the Republic in 1932 and which, run by Federico and the playwright Eduardo Ugarte, travelled the roads of Spain for four years, erecting its portable stage in village squares and introducing classical drama to people who had often never seen a play.

By the age of five or six, the future poet must have become aware that his father was one of the most powerful men in Fuente Vaqueros and that he himself, as the first-born son of such a potentate, was a privileged being. There are clear indications of this in 'My Village', as of Lorca's early awareness of poverty and suffering in the world.

One of the vignettes included in this early document is particularly significant. In Fuente Vaqueros there were people who still lived in conditions almost as abject as those that Horacio Hammick had found there forty years earlier. Among these unfortunate families was that of a little girl whom Federico had befriended. The child's father was a decrepit, rheumatic day labourer and the mother the exhausted victim of countless pregnancies. Federico visited the family frequently in their squalid home but was not allowed to do so on washing day, when all its members had to stay indoors, practically naked, while their only clothes hung out to dry. 'When I returned home on those occasions,' he wrote, 'I would look into the wardrobe, full of clean, fragrant clothes, and feel dreadfully anxious, with a dead weight on my heart.'

The adolescent author of 'My Village' affirms that knowing this family gave him his first awareness of the harsh reality often lurking behind the attractive façade of life in rural Andalusia. In particular, he sympathizes with the women, who often die from giving birth in disadvantageous circumstances to so many unwanted children. Meditating on the fate that has by now almost certainly overtaken his little friend, the poet becomes indignant: 'No one dares to ask for what he needs. No one dares – out of a sense of dignity or from timidity – to demand bread. And I who say this grew up among these thwarted lives. I protest against this mistreatment of those who work the land.'[122]

Of the characters recalled in 'My Village', the one described in most detail and for whom the poet feels the deepest affection is his friend 'The Shepherd', who is not identified by name. This was Salvador Cobos Rueda, a native of the village of Alomartes in the hills north of the Vega, who worked for Don Federico and was one of his most respected advisers.[123] Cobos, although always known in La Fuente as 'The Shepherd', did not in fact practise that profession. Whence the tag? We find a clue in 'My Village', where Lorca notes that his friend had been as a lad to the Alpujarras, the high mountain valleys described by Gerald Brenan in *South from Granada*, where many lowland flocks pass the summer.

Cobos lived close to Don Federico's first house in Calle de la Trinidad, and was virtually a member of the family.[124] In 'My Village' Lorca recalls the marvellous stories told to him by the Christlike 'old shepherd' (ghosts, saints, fairies, adventures with wolves in the mountains . . .). When Cobos began to talk, everyone in the kitchen would fall silent. When he prescribed a natural remedy, the doctor could be dispensed with. He knew the properties of herbs, and from thyme and hollyhocks prepared pain-killing ointments. In the stars he read when rain and mists might be expected. Cobos was a veritable compendium of folk wisdom. But one day he fell gravely ill. The doctors could do nothing, nor the physician heal himself. Federico, taken to see him, was greatly affected by the sight that met his eyes. That night 'The Shepherd' died. In 'My Village' Lorca provides a detailed account of the laying out of the corpse, of the funeral, and of his intense sorrow and confusion on that occasion. 'It was you who made me love Nature', the narrative ends – and there seems no reason to disbelieve the poet.

The contemplation of the corpse, of the sudden change worked by death on the features of his beloved friend, seems to have left a permanent mark on Lorca's sensibility. Throughout his work death is a constant presence or menace, and there is a tendency to dwell on the process of putrefaction. In his evocation of the corpse of his friend the bullfighter Ignacio Sánchez Mejías, fatally gored in 1934 – Lorca had refused to see the body – we may be justified in suspecting a reminiscence, conscious or not, of that of Cobos, 'The Shepherd' of Fuente Vaqueros:

¿Qué dicen? Un silencio con hedores reposa.
Estamos con un cuerpo presente que se esfuma,
con una forma clara que tuvo ruiseñores
y la vemos llenarse de agujeros sin fondo.* [125]

It is likely, moreover, that as a child Lorca saw other corpses, since in Spain, particularly in rural areas, it has never been the custom to hide the fact of death. In his lecture 'Play and Theory of the *Duende*',† the poet established a sharp distinction between the manner in which death is regarded in Spain and elsewhere. 'In all other countries death is the end,' he said, not without some exaggeration. 'When it arrives the curtains are pulled shut. But not in Spain [. . .] In Spain a dead man is more alive as a dead man than anywhere else in the world: his profile cuts like the edge of a barber's razor.' [126] 'My Village' shows that, from an early age, Lorca must have assimilated this way of experiencing death.

Francisco García Lorca refers, in his book on the poet, to the surprise registered by their mother when, years after the death of 'The Shepherd', Federico claimed that he remembered it perfectly. 'You couldn't possibly!' Vicenta Lorca had insisted. 'You were only a child then and I had to carry you in my arms.' But Federico, not to be done down, produced forthwith such a detailed account of the death and funeral of his friend that his mother could only exclaim in amazement: 'What a memory God has given you!' [127]

Lorca had, indeed, quite a remarkable memory, but on this occasion the feat was not so out of the ordinary as Francisco's account suggests, for when Cobos died on 23 October 1905 – he was fifty-five but presumably appeared older – Federico was in his eighth year. A granddaughter of 'The Shepherd' has confirmed, drawing on family tradition, how heartbroken the child was on that occasion. [128]

If Lorca had ever got around to finishing 'My Village', he would almost certainly have included some reference to the one-time schoolmaster of Fuente Vaqueros, Antonio Rodríguez Espinosa, who was present at his baptism and played an important part in his early life.

Born in the village of Gabia Grande, not far from Granada in the foothills of the Sierra Nevada, Rodríguez had taken up his first post, at Fuente Vaqueros, in January 1885. There he would remain until 1901, when he transferred to Jaén. [129] It may well be that he knew Vicenta Lorca in Granada

---

*   What do they say? A stinking silence rests.
      We are before a laid-out body fading away,
      before a noble form that had nightingales
      and that now we see filling with bottomless holes.

†   For Lorca's theory of the *duende*, see pp. 113–14.

before both moved to La Fuente, but, whether this was so or not, he became a firm friend to her, and to her husband, during his time in the village.

Antonio Rodríguez was an excellent teacher, and highly appreciated by pupils and parents alike. He belonged to a new breed of educators deeply influenced by the progressive ideas emanating from the celebrated lay college in Madrid, the Institución Libre de Enseñanza ('Free Teaching Institution'), founded in 1876 by Francisco Giner de los Ríos and other dissident pedagogues then at loggerheads with the authorities of the Bourbon monarchy, restored the previous year in the person of Alfonso XII, after the failure of the First Republic (1873–4). Throughout the nineteenth century the intolerant Spanish Church, still almost medieval in its attitudes, had virtually monopolized secondary education, vigorously opposing all encroachments on what it considered its exclusive territory. But now this privileged position was coming increasingly under attack, and not least from the Free Teaching Institution. Antonio Rodríguez Espinosa, like Giner de los Ríos, believed that school education should be practical and relevant to modern society. And the results showed that children reacted warmly to his approach.[130]

Lorca was only two and a half when Antonio Rodríguez left the village. The latter can hardly have been in any way the future poet's official teacher during this period therefore, as has sometimes been maintained, although it is certainly possible that he may have had some hand, as a friend of Vicenta Lorca, in starting Federico off on the alphabet.[131] There is a charming photograph of Rodríguez with his charges: in the centre of the front row, looking rather bewildered, sits Federico, his spruce costume, straw hat included, contrasting with the generally dowdy appearance of the other boys. Clearly he is there by invitation rather than as a pupil (see illustration 2).

If Federico did not attend Fuente Vaqueros primary school in the days of Antonio Rodríguez Espinosa, he began his education there some years later. But Don Antonio's successors lacked flair, and the picture Lorca draws of the school in 'My Village' is decidedly unflattering. There were compensations, however, and among them his friendship with two boys from poor families, with whom he exchanged sweets and chocolate and who ran to his assistance whenever trouble threatened. The proximity of the girls' school also helped to relieve the monotony:

Carlos, who was already quite grown up, whispered into my ear and said: 'If they stripped the girls naked and us as well, would you like it?' [. . .] Trembling and embarrassed I replied: 'Yes, yes, I'd like it very much.' And they all began whispering until the teacher, banging with his stick on the table, made us keep quiet. Amidst the scratching of pens on paper and the heavy breathing of the teacher we could hear the girls chanting with their virginal voices: 'Saint Helen, having embraced the Christian faith . . .'

How many hours of tedium and irritation I spent in the village school!

And how happy they were compared to those to come! My schoolfellows were beginning to feel the mystery of the flesh and they opened my eyes to the facts and to reality.[132]

Federico was never to be a good student, due partly, perhaps, to those endless months of boredom spent in a provincial classroom under the eye of an uninspiring teacher.

In his references to Fuente Vaqueros the poet liked to recall the abundance of water that defines the village where he spent his early childhood. La Fuente is not merely situated close to the meeting of the Genil and Cubillas and set in fields criss-crossed with irrigation channels, but built, almost literally, on water, for beneath the village are plentiful springs which, according to the locals, are connected to the Sierra Nevada. The drawback is that, when it rains heavily, the level of the subterranean water rises, increasing the humidity that pervades walls and floors.

In 1931, Fuente Vaqueros honoured Lorca by giving his name to the street in which he had lived from the age of four, Calle de la Iglesia. In his speech Federico praised the village and showed to what an extent he considered that his childhood there had moulded his poetic sensibility:

You may believe me when I say that I am deeply grateful, and that, when in Madrid or any other place they ask me [. . .] to say where I was born, I always reply that I saw the first light of day in Fuente Vaqueros, so that the fame that may come to me may also come to this delightful, modern and liberal village of La Fuente [. . .]. It's built on water. On all sides murmur the irrigation channels and grow the tall poplars where in summer the wind plays its soft melodies. At its very centre there's a fountain which wells up incessantly and beyond its rooftops rise the blue mountains around the Vega – but far off, distant, as if they preferred that their rocky slopes should not reach here, where a rich, fertile soil enables all sorts of fruits to thrive.[133]

Lorca's childhood years in Fuente Vaqueros were always to remain within him as a constant present, seemingly impervious to the action of time. He said once:

I love the countryside. I feel myself linked to it in all my emotions. My oldest childhood memories have the flavour of the earth. The meadows, the fields, have done wonders for me. The wild animals of the countryside, the livestock, the people living on the land, all these have a fascination that very few people grasp. I recall them now exactly as I knew them in my childhood. Were this not so I could not have written *Blood Wedding*. My earliest emotional experiences are associated with the land and the work on the land. That's why there's at the heart of my life what psychoanalysts would call an 'agrarian complex'.[134]

And on another occasion:

My whole childhood was centred on the village. Shepherds, fields, sky, solitude. Total simplicity. I'm often surprised when people think that the things in my work are daring improvisations of my own, a poet's audacities. Not at all. They're authentic details, and seem strange to a lot of people because it's not often that we approach life in such a simple, straightforward fashion: looking and listening. Such an easy thing, isn't it? [. . .] I have a huge storehouse of childhood recollections in which I can hear the people speaking. This is poetic memory, and I trust it implicitly.[135]

Unlike J. M. Synge, whose appropriation of the folk language of the west of Ireland was the result of conscious application, Federico was himself 'of the people', for in the Vega no linguistic and few social differences separated wealthy and poor, peasants and landowners. Lorca inherited all the vigour of a speech that springs from the earth and expresses itself with extraordinary spontaneity. Indeed, one has only to hear the inhabitants of the Vega talk and observe their colourful use of imagery to realize that the metaphorical language of Lorca's theatre and poetry, which seems (as he pointed out in the passage just quoted) so original, is rooted in an ancient, collective awareness of nature in which all things – trees, horses, mountains, the moon and the sun, rivers, flowers, human beings – are closely related and interdependent. Given these circumstances it is not surprising that if in later years the poet took pleasure in proclaiming that he was from the Kingdom of Granada, he habitually added, in order to be absolutely precise, that he came into the world in 'the heart of the Vega'.[136]

Paradise Lost

Lorca's La Fuente years came to an end towards 1907 when the family moved to the village of Asquerosa, situated 3 miles away on the other side of the Cubillas and where, in 1895, his father had bought a substantial house.[137] Nearby the enterprising investor had acquired a sizeable tract of land in what is known as the Vega de Zujaira, soon profitably planted with sugar-beet, which ran up to the walls of the San Pascual refinery of which he was a leading shareholder. Perhaps it was the desire to be closer to this and neighbouring properties that prompted the move to Asquerosa; another inducement may have been the greater proximity of the railway station, which was conveniently located at the edge of Don Federico's Zujaira estate and made access to Granada much more rapid than from Fuente Vaqueros.

Lorca went for at least a year to the primary school in Asquerosa, although there is no allusion to such attendance in his work, letters or interviews with journalists. Then, in June 1908, he reached his tenth birthday. That autumn, inexorably, he would have to begin the first year of his secondary education, which meant, in practice, enrolment at a college either in Granada or some other large centre.

And here Antonio Rodríguez Espinosa, primary teacher of Fuente Vaqueros until 1901, re-enters the picture. Don Antonio had remained in Jaén until 1903, when he was appointed headmaster of a school on the Mediterranean coast at Almería, some 70 miles from Granada.[138] He lived in this town for ten years, successfully running the various schools entrusted to his care before his removal to Madrid in 1913.[139]

In Almería, no doubt with a view to bringing in a little extra money (teachers in Spain were miserably paid at the time), Antonio Rodríguez had adopted the practice of taking in as boarders a small number of children registered at one or other of the town's schools, supervising their studies, providing some supplementary tuition and generally looking after their welfare in a friendly home atmosphere. The García Lorcas, who had not lost contact with their old friend, knew of this arrangement. And when the time came for Federico to begin his secondary education, it was decided that he should spend a period with Don Antonio in Almería, studying at a well-known private school there, enrolling at the local state college of secondary education (*Instituto*) – such enrolment was obligatory, although students could study privately – and being helped and coached by his mother's former colleague. Accordingly, on 28 August 1908, Federico applied for admission to the Almería Institute. [140] The entrance examination, which he passed, took place on 21 September. It comprised a short passage of dictation from *Don Quixote* and an elementary exercise in division.[141]

These were prosperous days for Almería, which then had some 50,000 inhabitants, due to the development of its iron ore mines and, particularly, to the massive export of fruit, mainly to England. Almería's relation with the latter was so close that it was common for the children of the well-to-do to be educated at English schools. Throughout the year a weekly boat service linked the town to Liverpool and London, and during the harvest of the area's famous grapes there were three or four boats daily.[142] It was inevitable, given these circumstances, that the need came to be felt in the town for a good private secondary school, the more so in view of the fact that the Institute was considered by the local bourgeoisie to be a dangerous hotbed of liberalism and 'progressive' ideas.[143] The College of Jesus (despite its name not a Jesuit establishment) was founded in 1888 to meet this demand, and it was here that the young Lorca began his secondary education.

We know little of the future poet's brief period in Almería, and most of our information comes from the largely unpublished memoirs of Antonio Rodríguez Espinosa, written when the teacher was already an old man.

When Federico arrived to live with Don Antonio, we learn from this document, two of his cousins from Fuente Vaqueros were already boarding with the teacher and his wife, a circumstance that presumably mitigated any homesickness. Each Sunday the kindly teacher took his charges on a trip into the countryside or to the sea, using these outings to impart what he liked to call 'a little practical knowledge'. Recalling those Sunday excursions, Rodríguez Espinosa commented that during them Federico never failed to answer a question. 'The answers could be right or wrong,' wrote the old teacher, 'but they were unfailingly rapid and ingenious.'[144]

The query arises whether Lorca's brief stay in Almería (there is no evidence that he ever returned) left any permanent impression. The only time the town is mentioned directly in his work occurs in the ballad 'The Gypsy Nun', where there is an allusion to the sweetmeats prepared in certain Granada convents from the citrus fruits for which Almería, with its subtropical climate, is celebrated.[145] Francisco García Lorca has suggested that in another of his brother's ballads, 'Thamar and Amnon', there may be a reminiscence of the almost African appearance of the town, whose Moorish fortress, walls and battlements, redolent of the Orient, struck Gerald Brenan, in 1920, 'like an illustration in a book of Eastern travel'.[146] In a letter to the writer José Bergamín, Lorca said that Almería, in the harshness of its climate and the saffron colour of its dust, made him think of Algeria;[147] and it can be added that the real events that inspired *Blood Wedding* took place, in 1928, 20 miles east of Almería, near the village of Níjar. Knowing as he did the barren, calcinated countryside, virtually bereft of rainfall, that lies just beyond the lush, densely vegetated oasis of the town's immediate surroundings, it would not have been difficult for the poet to imagine the setting in which the tragedy had occurred.

We do not know exactly how many months of the school year 1908–9 Lorca spent in Almería. The poet stated in 1928 that he fell seriously ill there and that, being almost at death's door, had to be rushed back to Asquerosa.[148] On another occasion he specified that what he had caught was a throat and mouth infection.[149] Federico's brother, for his part, has recalled the return to the village of the sufferer, his face still bloated.[150] While we cannot be sure, it seems that the illness probably struck in the spring of 1909.

That summer Don Federico García Rodríguez moved his family to Granada, where he had rented a spacious house in the centre of the town at 66 Acera del Darro (now number 46); and, on 15 May, Federico applied to the Director of the Granada General and Technical Institute for permission to be allowed to sit in June the examination for the subjects studied during the first year of his secondary education course: Castilian Language, General and European Geography, Notions of Arithmetic and Geometry, Religion (optional) and Calligraphy.[151] It was hardly surprising, given his recent illness, that he did not cover himself in academic laurels on this occasion, passsing in Castilian but failing in Geography and Notions of Arithmetic and Geometry. He did not sit Calligraphy or Religion.[152] In the September examinations he would manage to recoup some of the lost ground by passing Geography,[153] the only examination he sat, and during the year to dispose of the backlog in Calligraphy, Arithmetic and Geometry.[154]

Federico's childhood in the Vega had come to a brusque termination. The order of the day was now his education, and the vision of five more years poring over books did not enthral, far from it, Don Federico García Rodríguez's eldest son. Vicenta Lorca and her husband were determined, however, that both Federico and Francisco should have professional careers. And careers, they insisted, began with success at school.

2

Granada

Give him alms, woman, for nothing in life can equal the misery
of being blind in Granada.

F. A. de Icaza

In the summer of 1909, when the García Lorca family moved in from
Asquerosa to Granada, the famous city of the Alhambra – the last bastion
of Islam in Spain until it fell to Ferdinand and Isabella in 1492 – was a small
provincial capital of some 75,000 inhabitants.[1] A few years earlier Karl
Baedeker had called the city a 'living ruin', observing, not without sarcasm,
that if some of its principal thoroughfares had recently been 'furbished up
to a certain extent for the eyes of the visitor from foreign parts' the side
streets were filthy. 'The local aristocracy prefers to spend its rents in Madrid,'
Baedeker continued, adding that a 'large proportion' of the population
subsisted by begging. As for the recently inaugurated sugar-beet factories in
the Vega, he felt that it was still questionable whether the results would
justify the hopes placed in them.[2]

Such hopes proved to be more than justified, and soon after these words
were published Granada gave the impression of suddenly having come to
life after centuries of inertia. The profits from the sugar boom were flowing
in; businessmen and speculators could hardly believe their luck, and it was
generally agreed that the time had come to 'modernize' Granada and make
it more 'European'. A striking consequence of the new attitude was the
laying down, through the city's heart, of the wide, absolutely straight
thoroughfare baptized Gran Vía de Colón ('Columbus Avenue'). This jarred
with the introverted, private character of Granada, and was effected at the
expense of numerous buildings of historical and artistic interest, Moorish
and later, which were pulled down. Some wag quickly nicknamed the
offensive street 'Sugar Avenue', while Lorca was to say that it played a major
role in 'deforming the character of today's *granadinos*'.[3]

The fact is, however, that the construction of the Gran Vía de Colón was but the most recent expression of a process begun when Granada fell to the Christians.

The conditions imposed by Ferdinand and Isabella before the city surrendered had been pretty generous, and in tune with the spirit of compromise prevailing elsewhere in the peninsula in the years leading up to the final collapse of Islam there. There was initially no question that the defeated Moors – of whom there were perhaps some 300,000 in the kingdom of Granada – would be persecuted, expelled or forcibly converted to the religion of Christ; no question of their property being in jeopardy. But these promises were soon broken once it was borne in upon the Christians that, with the fall of the city, which completed the 'reconquest', the situation in the country had changed radically. The infidel had finally been routed! By the end of the century many noble Moorish families had fled to Africa, fearing the worst as forced conversions became the order of the day in Granada. In 1501 the *moriscos*, as the converted Moors were known, rose up against their oppressors, and this action gave Ferdinand and Isabella the excuse they needed for further breaking their word to the Granadine population. The Inquisition set to work in earnest and the situation grew steadily more tense. Then, in 1568, a full-scale Moorish revolt broke out. In Granada the rebels were quickly put down, but in the high valleys of the Alpujarras the fighting continued for two more years. The Moors, hopelessly outnumbered and poorly armed in comparison with the Castilians, could not hope to prevail, and after their defeat were exiled to other parts of Spain. Finally, in 1610, their definitive expulsion from the country was decreed.[4]

As for the Jews of Granada, it has been calculated that immediately before the city fell they numbered some 20,000. A hard-working, rich and cultured élite, their fate proved even worse than that of the Moors, despite the guarantees given to them by the 'Catholic Kings' in December 1491 – and despite the fact that the Granadine campaign had been in large part financed by Jewish money. The Sephardim were expelled from Spain *en masse*, with the exception of those who accepted immediate conversion to Christianity, by virtue of an edict of 31 March 1492. As for those *conversos* or New Christians who secretly continued to practise their Hebrew religion, the Inquisition took upon itself the task of gradually eradicating them.[5]

The fall of Granada meant the end of an era of almost 800 years of Moorish domination, and an inevitable decline. A kingdom had become a province, and if Seville, conquered 200 years earlier, had acquired, with the discovery of the New World, a fresh, buoyant personality, Granada, cut off from the sea and hemmed in by mountains, seemed to have lost its soul.[6]

While mentioning the fate of Granada's Moors and Jews, a word should be said about her Gypsies who, since the fourteenth century and until very recently, lived in the caves of the Sacromonte. In 1499 Ferdinand and Isabella issued an edict whereby the 'Egyptians' of Spain were required to abandon their itinerant ways and settle down in one place; and during the following centuries the Gypsies were never free from harassment. Despite this they survived, probably because at no time did they pose a threat to the established order. Their tribulations have been admirably documented by George Borrow in *The Zincali: An Account of the Gypsies of Spain* (1841), a book with which, in its Spanish translation by Manuel Azaña, Lorca may perhaps have been familiar.[7]

As a child the poet had known various Romany families in Fuente Vaqueros (where it is said they formed 10 per cent of the populace), and during his adolescence frequently visited the caves of the Sacromonte, where he made friends with the dancers and singers. *Gypsy Ballads* was to spring in part from Lorca's contact with these exotic people of Indian extraction who, despite their far-off origins, often seem more Andalusian than the Andalusians themselves.[8]

Lorca aligned himself firmly with those who considered that the fall of Muslim Granada had been a cultural calamity. Asked in 1936 for his opinion of that event, he remarked decisively:

It was a disastrous event, even though they may say the opposite in the schools. An admirable civilization, and a poetry, astronomy, architecture and sensitivity unique in the world – all were lost, to give way to an impoverished, cowed city, a 'misers' paradise'.[9]

They were strong words, and not everyone would agree with the poet's analysis of the situation prevailing in the city before its fall in 1492. But there can be no doubt that Lorca was absolutely sincere in his abhorrence of what happened once the city was in Christian hands. In 1931 he identified himself explicitly with the victims of Ferdinand's and Isabella's repression. 'I believe', he said in an interview, 'that being from Granada gives me a fellow feeling for those who are being persecuted. For the Gypsy, the Negro, the Jew . . . the *morisco*, whom all *granadinos* carry inside them.'[10] In saying this Lorca may have had in mind not only the Blacks he had seen in New York and Cuba, but the black slaves who had been common in Islamic Granada.[11]

The year 1492 is a key date in the history and consciousness of Granada for another reason, thanks to Christopher Columbus. The admiral had witnessed the fall of the city, and his historic agreement with Ferdinand and Isabella was signed in the encampment of Santa Fe, in the Vega, on 17 April 1492, three months after that event. On 3 August of the same year the *Santa*

María, the *Pinta* and the *Niña* set sail from Palos de la Frontera, and on the following 12 October Columbus disembarked in the New World, believing that he had found a hitherto unknown route to India. Lorca must have heard all about the great adventure as a child, for Santa Fe ('Cradle of the Spanish Empire'), the birthplace of his paternal grandparents, is only 4 miles from Fuente Vaqueros and through it passed the stagecoach linking the village to Granada – a stagecoach on which he must have travelled many times. Moreover it was in the town of Pinos Puente, not far from La Fuente, where, according to tradition, a messenger had caught up with the disconsolate Columbus who, after the monarchs' initial refusal to sponsor his projected voyage of discovery, was riding away from Granada. Columbus returned to Santa Fe and the agreement was duly signed.

The final collapse of Islam in Spain coincided, then, with the discovery and opening up of America: two related events which it has always been impossible to forget in Granada.

When the García Lorcas moved into their house in the Acera del Darro the city had not yet begun to spread into the Vega, and its last streets merged almost imperceptibly with the orchards, villas, farms and fields. Nothing could have been further removed from the sad spectacle offered today: all along the edge of the city stretches an unbroken wall of tall blocks which have destroyed not only many thousands of acres of fertile land but perspectives unique in the world. It all tends to prove that Lorca was right when, in his letters, he insisted on the philistine tendencies of his fellow *granadinos* and particularly of those with money.

The property rented by Federico García Rodríguez in the Acera del Darro, where the family was to live until 1916, approximates to what in England would be termed a terrace house. It had several floors, a vine-shaded patio with a diminutive fountain, and a garden at the end of which stood a small stable with a corral. Geraniums, violets and forget-me-nots abounded, and in the centre of the garden rose a luxurious magnolia tree. It was a house worthy of a rich landowner.[12]

Francisco García Lorca has pointed out that the family's move to Granada did not constitute a complete break with its former life in the Vega. Relatives and friends from Fuente Vaqueros or Asquerosa often dropped in, invited or otherwise; in the ample pantry were heaped fruits and vegetables of all kinds from Don Federico's estates; every summer the family used to spend several weeks in Asquerosa, and, most important perhaps, there were always servants from the Vega in attendance at 66 Acera del Darro.[13]

Among the latter the great favourite was Dolores Cuesta, who had been Francisco's wetnurse in Fuente Vaqueros. Illiterate, earthy, good-natured, an inexhaustible fund of country lore, Dolores left an indelible impression on Federico, and her exuberant personality and peasant speech are reflected in the Old Pagan Woman of *Yerma* and the Housekeeper in *Doña Rosita la soltera* ('Doña Rosita the Spinster'). [14] In a lecture on lullabies, Lorca was to express his deep appreciation of those peasant servants who, like Dolores, nourish the imagination of rich children with traditional music and poetry:

For a long time these wetnurses, maids and other lowly domestics have been performing the extraordinarily important task of taking ballads, songs and stories into aristocratic and bourgeois homes. The children of the rich know about Gerineldo, Don Bernardo, Thamar and the Lovers of Teruel* thanks to these admirable maids and nurses who come down from the mountains, or make their way along our rivers, to teach us our first Spanish history lesson and stamp on our souls the harsh Iberian motto: 'Alone you are, alone you will always be.' [15]

Aunt Isabel García Rodríguez, not yet married, also moved with the family to Granada. It was she who had given Federico his first guitar lessons back in the village, and the child felt for her a veneration that would deepen with the years. When Vicenta Lorca fell ill after giving birth, in October 1909, to Isabel, her last child, and was forced to spend several months convalescing in a Malaga clinic, Aunt Isabel and Dolores Cuesta took over the running of the household in her absence. Francisco García Lorca has suggested that the mild jurisdictional conflicts that arise between the Aunt and the Housekeeper in *Doña Rosita* may well derive from scenes between the two mother substitutes witnessed and enjoyed by Federico. [16]

Although we possess little documentary information about the poet's first years in Granada, we can be sure that such an observant and lively child would have lost no time in beginning to explore this fascinating city.

The Alhambra and its sister palace the Generalife are such universally celebrated symbols of delicate beauty and romance that it is almost impossible to write of them without falling into cliché – just as it was almost impossible in Lorca's day for a young Granadine poet to disenmesh himself from the tradition of nostalgic versifying which the palaces and their history have traditionally inspired. The Alhambra had first been 'discovered' by the Romantics after the publication in 1826 of Chateaubriand's *Le dernier Abencérage*, one of the great bestsellers of the time. The novel, which evokes the last days of Moorish Granada, appealed deeply to the rebellious spirit of the age. Three years later Victor Hugo included in *Les Orientales* the poem 'Grenade' which, clearly influenced by Chateaubriand, further whetted the appetites of many readers for a trip south:

---

* Gerineldo and Don Bernardo are personages in medieval ballads; Thamar is the biblical figure. The thirteenth-century Lovers of Teruel (Isabel de Segura and Juan Diego Martínez de Marcilla) died of grief at being separated and were buried in the same tomb. They have been the subject of plays by several Spanish dramatists, among them Tirso de Molina.

L'Alhambra! L'Alhambra! palais que les Génies
Ont doré comme un rêve et rempli d'harmonies,
Forteresse aux créneaux festonnés et croulants,
Où l'on entend la nuit de magiques syllabes,
Quand la lune, à travers les mille arceaux arabes,
Sème les murs de trèfles blancs!*[17]

Not long afterwards, Washington Irving, who had read, enthralled, about Granada when he was a boy on the banks of the Hudson, settled in the town. His *Legends of the Alhambra* (1832) enjoyed immense success and established the Moorish palace as one of the most admired monuments in Europe. The book can still be read with pleasure, and it is likely that Lorca already knew it as a child.

By mid-century the Alhambra was in fashion. Irving was followed by a throng of writers and aristocratic sightseers, many of whom published their impressions of Granada and its attractions. Among them we may mention Henry David Inglis, Théophile Gautier, George Borrow, Alexandre Dumas *père*, Baron Charles Davillier, Thomas Roscoe, Prosper Mérimée and Richard Ford. Nor did Granada escape the attentions of foreign composers. In 1845 Glinka spent several months in the city, striking up a friendship with a celebrated local guitarist, Francisco Rodríguez Murciano, who took the Russian to the caves of the Sacromonte and introduced him to the *cante jondo* or 'deep song' of the Gypsies – the primitive form of our modern flamenco. Glinka, fascinated by the possibilities for his own work afforded by Spanish folk music, began the experiments that led to his *Jota aragonesa* (1845) and *Summer Night in Madrid* (1849), which in turn sparked off a new interest on the part of the Russians in their own rich folk tradition, as well as a spate of Spanish-inspired, and usually superficial, pieces by foreign composers.[18] Lorca commented on this phenomenon in the lecture on *cante jondo* delivered in 1922: 'And so you see how the sad modulations and grave orientalism of our *cante* are imparted by Granada to Moscow, and how the melancholy of the Vela† is echoed by the mysterious bells of the Kremlin.'[19]

Of the composers attracted by Spain, Claude Debussy came closest to

---

* The Alhambra! The Alhambra! Palace that the Genies
  Gilded like a dream and filled with harmony,
  Fortress of festooned and crumbling battlements
  Where at night magic syllables resound
  When the moon, shining through a thousand Arab arches,
  Spangles the walls with white clover!

† The massive Vela Tower stands on the projecting prow of the Alcazaba and looks out over the plain. Its bell, known as La Vela, used to be rung at intervals during the night to regulate the complicated irrigation procedures of the Vega.

appreciating the essence of the country's folk music. In his numerous works of Spanish inspiration he rarely falls into pastiche, or degenerates to the level of merely transcribing ready-made melodies (both of which tendencies are present, to give but one example, in Rimsky-Korsakov's *Capriccio espagnol*). Debussy never visited Granada, but he felt powerfully drawn to the place. The love affair had begun in 1900 when, during the Paris Exhibition (whence proceeded Don Federico García Rodríguez's new steel plough), he had listened with delight to a group of Andalusian, perhaps Granadine, Gypsies sing *cante jondo*.[20] From that experience sprang, first, the work for two pianos *Lindaraja* (1901), whose title alludes to a Moorish princess who lived in the Alhambra. Next came *La Soirée dans Grenade*, published in 1903. The year 1910 saw the première of his orchestral *image*, *Ibéria*, redolent of Andalusia, and the publication, in the first book of *Préludes*, of *La Sérénade interrompue*, where Andalusia is again evoked. The second book of *Préludes*, brought out in 1913, contains *La Puerta del vino*, which owed its genesis to a picture postcard of the Alhambra showing the celebrated Moorish gateway.[21]

Lorca loved Debussy's music and played it with skill and sensitivity. He felt that in *La Soirée dans Grenade*, with its *habanera* rhythm, the Frenchman, almost miraculously, had captured to perfection the atmosphere of nocturnal Granada – the Granada of the Alhambra and the Generalife, with their pools bathed in moonlight.[22]

As for those Spanish composers who have felt a special fervour for Granada, the most noteworthy, before the advent of Manuel de Falla, was Isaac Albéniz, who wrote more than twenty piano pieces inspired by Granada. In 1908, Albéniz, then internationally famous as a composer and concert pianist, confided to Falla in Paris that, if he were ever able to return to Spain, he would live in one place and one place only: Granada, where, long ago, he had had a love affair with the daughter of the keeper of the Alhambra. But he died before he could return.[23]

And, of course, Granada has always had her painters. During the nineteenth century the Alhambra's charms were widely advertised in the engravings of Gustave Doré, David Roberts, John Lewis and many others, which achieved enormous popularity throughout Europe. At the end of the century the Catalan painter Santiago Rusiñol was a frequent visitor, and captured subtly the light, colours and shadows of the Alhambra's gardens and fountains. Rusiñol became a friend of the young Granadine thinker and novelist Angel Ganivet, and between their respective groups in Granada and Sitges (on the coast just south of Barcelona) were established links that presaged those later to be forged, in the 1920s, between Lorca and his companions in Granada and Salvador Dalí, and the writers and artists associated with the magnificent Sitges magazine *L'Amic de les Arts*.[24]

In Lorca's day a talented English painter, George ('Don Jorge') Apperley, from Ventnor in the Isle of Wight, carried on the tradition of the foreign artist beguiled by Granada. He settled in the hilly Albaicín quarter, opposite the Alhambra, married a beautiful Gypsy and produced a steady stream of pictures of Granadine inspiration which were much admired both in Spain and in Britain.[25]

No account of Lorca's Granada would be complete without a reference to the city's two rivers, the Darro and the Genil, both of which appear with some frequency in the poet's work. The Darro is the more unusual of the two, given the circumstance – lamented by Angel Ganivet – that it flows underground through the centre of the city, having been covered over during the nineteenth century. Why this apparent outrage? The main reason was to tame the beast into which the normally tranquil stream was liable to be transformed when freak cloudbursts broke on the hills where it rises, only ten miles away. When this happened the river would often wreak havoc, breaking its banks, flooding nearby streets and carrying away everything in its path. And so it was that, between 1854 and 1884, the municipal authorities implemented the works that condemned the rat-infested, gold-bearing Darro to perpetual darkness as it passed under the streets of Granada.[26]

When the García Lorcas settled into 66 Acera del Darro, the river still emerged from its gloomy prison some fifty yards away, passing directly in front of their house to join the Genil at the end of the street. The last section of its roof, as it descended from the Puerta Real, was steeply arched, so that from either side of the street passers-by could see only each other's heads. This vaulting was later removed. After the Civil War the remaining stretch of the Darro was also covered over, so that today the river is completely invisible – and inaudible – from the Plaza de Santa Ana until it trickles from the mouth of its tunnel into the Genil.

Of the latter, which runs to the south of the city, less need be said. The Singulis of the Romans, this much longer river rises in the Sierra Nevada, crosses the Vega and joins the Guadalquivir at Puente Genil. Just as part of the Darro's water is drawn off behind Granada to supply the fountains and pools of the Alhambra and Generalife, so a large volume of the Genil's is similarly deflected before reaching the city in order to feed the Acequia Gorda, a substantial irrigation channel built by the Arabs and still in perfect working order. It is only in its passage across the Vega that the Genil's stream begins to increase, due mainly to the contribution from its tributary the Cubillas. The two rivers meet, as has been said, close to Fuente Vaqueros, and their poplar-clad banks were the scene of Lorca's childhood excursions.

Alluding to the abundance of water with which Granada is supplied by the Darro and the snows of the Sierra Nevada, the poet computed that the town has 'two rivers, eighty belltowers, four thousand watercourses, fifty fountains, one thousand and one small jets and one hundred thousand inhabitants'.[27] Eighty years earlier Théophile Gautier had written a rapturous description of the Alhambra Wood in his *Voyage en Espagne*, whose chapter on Granada was much admired by Lorca and his friends. Never had the Frenchman seen such water, nor felt the heat of the south filter through such a canopy of green; nowhere else in Europe had he been so reminded of an African oasis:

Le bruit de l'eau qui gazouille se mêle au bourdonnement enroué de cent mille cigales ou grillons dont la musique ne se tait jamais et vous rappelle fortement, malgré le fraîcheur du lieu, aux idées méridionales et torrides. L'eau jaillit de toutes parts, sous le tronc des arbres, à travers les fentes des vieux murs. Plus il fait chaud, plus les sources sont abondantes, car c'est la neige que les alimente. Ce mélange d'eau, de neige et de feu, fait de Grenade un climat sans pareil au monde, un véritable paradis terrestre.[*][28]

The Sierra Nevada – the highest mountain range in Spain – dominates Granada and the Vega, and particularly at sundown provides an astonishing spectacle. This has been well described by Gerald Brenan in *South from Granada*. Brenan became acquainted in the twenties with the British colony that lived on the Alhambra Hill (in the best position, naturally), and found Charles Temple, ex-Lieutenant-Governor of the Nigerian Protectorate, one of the oddest members of that eccentric community. Temple had built a crackpot house close to the cemetery, and here each sunset a strangely English ceremony was enacted:

Every evening after tea, at the hour when the sun was getting ready to set, Mrs Temple would marshal her guests towards the veranda or, if it was cold, to the large window facing south, and pronounce in her slow, emphatic, careful voice, 'I don't think it will be long now.' We looked and waited. Gradually the smooth, undulating summits, which up to that moment had seemed remote and unterrestrial, began to turn a pale rose, just as though a beam of a Technicolor projector had been turned on them. 'There,' she said. 'Now.' At once a silence fell upon all of us, and we sat without moving, watching the rose flush deepen and then fade away. As soon as it

---

* The noise of the babbling water mingles with the hoarse buzzing of a hundred thousand cicadas or crickets whose music never stops and which brings one's ideas back forcibly, despite the coolness of the spot, to the torrid South. The water gushes out on all sides, from under the tree-trunks and through the cracks in the old walls. And the hotter the weather the more the springs well up, for they are fed by the melting snow. This mixture of water, snow and fire makes Granada's climate unique in the world, a true earthly paradise.

had completely gone everyone began talking again with the sense of relief felt by people who have just come out of church and without any allusion to what they have just witnessed.[29]

Lorca, while he may never have participated in Mrs Temple's evening rite, was addicted, like all true *granadinos*, to those magic sunsets, often the cause of his being late home for supper.[30]

Various writers, including the poet himself, have mentioned the locals' traditional apathy, their lack of interest in travelling and even their reluctance to climb up the hill to the Alhambra. Richard Ford, for instance (who, like Washington Irving, had the good fortune to live in the Moorish palace), noted in his *Handbook* that the place had been allowed to fall into a state of abandon after its occupation by the French during the Peninsular War, and commented sarcastically: 'Few *Granadinos* ever go there, or understand the all-absorbing interest, the concentrated devotion, which it excites in the stranger. Familiarity has bred in them the contempt with which the Bedouin regards the ruins of Palmyra.'[31] Perhaps the cause of such indifference lies in the extraordinary beauty of Granada's scenery, which tends to induce a markedly contemplative response in the spectator, encouraging him simply to stay sitting where he is – and to look.

Granada is often known among Spaniards as 'the city of the *carmen*'. The word, Arabic in origin, denotes a hillside villa with an enclosed garden hidden by high walls from inquisitive eyes, the architectural design expressing, originally, the Islamic notion of the inner paradise, a reflection of heaven. From the street outside, the garden is invisible; inside, amid a riot of vines, jasmine, fruit trees and geraniums, splashes the inevitable fountain. Lorca found in the title of a seventeenth-century composition by the Granadine poet Pedro Soto de Rojas the ideal definition of the *carmen*: 'Paraíso cerrado para muchos, jardines abiertos para pocos' ('A Paradise Closed to Many, Gardens Open to Few'). And in 1924 he declared that he adored Granada, 'but only to live there on a different plane, in a *carmen*. All the rest is a waste of time. To live close to what one feels deeply: the whitewashed wall, the fragrant myrtle, the fountain.'[32]

Lorca never ceased to ponder on the personality of Granada, and came to locate in what he called 'the aesthetic of the diminutive' – the love of small things, the care over detail – the essence of Granadine art, which expresses 'the retiring, introspective personality of the city'.[33] For the poet, Granada, severed from the sea, unlike Seville, is 'full of ideas but lacking in action',[34] and prefers to view the world 'through binoculars held the wrong way round'.[35] As for the Sierra Nevada, which dominates the city and Vega, the *granadino* admires it as pure form but would never think of climbing it.[36] Granada is 'the story of what happened earlier in Seville',[37] and in it one perceives a sense of absence, of something lost for ever.[38] Put another way, Granada's voice, for Lorca, is elegiac in tone, expressing 'the clash of East and West in its two palaces, both of them now alone and full of ghosts: the palace of the Emperor Charles V and the Alhambra'.[39] Because of these circumstances, the Granadine artist (typically a lonely, reserved creature with few friends, according to the poet) tends to produce small-scale, carefully wrought work. As a symbol of this sensibility, the poet singled out the infinitely subtle glazed tiles of the Alhambra, with their intricate arabesque patterns, which, in his opinion, influence all true Granadine artists.[40] Other examples of the same tendency, not mentioned by Lorca, can be found in the marquetry, ceramics and embroidery for which the locals are well known.

Corporative efforts on the part of Granada's artists and writers have never been lacking but, confirming the poet's thesis, they have tended to be short-lived. An exception was the Liceo Artístico y Literario, founded in 1833.[41] This association lasted for more than seventy years and during its early decades was one of the most active of its kind in Spain. Among its members and sympathizers were the novelist Pedro Antonio de Alarcón, author of *The Three-Cornered Hat*, the work that inspired Manuel de Falla's ballet of the same name and perhaps, too, some aspects of Lorca's *The Shoemaker's Prodigious Wife*; the Italian opera singer Giorgio Ronconi; and the writer of historical novels, in their day extremely popular, Manuel Fernández y González.

The last memorable event organized by the Liceo was the 'coronation' in 1889, as Spain's National Bard, of José Zorrilla, among whose works are to be found many poems of Granadine inspiration. Zorrilla was then seventy-two, and the 'coronation' proved to be an occasion of astonishing pomp and ceremony. Fittingly, the event took place in the Renaissance palace of the Emperor Charles V, next to the Alhambra. Once it was over, and Zorrilla had returned to Madrid (where he tried, unsuccessfully, to pawn his crown, only to find that it was made of imitation gold – that at least is how the story goes), the life of the Liceo languished, finally fizzling out completely some ten years later.

At the end of the nineteenth century, quite independently of the Liceo, a group of young writers had accreted around the figure of Angel Ganivet. This was a peripatetic gathering, which, discoursing as it went, used to make its way to the Fuente del Avellano ('Hazel-Tree Fountain'), near the banks of the Darro behind Granada. Ganivet, a diplomat by profession, was posted first to Antwerp, then to Helsinki and Riga (where he committed suicide in December 1898, at the age of thirty-three), and published, in 1896, a slim volume entitled *Granada la bella* ('Granada the Beautiful'). In it he expressed concern about the horrors being perpetrated in his native city by the property developers. The 'street-widening epidemic', as he termed it, was spreading, and local businessmen had fallen in love with the straight line, so at variance with Granada's true nature. The city, he had no doubt, was in mortal danger. Lorca, born in the year of Ganivet's death, knew this book well and took its message to heart. Ganivet, like him, believed that the essence of Granada was to be found in the small, the intimate, the delicate. He shrank from the sickly, outmoded orientalism of many Granadine poets (the example of Zorrilla had not helped), as would Lorca. And he dreamed of a future city where the old and the new would merge harmoniously, with prejudice to neither. 'My Granada is not that of today,' he wrote in the first page of his essay, 'but that which could and ought to exist, although I don't know if it ever will.'[42]

Lorca's generation, hard-working and ambitious, took up Ganivet's mantle and determined to do their best to work for that ideal Granada envisaged, not without pessimism, by the writer. A Granada that would preserve the best of the past but live firmly rooted in the modern age – what Lorca called 'a universal Granadinism'.[43]

Ganivet's suicide, coming as it did a few months after the traumatic loss of Cuba, Puerto Rico and the Philippines in 1898, and for this reason doubly symbolic; his dreams of a new Granada; the prestige of his truncated literary production, especially of the novel *The Labours of the Tireless Creator Pío Cid*: it all meant that creative *granadinos* of Lorca's generation recognized in him their spiritual guide, mentor and immediate forerunner. 'The most illustrious *granadino* of the nineteenth century,' the poet called him in 1935.[44] Without the precedent of Ganivet, in fact, it is probably fair to say that Lorca's attitude to the town that had become his second home, and to his own literary career, would have been considerably different.

3

School, Music, University

The liberal-minded Federico García Rodríguez, now installed with his family in Granada, had no intention of enrolling his two sons at a Catholic school.[1] Had this not been so, Federico and Francisco would almost certainly have been sent to the well-known establishment down the road, on the other side of the river Genil, run by the Piarist Fathers, which tended to be the first choice of middle-class Granadine families. After what we may assume was considerable deliberation, it was decided that the boys should be entrusted to the care of Vicenta Lorca's cousin Joaquín Alemán Barragán, who owned a small private school which, despite its name – the College of the Sacred Heart of Jesus – was free of clerical influence.

The school was situated in the little Placeta de Castillejos, at a stone's throw from the Cathedral. There Federico spent the remaining five years of his course, attending, in the mornings, the official classes at the Institute.

Francisco García Lorca early displayed a much greater aptitude than his brother for schoolwork, and became an outstanding student. Recalling those years in his book on the poet he records that their mother was forever nagging at Federico, trying to get him to concentrate on his lessons.[2] Joaquín Alemán's opinion, twenty years after the poet's death, was that, if Federico was a charming, companionable boy, he proved a quite hopeless pupil, spending his time filling exercise books with drawings and cartoons. This was perhaps something of an exaggeration.[3]

José Rodríguez Contreras, later a specialist in forensic medicine and a popular figure in Granada, had been born, like Lorca, in 1898, and was a classmate of his at the Institute. The Federico he remembered from those days was a shy boy who, because he came from the Vega, felt himself at something of a social disadvantage with the more sophisticated pupils with whom he now had to mix. It seems, too, that the young Lorca had to listen to jokes and innuendoes at his expense, and even that he was nicknamed 'Federica' because some of the boys found him effeminate. 'Federico was the worst in the class,' the doctor recalled, 'not because he lacked intelligence but because he didn't do a stroke of work. Often he wouldn't even turn up at school. Moreover, he had problems with one of the teachers, a pig of a man who simply couldn't stand him. Federico was always put in the back row.'[4]

In Lorca's New York poems there are some lines that may allude to these unpleasant experiences. In 'Poema doble del lago Eden' ('Double Poem of Lake Eden') we read:

> Quiero llorar porque me da la gana
> como lloran los niños del último banco,
> porque yo no soy un poeta, ni un hombre, ni una hoja,
> pero sí un pulso herido que ronda las cosas del otro lado.*[5]

While, in 'Infancia y muerte' ('Childhood and Death'), the poet apostrophizes his boyhood in the following terms:

> Niño vencido en el colegio y en el vals de la rosa herida
> asombrado con el alba oscura del vello sobre los muslos
> asombrado con su propio hombre que masticaba tabaco en su
>   costado izquierdo.†[6]

One of the teachers who crossed Lorca's path at this stage turns up, thinly disguised, as Don Martín in *Doña Rosita the Spinster*. This was Martín Scheroff y Aví, who taught Literature and Rhetoric at the College of the Sacred Heart of Jesus. Francisco García Lorca has recalled this likeable and pathetic figure. Already elderly when the brothers knew him, Don Martín was fussy about his appearance and carefully dyed his hair and moustache: an image of eternal youth and dash had to be projected. He lived alone, had published a collection of short stories, and contributed poems and theatre reviews to local newspapers and magazines, couching all of these literary effusions in an antiquated, overblown style.[7] In *Doña Rosita* Lorca conjures up the raggings meted out by the boys to Scheroff y Aví and his unfortunate colleagues, making Don Martín complain:

I've just given my Rhetoric class. It was pure hell. The talk was good: 'The Concept and Definition of Harmony', but the children couldn't care less. And what children! Because I'm disabled they respect me a little – only a pin on my chair from time to time, or a paper doll stuck on my back – but they do the most terrible things to my

---

*   I want to weep because I feel like it,
    as the children weep on the dunces' bench,
    because I'm not a poet, nor a man, nor a leaf,
    but a wounded pulse that probes the things on the other side.

†   Child defeated in school and in the waltz of the wounded rose,
    amazed by the dark dawn of the hair on his thighs,
    amazed by his own grown-up self chewing tobacco in his left side.

colleagues. They're the rich children, and since they pay we can't punish them. That's what the Head tells me.[8]

In this same passage there is a reference to the tribulations of a Latin teacher called Consuegra, who has just had a cat's turd strategically deposited on his chair. The name is real, and perhaps the incident too. About Consuegra, Francisco García Lorca has an interesting anecdote to tell. One day the two brothers were sitting chatting with him and Don Joaquín Alemán in a room on the top floor of the school where the headmaster, an inveterate canary and pigeon fancier, had installed various cages. Consuegra was extremely superstitious, and Federico, well aware of this, intentionally let fly the word 'snake', at which all sensitive Andalusians shudder. At that precise moment one of Don Joaquín's prize canaries emitted a piteous squeak and fell stone dead from its perch. Consuegra, convinced that the dreaded word had been responsible for the tragedy, began to repeat, staring at Federico, '*Now* do you see? *Now* do you see?' Francisco felt that, despite his brother's claim not to be superstitious, the incident left its mark.[9]

Another teacher, from the Institute this time, who impressed himself on Lorca's memory was the Castilian Language and Literature teacher, Manuel Gutiérrez Jiménez, who would recite verses from Zorrilla (the 'National Poet' crowned in Granada in 1889) as he charged round and round the classroom, finishing the performance with his tongue hanging out and frothing at the mouth.[10]

Lorca averred that, at the Institute, he was 'failed really badly several times'.[11] His records show, however, that he did not do nearly so poorly as he liked to make out later, and that, during the five years of the course, he was failed only four times, managing, in each of these cases, eventually to pass the relevant subject. But certainly he was no outstanding student, his file showing that in none of the twenty-eight examinations sat between 1909 and 1915 did he receive an 'Excellent', and in only twelve of them a 'Good'.[12]

One of the reasons, perhaps the main one, why Federico did not apply himself at school was that, soon after arriving in Granada, he discovered that, like so many members of his family on the García side, he had genuine musical ability, particularly as a pianist. He was elated, and spent hours every day at the keyboard. It has not been possible to document whether, as the poet was to maintain later, he had already begun to study music in Almería;[13] what we do know is that, when his parents eventually found him the right teacher (there had been a less satisfactory predecessor), he progressed at a dizzy speed.

Antonio Segura Mesa had been born in Granada in 1842, and was therefore already elderly when Lorca became his pupil. A shy, retiring individual, he had dreamt in his youth of being a great composer – but, alas, the dream had never become reality. A follower of Verdi, he had composed an opera in one act of biblical inspiration, *The Daughters of Jephthah* – a 'colossal opera', Lorca called it[14] – which, it seems, was booed off the stage during its première, which presumably took place in Granada. Don Martín in *Doña Rosita the Spinster* incorporates several details from Segura's career (as well as those deriving from Martín Scheroff y Aví), and among these we find this opera, now converted into a play entitled *The Daughter* (not *Daughters*) *of Jephthah*. Segura, a competent pianist, also composed music for *zarzuelas* – those light-hearted operettas that correspond, roughly, to a Spanish version of Gilbert and Sullivan – and, before Lorca came his way, had taught two outstanding local musicians: Angel Barrios and Paco Alonso.[15]

Lorca wrote that it was Antonio Segura who 'initiated' him into the methodical study of folk music but, unfortunately, we have no information whatsoever as to how that initiation, vital in the poet's career, was implemented.[16]

Federico came to revere the old teacher who, as well as stimulating his innate musical talent and ensuring that he acquired an excellent piano technique and solid knowledge of harmony, took him into his confidence and recounted the ups and downs of his life as a less than successful composer. 'The fact that I haven't reached the stars doesn't mean that the stars don't exist,' he would chuckle, and Lorca never tired of repeating the phrase, 'with religious fervour', to his friends.[17]

Aunt Isabel García Rodríguez, from whom Federico had received his first guitar lessons as a child in the Vega, liked to recall in later years Antonio Segura's daily visits to the García Lorca household in the Acera del Darro. On one occasion, when Federico had performed with particular brilliance, the teacher exclaimed to Doña Vicenta as he was leaving: 'Please embrace your son on my behalf. It wouldn't be correct for me to do so. He plays divinely!' It was little wonder that Federico found it difficult to concentrate on his books.[18]

Lorca's parents had made up their minds that he and his brother should have sensible professional careers. As a result Federico had no option but to resign himself, after the misery of his school years, to entering Granada University, no matter how strongly he now wished to devote himself exclusively to music. Accordingly, in October 1914, he put his name down for the preparatory course common to the Faculty of Philosophy and Letters and that of Law. They were really the only possible options open to him, for the other Faculties – Medicine, Science and Pharmacy – were, given Lorca's interests and temperament, unthinkable.

At the end of October 1914 Federico passed the first part of his final secondary education examination, but failed the second. In February 1915 he successfully repeated the latter. His schooldays were over.[19]

Granada University could hardly claim, in those days, to be a distinguished seat of learning. Founded by the Emperor Charles V in 1526, with the purpose of disseminating Christian and European culture where only recently Islam had held sway, the University, after periods of splendour, had reached a low ebb by the beginning of the twentieth century, particularly in Philosophy and Letters. There was little research, little innovation of any kind. The muscles of the place had grown stiff and heavy from lack of exercise.

But despite the prevailing atmosphere of stagnation, a few excellent new academics were making their presence felt by the time Lorca began his studies there. Among them were Martín Domínguez Berrueta, Professor of the Theory of Literature and the Arts, and Fernando de los Ríos Urruti, Professor of Political and Comparative Law. Both teachers were to exert a considerable influence on the future poet.

Domínguez Berrueta had been born in 1869 at Salamanca. His mother was from Burgos, and Berrueta spent many holidays there during his youth, coming to love passionately the old Castilian city so closely associated with the medieval hero El Cid and on whose exquisite Gothic cathedral his uncle was the local authority. Don Martín always considered himself a true son of Burgos: his birth in Salamanca had been a mere accident.[20]

Berrueta read Philosophy and Letters at Salamanca and, in 1893, published a doctoral thesis on St John of the Cross – a mere pamphlet by today's standards. From 1907 he lectured at his Alma Mater, editing, at the same time, a local Catholic newspaper, *El Lábaro*, of moderately liberal inclination. Berrueta proved a pugnacious journalist, with strong opinions, and was soon locked in controversy with numerous adversaries of the paper's editorial line, among them no less a person than the formidable philosopher, author of *The Tragic Sense of Life*, Miguel de Unamuno. The day inevitably came when Berrueta went too far. He had offended ultra-conservative Catholics by supporting the separation of Church and State, and the Bishop of Salamanca decided that enough was enough. In 1910 he had no option but to resign his editorship. Shortly afterwards, in May 1911, he was appointed to the Chair of Theory of Literature and the Arts at Granada University, a post he held until his early death in 1920, from cancer, at the age of fifty-one.[21]

Don Martín had been deeply influenced by the liberal ideas emanating from the Free Teaching Institution in Madrid. He saw clearly that Spanish universities were out of touch with the needs of contemporary society, and in particular he deplored the lack of contact, of give and take, between students and teachers, the blame for which, he was quite certain, lay with the latter. Nothing could be done to improve the situation, he maintained, until this barrier was broken down and students were able to enjoy a more personal relationship with their teachers. What he was groping towards, in fact, was the tutorial system, then unknown in Spain.[22]

The Granada chair gave Berrueta the opportunity he needed to put his ideas into practice, and he did so with characteristic verve, both in class and outside, making, as he went, many friends and not a few enemies. Towards his students he was both father and comrade, and they could always be assured of a welcome at his flat, where his charming wife added a warm maternal touch.

Don Martín's most original contribution to the practical education of his students was undoubtedly the study trips he organized each spring and summer from 1913 onwards. These became famous at a time when such excursions were all but unheard of in Spain. Berrueta, who knew Castile inside out, was just the person to take students there, and the forays were much appreciated by his charges.

Wildly enthusiastic, emotional, somewhat over-emphatic and even pompous in the expression of his views, capable of reacting furiously against those who disagreed with him, Berrueta was possessed of a special gift for stimulating young people's interest in the arts. He had his adversaries among these, certainly, but they were in a minority, and most of the students who attended his classes – they were never numerous – felt nothing but gratitude to this passionate, argumentative man.[23]

Fernando de los Ríos, who took up his chair at Granada in March 1911, a few months earlier than Berrueta, was cast in a different mould and, as an intellectual, stood head and shoulders above the latter, ten years his senior. An Andalusian from Ronda, in Malaga, where he had been born in 1879, De los Ríos came from a liberal, middle-class family, his mother being a relative of Francisco Giner de los Ríos, founder of the Free Teaching Institution in Madrid, who had advised her that she should settle in the capital to see to her children's education. She took heed, and so it happened that Fernando became a pupil at the famous school.[24]

The influence of Francisco Giner de los Ríos on the boy's development was decisive, and Fernando came to see himself eventually as the 'spiritual grandson' of the great teacher.[25] The school convinced him that Spain was desperately in need of a moral and intellectual revolution – and that he had a part to play in the great adventure. These were the days of the 'Disaster' of 1898, when Spain lost Cuba, Puerto Rico and the Philippines in an encounter with the United States Navy that was as decisive as it was brief. The event produced a deep depression in the country. In 1926 Fernando de los Ríos commented in a lecture:

It will be difficult for those listening to me to appreciate the terrible distress of mind felt by Spaniards in 1898; difficult for the young people listening to me to appreciate the impact made on us mere children, who had just gone up to university, by that tremendous defeat, a defeat for which today we are immensely grateful, because in 1898 was found the psychological key to the intellectual, and even economic, renewal of Spain.[26]

It was Francisco Giner de los Ríos who, the lecturer insisted, found that key; Giner who, more perceptively than anyone else, realized that the defeat could have a cathartic effect and that, free now of the last vestiges of its American empire (some remained in Africa), Spain could at last attend to her own inner needs and put her house in order.

When he finished his studies at the Free Teaching Institution, Fernando de los Ríos went to Germany on a scholarship made available by the Government Council for the Broadening of Studies, set up in 1907. There he made friends with other young Spanish scholars and came into contact with so-called Neo-Kantian Socialism, which deeply impressed him. When he returned to Spain he was a confirmed 'European', and more convinced than ever that the clue to Spain's rebirth lay in education. 'When between 1906 and 1909 my generation returned after having broadened our studies in France, England and Germany,' he explained later, 'we came back with such fervour and enthusiasm that each of us felt himself to be a missionary dedicated to an ideal which collectively we were to realize in our own country: the work of cultural reconstruction which we longed to begin.'[27]

Fernando de los Ríos and his similarly idealistic companions would later come to be known as 'The Generation of 1914', and there can be no doubt that their contribution to that 'cultural reconstruction' was outstanding. In De los Ríos's case the contribution was both academic and political. In 1918 he joined the Spanish Workers' Socialist Party, founded by Pablo Iglesias, became a Member of Parliament for Granada, and, on the advent of the Second Republic in 1931, was, first, Minister of Justice and then Minister of Education. Fernando de los Ríos was one of the great men of the Spain that disappeared with the Civil War.[28]

Shortly after Lorca's death De los Ríos evoked his first meeting with the poet, which, unless his memory played him false, had taken place in the Granada Arts Club, of which he was then President and which we know Federico joined in March 1915, halfway through his first year at the University. One day, almost certainly that same year, Don Fernando was intrigued to hear someone launching into a Beethoven sonata on the Club's piano, and went down to inspect. At the instrument sat a young man with jet-black hair, impeccably dressed, who proceeded to introduce himself. It was Lorca. From that moment Federico became one of Don Fernando's protégés, and was a frequent visitor to his flat on the Paseo de la Bomba, overlooking the river Genil. No doubt they also coincided in the Law Faculty, where the famous professor can hardly have been impressed by Federico's progress as an undergraduate.[29]

Apart from Martín Domínguez Berrueta and Fernando de los Ríos, in their different ways two almost guru-like personalities, no other teachers seem particularly to have impressed or attracted Lorca. The University Librarian, however, was a kindred spirit who enjoyed recommending books to his young friends and, after closing hours, sharing his forty years' experience 'enchained like Prometheus', he would say, 'in this den of learning'. A delightful den, certainly, that looked on to the somewhat overgrown Botanical Garden, where cicadas sawed all day in the summer heat and, in the spring, nightingales sang.[30]

We have little information about Lorca's preparatory year, 1914–15, at the University. The records show that he passed the three subjects studied, obtaining a 'Good' in Spanish Language and Literature and a simple 'Pass' in Fundamental Logic and Spanish History. After this minor achievement he signed on simultaneously in both the Law and the Philosophy and Letters Faculties. Such double enrolment was a practice common at the time, leaving open more professional possibilities for the future; and, since the workload was hardly excessive, many students succeeded in obtaining both degrees.[31]

Lorca's university career, like his school record, was far from brilliant, and if in 1915–16 he worked with relative seriousness in both Faculties, in the next two or three years he hardly bothered to sit an examination.[32] It is not surprising, therefore, that Doña Vicenta should have grown increasingly dissatisfied, rounding every so often on Federico's friends, whom she accused of distracting him from his studies; nor that Don Federico, immensely pleased with the academic progress of Francisco, should often despair of his elder son.[33]

During his early university days Lorca was, above all, the talented young pianist, for whom both his friends and teacher were forecasting an outstanding musical career. Under Antonio Segura's guidance he had begun to compose, and several short works, now apparently lost, convinced his listeners that here was no run-of-the-mill aptitude. What few of Federico's companions could have guessed during 1915, however, was that 'The Musician', as they called him, was also a poet.

One of those in the know was the journalist Constantino Ruiz Carnero, who inscribed a book published in the summer of that year thus: 'For my friend Federico García Lorca, inspired musician, intense prose-writer and fine poet'.[34] None of these early literary effusions seems to have survived. During the academic year 1915–16 Lorca's literary vocation became stronger under the influence of Martín Domínguez Berrueta, who was in the habit of taking his class to study monuments and places of interest in Granada during the course. An incurable romantic, Don Martín had a predilection for convents, preferably of the enclosed-order variety. And he was a great authority on the Cathedral. During the year Lorca accompanied Berrueta frequently on these visits, deepening daily his knowledge of the city, its history and its architecture.[35]

Then, on 26 May 1916, as the university session drew to its close, Antonio Segura died, at the age of seventy-four. Suddenly, at a critical point in his life, Federico had lost a great friend, teacher and ally. His heart set on a musical career, and hoping to continue his studies in Paris, Lorca badly needed Don Antonio's support in his struggle to persuade his parents to allow him off the university hook and to devote himself to his art. Now that Segura had died everything changed for the worse. Lorca's father, predictably, refused to countenance the possibility of his son's departure for France: no doubt he was not convinced that Federico had a genuine vocation for music, and anyway he felt strongly that, first, his son should have a degree to fall back on in case things did not work out. It was the sort of practical attitude to be expected of the rich landowner Don Federico García Rodríguez.[36]

In an 'Autobiographical Note' written in New York in 1929, Lorca referred to this moment in his life: 'Since his parents refused to allow him to move to Paris to continue his musical studies, and his music teacher died,' he stated, 'García Lorca turned his creative urges to poetry.'[37]

The process may have been assisted by the fact that, on 6 June 1916, less than two weeks after the death of Antonio Segura, Lorca set out for Baeza, in northern Andalusia, on his first study trip with Domínguez Berrueta. As well as Don Martín and Lorca, the group comprised the Professor of Fundamental Logic at Granada University, Alberto Gómez Izquierdo – a corpulent, genial cleric – and five of Federico's deserving companions.[38]

During the trip to Baeza the group met the distinguished poet Antonio Machado, who, since 1912, the year in which he lost his young wife Leonor in Soria, had been teaching there at the Institute. Machado was friendly with Berrueta and admired his energy, liberalism and enterprise. As a result, and discarding as best he could his habitual aloofness, he made an effort to be pleasant to the visiting students. On 10 June they met at the Institute, where Machado gave a reading from his by then famous book of poems *Campos de Castilla* ('Fields of Castile', more or less, although a windswept Castilian field bears little resemblance to those elsewhere), as well as reciting some verses by his friend the great Nicaraguan poet Rubén Darío, who had died that February. The occasion was a notable success. That night it was Federico's turn to perform, in his capacity as the musician of the group, and he did so with his customary energy, playing a selection of classical pieces and several of his own compositions of Andalusian inspiration.[39]

From Baeza the group proceeded to Cordova, where they spent three days. Berrueta kept his students on the move on these trips, and reports appearing in the local press indicate that, in Cordova, not a moment was wasted. The great mosque was the object of frequent visits by day and night, while the exhibition of the Sevillian painter Juan Valdés Leal (1630–91) riveted Lorca's attention, no doubt because of the obsession with death that dominates the artist's canvases. It was the first time that Federico had seen the original of Valdés Leal's *Finis Gloriae Mundi* (on loan from the Charity Hospital at Seville), with its putrescent, worm-infested bishop, and the experience was unforgettable. Later the poet said that the painting constitutes a quintessential expression of the Spanish preoccupation with mortality.[40]

The excursion ended with a brief visit to the beautiful town of Ronda, in the province of Malaga (the birthplace of Fernando de los Ríos) celebrated by Rainer Maria Rilke.[41]

This short Andalusian tour had been planned merely as an appetizer for the much more ambitious trip to take place that summer. But Berrueta fell ill shortly after the group returned to Granada, and the visit had to be postponed until the autumn.

In Baeza, Federico had met Lorenzo Martínez Fuset, the son of a comfortably off lawyer from the nearby town of Ubeda. A year younger than Lorca, Martínez Fuset, who was studying at the Institute in Granada, felt passionately about music and literature and was almost literally swept off his feet by the poet, whom he had taken proudly to meet his family. Federico played for them a tango he had recently composed, promising to forward a copy of the score when he returned to Granada. But the copy never arrived, despite Fuset's frequent remonstrances during that summer and autumn. Of their correspondence, which was maintained over several years, only Fuset's letters seem to have survived. They show that the relationship, on his side at least, was intense. Fuset wanted to believe that he was Federico's best friend, his only soul companion, and jealousy frequently broke the surface of his fervent missives. All his life Lorca would have to bear with this sort of reaction.[42]

During the summer of 1916 the García Lorcas left their house in the Acera del Darro, where they had lived since their arrival in Granada, and moved temporarily into 34 Gran Vía – the aggressively straight main street so much disliked by Angel Ganivet. Opposite their flat lived an extremely pretty, zany young woman, Amelia Agustina González Blanco, known as 'La Zapatera' because she kept a shoe shop in the Calle de Mesones. At a time when few women in Spain had anything to do with politics, Amelia was both a suffragette and a feminist, and had founded a political party called 'The Complete Humanist' (*El Entero Humanista*) whose motto was 'Peace and Nourishment' and which held out, among other things, for the revision of the alphabet along more rational lines. Amelia was to put herself up as a municipal candidate towards 1920, but failed, no doubt inevitably, to be elected. Martínez Fuset's letters show that Federico had told him about this unusual person, who clearly fascinated him during 1916 and 1917.[43]

On 15 October 1916 Berrueta's second trip of the year finally set out. The government had made a grant towards the cost of the expedition, and enthusiasm was running high because an ambitious one had been planned, which would take the group to Madrid, El Escorial, Avila, Salamanca, Zamora, Santiago de Compostela, La Coruña, Lugo, León, Burgos and Segovia. The tour proved a great success. Among Lorca's papers are various jottings from these weeks, some of which, touched up later, appeared in his first book, *Impresiones y paisajes* ('Impressions and Landscapes') (1918), largely an account of his excursions with Berrueta.

In Salamanca, Don Martín's home town, the *granadinos* met Miguel de Unamuno, although there is no reference to the great occasion in *Impressions and Landscapes*.[44] From there the group proceeded, via Zamora, to Galicia, in the north-west corner of the peninsula, the Ireland of Spain. Lorca was enchanted. In an evocation of the trip published the following year he recalled the luminous, green meadows of these parts and observed that it was easy, seeing such a landscape, to understand why the poetry and music of Galicia have always been tinged with sadness.[45]

Berrueta and his charges spent three days in Santiago de Compostela, visiting with their habitual thoroughness the many sights of the old, granite-built city, goal of one of the most famous of all Europe's medieval pilgrimages. The local press, as that elsewhere, intoned Berrueta's praises, and one newspaper called Lorca 'a disciple of the unfortunate Enrique Granados'.[46] The famous pianist and composer had just gone down in the English Channel with HMS *Sussex*, torpedoed by a German submarine, and the comment reminds us that a terrible war was then raging on the other side of the Pyrenees, a war that divided the inhabitants of a neutral Spain into two fiercely arguing bands of germanophiles and supporters of the Allies.

One of the group's most memorable visits in Santiago was to the Conjo Mental Asylum, where they conversed with some bizarre inmates. The student Ricardo Gómez Ortega remembered one of these patients in particular – a gentle, shy man, well versed in philosophy and literature, who, as they discovered later, had killed his wife in a fit of madness and cut her up into small pieces.[47]

Another visit was to the miserably decrepit orphanage of Santo Domingo de Bonaval. This made a deep impression on the young Lorca. In an indignant passage in *Impressions and Landscapes* he evokes the grim building, the pathetic appearance of the unfortunate children deposited there, the smell of bad food, the damp and the decay. The poet's eye fixes on the massive, worm-eaten door of the sombre establishment and he voices the hope that, some day, it will fall on a commission of municipal do-gooders, making with such unpalatable ingredients 'an excellent omelette of the kind so necessary in Spain'. This note of protest, which it is hard not to relate to the influence of both Berrueta and Fernando de los Ríos, is characteristic of Lorca's early writings – and can be heard often in his later work.[48]

After their stay in Santiago de Compostela the group proceeded to Lugo and León and, finally, reached Burgos, the ultimate object of all Berrueta's excursions. The professor's mother, as has been remarked, was from Burgos, and he had spent frequent periods in the city as a child. We may add that while still a young man he had published his first literary efforts in the leading local newspaper, *El Diario de Burgos*, and that, from 1908, had helped with the summer schools organized in the city by Ernest Mérimée, of the University of Toulouse.[49] It may have been Berrueta's commerce with these young French students that opened his eyes to the cultural value of study trips. For many reasons, anyway, Don Martín felt closely identified with Burgos and cared deeply about the place and its history. And it was natural that he should do his utmost to ignite a similar fervour in his pupils. But in 1916 the group's visit was brief, and on 8 November they were back in Granada.[50]

This contact with other parts of Spain exerted a profound influence on Lorca, as *Impressions and Landscapes* testifies. And it seems undeniable that it was during the trip that he began to feel convinced that he had a literary vocation as well as a musical one.

The first result of that realization to appear in print was a short piece of poetic prose, 'Fantasía simbólica', published in February 1917 in a special issue of the Granada Arts Club's bulletin dedicated to José Zorrilla on the occasion of the centenary of his birth.[51] The piece demonstrates that, in Lorca, the dramatic tendency was present from the beginning, for it constitutes, really, a little play – not intended for performance – in which the author seeks to define the personality of Granada. It is significant that in the first line of the first text published by the poet we should find the word 'romantic' ('The city sleeps lulled by the music of its romantic rivers'): at this time Lorca was losing no opportunity to profess himself a Romantic, and the adjective is applied lavishly, too lavishly, throughout *Impressions and Landscapes*. The characters of 'Fantasía simbólica' are voices (those of the Vela Bell, Zorrilla, the river Darro, Angel Ganivet, Granada itself), and the piece shows that, in the seven and a half years he had been living in the city, Lorca had been unable to resist assimilating the Romantic notion of the place, with its insistence on the brilliant Moorish past and 'mysteriousness' of Granada, its melancholy at the loss of a culture as rich as it was varied, and so forth. The poet soon banished such clichés from his work, but his view of Granada remained fundamentally the same and was to find its finest expression in *Doña Rosita the Spinster*.

'Fantasía simbólica' reveals, implicitly, an impatience with contemporary Granada. Who now loves the city with the intensity of a Zorrilla, a Ganivet, asks the adolescent writer? The poet and his friends felt themselves to be the spiritual heirs of Ganivet if not of the verbose Zorrilla, and believed that it was their duty to raise Granada back to a level of cultural pre-eminence. We can see with hindsight that they were well equipped for the task, for when Lorca began his literary career there was in the town a remarkable group of like-minded and highly talented young people, many of whom were to make an outstanding contribution not only to Granada but to Spain. They deserve a chapter to themselves.

4

The *Rinconcillo* of the Café Alameda

On 11 November 1911 an event had taken place in Granada that provoked lively debate: the first performance, by the María Guerrero theatre company, of *El alcázar de las perlas* ('The Castle of Pearls'), a verse play by the Almerian poet Francisco Villaespesa, then at the height of his fame but today almost forgotten. The theme of the work is the mythical origin of the Alhambra, and some of the lines, such as the song about Granada's fountains, were immediate hits with the audience:

> Las fuentes de Granada . . .
> ¿Habéis sentido
> en la noche de estrellas perfumada,
> algo mas doloroso que su triste gemido?
> Todo reposa en vago encantamiento
> en la plata fluida de la luna.* 1

Villaespesa declared that his intention had been to write the play as a Granadine Arab might have done. The notion, which now appears ludicrous, indicates the extent to which, two years after the García Lorcas moved to Granada in 1909, the threadbare clichés that had gathered around the topic of the city's Moorish past still held sway.[2]

Federico — then aged thirteen — had attended the opening night, accompanied by his friend the future painter Manuel Angeles Ortiz, and Francisco García Lorca has recalled that his brother, deeply impressed by the play, afterwards proceeded to dress up one of their maids in Moorish

---

* The fountains of Granada . . .
Have you ever heard,
in the perfumed, starry night,
anything more sorrowful than their sad moan?
All reposes in a vague enchantment
in the fluid silver of the moon.

garb and persuaded her to recite, over and over, Villaespesa's most evocative lines – probably the ones quoted.[3]

It became clear not long afterwards that the performance of *The Castle of Pearls* had been a significant event in the literary history of Granada, heralding the definitive decline of the pseudo-orientalism that for all too long had been stifling fresh initiatives. The fad did not die out all at once, though, and in 1914 there blew up in the local press a furious debate on the old and new values. This was initiated by a young journalist on *El Defensor de Granada*, Constantino Ruiz Carnero, who was to become one of Lorca's most intimate friends. Ruiz lashed out against Granada's narrow-minded, trivial literary establishment; made the point that in such an atmosphere honest criticism was nigh impossible; and lamented the increasingly bourgeois attitudes of the Arts Club, which was now fit, he said, only for an agreeable evening's chess. Ruiz Carnero looked over the books that had appeared in Granada between 1909 and 1914. They were a poor bunch, he concluded, and contaminated by the same provincialism as always. Granadine poetry still moved within the vicious circle of introspection and obsession with past happiness that for so long had characterized it. The panorama was bleak.[4]

Pricked into action by Ruiz Carnero's articles, a far more aggressive young journalist now entered the lists. This was José Mora Guarnido, soon a close friend of Lorca and later one of his first, and most perceptive, biographers. Mora was born in 1894 in the town of Alhama, not far from the Vega, the son of a schoolmaster, and had begun to write in the Granada newpapers around 1913. He was not only intensely combative, but utterly fearless in the expression of his opinions. He hated passionately the 'Alhambra poets', despised Villaespesa and, where the Granadine writers of the day were concerned, had conceived a particular scorn for the poet Manuel de Góngora, blue-eyed boy of the Arts Club. For weeks a violent polemic between Mora and Góngora raged in the local press and, when it was all over, the paladins of the new order felt convinced that they had prevailed and that Romantic Granada ('Pearl of the Orient', 'Sultan of Andalusia', etc.) had finally had its day.[5]

When Lorca joined the Arts Club in March 1915 the Mora–Góngora row had fizzled out. Federico had already met Mora by that time, and must have been fully aware of the dissensions that were rending the association. But Fernando de los Ríos was its President and, deficiencies apart, there could be no doubt that the Club was making a contribution to the cultural life of the city.

The aspirations of Ruiz Carnero, Mora Guarnido and other like-minded young men found brief expression in the monthly magazine they published in 1915, entitled *Granada*, which ran valiantly for six numbers. Lorca said in 1928 that the magazine expressed 'all that was pure and youthful in the city', while Mora Guarnido recalled years later in Montevideo that it represented faithfully the ideals of his generation.[6]

The staff of the magazine and their friends used to meet each evening in the Café Alameda, situated in the Plaza del Campillo. Mora Guarnido sets the scene:

In the morning and until the early part of the afternoon its clients were tough characters from the abattoirs and the fish and general supplies market, chaps 'with hair on their chests', as the silly expression has it, back and forth on their business; in the afternoon and evening arrived the small-time bullfighters, the flamenco set, the guitarists and singers from the *café chantant* La Montillana, situated nearby, the pimps' chums and frequenters of La Manigua (the red-light district), and the audience from the Cervantes Theatre opposite, where companies specializing in low-brow entertainment would put on moral operettas for family consumption early in the evening and, late at night, pornographic works for those prudent gentlemen who like from time to time to let their hair down a bit. The odd thing is that, despite such a heterogeneous clientele, the café maintained in permanent session a quintet formed of piano and strings which, every evening until midnight, gave concerts of classical music. And, even more odd, the clientele – contrary to what is often said about the public's ability to appreciate – listened to such concerts with pleasure and respect.[7]

At the back of the café, behind the little dais on which the quintet performed, was a recess wide enough to hold two or three tables. It was here that Mora and his fellow collaborators on the magazine met. Despite the ephemeral nature of that publishing venture, the group continued to frequent the *rinconcillo* ('little corner') of the Alameda, and eventually, as it expanded, became known by this name. The *Rinconcillo* had its heyday between 1915 and, approximately, 1922. After that many of its members left for Madrid and elsewhere, and it began to disintegrate.

The high priest of the gathering was the brilliant and eccentric Francisco ('Paquito') Soriano Lapresa (1893–1934), who had something of the wit, appearance, mannerisms and reputation of a Granadine Oscar Wilde. An object of heated debate in the town, Soriano scandalized many of the place's more straight-laced worthies. Tall, extremely stout, with lank, black hair, thick sensual lips and a pale, moon-like face, immaculately if extravagantly dressed – he looked, and was, the perfect dandy. Moreover he had private means and could afford to indulge his whims, which were as expensive and wide-ranging as the sweep of his interests, which extended from contemporary music and poetry to painting, archaeology, oriental languages and literature. His library, by all accounts, was fabulous, and several *rinconcillistas*, including Lorca, later recalled with gratitude the generosity with which their obese friend was prepared to lend books. Soriano's collection of erotica was particularly frequented by his companions, and he read modern French poetry avidly. It was bruited in Granada that his interest in erotic literature was not merely passive; that strange orgies, perhaps sado-masochistic in character, took place at his house.

Despite being an aesthete Soriano was interested in politics and joined the Granada branch of the Socialist Party, helping to organize the cultural section of the Workers' Club. He was, certainly, one of the most interesting and original figures in Granada, and it is not surprising that his influence on the other members of the *Rinconcillo* came to be considerable. Lorca, four years his junior, admired him intensely and owed him a great deal.[8]

The friendship, nevertheless, had its ups and downs. Manuel Angeles Ortiz, the painter, had an interesting story to tell. According to him Paquito Soriano, in 1918 or 1919 – the date is impossible to determine – took a fancy to Concha García Lorca, Federico's sister, who was then sixteen or so. Don Federico and his wife disapproved, it seems, of Soriano's pretensions, and he was given the cold shoulder. The aesthete, deeply offended, blamed Federico, and, if Angeles Ortiz's account is to be trusted, took his revenge by telling people that the poet was homosexual. Ortiz recalled that Lorca was deeply upset by what he considered Soriano's betrayal.[9]

Melchor Fernández Almagro (1893–1966), born in Granada the same year as Soriano, was another leading light of the *Rinconcillo* and later became a distinguished member of the Spanish cultural establishment, producing important books on literary and historical topics, a large corpus of good theatre criticism published in newspapers and magazines, and eventually being elected to both Royal Academies (Language and History).

Melchor had fallen under the spell, as a child, of Angel Ganivet's little book *Granada la bella* ('Granada the Beautiful'), and became an outstanding authority on the city. 'He had a prodigious memory,' writes Francisco García Lorca, 'and there wasn't an anecdote, event, imputation, piece of gossip or love tangle that he didn't have at his fingertips – and the people involved could be dead or alive.'[10] Fernández Almagro was one of the first to perceive Lorca's literary potential and, as co-editor of the Arts Club's special Zorrilla issue in 1917, it was probably 'Melchorito', as Lorca liked to call him, who secured the latter's collaboration on that occasion.

Melchor was also one of the first *rinconcillistas* to settle permanently in Madrid, moving there in 1918 to work at the Post Office. In the capital he took it upon himself, like a literary St John the Baptist, to prepare the ground for Lorca's imminent arrival, and he succeeded in creating among his many new friends considerable curiosity concerning the Granadine prodigy about to be unleashed on Madrid. When, in 1919, Lorca made his first exploratory trip to the capital, Melchor would be his principal cicerone. And the long correspondence exchanged between the two (1921–34) is eloquent of the deep affection felt by Lorca for his older friend, and of his respect for Melchor's judgement in literary matters. Federico turned to him again and again when he found himself in need of advice, and Fernández Almagro was often the first to be informed of a new literary project. Melchor understood Lorca's work better than almost any other contemporary critic, and his articles merited the poet's deep appreciation.

Tied to his Post Office desk in Madrid, and hard at work on literary projects during his free hours, Fernández Almagro could not return to Granada with the frequency he would have wished. But this did not prevent him from keeping in close touch with what was going on in the town, from contributing articles to Granada newspapers and magazines and, every so often, from commenting in the Madrid press on the cultural initiatives of the friends he had left behind. 'Consul General of the *Rinconcillo* in Madrid', the latter baptized him accordingly.[11]

Another member of the group who was to make his mark on contemporary Spanish society was Antonio Gallego Burín (1895–1961), who is remembered as Granada's most energetic mayor in the post-war period. Gallego Burín had been a precocious child, and early developed a passionate interest in the arts and in history, publishing his first articles at the age of fourteen in the local press. Fernández Almagro has recalled in his memoirs, *Viaje al siglo XX* ('Journey into the Twentieth Century'), his first meeting, as a child, with Gallego Burín, and their shared interest in 'Granada things'. Gallego Burín was already by then an avid reader of guidebooks to the town and in 1942 was himself to publish one of the best such volumes ever to appear.[12]

Gallego Burín proved a brilliant student and, before the arrival on the scene of Lorca, was Martín Domínguez Berrueta's star pupil, taking part in one of the latter's first study trips, in 1914. In 1915 he was given a small post at the National Library in Madrid, but a few months later was back in Granada to work in the archives of the local delegation of the Ministry of Finance. Gallego Burín later confirmed that he was one of those *granadinos* incapable of living away from his native surroundings. He knew only too well that his inability to wrench himself free of the town's grip could prove fatal to his career, but, realizing he was powerless, eventually accepted the inevitable.[13]

Gallego Burín was more politically minded than most of the *rinconcillistas*, and had become interested, in 1915, in the debate on the possibility of a federal Spain then being aired in the press. In December 1918 he founded the magazine *Renovación* in order to propagate his federalist ideas, which he felt could be beneficially applied to Andalusia. It lasted for thirty-four numbers, and expired in November 1919. Various *rinconcillistas* contributed to it, and in its inaugural issue appeared what seems to have been Lorca's first published poem, 'Crisantemos blancos' ('White Chrysanthemums'), which, owing to the fact that no complete set of the magazine is known to exist, has not been recovered.[14]

Gallego Burín suffered from precarious health, but this rarely succeeded in diminishing his extraordinary energy. In Granada his capacity for hard work, and his ability for taking on new appointments, became famous – and this in a town where, as he himself commented, little effort is spared to kill individual enterprise.[15] In Gallego Burín Lorca found a loyal friend, and their correspondence shows that the poet felt he could always rely on him for information and advice.

Then there was the Arabist José Navarro Pardo (1890–1971), a lecturer in the Philosophy and Letters Faculty. 'I suppose Hebrew and Arabic are dead simple with Navarro?' we find Lorca asking Gallego Burín in August 1920, at a moment when he was worried about finishing his Arts degree. 'When will I ever know Hebrew or Arabic? (They ought to pass me immediately!)' he added.[16]

Miguel Pizarro Zambrano (1897–1956), one of the founders of the magazine *Granada* in 1915, was the 'eternal adolescent' of the group, a hypersensitive individual with a burning desire to live to the full both the intellectual and the sensual life. Pizarro used to fall in love every day with a different girl – almost always from a prudent distance – and kept his companions in the *Rinconcillo* closely informed of the progress, or lack of progress, of his amatory comings and goings. As one might expect of someone with such a surname, he was a born adventurer, constantly in search of fresh horizons, sensations and experiences. In 1919, a year after Melchor Fernández Almagro, he moved to Madrid, where he worked on the great liberal newspaper *El Sol*. Then, in 1922, he fulfilled his ambition of visiting Japan, where he spent eight years on and off teaching at Osaka University, sending back charming letters to Lorca and other friends and managing every so often to return to Spain for long holidays.[17]

Lorca was fascinated by Pizarro's carefree attitude to life, and by the determination of this 'exquisite lover' of myriad moods, this 'arrow without a target', to taste all the pleasures the world had to offer. It was a programme little different from Federico's own, but implemented with much greater abandon.[18]

The journalist Constantino Ruiz Carnero (1890–1936) has already been mentioned in passing. Small in stature, fat, homosexual, prematurely bald, witty and enthusiastic, Ruiz, according to some contemporary comments published by his great friend José Mora Guarnido, 'hates working at night but has got so used to it that he has now forgotten how to work by day'.[19]

57

Appointed editor of *El Defensor de Granada* in the mid-twenties, Ruiz Carnero was a passionate Republican and enemy of the dictatorial regime of General Primo de Rivera. Under his direction, *El Defensor* became the chief mouthpiece of democracy in Granada and, where Lorca was concerned, chronicled the poet's career with pride. Lorca knew, and it was almost certainly important to him, that, where *El Defensor* was concerned, he was a prophet in his own country.

A few words should be added about José Mora Guarnido who, like Melchor Fernández Almagro, moved early to Madrid to pursue his career as a journalist. Four years older than Lorca, he exerted a certain fascination over the poet at a time when the latter's vocation was shifting from music to literature. Once established in the capital, Mora joined Melchor in spreading the good news about Lorca's imminent arrival. Then, in 1923, he left Spain, never to return, and settled in Montevideo. Mora's book on the poet, published in 1958, is extremely valuable for the Granadine background to the poet's work, despite the occasional slips of memory.[20]

The acknowledged philologist of the *Rinconcillo* was the shabbily dressed, lanky and bespectacled José Fernández-Montesinos (1897–1972), whose fervid admiration for the plays of Lope de Vega spread to the other members of the group, including Lorca. Like Fernández Almagro, Pizarro and Mora Guarnido, Fernández Montesinos was one of the first *rinconcillistas* to leave Granada for Madrid. No sooner had he finished his BA in 1916 than he moved to the capital where, between 1917 and 1920, he worked in the Lexicography section of the Centre for Historical Studies, under the direction of the great historian Américo Castro. Then, in 1920, he took up a teaching post in Hamburg, as *Lektor* at the Institute of Iberian and Latin-American Studies, and disappeared for the moment from view.[21]

An intimate (and childhood) friend of the poet who frequented the *Rinconcillo* was José María García Carrillo, who lived in the Acera del Darro next door to the García Lorcas' first house in Granada, and whose brother Francisco achieved local renown as a pianist. José María, a quantity surveyor by trade, was a Bohemian dilettante of the arts, an engaging, imaginative camp faun, quite unashamed of his homosexual proclivities, and the few extracts of Lorca's letters to him that have been found show that between the two there existed a deep understanding. The lack of documentation makes it impossible to assess to what extent José María García Carrillo influenced the poet's life, although some witnesses to that friendship have stated that it was exultant and that, whenever Lorca returned to Granada, the first people he saw were 'Pepe' and his other homosexual friend, Constantino Ruiz Carnero, with both of whom he exchanged his latest confidences. It is a tragedy that neither Ruiz Carnero, who was shot by the rebels at the beginning of the Civil War, nor García Carrillo, seem to have left any written testimony of their relationship with the poet.[22]

The *Rinconcillo* had two excellent painters: Manuel Angeles Ortiz and Ismael González de la Serna. Angeles Ortiz (1895–1984) was from Jaén, in northern Andalusia. His mother had moved to Granada when he was still a child (he was illegitimate), and the town and its surroundings were to be the central, obsessive theme of all his work.

Angeles Ortiz had met Lorca for the first time in Asquerosa, when the future poet was still in short trousers, and the two immediately began a friendship which grew when the Garcías moved to Granada. In 1912 he moved to Madrid to study with the Valencian artist Cecilio Pla. At that time the news was beginning to trickle through to the capital that, in Paris, exciting ground was being broken by an army of young, innovative artists. The name of Pablo Picasso was in the air. An Andalusian painter triumphant in Paris! In Madrid the established artists of the day – Zuloaga, Sorolla, Gutiérrez Solana – stood outside the new trends, and young artists like Ortiz longed to settle in the French capital.

Ortiz came and went between Madrid and Granada. In 1919 he married a Granadine Gypsy girl, Francisca Alarcón Cortés, whom he had met some years earlier at the studio of his teacher José Larrocha. The couple's happiness was short-lived, for Francisca died in 1922. Manuel, shattered by the loss of his young wife, left for Paris in November 1922. There he soon met and became friends with Picasso, and under the latter's influence veered in the direction of cubism. These were years of success for the young artist, who under Picasso's patronage became a sought-after portrait painter. The handsome Andalusian's pictures won him not only money but many favours with the ladies, among whom Ortiz's conquests became proverbial, as Luis Buñuel was to recall in his memoirs, referring to him as 'the darling of the salons'.[23]

González de la Serna (1898–1968) was by all accounts an inveterate Bohemian and absolutely indifferent to the adverse opinions that his flamboyant dress and manners elicited in Granada. From 1914 onwards his work, published in local magazines and exhibited at the Arts Club, had attracted the attention of the more perceptive of the town's few art critics for its refusal to make concessions to the 'Alhambra School'. González de la Serna designed the cover of Lorca's first book, *Impressions and Landscapes* (a naïve bucolic scene with an art nouveau flavour), and shortly afterwards, preceding Manuel Angeles Ortiz, betook himself to Paris. There he remained until his death, becoming one of the best-known members of the so-called Spanish School in the French capital.[24]

The *Rinconcillo* also had its sculptor, Juan Cristóbal González Quesada

(1898–1961), an adolescent prodigy who became famous in Madrid; its engraver, Hermenegildo Lanz (1893–1949); its composer and guitarist, Angel Barrios (1882–1964) and another guitarist, destined for international fame, Andrés Segovia (1893–1987), who, like Manuel Angeles Ortiz, was from Jaén but lived in Granada, and often dropped in when he was not on tour; its members destined for diplomatic careers – Luis Mariscal (1895–1941), Francisco García Lorca (1902–1976), Juan de Dios Egea (1888–1970?) and Francisco Campos Aravaca (1893–1948); and a hard to classify local 'character', Ramón Pérez Roda (1887–1943), much appreciated by the *rinconcillistas* because of his expulsion from a Jesuit college on the accusation of heresy. (Pérez Roda was an excellent mathematician, an authority on England and an admirer of Byron, Shelley, Rubén Darío, Ravel and Oscar Wilde – Wilde's works had begun to be published in Spain in 1917 – and Lorca, his interest perhaps stimulated by Pérez Roda, acquired a copy of the first Madrid edition of *De Profundis* (1919), which he seems to have read carefully.)[25]

This was the nucleus of the *Rinconcillo*. Many other young Granadine writers, artists and intellectuals came and went, leaving little trace. It was an open, informal arrangement, with no dogma and no membership cards.

Visiting Spanish writers and artists not infrequently found their way to the gathering. There were 'honorary members', such as Manuel de Falla and Fernando de los Ríos, who joined the group from time to time. And foreign writers, artists and musicians who, passing through the town, were adopted and taken on privileged tours of secret Granada. Among the latter were H. G. Wells, Rudyard Kipling, Wanda Landowska, Artur Rubinstein and the Swedish Hispanist Carl Sam Osberg, who, until he happened to chance on the *Rinconcillo*, had wandered around Granada like a lost soul.[26] One day a young Japanese diplomat, Nakayama Koichi, turned up, and José Mora Guarnido has recalled that the *rinconcillistas* pestered the poor lad mercilessly with questions about the sexual mores of his compatriots, finding him woefully under-informed on the subject. The *Rinconcillo* had its Englishman, too, a student called Charles Montague Evans who spent several months in Granada in 1922 and spoke, many years later, of those impassioned late-night discussions in the 'corner' of the Café Alameda.[27]

One of the favourite activities of the *Rinconcillo* was the fixing of commemorative plaques to the walls of houses where famous artists and writers, Granadine or otherwise, had lived. Thus were honoured Théophile Gautier, Isaac Albéniz, Glinka and the seventeenth-century local poet Pedro Soto de Rojas.[28] The members were not above concocting the occasional hoax, and in this line their finest achievement was the creation of an apocryphal poet, Isidoro Capdepón Fernández, in whose person were fused all those characteristics of the Granadine artistic stereotypes that the friends most deplored. This fictional Capdepón had emigrated as a young man to South America, where he achieved some celebrity, returning in ripe old age to his native Granada. There, in a style redolent of nineteenth-century bombast, he continued to write verse, some of which the *rinconcillistas* succeeded in placing, as authentic, in the local press. Capdepón's fame eventually spread to Madrid where, participating in the propagation of the amusing deception, Melchor Fernández Almagro and others published articles on the bard in respectable journals, even suggesting that he should be elected to the Royal Academy. Lorca took part in the composition of Capdepón's effusions, several of which are perfect gems of parody.[29]

The average date of birth of the seventeen most regular members of the *Rinconcillo* was approximately 1893, and for Lorca the support and encouragement of these companions, in the main slightly older than himself, proved vital. The poet's life and work would have been very different had he not coincided in Granada with such an intelligent, creative and unconventional group.

5
Juvenilia

In the spring and summer of 1917 Lorca accompanied Martín Domínguez Berrueta on two more study trips. The first was a repeat visit to Baeza, where they met Antonio Machado again and Federico became friends with a talented young pianist, María del Reposo Urquía, daughter of the principal of the local Institute of Secondary Education. The summer trip, as usual, was longer, and based this time on Burgos. It began on 15 July. After three weeks the rest of the party returned to Granada while Federico, perhaps because his parents were better off than those of his companions, stayed on for an extra month alone with Don Martín.[1]

The seven weeks spent in Burgos made a lasting impression on Lorca. One of the most interesting visits was to the Royal Monastery of Las Huelgas, on the outskirts of the city, founded by Alfonso VIII of Castile, the king remembered for a resounding victory over the Moors at the battle of Las Navas de Tolosa in 1212. Both Federico and his companion Luis Mariscal commented on this visit in the local press, and it is noticeable that, while the latter concentrated on the historical aspects of the venerable pile, Lorca was more interested in the motives that might have induced the present incumbents of Las Huelgas to renounce the world and its ways. He had no doubt, he wrote, that emotional conflicts were at the heart of the nuns' abnegation, nor that the monastic life represents a rejection of God's gifts of life and love. The article must have been found offensive by some of the readers of *El Diario de Burgos*.[2]

The group's visit to the Benedictine monastery of Santo Domingo de Silos and the Charterhouse of Miraflores confirmed Lorca in his analysis of the monastic rejection of the world, and in *Impressions and Landscapes* he recounted a poignant scene which he claimed had occurred there. Among the various bizarre personages living in the abbey was a monk who had entered the order in middle age to atone, it was hinted darkly, for a particularly disordered life. One afternoon, tired of the Gregorian chant for which the monastery is renowned, Federico climbed up to the organ and began to play the opening bars of the *Allegretto* of Beethoven's Seventh Symphony. Hardly had he begun when the monk in question burst in. 'Don't stop! Don't stop!' he begged. But Lorca could only remember a little more, and the instrument fell silent. The monk, as if in a trance, was staring into the far distance with eyes that expressed, wrote the poet, 'all the bitterness of a spirit which had just awakened out of a fictitious dream'. Later, once he had regained his calm, the unfortunate man explained all: he had been a passionate lover of music, and, fearing that such an attachment was having a deleterious effect on his spiritual life, had decided to renounce it for ever. And where better than at Silos, with its spartan plainsong, to escape from the allurements of the goddess? But now this young musician from Granada had unwittingly reminded him of all that he had renounced![3] That the impromptu concert really took place there is no doubt (two of Lorca's companions later recalled that they were present in the church), and it seems that Lorca did not invent the rest.[4]

Alone with Berrueta in Burgos, Lorca published two more articles in the local press and announced that he was working on a book to be called *Caminatas románticas por la Vieja España* or *Romantic Wanderings in Old Spain*.[5]

One of the articles, 'Rules in Music', opens a window on to the workings of Lorca's mind at this time. In it he argued, with a vehemence worthy of Berrueta, that, in art, rules, while necessary for beginners, exist thereafter only for the mediocre. The true artist works by intuition, not by rule, and, so far as music is concerned, what a composer needs, after acquiring the rudiments, is an original imagination and a passionate heart. The only acceptable reaction to music, Lorca insisted, is to say, 'I like this' or 'I don't like that', never, 'This is good, that is bad.' He reminded his readers that Beethoven, in his day, had fallen foul of the self-appointed guardians of musical decorum, and finished with what was undoubtedly an allusion to his recent experience in the organ loft of Silos:

I know people who have given up listening to music because their feelings overwhelm them. An art capable of such an effect transcends such rules. The night has no rules, nor the day. But, of course, very few people will be affected so tragically by music . . . It is a vampire which slowly devours the brain and the heart.

Rebelliousness; a boundless confidence in his own view of music; a deep admiration for the Nicaraguan poet Rubén Darío and for the European avant-garde; sarcasm; humour; enthusiasm . . . this early article shows that the Lorca then staying with Berrueta in Burgos had few doubts about his own vocation as a true and revolutionary artist.[6]

Lorca was deeply in love at the time – or imagined that he was – with María Luisa Egea González, the daughter of a wealthy businessman from the village of Alomartes, not far from the Vega, whose brother, Juan de Dios Egea, was one of the members of the *Rinconcillo*. Four or five years older than Federico, the blonde María Luisa was an accomplished pianist and, according to Manuel Angeles Ortiz, extremely beautiful. Lorca's feelings for her, perhaps never declared, tormented him during his stay in Burgos, and he wrote about them in his letters to José Fernández-Montesinos, which apparently are not extant. From one of Montesinos's replies we know that Federico had told him that María Luisa was 'cold'. Montesinos, a consummate philanderer, wanted to know what the poet meant by 'cold'. He tried to console his friend, but not, apparently, with great success.[7] Lorenzo Martínez Fuset was also aware that Lorca was passing through a time of emotional upheaval and repeatedly begged him to clarify the enigmatic hints contained in his letters.[8]

When Lorca arrived back in Granada at the beginning of September, the *rinconcillistas* were amazed to discover that a change was fast taking place in the direction of his artistic vocation. No longer exclusively the musician of the group, Federico was working feverishly on a book of impressions of Castile as well as writing poetry, prose pieces of a metaphysical cast and even little plays. Evidently something extraordinary was happening.[9]

During the visit to the Charterhouse of Miraflores in Burgos, Federico, who was appalled by the asceticism and, as he saw it, hypocrisy of the Carthusian rule, had greatly admired the celebrated head of St Bruno by the seventeenth-century Portuguese sculptor Manuel Pereira. Some weeks later Berrueta published in *La Esfera*, a leading high-quality Madrid art magazine, a rapturous article on the sculpture,[10] while at the same time Lorca wrote for inclusion in his book on Old Castile a similarly eulogistic piece on the work, which he now read to the *Rinconcillo*. The reaction of the latter was largely hostile. Berrueta was anathema to the group, who considered him bombastic, pedantic and uncritical – in short, something of a fake – and believed that Federico had fallen far too much under his influence. José Mora Guarnido was particularly outspoken. Federico's pages on the sculpture, he said, were little more than a rehash of Berrueta's opinions. They lacked authenticity. They should be scrapped. Lorca, stunned by this reaction, thought again. The passage was rewritten, and when *Impressions and Landscapes* appeared the following spring the section on Pereira's St Bruno, far from a paean, constituted a vicious attack with, to make matters worse, a veiled allusion to Berrueta's 'ecstatic' response to the work. Don Martín was dismayed and deeply hurt by this betrayal.[11]

Contrary to his later practice Lorca dated his early literary efforts with precision, and these give us an almost day-to-day insight into his state of mind: a state of mind whose components are a growing rebellion against the Catholic religion in which the poet had been reared, and an all-pervasive sexual malaise.

The rebellion was almost Swinburnian in its intensity. Lorca, while retaining his admiration for Jesus, had come to feel a passionate hatred for the Christian God. In a poem dated 17 December 1917 we find the following lines, which express the mood of the moment:

> Este es reino del dolor
> Y no existe el Dios de Amor
> Que nos pintan.
> Contemplando los cielos
> Se adivina el imposible de Dios
> Dios que es eterno mudo
> Dios inconsciente, rudo,
> El abismo.
> El Dios que dice el Cristo
> Que habita en los cielos es injusto.
> Truena sobre los buenos
> Truena sobre los malos
> Inclemente . . .*12

In one of the prose pieces Lorca called *Místicas*, in which he expressed his religious doubts, the poet asked himself this autumn of 1917: 'Might it not be that we were made to serve as playthings for the Most High?' He finds the evidence of the Old Testament overwhelming in this respect, continuing: 'It seems that we are destined to be moved by the hands of the inflexible God who keeps us for his amusement.'13 Man is under the constant threat of punishment and, as a result, whatever love he may pretend to feel for his Father in Heaven is likely to be a disguise for fear. The young Lorca cannot forgive this God for having created a world in which suffering is the norm. Again and again throughout the juvenilia – verse and prose –

---

* This is the kingdom of sorrow
And the God of Love they paint for us
Does not exist.
Contemplating the sky
We guess the impossibility of God,
God the eternally mute,
God the unfeeling, the uncouth,
The abyss.
The God who Christ says lives
In Heaven is unjust.
He thunders on the good
He thunders on the bad
Harshly . . .

the poet repeats the same insistent questions concerning the nature of Man's relation to the Christian God. And again and again he voices his protest against the Tyrant, who is an enemy not only of mankind but of his own Son,[14] a son who for Lorca is the supreme expression of charity, of pity and compassion:

He was love itself. He preached the sweetness of tears and the joy of brotherhood . . . He condemned hatred and lies. He spread His melancholy – the melancholy of a failure – across the mountains, the woods and the beaches. He was lily and lake, immensity and wild flower. He was the heart and the wonder of the unknown. He saw and He wept. His eyes looked and convinced. He used His long journeys through the countryside to urge all creatures to love each other. He explained about equality and became incensed about poverty . . . for that reason the humble loved Him . . . and then He moved on.[15]

The writings of this period show that Lorca now believed that Christ's example and sacrifice had been useless. And that, if mankind does not wish to heed His message of love, a large share of the blame must fall on the shoulders of the 'official' representatives of the Saviour on earth, starting with the Pope, for whom the young poet feels the utmost scorn. The churchmen constantly betray Christ, we are told repeatedly, and Lorca's hatred of these (as he saw them) celibate hypocrites was now virulent. Quite clearly he felt that they had blighted his own life. 'The world that has been educated by you', he wrote that autumn, at the end of a typical anticlerical tirade, 'is an imbecilic world with clipped wings.'[16]

Lorca had also come to loathe militarism at a time when the Spanish press was full of accounts of the bloody fighting on the other side of the Pyrenees and the lives of Spain's soldiers were being squandered in the futile, never-ending war in the Moroccan protectorate against the forces of Abd el-Krim. In an essay entitled 'Patriotism', dated 27 October 1917, he lashes out against those responsible for beguiling children with false notions of patriotism incompatible with charity. The alliance of sword and cross, so prevalent in Spain's history, particularly appals the poet, and in the adulation of the national flag he finds a blatant negation of the God of Love. Worst of all, the name of Jesus, used for spurious nationalistic purposes, has given rise to innumerable atrocities. 'To hide her evils Spain chose Christ Crucified,' Lorca complains. 'That is why we can still see His defiled image in every corner. In the name of Jesus was consummated the terrible crime of the Inquisition. In the name of Jesus science was banished from our land.' To all this the only solution lies in a new form of education, whose fundamental purpose will be to liberate the young from fear and hatred. Here we sense the strong influence of Martín Domínguez Berrueta and Fernando de los Ríos:

We ought, in the schools, to produce citizens who love peace and know the message of the Gospel. We ought to produce men who are unaware of the existence of the wretched Ferdinand the Holy, of Isabella the Fanatic, of Charles the Inflexible, of Peters and Philips and Alfonsos and Ramiros. We ought to inspire our children by telling them that Spain was the cradle of Theresa the Admirable, of John the Marvellous,* of Don Quixote the Divine and of our many poets [. . .] We must extirpate false patriotic ideas from the minds of our youth, just as we must extirpate from those of the false patriots, out of love for our mothers, the concept of the nation as Mother. How could she ever be our mother if, as you tell us, we have to give the last drop of our blood for her! [. . .] We must be the sons of the true fatherland: the fatherland of love and equality.[17]

Lorca's early work has an evangelical root, revealing a strong tendency on the part of the young poet to identify with Christ. This aspect of the juvenilia comes out strongly in the unfinished play *Christ. A Religious Tragedy*, whose first draft probably belongs to the period 1917–18. In this work Jesus is nineteen – Lorca's age when he wrote it; Christ's evangelical vocation, which conflicts with his family's wishes for his future, reminds us that the poet's parents insisted on his acquiring a university degree, despite his artistic calling; Jesus, as a boy, 'would slowly follow an ant', and we recall Lorca's claim that, as a child in Fuente Vaqueros, he often talked to these insects; Christ, like the child Federico, spends hours and hours chatting to people in the village, and often his family has to go and look for him; Jesus declares that his soul is 'sad from birth', that he is 'made for suffering', and these are the sentiments that recur in many of Lorca's early poems; and, perhaps especially, this Jesus, like Federico, is sunk in a sea of erotic despair.

The most moving moment in the unfinished tragedy occurs when Jesus tries to explain to his mother his inability to reciprocate Esther's feelings. Try as he will he cannot react erotically to her. Jesus and Esther are prototypes of other couples in Lorca's work who are trapped in a prison of frustrated desire. But only in *Christ* do we witness the sorrow of a mother who realizes that her son is not as other men. 'Oh God, take from my son the infinite bitterness lodged in his heart!' exclaims Mary. And we wonder if the adolescent Lorca did not have his own mother in mind as he was writing; for Doña Vicenta, inevitably, must have already realized that her elder son, for all his talents, charm and popularity, was, deep down, a tormented soul.[18]

The Lorca who appears in these first poems is obsessed by sexual love. Both the compositions written in the first person – by far the majority – and those in which the poet projects his feelings on to other personages, treat

---

* The reference is to St Theresa of Avila (1515–82) and St John of God (1495–1550), founder of the Order of Charity.

insistently of the 'sex we search for in vain', of 'anxious urges to embrace', of flesh and mouths 'thirsty for love', of 'a hungry yearning for kisses of fire'. Lorca and the figures who populate his early poems seem to have only one concern: to experience Dionysian love.

The search is accompanied by an ever-present sense of sin. Lorca may express in these poems his vehement rejection of Catholic sexual morality, but the system is built into the very fibre of his being and, try as he will to be free, he is a victim of an inner enemy that makes the achievement of a relaxed attitude to sex impossible – an attitude, moreover, that it was difficult for everyone to achieve at the time, and even more so in a city as reactionary as Granada. It was little wonder that the dream of escaping to France, so free in its love-making, occupied the minds of many young Spaniards, including Lorca, during the twenties and thirties.

There was one great consolation: to have found in the work of the Nicaraguan poet Rubén Darío a sensibility strongly akin to his own – so akin, in fact, that Darío's was to prove the major literary influence on the young Lorca during this formative period. With its incorporation of French *fin-de-siècle* themes and innovations, its refined eroticism, its musicality and its exoticism, Darío's work came as a breath of spring air to a Spain where poetry had become stiflingly trite and academic. His revolution, known as *modernismo*, was compared by Lorca's friend and fellow poet Dámaso Alonso to that effected in the sixteenth century by Garcilaso de la Vega, who incorporated Italian Renaissance modes of feeling and expression into his poetry; and other poets of Lorca's generation attested similarly to the influence of Darío on their lives and work. For these young men, in fact, it was impossible to ignore Darío, however strongly they might react later against the Central American's verbal excesses and gaudy imagery.[19]

Lorca knew his Darío well, and referred to him often in the poems and other writings of this period, admiring his scorn for the philistines, disregard for conventional notions of poetic decorum and refusal to be classified as belonging to this or that 'school'. Faith in art; individualism; allegiance, among the gods, to Dionysus; the sense of the deep mystery of life; intellectual curiosity; astonishing creative energy; a capacity for wonder and admiration; pantheistic fervour; sincerity; terror of death; underlying Christian unease: all these qualities awoke a deep response in the young Lorca and spoke powerfully to his condition. It is not strange, therefore, that everywhere in this early work the presence of Rubén is palpable.

Darío's attempt to effect a synthesis of the Apollonian and the Dionysian, the pagan and the Christian, had a particular relevance for Federico, struggling as he was against the shame and guilt generated by a religion that rejected the flesh. When, therefore, in the prologue to *Impressions and*

Landscapes, the *granadino* insisted on the need to be both 'religious and profane', to 'combine the mysticism of a severe Gothic cathedral with the wonder of pagan Greece', we can be sure that he had in mind Darío's poem 'Divina Psiquis', in which the poet likens his soul to a butterfly flitting between pagan ruins and a cathedral.[20] Moreover, Darío's deep admiration for Paul Verlaine, whom he had met briefly in Paris in 1893, undoubtedly strengthened that felt by Lorca for 'le pauvre Lélian'. In Federico's early work there are numerous allusions to Verlaine, of whom Darío observed in his book *Los raros* – studies of nineteenth-century 'eccentric' writers, in the main French – that 'rarely has a human brain been bitten with more violence and venom by the serpent of sex'.[21] Lorca knew this book by Darío well and it must have drawn him even closer to the French poet.[22]

For Lorca, as for Darío, ancient Greece stands for an attitude to life far superior to that of conventional Christianity, principally because the Greek deities, unlike the Christian God, not only do not condemn eroticism but revel in it themselves. Moreover, Lorca cannot have been indifferent to the notion of ancient Greece as a haven of homosexual freedom. In 'La religión del porvenir' ('The Religion of the Future'), dated 10 January 1918, the poet, showing that he has been delving enthusiastically into Hesiod's *Theogony*, praises the 'celestial religion' of 'warm Greece' and looks forward to the day of its resurrection, when:

> Las estatuas de nuestros jardines
> Vida tendrán
> Los Apolos entre los jazmines
> Suspirarán.
>
> En los parques dulces y brumosos
> Sensualidad
> Pondrá en los labios de los esposos
> Diafanidad.*[23]

From the end of 1917, poems with the twin themes of lost love and despair of achieving future amorous fulfilment become more and more frequent. They are weak, almost self-pitying effusions, to be sure, in a *modernista* register that the poet soon abandoned, but they have, undoubtedly, a basis

---

* The statues in our gardens
Will come to life,
The Apollos among the jasmine
Will sigh.

In the parks, sweet and misty,
Sensuality
Will place on the lips of husbands and wives
Diaphanousness.

in lived experience. In one poem, 'Romanzas con palabras' ('Romances with Words'), dated 31 March 1918, Lorca apostrophizes his 'tragic wedding, with no bride and no altar', and proceeds to evoke the separation or rejection that has reduced him to absolute hopelessness:

> Un velo blanco de desposada
> Cubre a la novia que nunca veré
> Ella era dulce y vaga y sentida
> Era sagrario donde iba mi vida
> Pero una noche callada y dormida
> Como princesa de cuento se fue
> Yo fui sombra de amor doloroso
> Juglar extraño de un extraño amor [. . .]
> Y fui por los caminos
> Cansado y doloroso
> Juglar extraño de un extraño amor
> En busca de la novia
> Que se fue aquella noche
> En que apuré mi cáliz de dolor . . .*24

Several of the poems of this period hint that, if the young Lorca felt that he would never again find love, this was largely due to his conviction that he was unattractive to women. In 'Carnaval' (February 1918), for example, we are assured that the 'roses that smell of Woman' wither in his lachrymose presence.25 In 'Canción menor' (December 1918), the poet – 'grotesque and without a solution' – compares himself to two famous frustrated lovers: Don Quixote and Cyrano de Bergerac.26 And in composition after composition we find him expressing feelings of clumsiness, impotence and absolute discouragement in regard to his chances of ever achieving erotic fulfilment. These feelings are early projected on to other personages. In the poem 'Viejo sátiro' ('Old Satyr'), dated 25 December 1917, appears a 'little old bent man

> *   A white bride's veil
>   Covers the fiancée I'll never behold.
>   She was sweet and vague and sensitive,
>   The sacrament house of my life,
>   But one night, when all was silent and asleep,
>   Like a fairy-tale princess she left for ever.
>   I was a shadow of sorrowful love,
>   A strange minstrel singing a strange love [. . .]
>   And I went down the roads,
>   Tired and sorrowful,
>   A strange minstrel singing a strange love
>   In search of the fiancée
>   Who left that night
>   When I drained dry my cup of sorrow . . .

(The manuscript is unpunctuated. Commas and full-stops have been added for the sake of clarity, as in the English versions of the other poems quoted in this chapter.)

with silver hair' who, despite his advanced years, will continue to dream about 'unbridled sex' until, 'an old satyr in a threadbare mackintosh' (an allusion, surely, to Verlaine), he will succumb in some dingy hospital.[27] Lorca paints a similarly dismal picture of Beethoven.[28] Pierrot, abandoned by Columbine, appears in several poems, at times explicitly identified with the poet.[29] In another poem, 'Elegía' (December 1918), Lorca augurs a loveless life for an unmarried Granadine beauty, Maravillas Pareja, spied on by him and his friends.[30] Joan the Mad, to whom the poet also addresses an elegy, is a victim of her unrequited passion for her husband, Philippe le Bel.[31] These and other similar figures who appear in the juvenilia are the prototypes of a long series of characters for whom, in Lorca's mature work, the search for love, always fruitless, constitutes the principal driving force in their lives.

Lorca's production at this time, then, reveals a tremendous conflict raging in his psyche between God and Dionysus, between the urges and promptings of the libido and the repressive forces deriving from the Catholic attitude to sexuality. It strongly suggests, too, that, somewhere along the line, Federico tasted, precociously, the bitter pill of unhappy love. An unhappy love first experienced, it seems, during his childhood and later in his thwarted relationship with the 'cold' María Luisa Egea González.

Don Federico García Rodríguez was perplexed and disturbed by the sudden flowering of his eldest son's literary vocation. Moreover, it was clear that he was going to be expected to foot the printer's bill for *Impressions and Landscapes*, which was ready to go to press in early 1918. Did the book deserve to be published? Was its prose any good? The landowner decided to consult various people qualified to pass judgement, among them Luis Seco de Lucena, editor of *El Defensor de Granada*; a cultured businessman, Miguel Cerón Rubio, who admired Federico, and Andrés Segovia, then twenty-three and already a much respected figure in the town. After a careful perusal of the manuscript, the three were unanimous that the book should be allowed to appear. 'We liked it,' Andrés Segovia recalled many years later. 'We spoke to Don Federico at once and told him that, in our view, his son had a great talent as a writer and a splendid future.' Federico García Rodríguez accepted the ruling of his triumvirate, and generously undertook to finance the book.[32]

On 17 March 1917, with *Impressions and Landscapes* at the printer's, Lorca gave a reading from the work in the Arts Club. The evening was a great success, to judge from the notices that appeared in the local press, particularly in the *Noticiero Granadino*:

Federico García Lorca has as well as his natural abilities a solid cultural grounding and other qualities which assure him an enviable position in the Republic of Letters. Letters only? No. Listen to him play the piano, particularly the most select classical pieces, and you will appreciate in him not only someone with an excellent technique, but the Romantic, the man whose soul vibrates to the rhythm of the sweet strains of music.

Listen to his views on whatever painting you wish, in whatever style: you will be forced to concede that here is a conscientious critic, and in his face you will see reflected the depth of his feelings. To hear him talk about architecture is to include him at once in the band of 'true artists'.[33]

José Murciano, a friend of Federico's interested in Oriental mysticism, also published an account of the evening, underlining the poet's ability as a performer. 'Throughout the time the author's clear and harmonious voice filled the room,' he wrote, 'we might say that he played with the audience, sometimes moving it intensely with his descriptions of sadness or misery; sometimes with a humour full of charm and perspicacity. We didn't know whether to laugh or to cry.' Murciano made the point at the end of his article that soon Lorca would escape from his Granadine cage. The town, he assured his readers, was too small and constricting to hold for long such a rare artist. He was right.[34]

Impressions and Landscapes went on sale in the second week of April 1918. To the Castilian evocations, which form the core of the book, and those of Baeza, Lorca had added some impressionistic sketches of Granada, some meditations on gardens and a medley of pages on various topics. The book was reviewed in the local newspapers, and it was generally agreed that a talented new writer had appeared on the scene.[35] *Impressions and Landscapes* could not hope for any success nationally, however, and Lorca foresaw in his prologue that, after a few days in the windows of local bookshops, it would disappear from sight for ever, the victim of the most absolute public indifference. The prognostication was right on target, and not long after publication the poet withdrew the book, the hundreds of unsold copies being stacked in the family attic.[36] Lorca said in Cuba in 1930 that the book had been reviewed by Miguel de Unamuno. 'Nobody taught me so much about the art of writing as Unamuno did on that occasion,' the poet claimed. But the philosopher was an incredibly prolific generator of articles – they appeared in dozens of newspapers and magazines, Spanish and foreign – and the piece has not yet been traced.[37]

When Berrueta and Lorca's companions on the study trips saw *Impressions and Landscapes* their reaction was, first, one of amazement, then of outrage. Lorca had not invited Berrueta to contribute a prologue to the book, as had originally been announced; in the text there was no indication whatsoever of the author's debt to the professor; the pages on Pereira's head of St Bruno were profoundly hypocritical; the work was effusively dedicated to Lorca's old piano teacher, Antonio Segura Mesa, not to Berrueta; and, as a final insult, the latter was mentioned only at the very end of the book, in an appended dedication that read: 'To my dear teacher Don Martín Domínguez Berrueta and to my dear companions who accompanied me on my trips'. The latters' names followed. One of them, Ricardo Gómez Ortega, rounded furiously on Lorca for what he considered the poet's appalling behaviour towards Berrueta, insisting moreover that it wasn't that *they* and Don Martín had accompanied Lorca, as the note implied, but that *he* had accompanied *them*.[38]

Shortly after the publication of the book, Federico, with a further display of insensitivity, took Berrueta a signed copy and a few days later, as a result of some slighting allusion to the fledgling writer's relationship with the professor, that appeared in the newspaper *La Publicidad*, came the final rupture. Berrueta, cut to the quick, returned his copy of the book, and explained in a hurt letter of 3 May 1918 that, in view of Federico's lack of vigorous reaction to the comments in *La Publicidad*, he had no option but to end their friendship.[39]

The two never talked again and even the relations existing between the poet's family and the Berruetas, until then excellent, were broken off. It was a highly unpleasant situation, and Don Martín never recovered from the bitter disappointment that Lorca's rejection and betrayal had occasioned him.[40]

But if *Impressions and Landscapes* estranged Lorca and Berrueta, it also made new friends for the author. One of the most interesting of these was a young Andalusian poet called Adriano del Valle y Rossi, with whom Federico's Uncle Enrique had become acquainted recently in Seville. Valle had read *Impressions and Landscapes* and, discovering that Enrique García Rodríguez was the author's uncle, had begged the latter to put them in touch. This Enrique willingly did, and the result was a relationship important at this time in Federico's life. Valle, although already bald when he and Lorca began to correspond, was the same age as the *granadino*, twenty, and a fervent disciple of Rubén Darío. Moreover Federico had some acquaintance with his work, for Valle was a regular contributor to various small magazines in Granada. In his first letter (May 1918) Adriano confessed himself an ardent francophile, asked Federico whether he supported the Germans or the French in the war and poured lavish praise on *Impressions and Landscapes*, in which, he said, he had sensed the presence of Rubén Darío, which was undoubtedly true.[41]

Lorca replied immediately, and the letter deserves to be quoted almost in full, despite the difficulty of rendering it into readable English – it is couched in deliberately *modernista* style – because it gives us an important glimpse into the poet's feelings at this time and reveals that he was already acutely aware of his sexual differentness and the discrepancy between his private and public selves:

Today. May in time, October inside my head

PEACE

Friend: I was delighted to receive your letter, and you can be sure that it gave me moments of deep satisfaction. I am not now introducing myself to you as anything other than a companion (a sad companion, to tell the truth) who has read some of your delightful poems. I am a simple youth, passionate and silent, who almost, almost like the wonderful Verlaine, carries inside him a lily that cannot be watered and who presents to the imbecilic eyes of those who look at him the image of a deep red rose with the sexual tinge of an April peony, which isn't the truth of my feelings. I appear to people (those things called people, as [*unreadable word*] says) like an Oriental drunk on the full moon and feel, in point of fact, like a Chopinesque Gerineldo* in an odious and despicable time of Kaisers and La Ciervas† (I hope they all drop dead!). My physical appearance and poems give the impression of tremendous passion, yet in the depths of my being there is a powerful desire to be a little child, very humble and very retiring. Ahead I see many problems, many eyes which will imprison me, many difficulties in the battle between heart and head, and my emotional flowering wants to take possession of its sunlit garden and I make an effort to enjoy playing with the paper dolls and toys of my childhood, and sometimes I lie on my back on the floor and play *comadricas* with my baby sister (I adore her)‡ . . . but the phantom that lives within us and which hates us pushes me forward. And we have to carry on because it's our lot to grow old and die, but I don't want to listen to the phantom promptings . . . and yet every day that passes I have another doubt and another cause for dejection, the dejection of the enigma of oneself! We all have a desire not to suffer and to be good, Adriano, but which the strength of temptation and the overwhelming tragedy of our physiology take it upon themselves to destroy . . . I believe that we are surrounded by the souls of those who died and that it is they who prompt our sorrows and they who propel us into the kingdom inhabited by the blue-and-white virgin called Melancholy – that is to say, the kingdom of poetry (I can conceive of no poetry other than the lyrical). I entered it a long time ago now – I was ten and I fell in love. Then I became totally engulfed on taking up the unique religion of Music and clothing myself in the mantles of passion that She bestows on those who love her. Then I entered the kingdom of Poetry and was anointed with love for all things. I am a decent fellow, in sum, and open my heart to everyone . . . Naturally, I am a great admirer of France and hate militarism with all my soul, but really all I feel is a vast yearning for Humanity. Why struggle against the flesh while the fearsome problem of the soul is uppermost? I love Venus passionately, but more, much more, the question 'And the heart?' . . . and, especially,

---

* See footnote p. 31.

† An allusion to Juan de la Cierva, the conservative politician, who was considered responsible, as Minister of the Interior, for the brutal repression of the Barcelona riots of 1909.

‡ A game in which the gossip of neighbours was imitated. Isabel García Lorca, as has been pointed out, was born in 1909.

I view myself as did the curious and authentic Peer Gynt with the button-maker . . . I want to be my true self.

As regards the things I am writing, well, all I can tell you is that I am working very hard, writing lots of poetry and composing music. I have three books ready (two of them of poems) and hope to continue working. As for music, I am devoting myself at the moment to copying down the splendid inner polyphony of the folk music of Granada.

As regards my first book, thanks for your praise. If you want to review it you don't have to ask me, because once the book is out there in the world it no longer belongs to me but to everyone . . . In my book (which is very bad) there is only the deep feeling that constantly wells up from my sadness and the sorrow I feel on observing Nature . . . I don't know if you'll understand the extent to which my heart is sincere, passionate and humble. It's enough for me to know that your spirit is that of a poet. And if you should fail to see the pale light of my soul that I'm putting in this letter, or if you should laugh, well, all I'd be left with would be the intimate bitterness of having showed part of my inner reliquary to another soul that shut its eyes and smiled sceptically. Naturally I rule this out.

I am a great Romantic, and that's my principal pride. In a century of Zeppelins and idiotic deaths, I weep at my piano dreaming of the Handelian mist. I write verses very much my own, praising equally Christ and Buddha, Muhammad and Pan. For lyre I have my piano and, instead of ink, the sweat of desire, the yellow pollen of my inner lily and my great love. We must kill the 'foppish bourgeois pups' and wipe the laughter off the mouths of those who love Harmony. We must love the moon on the lake of our souls and fashion our religious meditations over the magnificent abyss of flaring sunsets . . . because colour is the eye's music . . . Here I shall put down my pen to climb into the merciful ship of Sleep. Now you know what I'm like in part at least of my life . . . [42]

Despite its bombast and self-conscious appropriation of *modernista* idiom, this is one of the most revealing letters by the young Lorca that has been preserved, and shows that by May 1918 he was fully aware of being sexually 'different' (red rose outside, lily 'impossible to water' within). The allusion to Paul Verlaine, moreover, may suggest that at this time the poet diagnosed his condition as a form of bisexuality, for it is difficult to imagine that from Francisco Soriano Lapresa, such an authority on contemporary French poetry and things decadent, Federico had not informed himself well about Verlaine's ambivalent love life and his passionate relationships with Arthur Rimbaud and various women.

In Baeza, the publication of *Impressions and Landscapes* had been awaited with great impatience both by María del Reposo Urquía, to whom Lorca had dedicated the chapter on the town, and Lorenzo Martínez Fuset. A letter from the latter (9 May 1918) shows that Federico was considering the possibility at this time of taking copies there personally for Antonio Machado and his friends. 'I have spoken to Machado,' wrote Fuset. 'His modesty knows no bounds, and when I showed him your letter he said immediately that he could never be the reason for such a trip; none the less, that he'd be delighted to see you. He asked me to get you to send him a copy.' Machado had told Fuset that, in his opinion, Lorca should devote himself fully to music, for which he had obvious talent, give up the study of law ('to be an artist is to be unsystematic') and that Granada was too small for him. Federico must have been flattered that the great poet was taking an interest in his future.[43]

A few days later Lorca confessed to Lorenzo that he was in love, without telling him the name of the girl. When Fuset received his inscribed copy of *Impressions and Landscapes*, however, and saw the printed dedication to María Luisa Egea, he could no longer entertain any doubts as to the identity of the lady in question. 'María Luisa!' he exclaimed. 'I can almost see her in her little room in the Gran Vía.'[44] But the 'cold' María Luisa did not reciprocate the poet's feelings, despite the dedication, and shortly afterwards moved to Madrid.[45]

This summer of 1918 Lorca got to know another Granadine beauty, Emilia Llanos Medina, a forceful brunette ten years older than himself. The meeting occurred (Emilia recorded the date in her diary) on 18 August, shortly after Federico returned to town following a spell in Asquerosa. The personality and physical attractions of Emilia made an immediate impact on the poet, and ten days later he took her a copy of *Impressions and Landscapes* with a suitably overblown inscription. It was the beginning of a close friendship that continued until the death of the poet, and which, after this, was gradually transformed, in Emilia's mind, into the great lost love of her life.[46]

In the early days of their relationship, the two met almost daily. On 4 September 1918 Federico gave Emilia a present of a copy of *Hamlet*, a play that obsessed him at the time, and over the following weeks lent or gave her books by Tagore, Oscar Wilde, Maeterlinck, Ibsen (Emilia remembered that Lorca liked especially *The Wild Duck*), Juan Ramón Jiménez's famous book about his donkey, *Platero and I*, and Edgar Rod's novel *The Silence*, whose theme, significantly, is the love that cannot declare itself, the unknown passion of a man who suffers without speaking.[47]

Emilia lived with her sister near the Alhambra, in a house with a charming garden full of cats and flowers. Federico was delighted with his new friend's servant, an extremely vivacious and talkative country girl called Dolores Cebrián, whose anecdotes and earthy language never failed to make him roar with laughter. Many of these expressions turned up later in *The Shoemaker's Prodigious Wife*, as Dolores was proud to proclaim.[48]

Lorca's university career was at a standstill at this time, and matters were not helped by his rupture with Berrueta. In fact the poet sat no examinations, in either Faculty, in 1917–18 and 1918–19, and probably hardly attended lectures.[49] Only when Don Martín died in the summer of 1920 would Federico decide to please his father and to renew his 'shipwrecked arts course'.[50]

Lorca felt remorse over his behaviour towards Berrueta and, although he tended to blame José Mora Guarnido for what had happened, knew perfectly well that he himself had been the principal cause of that sad business. In later years he did his best to make amends, and was careful to acknowledge his debt to Don Martín – a debt that was, after all, very real. Berrueta's insistence on the individual response to works of art had found a very personal echo in the young poet, while his contagious enthusiasm and support had proved vital at a critical moment in Lorca's life, when, with his musical career frustrated, his literary vocation had begun to assert itself. The poet claimed in later years that the time he spent in Burgos with Berrueta had been decisive in shaping his future, and that in the old Castilian city he had found the 'narrow door' through which he had to pass in order to know himself as he was. There seems little reason why we should doubt his word.[51]

6

The Residencia de Estudiantes. Martínez Sierra

Une forte citadelle de l'humanisme espagnol, c'est la Residencia de Estudiantes.

Roger Martin du Gard[1]

It was time for the bird to fly from its cage, as José Murciano had predicted. Almost certainly through the influence of Fernando de los Ríos, Lorca's parents decided to allow Federico – who had been declared 'totally unfit' for military service because he presented 'light symptoms of spinal sclerosis' – to spend a year at Madrid's famous university hostel, the Residencia de Estudiantes, beginning that autumn. Accordingly, at the end of April or beginning of May 1919, Lorca arrived in the capital to arrange matters, armed with a letter of introduction from De los Ríos to the young warden, Alberto Jiménez Fraud, an Andalusian from Malaga.[2]

The Residencia was the spiritual offspring of the liberal Institución Libre de Enseñanza ('Free Teaching Institution'), already mentioned, which had been founded in 1876 by Francisco Giner de los Ríos. Alberto Jiménez Fraud had taught at the Institución Libre for three years, in the closest collaboration with Giner and the great scholar Manuel Bartolomé Cossío (whose daughter Natalia he was to marry), and been deeply affected by the spirit that pervaded that most admirable of schools. Giner's obsession with the intellectual, moral and material advancement of Spain, his humanity and his conviction that only the creation of a select minority of cultured men and women devoted to the betterment of the country could bring about a change in the latter's fortunes – this idealism exerted a profound influence on Jiménez Fraud, whose vocation as a teacher and guide to the young soon became manifest. Between 1907 and 1909 he spent several months in England, where he took a lively interest in the Oxbridge college system. And when, in 1910, Giner invited him to take charge of a small, experimental students' hall of residence to be set up in Madrid, he accepted the challenge with alacrity. He was then twenty-six.[3]

The Residencia de Estudiantes, as it was called, simply, in the laconic style of its begetters, opened that autumn in Fortuny Street, not far from the then northernmost reaches of the Paseo de la Castellana, the great avenue that cuts Madrid in two. It had only fifteen bedrooms and seventeen students, an inauspicious beginning to one of the most exciting educational experiments in the history of modern Spain. At the time there was nothing in the country corresponding to the British notion of a residential college or hall of residence. Students from the provinces who went up to Madrid University normally lived in digs, and such accommodation tended to be extremely unsatisfactory. The new hostel set out to correct some of these deficiencies: to provide comfortable lodgings and unofficial tutorial advice and to bring students into contact with persons from other disciplines, thereby broadening their outlook. Jiménez Fraud, like Giner, was convinced that the excessive specialization of university studies was detrimental to education in the broad sense, and all his life would labour to build bridges between the sciences and the humanities. From its earliest days the Residencia installed modest laboratories (research in Spain had reached an absolute nadir), and Jiménez Fraud selected the students carefully to ensure that there was always a balance between the 'two cultures'. Stress was laid on the importance of communal effort and personal responsibility; and a marked austerity was apparent in the running – and decoration – of the house. The warden and his collaborators felt themselves to be missionaries in the cause of a new Spain, and for twenty-seven years – until the Civil War brought the adventure to an end – the Residencia produced a constant stream of young men imbued with the ideals of its founders.[4]

From the outset Jiménez Fraud received the support of distinguished patrons. The young King Alfonso XIII (who had ascended the throne in 1902) visited it in 1911; Miguel de Unamuno came often; José Ortega y Gasset sat on the board, and the poet Juan Ramón Jiménez was a resident until his marriage in 1919. Very soon, as the demand for rooms rocketed, it became obvious that more spacious premises would have to be found – or built. In view of the spectacular success of the venture, and the certainty that expansion would continue, it was decided to take the latter course.

The site chosen was known as Los Altos del Hipódromo, a group of low hillocks situated to the right of what was then the northern end of the Paseo de la Castellana, and which later became the Plaza de San Juan de la Cruz. Here Madrid terminated and the countryside began. In the middle of the broad thoroughfare stood the equestrian statue of Isabel the Catholic (moved afterwards to the foot of the first hill), around which the number 8 tram circled before returning to the city centre. On the east side was the redbrick School for the Deaf and Dumb (today the Technical School of the Army) and, a little further on, where now rise the government buildings known as the New Ministries, begun under the Republic, stretched the sward of the racecourse.

On one of the hillocks had been constructed, in the nineteenth century, the Palace of Industry and the Fine Arts, now the National History Museum; while, behind this building, was the eminence known popularly as the Cerro del Viento ('Windy Hill'), to the east of which stretched the dry, open wastes of the Castilian plains. It was here that Jiménez Fraud and his collaborators decided to construct the new halls of residence. The site, almost in the open countryside, with stunning views, to the north, of the Sierra de Guadarrama, but only twenty minutes by tram from the centre of a Madrid which then had considerably less than a million inhabitants, was indeed ideal. 'When I saw it, now belonging to the Residencia,' wrote Jiménez Fraud years later, 'I felt certain that we had reached harbour.'[5]

The architect chosen to design the halls was Antonio Flórez, who had been a pupil at the Free Teaching Institution before continuing his studies in Rome. Flórez conceived a group of brick buildings in the style known as *neo-mudéjar*, inspired by that of the Moorish builders working under the Christians after 1492. The first two, absolutely identical, were erected side-by-side along an east–west axis. They were slim, three-storeyed constructions, with charming turrets, prominent wooden eaves and twenty-four double bedrooms with large windows facing south. There was a generous provision of showers and baths, and Flórez had done his calculations carefully to ensure that both buildings received a maximum of light throughout the year.[6] The third hall, lower than the first two, comprised fifty bedrooms, as well as the administrative nucleus of the hostel, the dining room and ample salon where, in the 1920s – the great days of the Residencia – numerous lectures and concerts were given, and the students rubbed shoulders with many of the most outstanding representatives of contemporary Spanish, American and European culture.

The first three buildings were completed in record time, and the new Residencia opened in 1915. The fourth and fifth, built, like the third, along a north–south axis, were the work of a different architect, Francisco Luque, and were completed the following year. They respected the style adopted by Flórez. The fourth, with its two handsome towers, was soon baptized 'The Transatlantic', from the wooden balustrade that runs the length of the façade at first-floor level and calls to mind, in effect, the railing of an ocean liner. In the basement and on the ground floor were installed the Residencia's laboratories, which became increasingly efficient under the direction of men such as Dr Juan Negrín, head of the General Physiology Laboratory, and the future Nobel Prize-winner for Medicine, Dr Severo Ochoa.[7]

The group of buildings had a sober beauty unmistakably reminiscent of Andalusia. Juan Ramón Jiménez participated actively in the planning of the gardens, in the choice of trees, bushes and flowers. Under the poet's guidance numerous poplars and irises were planted beside the little canal that ran through the premises in front of the buildings (now, alas, covered over) while, in the space between the first two halls, Juan Ramón put down oleanders (three red, one white), surrounding them with box hedges. The poet was delighted with the results of his efforts, and, imagining how a few years later the wind would rustle the leaves of his trees, renamed the site 'La Colina de los Chopos' or 'Poplar Hill'.[8]

The interiors of the buildings were austere, continuing the tradition of the original hostel. All the furniture was of pinewood (with the exception of the rather uncomfortable cane chairs), touches of colour being provided by reproductions of paintings, glazed tiles and Talavera pottery. The bedrooms had a slightly monastic air. And, of course, the place was kept spotless. In a country where floors have habitually been used as substitute dustbins, those of the 'Resi' (as the place was known familiarly) were sacrosanct, and Lorca was to recall the intense shame he felt when once Don Alberto saw him drop a cigarette end in a passageway. The warden, without saying a word, had bent down, picked up the butt and deposited it in an ashtray, while the poet looked on in agony.[9]

Once the five buildings were completed, the Residencia was able to accommodate 150 students, a figure that remained practically constant until 1936 and made it possible for all the occupants to know each other by name. It was a community of ideal proportions.[10]

The majority of the residents were students of medicine, attracted by the laboratories and the supplementary instruction provided in these. They were followed by the industrial engineers, whose School was situated in a wing of the nearby Natural History Museum. As for the accusation of social élitism sometimes levelled at the Residencia, it is true that the overwhelming majority of the students came, inevitably, from middle-class backgrounds – inevitably, because of the backwardness of Spanish education. The Board was acutely aware of this circumstance, however, and strove to make places available to the less privileged.[11]

One of Alberto Jiménez Fraud's principal endeavours was to persuade distinguished men and women to lecture to his students. From the moment the 'Resi' moved to its new buildings this activity increased notably. The complete list of the visitors to 'Poplar Hill' would occupy several paragraphs, the lecturers including H. G. Wells, G. K. Chesterton, Albert Einstein, Marie

Curie, Paul Valéry, Howard Carter, Le Corbusier, Sir Arthur Eddington, Louis Aragon, Sir Leonard Woolley, François Mauriac, Blaise Cendrars, Leo Frobenius, Paul Claudel, Georges Duhamel, Hilaire Belloc, Henri Bergson, John Maynard Keynes and General Bruce.

Music at the Residencia was of a high quality, too. Numerous distinguished musicians – composers and performers – were invited, among them Manuel de Falla, Andrés Segovia, Wanda Landowska, Ricardo Viñes, Darius Milhaud, Igor Stravinsky, Francis Poulenc and Maurice Ravel. In the salon were heard for the first time works by the new Spanish composers known as 'The Eight' (Salvador Bacarisse, Julián Bautista, Rosa García Ascot, Ernesto and Rodolfo Halffter, Juan José Mantecón, Gustavo Pittaluga and Fernando Remacha), while among the lecturers on musical topics were Adolfo Salazar, an outstanding music critic and talented composer who became a close friend of Lorca, and the future Professor of Spanish at Cambridge University, John Brande Trend.

Trend (1887–1958) was quite well known by 1920 in England as a musicologist – he contributed to *The Times, The Times Literary Supplement, Music and Letters* and the *Athenaeum* – and was also a fervent hispanophile, although not yet a professional hispanist. Shortish, prematurely thin on top, timid and amiable, with an engaging stutter that did not improve his Castilian, he wrote several books on things Spanish, the best of which is probably *The Origins of Modern Spain* (1934).

Trend was astonished and delighted by the atmosphere he found at the Residencia, and in his book *A Picture of Modern Spain, Men and Music* (1921) stressed the tremendous influence exerted on the thinking of Alberto Jiménez Fraud and his colleagues by English educational methods, particularly the tutorial system. 'Oxford and Cambridge in Madrid', Trend termed the experiment, and went on to say that the principal aim of the Residencia was 'to awaken curiosity – a faculty lacking in many Spaniards – to arouse a desire to learn and the power to form personal judgements instead of accepting what other people say'.[12]

In a country woefully short on modern libraries, the 'Resi' had an excellent one which, presided over by a portrait of Goethe, occupied the whole ground floor of the fifth pavilion and was constantly expanding. Trend had suffered at the hands of Spanish librarians, and a priest at the University of Seville had actually refused to allow him to see the catalogue. ' "See the catalogue!" he said, in a horror-struck voice; "see the *catalogue*"!' Here things were different, and the shy Englishman discovered that not only could the residents see the catalogue and browse, but sit and read in comfort until late at night and even take the books to their rooms.[13] There were numerous foreign journals and magazines.[14] And, perhaps most heartening of all, Trend also discovered that the Residencia itself published books, corresponding in a modest way to the university presses of Oxford and Cambridge.[15]

Not all was plain sailing, however, and the hostel had its detractors, who found the liberal, lay spirit that pervaded the house intolerable. 'In the Residencia there were Catholics and non-Catholics, and Don Alberto never permitted discussions on the subject,' recalled the historian Américo Castro. 'But there was no chapel, and this provoked extreme anger, because in Spain, apparently, it was not enough to be dignified and fully human, in any one of the innumerable varieties of these modes.'[16] General Miguel Primo de Rivera's right-wing coup in 1923 was to make things more difficult for the Residencia: the Board was sacked and replaced with men of a conservative cast of mind, some of them mortal enemies of everything the place stood for. But Alberto Jiménez Fraud had powerful friends in high places, and these helped to pour oil on the troubled waters so that, when the Republic arrived in 1931, the Residencia was still thriving.[17]

As the emblem of the hostel was adopted a drawing of the fifth-century BC Athenian sculpture known as *The Blond Athlete*, which represents the head of a handsome youth with curly hair. No doubt the work was felt by Don Alberto and his collaborators to express the ideal of the 'perfect citizen'. *Mens sana in corpore sano*, if not explicitly the motto of the house, was virtually so in practice. Football, tennis, running, sunbathing, hockey – there was an unmistakably sporty atmosphere about the Residencia inspired not a little by what Don Alberto had seen in England. And the vast quantities of tea consumed in the rooms (alcohol was forbidden) was another indication of British influence.

When Lorca arrived in Madrid that spring of 1919, installed himself in a cheap *pensión*, and visited the Residencia de Estudiantes for the first time, Juan Ramón Jiménez's dream of a few years earlier was beginning to take shape. The poplars were doing well, the bushes and plants maturing, and what had previously been a bare Castilian hillside was now an oasis of water, flowers and luxuriant verdure. The young poet was enchanted. As for his interview with Alberto Jiménez Fraud, the latter remembered years later the immediate impression made on him by the vehement, dark-eyed *granadino* with his lank hair and impeccable suit and tie. The poet was clearly a perfect candidate for a place at the Residencia, and a room was immediately guaranteed for the academic year starting the following autumn.[18]

The members of the *Rinconcillo* who had been impatiently awaiting Lorca's arrival in Madrid – José Mora Guarnido, Melchor Fernández Almagro, José Fernández-Montesinos and Miguel Pizarro – were delighted with the impact Federico made on their friends in the capital. Mora was present when Lorca gave a reading of his work in the Residencia. 'The minstrel's success was devastating,' he wrote.[19] Part of it was no doubt due to Lorca's skill at the keyboard, for it is difficult to believe that, on what were presumably several visits to the Residencia during his stay in the capital, the poet missed the opportunity to perform on the excellent Pleyel which occupied a corner of the lecture room.

Mora introduced Federico to his circle of friends at the Ateneo (Madrid's celebrated Arts Club) and to other young writers and poets – people such as the philologists Angel del Río and Amado Alonso and the poets Guillermo de Torre, Gerardo Diego, Pedro Salinas and José de Ciria y Escalante. These contacts must have proved highly stimulating, particularly, perhaps, the introduction to Torre, who, at the age of nineteen, was fast becoming the leader of a new avant-garde movement called *ultraísmo*, a derivative of the artistic innovations then taking place in Europe, especially in France. The gurus of the group, among Spanish writers, were the Seville polyglot and translator Rafael Cansinos Asséns (1883–1964), a relative of Rita Hayworth, and the younger Ramón Gómez de la Serna (1888–1963); while, outside, they admired people like Apollinaire, whose calligrammes were beginning to catch on in Spain, Pierre Reverdy, Jean Cocteau, Pablo Picasso, Juan Gris, Sergei Diaghilev (who had been in Spain with his Ballets Russes in 1916 and 1917), Emilio Marinetti – the Futurist Manifesto was much appreciated by the *ultraístas* – and the Chilean poet Vicente Huidobro, who had spent five months in Madrid in 1918 preaching the good news of Dada and Cubism. The *ultraístas* – whose manifesto, written by Torre, was published in 1920 – devoured the French literary magazines of the day, despised sentimentality and believed that the new art should express the spirit of an age represented by the Tour Eiffel, machines, skating rinks, dynamos, ragtime and foxtrots, fast motor cars, radio, aeroplanes, telegraphy, transatlantic steamers, photography – that sort of thing. Torre and his companions – among them the poets Eugenio Montes, Pedro Garfias, Isaac del Vando Villar, Humberto Rivas and the Argentinian Jorge Luis Borges, then living in Madrid – had taken to heart Gómez de la Serna's recommendation that the modern artist should hurl a stone at the eye of the moon (the moon as symbol of Romantic sentimentality); and, where literature was concerned, the revolution they called for, and sought to implement, was to be not just thematic but lexical and typographical. Conservatism was the only heresy detested by the iconoclastic band, and they were determined to ensure that Rubén Darío and the *modernistas* had had their day. Lorca did not get deeply involved in *ultra*, but there can be no doubt that this friendship with Torre and his group proved highly beneficial to his poetry which, from the moment he arrived in the capital, began to shed its long-winded exuberance, excessive subjectivity and *modernista* throwbacks.[20]

It is likely that, during this first visit to the Residencia, Lorca initiated at least two friendships that were to prove extremely rewarding: with José ('Pepín') Bello and the future film director Luis Buñuel, both of whom were from Aragon.

José Bello, born in 1904 in the town of Huesca, was the son of a well-known and prosperous engineer and one of the first students to stay at the Residencia, which he entered in 1915 (a certain number of rooms were reserved for those still completing their secondary education), four years before Lorca, staying until the end of the 1923–4 academic year.[21] All those who knew Pepín at the 'Resi' have spoken of his extraordinary charm, wit and inventiveness. 'Excellent fellow, unpredictable [. . .] a medical student who never passed an exam,' recalls Buñuel in his memoirs; 'neither painter nor poet, Pepín Bello was only this: our inseparable friend.'[22] Buñuel's comments were a bit unfair, for Bello did in fact pass some examinations, although he never finished his degree, and had an innate artistic flair which, because he was a born dilettante, he never bothered to develop. Like Yorick, Pepín could always be counted on to set the table in a roar, and was to become one of Lorca's closest, most stimulating and loyal friends.

Born in the village of Calanda in 1900, Buñuel had arrived at the Residencia in 1917, immediately after finishing his secondary education in Saragossa. His elderly father was relatively generous (he had made his fortune in Cuba), and Buñuel, the first of five children, was able to count fully on the indulgence of his adoring, and much younger mother, who catered to his every whim. The latter had experienced vast relief, after seeing the horrors of Madrid's boarding houses, on being directed to the hall of residence presided over by Alberto Jiménez Fraud: here, she had decided immediately, her darling boy would be in safe hands.[23]

Buñuel conformed more obviously than Bello to the notion other Spaniards have of the Aragonese – that is, he was aggressively tough, stubborn and self-reliant. He began his chequered academic career by enrolling in the Department of Agricultural Engineering at Madrid University, changing almost immediately to Industrial Engineering. This also failed to rouse his enthusiasm. Next came the Natural Sciences, and for a year he devoted himself to the study of Entomology. (Buñuel would always be fascinated by insects and small creatures: the ants and the death's-head moth in *Un Chien andalou* and the scorpion sequence at the beginning of *L'Age d'or* are but three examples.) Finally he switched to the Faculty of Philosophy and Letters, taking a degree in History in 1924.[24]

Buñuel soon acquired a reputation as one of the most original characters staying at the Residencia. A sports addict, he could be seen each morning, irrespective of weather conditions, in shorts and often barefoot, running, jumping, doing press-ups, pummelling a punch-ball or throwing his javelin. On a famous occasion he scaled the façade of one of the halls; he was immeasurably proud of his torso, considered by the famous Doctor Marañón as a perfect specimen in its line; he fancied himself as a boxer (this gave him the chance to show off his splendid physique), although, despite the combative image he worked so hard to project, he was no genuine pugilist; but the strength of his arm and stomach muscles afforded him endless satisfaction.[25] Buñuel soon became involved in the activities of the *ultraístas* and developed a deep admiration for Ramón Gómez de la Serna; the latter's witty, metaphorical definitions, which he termed *greguerías*, were all the rage at this time, and his well-attended literary cenacle, Pombo, which met each Saturday night near the Puerta del Sol, was the most famous gathering of its kind in Madrid. There Buñuel was in his element.[26]

Lorca had arrived in Madrid with a letter of introduction to Juan Ramón Jiménez from Fernando de los Ríos. Juan Ramón was then thirty-eight. He and Antonio Machado were the most famous poets in Spain. Federico knew the work of his fellow Andalusian well (Jiménez was from Moguer, in Huelva), and his early poetry had been influenced to some extent by that of the older man. The meeting was a success, and Juan Ramón decided to take the *granadino* under his wing. ' "Your" poet came,' he wrote to Fernando de los Ríos (21 June 1919),

and greatly impressed me. It seems to me that he has an outstanding temperament and a virtue in my view essential in art: enthusiasm. He read to me various very beautiful compositions – a bit long, perhaps, but concision will come of its own accord. I would be delighted not to lose sight of him.[27]

Federico was back in Granada by this time after his exploratory visit to Madrid (he must have been elated to think that in a few months he would be settling in at the Residencia), and no doubt Fernando de los Ríos at once conveyed to him the encouraging words from the great poet. A few days earlier, moreover, Lorca had had another occasion, quite spectacular this time, to witness the effect of his recitations on an established literary figure. On 16 June the Arts Club had held a reception in the gardens of the Generalife in honour of Don Fernando, its ex-President, on the occasion of the latter's election as a socialist Member of Parliament for Granada. During the festivities Angel Barrios performed on the guitar, while Lorca and another Granadine poet, Alberto Alvarez de Cienfuegos, today little remembered, recited.[28]

Among the guests were Gregorio Martínez Sierra, the man of letters and theatre impresario, and his leading actress (and mistress) Catalina Bárcena, who had arrived a few days earlier with their company to perform during the Corpus Christi celebrations.[29] Martínez Sierra had built up for himself a solid reputation as a dramatist, novelist and, to a lesser degree, poet. At the beginning of the century he had founded the Madrid literary magazines *Helios* (1903) and *Renacimiento* (1907), which played a vital role in the dissemination of contemporary European culture in Spain. Now, in 1919, he headed two publishing ventures and ran his own theatre company. A passion for the theatre had been one of the earliest manifestations of his interest in the arts, and it was a passion shared by his wife María, whom he had married in 1900. Both deeply admired modern French literature and art, spoke the language well and had made many visits to Paris, where they frequented the avant-garde theatre: Paul Fort's Théâtre d'Art, Aurélien Lugné-Poe's Théâtre de l'Oeuvre and Jacques Rouché's Théâtre des Arts.[30]

Only many years later would it become known that Martínez Sierra's extraordinary productivity at this time – plays poured from his pen – was due largely to the fact that most of the work published under his name was written by his highly talented wife, from whom he separated definitively in 1922.

In 1916 Martínez Sierra had established his company in Madrid's Teatro Eslava, situated in the Calle del Arenal, a stone's throw from the Opera House. Between that year and 1919 the Eslava had become the most innovative theatre in the capital, despite the physical limitations of the stage, which was only twelve feet deep, and the lack of adequate machinery. Among the great successes of this period were productions of Zorrilla's *Don Juan Tenorio* (1916); *La Dame aux camélias, The Taming of the Shrew* and *The Doll's House*, all in 1917; and various plays by the Martínez Sierras themselves.[31]

Martínez Sierra's taste was essentially eclectic and, if he loved the classical theatre, as an impresario he also felt enthusiasm for pantomime, farce, ballet and music. He considered that the theatre should be a meeting place for all the arts, and sought to put this belief into practice. Many of the works produced in the Eslava had musical accompaniments – by Joaquín Turina and Manuel de Falla, among others – and it was no accident that Falla's *El corregidor y la molinera* ('The Magistrate and the Miller's Wife'), prototype of *The Three-Cornered Hat*, was first played at the Eslava, in 1917.[32]

Martínez Sierra had declared war on the slavish realism that still pervaded the Spanish theatre. And it was in the scenery of his productions that the most obvious expression of this rebellion could be appreciated. To achieve his revolution he called on the services of three outstanding artists, who with their work at the Eslava transformed the art of scenery design as it was then habitually practised in Spain. These were the German Siegfried Bürmann, who had studied with Max Reinhardt at the Deutsches Theater in Berlin; the Uruguayan Rafael Pérez Barradas, who had travelled to Europe in 1912 and made his way to Spain in 1916; and, especially, the Catalan Manuel Fontanals.[33]

Gregorio Martínez Sierra was reaching the pinnacle of his career as a theatre producer at this time, so Lorca must have been flattered when he and Catalina Bárcena, deeply impressed by his recital, begged him to give them a private hearing. Accompanied by his friend Miguel Cerón, Federico led the distinguished couple to the top floor of a nearby tower – one of those Romantic elevations sung endlessly by the pseudo-poets of Granada and immortalized by Washington Irving – and there recited various poems, among them a composition, now apparently lost, which recounted, in a mixture of narrative verse and dialogue, the story of an injured butterfly which falls to the ground and is tended by a colony of cockroaches, one of whom falls in love with the beguiling creature and dies heartbroken when the latter recovers the use of its wings and flies away.[34] When Lorca finished reciting, Catalina Bárcena was in tears and Martínez Sierra beside himself with excitement. 'Pure theatre! Wonderful!' he exclaimed, if we are to believe Miguel Cerón's later account, going on to assure Federico that, if he succeeded in transforming the poem into a play, the Eslava would produce it forthwith. Forty-five years later Cerón retained a clear impression of that emotional scene: Catalina Bárcena's tears, Martínez Sierra's enthusiasm, Federico's jubilant acceptance of the offer – and his own satisfaction at seeing the impression his friend had made on the famous couple.[35]

But the metamorphosis of poem into play proved no easy task. That summer Cerón received several urgent communications from Martínez Sierra. Was Federico working on the project? Would he have it ready by the autumn? Would Cerón please do his best to ensure that the poet kept his nose to the grindstone? It seems that Don Gregorio hoped to produce the play before Christmas, but, if that were so, he was to be disappointed.[36] 'Late but in time' would always be Lorca's motto where deadlines were concerned.

7

The Butterfly's Evil Spell

If, in the summer of 1919, after his visit to Madrid, Lorca had the good fortune to meet and impress Gregorio Martínez Sierra, that autumn an even more vital relationship was initiated – with Manuel de Falla, who settled permanently in the town the following year.

Long before he came to know Granada personally, Falla, who was born at Cadiz in 1876, felt himself powerfully attracted to the place. His opera *La vida breve* (1904–5) was set there, and unfolded the tragic story of the love of a Gypsy girl from the hilly Albaicín quarter for a fickle, downtown Don Juan. Then in Paris, where he lived from 1907 to 1914, circumstances served to strengthen Falla's desire to know Granada. In the first place he met there the Granadine guitarist and composer Angel Barrios (one of the occasional participants in the *Rinconcillo*), whose father ran El Polinario, a celebrated tavern next to the Alhambra, haunt of artists and poets. Barrios undoubtedly fanned Falla's enthusiasm for the town he had not yet visited.[1] So too did Isaac Albéniz, then one of the darlings of Parisian high society, who had composed numerous pieces of Granadine inspiration.[2] Falla probably knew *La Soirée dans Grenade* before he met Debussy, but, whether this was so or not, his friendship with the French composer almost certainly deepened his urge to see the Alhambra (which Debussy never visited). Then, in 1911, Falla had come across a delightful book, *Granada. Guía emocional* ('An Emotional Guide to Granada'), published that year in Paris by Garnier and illustrated with excellent photographs. Although attributed to the ubiquitous Gregorio Martínez Sierra, the volume was almost certainly the work of his wife María. The composer was enthralled.[3] Two years later, in 1913, he met the couple in Paris. They got on well, and when Falla returned to Spain in 1914, fleeing from the war, he soon began to work with them.

In her book *Gregorio y yo* ('Gregorio and I'), published in 1953, María Martínez Sierra recalled nostalgically the ups and downs of her friendship with Falla and how she had accompanied the composer on his first visit to Granada, which took place some time between the autumn of 1914 and the first months of 1915. The ballet *El amor brujo* ('Love the Magician'), composed at great speed immediately after the visit, is set 'in a cave', and was undoubtedly inspired by the celebrated cave-dwellings of the Gypsy quarter of the Sacromonte, with which, it seems fair to assume, Falla became acquainted during his stay.[4]

El amor brujo opened in Madrid on 15 April 1915. Almost exactly a year later, on 9 April 1916, the capital saw the first performance of *Noches en los jardines de España* ('Nights in the Gardens of Spain'), which was followed by another that June, this time with Falla himself at the piano, in the Palace of Charles V at Granada, close to the gardens of the Generalife which had inspired the first movement of these 'symphonic impressions'.[5] Was the young Lorca, who a month earlier had lost his piano teacher, Antonio Segura, among the audience that evening in the spectacular, open-air auditorium of the unfinished Renaissance palace? There seems to be no record of his attendance, but it is difficult to believe that he would have missed such an exceptional occasion. At all events, the members of the *Rinconcillo*, many of whom were passionately interested in music, can hardly have been unaware of the presence among them of the great composer.

Falla was accompanied on this brief visit by Sergei Diaghilev and Léonide Massine who, with Igor Stravinsky, had recently arrived in Spain (the latter to conduct the Spanish premières of *The Firebird* and *Petrushka*). Diaghilev was at the first performance of *Nights in the Gardens of Spain* in Madrid, and had immediately conceived the notion of turning it into a ballet. Hence the Russian's trip to Granada with Falla: he wanted to see the Alhambra and Generalife with his own eyes, to hear the murmur of the fountains with his own ears. He did so, but the projected ballet of *Nights in the Gardens of Spain* never got off the ground.[6]

Falla's pantomime *The Magistrate and the Miller's Wife* – prototype of *The Three-Cornered Hat* – produced by Gregorio Martínez Sierra in 1917, was partly inspired by Granada, for the plot derives from the novel *El sombrero de tres picos* (1874) by Pedro Antonio de Alarcón. Several of the themes that appear in *The Three-Cornered Hat*, moreover, are from Granadine folk songs.[7]

An indication of the almost obsessive presence of Granada in Falla's work before he settled in the town is the insistence with which the haunting melody of the 'Zorongo gitano' – a Gypsy song from the Sacromonte – recurs in his music. The 'Zorongo' had been quoted fleetingly in the last part of Albéniz's *La vega* (1897), a work Falla must surely have known before moving to Paris in 1907. It appears for the first time in Falla's music – little more than a vague insinuation – in *La vida breve*; we hear it again in *Love the Magician*; and finally it becomes a leitmotif in *Nights in the Gardens of Spain*. Lorca was not only fully aware of the fascination that the 'Zorongo' held for Falla, but himself loved this song, which he later recorded for His Master's Voice with the dancer and singer Encarnación López Júlvez and incorporated into his play *The Shoemaker's Prodigious Wife*.[8]

Given his love for Granada before he had visited the Alhambra or seen the beauty of the Vega and the Sierra Nevada, it is not surprising that, once he experienced the reality of the fabled town, Falla pondered on the possibility of settling there. The decision began to take shape in the summer of 1919. On 22 July, Diaghilev's production of *The Three-Cornered Hat*, with sets and costumes by Picasso, opened at London's suitably named Alhambra Theatre. A few hours earlier Falla had received a telegram from Madrid informing him that his mother was critically ill. He left for Spain before the curtain rose and when he reached home his mother was already dead. Earlier in the year he had lost his father.[9] Falla disliked Madrid and, now that he was alone, felt free to consider moving elsewhere. The idea of Granada floated constantly into his mind, and finally he wrote to his friend Angel Barrios inquiring about lodgings close to the Moorish palaces. The guitarist informed him that the Pensión Alhambra had good rooms at a moderate price, and set the composer's mind at rest about the typhus scare that had recently been exaggerated in some of the newspapers. Thus reassured, Falla arrived in Granada in the middle of September, accompanied by his sister María del Carmen and the painter Daniel Vázquez Díaz and his family.[10]

After a few weeks in the Pensión Alhambra, Falla moved across the street to another similar establishment, the Pensión Carmona (where Malcolm Lowry was to meet Jan Gabrial in 1933, and Yvonne Firmin stays in *Under the Volcano*). Here, on a blustery afternoon in September 1919, John B. Trend made the acquaintance of the composer. In *A Picture of Modern Spain* the musicologist described that encounter, which signalled the beginning of a life-long friendship broken only by the death of Falla in 1946:

It was the first suggestion of autumn. The tops of the Duke of Wellington's elm trees swayed in a high wind,* and the pomegranate under which we were dining dropped pips in luscious, sticky envelopes on to the tablecloth. Suddenly there was a burst of rain, and every man seized his bread, plate and glass and ran for the house; I never realized the possibilities of a romantic situation so thoroughly as when I trod lightly

---

* Here Trend, following popular belief, is wrong. The Duke of Wellington never visited Granada and was in no way involved in the planting of the magnificent elms of the Alhambra Wood.

on a rotten quince which was lying on the garden path. Sr de Falla described the whole episode as a mixture of 'La Soirée dans Grenade' and 'Jardins sous la pluie'.[11]

Through Angel Barrios, Falla entered into contact with the group of artists, writers and music-lovers who frequented El Polinario, down the street from the Carmona and today transformed into the Angel Barrios Museum. It was here that occurred a picturesque episode engagingly described by Trend:

One evening Sr de Falla took me to a house just outside the Alhambra. In the *patio* the fountain had been muffled with a towel, but not altogether silenced; there was a light murmur of water running into the tank. Don Angel Barrios [. . .] sat there collarless and comfortable with a guitar across his knees. He had tuned it in flats so that in some odd way it harmonized with the running water, and was extemporizing with amazing resource and variety. Then his father joined us, and Sr de Falla asked him if he could remember any old songs. The old gentleman sat there with eyes half closed, while the guitar kept up a constantly varied 'till ready', chiefly in D flat and in B flat minor, sliding down with the characteristic 'false relation' to F major. Now and again he lifted up his voice and sang one of those queer, wavering melodies of *cante flamenco*, with their strange rhythms and flourishes characteristic of Andalucia, while Sr Barrios accompanied, sometimes thrumming simple chords, sometimes producing a sort of orchestral 'melodrama', sometimes playing a counterpoint, sometimes treating the song as a recitative and punctuating it with staccato chords. Sr de Falla wrote down those which pleased him, or those which it was possible to express in staff-notation, for one of the best of them was full of 'neutral thirds and sixths' – intervals unknown and inexpressible in modern music.[12]

We do not know in precisely what circumstances Falla and Lorca met that autumn, but they had certainly begun their friendship before the composer returned to Madrid. Trend describes a memorable occasion at which the poet and Falla were present. After a concert given in honour of Falla at the Arts Club by Angel Barrios's Trío Iberia, the Englishman accompanied a group of Granadine acquaintances up the steep streets of the Albaicín to the magnificent villa (the Carmen de Alonso Cano) owned by Fernando Vílchez, already a good friend of Lorca and soon to be of Falla. There in the garden, beneath the stars, the musicians had repeated part of their programme:

Before leaving the Carmen, our host made us follow him upstairs to another veranda, just below the roof. Here we were above the tops of the cypresses, and a vast panorama presented itself: the curved backs of the Sierra Nevada, the shadowy outline of the Alhambra Hill and its palaces, the greenish violet of the white walls bathed in moonlight with the rose-coloured blotches of the not too frequent lamps, the distant chimes, the bells to regulate irrigation,* the gentle murmur of falling water. We shouted for the music of Falla. And then, when the musicians had played

---

* A reference to the bell of the Tower of the Vela (see footnote on p. 32).

till they were tired, a poet recited in a ringing voice an ode to the city of Granada. His voice rose as image succeeded image and his astonishing flow of rhetoric fell upon the stillness. What did it matter, he concluded, that the glories of the Alhambra were departed if it were possible to live again such nights as this, equal to, if not surpassing, any of the Thousand and One! He ended, and 'the silence surged softly backwards'. Then the clock struck four, and we stumbled down into the town over the ungainly cobbles and climbed up to the Alhambra.[13]

The poet, as Trend made clear in his many subsequent versions of this description, was Federico García Lorca.[14]

Falla also remembered having met Lorca during his stay in Granada that year, telling his biographer Jaime Pahissa that the poet was introduced to him as one of the town's curiosities, as a 'precocious child of poetry'.[15]

Before he returned to Madrid, Falla was visited by the Princesse de Polignac, who some eight months earlier had commissioned him to compose a work for her Parisian salon. The princess – by birth Winnaretta Éugenie Singer – was born in 1865, daughter of the Singer of sewing-machine fame and fortune, whose millions she inherited. In 1883 she had married Prince Edmond de Polignac, thirty years older than herself, an elegant society figure, original composer of experimental music, brilliant conversationalist, wit, notorious homosexual and friend of Proust (who incorporated elements of his personality into various characters appearing in *A la Recherche du temps perdu*). Winnaretta, for her part, was a person of indomitable will, discreetly lesbian, an impressionist painter in the mode of her idol, Manet, a good pianist and a passionate devotee of contemporary music. By the time Falla met her the Princesse de Polignac was one of the leading hostesses in Paris. Friend and defender of Debussy (who baptized her 'Madame Machine à Coudre'), Satie, Fauré, Stravinsky and Chabrier, she also helped and cosseted numerous artists and writers, among them Proust, Cocteau and Picasso.[16]

Winnaretta was interested in modern Spanish music, and Falla had begun to attend her soirées in 1908. Ten years later she decided to commission a work from '*le petit espagnol tout noir*', as Paul Dukas had described Falla,[17] and it was finally agreed between them that the subject of the composition should be the famous episode of Master Peter's puppet show in *Don Quixote*. Falla and Winnaretta discoursed at length in Granada on the pros and cons of the projected work, and the composer introduced his guest to the delights of the Alhambra and the Generalife. One night, under a full moon, Andrés Segovia, already fast becoming Spain's most celebrated classical guitarist, played for them beside one of the Moorish pools. 'I can never forget the incomparable beauty of those gardens steeped in music and moonlight', the Princess stated emphatically years later.[18]

Falla's brief stay in Granada was a great success and before returning to Madrid he decided that, as soon as possible, he would settle permanently in the town. The search for a suitable house – it had to be a *carmen*, preferably on the Alhambra Hill – got under way immediately, with Angel Barrios directing operations, but, as it turned out, it would not be possible until the following September for the maestro to disengage himself from the trammels of the capital.[19]

During the autumn of 1919 Lorca worked away in Granada at his play for Gregorio Martínez Sierra and, at the end of November, travelled up to Madrid for his first session at the Residencia de Estudiantes, where his friendship with Luis Buñuel grew closer. In his autobiography, *Mon dernier soupir*, published towards the end of his life and not always entirely trustworthy, Buñuel paints an engaging picture of those days, referring to his visits to the brothels of Madrid ('beyond a doubt the best in the world'), his delight in beating up homosexuals outside public urinals (a proclivity which he soon abandoned), his experiments with hypnosis, his practical jokes (which included emptying pails of water under people's doors), his passion for jazz and his contacts with the avant-garde groups then beginning to spring up in the capital. Buñuel had money (he would have much more when his father died in 1923) – and it told on his behaviour.[20]

In the same book Buñuel recalls his friendship with Lorca in the 'Resi' and gives the poet credit for having opened his eyes and ears to the appreciation of poetry – an appreciation, it must be said, that never developed beyond the rudiments. The friendship had its crises. According to Buñuel one of the 'residents', a Basque by the name of Martín Domínguez, began to spread the rumour (no date is supplied) that Lorca was a homosexual. Buñuel, shocked – by his own admission he greatly disliked 'pederasts' – immediately accosted the poet, with his habitual Aragonese bluntness, and demanded satisfaction. Was he or was he not a homosexual? 'You and I have finished forever,' was Lorca's only reply as he rose and left. 'He was cut to the quick,' comments Buñuel. The recollection, on whose accuracy it is impossible to check, no doubt tells us more about the film director than the poet. That Buñuel was deeply disturbed about homosexuality there can be no doubt, and it is significant that neither in his memoirs nor in any of his many statements to the press did he ever refer to the fact that his younger brother Alfonso turned out very obviously gay.[21]

Many of the poet's former companions at the Residencia have been extremely reticent about his homosexuality, often denying that they were ever aware of the poet's 'problem'. What is beyond doubt is that, given the mores prevailing in Spain at the time, the majority of people with such inclinations went to inordinate lengths to mask their true feelings. Lorca was no exception to the rule. None the less his homosexuality was immediately apparent to many people. For example to the Andalusian painter and poet José Moreno Villa, who lived at the Residencia and served as a sort of cushion between the students and Alberto Jiménez Fraud. 'Not all the students liked him,' wrote Moreno Villa in his autobiography *Vida en claro*, published in Mexico in 1944. 'Some sensed his weakness and distanced themselves. Nevertheless, when he opened the piano and began to sing, all resistance was in vain.' That Moreno Villa provided no further details was itself symptomatic of the reserve that even today makes it so difficult to research the life of a homosexual artist in Spanish-speaking communities.[22]

If neither Buñuel nor Pepín Bello recorded their first meeting with Lorca, a little more information is forthcoming about the poet's early days at the Residencia from the diary of the poet Emilio Prados, whom Federico had first met in the summer of 1912 at the latter's home town of Malaga, where he was born in 1899.[23] Prados, who from childhood had suffered from tuberculosis of the chest, was an extraordinarily sensitive young man, deeply introspective and anxious. In the pages of his *Intimate Diary*, written sporadically between 1919 and 1921, he gave vent to his misery, returning again and again to the collapse of his love affair with Blanca, the muse of his first poems, and expressing an almost suicidal self-loathing. Prados believed for a while that in Lorca he had at last found the perfect friend. The diary shows that he had poured his troubles into the *granadino*'s understanding ear, and that they had discussed at length their aspirations in life, finding these to be identical (literary fame and the desire to contribute to a more just society). 'His political ideals,' jotted down Prados, 'at variance with his privileged social position, are the same as mine, and this makes me love him more.'[24] These observations have their interest, for we know from other sources that Lorca was in no way indifferent to fame (whatever he may have said on occasion to the contrary) and that, in his earliest writings, the concern with social injustice was already a crucial theme.

Other passages in Prados's diary reveal that, in their long discussions, the two friends sketched out a programme for the implementation of their political ideals. In an undated entry we find Prados writing:

I wish he were here now so that we could organize the promotion of our common ideals, which I yearn to see put into practice. I would give all my blood to see humanity united in love, with total equality for everyone. It horrifies me to think how much starvation and suffering could be changed into happiness. Anyway, when Federico comes we will work enthusiastically for the cause.[25]

Prados, however, soon became disillusioned with Lorca, complaining in his diary of the poet's lack of understanding of his problems. Soon afterwards he left for a clinic in Switzerland (his tuberculosis had grown worse), and there he worried over the breakdown of his relationship with Federico. What had happened? The diary is not explicit on this point. Perhaps Prados, who repeats that he had 'opened his soul' to Lorca, asked too much of his friend, who may have found his insistence cloying.[26] All was patched up, anyway, when Prados returned not long afterwards to Spain. For Lorca, Emilio – like the latter's close friend, the poet Manuel Altolaguirre – would always represent Malaga. And both were to play an important part in his life, not least by bringing out in Prados's publishing house, in 1927, his book *Canciones* ('Songs'), and several of his poems in their review *Litoral*, one of the most important Spanish literary magazines of the 1920s. But that would be six or seven years later.

During his first months at the Residencia, Federico frequently saw the members of the *Rinconcillo* who were now established in the capital – José Fernández-Montesinos, José Mora Guarnido, Melchor Fernández Almagro and Miguel Pizarro – and was often to be found in the studio of Manuel Angeles Ortiz. There, while the painter worked at his easel, the poet wrote a substantial part of the play commissioned by Gregorio Martínez Sierra.[27]

Lorca returned for the Christmas holidays to Granada, where he received several urgent communications from Don Gregorio, among them a letter which shows that the impresario's original intention had been that the play should be performed by puppets, not actors. Rafael Pérez Barradas had already done the designs, Martínez Sierra assured the poet, and the next day some of the costumes would be tried. But *when* would the poet send him the complete script? Martínez Sierra did not like to be kept waiting.[28] Given such insistence Lorca strove to finish the play, which, after last-minute hesitations about the title and the scenery, was finally staged, as *El maleficio de la mariposa* ('The Butterfly's Evil Spell'), on the night of 22 March 1920.

Federico was extremely uneasy in the days preceding the première, and Mora Guarnido recalls that he toyed with the idea of withdrawing the play. The other *rinconcillistas* resident in Madrid were summoned to give their verdict. There was a division of opinion, but finally Mora's insistence that the show must at all costs go on won the day. Better to take the risk of a flop than miss the opportunity of having a play staged at the avant-garde Eslava, a break for which many an older dramatist would give his right arm. Federico allowed himself to be convinced.[29]

Melchor Fernández Almagro was present at the rehearsals. For him one of the great attractions of the work lay in its exploitation of the ballet. And who better than the splendid dancer Encarnación López Júlvez, 'La Argentinita', to perform, to the strains of Grieg, the fragile steps of the injured butterfly? Melchor felt sure that Encarnación's dance in the culminating moments of the play guaranteed the success of the production.[30]

The Prologue to *The Butterfly's Evil Spell* is an arresting text, particularly in the deep – and explicitly acknowledged – debt it reveals to *A Midsummer Night's Dream*. An unpublished poem written on 23 October 1917 confirms that, for the young Lorca, Shakespeare's theme in this play is that love, falling in love, is purely fortuitous, the product of mere chance: we fall asleep, and a fairy sees to it that we desire the first person that passes.[31] Ten years later, in a key passage of his experimental play *The Public*, Lorca would refer again to *A Midsummer Night's Dream*. 'If love is pure chance and Titania, Queen of the Fairies, falls in love with an ass,' argues the Conjuror, 'it would hardly be surprising if, by the same procedure, Gonzalo drank in the music-hall with a boy dressed in white on his knee.'[32] Nor, we may add, if a cockroach should have the misfortune to fall in love with a beautiful injured butterfly which has fallen into its meadow.

Lorca clearly projected his own erotic longings, fears and metaphysical doubts on to the despairing orthopteran, for the insect's complaints echo almost word for word those expressed by the poet, in the first person, in numerous compositions of the juvenilia, for example 'Alba' ('Dawn') or 'Canción menor' ('Little Song').[33] The play is a thin disguise for the expression of the poet's own unhappiness, and it is noticeable that, for his failed lover, Lorca has chosen an insect universally considered repugnant. The message seems to be that only the beautiful are lovable, and one is reminded of other instances in the early work where the poet regrets his clumsiness and lack, as he sees it, of physical attractiveness.

When, on the night of 22 March 1920, the curtain went up on *The Butterfly's Evil Spell*, neither 'La Argentinita', nor Catalina Bárcena (in the role of the Cockroach), nor Grieg, nor Mignoni's colourful set, nor Barradas's costumes, nor Martínez Sierra's direction, nor the several merits of the little verse play itself, could overcome the rooted hostility of the audience. Lorca's friends, present in strength – among them José Bello, Manuel Angeles Ortiz and the beautiful María Luisa Egea, of whom the poet had declared himself so enamoured a few years earlier[34] – had organized an enthusiastic claque, but all in vain. The enemy prevailed and the performance of Federico's first dramatic work was a fiasco. From the moment the actors began to speak the protests erupted, and it soon became clear that a section of the audience was determined to wreck the show. Boos, catcalls, insults and witticisms, foot-stamping – the hullaballoo was deafening. A particularly ferocious outcry was provoked by the Scorpion's reference to his eating habits. When he exclaimed, 'I've just eaten a worm. It was delicious! Soft and sweet. Scrumptious!' some wag shouted, 'Pour

Zotal* on him!' and the theatre rocked with mirth. The first act ended in uproar. The second fared hardly better, although it seems that while 'La Argentinita' danced the audience calmed down a little. When the final curtain fell it was clear that Madrid was not yet ready (and no doubt never would be) for a verse play concerning the amorous misfortunes of cockroaches.[35]

In Granada, the poet's family eagerly awaited news. At last, at one in the morning, a telegram arrived. It was from a close acquaintance of Lorca's father and stated simply: 'Play not a success. All agree Federico a great poet.'[36]

Next day almost all the Madrid press referred, in a few dismissive lines, to the failure of The Butterfly's Evil Spell, noting at the same time that the farce about student life that followed it had gone down excellently with the audience. Some critics were honest enough to admit that, because of the din, they had been unable to hear the work; several said that the play, if it contained some good poetry, was intrinsically undramatic; others made a big thing of trying to identify what they considered to be the literary sources of the production – among the candidates proposed were Rostand's Chantecler, Le Roman de la Rose, Diaghilev's ballet Le Spectre de la Rose (recently performed in Madrid), Manuel Linares Rivas's El caballero lobo, the medieval fable Calila y Dimna . . . None of the critics took into account the ironic or humorous elements in the play, or attempted to analyse its theme, while several rejected the notion that such repugnant creatures as cockroaches could properly be dramatis personae (a misgiving Lorca had pre-empted in his Prologue). It was, in short, a pretty poor performance by audience and critics alike.[37]

According to several witnesses Lorca took the reverse well, going after the show to the famous café La Granja del Henar, in the Calle de Alcalá, to review the events of the evening. The poet Rafael Alberti, whose friendship with Lorca began a few years later, recalled that Federico told him in fits of laughter about the disastrous first night;[38] while as late as 1935 Lorca was still insisting that his reaction to the misfortune had been to have a good laugh.[39] It may well be, however, that, deep down, the evening left its mark, for afterwards the poet stated publicly on various occasions that his first play was Mariana Pineda, which had its première in 1927, conveniently forgetting to mention his unpleasant experience at the Eslava seven years earlier.

* A well-known brand of insecticide.

8

New Directions

Family Pressures and *Book of Poems*

It was patently obvious by this time that, if Francisco García Lorca was now embarked on a distinguished academic career, no such hopes could be entertained for his brother. The commercial failure of both *Impressions and Landscapes* and *The Butterfly's Evil Spell* had not strengthened Don Federico García Rodríguez's belief in the capacity of his eldest son to earn his living by his pen, and strong paternal pressure would be applied until, finally, Federico managed to get a degree. Nor would it stop there.

When Martín Domínguez Berrueta died in the summer of 1920 and the embarrassment of meeting him in the University was thereby removed, the poet decided to placate his parents by making the gesture of resuming his BA studies. That summer he wrote from Asquerosa to Antonio Gallego Burín, who had recently been appointed to a lectureship in the Faculty of Philosophy and Letters at Granada University, and asked for advice. His father had just told him that if he made an effort to sit some subjects in September he would let him return afterwards to Madrid. This was good news. Lorca pestered Gallego with a series of questions about how best to tackle the onerous task. What subjects should he prepare? It was clear that Federico hoped to struggle through on a minimum of work and with maximum help from his friends in the Faculty.[1]

At the same time the poet wrote to another friend, José Fernández-Montesinos, in Madrid, asking him to lend him an essay he had written on Lope de Vega which he wanted to submit, as his own, to the Spanish Literature (Research Course) examination. Fernández-Montesinos acceded rather indignantly to the request – and on the strength of his contribution Lorca not only passed his examination but won a prize. He also sailed through Universal History but was failed in History of the Castilian Language, a circumstance that brought down the scorn and ire of the

Rinconcillo on the head of the professor responsible, who received an outraged letter from the group.[2]

Lorca's university records show that on 30 October 1920 he transferred from the Faculty of Philosophy and Letters in Granada to that of Madrid University. It seems, therefore, that his success in the two subjects had been sufficient to persuade his father to let him return to the capital, with the condition that he attend classes there. There is no evidence, however, that he ever set foot in the University.[3]

Installed that autumn for his second session at the Residencia de Estudiantes, Federico kept his parents informed about his projects. He was producing poetry, he assured them, and exploring the possibility of having a book published. Several letters from Vicenta Lorca to her son at this time show that she now approved fully of his determination to have a literary career, and identified closely with his plans. By the spring of 1921 the idea of the book had advanced considerably, and we find Doña Vicenta writing:

You haven't told us to whom you've given the book, and if it will take them a long time to publish it; you'll appreciate that, as a woman and moreover as your mother, I'm more interested in all these things than anyone else. We think it's a good idea for you to publish the book yourself, for you know that your father is happy (provided that you all work) to help you in whatever way is necessary. We are delighted that you feel you have the strength to recognize that you possess the abilities and faculties of a pure, exquisite artist; because that way you'll hurl yourself with great courage into the fray that awaits you, without being put out by the criticisms of the ignorant, or the malevolence of those who envy you, who in such cases almost always abound. I pray to the Virgin that everything will work out very well for you and that you'll stay calm so that nothing upsets you for any reason at all.[4]

Lorca was in the happy position, therefore, of knowing that his parents not only approved of his plan to publish his poems but that they would make available the necessary funds to defray the printing costs. He could count, moreover, on the assistance, and perceptiveness, of his brother who, out of the mass of manuscripts that had now accumulated, helped him to compile an anthology of his best verse.[5]

Federico's mother had inquired as to the publisher of the poems. These were confided to a friend of Lorca's, Gabriel García Maroto, who ran a small printing establishment in Madrid. Born in the town of La Solana, in Don Quixote's country La Mancha, south of Madrid, in 1889, Maroto (who, like Lorca, was known by his second surname, far less common than García) had been living in the capital since 1909. He was not only a printer, but a painter, a critic, a poet and, in the words of José Mora Guarnido, 'a fine human being', albeit somewhat irascible.[6]

Mora Guarnido relates that Maroto had virtually to wrench the manuscript from Lorca's grasp, so loath was the latter to hand it over for publication.[7] Once it was in his possession Maroto made a typewritten copy of the poems and asked Lorca to correct this, dating each composition as he went.[8] Federico obliged, but it is almost certain that he did not proof-read the book, which appeared full of errata. The printing, which cost Don Federico 1,700 pesetas – a considerable sum in those days – was completed on 15 June 1921.[9] *Libro de poemas* ('Book of Poems') had 229 pages, was attractively produced, contained 70 poems dated between 1918 and 1920 and was dedicated to Francisco García Lorca.

José Mora Guarnido had continued to follow Lorca's artistic development with fascination and pride. On 1 July 1921 he announced the good news of the forthcoming book in the columns of the *Noticiero Granadino*, using the opportunity to rail at the philistinism of his fellow *granadinos*. Mora Guarnido expressed the view that the volume might well be the harbinger of a poetic awakening in Spain.[10]

Mora Guarnido's review was written for exclusively Granadine consumption. Of much more consequence was one that appeared in the leading Madrid daily, *El Sol*, on 30 July by Adolfo Salazar, already the country's most distinguished music critic and by this time a firm friend of Federico. The review, entitled 'A New Poet. Federico G. Lorca', no doubt made some impact, although the fact that the book had appeared in the middle of the summer holidays did not help. Salazar pointed out that *Book of Poems* was a transitional work, a *dignus est intrare*, and that, before publishing his current production, Lorca had wanted to set out a representative selection of his earlier verse, showing its evolution. The poet had informed Salazar of his intention of bringing out in the autumn a book of his recent poems, and the critic commented that, in point of fact, the later compositions of the present volume under review, which were from 1920, had a 'modern profile' that distinguished them sharply from the earlier ones. Reading between the lines it was clear that, in Salazar's view, the contact of the Granadine poet with the new trends then making themselves felt in Madrid was having a beneficial effect on his work.[11]

The book received, so far as we know, only two other reviews, by Cipriano Rivas Cherif and Guillermo de Torre.[12] Both these critics had noticed the pantheism that suffuses *Book of Poems*. Torre, by now firmly established as high priest of the *ultraísta* movement, reproached the poet for his moments of excessive sentimentality, deriving from the Romantics, which in his view marred many of the poems. Nevertheless he praised Lorca's flair for arresting metaphor, giving some examples, and ended by auguring that, once the *granadino* shed the out-of-date elements of his art, he would be 'a genuine poet of the avant-garde'. Torre was unrelenting in his efforts at this time to persuade Lorca to identify himself fully with the aims and techniques of *ultraísmo*,[13] but Federico remained resolutely on the fringes of the movement, taking from it only what he considered absolutely necessary to his own poetry. The determination of the *ultraístas* to eradicate the last remnants of Romantic and post-Romantic sentimentality, and their insistence on the primacy of the poetic image, certainly influenced Lorca, who even before he became fully immersed in the literary life of Madrid had come to see the dangers of his tendency to excessive verbal exuberance.

Federico was delighted with Salazar's review – and with the long letter from the critic (29 July 1921) in which the latter voiced some misgivings about *Book of Poems* which he had tactfully omitted in *El Sol*.[14] Lorca agreed with these and explained in his reply (2 August 1921) that, if in the book he had not yet found himself, he now felt that he was on the right road, 'the ineffable road full of daisies and multicoloured lizards'.[15]

Although Salazar's glowing review had appeared on the front page of one of Spain's leading newspapers, Lorca's parents were, apparently, still not satisfied. The poet confided to the critic that his mother and father considered him a failure because the book was not being widely noticed, and asked him to find out if there had been any other articles. If more were to appear, he felt sure, his parents would forgive him for not having sat any subjects that summer at the University and would let him get on in peace with his poetry which, he assured Salazar, 'seems to me the best and most exquisite that I have yet produced'.[16]

The 'ineffable road' the poet believed he had found was that of the *suite*, which he began to elaborate towards the end of 1920, that is during the period to which belong the last compositions of *Book of Poems*, and which consisted of a sequence of thematically linked short poems constructed on the analogy of the musical suite of the seventeenth and eighteenth centuries. Lorca also thought of calling his projected collection 'El libro de diferencias', a direct allusion to the musical variations or 'differences' of sixteenth-century composers for the *vihuela* such as Antonio de Cabezón, Luis Milán and Alfonso Mudarra.*[17]

Despite his optimism, Lorca did not succeed in publishing his *Suites* that autumn – or ever, although they were to occupy him intensely between 1920 and 1923 and he referred frequently to their forthcoming publication in later statements and letters. Only in 1983, forty-seven years after the poet's death, was the book of *Suites* 'reconstructed', thanks to the patient work of André Belamich. The volume published by the French hispanist contained more than two thousand lines which, added to the few *suites* published by

---

* The *vihuela*, strung and played like the lute, had a body similar to that of the guitar.

Lorca in reviews and in the slim volume of *Primeras canciones* ('First Songs'), in 1936, make up a highly impressive body of verse.[18]

Contrary to the view of the French editor of *Suites*, however, it does not seem possible to maintain that these poems show any notable thematic development, as such, in Lorca's work. (Belamich finds in them 'the starting point of the great black river, meditative and visionary, radically pessimistic, which, running beneath *Songs* and *Gypsy Ballads*, would flood *Poet in New York* and, later, the *Diwan of the Tamarit*'.)[19] In them, rather, we find the same preoccupations that pervade all the early work of the poet, and the originality of the *suites* lies less in their themes than in their structure and poetic language. Here, certainly, the poet had achieved a notable advance on his previous production.

In the *suites* composed during the summer of 1921, allusions to the definitive loss and frustration of love are ubiquitous, and the theme of irretrievable childhood recurs insistently. In the poem 'Canción bajo lágrimas' ('Song under Tears'), for example, from the *suite* entitled 'Momentos de canción' ('Moments of Song'), dated 10 July 1921, both themes fuse, as they had done in lines written four years earlier:

> En aquel sitio,
> muchachita de la fuente,
> que hay junto al río,
> te quitaré la rosa
> que te dio mi amigo,
> y en aquel sitio,
> muchachita de la fuente,
> yo te daré mi lirio.
> ¿Por qué he llorado tanto?
> ¡Es todo tan sencillo! . . .
> Esto lo haré ¿no sabes?
> cuando vuelva a ser niño,
> ¡ay! ¡ay!
> cuando vuelva a ser niño.*[20]

> *   In that place,
>   little girl of the fountain,
>   close to the river,
>   I'll take from you the rose
>   my friend gave to you,
>   and in that place,
>   little girl of the fountain,
>   I'll give you my iris.
>   Why have I wept so much?
>   Everything is so easy! . . .
>   I'll do it, do you see?,
>   when I'm a child again,
>   Ay! Ay!
>   when I'm a child again.

In various of Lorca's early poems the iris appears, as here, in contrast to the rose (or carnation), floral emblems of heterosexual love.[21] Can we doubt that in this little poem Lorca is indicating again – as in his epistolary confidence to Adriano del Valle in 1918 – his feeling of sexual margination?

Adolfo Salazar's friendship had become extremely important to Lorca by this time. Salazar was more at ease than the poet with his homosexuality (by all accounts very obvious), and those letters of Lorca to him that have come to light, which form only a tiny part of the correspondence, suggest that the two understood each other well. On 2 August 1921, shortly after Salazar's review of *Book of Poems* had appeared, the poet confided: 'I see that my life is already shackling me with its chains. Life is right, quite right, but . . . what a shame about my poor wings! What a shame about my desiccated childhood!'[22] Although the poet did not tell his friend, he was composing at this moment his 'Suite del regreso' ('Suite of the Return'), which, dated 4 August 1921, is without doubt the best and most personal poem we know from that summer. The *suite* begins:

> El Regreso
>
> Yo vuelvo
> por mis alas.
>
> ¡Dejadme volver!
>
> ¡Quiero morirme siendo
> amanecer!
>
> ¡Quiero morirme siendo
> ayer!
>
> Yo vuelvo
> por mis alas.
>
> ¡Dejadme retornar!
>
> Quiero morirme siendo
> manantial.
>
> Quiero morirme fuera
> de la mar.*[23]

> * The Return
>
> I am returning
> for my wings.
>
> Let me return!
>
> I want to die being
> the dawn!
>
> I want to die being
> yesterday!

The first version of these lines, scrapped by the poet, was more explicit in its reference to the lost paradise of childhood:

El Camino Conocido

Yo vuelvo hacia atrás.

¡Dejadme que retorne
a mi manantial!

Yo no quiero perderme
por el mar.

Me voy a la brisa pura
de mi primera edad
a que mi madre me prenda
una rosa en el ojal.*24

While each of the ten 'variations' or 'differences' of the *suite* develops the theme of the poet's lost childhood paradise, it is the section 'Realidad' ('Reality') that most strikes our attention. Here again is the figure of the mother who, one dark winter afternoon, reads aloud, by the fireside, the ending of *Hernani*, when Doña Sol dies 'like a yellow swan/of melancholy'. The poet reflects gloomily:

Yo debí cortar
mi rosa aquel día,
pura apasionada
de color sombría

—————

I am returning
for my wings.

Let me return!

I want to die being
a spring of water.

I want to die away
from the sea.

*   The Known Way

I am returning.

Let me return
to my spring of water!

I don't want to get lost
in the sea.

I'm leaving for the pure breeze
of my first years,
so my mother may put
a rose in my button-hole.

al par que los troncos
dorados ardían.*25

In the last two sections of the *suite* the poet expresses his sense of the futility of life without love, and remembers again the girl he has lost forever. A mother fixation and an obsession with lost or impossible love: the theme recurs frequently in many other poems written at the time.

During the summer of 1921, perhaps for light relief, Lorca took flamenco guitar lessons with two Gypsies from Fuente Vaqueros. 'Flamenco seems to me to be one of the greatest inventions of the Spanish people,' he wrote enthusiastically to Adolfo Salazar. Already, he claimed, he was able to accompany *fandangos, peteneras, tarantos, bulerías* and *romeras*. The two Gypsies 'sing and play fabulously, reaching the very depths of popular sentiment', continued the poet; 'it's no wonder that I'm enjoying myself'.26 It is the first indication we have of a new interest on the part of Lorca in this variety of the folk music of Andalusia, whose unspoiled form is often known as *cante jondo* or 'deep song' – an interest that was to lead to his *Poem of Cante Jondo* and *Gypsy Ballads*. We possess no information on the first discussions that took place between Manuel de Falla and Lorca on the subject of this primitive music, in whose conservation the Gypsies of Andalusia have played such an important part, although Miguel Cerón recalled that two years before the celebration of the Festival of Cante Jondo, in 1922, the composer and the poet were already visiting together the caves of the Sacromonte – the caves evoked by Falla in *Love the Magician* – and had become friends with several flamenco singers and guitarists.27

If Manuel de Falla was fascinated by this music, then still rejected by the cultural establishment, the great philologist Ramón Menéndez Pidal was concerning himself, at the time the composer settled in Granada, with the transcription of the words of popular ballads still surviving in the oral tradition. In 1920 Pidal had visited Granada and was accompanied by Lorca in his investigations among the Gypsies of the Albaicín and Sacromonte. Pidal later wrote that, on that occasion, the poet had shown himself deeply interested in the subject. From one of the García Lorcas' servants Pidal copied down several ballads, and Federico sent him others. It seems fair to assume that the learned philologist's stay in Granada, added to the fact of

* I should have cut
  my rose that day,
  pure, passionate,
  sombre-hued,
  while the golden
  logs burned.

Falla's presence, reinforced Lorca's interest both in folk music in general and in that of the local Gypsies in particular.[28]

That busy summer of 1921 Lorca also began to write a puppet play. He and Adolfo Salazar had discussed the possibility of working together on the project, which would aim at resurrecting the almost extinguished tradition of the Andalusian *guignol*. Federico now told Salazar that he had been questioning people in Asquerosa about the often ribald puppet shows that used to delight the children of the Vega, and that had stimulated his own poetic imagination. 'The things the old folk remember are spicy in the extreme and you'd kill yourself laughing,' wrote the poet.

Just imagine that in one of the scenes a cobbler called Currito from Puerto de Santa María wishes to measure Doña Rosita for some boots, and she doesn't want to for fear of Cristóbal,* but Currito is cunning and convinces her by singing this verse in her ear:

> Rosita, what I'd give for a look
> at the tip of your toe!
> If I got hold of you
> We'd soon see . . .

to a tune of the most delightful vulgarity. But then Cristóbal comes and kills him with two blows of his cudgel.[29]

This was the point of departure for the guignolesque *The Tragicomedy of Don Cristóbal and Señorita Rosita*, which the poet finished the following year. A letter written by Salazar to Federico during the summer (13 August 1921) suggests that the two friends had discussed the possibility that their project might interest Diaghilev. 'How Massine would do this!' exclaimed Salazar, after praising the scene Lorca had described and insisting that the play should also include one in which a barber shaves Cristóbal. (The poet took the hint and incorporated this into his *Tragicomedy*.) 'It's essential that we have two versions,' continued Salazar. 'One purely for ballet. If we could interest the Russians it would be fantastic.'[30] But it was one of the many Lorca projects that did not mature.

As the summer of 1921 drew to a close Federico probably felt reasonably optimistic about his literary vocation. Moreover, Juan Ramón Jiménez had just brought out some fragments from the *suites* in his review *Indice*, thereby honouring his promise to do what he could to foster the young poet's career. It was the first indication to appear in print of the new direction that Lorca's poetry was now taking.[31]

Meanwhile Federico had almost completely neglected his university studies, and no doubt his parents lost no opportunity to nag at him. He

---

* The Spanish equivalent of Punch.

enrolled towards the end of the holidays for examinations in Arabic, Palaeography and Bibliology but, characteristically, failed to turn up on the appointed days in September.[32] From this moment on the poet never again attempted to complete his BA course in Philosophy and Letters, although he made up his mind to finish Law, by hook or by crook, and that autumn resumed with an unwonted seriousness his studies in the Faculty.[33]

Falla and *Cante jondo*

Manuel de Falla had returned to Granada in September 1920 and, after spending brief periods in several houses near the Alhambra, had finally moved with his sister into a charming *carmen* at 11 Calle de Antequeruela Alta, which enjoyed splendid views over the Vega and towards the Sierra Nevada. There the composer would live until the end of the Civil War in 1939.

It needs little imagination to grasp the effect that Falla's presence in Granada exerted on the artistic life of the place, or the particular enthusiasm it provoked among the members of the *Rinconcillo*. Falla was by this time internationally recognized as Spain's finest composer, and his decision to live in the town meant that Granada suddenly became an important name on the musical map of Europe. It was not long before Lorca and his friends discovered, moreover, that Falla was a person of profound modesty and humanity who, provided that his working hours were respected, enjoyed meeting and helping other people.

It so happened that Don Manuel's maid was an aunt of the García Lorcas' cook, and this circumstance ensured that a constant flow of information concerning the composer's habits and idiosyncrasies was transmitted to Federico and his family, who were duly enlightened as to Falla's hatred of flies, his loathing of noise, his obsession with cleanliness, his abstemiousness, his compulsive attendance at mass . . . The composer had recently abandoned his moustache, and his head, already bald, had a monk-like quality and looked as though it had been carved out of ivory. Falla's expression, though he had a ready smile, was frequently grave, and every so often he would drift away into a brown study, only to return a moment later to listen attentively to what was being said. Timid Falla certainly was, but no one who observed him closely, or knew his music, could fail to sense his intense fervour of spirit.[34]

José Mora Guarnido suspected that if Falla had arrived in Granada a few years earlier, when Lorca was hesitating between music and literature, the balance might well have been tipped in favour of the former. It is possible, certainly, that if the composer's advent had coincided with the death of

Federico's teacher Antonio Segura Mesa, in 1916, all might have been different.[35] Lorca claimed that it was Segura who had initiated him in 'the science of folklore'.[36] If such was the case, it fell to Falla to complete the process. Federico was already a serious student of folk music by the time the two met, although Falla's knowledge of the subject, which he put at the poet's disposal, was undoubtedly much wider. Lorca soon became a frequent visitor at Falla's *carmen*, where the maestro came to regard him with an almost paternal affection, marvelling at his multiple gifts and not least his ability at the keyboard. Nor was it a question of a one-way influence, for if Federico learned and grew under Falla's benign guidance, Don Manuel was in turn encouraged by the poet's friendship and enthusiasm for his work.

It is not certain to whom should be attributed the original idea of holding a festival of *cante jondo* in Granada, although the leading candidate is Falla's close friend (and Lorca's), Miguel Cerón Rubio. According to the latter – a man not given to immodesty – he had the brainwave after numerous discussions with Falla and others at the lovely *carmen* of their friend Fernando Vílchez in the Albaicín, where the decline of authentic flamenco was a frequent topic of conversation. One day, as the group racked their brains in search of some way in which they could help, Cerón came up with the suggestion that perhaps a great competition should be organized in Granada, in which exponents of *cante jondo* – genuine flamenco – from throughout Andalusia could participate. In this way the attention of the artistic world, at home and abroad, would be focused on the rare musical heritage of the south of Spain.[37]

It was agreed by all the friends that the suggestion was brilliant, but that the idea had no chance of success without the sponsorship of the Arts Club. This backing was guaranteed soon afterwards. The ideal date for the venue, it was decided, would be the following June, during the Corpus Christi festivities. Miguel Cerón, whether or not the original begetter of the project, immediately became its principal organizer.[38]

In November 1921, Lorca, in the midst of the preparations for the great event, in which he had become deeply involved, wrote a series of poems inspired by *cante jondo*. Their publication, he informed Adolfo Salazar confidently on 1 January 1922, would coincide with the celebration of the festival, although the poet was being over-optimistic for they were not to appear in book form until 1931. 'The poem is full of Gypsies, oil lamps and forges,' he wrote,

and there are even allusions to Zoroaster. It's the first expression of a *new orientation of mine* and I don't yet know what to say to you about it [. . .] but it certainly breaks new ground! The only person already in the know is Falla and he's really enthusiastic![39]

The *Poema del cante jondo* signified, certainly, a new direction in the poet's work. In these compositions Lorca makes no attempt to imitate the words of the often illiterate *cante jondo* singers, as so many poets had done in the nineteenth century and even well into the twentieth. Nor does he write in the ubiquitous first person of the songs. What he attempts to do, rather, is to create in the mind of the reader – or the listener, for Lorca is a minstrel and conceives of poetry principally as oral communication – the sensation that he can 'see' the primitive sources (those 'remote lands of sorrow') from which wells up the anguish of *cante jondo*, and to follow the song imaginatively from its first note until the voice of the *cantaor* ('singer') dies away.

Some months earlier, Miguel Cerón had witnessed a scene that was to inspire the opening section of the 'Poema de la siguiriya', the first poem of the collection. 'One moonlit night,' he recalled over forty years later,

Federico, Falla and I walked up to the Silla del Moro* behind the Alhambra, following the track that twisted its way through an olive grove. A breeze was moving the branches of the trees, through which the moonbeams filtered. Suddenly Federico stopped, as if he had seen something unusual. 'The olives are opening and shutting like a fan,' he exclaimed.[40]

The poet drew on that vision in the first lines of his poem:

> El campo
> de olivos
> se abre y se cierra
> como un abanico.
> Sobre el olivar
> hay un cielo hundido
> y una lluvia oscura
> de luceros fríos.†[41]

In each of the four sections of the book, inspired by the *cante jondo* forms known as the *siguiriya*, the *soleá*, the *saeta* and the *petenera*, Lorca embodied in a woman the song evoked – a woman representing the anguish expressed in this primitive music. Death, unhappy love, despair: here are the themes

---

* The 'Moor's Seat', a tower, recently restored, that commands a splendid view of the Generalife, Alhambra and Vega beyond.

> † The field
> of olives
> opens and shuts
> like a fan.
> Over the olive grove
> is a sunken sky
> and a dark rain
> of cold evening-stars.

of these poems, in which, every so often, as in the *suites* (whose structure they follow), we find a brief snatch of direct speech – a reminder that in Lorca's poetry the dramatic element is rarely lacking. The section 'Encuentro' ('Meeting') in *La soleá*, with its Christological allusion, is a good example. The narrator addresses the beloved:

> Ni tú ni yo estamos
> en disposición
> de encontrarnos.
> Tú . . . por lo que ya sabes,
> ¡Yo la he querido tanto!
> Sigue esa veredita.
> En las manos,
> tengo los agujeros
> de los clavos.
> ¿No ves cómo me estoy
> desangrando?
> No mires nunca atrás,
> vete despacio
> y reza como yo
> a San Cayetano,
> que ni tú ni yo estamos
> en disposición
> de encontrarnos.*42

This is a mythical, chthonic, anthropomorphic world where death reigns supreme, and the densely metaphorical language shows again that, though the poet never allied himself closely with the *ultraístas*, he undoubtedly sharpened through his contact with them and their work his innate image-making capacity.

> * Neither you nor I
> are ready
> to meet.
> You . . . you know why.
> I loved her so much!
> Follow this path.
> In my hands
> I have the holes
> of the nails.
> Can't you see how I am
> bleeding to death?
> Don't look back once!
> Go slowly
> and pray like me
> to Saint Cayetano,
> for neither you nor I
> are ready
> to meet.

At the same time that he worked on the poems, Lorca was putting together, under the guidance of Falla, a lecture on *cante jondo* to be delivered as part of the propaganda build-up to the competition. Entitled '*Cante jondo*. Primitive Andalusian Song', the talk was given on 19 February 1922 in the Arts Club and revealed how far Lorca had travelled since he began, not very long ago, his exploration of this strand in the Andalusian musical heritage. Clearly the 'discovery' or, better, 'rediscovery', of *cante jondo* was having a profoundly liberating influence on Lorca's poetic imagination.

In his lecture Lorca acknowledged explicitly his debt to Falla's research into the origins and evolution of *cante jondo* and the latter's musical structure. Falla had sketched out by this time a study of the same subject, which was published anonymously just before the competition began in June, and there is no doubt that much of Lorca's talk derived from this source.[43]

Lorca felt sure that it was the Gypsies of Andalusia who had given *cante jondo* its 'definitive shape', whatever earlier influences went into its making – the adoption by the Church of the Byzantine liturgical chant, for example, or the Moorish invasion of AD 711. Following Falla closely he argued that the *siguiriya gitana* is the archetypal form of the genre, and that these songs constitute the 'thread that joins us to the impenetrable Orient'. The lecture reveals that the poet, who had known Gypsies from his early days in Fuente Vaqueros, had come to believe that in this primitive music, with its unmistakably Eastern quality, its quarter tones and its pathos, are expressed the very depths of the Andalusian soul (hence the designation 'deep song'). His study of *cante jondo* had led Lorca to the conclusion, moreover, that Andalusians are 'a sad people, a static people', and not at all the merry, extroverted songsters that they often lead foreigners to believe. Not only the music of *cante jondo* but its words had made him see this. In the second part of his lecture, much more original than the first, he subjected to scrutiny the little verses, known as *coplas*, used by the singers of *cante jondo* and which undergo constant variation. Speaking now as a young poet in contact with the avant-garde tendencies of Madrid, themselves inspired by the latest trends in Europe, Lorca told his audience that he and his friends found these verses astonishing – for their concision, their subtle gradations of anguish (*pena*), their striking imagery and their obsession with death.

Lorca also mentioned another feature of the *coplas* that had caught his attention. It is what he called their 'pantheism', their tendency to personify what the modern mind would consider inanimate objects or forces. He quoted some examples:

Todas las mañanas voy
a preguntarle al romero
si el mal de amor tiene cura
porque yo me estoy muriendo.*

    Subí a la muralla;
    me respondió el viento:
    ¿para qué tantos suspiritos
    si ya no hay remedio?†

It seems certain that Lorca's careful study of *cante jondo* in 1921 and 1922 revived what he called the 'poetic memory' of his childhood in the Vega of Granada, when he used to speak to the insects and, as he said, assign, like all children, 'to each thing, piece of furniture, object, tree or stone, its personality'.[44] Another important find which the poet claimed in his lecture to have made recently was that of the *Poesías asiáticas* ('Asian Poems') of Gaspar María de Nava Alvarez, an anthology of Arabic, Persian and Turkish verse translated into Spanish from English versions of the originals, and first published in Paris in 1833. Lorca had perceived a strong connection, both linguistic and thematic, between the poems in Nava Alvarez's collection and the *coplas* of Andalusian *cante jondo*. The anthology seemed to him further proof, that is, of the Oriental basis of *cante jondo*.

It cannot be doubted, given the evidence of this lecture, and of the poems thematically linked to *cante jondo* that Lorca had already composed by the date of its delivery, that the poet now identified himself closely with the flamenco singers or *cantaores* of Andalusia, 'mediums' through whom, in his view, the people express their deepest feelings and no doubt, too, their collective unconscious.[45]

Lorca well knew by the spring of 1922, moreover, that he too, like the *cantaor* in a moment of particularly intense inspiration, often possessed the mysterious communicative power known as *duende*, although it seems that he became fully aware of the implications of the expression 'to have *duende*' only after he had written his lecture on *cante jondo*, where he does not mention it. The insight may well have come during the June competition. But what is *duende*? In his famous lecture on the subject, first delivered in 1933, the poet attributed to the great Gypsy singer Manuel Torre, present

*   Every morning I go
    to ask the rosemary
    if there's a cure for lovesickness
    because I'm dying from it.

†   I climbed on top of the rampart;
    the wind replied to me:
    Why all this silly sighing
    if nothing can now be done?

at the 1922 competition, a penetrating observation made while listening to Manuel de Falla play *Nights in the Gardens of Spain*. 'Whatever has black sounds has *duende*,' Torre had said. For Lorca, *duende* (which in normal usage means a poltergeist-like spirit) came to denote a form of Dionysian inspiration always related to anguish, mystery and death, and which animates particularly the artist who performs in public – the musician, the dancer, or the poet who recites his work to a live audience, as was so often his own case. While *duende* may appear anywhere, Lorca was convinced that Spain is the country it prefers: Spain, where the national *fiesta* (not to be confused with a sport) is the sacrificial ceremony of the bull-fight. Without *duende*, as Lorca explained, the singing of the *cantaor*, while it may be technically perfect, will lack edge, and fail to send shivers down the listener's spine.[46]

Lorca's 1922 lecture on *cante jondo* served as a preliminary to three months of frantic activity on the part of the organizers of the competition to get everything ready on time for June. A publicity campaign was mounted to ensure that up and down the country the flamenco singers knew about the competition; invitations were sent to foreign musicians, artists and writers; and a fierce debate got under way in both the local and the national press about the merits or otherwise of *cante jondo* and the wisdom of holding the event. In Granada it was said that the competition would leave the municipal coffers empty and that, on account of the expenditure involved, the other attractions of the Corpus Christi celebrations would suffer. As a result, the Town Council failed to respond with the generous financial assistance that might have been expected, and refused, for example, to sponsor the attendance at the festival of Maurice Ravel and Igor Stravinsky, both of whom had expressed a lively interest in being present. Manuel de Falla was outraged by this meanness.[47]

Don Manuel, Federico and Francisco García Lorca took a break from the hectic preparations for the competition and spent that Holy Week, which began on 9 April, in Seville. During their stay they ran into the Cuban poet and diplomat José María Chacón y Calvo, who was to become a close friend of Federico in Madrid. 'To meet Lorca in Seville in the middle of those religious processions', Chacón told an audience in Cuba eight years later, 'was like meeting the very stuff of poetry.'[48]

And then it was June. The Cante Jondo Festival was just around the corner and the excitement in Granada mounted day by day. At the beginning of the month Lorca took part in the concert that concluded the events leading up to the great event. It was given in the little pseudo-Moorish theatre of the famous Alhambra Palace Hotel, just up the steep street from Falla's *carmen*, and comprised the reading, by Antonio Gallego Burín, of the maestro's anonymous pamphlet on *cante jondo*; a recital by the Granada flamenco guitarist Manuel Jofré; Lorca's recitation of several compositions from his *Poem of Cante Jondo*; and, to round off the evening, Andrés Segovia doing something unheard of – showing that, when he felt in the mood, he too was capable of playing flamenco, a genre for which he had little real affection. The following day the newspapers agreed that Lorca had been the star turn of the evening, and the *El Defensor de Granada* went so far as to prophesy that soon the young poet would become a national celebrity.[49]

The competition was held on 13 and 14 June, in the Alhambra's Plaza de los Aljibes, which had been decorated by the Basque painter Ignacio Zuloaga. Here on both nights a massive and gaily dressed audience filled the precinct to bursting point. Among the numerous foreigners present was John B. Trend who, since his first visit to Falla in 1919, had become a firm friend of the composer. Trend published an account of those two unforgettable evenings (on the second of which there was a downpour) when he returned to England. He had been deeply impressed by the scene. 'Wherever one looked there were exquisite figures in gay, flowered shawls and high combs,' he wrote in the *Nation and the Athenaeum*, 'while many had put on the silks and satins of bygone days, and appeared in the fashion of the thirties and forties – the Spain of Prosper Mérimée and Théophile Gautier, of Borrow and of Ford.'[50]

The great surprise of the competition was the performance of Diego Bermúdez Cañete, 'el Tenazas' ('Pincers'), an old *cantaor*, almost forgotten, who, so it was said, had walked to Granada all the way from Puente Genil, in the province of Cordova, a cross-country hike of some 80 miles. Bermúdez sang the first night with powerful *duende* and carried all before him. The second evening, however, after a day's tippling (sponsored, some averred, by his rivals), 'el Tenazas' was not in such inspired form. None the less he was awarded a thousand pesetas for his first night's achievement. Another prize-winner was the eleven-year-old Manuel Ortega, 'el Caracol' ('The Snail'), destined to become one of the greatest *cantaores* of the century.[51]

The festival over, Manuel de Falla returned with relief to the seclusion of his *carmen*. 'You could not imagine', he wrote to Trend on 7 July 1922, 'the extent to which my work and other things put off till later piled up during the long and laborious preparations for the competition.'[52] Falla was scandalized by the fact that the competition left in its aftermath an ugly discussion about what should be done with the profits that had accrued as a result of the venture's undoubted success. The punctilious composer decided that he had had enough, and henceforth largely avoided the Arts Club.[53] From this moment, too, the Andalusian elements in his work were drastically reduced.

The effect on Lorca was the opposite, and the competition, with the further insights it entailed for the poet into *cante jondo*, confirmed the broadly Andalusian direction of his work at this time, which would lead soon afterwards to his first 'Gypsy' ballads.

9

1922–3

Puppetry

Lorca had not forgotten his plans to resuscitate the Andalusian puppet theatre with the collaboration of Adolfo Salazar, although these had been shelved during the hustle and bustle of the preparations for the Cante Jondo Festival. Falla was enthusiastic about the project and, as Federico reported to Salazar at the beginning of 1922, had promised to provide the music, assuring the poet that he would be able to persuade Stravinsky and Ravel to participate. Don Manuel, who was still at work on his *Master Peter's Puppet Show* for the Princesse de Polignac, felt sure that they could take their 'Granada Puppet Theatre' to Europe and South America. Lorca was delighted, and urged Salazar to get to work seriously on their joint play, which would form part of the repertory.[1] Unfortunately we possess very little further information on the subject: no letters from Salazar are among the poet's surviving papers, and those the critic wrote at this time to Falla add nothing.[2]

During the summer of 1922 the García Lorcas made their annual visit out to Asquerosa where, on 5 August, the poet finished the first draft of his 'guignolesque farce', *The Tragicomedy of Don Cristóbal and Señorita Rosita*, begun the previous year.[3] Federico wrote excitedly to Falla, who, it seems, had agreed to write the music for the play,[4] about their projected puppet theatre which now, more realistically, they planned to take to the Alpujarras, the high mountain region south of Granada (in one of whose villages, Yegen, Gerald Brenan was installed and busily acquainting himself with Spanish literature and life).[5]

The Tragicomedy of Don Cristóbal and Señorita Rosita, which the poet later reworked considerably, was a notable advance on *The Butterfly's Evil Spell*. Lorca, now writing within the Andalusian tradition, had begun to find his authentic voice as a dramatist. The play contains several elements characteristic of the poet's mature work: the subtle exploitation of folk songs; witty, incisive dialogues modelled on the speech habits of the countryfolk of the Granadine plain; the theme of society's suppression of individual liberty. Despite the happy ending of the puppet farce, Rosita's words on love (as she embroiders) anticipate those of Lorca's great protagonists, while looking back to his earliest prose and poems:

Between priests and fathers we girls have a miserable life. (*She sits down to embroider.*) Every afternoon – three, four – the priest tells us: You're going to be sent to Hell! You'll be done to a frizzle! Worse than dogs [. . .] But I say dogs marry whom they wish and have a good time! How I'd like to be a dog! If I obey my father – four, five – life will be a hell on earth, and if I don't, I'll be sent to the other one up there [. . .] The priests also could shut up and not talk so much.[6]

Currito, too, foreshadows Lorca's later protagonists. Because he is a rover he loses Rosita, his great love, for ever. In Lorca, he who hesitates in matters of the heart is lost – always.

That summer the poet also continued work on his *suites*, informing Melchor Fernández Almagro of his progress. In Madrid Melchor had been seeing a lot of Guillermo de Torre, who had just completed a book of *ultraísta* poems, with the suitably modern title of *Hélices* ('Propellors'), and was about to leave on a visit to Paris. He and Fernández Almagro had discussed Lorca. 'I needn't tell you,' wrote Melchor (4 August 1922), 'that he has the high regard for you that you deserve. He says regretfully, however, that "Lorca doesn't want to become a fully fledged *ultraísta*".'[7] Torre knew by now that Federico was his own man and constitutionally incapable of identifying himself closely with any *ism*, whatever broad sympathy he might feel towards it.

Lorca and Falla did not succeed in taking their projected puppet theatre that autumn to the Alpujarras. The main reason was that, in September, coached by his brother Francisco (who finished his Law degree this year) and with the indulgence of understanding professors, Lorca managed to pass all his outstanding Law subjects with the exception of two.[8] Completion of his degree was within reach and he decided to make one last effort. 'I'll finish my degree in January,' he wrote confidently to Melchor Fernández Almagro. 'Then my dear Pappa will allow me to travel. I plan to go to Italy.'[9] There could be no question for the moment, therefore, of either making a trip to the Alpujarras or of returning to the Residencia de Estudiantes. All of this would have to wait for the New Year.

Nothing daunted, Falla and Lorca thought up a substitute for the trip to the Alpujarras. The idea was to organize a puppet show in the García Lorcas' spacious flat on 6 January, the Day of the Kings (that is, the Three Wise Men), when Spanish children traditionally receive presents. This time all went well, and the performance proved unforgettable for the children – and adults – present. The programme consisted of the interlude *The Two Talkers*, then still attributed to Cervantes; a tiny puppet play by Lorca, *The Girl who Waters the Pot of Basil and the Inquisitive Prince*, adapted from an old Andalusian story; and the thirteenth-century *Mystery Play of the Three Wise Men*. The musical accompaniments, performed by a small orchestra under the direction of Falla, were elaborate and varied. They included excerpts from Stravinsky's *L'Histoire du soldat* and Albéniz's *La vega*, Debussy's *Sérénade de la poupée*, a berceuse by Ravel and several early Spanish pieces. Isabel García Lorca, then thirteen, and her ten-year-old friend Laura, daughter of Fernando de los Ríos, sang two songs. The puppets were the work of the engraver Hermenegildo Lanz.[10]

Both Falla and Lorca remembered the occasion with nostalgia years afterwards. Federico had been impressed by the care with which Don Manuel prepared himself for the performance, recalling in 1933:

Three days before our theatre opened I went to Falla's house and heard him playing the piano. I knocked on the door. He didn't hear me. I knocked more loudly. Finally I entered. The maestro was seated at the instrument with a score by Albéniz in front of him.
'What are you doing, maestro?'
'I'm getting ready for the concert in your theatre.'
That's Falla: in order to amuse some mere children he was going to the trouble of getting everything just right. Because that's Falla's way: the awareness of and search for perfection.[11]

In Buenos Aires, a year later, at the beginning of a performance of *The Tragicomedy of Don Cristóbal and Señorita Rosita*, the puppet Cristóbal recalled:

Ladies and Gentleman: This is not the first time that I, Don Cristóbal, the drunken puppet who marries Señorita Rosita, come on to the stage on the arm of Federico García Lorca, the little stage where I live forever and never die. The first time was in the poet's house – do you remember, Federico? It was springtime in Granada,* and the salon of your house was full of children who said: 'The puppets are real, but why do they stay so small and not grow bigger?' The great Manuel de Falla was at the piano, and there Stravinsky's *L'Histoire du soldat* received its first performance in Spain.† I still remember the smiling faces of the little newspaper boys, mere children, whom Federico had invited upstairs, surrounded by the curls and ribbons of the rich children.[12]

Not since his childhood days in the Vega had Lorca put on a puppet play of his own, and the success of the venture probably encouraged him to seek

---

* Not strictly true. Spring does not arrive in Granada as early as January.
† Partial performance, that is.

the means of producing, in a proper theatre, his much more ambitious *The Tragicomedy of Don Cristóbal and Señorita Rosita.*

For Falla, too, the experience had its importance, since at this time he was at last finishing his *Master Peter's Puppet Show* for the patient Princesse de Polignac. In its orchestral version the work was first played at Seville, on 21 March 1923,[13] and, in its complete form, after many rehearsals, in the Princess's Parisian salon on 25 June following. All went even better than expected on the latter occasion, with a brilliant performance on the harpsichord by Wanda Landowska. Several of the *rinconcillistas* then resident in Paris contributed to the success of the evening, among them Manuel Angeles Ortiz, who designed the proscenium arch, various elements of the set and many of the costumes. The heads of the puppets, like those of Lorca's theatre, were the work of Hermenegildo Lanz. That night in Winnaretta's salon, which was filled with the *crème de la crème* of Parisian high society, the old and new arts of Spain fused in fluid symbiosis, as they were to do in some of the best work by Lorca.[14]

At the end of January 1923 Federico completed his Law degree, and must have felt immense relief at having proved himself at last in the eyes of his parents. From this moment on, according to Francisco, he never again mentioned the subject of his university career – or was seen to open a law book.[15] The poet was now twenty-three and, having fulfilled his academic obligations, expected that, as promised, his father would let him travel to Italy. But it was not to be, and in May we find him complaining in a letter to Falla that his parents have refused to allow him to join the composer in Rome. Why the veto? We do not know, although it can be surmised that Don Federico was now insisting that it was his elder son's duty to set about finding employment.[16]

But if the poet did not succeed in getting to Italy, at least he was able to persuade his parents to allow him to return that spring for a spell at the Residencia de Estudiantes, after an absence of a year and a half. There he met Salvador Dalí, and embarked on a friendship that was to have a profound influence on his life.

A Catalan Genius in Madrid

Born in Figueras, in the Catalan province of Gerona, in 1904, Dalí had been admitted to Madrid's famous Academy of Fine Arts in September 1922.[17] He was accompanied on that first visit to the capital by his father, Salvador Dalí y Cusí, a prosperous notary, and his young sister Ana María. The Dalís had been recommended to Alberto Jiménez Fraud by the playwright Eduardo Marquina, a friend of the family, and they took straightaway to the atmosphere of the Residencia de Estudiantes, where Don Alberto provided them with accommodation during their stay.[18]

The eighteen-year-old Dalí who arrived at the 'Resi' in the autumn of 1922 was by any standards an arresting figure. Extremely slim, he wore his jet-black hair down to the shoulders (in imitation of the self-portrait by Raphael), exaggeratedly long sideburns that set off the olive-coloured cheeks of his oval face, a voluminous wide-brimmed hat, a floppy bow-tie and a jacket that reached to his knees. A flamboyant cape brushed the ground as he swept past on legs sheathed in leather gaiters. The future master exhibitionist hardly spoke, and wore an air of haughty superiority with which he contrived to mask his pathological timidity and tendency to blush furiously at the least inquiry. Dalí was ludicrously unpractical, finding even the most apparently straightforward everyday tasks beyond him. Other characteristics noted by those who came to know him then were his tendency to be influenced by anyone with strong views; his sardonic, deadpan sense of humour; his complete lack of interest in women; his financial affluence (thanks to an indulgent father); his close knowledge of the work of Picasso at a time when, in Madrid, ignorance about the latter was almost universal; and his prodigious capacity for hard work. Few if any of the residents can have known, however, that Dalí was intensely anal in character (his scatological obsessions were to horrify the surrealists a few years later) and terrified of venereal disease and impotence, or that he had recently been steeping himself in Nietzsche and was coming to think of himself as an artistic Zarathustra, destined to do battle with the world. He was also immersed in Freud's *The Psychopathology of Everyday Life*, which had just been published in Madrid ('The book was one of the most important discoveries of my life'), had outgrown his impressionist phase and was executing his first cubist canvasses under the influence, principally, of Juan Gris.[19]

Before long Dalí was 'discovered', as he relates in his *Secret Life*, the first edition of which, in English, was published in New York in 1942:

One day, when I was out, the chamber maid had left my door open, and Pepín Bello, happening to pass by, saw my two cubist paintings. He could not wait to divulge the discovery to the members of the group. These knew me by sight, and I was even the butt of their caustic humour. They called me 'the musician', or 'the artist', or 'the Pole'. My anti-European way of dressing had made them judge me unfavourably, as a rather commonplace, more or less hairy romantic residue. My serious, studious air, totally lacking in humour, made me appear to their sarcastic eyes a lamentable being, stigmatized with mental deficiency, and at best picturesque. Nothing indeed could contrast more violently with their British-style tailored suits and golf jackets than my velvet jackets and my flowing bow-ties; nothing could be more diametrically opposed than my long tangled hair, falling down to my shoulders, and their smartly trimmed hair, regularly worked over by the barbers of the Ritz or the Palace. At the time I became acquainted with the group, particularly, they were all possessed by a complex of dandyism combined with cynicism, which they displayed with accomplished worldliness. This inspired me at first with such great awe that each time they came to see me in my room I thought I would faint.[20]

Dalí, now that he stood revealed as a marvellously talented modern painter, was immediately taken up by the group, and in so far as he was capable of belonging to anything, became part of it. Four months after his arrival in Madrid he had abandoned his Bohemian uniform and transformed himself into a slick young man-about-town. With his hair now done in the manner of Rudolph Valentino he frequented Madrid's most distinguished hotels, the Palace and the Ritz, tasted the delights of double vodkas and olives and revelled in the syncopated rhythms of the Black jazz orchestra then thrilling the public that flocked to the fashionable Rector's Club, on the ground floor of the Palace. 'For us money did not count,' wrote Dalí – and Buñuel and Pepín Bello, also *habitués* of the Rector's Club, could have borne him out;'we were really of a limitless magnificence and generosity with the money earned by our parents' labours.'[21]

The Dalí that Lorca met in the early months of 1923 was a violent rebel against conformity in all its manifestations and an avowed enemy of sentimentality and religion, although the influence of Catholicism on his sensibility had been stronger and more permanent than he would have been prepared to allow at the time. Unfortunately, neither Lorca nor Dalí seems to have left a contemporary record of their first meeting. The earliest letters from Salvador preserved among the poet's papers are from 1925 and, in the absence of Federico's to Dalí – there were probably several dozen – it is impossible to reconstruct accurately the development of their friendship up to that year. We can safely assume, however, that from the moment Lorca set eyes on Dalí, six years younger than himself, he was fascinated by the young Catalan's looks, personality and talent. As for Salvador, a passage from the *Secret Life* gives us to understand that he recognized immediately the charisma and multifarious genius of the poet:

Although I realized at once that my new friends were going to take everything from me without being able to give me anything in return – for in reality of truth they possessed nothing of which I did not possess twice, three times, a hundred times as much – on the other hand, the personality of Federico García Lorca produced an immense impression on me. The poetic phenomenon in its entirety and 'in the raw' presented itself before me suddenly in flesh and bone, confused, blood-red, viscous and sublime, quivering with a thousand fires of darkness and of subterranean biology, like all matter endowed with the originality of its own form. I reacted, and immediately I adopted a rigorous attitude *against* the 'poetic cosmos'. I would say nothing that was indefinable, nothing of which a 'contour' or a 'law' could not be established, nothing that one could not 'eat' (this was even then my favourite expression). And when I felt the incendiary and communicative form of the poetry of the great Federico rise in wild, dishevelled flames I tried to beat them down with the olive branch of my premature anti-Faustian old age.[22]

It seems fair to assume that by the time Lorca met Dalí that spring, the painter and Buñuel were already on good terms, although there is no hard evidence for this either in Dalí's *Secret Life* or Buñuel's much later *Mon dernier Soupir*, both of which lack chronological precision. At all events we know that, before long, Buñuel, Dalí and Lorca were almost inseparable and formed with Pepín Bello the nucleus of one of the most lively groups at the 'Resi'. As for Lorca's sexual passion for the painter, about which Dalí is less than explicit in the *Secret Life*, it seems beyond a doubt that this did not develop until a few years later. What may be mentioned here is the jealousy which, on Dalí's own admission, Lorca's social brilliance could provoke in him and which presumably dated from the early days of their relationship:

During this time I knew several elegant women on whom my hateful cynicism desperately grazed for moral and erotic fodder. I avoided Lorca and the group, which grew to be his group more and more. This was the culminating moment of his irresistible personal influence – and the only moment in my life when I thought I glimpsed the torture that jealousy can be. Sometimes we would be walking, the whole group of us, along El Paseo de la Castellana on our way to the café where we held our usual literary meetings and where I knew Lorca would shine like a mad and fiery diamond. Suddenly I would set off at a run, and no one would see me for three days . . . No one has ever been able to tear from me the secret of those flights, and I don't intend to unveil it now – at least not yet . . . [23]

That admission was published in 1942, and Dalí never revealed any more details about the disappearances in question. As for Buñuel, who lost his father in May 1923 and was now the proud head of his large family, he was engaged at this time in organizing, after what he claimed had been a vision, the 'Noble Order of Toledo', whose purpose was to promote the love of the marvellous city on the Tagus 50 miles from the capital (a city rich in Roman, Visigothic, Moorish, Jewish and Christian history), which he venerated. Among the co-founders of the Order were Federico and Francisco García Lorca, Rafael Sánchez Ventura, the poet Pedro Garfias and Pepín Bello. Buñuel, naturally, named himself Grand Master of the Order, and the rest of the members belonged to categories ranging from Knights to Squires and, most menial of all, the 'Guests of the Guests of the Squires'. Dalí was a Knight; Manuel Angeles Ortiz and the poet José María Hinojosa were Squires; and Buñuel appointed José Moreno Villa to the less than exalted post of 'Head of the Guests of the Squires'. The qualifications for admission to the Order were minimal: one had simply to love Toledo unconditionally and get drunk there for at least one whole night, wandering through the streets. Anyone with the pathetic habit of going to bed early could never hope to rise above the level of squiredom.

Buñuel had been fascinated since his childhood by disguises, as had Lorca and Dalí, and his enthusiasm was contagious. The members of the Order of Toledo enjoyed dressing up, and would appear in the most varied and at times outrageous outfits. Buñuel indulged to the full his compulsive need to disguise himself as a priest, and Dalí could always be relied upon to cut an eye-catching figure on their visits to Toledo. Buñuel's move to Paris at the beginning of 1925 in no way meant the dismantling of the Order; on the contrary, from that moment its membership grew until the Civil War began in 1936, and included several French writers and film people, among them René Crevel, Pierre Unik and Georges Sadoul. Buñuel would remain faithful to Toledo until the end of his life, and in his memoirs recalls with unashamed nostalgia several of the Order's nocturnal pranks in the magic city, some of them involving Lorca.[24]

Comic Opera and Other Projects

The poet was engaged during the spring of 1923 on a new project with Falla: the composition of a comic opera. To explain the genesis of this venture we need to go back three years, when Falla settled in Granada. The composer had recently abandoned work on a comic opera, *Fuego fatuo* ('Will o' the Wisp'), based on the music of Chopin and with María Martínez Sierra as librettist. According to María, the intensely Catholic Falla, with the score of two acts almost finished, had become deeply worried about the possible immorality of the plot of the work, which concerned the love of two women – one 'good', the other 'bad' – for the same man, a young composer. Finally Falla had opted out, to María's intense annoyance. Then something similar had happened with the conversion into an opera of the Martínez Sierras' play *Don Juan de España*, to which Falla had agreed to put music. Don Juan! Hardly a theme, to be sure, for the sin-obsessed, anchorite composer from Cadiz, who again beat a retreat. As a result of these contretemps, the professional relationship between Falla and his former friends came to an abrupt halt.[25]

It is likely that, as he got to know Federico better, Falla realized that here might be an excellent substitute librettist for María Martínez Sierra – for Lorca had not only a good knowledge of harmony but some years earlier had himself attempted to compose (in collaboration with José Mora Guarnido) some fragments of *zarzuela*, and understood something, therefore, of the complicated business of matching words to music.[26] Why, the composer may have thought, should he and Lorca not work together on a comic opera to replace *Will o' the Wisp*? It is also possible, of course, that it may have been Lorca who suggested the idea, although we have no documentary evidence on the matter.

It seems that Lorca began work on a synopsis of the opera – to be called *Lola, la comedianta* ('Lola, the Actress') – at the beginning of 1923. Falla must have approved of the synopsis, for to Lorca's manuscript he added marginal indications concerning the music required. Nor, on the face of it, was there much reason why the composer should baulk at the plot, for this was to be a comic opera, after all, and if Lorca's Lola got a kick out of toying with men's feelings, surely such behaviour need not be taken too seriously. But Falla was always serious, and the poet ought to have foreseen the dangers. Encouraged by the maestro's initial response, however, he got down to work in earnest on the libretto and, by the beginning of May 1923, wrote enthusiastically to Falla in Rome about his progress, looking forward to the day when they could take their opera together to the 'Holy City'.[27]

When Falla returned to Granada Federico showed him what he had done, and that summer, in Asquerosa (where Don Manuel paid him a visit) the poet continued the work. On 18 August, replying to a letter from Lorca, Falla gave him to understand that soon he would resolve the remaining musical problems, and added various details, suggesting that he was in earnest.[28] Over the next months Federico continued with the libretto, and, in mid-October, was able to inform Melchor Fernández Almagro that it was almost finished.[29]

Between then and the following summer we hear no more of the project. In August 1924 Lorca informed Melchor that 'Falla the Angelical will start work on my operetta in a few days.' But then a curtain of silence fell on the project.[30] There is no evidence to suggest that Falla ever began scoring *Lola*. What had happened? It is possible that, as he became increasingly aware of the cynicism of Lorca's actress, he had second, and third, thoughts about the morality of the work, thoughts that he may never have conveyed to the poet. To exploit other people in matters of love was anathema to Falla (perhaps his own unhappy love life played a part in this) and, in fact, it seems likely that he had decided that the projected work might be morally reprehensible, comic opera or no comic opera. But, whatever his reasons, the collaboration fell through – and was never resumed.

Nor had the joint project to organize a puppet theatre borne fruit. Lorca and the maestro had hoped to stage a new puppet show that September, with music by Falla and the participation of Adolfo Salazar and the young composer Ernesto Halffter, one of Don Manuel's protégés whom Federico had got to know in Madrid. But this second performance by the 'Granada Puppet Theatre' never took place.[31]

At the same time Lorca had been in contact with Gregorio Martínez Sierra, who apparently, despite the failure of *The Butterfly's Evil Spell*, still had faith in the poet. A letter to Federico from the celebrated impresario (31 August 1923) shows that there was a plan afoot to produce *The Tragicomedy of Don Cristóbal and Señorita Rosita* at the Theatre Eslava. Don Gregorio expressed himself somewhat unconvinced that Lorca would finish his play (remembering, no doubt, how things had gone in 1919–20), and thought that under the Persian jasmine where Federico alleged that he was working it would be impossible to concentrate. Lorca did finish the play, but it was never performed at the Eslava, or anywhere else, for that matter, in his lifetime.[32]

Despite the time and energy expended on these projects, Lorca continued to work intensely, during the summer of 1923, on his *suites*, in particular on the ambitious composition *El jardín de las toronjas de luna* ('The Garden of the Moon-Grapefruits') which, as the poet explained, 'is the garden of possibilities, the garden of that which does not exist but which could have and (at times) should have existed, the garden of the processions that passed by without been seen and of the children who were never born'.[33] In the prose prologue to the second, much longer version of this poem, the poet explains:

I am setting off on a long voyage [. . .] I wish to visit the static world where dwell all my lost possibilities and landscapes. I wish to enter dispassionately but alertly the garden of the seeds that did not germinate and of the processions of the blind, in search of the love which I never experienced but which was mine . . . [34]

For André Belamich, Lorca expressed in this poem his deepest anguish concerning his homosexuality. It is difficult not to agree.[35]

Three sections reconstructed from the original manuscripts by Belamich especially attract the interest of the biographer: 'Arco de lunas' ('Arc of Moons'), ['Altas torres'] (['High towers']) and 'Encuentro' ('Meeting').

In the first of these appear the poet's unborn children:

Arco de lunas

Un arco de lunas negras
sobre el mar sin movimiento.

Mis hijos que no han nacido
me persiguen.

'Padre, no corras, espera
¡el más chico viene muerto!'

Se cuelgan de mis pupilas.
Canta el gallo.

El mar hecho piedra ríe
su última risa de olas.
'¡¡Padre, no corras!!' . . .
Mis gritos
se hacen nardos.*36

The snatch of dialogue contained in the second, untitled, poem suggests that the poet has now realized that not only is marriage impossible for him but that he no longer wants it:

Altas torres.
Largos ríos.

HADA
Toma el anillo de bodas
que llevaron tus abuelos.
Cien manos bajo la tierra
lo echaron de menos.

YO
Voy a sentir en mis manos
una inmensa flor de dedos
y el símbolo del anillo.
¡No lo quiero!

Altas torres.
Largos ríos.†37

* Arc of Moons

An arc of black moons
over the motionless sea.
My unborn children
are chasing me.

'Father, don't run, wait,
the youngest is dead!'
They hang from my pupils.
The cock crows.

The sea, turned into stone, laughs
its last laugh full of waves.
'Father, don't run!' . . .
My shouts
turn into spikenards.

† High towers.
Long rivers.

FAIRY
Take the wedding-ring
that your grandparents wore.
A hundred hands under the earth
missed it.

In 'Encuentro', perhaps one of Lorca's most moving poems, the 'I' converses with the woman who could have been his companion:

Encuentro

Flor de sol.
Flor de río.

YO
¿Eras tú? Tienes el pecho
iluminado, y no te he visto.

ELLA
¡Cuántas veces te han rozado
las cintas de mi vestido!

YO
Sin abrir, oigo en tu garganta
las blancas voces de mis hijos.

ELLA
Tus hijos flotan en mis ojos
como diamantes amarillos.

YO
¿Eras tú? ¿Por dónde arrastrabas
esas trenzas sin fin, amor mío?

ELLA
En la luna ¿te ríes? entonces
alrededor de la flor del narciso.

YO
En mi pecho se agita sonámbula
una sierpe de besos antiguos.

ELLA
Los instantes abiertos clavaban
sus raíces sobre mis suspiros.

YO
Enlazados por la misma brisa
frente a frente, ¡no nos conocimos!

ELLA
El ramaje se espesa, vete pronto,
¡ninguno de los dos hemos nacido!

I
I shall feel on my hands
an immense flower of fingers
and the symbol of the ring.
I don't want it!

High towers.
Long rivers.

Flor de sol.
Flor de río.*[38]

Not often in Lorca's work do we hear confidences as intimate as these, and it is not surprising to find him writing to his friend the poet José de Ciria y Escalante at the end of July: 'Every day I suffer more as I realize that I must immediately publish my *suites*'.[39] The comment implies, moreover, that Lorca considered that the long cycle of poems was now complete, and it is a fact that from that August he turned to other tasks. As for the

---

* Meeting

Flower of sun.
Flower of river.

I
Was it you? Your breast
is shining and I didn't see you.

SHE
How often the ribbons
Of my dress brushed you!

I
Unopened, I hear in your throat
the white voices of my children.

SHE
Your children float in my eyes
like yellow diamonds.

I
Was it you? Where did you drag
these endless tresses, my love?

SHE
In the moon – you laugh? –
around the narcissus flower, then.

I
In my heart stirs restlessly
a serpent of past kisses.

SHE
The open seconds nailed
their roots in my sighs.

I
Entwined by the same breeze,
face to face, we did not recognize each other!

SHE
The foliage grows dark, go quickly,
neither of us has yet been born!

Flower of sun.
Flower of river.

'immediate publication' of the *suites*, it was just another example of wishful thinking, and there is no evidence that the poet had discussed the matter either with his long-suffering father, who had financed his two previous books, or with any publisher.

To round off the summer of 1923 the García Lorcas made their usual visit to Malaga where, as always, they stayed at the Hernán Cortés hotel, on the very edge of the Mediterranean. It had been agreed that Falla, with his sister and other friends, would join the family at the seaside, and Federico and Francisco wrote urging the composer to keep his word. But Don Manuel was held up in Granada.[40]

On 13 September, while the family were still in Malaga, General Miguel Primo de Rivera, Captain General of Catalonia, launched a successful coup against the relatively progressive government of the day, alleging that military intervention was necessary in order 'to save the Fatherland' from the inefficiency of the politicians. Primo de Rivera appointed himself President of a military directorate; the state of war was proclaimed, with the consequent suppression of public liberties and the imposition of press censorship; the parliament was abolished; the left-wing trade unions, with the exception of the socialists, were proscribed, and the legally constituted town councils were replaced by *juntas* named by the military authorities. King Alfonso XIII, who favoured the Army, accepted the new situation, thereby incurring the wrath of the proletariat, the democratic political establishment and the intellectuals. Primo de Rivera had announced, on seizing power, that his intervention would be merely provisional. In fact the paternalistic and fairly benevolent dictatorship was to last for seven years.

By the time of the coup another major project had begun to take shape in Lorca's mind: a play about the Granadine heroine Mariana Pineda, who had been executed in 1831 at the age of twenty-seven by the repressive regime of Ferdinand VII, on the charge of having embroidered a flag for the town's liberal conspirators. Lorca had become acquainted as a child in Fuente Vaqueros with the story of Mariana Pineda, about whom ballads still circulated and whose sad end was recalled by old people in the village. Gradually Mariana had become an obsession with him, and when, in 1909, the family moved to Granada, the heroine's nearby statue, in the square that bears her name, had further stimulated the boy's interest in the reputedly beautiful victim of that tyrannical king.[41]

Lorca, as he explained in a letter to Fernández Almagro, written just before Primo de Rivera's coup, was fascinated by Mariana's love life. From the ballad about her that he had learned as a child he guessed that the young widow was passionate; the stories he had heard confirmed this, and he had always assumed that, if Mariana embroidered a flag for the liberals, it was as much for the sake of love as from a fervent belief in democracy. 'She became a martyr for Liberty,' Lorca wrote to Melchor, 'being, in reality (as, moreover, one gathers from the historical accounts) a *victim* of her own enamoured and crazed heart. She was a Juliet without a Romeo, closer to the madrigal than to the ode.' Lorca was determined to find out more about Mariana's private life. Was she in love with her cousin, Fernando Alvarez de Sotomayor, whose escape from Granada gaol she had helped to engineer? The researchers had never succeeded in establishing the truth, but tradition had no doubts about it – and the poet was more interested in tradition than in the strict historicity of the matter.[42]

Melchor replied to Lorca's letter shortly after the right-wing coup. He considered the latter an 'enormously regressive' step. 'The people of Spain continue in a state of unbelievable apathy,' he wrote. 'They have seen what chaos is to ensue – and don't turn a hair. What blindness! We are paying for historical sins difficult to remit [. . .] What a splendid autumn it would be but for Primo de Rivera.' As for Federico's projected play on Mariana Pineda, Melchor's enthusiasm knew no bounds: the subject was excellent and Lorca's approach to it – to express the poetic, and not the slavishly historical, truth – seemed to him the correct, indeed the only, one. Melchor recognized, moreover, that the seizure of Spain's political helm by yet another reactionary general favoured the 'exaltation' of the figure of Mariana Pineda, for Primo de Rivera's accession to power was the return of the nineteenth century, which 'our parents have been unable to surmount'.[43]

Lorca confided his project to another friend, Antonio Gallego Burín, like Fernández Almagro an authority on Granada, and himself, as it happened, hard at work on a book about Mariana Pineda. Federico informed Gallego that he had already mentioned his idea to Gregorio Martínez Sierra and Catalina Bárcena, and that the couple had responded favourably. From Gallego the poet required merely some bibliographical advice about Granada at the time of Mariana's activities and, in particular, information concerning her persecutor, the sinister Pedrosa, Ferdinand VII's police chief in the town.[44]

Encouraged by his two friends, Lorca worked fast, as was his way when he got the bit between his teeth, reading a first draft of the play to José Mora Guarnido before the end of the year.[45] This version appears not to be extant. The text was later revised considerably, some of the changes being counselled, almost certainly, by the adverse political conditions then prevailing in Spain, among them strict censorship. For four years Lorca would spare no effort to see *Mariana Pineda* produced – four years of constant disappointments and procrastinations, which, at moments, almost drove the poet to despair.

Meanwhile, that autumn of 1923, as Spanish society gradually adapted to the restrictions imposed on it by Primo de Rivera, Federico's many friends in the capital eagerly awaited his return to the Residencia de Estudiantes, which it seems he finally achieved only in November.[46] A month earlier Melchor Fernández Almagro had published, in the leading Madrid review *España*, a penetrating article on the *granadino*'s poetic world, hailing Lorca as 'the great revelation' among contemporary Spanish poets, despite the fact that to date he had published only one book of verse.[47] Melchor, who understood better than almost anyone else the workings of Federico's mind, was to prove one of his most subtle critics.

By the time Federico returned to Madrid Salvador Dalí had been sent down for a year from the Academy of Fine Arts for his alleged participation in a rumpus concerning the election of a new professor, and had almost certainly returned to Figueras. Lorca would not see the painter again until the autumn of 1924, and there is no indication that they corresponded during Dalí's absence.[48]

10

1924–5

Gypsy Ballads

Gregorio Martínez Sierra had undertaken to produce the new version of *The Tragicomedy of Don Cristóbal and Señorita Rosita* on which the poet was working. But nothing came of the project. He had also expressed his willingness to put on *Mariana Pineda*, but here too difficulties arose and, in June 1924, Federico told Falla that the production had been postponed and that he was rewriting the play.[1]

Shortly afterwards Lorca returned to Granada accompanied by the poet Juan Ramón Jiménez and his wife Zenobia, who had expressed an urge to visit the Alhambra and Generalife under Federico's expert guidance. They were unforgettable days, as much for the García Lorcas and their friends as for the Jiménezes. At first, to be sure, there were some problems: the hypersensitive, fastidious Juan Ramón disliked the hotel, and another had to be found; the food upset his delicate stomach; and it can safely be assumed that the note in *El Defensor de Granada* announcing his arrival hardly improved his humour, for the printer's imps had seen to it that his name figured as 'Juan Ramírez Jiménez'. But these were trifles compared with the positive aspects of the visit.[2]

Juan Ramón and his muse could not have been better looked after. The García Lorcas, Fernando and Gloria de los Ríos and their daughter Laura, Manuel de Falla and his sister María del Carmen, Miguel Cerón, Lorca's friend Emilia Llanos (whose beauty and bearing deeply impressed Juan Ramón), the painter Manuel Angeles Ortiz, just back from Paris – they all took infinite pains to ensure the success of the visit.

Jiménez loved the gardens and fountains of Granada but disapproved strongly of the modern innovations he had seen in the town. Back in Madrid he wrote to Federico (20 July 1924) complaining about 'the appalling, boastful, aggressive buildings thrown up on Granadine plain and hill by a pride bloated with money, in the most beautiful spots in line and colour of that imponderable and universal landscape'.[3] Juan Ramón was only confirming the view of the local capitalists held by Federico, Melchor Fernández Almagro and the other *rinconcillistas* and, before them, Angel Ganivet.

After the Jiménezes left, the García Lorcas moved out to their summer quarters at Asquerosa, where Federico set to work with the vigour he always deployed during the summer months. On 29 July he took his notebook and, under the general heading of *Romancero gitano* ('Gypsy Ballads') wrote a decisive figure '1' at the top of the page and copied out, without a title, the 'Romance de la luna, luna' ('Ballad of the Moon, Moon'), which had been written the previous year and, according to the poet, was the first of the series.[4] On other pages of the same notebook Lorca wrote, on 30 July, the 'Romance de la pena negra' ('Ballad of Black Anguish') and, on 20 August, without a title, 'La monja gitana' ('The Gypsy Nun').[5] At around the same time he sent Fernández Almagro another ballad (it is not clear which) and promised, if his friend replied quickly, to let him have the 'Romance sonámbulo' ('Sleepwalking Ballad').[6] It is possible that Lorca also wrote during these weeks the 'Romance de la Guardia Civil Española' ('Ballad of the Spanish Civil Guard').[7] The summer of 1924, then, saw the crystallization, as a projected book, of the *Gypsy Ballads*, which derived directly from the *cante jondo* cycle written in November 1921 during the preparations for the competition.

It is not necessary to return to the real-life, non-literary circumstances that linked Lorca (first in Fuente Vaqueros, then in Granada itself) to the world of the Andalusian Gypsy. Nor need we refer again to the poet's concept of the Gypsy contribution to the creation of *cante jondo*, deriving in the main from Manuel de Falla. For Lorca, by the time he gave his lecture on *cante jondo* in 1922, the Gypsy was coming to symbolize the deepest elements in the Andalusian psyche. In *Gypsy Ballads* this process reaches its logical poetic conclusion.

Certainly there has been a great deal of confusion about Lorca's Gypsies. The poet himself was well aware of the problems involved, and on several occasions felt obliged to explain what he had sought to achieve in the ballads. In 1931, for example, he stated:

Gypsy Ballads is only Gypsy in one or two passages at the beginning. Really it forms an Andalusian retable* expressing Andalusia in all its variety. At least that's how I see it. It's an Andalusian song in which the Gypsies serve as the refrain. What I do is to bring together all the various local elements and give them the most visually

---

* The Spanish *retablo* means both retable (or reredos) and the portable stage of the puppeteer. Perhaps Lorca has both senses in mind.

striking label. The ballads appear to have several different protagonists. But in fact there is only one: Granada.[8]

This definition the poet later completed with some written precisions:

Although it is called Gypsy, the book as a whole is the poem of Andalusia, and I call it Gypsy because the Gypsy is the most distinguished, profound and aristocratic element of my country, the one most representative of its way of being and which best preserves the fire, blood and alphabet of Andalusian and universal truth.

The book, therefore, is a retable expressing Andalusia, with Gypsies, horses, archangels, planets, its Jewish breeze, its Roman breeze, rivers, crimes, the everyday touch of the smuggler and the celestial touch of the naked children of Cordova who tease Saint Raphael.* A book in which the *visible* Andalusia is hardly mentioned but in which palpitates the invisible one. And now I am going to be explicit. It is an anti-picturesque, anti-folkloric, anti-flamenco book, with not a single short jacket, bullfighter's suit of lights, wide-brimmed sombrero or tambourine;† where the figures move against primeval backdrops and there is just one protagonist, Anguish, great and dark as a summer's sky, which filters into the marrow of the bones and the sap of the trees and has nothing in common with melancholy, or with nostalgia, or any other affliction or distress of the soul.[9]

The principal actor of *Gypsy Ballads* then – the poet leaves us in no doubt about it – is a personage called both Anguish (*Pena*) and Granada. And in these poems, despite their dazzling surface and throbbing vitality, what Lorca is really expressing is his view of Granada, and, by extension, his own underlying sense of doom and foreboding.

It was a brilliant idea on the part of the poet to give epic expression to the traditional struggle between the Gypsies of Andalusia and the Civil Guard, the rural paramilitary police force founded in 1842 by the Duke of Ahumada to put down banditry, and whose patent-leather three-cornered hats are among the most famous symbols of Spain. In Granada itself not only have vendettas among Gypsy families been common – they are reflected in the ballads 'Reyerta' ('Affray') and 'Muerte de Antoñito el Camborio' ('The Death of Antoñito el Camborio') – but the frequent bloody encounters between the Romany and the Civil Guard have left their imprint on the collective unconscious of the town. At the beginning of November 1919, for example, *El Defensor de Granada* reported that Gypsies had killed two Civil Guards in the Sierra Nevada. The culprits were soon apprehended and taken to Granada, handcuffed, on muleback. Lorca and Manuel Angeles Ortiz saw their arrival. The Gypsies had been brutally beaten by the Guards and their faces were bruised purple from the blows. Sickened at the sight, Ortiz had fainted and been carried inside the Café Alameda, where the

---

* St Raphael is the unofficial patron saint of Cordova.
† Here Lorca was being forgetful, for in 'Preciosa and the Wind', the Gypsy girl plays a tambourine by the shore.

Rinconcillo met. The painter never forgot that scene. Nor, we may surmise, did Lorca, who perhaps had it in mind when he wrote the 'Canción del gitano apaleado' ('Song of the Beaten Gypsy') with which, in July 1925, he completed his brief 'Scene of the Lieutenant-Colonel of the Civil Guard' included in *Poem of Cante Jondo*.[10]

As for the ballad form in itself (octosyllabic lines with the same assonance throughout in the even ones), it was not surprising that Lorca, a born minstrel with a rare gift for reciting his poems, should have felt powerfully attracted by the genre, in both its literary and oral traditions, a genre termed by Juan Ramón Jiménez the 'river of the Spanish language', and whose history, in the view of Lorca's friend the poet Pedro Salinas, is, in good part, 'that of Spanish literature itself'.[11] Lorca explained that, since 1919, he had been deeply attracted to the ballad, feeling that it was the verse form best suited to his temperament. It had been traditionally of narrative character, and what he wished to do was to fuse this strain with a lyrical component (Juan Ramón Jiménez had recently written lyrical ballads) in order to produce a new synthesis.[12]

Each of the four 'Gypsy' ballads which we know with certainty had been written by the end of the summer of 1924 evoke a Granadine atmosphere, confirming the poet's statement about the 'protagonist' of the collection. 'The Gypsy Nun' and 'Ballad of the Moon, Moon' conjure up the Albaicín quarter; 'Sleepwalking Ballad', the Alhambra Wood and the Generalife; and the 'Ballad of Black Anguish', despite being assigned by the poet to the province of Jaén, perhaps suggests the Sacromonte.[13] The poems treat the themes of erotic frustration and death. Soledad Montoya, the protagonist of the 'Ballad of Black Anguish' and, according to the poet, 'the embodiment of Anguish with no solution',[14] is one of Lorca's most memorable and pathetic figures, and with the eponymous Gypsy nun forms yet another link in the chain of sexually thwarted women that stretches from Joan the Mad and other figures of the early work to the daughters of Bernarda Alba.

Around the eighteen poems of *Gypsy Ballads*, almost all of them written between 1924 and 1927, there has grown up a huge bibliography in many languages. Beyond any doubt it is the most widely read, most often recited, most studied and most celebrated book of poems in the whole of Spanish literature. From the mythical roots of Lorca's Gypsy world to the identity in 'real life' of some of its characters (such as the English consul of 'Preciosa and the Wind', Soledad Montoya or Antoñito 'el Camborio'); from the numerous folkloric reminiscences embedded in these verses (and the not infrequent literary ones) to the symbolic value in them of the moon, fish, bulls, flowers or the colour green; from the recondite allusions to Mithras and Manichaeism to the references to Christ; from the function of the assonating rhymes to that of the punctuation: there is hardly an aspect of this poetry that has not been worked over by Spanish and foreign critics and scholars. The circumstance proves that, despite the label of 'provincialism' sometimes hung around the neck of *Gypsy Ballads*, the poems rise above the narrow local limits of their origins.

The Shoemaker's Prodigious Wife and *Mariana Pineda*

Federico was not only at work on his ballads during the summer of 1924. In a letter to Melchor Fernández Almagro written, it appears, at this time (Lorca hardly ever dated his correspondence), occurs the first known reference to *The Shoemaker's Prodigious Wife*, whose opening act the poet stated he had completed. The play, Lorca assured Melchor, was in the line of the Andalusian puppet tradition, and would be enlivened with flute and guitar music.[15] The theme of the elderly man married to a young, attractive wife is, of course, an old one, and Lorca was no doubt familiar with many of the precedents, Spanish and otherwise. A manuscript that appears to be an early sketch of the play, written in the style of a folk tale ('Once upon a time there was a shoemaker . . .'), suggests, read alongside the list of characters included in Lorca's letter to Fernández Almagro, that in his mind were echoing, particularly, reminiscences of Cervantes's *Exemplary Novels* and of Alarcón's novel *The Three-Cornered Hat*: reminiscences most likely prompted by the poet's close knowledge of Falla's ballet *The Three-Cornered Hat* and his tiny opera *Master Peter's Puppet Show*.[16]

Not so obvious, though, are the elements taken from the poet's Granadine background. It was mentioned earlier that the 'shocking green dress' in which the 'prodigious' young wife appears at the beginning of the play, and which crops up again in *The House of Bernarda Alba*, is an allusion to the one belonging to Federico's cousin Clotilde García Picossi, in Fuente Vaqueros. The 'ancient polka' rendered in the street on a flute accompanied by a guitar, and which so pleases the *zapatera*, used to be played on a clarinet in the village (so the poet assured his friends) by a certain Pepe 'The Painter'.[17] The Mayor is based on the one nicknamed 'el Pongao', who when Lorca lived in Fuente Vaqueros headed the corporation of the nearby village of Chauchina (home town, too, of the real-life Camborio family, who acquire mythical status in *Gypsy Ballads*).[18] As for the Child, he clearly reflects aspects of the author: the love he feels for the *zapatera* reminds us of Federico's for his older female cousins, especially Clotilde García Picossi, Mercedes Delgado García and Aurelia González García, while his excitement when the ballad-singer arrives is an obvious allusion to Lorca's own on that momentous occasion in Fuente Vaqueros when the strolling players erected their stage in the village square. Moreover, when the Child, anxious to protect his friend from the nastiness of her neighbours, offers to fetch the 'big sword' belonging to his grandfather ('the one who went to the war'), Federico is recalling a true detail from his own childhood.[19] As for the *zapatera*'s terrible tongue, the poet had to the forefront of his mind the colourful outbursts of Emilia Llanos's maid, Dolores Cebrián, when irritated by her suitor, as well, no doubt, as those of the peasant servants in his own home.[20]

The Shoemaker's Prodigious Wife was destined to be one of the poet's most successful works and to be produced, in his lifetime, more than any other of his plays. In it Lorca connected again, as he had done in *The Tragicomedy of Don Cristóbal and Señorita Rosita*, with the Andalusian popular tradition within which his childhood had developed. And the result was a work of perfect balance and symmetry. Music and snatches of verse taken directly from folk tradition, or invented in accordance with that tradition, and the richly metaphorical language of the Vega: these were to be fundamental elements in the later rural tragedies. As for the theme of the work, here again, despite the guignolesque, farcical aspects and the humour of the play, we find yet another variant of Lorca's omnipresent obsession with amorous frustration and sterility.

In the autumn of 1924 Lorca returned to the Residencia de Estudiantes. There he resumed his friendship with Salvador Dalí, who after his year's rustication had been allowed to return to the Academy of Fine Arts,[21] and contacted Gregorio Martínez Sierra, whom he still saw as his saviour, informing him of his progress on *The Shoemaker's Prodigious Wife* and the revised version of *Mariana Pineda*. In November he wrote euphorically to his parents to say that both plays had made a strong impression on the great man, especially *Mariana Pineda*, while the dramatist Eduardo Marquina had gone so far as to say that he would cut off his right hand if *Mariana* were not successful throughout the Spanish-speaking world! There were problems, however, and because of Primo de Rivera's censorship the work could not be staged straightaway. The plan was to have the play ready to be performed at the first favourable moment. 'I believe, and everyone believes the same,' continued Federico,

that this year it will be produced; and I'm convinced that the work's success won't lie, and *should not lie*, as Don Fernando [de los Ríos] would wish, in its political aspects, because it's a *work of pure art*, a tragedy I've written, as you know, without a political slant. I want its success to be a *poetical* one – and it will be! – no matter when it is produced.

As for *The Shoemaker's Prodigious Wife*, Lorca assured his parents that it was almost finished and that it too would soon be performed, not least because the role of the *zapatera* admirably suited Martínez Sierra's mistress, the actress Catalina Bárcena. 'If I make a hit in the theatre, all the doors will open wide for me,' the poet ended his missive home.[22] No doubt he needed to convince himself, as well as his parents, that his literary career was advancing and that, despite the difficulties, it would not be long before he achieved a breakthrough as a dramatist. The reality was going to be even harder than he could have imagined, however: *Mariana Pineda* was not produced until the summer of 1927 and *The Shoemaker's Prodigious Wife* until December 1930, after the poet's return from New York and Cuba.

It seems that it was during this autumn at the Residencia that Lorca first met a handsome young poet who was beginning to make a reputation for himself in Madrid. Rafael Alberti, like Federico, was an Andalusian, but from another, very different, province – Cadiz. He was born in 1902 in Puerto de Santa María, and his passionate love of his native sea and nostalgia for his childhood were reflected in the poems that, in 1925, appeared under the title *Marinero en tierra* ('Mariner Ashore'). Alberti had heard a lot about Lorca and knew his *Book of Poems*, while Federico must have read his fellow Andalusian's verses in the small magazines of the day. The time was ripe, therefore, for a friendship that was to prove stimulating to both poets.

Alberti's first love had been painting, but when he and Lorca met he had already taken the decision to devote his energies fully to poetry. Federico begged him to celebrate the occasion of their meeting by painting one last picture for him, and Alberti agreed. In his autobiography *La arboleda perdida* (1959) – the 'lost grove' of the title is a submerged wood in his childhood paradise by the sea – Alberti evoked his first impressions of Lorca. The poet had invited him to supper (he himself was not a 'resident', but lived nearby) and, afterwards, in the garden, had recited for him the almost hypnotic 'Sleepwalking Ballad':

> Verde que te quiero verde.
> Verde viento, verdes ramas.
> El barco sobre la mar
> y el caballo en la montaña . . . *

Alberti never forgot these first hours with Lorca. The recitation was accompanied by the murmur of the Residencia's poplars, and when they parted late that night it was to be as 'cousins' (*primos*) for ever. (In Andalusian Gypsy terminology to call someone a 'cousin' is to express

---

*   Green how I love you deeply green.
    Green wind, green branches.
    The ship on the sea
    and the horse on the mountain . . .

particularly deep affection.) To a certain extent Alberti and Lorca were to be poetic rivals and, if we can believe Salvador Dalí, Lorca was at times jealous of the younger, blond poet from Puerto de Santa María whose charisma, if different from his own, was nevertheless considerable.[23]

Alberti was soon a frequent visitor to the Residencia, and in his autobiography recalls Lorca's impromptu folk song sessions, already by that time famous. Sometimes Federico would hold competitions:

'Where is this one from? Let's see if anyone knows,' the poet would ask, singing and accompanying himself:

> The lads from Monleón
> went off early to plough,
> alas! alas!
> went off early to plough.

In those days, when there was growing research into, and a new fervour for, the old songs and ballads, it was not difficult to know where they came from.

'From the Salamanca area,' someone would reply, no sooner had the tragic bull-fighting ballad got under way.

'Correct, well done,' Federico would agree, at once serious and burlesque, adding, with a pedagogical intonation: 'And it was included in his songbook by the priest Don Dámaso Ledesma.'[24]

Alberti was also familiar with the game called *anaglifos*, invented by the 'residents', which consisted in choosing three nouns, the first of which had to be repeated twice, the second to be *gallina* ('hen') and the last to shock by its phonetic unexpectedness or total lack of logical connection with the preceding words.[25] José Moreno Villa gives various examples, of which one will suffice:

> El té
> el té
> la gallina
> y el Teotocópuli.*

The fact that this particular *anaglifo* began by referring to tea was no doubt an allusion to the vast quantities of the beverage drunk in the Residencia, in accordance with the English influence that pervaded the hostel. As for the associations between tea, hens and El Greco, that is anyone's guess.[26]

Another fad in the Residencia was the application of the adjective *putrefacto* ('putrid', 'putrescent') to whatever was considered bourgeois, out-of-date or artistically fetid. No one seems sure who first put the term

---

* The tea
the tea
the hen
and Theotocopulous.

into currency, although Pepín Bello, renowned for his original ideas, is the leading candidate for the distinction. By 1925 the word was all the rage. Dalí did a special line in *putrefactos*, drawing them in a wide variety of shapes and sizes. 'Some wore scarfs, coughed a lot and sat alone on street benches,' writes Alberti.

Others were elegant, with a flower in their buttonhole, carried a stick and were accompanied by a little *beasty*. There were Academy-member *putrefactos*, and *putrefactos* who were putrid without being in the Academy.* They came in all genders – masculine, feminine, neuter and epicene. And were of all ages.[27]

Dalí and Lorca planned an amusing book on the species which never came to fruition, despite Salvador's strenuous efforts to get the poet to remit the promised texts, and for several years the *putrefactos* were a constant theme of the Catalan's letters.[28]

As for the presence of the Residencia in Lorca's work, many of the poems written between 1921 and 1924 and later included in the slim volume *Canciones* ('Songs'), published in 1927, reflect the atmosphere of the hostel, with its tea-drinking sessions, its humour and its camaraderie. Several of the compositions are dedicated to 'residents' and other friends who regularly visited the house – among them José ('Pepín') Bello, Luis Buñuel, José Fernández-Montesinos, the Englishman Campbell ('Colin') Hackforth-Jones (whom Lorca would see again in New York), Rafael Alberti, José Bergamín and the young musicians Ernesto Halffter and Gustavo Durán – while 'Nocturnos de la ventana' ('Nocturnes of the Window') is explicitly ascribed to the 'Resi', the window in question being that of the poet's room.

It seems that it was during the 1924 autumn session at the Residencia that José Moreno Villa unwittingly provided Lorca with one of the central ideas for his play *Doña Rosita the Spinster* when he told the poet, Dalí and Pepín Bello about his discovery, in an early nineteenth-century French book on roses, of a remarkable species, the *rosa mutabilis*, which is red when it opens in the morning, flushes a deeper carmine at midday, turns white in the afternoon and dies the same night. Lorca was deeply impressed by this colourful variant on the *topos* of the rose as symbol of passing time and love's brevity, and said later that, by the time Moreno Villa had finished, he had composed the play in his head, although it was several years before he actually wrote it down.[29] The poet had apparently forgotten, however, that he had already begun to think about the play two years earlier, in 1922, when he had sketched out a list of characters.[30]

---

* The Royal Spanish Academy of the Language, to give it its full title, was founded in 1713. Its members were considered staid and unimaginative by Lorca and his friends at the Residencia.

Federico spent Christmas in Granada with his family, as usual. There he received a letter from Juan Vicéns, one of his friends at the Residencia and, like Buñuel and Pepín Bello, an Aragonese. 'I suppose you'll be returning to Madrid to see Buñuel off,' he wrote. But he supposed wrong, and when Buñuel left for Paris the poet was still in Granada where, on 25 January, he dated the 'definitive' manuscript of *Mariana Pineda*.[31] Referring in 1927 to the early drafts of the play, Lorca said that he had 'three completely different versions of the drama, the first of them absolutely unviable as theatre', and went on:

The one I'm staging implies a fusion, a synchronization. It has two planes: the first is broad, synthetic, and over it the attention of the audience can hover without complications. The second – the deep meaning – will be grasped only by part of the audience.[32]

What was the poet intimating here? That the play had a 'secret' accessible only to an initiated minority? The 'deep meaning' of *Mariana Pineda* could hardly be an attack against the Primo de Rivera dictatorship, for the work had begun to take shape months before the *coup d'état* of September 1923. And, in fact, while liberty, political and personal, is the theme of *Mariana*, there are few allusions in the play that could be taken as deliberate references to Primo de Rivera's Spain. It seems probable, rather, that Lorca was alluding to his treatment of love in the work. Mariana is, above all, a woman in love. From the opening scene of the play we know that, if she has taken it upon herself to risk embroidering a liberal flag (a highly dangerous activity in those days), it is in order to please the man in her life. Mariana is well aware that only with the collapse of Ferdinand VII's odious regime and the return to democracy will she be able to live happily with Pedro. Moreover, she is far from sharing the political naïvety of the conspirators, and has little faith that they will be backed by the masses or that there are any 'liberal bands' waiting to hurry to the rescue. What she cares about is Pedro. And Pedro proves to be all hot air and no action. The love that the widowed Mariana feels for the pusillanimous liberal captain absorbs her to such an extent that she neglects her children, as she herself recognizes. Moreover, Mariana is bitterly conscious that she is now over thirty. We sense that, in Pedro, she sees her last hope for finding happiness. For this reason she will stop at nothing. And certainly not at embroidering a liberal flag.

Another possible aspect of the 'double meaning' of the play could be the cynical view of the Granadine bourgeoisie and aristocracy that the work transmits. No one moves a finger to intervene on Mariana's behalf. Before the execution the streets of Granada are empty and the heroine, alone in her cell, knows in her heart that neither Pedro nor anyone else will attempt to save her. When Fernando confirms this, he is forced to witness the transformation of Mariana, who, accepting her fate and refusing to escape the scaffold by naming the conspirators, decides to go to the sacrifice with dignity. The critics have paid too little attention to Fernando, another failed Lorca lover, whose 'bitter passion' for Mariana is so reminiscent of the Cockroach's in *The Butterfly's Evil Spell* that we may be forgiven for sensing a close identification on the part of the author with his character.[33] Mariana's final words to Fernando offer little consolation:

> ¡A ti debí quererte más que a nadie en el mundo,
> si el corazón no fuera nuestro gran enemigo!
> Corazón, ¡por qué mandas en mí si yo no quiero!*[34]

Gregorio Martínez Sierra was still assuring Federico in March 1925 that he would soon produce both *Mariana Pineda* and *The Shoemaker's Prodigious Wife*; and suggested, to the poet's irritation, that the plays first be given a run in the provinces that summer to see how they fared. Lorca told his parents that he would insist that Martínez Sierra produce them initially in Madrid and nowhere else, and that he was about to make this perfectly clear to the impresario. If the latter said no, he was determined to give the plays to another company. Despite all the setbacks and delays, however, Federico continued to believe in the good intentions of Martínez Sierra, whom he still felt was 'the best producer in Spain'.[35]

In Cadaqués with Dalí

Meanwhile, Lorca had received two tempting invitations: to give a poetry recital at the Athenaeum in Barcelona and, taking advantage of this visit, to spend Holy Week with Salvador Dalí and his family in Figueras and Cadaqués. Delighted, he accepted both.[36]

Holy Week began that year on 5 April. Some days earlier, Ana María Dalí, then seventeen, and her father had travelled down to their holiday house by the sea at Cadaqués to prepare for the arrival of their guest. Salvador and Federico turned up at lunchtime, and Ana María was enchanted by the poet. 'When we got to the dessert,' she writes, 'we were such good friends that it was as though we had always known one another.'[37]

Cadaqués, one of the most attractive towns on the Costa Brava, is cut off from the rest of Spain by the impressive mountain barrier of the Pení, which rises to a height of over 2000 feet, and at the time of Lorca's visit could be

---

* I should have loved you more than anyone else in the world,
  if our hearts weren't our worst enemies!
  Heart, why do you control me when I don't want you to!

reached only by horse-drawn cart: a tiny Mediterranean paradise, as yet hardly touched by tourism. The Dalí villa was situated on the edge of the pebbled beach of Es Llané, only a few yards from the water. The houses that today surround it did not exist then, nor did the street that now passes in front of the eucalyptus-shaded terrace, preventing the direct access to the beach previously enjoyed by the family. In 1925 the villa stood almost alone, and on days of *calma blanca* ('white calm'), when not a ripple stirred the surface of the bay, the building would be reflected as if in a mirror.

The poet was delighted with the town, the Dalí family, and the local characters to whom Salvador introduced him. Among the latter the most notable was undoubtedly Lydia Noguer, who might have been fifty when Lorca met her although her age was indeterminate. As a young woman Lydia had kept a boarding house in Cadaqués where Picasso and Derain stayed. Later her mind went – as would those of her two fishermen sons – and her always vivid imagination, freed from the constraints of reason, had flowered with a tropical luxuriance. The woman's torrential conversation, shot through with extraordinary insights and oracular pronouncements, fascinated Lorca, who listened to her in astonishment. Later, in his letters to Ana María Dalí, he rarely failed to inquire about Lydia, while Salvador kept the poet up to date concerning her latest crack-brained effusions.[38]

Encouraged by Salvador, Lorca read *Mariana Pineda* to the Dalís and some selected friends. The event proved a great success. Ana María was in tears when Federico finished, and Dalí senior beside himself with enthusiasm, exclaiming that Lorca was the greatest poet of the century.[39] The truth no doubt was that the lines, read and 'acted' by Lorca himself, seemed better than they were – less naïve, less laboured and less antiquated. The poet, utterly at home with his hosts, unfolded during his brief stay the rich tapestry of his many talents – impromptu poetry recitals, anecdotes, mimicry, tricks and even the occasional bout of sulking for good measure – and the Dalís were fascinated.[40]

There were boat trips, which produced in Federico, terrified as he was of drowning, a mixture of delight and apprehension. In his letters to Ana María he referred later, exaggerating no doubt, to some scare that had occurred on one of these outings. 'How often I have recalled that very real danger of shipwreck that we ran at Cape Creus,' he wrote to her the following autumn. 'And how delicious that rabbit tasted that we ate with salt and *sand* at the foot of the Orange Eagle!'[41] Cape Creus, which, as Dalí later wrote in his *Secret Life*, 'is exactly the epic spot where the mountains of the Pyrenees come down into the sea, in a grandiose geological delirium',[42] had already exerted a deep influence on the young painter's ideas and art, and was to be one of the protagonists of his future pictorial work. Dalí was deeply impressed by what he called 'the elementary and planetary violence of the most diverse and the most paradoxically assembled rocks',[43] identified locally as The Camel, The Eagle, The Anvil, The Dead Woman, The Monk, The Lion's Head and so forth, and which undergo surprising transformations in the changing Mediterranean light and depending on the vantage point of the viewer. In these crags and rocks, later filmed by Buñuel in *L'Age d'or* (1930), Dalí discovered his principle of 'paranoiac metamorphosis', and it is not surprising that the painter introduced Lorca with particular pride to Cape Creus, whose 'stirring' forms belie the apparently motionless character of the rugged promontory.[44]

Lorca took part enthusiastically in Cadaqués's traditional Holy Week festivities, guzzling the delicious sweetmeats produced for the occasion and following the processions. One day Dalí took him to Gerona, to see the Easter ceremonies for which the cathedral is renowned. 'I have spent a magnificent Holy Week, with mass in Gerona Cathedral and the murmur of Latin waves,' Lorca wrote in a postcard to Manuel de Falla.[45] Other friends received equally enthusiastic communications, among them the poet Jorge Guillén,[46] and, in Granada, Fernando Vílchez. To the latter Lorca confided that, after Granada's Vega, nothing could be more beautiful than the region of the Ampurdán.[47] It was a view that must have pleased Salvador who, recalling his childhood, was to write that his native plain's 'unique geology, with its enormous vigour, was later to fashion the entire aesthetic of the philosophy of the Dalinian landscape'.[48] Dalí also took Lorca to see the famous ruins of the Greek and Roman trading port of Ampurias, on the shore of the Bay of Rosas, from which the Ampurdán takes its name. These the poet found fascinating, especially a large mosaic representing the sacrifice of Iphigenia, which immediately inspired him to write something on the subject.[49]

Salvador was determined to show Lorca off not only to the locals but to his friends in Barcelona, and invited a group of them to spend a day in Cadaqués. It proved an important event for the poet – his first contact with the intellectual and artistic life of the Catalan capital. Among those who responded to Dalí's imperious summons was the poet Josep Maria de Sagarra, who was to become a good friend of Federico and whom he saw again a few days later in Barcelona.[50]

Dalí was well aware of Federico's obsessive fear of death and of one of his strangest compulsions: the need to act out his own demise and burial. The earliest record of this ceremony is from 1918 when, with the *rinconcillistas* Manuel Angeles Ortiz, Angel Barrios and Miguel Pizarro, Lorca devised a 'film', made with a sequence of stills, called *The History of the Treasure*, in which, dressed as Moors, they enacted the assassination of the guardian of a hoard of gold – the guardian being played by the poet.[51] Luis Domínguez Guilarte, the son of Martin Domínguez Berrueta, witnessed a similar scene when, during Carnival in Granada, Lorca once decked himself out as a bullfighter who had just been mortally gored, and persuaded some friends to carry him home, oozing blood, on their shoulders. So realistic was the scene that the boy thought that Federico had really been injured, and was immensely relieved when the poet suddenly 'resuscitated' and jumped up laughing and gesticulating.[52] When Lorca moved to Madrid he often put on similar performances for the edification of his companions in the Residencia. Dalí, who shared the poet's fear of death, was deeply impressed. Years later he recalled:

I remember his death-like, terrible expression as, stretched on his bed, he parodied the different stages of his own slow decomposition. In this game the process of putrefaction lasted for five days. Then he would describe his coffin, the positioning of the corpse, and, in detail, the scene of the shutting of the coffin and the progress of the funeral procession through the streets, full of potholes, of his native Granada. Then, when he was sure that he had provoked in us a sufficient unease, he would jump up and break out into wild laughter, showing his white teeth; finally, he would push us towards the door and go back to bed, there to sleep tranquilly, liberated from his anxiety.[53]

It occurred to Dalí to paint Lorca in this corpse-imitating posture, and during what was clearly an action-crammed Holy Week in Figueras and Cadaqués he found time to make some preliminary sketches, while his sister Ana María photographed Federico in his recumbent pose. On the basis of these drawings and photographs Salvador began a picture, completed in 1926, in which the influence of the dream world of the surrealists was already apparent. Entitled (in Catalan) *Natura morta (Invitació al son)* – 'Still Life (Invitation to Sleep)'* – the painting was included in Dalí's one-man exhibition held at the Dalmau Gallery in Barcelona at the end of 1926. In the brightly coloured picture the head of the poet, in the form of an heroic sculpture lying on its side, is unmistakable. Beside it Dalí placed one of his triangular *aparells* or 'gadgets', soon to proliferate in his work: with their round central orifice and spindly legs, suggestive of tottering, it seems possible that, in a context of impotence, frustration or sterility, Dalí intended these objects to represent the female sexuality both he and Lorca feared. In the background, behind the poet's head and between two barriers, there is an aeroplane – an allusion, no doubt, to the precision and asepticism of the machine age, whose praises other poets and artists were entoning at the time, following the example of Marinetti (see illustrations 7 and 8).

This was to be the first of a substantial series of paintings and drawings

* Or, 'to Dream' – the word has both meanings.

in which Lorca's head appeared. From the moment of the poet's visit to Cadaqués that spring, in fact, his presence in Dalí's work began to become almost obsessive, displacing that of Ana María, whose ample contours had filled the pictures of the immediately preceding period.

The day before he returned to Figueras with the Dalís, Lorca wrote an enthusiastic letter home. His stay in Cadaqués would prove unforgettable, he stated emphatically; Ana María was by far the most attractive girl he had ever met; he had been invited to read *Mariana Pineda* to the members of the Figueras Arts Club; the following Thursday or Friday he was to give his recital in Barcelona; in Cadaqués the Dalís had made him a cake with his name, and some lines from his poems, inscribed on it . . . He was having a fabulous time.[54]

The poet made a great hit in Figueras, giving a well-attended reading of *Mariana Pineda*, not at the Arts Club, but in the ample salon of Don Salvador Dalí's law chambers and, at the lunch organized by the Club, a poetry recital. Finally, as a last gesture of appreciation, Don Salvador arranged for the poet's benefit an open-air performance of the Catalan folk songs known as *sardanas*, which are rendered traditionally by a *cobla*, a band comprising a flageolet, two *tenoras* (a sort of oboe), a small drum, two cornets, a double-bass, two *tiples* (a variety of guitar) and two bugle-style instruments called *fiscornos*. All of this was quite new to the poet, who, despite the fact that he was relatively well versed in Catalan folk music, had never before had the opportunity of hearing a *cobla*. It was a memorable evening.[55]

The festive week over, Lorca and Dalí set off for Barcelona, where they stayed for a couple of days at the house of Salvador's uncle, Anselmo Doménech, brother of the painter's mother (who had died in 1921).[56]

Barcelona

Lorca was thrilled and exhilarated by Barcelona. Much more European than Madrid, more alive to new tendencies in the arts, more 'sexy' (the Barrio Chino or red-light district was famous), with a medieval quarter unmatched by anything in the capital (only a village in the Middle Ages), the city was like a Spanish, small-scale version of Paris, with the added advantage of being a Mediterranean port. Lorca never forgot these first impressions. At the beginning of the following year he wrote to Melchor Fernández Almagro, whose adverse reaction to Saragossa he said he shared:

But Barcelona's a different matter, isn't it? There you have the Mediterranean, spirit, adventure, the promise of perfect love. There are palm trees, people from all over the world, unusual commerical advertisements, Gothic towers and a rich urban flood-tide of typewriters. How good I feel there, with that style and that *passion*!

I'm not surprised that they remember me, because I got on splendidly with all of them and my poetry was appreciated more than it deserves.

The poet went on to say that he considered himself a 'rabid supporter of Catalonia' – then suffering under the centralist policies of General Primo de Rivera – and that he sympathized with a people 'so sick of Castile'.[57] In March 1924, before he had ever set foot in Catalonia, the poet, along with many other writers, had added his name to a manifesto sent to the government in protest against attempts to limit the use of the Catalan language; since then his dislike of the regime had grown, and now his personal contact with Catalan culture confirmed him in the scorn he already felt for Primo de Rivera.[58]

It was true, as Federico told Fernández Almagro, that he had been made much of in Barcelona. In the Athenaeum Club he gave an informal reading of *Mariana Pineda* and some as yet unpublished poems from *Gypsy Ballads*. Salvador's friends who had visited them in Cadaqués were there, and some other figures from the literary and art worlds, but it was not a genuinely public occasion. The recital had not been advertised and, so far as we know, no comment appeared in the press. Lorca was not yet the famous poet he was soon to become.[59] After the recital the group went to dine in a celebrated Bohemian restaurant, the Canari de la Garriga, which had been frequented, at the turn of the century, by the most notable writers and artists of the day, including Picasso, and was still the haunt of the Barcelona late-night intelligentsia. It was a fitting venue for the occasion, and the uproarious evening was to be the predecessor of the many in which the poet would participate when he returned to Barcelona in 1927 and afterwards. Lorca, Dalí and the rest of the company made the requisite entries in the visitors' book. Dalí produced an amusing caricature of Picasso and signed himself 'ex-prisoner', a reference to the two occasions when, as an adolescent in Figueras, he had been arrested and, particularly, to his brief incarceration in 1923 as a result, in part, of the rumpus in the Academy of Fine Arts which had led to his year's suspension. Lorca, following suit, styled himself 'potential prisoner', adding, in Catalan, 'Long Live Free Catalonia!'[60]

This first visit to Catalonia made a deep impression on Federico. Cadaqués remained in his mind with crystal clarity over the next two years as an image of perfect, classical beauty, of harmony and of creativity. The painter and Cadaqués were now inseparably linked for him, and shortly after returning to Madrid he began work on his great *Ode to Salvador Dalí*. Lorca's letters to Ana María show the extent to which the brief but intensely lived holiday had left its mark. Not a detail had escaped the poet, and his nostalgia had an absolutely authentic ring.[61]

Surrealism and Summer without Dalí

Lorca and Dalí missed the lecture on surrealism given by Louis Aragon at the Residencia de Estudiantes on 18 April 1925. But they must have received a full account of it from their friends, and may even have been able to read it, for it was normal practice for visiting speakers to present a copy of their talks to the warden. Moreover, excerpts were published shortly afterwards in Paris in the June 1925 issue of *La Révolution surréaliste*, which it is likely reached the Residencia.

Aragon, using the 'insolent tone', which, as he explained to his audience, he enjoyed employing on such occasions, had launched a ferocious attack against contemporary Western society, against 'the great intellectual powers – universities, religions, governments – which divide out the world among themselves and which, from his infancy, separate the individual from himself according to a sinister pre-established plan'. He assured his listeners that 'the old Christian era' was over and that he had come to Madrid to preach the good news of the advent of surrealism, 'the arrival of a new spirit of rebellion, a spirit determined to attack everything':

We shall awaken everywhere the germs of confusion and unease. We are the agitators of the spirit. All barricades are valid, all barriers against your accursed pleasures. Jews, leave your ghettos! Starve the people, so that they know at last the taste of the bread of hunger! Move yourself, India of the thousand arms, great legendary Brahma! It is your turn, Egypt! And let the drug traffickers hurl themselves at our terrified countries. Let far-off America crumble under the weight of her buildings amidst her absurd prohibitions. Rebel, world. Look how dry the ground is, how ready for all the fires. Like straw, one might say.[62]

It seems that no Madrid newspaper commented on or reproduced extracts from Aragon's lecture, which had been delivered in French. None the less, the fact could not be denied: surrealism, in the person of one of its fiercest advocates, had made its debut in the Spanish capital – and a fittingly provocative debut at that.

Before Aragon's arrival in Madrid, moreover, Lorca must already have been familiar with the theories underlying the new Paris-based movement. It is almost certain, for example, that in the December 1924 issue of Ortega y Gasset's *Revista de Occidente* he would have read Fernando Vela's critical analysis of Breton's *Manifeste* (in its seventh edition by that October),[63] while we know for a fact that he had a copy of his friend Guillermo de Torre's comprehensive *Literaturas europeas de vanguardia*, published in May 1925, which contained a detailed account of the origins and development of surrealism. Probably Lorca also discussed the latter personally with Torre, that tireless fan of the European avant-garde, and with Dalí, fast veering in the direction of the new movement.[64]

On 28 May the first exhibition held by the Iberian Society of Artists opened in Madrid. The principal purpose of the association, of which Lorca was a member, was to promote contacts between the arts of Catalonia and the rest of Spain. Several of the exhibitors were personal friends of the poet – for example Benjamín Palencia, José Moreno Villa and the sculptor Angel Ferrant, while, naturally, Lorca must have been especially interested in the Dalís: *Naturaleza muerta*, later known as *Syphon and Bottle of Rum*, and *Female Nude*, both of which the painter gave to Federico; *Seated Girl Seen from Behind*; and a remarkable portrait of Luis Buñuel, with elongated, pointed clouds imitating, at the suggestion of the Aragonese, those in Mantegna's *Death of the Virgin* in the Prado, and one of which, almost aimed at Buñuel's right eye, perhaps predicts the opening scene of *Un Chien andalou*.[65]

Shortly afterwards Dalí returned to Cadaqués for the summer and Federico to Granada. As usual the García Lorcas moved out to Asquerosa, and soon the poet was writing to Melchor Fernández Almagro to tell him about his work in progress. With perhaps an allusion to D'Annunzio (*o rinnovarsi o morire*), Lorca expressed his gratitude for the process of renewal which he felt sure was taking place within him, and as a result of which he was composing a series of strange, prose 'dialogues', all of which ended with a song and which he found 'by dint of their superficiality deeply profound'. This summer he had already written *La doncella, el marinero y el estudiante* ('The Maiden, the Sailor and the Student'); *El loco y la loca* ('The Madman and Mad Woman'); *El teniente coronel de la Guardía Civil* ('The Scene of the Lieutenant-Colonel of the Civil Guard'); *Diálogo de la bicicleta de Filadelfia* ('The Dialogue of the Philadelphia Bicycle'), and was at work on *Diálogo de la danza* ('The Dialogue of the Dance'). 'Pure poetry. Naked,' he termed these pieces, alluding to the debate, much in the air at the time, on the subject of *poésie pure* and the 'dehumanization' of art. 'I believe that they're genuinely interesting,' he went on. 'They're more *universal* than the rest of my work . . . (which, between brackets, I find unacceptable).'[66]

Of these titles, 'The Dialogue of the Dance' is unknown and only a few fragments of 'The Madman and Mad Woman' are preserved among the poet's papers. 'The Dialogue of the Philadelphia Bicycle' can almost certainly be identified with 'Buster Keaton's Stroll', undoubtedly the most important of the extant pieces, which amply justifies Lorca's feeling that the 'dialogues' were more 'universal' than his earlier work, if by 'universal' he understood less recognisably Andalusian or even Spanish in flavour. Dalí and Lorca, like Rafael Alberti and other friends more or less connected to the Residencia de Estudiantes, were avid cinema-goers, and passionate admirers of Buster.

'It seems that Buster Keaton has made a film on the sea-bed with his straw hat on top of his diver's helmet,' Dalí wrote to Lorca towards the end of this summer. The reference was to *The Navigator*, made the year before.[67] With another letter Dalí sent Federico a charming *collage* entitled *The Marriage of Buster Keaton*, comprising a series of press cuttings (photos of Buster and accounts of his courtship of Natalia Talmadge), snippets from works on astronomy and Dalinian additions.[68] Some years later Salvador was to attempt an emulation of Keaton's subaquatic feat when, in July 1936, at the International Surrealist Exhibition in London, he attempted to give a lecture wearing a diver's suit, and was almost asphyxiated in the process.[69] 'Forerunners of the irrational', Dalí called Keaton, Mack Sennett and Harry Langdon in his *Secret Life*.[70]

'Buster Keaton's Stroll', despite its extreme brevity, can be seen with hindsight to have been an important landmark in Lorca's development as a writer, looking forward in various ways to *Poet in New York*, *The Public* and *When Five Years Pass*. The setting (the outskirts of Philadelphia), the Pathé News cockerel, the Black who chews a straw hat among old tyres and petrol tins, the aggressively liberated Modern Woman, the insensitivity of an immense, materialistic country – all of this is an intimation of what was to come a few years later when Lorca escaped to New York.

Lorca's Buster Keaton, it has been suggested, incorporates the anxieties and preoccupations of the poet.[71] There is some justification for such a view, certainly. Buster's melancholy eyes, for example, particularly caught Lorca's attention ('infinite and sad like those of a newly born animal' he calls them),[72] and remind us of the many descriptions of the poet's own eyes left by friends and perceptive observers; while Buster's encounter with the All-American Girl points up both the protagonist's absolute incapacity to cope with such a brazen assault on his virility and his longing to be someone else:

I wish I could be different. But I can't, even though I'd like to. Because, where could I leave my hat? Where could I leave my bow-tie and my moiré one? What a shame![73]

If 'Buster Keaton's Stroll' constitutes a little tribute to the silent screen (and heralds Lorca's New York filmscript, *Trip to the Moon*), 'The Maiden, the Sailor and the Student' conjures up Malaga – Lorca's friends the poets Emilio Prados and Manuel Altolaguirre, both from there, appear, unexpectedly, at the end – and, especially, Cadaqués. The balcony where the 'dialogues' take place recalls the window of the Dalís' villa, as it does a work by Salvador, *Venus and the Sailor*, painted that year; while the indication 'a motorboat bedecked with flags crosses the bay, leaving behind its stuttering song' evokes not only this painting, as well as many of Dalí's drawings of the period, but, more concretely, Lorca's letter of May 1925 to

Ana María Dalí in which the poet 'imagines' the scene on the village shore: 'The silver fish come up to take the moon and you bathe your tresses in the water while the stuttering song of the motorboats comes and goes.' The days in Cadaqués, and the constant contact with Dalí, were already influencing Lorca's approach to his work.[74]

Moreover it is certain that the poet's feelings for Dalí had grown more intense as a result of the visit to Figueras and Cadaqués, and that, as he continued to work on the ode to his friend, he was greatly missing Salvador. In another letter to Fernández Almagro he spoke of his urgent need to get out of Spain, to Europe, to Italy, anywhere. Once again Federico was at loggerheads with his parents, who would not allow him to leave Granada – a Granada that now, after Cadaqués, seemed intolerable to him:

Granada is horrible. This isn't Andalusia. Andalusia is different [. . .] It's its people . . . and here they're Galicians.* I'm Andalusian through and through and I long for Malaga, Cordova, for Sanlúcar la Mayor, for Algeciras, for the authenticity and harmony of Cadiz, for Alcalá de los Gazules, for what is *intimately* Andalusian. The real Granada is the one that has disappeared for ever [. . .] The other Andalusia is alive; Malaga, for example.[75]

To get out of Primo de Rivera's Spain, with its stifling sexual morality, its censorship and its taboos, its constant harassment of non-conformers and intellectuals and its pettiness; to achieve financial independence, by getting a teaching job if necessary, perhaps as a 'Lector' in a department of Spanish somewhere: these had become vital goals for the poet who, at the age of twenty-seven, was still totally dependent on his parents and had hardly yet earned a penny from his work. It was natural that Lorca should dream of getting to Europe – not least because there it might be easier for him to come to terms with his homosexuality – and his urge to do so may have been stimulated by a note from Dalí in which the latter informed him that he had received cards from Paris signed by various friends – Buñuel, Juan Vicéns, the Malaga poet José María Hinojosa and José Moreno Villa.[76]

To another friend, also homosexual, the painter Benjamín Palencia, Federico confessed at this time that he was in a deep depression, indeed passing through one of the most severe crises he had known. He felt that both his literary career and his love-life were collapsing around him. 'I believe in nobody. I don't like anybody,' he wrote, going on to express, in metaphorical terms impossible to render meaningfully in English – and whose sense Palencia quite failed to grasp, as his reply showed – his longing for a stable relationship. The poet hoped soon to escape to his beloved

---

* After the expulsion of the Jews and Moors, much of the province of Granada was, in fact, repopulated with people from the north and north-west of the country, so perhaps Lorca's complaint was justified in part.

Malaga, where Dionysus 'grazes your head with his twisted horns and your soul turns the colour of wine' (of red wine, no doubt). There, by the Latin sea, the poet thought that perhaps he might succeed in recapturing his former belief in fatalism, which he had lost in Madrid, and come again to accept that '*What will be will be. And that's all!*'[77]

Another letter sent earlier that summer to Palencia leaves little doubt that the principal cause of Federico's depression was his feelings for Dalí. 'I haven't forgotten the Barcelona business,' Lorca had written. 'It's the only possibility I have of being able to see our friend Dalí this summer.'[78] What the 'business' in question was is not known. The poet announced in the same letter that Dalí would soon visit him in Granada, but Salvador, now feverishly preparing for his first one-man exhibition, to be held at the Dalmau Gallery in Barcelona, soon disabused the poet as to the possibility of his being able to leave Catalonia.[79]

At the end of the summer Federico accompanied his family to his longed-for Malaga. There he wrote to Ana María Dalí that the change of environment had cured him completely, which was probably an exaggeration. 'I can state that Malaga has saved my life,' he wrote. 'As a result I was able to finish my *Iphigenia*, of which I shall send you an extract.' But Ana María never received her extract, and about this work (play or poem?) no further information has come to light.[80]

And the poet's frustrating attempts to find a producer for *The Shoemaker's Prodigious Wife* and *Mariana Pineda*? Things were still moving with painful slowness. On 10 September 1925 Eduardo Marquina wrote to say that that very day he would be in touch with the actress Margarita Xirgu, recommending that she put on *Mariana Pineda*. Marquina undertook to do everything in his power to help.[81] This seemed like good news, for the dramatist, much in vogue at the time, was highly thought of by the famous Catalan actress, who had played many of his heroines. But Federico's hopes were soon to be dashed again.

Then, on 14 November 1925, Dalí's exhibition opened in Barcelona. It was an immediate and resounding hit. Seventeen paintings and five drawings were shown, most of them among the twenty-one-year-old painter's recent production, and the critics were unanimous in their praise. Dalí wrote to Federico ecstatically to tell him that the exhibition had been 'a complete success', enclosing cuttings of only the more stringent reviews because in his opinion the others, 'unconditionally enthusiastic', lacked interest. 'And what are *you* up to? Drawing?' inquired the painter, impishly, going on, 'Don't you fail to write to me – you, the only interesting man I've ever known.' The letter was accompanied by a drawing of a *picador* goading a bull and bearing a significant inscription: 'For Federico García Lorca, with all the tenderness of his little son (*hijito*) Dalí, 1925'.[82] We may assume that, on receiving communications such as this, the poet's urge to get away from Granada and see Salvador must have been overwhelming, and his sense of frustration intensified. But, dependent as he was on the parental purse, there was little Lorca could do for the moment to change the situation. All he could hope was that soon, somehow, he would get the breakthrough in the theatre he so vitally needed if he was ever to achieve some freedom of action.

I I

1926

In January Melchor Fernández Almagro was sent to Barcelona by his newspaper *La Epoca* to report on the celebrations being held in honour of the Catalan painter and writer Santiago Rusiñol.[1] On his way back he wrote to Lorca from Saragossa, and the letter sparked off a detailed reply from the poet in which, after expressing his enthusiasm for Barcelona in particular and Catalonia in general, he added that he was in constant touch with what was going on there thanks to Dalí, his 'inseparable companion', with whom he was then sustaining an 'abundant correspondence' and whom he planned to visit soon to sit for a portrait – perhaps *Still Life (Invitation to Sleep)*, mentioned earlier, inspired by the poet's enactments of his own death. Referring to *Poem of Cante Jondo, Suites* and *Songs*, Lorca told his friend that he had revised these three collections carefully and that they had now reached the required state of what he called 'poetic purity', particularly *Songs*, with which he expressed himself much pleased. But once again it was more a question of wishful thinking than of a concrete publishing programme. In fact, *Songs* did not appear until 1927 while *Poem of Cante Jondo* would have to wait until 1931 and *Suites* until forty years after Lorca's death. Federico was still champing at the bit, desperate to escape from Granada, and in the same letter told Melchor that he wanted to get back to Madrid as soon as possible. He then hoped to move on to Figueras, continuing thence to Toulouse, where his brother would soon arrive from Bordeaux.[2]

Francisco had been working on his Law doctorate since graduating, brilliantly, in 1922, and often stayed at the Residencia de Estudiantes. Supported by Fernando de los Ríos he had now applied successfully for a government grant to enable him to spend the 1925–6 academic session in France, enrolling first at the University of Bordeaux, then at the University of Toulouse. The contrast between Francisco's university career, which made his parents purr with contentment, and Federico's apparent inability to get his plays staged or work published, could not have been more glaring, and must have preyed constantly on the poet's mind. Francisco was doing wonderfully and he, Federico, was a disaster! Lorca must also have pondered on the irony whereby while *he* was racked by sexual anxiety and condemned to live with socially unacceptable drives, Francisco – 'the handsome member of the family', as Federico often pointed out, and it was true – was ebulliently heterosexual and a great success with the ladies. None of this seems to have made Lorca resentful (Federico was not the resentful type), and there is ample evidence to show that he loved his younger brother, whose literary judgement – and talent – he respected. It must have irked the poet, however, that Francisco had succeeded in getting out of Spain with both grant and parental blessing while he, still financially dependent on his father, was chained Prometheus-like to his desk in Granada. A letter Federico wrote to Francisco in France at this time confirms that he was determined to leave Spain as soon as he could – just as soon, that is, as he could effect the publication of his three books of poetry and see to the production of *Mariana Pineda*. But even as he penned the letter he must have realized that it was not going to be so easy.[3]

With his letter to Melchor Lorca enclosed the second scene of the third act of his *Amor de don Perlimplín con Belisa en su jardín* ('The Love of Don Perlimplín for Belisa in His Garden'), on which he had begun work during the summer of 1925. The fact that this was the penultimate scene of the tiny play, and that it corresponds almost exactly to that contained in the 1928 typescript (the manuscript is missing), suggests that, by the beginning of 1926, the work was virtually finished.[4]

Don Perlimplín is one of Lorca's dramatic masterpieces, and constitutes, despite its farcical and grotesque elements, a penetrating exploration of the theme of sexual impotence, being much more than a variation on the well-tried subject of the marriage of an old man to a young woman. Perlimplín, indeed, can hardly be considered old. He is exactly fifty and, if a virgin and impotent, the reasons are strictly psychological and almost certainly connected with castration anxiety and fear of his dominant mother, now dead. He himself has no doubt why he is terrified of women:

When I was a child a woman strangled her husband. He was a cobbler. I can't forget it. I've never wanted to marry. I have enough with my books.[5]

Perhaps the most interesting aspect of the play is Perlimplín's reaction to his wedding-night discovery of his impotence, and his decision to exact an imaginative and subtle form of revenge before committing suicide. When he disguises himself as a young gallant in a red cloak, Perlimplín not only delights Belisa but becomes sexually potent – we must surely take at its face value Belisa's claim that she has felt not only the heat but the *weight* of her 'delicious youth'.[6] The full awareness that only by way of fantasy can he achieve potency is the bitter pill that marriage has forced Perlimplín to swallow, and the realization is mortal. His self-stabbing is no doubt open to different interpretations, but Perlimplín himself seems quite clear about his motives: he dies to free himself from the 'dark nightmare' of Belisa's grandiose body which, he exclaims, he would never have been able to 'decipher'. And he dies, too, to free her.[7]

In the death of Perlimplín, as in that of Mariana Pineda, it is not difficult to find a Christological dimension. Perlimplín tells Belisa that he is going to sacrifice himself on her behalf, and the stage directions for Act III state that his dining-room table has the appearance of a primitive painting of the Last Supper. The red cloak of Perlimplín's alter ego can perhaps be related to the purple mantle of Christ's passion; while, in making the servant Marcolfa tell Belisa that now she is 'clothed in the glorious blood of the master', Lorca is surely alluding to the Crucifixion.[8] All of which indicates yet again the degree to which the poet's religious obsessions, which had so struck Salvador Dalí – 'you are a Christian tempest and you need my paganism', the painter wrote to him in 1928[9] – continued to operate.

At some point, if we can believe Buñuel's memoirs, Dalí, who was wildly enthusiastic about *Don Perlimplín*, persuaded a reluctant Lorca to read the play to the budding film director during one of the latter's visits to Madrid. Halfway through Buñuel could stomach no more. 'It's a load of rubbish!' he exclaimed, banging on the table. 'Buñuel's right,' Dalí now agreed. 'It's a load of rubbish.' According to Buñuel's account, Lorca turned pale and closed the manuscript. There is no way of checking on this anecdote however, and when Dalí was questioned on the same subject in 1980 he did not remember the occasion.[10]

Lorca was becoming increasingly angry, in the opening months of 1926, at the apparent refusal of Eduardo Marquina and Gregorio Martínez Sierra to interest themselves further in the fate of *Mariana Pineda*. It was some six months since Marquina had given his word to use his influence with Margarita Xirgu, yet it appeared that the actress had not yet even read the play. As for Martínez Sierra, he had now flatly refused to produce *Mariana*. Lorca was furious at what he considered this betrayal, calling Don Gregorio a 'bastard' in a letter to Melchor Fernández Almagro and vowing revenge. Moreover, things were faring no better with *The Shoemaker's Prodigious Wife*.[11]

Lorca's friends were worried about the situation, realizing that the poet badly needed some good luck. Buñuel wrote from France (2 February 1926), playfully upbraiding Federico for having forgotten him and suggesting that he should visit Paris. 'What a pity you can't come,' he wrote,

or, at least, have a change of air! Of all the people I know you are the one who would derive the most benefit from it. At least I could see you all the time and renew our old friendship. I always remember the intense moments we shared over several years.[12]

The letter can only have served to strengthen Lorca's conviction that he must escape from Spain. Buñuel was brimful of projects at the time, as he told another friend: a book on the cinema was on the way, he boasted (rather too confidently, for it was never published); he was going to 'help' Jean Epstein with his film *The Fall of the House of Usher* – which he did; and he was beginning to wonder if, in two years or so, he might not himself become a film director.[13]

Meanwhile, in Granada, at the beginning of the year, Lorca and his friends had inaugurated the Scientific and Artistic Athenaeum as a slap in the face for the Arts Club, considered by the *Rinconcillo* as now irremediably moribund. It fell to the poet to deliver the inaugural address, given on 13 February. Entitled 'The Poetic Image in Don Luis de Góngora', the lecture was the result of a profound meditation on the aesthetic of the author of the *Soledades*, an aesthetic which coincided so closely, in Lorca's view, with contemporary trends, by dint of its objectivity and cult of the image, that Góngora (1561–1627) ought to be considered the 'father of modern poetry' and Mallarmé his 'best disciple' – despite the fact that the French poet almost certainly did not know the work of the Andalusian.

In this lecture, later to be recognized as one of the basic documents of Spanish poetic theory in the 1920s, Lorca expresses his admiration for Góngora's pursuit of 'objective beauty, beauty pure and useless', free of personal confessions and sentimentality; for his fashioning of a highly original mode of linguistic expression, 'a new model of the language'; and for the self-imposed *limitations* within which the poet chose to work, his efforts to control and shape the metaphorical exuberance of his extravagant imagination. Góngora, he notes, hated those 'obscure forces' of the mind that defy encapsulation, seeking above all clarity, measure and order. And if the *Soledades* are difficult, this is not the result of a deliberate, perverse pursuit of obscurity for the sake of obscurity, but of the imperious task the poet had set himself of finding 'new perspectives'.

But if Lorca considered Góngora eminently worthy of the attentions of modern poets, this was particularly on account of his extraordinary use of metaphor, itself deriving in large measure from that Andalusian speech which Lorca, too, had inherited. And the impression is inevitable that here, as in his 1922 lecture on *cante jondo*, Lorca is really glossing his own work and practice. One passage in particular strikes the attention when Lorca comments that Góngora

harmonizes and makes tangible – at times almost violently – the most dissimilar worlds. In his hands there is neither disorder nor disproportion. As if they were playthings, he picks up seas and geographical realms and furious winds, and merges astronomical sensations with tiny details drawn from the domain of the infinitesimally small, with a notion of masses and materials unknown in Poetry until he invented them.[14]

Several years later Lorca referred in almost identical terms to his own poetry, to the 'taste for mixing astronomical images with insects and ordinary things which are the hallmark of my poetic temperament', asserting that such a tendency was already identifiable in his work by 1919.[15]

It is clear, therefore, that, at a time when the revaluation of the long-despised Góngora, on the eve of the tercentenary of his death, was only beginning to gather pace, Lorca had already found in the author of the *Soledades* many points of contact, not only with his own poetry but with contemporary art in general. And, as he prepared his lecture, there can be no doubt that the poet had in mind not only his many conversations with Salvador Dalí on the 'objectivity' of modern art, which Dalí was then proclaiming fanatically and which José Ortega y Gasset analysed at this time in his *The Dehumanization of Art*,[16] but also the ode in honour of the painter that he had almost finished, and another long poem, 'La Sirena y el carabinero' ('The Siren and the Coastguard'), whose twenty-four extant lines move within the same orbit.[17]

For months Dalí had been complaining in his letters to Lorca about not being allowed to see *his* ode as a whole but only extracts here and there, served as if from an eye-dropper.[18] The painter's curiosity and vanity were finally and fully satisfied when the poem was published, entitled *Ode to Salvador Dalí* (its original title had been *Didactic Ode to Salvador Dalí*), in the April 1926 issue of the *Revista de Occidente*.

The ode constitutes not only a fervent affirmation of Lorca's friendship with Dalí but an appraisal of contemporary painting as represented in Spain by his friend. Lorca admired in Dalí's work – as in that of his cubist predecessors – its symmetry, objectivity and lack of sentimentality, its flight from both outmoded realism and the 'impressionist mist'. At the end of the first section of the poem (written in classical, measured alexandrines, as befitted its theme) we find the verse:

> Un deseo de formas y límites nos gana.
> Viene el hombre que mide con el metro amarillo.

Venus es una blanca naturaleza muerta
y los coleccionistas de mariposas huyen.*[19]

The poet identifies with the new aesthetics, then. And the ode is both an exegesis and an example of cubist tenets. The sea and houses of Cadaqués, where Picasso and Derain (the latter after his fauvist period) had executed some of their first cubist works, represent for the poet, as for Dalí, the classical idea of harmony, sobriety, light, and sharp contours:

Cadaqués, en el fiel del agua y la colina,
eleva escalinatas y oculta caracolas.
Las flautas de madera pacifican el aire.
Un viejo dios silvestre da frutos a los niños.

Sus pescadores duermen, sin ensueño, en la arena.
En alta mar les sirve de brújula una rosa.
El horizonte virgen de pañuelos heridos
junta los grandes vidrios del pez y de la luna.†[20]

The poet praises in Dalí his 'desire for an eternity with boundaries', his determination to avoid 'the dark forest of incredible forms', his wish for precision and order and his 'love of whatever can be explained'. These are precisely the same qualities Lorca admired in Góngora. Dalí, like the great Cordovan poet, shuns all vagueness and searches for the light:

Al coger tu paleta, con un tiro en un ala,
pides la luz que anima la copa del olivo.
Ancha luz de Minerva, constructora de andamios,
donde no cabe el sueño ni su flora inexacta.

Pides la luz antigua que se queda en la frente,
sin bajar a la boca ni al corazón del hombre.

---

* A desire for forms and limits takes hold of us.
The man who measures with the yellow ruler is coming.
Venus is a white still-life
and the butterfly collectors flee.

† Cadaqués, balanced between the water and the hill,
raises steps and hides seashells.
The wooden flutes still the air.
An old sylvan god gives fruit to the children.

Her fishermen sleep, undreaming, on the sand.
On the high sea a rose serves them as compass.
The horizon, free of wounded handkerchiefs,
merges the large crystals of fish and moon.

> Luz que temen las vides entrañables de Baco
> y la fuerza sin orden que lleva el agua curva.*[21]

And again:

> Amas una materia definida y exacta
> donde el hongo no pueda poner su campamento.
> Amas la arquitectura que construye en lo ausente
> y admites la bandera como una simple broma.†[22]

As for the friendship that unites painter and poet, Lorca makes a point of stressing that, for both of them, what counts is love, human warmth and play – and not, exclusively, devotion to art:

> Pero ante todo canto un común pensamiento
> que nos une en las horas oscuras y doradas.
> No es el Arte la luz que nos ciega los ojos.
> Es primero el amor, la amistad o la esgrima.
>
> Es primero que el cuadro que paciente dibujas
> el seno‡ de Teresa, la de cutis insomne,
> el apretado bucle de Matilde la ingrata,
> nuestra amistad pintada como un juego de oca.§[23]

The *Ode to Salvador Dalí* is perhaps the finest paean to friendship ever written in Spanish, and the fact that it had appeared in one of the most

---

* On taking your palette, with its bullet hole in one wing,
You ask for the light that animates the top of the olive.
The broad light of Minerva, the constructor of scaffolds,
where there's no room for dreams or their inexact flora.

You ask for the ancient light that lodges in the brain
without descending to the mouth or heart.
The light feared by Bacchus' impassioned vines
and the disordered strength of the curved water.

† You love a clearly defined and precise material
where the toadstool cannot set up camp.
You love the architecture that builds where there is nothing
and you admit the flag only as a joke.

‡ The manuscript, preserved in the Fundación Federico García Lorca, shows that the poet first wrote *culo* ('backside') and then thought better. By this time he was well aware of Dalí's preference for buttocks over breasts.

§ But above all I sing a shared way of thinking
which unites us in both the dark and the golden hours.
Art is not the light that blinds our eyes.
But, first, it's love, friendship, fencing.

More important than the picture you draw so patiently
are the breasts of Theresa of the sleepless skin,
the tight ringlet of Matilde the ungrateful,
our friendship painted like a game of snakes and ladders.

important journals in Europe filled the painter with pride, as he recalled in 1980.[24] Nor did the poem fail to attract the attention of the critics, among them the French hispanist Jean Cassou who, on 1 July 1926, praised it highly in the *Mercure de France*, finding it 'the most dazzling manifestation of a sensibility quite new in Spain'. For Cassou the ode was a further indication of the influence of cubism on the other side of the Pyrenees. 'This taste for construction and precision,' he predicted, 'which moreover appears in several of the young writers associated with the *Revista de Occidente*, is going to spread to poetry, and one may consider, as a demonstration and example of this, García Lorca's very beautiful and very important poem.'[25] Lorca was by no means indifferent to such praise, asking Jorge Guillén if he had seen Cassou's piece.[26]

During February and March 1926 Dalí, while anxiously waiting to see the ode in print, kept pestering Federico to send him his promised introduction to their *Book of Putrescent Philistines*, since he wanted to get their joint effort to the printer as soon as possible. Might it not be a good idea to include, as well, 'Buster Keaton's Stroll', he asked? But even this possibility did not now seem to appeal to the poet. His reply to Dalí is not known, but it must have been convincing, for thereafter the matter was dropped.[27]

In the middle of March 1926, on the eve of publication of the ode, Federico finally got away from home and settled in once again at the Residencia, doubtless with extreme relief – he had not been in Madrid since the previous summer, and was finding Granada intolerably oppressive. Ahead of him stretched the pleasant prospect of three or four months' immersion in the life of the capital and of re-establishing contact with Dalí, whose arrival back in Madrid was expected at any moment.[28]

On 8 April Lorca was in the Castilian city of Valladolid, which he had apparently not visited since his trip there ten years earlier with Berrueta, to give a poetry reading to the Arts Club. He was introduced by Jorge Guillén, Professor of Literature at the University, with whom he had been corresponding regularly since 1925 and whose poetry and critical acumen he much admired. Guillén's introductory address was no improvisation but, rather, a considered appraisal of Lorca's poetic genius. Read now it can be seen to be a text of extraordinary power and intuition. That the audience was about to hear a 'great poet' Guillén had no doubt, nor that one of Lorca's most outstanding strengths was his ability to throw bridges across the gap normally separating poetry for a select minority from poetry for a wide public. 'This is the great secret of Federico García Lorca,' Guillén insisted. 'His poetry, at once traditional and highly novel, while always of the highest quality, demands public recitation in order fully to be itself.

(Another lost tradition.) And the public understands it and likes it – very much indeed.'

Guillén stressed that one of the reasons why to date Lorca had published only one book of verse lay, precisely, in the jongleuresque nature of the Granadine poet's personality, in his need to communicate his work orally to a live audience. And if Lorca had already acquired among his friends a 'private celebrity', Guillén was certain that he was 'fatally condemned' to achieve widespread public acceptance before long, and assured the audience that evening that they – and he – were privileged to have among them a great poet not yet universally recognized as such, but who was about to step firmly into the pages of history. 'Some day,' he concluded, 'we shall be able to say: we perceived in Federico García Lorca the famous poet that he was to become.'[29]

The recital was a huge success. In the audience was Guillermo de Torre, who had known Lorca from his earliest days in Madrid and was now the leading Spanish authority on avant-garde European literature. 'I was able to ascertain,' Torre wrote later, 'with the satisfaction of the incense-bearer, that our enthusiasm, that of his [Lorca's] oldest friends, could be shared by unprepared folk who were in no way close to him.'[30] Valladolid's leading newspaper, *El Norte de Castilla*, which had an excellent literary page, reproduced Guillén's introduction in full and published a rave notice of the recital. Lorca had read poems from his three 'forthcoming books' (*Songs, Poem of Cante Jondo* and *Suites*) and also, it seems, an extract or extracts from *Ode to Salvador Dalí*. News of the triumphant evening quickly reached Granada, where *El Defensor*, always alert to the progress of the local prodigy, printed Guillén's text and proudly commented on Lorca's growing fame.[31]

Meanwhile, on 11 April, Salvador Dalí had set off from Figueras on a short, Holy Week visit to Paris and Brussels, accompanied by his sister and step-mother. The finance was provided by Dalí senior, who was elated by the success of his son's recent exhibition in Barcelona, a success, he wrote in his diary, that had outstripped all his expectations.[32] Luis Buñuel was at the station to meet the group, and found Salvador in a state of febrile excitement. Paris! At last he had set foot in the Mecca of Art! During his stay Dalí met several members of the colony of Spanish painters resident in the French capital and now enjoying considerable standing: Hernando Viñes, Ismael González de la Serna (who had designed the cover of Lorca's first book, *Impressions and Landscapes*, eight years earlier), Francisco Bores and others. Manuel Angeles Ortiz took him to see Picasso. 'When I arrived at Picasso's on Rue de la Boétie,' Dalí recalled in his *Secret Life*, 'I was as deeply moved and as full of respect as though I were having an audience with the Pope. "I have come to see you," I said, "before visiting the Louvre." "You're quite right," he answered.'[33]

It was a lightning visit – two weeks divided between Paris and Brussels – but long enough to serve as a sharp spur to Dalí's burning ambition. From this moment the painter's obsession was to settle in Paris as quickly as possible.

In May Dalí was back in Madrid for the first time, it seems, since the previous summer. He and Lorca had not seen each other for nearly a year although they had corresponded regularly, and we may assume they had a lot to say to each other.* It is likely that it was during these weeks that took place, perhaps at the Residencia, a scene not recounted in Dalí's *Secret Life* and evoked by the painter for the first time in an interview with Alain Bosquet published in 1966. Asked about his relations with Lorca during the period when the latter was working on his *Ode to Salvador Dalí*, the painter replied:

He was a pederast, as is well known, and madly in love with me. He tried on two occasions to . . . me. That upset me a lot because I was not a pederast, and had no intention of giving in. It hurt, moreover. And so nothing happened. But I was very flattered from the point of view of my personal prestige. Deep down I said to myself that he was a very great poet and that I owed him a little bit of the Divine Dalí's arseho . . . !†

Dalí went on to claim that, as a result of his refusal, the poet was driven, in despair, to 'sacrifice' there and then a young woman of their acquaintance, the first with whom he had intercourse.[34] Years later, in 1986, the painter explained that the girl in question, who from Lorca's point of view had the advantage of being virtually without breasts ('Federico hated breasts'), was one of his companions at the Academy of Fine Arts.[35]

Dalí has always been consistent in his allusions to Lorca's attempts to sodomize him. Moreover, if we are to believe Santos Torroella, the leading authority on Dalí's 'Lorca period', the painter never lied when talking about the really fundamental experiences of his life, although he may not have told all. The same critic has no doubt that Dalí's paranoia was the product of the tremendous resistance of the painter against his homosexual tendencies, nor that the potent attraction that Lorca came to exert over him was the cause, finally, of a certain distancing on Dalí's part, due to fear, a distancing

---

* At the time of writing, Lorca's letters to Dalí (there were probably thirty or forty) have still not come to light, although those from Dalí to the poet have now been published.

† Il était pédéraste, comme on sait, et follement amoureux de moi. Il a essayé par deux fois de m' . . . Cela me gênait beaucoup, car moi, je n'étais pas pédéraste, et je ne tenais pas à céder. De plus, cela me faisait mal. Ainsi, la chose n'a pas eu lieu. Mais je me sentais fort flatté au point de vue du prestige. C'est que, au fond de moi-même, je me disais qu'il était un très grand poète et que je lui devais un petit peu du trou de c . . . du Divin Dalí!

facilitated by the fact that the two were separated in space and that, not long afterwards, when Lorca was in America, Dalí met Gala.[36]

There seems little doubt, in fact, that Lorca's passion for the painter did indeed lead to various attempts at anal intercourse. The first instance may have been prompted by Lorca's despair on learning from Salvador that he was about to ensure his definitive dismissal from the Academy. There, on 14 June 1926, the painter deliberately caused a tremendous scene, refusing, before a large audience, to be examined by the board, which he declared incompetent to sit in judgement on someone of his genius, and announcing his withdrawal. His dismissal was instantaneous.[37] In his *Secret Life* we are given the painter's reasons for his gesture:

The motives for my action were simple: I wanted to have done with the School of Fine Arts and with the orgiastic life of Madrid once and for all; I wanted to be forced to escape all that and come back to Figueras to work for a year, after which I would try to convince my father that my studies should be continued in Paris. Once there, with the work that I should take, I would definitively seize power![38]

Thus ended Dalí's academic career. A few days later he returned to Figueras, where he was awaited by a father sick with anxiety and mortification. Federico's reaction to his friend's decisive action is not on record, but it must have been one of consternation, for Dalí, with his sights firmly set on Paris, had left Madrid with no intention whatsoever of returning.

Lorca spent the summer with his family between Asquerosa, Granada and Lanjarón – a spa in the lower part of the Alpujarras, where his mother, suffering from a liver complaint, had been urged by her doctor to take the waters.[39] The poet continued to work on *Gypsy Ballads*, telling Jorge Guillén that he hoped soon to finish the book.[40] But what was most on his mind was the fate of *Mariana Pineda*. In Madrid he had made the point of establishing personal contact with Margarita Xirgu and had given her a copy of the play. Impressed by the poet's personality, the actress had promised to read the work, and to communicate her reactions.[41] But had she read it? The expected letter did not arrive, and at the end of the summer Lorca wrote in despair to Eduardo Marquina. His parents, he said, were constantly nagging at him, seeing '*nothing practical*' in his literary efforts and always comparing him unfavourably with his brother Francisco who, despite being four years younger, was now crowned with academic laurels and the blue-eyed boy of the family. What should he do? Write to Margarita? Give up hope?[42]

Spaniards are not good letter-writers, and Lorca received no reply to this plea, nor to a second one.[43] To be fair, it may well be that Marquina, who habitually spent his summer holidays in Cadaqués, may not have received them till later. The poet, at all events, was somewhat encouraged by an interview with the famous – and today almost totally forgotten – playwright published in the Madrid magazine *La Esfera* on 31 July 1926. In this Marquina commented on the injustice whereby competent new dramatists were finding it almost impossible to have their work produced, because impresarios were interested only in guaranteeing profits. 'At this moment I am trying to convince them to accept a play by García Lorca,' Marquina was quoted as saying; 'the problem is that from a new author they all demand a masterpiece.' While he did not say so explicitly, Marquina must have realized that *Mariana Pineda* certainly did not fall into that category.[44]

Meanwhile, the possibility of turning his hand to an academic career again became an obsession with Lorca. At the beginning of September he wrote to Jorge Guillén to inform him of his determination to be a literature teacher. But how in heaven's name to achieve this? Where to start? Surely Guillén, who was in the business himself, could advise him, along with their mutual friend the poet Pedro Salinas, then teaching at Seville University?

The letter was written from the Huerta de San Vicente, the charming property that the poet's father had recently bought on the outskirts of Granada and renamed in honour of his wife Vicenta. The building (the word *huerta* implies a combination of farmhouse, orchard and market garden) was typical of the villas that dot the Vega, and grew with a complete naturalness out of the exuberant vegetation that surrounded its white walls. From the balcony of his bedroom window, the poet could look out across the fields to the snow-covered peaks and slopes of the Sierra Nevada, and up over the town to the Alhambra. It was a paradise. 'There's so much jasmine and nightshade in the garden', he told Guillén, 'that we all wake up with lyrical headaches.'[45]

Guillén was delighted with Federico's decision. *Of course* he could be a literature teacher, he assured him. But he must begin by changing his habits and taking methodical notes of his reading (Guillén was method itself), perusing, as well, 'the historians and scholars who have commented on these texts, boiling them down to notes'. He must acquire a card index! Work in earnest! All of which, the professor-poet felt sure, would make a deep impression on Don Federico and Doña Vicenta.[46] Back went another letter from Lorca, criss-crossed with questions. Should he stay in Granada while preparing for the examination that would afford him entrance to the academic profession? How long would it all take? Might it not be a good idea first to give Spanish conversation classes in Paris? Meanwhile, he promised, he had ordered the card index and was ready to begin. What fantastic notes the box was going to contain, all neatly arranged! And how splendid to have a job and to be free of his dependence on his parents! The letter breathed euphoria through its every pore, and Lorca even tried to hoodwink Guillén, of whom he was always slightly in awe, that now that his career had been decided he wanted to marry and settle down.[47] But he must have known in his heart of hearts that he was not made of the stuff of professors of literature, that he would never have a Chair and that, if in a moment of optimism he had ordered a filing box, this was not destined to hold his annotated cards. The poet's life was to progress down a different road – and in doing so provide the professional note-takers with an inexhaustible fund of materials for classification and analysis.

St Sebastian

During the summer Dalí painted enthusiastically in Cadaqués, and kept Lorca informed about his progress and current thinking. The two letters to the poet that have been preserved from these months show that a new obsession was now increasingly occupying Salvador: the martyrdom of St Sebastian. Dalí reminded Lorca that St Sebastian is the patron of Cadaqués and, from one of his remarks, it seems that during Federico's visit in 1925 the two may have climbed up to the saint's sanctuary on the mountain behind the town. Dalí was clearly attracted by the sado-masochistic and homosexual implications of the martyrdom's iconography, and asked the poet if he had not noticed that St Sebastian's buttocks are never wounded by the arrows – a recondite allusion, surely, to anal intercourse and the painter's resistance to his friend's desires.[48] At this time Lorca, for his part, was assembling material for three lectures on 'The Myth of St Sebastian', to be illustrated with slides, and in September wrote to Jorge Guillén in Valladolid asking him for a photograph of Berruguete's sculpture of the martyr, which is preserved in the city's fine museum.[49] That Lorca admired the work is hardly surprising, for Berruguete's St Sebastian is a beautiful, languid youth with an uncanny resemblance to Lord Alfred Douglas.

By this summer Dalí (not yet immersed in surrealism) had come to see St Sebastian as an embodiment of the Holy Objectivity to which he felt contemporary art should aspire. The saint's impassivity, serenity and detachment as his flesh is pierced by the arrows – they were the very qualities the painter aspired to express in his own life and work, as he explained to Federico.[50] How fitting, we may add, that St Sebastian should preside over Cadaqués, whose classical sobriety and equilibrium Dalí never failed to praise in his letters to the poet or in his subsequent memoirs.

Lorca had written to tell Dalí about his problems with his family and decision to become a teacher of literature. The painter was horrified. Federico a teacher? Never! Salvador advised the poet to work on his father and make him see the futility of such ludicrous aspirations. Surely Don Federico must realize that, relieved of anxiety about the future, about getting a job, having security and all such silliness, his son could produce the poetry and plays that would make him famous and economically viable? It seemed obvious to Dalí; and, although we do not know what Lorca wrote in reply, Salvador's indignation must have helped to convince the poet that filing boxes were not, after all, in his line, whatever the prudent Jorge Guillén might think about the matter.[51]

In October Dalí exhibited two paintings at the 1926 Autumn Salon in Barcelona, *Noia cosint* ('Girl Sewing') and *Natura morta* ('Still Life'), which were much appreciated by the critics and, in the opinion of Sebastià Gasch, soon to be a close friend of Lorca, constituted the highlights of the show.[52] *Natura morta*, later to be renamed, in Catalan, *Peix i balcó* ('Fish and Window') or *Naturaleza muerta al claro de luna* ('Still Life by Moonlight'), is closely related in theme to the painting *Still Life (Invitation to Sleep)* already discussed. In the more recent work the severed and fused heads of Salvador and Federico lie on a moonlit table in the Dalís' sitting room at Cadaqués beside a guitar, the artist's palette, some fish and a fishing net.[53] Another painting from this period, *Natura morta al claro de luna malva* ('Still Life by Mauve Moonlight'), not exhibited in 1926, repeated the same motifs with greater complexity.[54] Whether Lorca was aware of the extent to which he was now present in his friend's work we do not know.

On 17 October the new Granada Arts Club opened its 1926–7 session. Lorca delivered the inaugural lecture, talking about the seventeenth-century Granadine poet Pedro Soto de Rojas, author of the long allegorical work *Paraíso cerrado para muchos, jardines abiertos para pocos* ('A Paradise Closed to Many, Gardens Open to Few'). The theme of the lecture, mentioned earlier, was that Granadine art expresses a love of the small, the delicate and the intimate, shunning the grandiose. Lorca's admiration for Soto de Rojas at this time was inseparable from that which he felt for Góngora, the latter's master, and once again he wanted to demonstrate the relevance of such poetry to the 'dehumanizing' tendency of contemporary art, with its stress on objectivity and its flight from sentimentality.[55]

Emilio Prados, the poet's friend from Malaga, was spending some days in Granada with him at this time, and took part in the series of events organized by Federico and his group in honour of Soto de Rojas. The principal reason for the visit, however, was to persuade Lorca to allow him to publish, in Malaga, the three books of poems which the poet had started to announce at the beginning of the year: *Suites, Poem of Cante Jondo* and *Songs*. Prados left with the relevant manuscripts under his arm, and it seems that it was also agreed that he should publish a luxury edition of the *Ode to Salvador Dalí*. But in the event the only work brought out by the Malaga poet was *Songs*, which appeared the following year.[56]

Shortly after Prados's departure, Federico raised again with Melchor Fernández Almagro the 'ugly matter' of *Mariana Pineda*, begging him to visit Eduardo Marquina (who had still not replied) and find out what was happening. The letter, written in a tone of taut urgency, made it clear that Lorca no longer trusted the playwright. He had convinced himself that, secretly, Marquina would prefer that the play were not produced, and he now even doubted the sincerity of his statement in *La Esfera*, in which he had mentioned his efforts on its behalf. Lorca still saw his professional salvation in the successful staging of the play. 'If *Mariana* were produced I would gain everything with my family,' he ended.[57]

Fernández Almagro did not let his friend down – he never did – and immediately saw, not Marquina (who apparently had not yet returned to Madrid from Cadaqués), but Margarita Xirgu herself. On 8 November he was able to send Federico an excellent piece of news: the actress had read, and liked, *Mariana Pineda* and had assured him that it was her intention to produce it, either at the end of her current season in Madrid or the following April in Barcelona. Melchor felt sure that Margarita had spoken to him with absolute sincerity.[58] The news was splendid, certainly, although it would be some months before Lorca, after years of disappointment, allowed himself to be convinced that the play was going to be produced at last.

At the end of November 1926 the first number of *Litoral*, a new literary magazine edited by Emilio Prados and Manuel Altolaguirre, appeared in Malaga. It contained, in pride of place, three of Lorca's 'Gypsy ballads' – 'St Michael', 'The Arrest of Antoñito el Camborio' and 'Preciosa and the Wind' – unfortunately with several printing errors which threw the poet into a fit of excessive irritation. Lorca claimed in a letter to Guillén that Prados had promised to send him a proof of the poems but, on the face of it, this seems unlikely.[59] He immediately dashed off a telegram of protest to Malaga, which brought a pained rejoinder from Prados in which the latter blamed the mistakes on Lorca's illegible handwriting. Determined not to have to deal a second time with such an outburst, Prados returned the manuscripts of the three books accompanied by a typescript copy he had had made of the poems, insisting that Lorca himself correct the latter, likewise in typescript, and send it back to him. Prados also asked Lorca to let him publish *Gypsy Ballads*, as the first volume in a series to include Rafael Alberti's *La amante*, José Bergamín's *Caracteres* and Luis Cernuda's *Perfil del aire*.[60] But Federico had decided to withhold *Gypsy Ballads* for a little longer.

If, at the end of 1926, Lorca did not yet quite believe that soon the curtain would rise on *Mariana Pineda*, he had various other projects well under way and a solid body of poetry ready to go to the printers. Apart from Prados's commitment to publish *Songs, Poem of Cante Jondo* and *Suites, Gypsy Ballads* was virtually finished, while the poet's folders also contained drafts of *The Shoemaker's Prodigious Wife, Don Perlimplín* and *The Tragicomedy of Don Cristóbal and Señorita Rosita*. There was little room for dejection, and Federico may well have sensed that 1927 was to be his year of breakthrough.

12

A Decisive Year

Idyll with Dalí

Between 31 December 1926 and 14 January 1927 Dalí held his second one-man exhibition at the Dalmau Gallery. It was an outstanding success. Of the twenty-three paintings shown, at least four were concerned with the obsessive theme of Lorca. In *Composició amb tres figures. 'Acadèmia neocubista'* – 'Composition with Three Figures. "Neocubist Academy" ' – appears a recumbent heroic head which casts, as its shadow, the poet's profile.[1] The Lorca implications of *Still Life (Invitation to Sleep)* have already been mentioned. *Taula devant el mar* ('Table by the Sea') has been identified as the picture later renamed *Homenaje a Eric Satie* ('Homage to Eric Satie'): here the blue shadow of the heroic head undoubtedly represents that of Lorca.[2] In *Arlequí* ('Harlequin'), later called *Cabeza amiba* ('Amoebaean Head'), the silhouette of the poet's head is particularly arresting.[3] Finally, it is possible that one of the three paintings entitled *Natura morta* was the picture of the same name hung in the 1926 Autumn Salon at Barcelona, later called *Peix i balcó* ('Fish and Window'), in which case there was a fifth painting in the exhibition reflecting the same theme.[4] These Lorca-inspired works (and there are many others from the same period) show that, if the poet was now obsessed with Dalí, the latter was in no way indifferent to Federico; and it is tempting to relate them to a passage in Dalí's *Secret Life* where the painter, referring to Lautréamont's *Les Chants de Maldoror*, of which an excellent Spanish translation by Julio Gómez de la Serna had appeared in Madrid in 1925, recalled:

The shadow of Maldoror hovered over my life, and it was just at this period that for the duration of an eclipse precisely another shadow, that of Federico García Lorca, came and darkened the virginal originality of my spirit and of my flesh.[5]

In the paintings and drawings of Dalí's 'Lorca period' (1925–7), as Santos Torroella has termed it, we find, in effect, that the artist's head is often accompanied by the shadow, silhouette or superimposition of that of the poet. Again and again the same motif recurs: Dalí's oval face and characteristic little sticky-out ears, juxtaposed with Lorca's broad head, the ears of which, also prominent, contrast, in their chunkiness, with the painter's. Unmistakable, too, is the poet's jaw.[6]

Dalí was euphoric about the success of his exhibition, which had attracted interest even in the United States, where the Pittsburgh Museum of Modern Art acquired *Cesta de pan* ('Basket of Bread'). In a press clipping that he proudly sent to Lorca, the artist was described as 'one of the most formidable personalities of modern Catalan painting'. No doubt Salvador was beginning to feel that his conquest of Paris was now inevitable.[7]

Meanwhile, in Granada, Federico and his group were busily preparing to launch a literary review. For months Lorca had been pestering his literary friends, among them Jorge Guillén, Guillermo de Torre, José Bergamín, José María de Cossío and Melchor Fernández Almagro for poems and articles. And now, at last, his efforts were about to bear fruit.[8] The review was to appear as the literary supplement of *El Defensor de Granada* and be called *El gallo del Defensor* ('The Cockerel of the *Defensor*'), a title which did not please Dalí and was later modified to, simply, *gallo* (without a capital).[9]

From Dalí the poet requested a drawing of a cockerel to embellish the magazine's cover. This the painter dutifully supplied in February 1927, informing Federico at the same time that he had just begun, of all things, his military service. 'No travelling for the moment!' he wrote. 'But this summer we have got to spend three months together in Cadaqués. It's fated, well, fated no, but certain.' With his letter Dalí included an extravagant greetings card, bought no doubt in some Figueras stationery shop, in which a winged mermaid, with the upper part of her body discreetly clothed, offers, lovingly, a large bowl of fruits. Beneath the drawing are printed the following lines:

A mi Prenda Adorada

Si una muestra no te diera
de mi amor y simpatía
en verdad amada mía
poco atento pareciera;
dígnate pues placentera
aceptar lo que te ofrezca,
alma, vida y corazón.
Con un cariño igual
un amor extenso y sin fin,

y solo me siento feliz
cuando a tu lado puedo estar.*

Dalí had modified the sense of the line 'un amor extenso y sin fin' ('Love wide and without end'), underlining 'extenso' and 'sin' ('without') and adding to the latter preposition an asterisk whose corresponding manuscript note read 'instead of *without* read *with*, signed Saint Sebastian'. What did the painter intend by these personal additions to the charmingly ludicrous piece of printed doggerel? To express his rejection of the romantic notion of love beyond death while, at the same time, affirming his love for Lorca in the here and now? To suggest that, sooner or later, and perhaps sooner, their relationship would have to end? Only Dalí could have given us satisfactory answers to these questions. The letter ended with an allusion to the article on St Sebastian on which Salvador, now a writer as well as a painter, as he frequently reminds Lorca in his letters, was currently working:

I want a really long letter from you, mon cher! . . . In my Saint Sebastian I remember you a lot and at times I think it's you . . . We'll see if it turns out that Saint Sebastian is you! . . . but for the moment allow me to use his name to sign.
A big hug
from
your Saint Sebastian[10]

By the end of January 1927 Lorca was still without word of Margarita Xirgu, and had convinced himself that the great actress was never going to produce *Mariana Pineda*. But Melchor Fernández Almagro, to whom he confided his misgivings, soon reassured him. Margarita was certainly going to put on the play, he wrote on 2 February, but things would no doubt move faster if Lorca could escape to Madrid and see the actress personally.[11] Then, on 13 February, Cipriano Rivas Cherif confirmed the good news, informing Federico, officially, that Margarita had committed herself to producing *Mariana Pineda* that summer in Barcelona, and that she would open the following winter season in Madrid with the play.[12]

---

*   To My Beloved

If I didn't give you a sign
of my love and friendship,
in truth, my love,
I'd hardly seem attentive.
Have the goodness, therefore,
to accept what I offer you:
soul, life and heart.
With an unequalled affection
love wide and without end,
I only feel happy
when I can be by your side.

No sooner did he receive this excellent news (which meant that, as Dalí had prophesied, the two would certainly meet that summer), than Lorca began to worry about the immaturity or old-fashionedness of the play. 'Three years ago the idea of writing a Romantic drama pleased me immensely,' he wrote to Jorge Guillén. 'But now I see it as marginal to my work.'[13] There could be no turning back at this point, however, and, as in the case of *The Butterfly's Evil Spell* seven years earlier, the poet would have to go through with the experience, doing his best to ensure that, despite the play's weaknesses, the production was as good as possible.

On 12 February, the day before he received the cheering letter from Cipriano Rivas Cherif, Lorca had another pleasant surprise: the arrival from Malaga of the first batch of proofs of *Songs*. It seemed that, at last, the tide was beginning to turn in his favour.[14]

The year 1927 was to be remembered as the year of the Góngora tercentenary celebrations and, as well as the lecture on the author of the *Soledades* which Lorca already had to his credit, he was now working (as was Rafael Alberti) on a poem in honour of the great ma... During February Alberti sent Federico a fragment of his *Soledad tercera (parafrasis incompleta)* – 'Third Solitude (Incomplete Paraphrase)' – while Federico posted off to Guillén some excerpts from his incipient 'Soledad insegura' ('Uncertain Solitude').[15] Unlike Alberti, who in his poem succeeded in elaborating an extraordinary imitation of Góngora's intricate syntax, Lorca aimed at capturing the spirit rather than the letter of the Cordovan poet, a purpose of which Guillén approved.[16] He soon realized, however, that his 'Soledad insegura' would never be completed, and that, really, such a project was something of an 'irreverence'.[17] Several journals brought out special Góngora issues during the year, but while Alberti's poem appeared in Emilio Prados's *Litoral*, Lorca chose to push his effort into a folder, where it remained.

At the end of March, following Melchor's advice, Federico returned to Madrid, after an absence of eight months, to read *Mariana Pineda* to Margarita Xirgu and her company and settle details of the play's forthcoming première in Barcelona. Present at the reading were Melchor Fernández Almagro, Cipriano Rivas Cherif and the latter's forbidding brother-in-law Manuel Azaña, head of the Athenaeum Club, and, a few years later, Prime Minister and President of the Republic.[18]

The Dalís, remembering Lorca's readings of the play in 1925, were delighted to hear that *Mariana Pineda* was to have its first performance in Barcelona. Salvador had always assumed that he would design the sets, and now he wrote excitedly to Lorca with a series of 'general indications' concerning the stage design. Doubtless Margarita Xirgu had already given her approval by this time to the collaboration of the painter, who awaited Lorca's arrival in Barcelona with impatience.[19]

After spending Holy Week in Granada,[20] Federico packed his bags for the great adventure: with *Mariana Pineda* about to be produced at last he had begun to win the now several-years-old running battle with his parents on the subject of his future. The exact date of his arrival in Barcelona is not known, but it must have been at the end of April or beginning of May 1927.

During May and June Lorca came and went between Barcelona, Figueras and Cadaqués as preparations pushed ahead for the première, scheduled to take place at the end of Margarita Xirgu's season, which had opened on 16 April and was to continue until early July.[21]

Lorca lived these months with great intensity, free of his parents' vigilance and carping. The art critic Sebastià Gasch has described his first meeting with Federico that summer. Gasch was a close friend of the painter and stage designer Rafael Pérez Barradas, who had been living in Barcelona since 1925 after his period in Madrid. Despite the near poverty in which he now eked out his existence, Barradas continued to demonstrate the faith in life and art which had always characterized him, and every Sunday held open house at his decrepit flat in the suburb of Hospitalet. One day Gasch received a note from the painter, inviting him to meet his friend Federico García Lorca. The name rang no bell in Gasch's head, but he accepted the invitation none the less. He never regretted it. Lorca delighted him with his mixed array of talents, his combination of extraordinary sensitivity and Andalusian vehemence ('he breathed "South" through every pore'), his charm. That afternoon Federico presented his new friend with a copy of *Songs*. Gasch read it at a sitting and saw at once that Lorca was an outstanding poet. Within a few days they were inseparable and Sebastià became Lorca's principal cicerone, after Dalí, in the city, taking him to his favourite haunts in the Gothic quarter and introducing him to his many artist and writer friends.[22]

One weekend Lorca went down the coast to Sitges with Dalí and Gasch to meet Josep Carbonell, editor of Catalonia's leading avant-garde review, *L'Amic de les Arts* ('The Friend of the Arts'). Seated at Carbonell's piano the poet improvised one of his by now celebrated folksong sessions. The company, according to Gasch, was 'electrified'.[23]

Gasch records various anecdotes relating to Lorca's stay in Barcelona. One day, for example, he accompanied Federico to the Athenaeum Club, introducing him there to some of the members of the day's 'most famous and feared cenacle':

After the *de rigueur* introductions and a few polite words, one of the members asked

Lorca in the same tone that he would have used to speak to a foreigner: 'And where are you from, young man?'

At that time, in the middle of General Primo de Rivera's dictatorship, Catalan nationalism had acquired a ferocious intransigence. Lorca, on whom there were no flies and who understood at once the ultranationalist intention behind the question, raised his arm solemnly – as he would do habitually when about to make some significant statement – and replied in a tone half challenging, half proud: 'I am from the Kingdom of Granada!'[24]

If this story illustrates Lorca's pride in his Granadine origins, another points up the gulf that separated Lorca and Dalí on the question of religion ('You're a strange, religious spirit,' Dalí had written in March 1926. 'You're strange. I can't relate you to anything with known dimensions.'):[25]

One night, after supper, Dalí, Federico and the present writer entered a cabaret in the Plaza del Teatro which, if I remember correctly, was called *Monaco*. After a lively conversation, in the course of which Dalí expatiated on the need to adapt classical music to jazz, Lorca got up and took his leave of us saying: 'I'm off. I want to go to bed early. Tomorrow I'm going to attend solemn high mass in the Cathedral.' 'What a perfume of ancient splendour!' he added, showing the whites of his eyes, while over his delicate lips there strayed a slight smile.

'I'm more interested in this olive,' Dalí broke in, pointing with his forefinger to one on the table.

Dalí's obsession with the 'micrographically small' and his profound anti-Catholicism lost no opportunity at the time to voice themselves.[26]

Lorca was delighted with Dalí's designs for *Mariana Pineda*, and admired especially his friend's intuitive understanding of an Andalusia he had not yet visited – an understanding, as Lorca wrote to Manuel de Falla, that came from looking at photographs and from their 'hours and hours' of conversation.[27] Rafael Moragas, a journalist on the Barcelona newspaper *La Noche*, visited the Theatre Goya one afternoon to see the dress rehearsal of *Mariana Pineda* and interview Lorca and Dalí. He found the poet full of gratitude towards Margarita Xirgu, not only for accepting the play in the first place but for her sensitive embodiment of the heroine. Dalí was busy putting the final touches to the sets, and Moragas felt sure that these were going to cause a sensation.[28]

At last, on the night of 24 June, the curtain went up on *Mariana Pineda*. The première was a considerable success, and the audience demanded that the author appear on the stage with Margarita Xirgu at the end of each act, when both received an enthusiastic ovation. That night Dalí and Lorca sent a telegram to Melchor Fernández Almagro in Madrid. It read simply: 'GREAT SUCCESS MARIANA PINEDA. BEST WISHES.' Doubtless Lorca's family received a similar communication, and we may surmise that his parents were as

relieved as he was that, after so many years of frustration and disappointment, the play had at last got off the ground.[29]

Lorca knew, however, that *Mariana Pineda* could have only a short run,
for Margarita Xirgu's season in Barcelona would end on 3 July. The play
was performed six times in all, coming off on 28 June.[30]

The press reaction to *Mariana Pineda* was generally indulgent, and the
majority of the critics grasped Lorca's intention that the work should have
the feel of a story recounted in the broadsheets of the nineteenth-century
ballad-singers or, more precisely, of the etchings of the period, in accordance
with its subtitle, 'A Print in Three Acts'. With the purpose of emphasizing
the analogy with framed etchings, Dalí had conceived sets that gave the
impression of a stage within a stage.[31] His designs were warmly praised by
the critics (for their simplicity and sober use of colour), although a few
dissidents felt that their modernism was incompatible with the period
costumes.[32]

Various critics noted the psychological subtlety with which the poet had
delineated his heroine, but none of them plumbed the thematic depths of
the play. Only later, with hindsight, would it become apparent to what
extent *Mariana Pineda* expressed Lorca's characteristic preoccupations with
frustrated love and death.

Margarita Xirgu, whose performance all the critics praised, was as
delighted as Federico with the play's success, and repeated her promise to
open her autumn season in Madrid with it that October. When the two
separated at the beginning of July the poet had the satisfaction of knowing
that his career as a dramatist was genuinely under way, while the actress
was convinced that in Lorca she had found a playwright of undoubted talent
capable of producing work far superior to *Mariana Pineda*. Echoes of the
success soon reached Madrid and Granada, as they did of Lorca's impact
on the many Catalan writers and artists with whom he was now associating
in Barcelona.[33]

Some time before the première of *Mariana Pineda* the poet had sprung a
surprise on his Catalan friends: the revelation that, as well as poet, dramatist
and musician he was also gifted at drawing. In the Oro del Rhin, one of
Barcelona's best-known cafés, he had shown Gasch a selection of his work,
mainly recent, and the art critic was astonished by its quality.[34] We do not
know whose idea it was to persuade Josep Dalmau, with whom both Gasch
and Dalí were intimate, to mount a small exhibition of Lorca's coloured
drawings in his gallery, but the fact is that Dalmau – who Dalí said looked
as if he had just stepped out of a painting by El Greco[35] – agreed to
collaborate. Between 25 June and 2 July, twenty-four Lorca drawings were
exhibited, only nine of which can be identified today with any certainty.[36]

These, along with other drawings from the same period, reveal the extent to which the poet's friendship with Dalí was influencing his work – with a Dalí ever more attracted by surrealism and the lure of the unconscious.

Among the drawings exhibited, that entitled *El beso* ('The Kiss') alludes directly to the series by Dalí in which the heads of both friends are juxtaposed or fused. The drawing, for which the poet employed Indian ink, coloured pencils and gouache, almost certainly represents Lorca's head on which that of Dalí has been superimposed, the lips of both faces meeting in the kiss of the title. The shadow of Lorca's head, in red, is a direct quotation from Dalí's *Dona de Barcelona* ('Barcelona Lady') – clearly a lady of the streets – and *Naturaleza muerta al claro de luna* ('Still Life by Moonlight'), in both of which the painter's and Federico's heads merge; and Lorca was probably amused by the fact that the significance of his drawing was lost on everyone but himself and Salvador.[37]

In another drawing almost certainly from this summer and possibly also included in the Dalmau exhibition, Federico portrayed Dalí sitting at the foot of a high tower, beneath a yellow crescent moon, with white egg-shaped cap and white robe, his palette in his right hand (a very obviously phallic finger emerging from the hole), a little red fish affixed to the end of each finger of the left and, in the centre of his chest, pointing upwards, a large, red, vertical fish, which the artist wears as if it were a badge. 'Lorca saw me as the incarnation of life, with a hat like one of the Dioscuri. Each finger of my right hand has been converted into a fish-chromosome,' commented Dalí years later.[38] The idea that Lorca and Dalí were twin souls, like Castor and Pollux, had evidently occurred to them, and the poet was to draw a journalist's attention to this special kinship when, in 1935, he met Salvador again after seven years' separation and found that they still understood each other perfectly.[39]

Lorca's exhibition passed almost unnoticed, and left hardly a trace in the Barcelona press. The poet, however, was quite content, for it had never occurred to him that his work was going to take the art world by storm. 'I held an exhibition of my drawings, *forced* by everyone,' he wrote excitedly to Falla; 'and I sold four!'[40]

The last performance of *Mariana Pineda* and the closing of the exhibition coincided, on 3 July. Shortly afterwards Federico's friends in Barcelona organized a multitudinous banquet to celebrate the twin successes of *Mariana Pineda* and Lorca's public début as an artist.[41] Then the poet retired with Dalí to Cadaqués, where he spent the rest of the month.

During the spring and summer of 1927 two drawings by Dalí on the theme of his relationship with Lorca were published. The first, entitled *La playa* ('The Beach'), accompanied a selection of poems by Lorca on the front page of the April issue of *Verso y prosa*, an important literary review edited in Murcia by Juan Guerrero Ruiz, and constituted another variation on the motif of the fused heads of painter and poet:

BOLETIN DE LA JOVEN LITERATURA

MURCIA - 1927 - ABRIL

SALVADOR DALÍ La playa

The second drawing, entitled *El poeta en la platja d'Empúries* ('The Poet on the Beach at Ampurias') (see over), was published in the 30 June 1927 issue of *L'Amic de les Arts*, where it accompanied Lorca's ballad 'Reyerta de gitanos' ('Gypsy Feud').

As can readily be appreciated, the two drawings are closely linked in theme. The setting is the same. (Lorca and Dalí probably repeated their 1925 visit to Ampurias this summer.) In each there are a severed head and, in *The Beach*, Lorca's is unmistakable, as is the silhouette of Dalí's. The severed arm of the second drawing is identical to those which appear in the

ȆL POETA EN LA PLATJA D'EMPÚRIES
VIST PER SALVADOR DALÍ

first. In both drawings we find examples of the triangular gadgets so frequent in Dalí's work of this period and which, as has been suggested, may perhaps be understood as allusions to the female genitals so disturbing to both friends. On the back of Federico's right hand, in the second drawing, as on the inside wrists of the severed ones lying on the beach in both drawings, Dalí has drawn the vein motif which occurs in other works of his 'Lorca period'.

The two drawings, published in association with poems by Lorca (a circumstance due, doubtless, to an arrangement agreed on by poet and artist), contained personal allusions whose full significance was known only to the two. This is confirmed by a photograph of Federico, taken in Barcelona, in which the poet purposely assumed the same posture as that given to him by Dalí in the second drawing reproduced – a drawing the poet must have known before it appeared in *L'Amic de les Arts*. To the photograph (see illustration 9) Lorca added, in ink, various references to the Dalí drawing in question, as well as to the theme of St Sebastian. This photograph, which the poet sent to Dalí in Figueras, was probably taken when Lorca arrived in Barcelona at the end of April or beginning of May 1927. 'Hullo there, my boy! Here I am!' announces Federico, whose head is surrounded by a halo identical to that of St Sebastian in another drawing by the poet of the arrow-pierced martyr (see illustration 12). Beneath his feet, Lorca has sketched a capital recalling both the description of the saint's posture in Dalí's *Saint Sebastian* ('His feet rested on a broken capital') – which he read that summer – and Mantegna's painting of the same saint (see illustration 11). On the back of his left hand the poet has imitated clearly the vein motif appearing in both Dalí drawings. At the right of the photograph, next to the capital, he has drawn a severed head, while, on the left, we find a 'gadget' of Dalinian inspiration but in pure Lorca style, alluding, undoubtedly, to that appearing in *The Beach*. The motif emerging from the capital and climbing up the left side of the photograph may be a reference to the severed arms figuring in numerous Dalís from this period, while the object sketched in the left-hand bottom corner is similar to the fish that appears in *The Beach* (between the flowerpot and the 'gadget') and other Dalí paintings and drawings. Covering the lower part of his body, finally, it can be seen that Lorca has drawn the silhouette of a face whose expression is suggestive of extreme sadness. An allusion to his erotic despair?

We should also take into account two outstanding paintings begun by Dalí this summer while Lorca was in Catalonia. They are *La miel es más dulce que la sangre* ('Honey is Sweeter Than Blood') and *Cenicitas* ('Little Ashes'). The first of these works was originally entitled, in Catalan, *El bosc d'aparatus* or *El bosc d'aparells* ('The Wood of Gadgets'), thanks, Dalí said, to a suggestion from Lorca.[42] The later, definitive, title was the product of the wild imagination of Lydia Noguer, Dalí's crazy friend in Cadaqués.[43] As for *Little Ashes* (which hangs today in Madrid's Museum of Contemporary Art), it was first called *El naixement de Venus* ('The Birth of Venus') and then *Els esforços estérils* ('Sterile Efforts').[44]

According to Dalí, Lorca said to him as he worked that summer on *Honey is Sweeter Than Blood*: 'Inscribe my name on this picture so that it may mean something to the world.'[45] The painting (see illustration 13) was exhibited at Barcelona's Autumn Salon in 1927 and belonged later to Dalí's great friend in Paris, the couturière 'Coco' Chanel. Today its whereabouts is unknown. In it Lorca's head, which casts the shadow of Dalí's, appears half buried in the sand beside a decapitated female dummy and a rotting, fly-infested donkey. (Dalí was obsessed by rotting donkeys at this time, and made sure, two years later, that one appeared in his and Buñuel's film *Un Chien andalou*.) Lorca's left eye, the only one visible, is fixed in a glassy stare. Nearby lies another severed head, almost certainly Dalí's, separated from the poet's by an attenuated, disembodied arm, and a rotting corpse, which, it has been argued, represents Buñuel.[46] From both mouths comes a trickle of blood. Across the canvas, among the objects that litter the spectral beach, Dalí has placed numerous examples of his triangular and other 'gadgets', forming the 'wood' of Lorca's suggested title.

It seems certain that the heads in *Little Ashes* represent those of Dalí and Lorca. The subject of the painting, suggested clearly by the second title, *Sterile Efforts*, is almost certainly that of sexual impotence. The work contains one of Dalí's most alluring female nudes, albeit decapitated, seen from behind. The artist, a self-confessed worshipper of the female bottom (whose ideal version he was to find in those of the callipygean Gala, in 1929), always insisted on his loathing of breasts and women's genitals, his distaste for 'normal' intercourse, and preference, among the body's orifices, for the anus.[47] *Little Ashes*, in which Lorca's head is represented with eyes closed (asleep or dead?) beside the sea – suggesting, perhaps, the poet's unconcern at the torment unleashed in Dalí's brain by the contemplation of his ideal female posterior – seems, therefore, to be yet another expression of the conflicts that during this period threatened to reduce Dalí to a state of mental paralysis.[48]

Taking together the evidence of Dalí's letters to Lorca and the presence of the poet in his work at this time, we may fairly conclude, that, by 1927, Salvador was much more emotionally involved with Federico than he would later be prepared to admit.

There can be no doubt that Lorca knew Dalí's *Saint Sebastian* before it appeared, in Catalan, in the 31 July 1927 issue of *L'Amic de les Arts*, dedicated to himself, nor that he had discussed it in detail with Salvador. The piece moved him powerfully, not only because of its allusions to their friendship but because of its extreme stylistic novelty. Dalí was a strikingly original painter: now he had shown that he was also a writer of considerable talent (as the poet had told him some years previously).[49] *Saint Sebastian* is a fact of such importance in Lorca's biography that no excuse need be made for providing a translation of it here:

Saint Sebastian

Irony

Heraclitus, in a passage quoted by Themistius, tells us that Nature likes to hide herself. Alberto Savinio believes that her hiding of herself is an expression of self-modesty.* It is an ethical matter – he tells us – since this modesty is born out of the relationship between Nature and Man. And in this he discovers the prime cause that engenders irony.

Enriquet, the Cadaqués fisherman, told me these same things in his own language one day when, looking at a painting of mine that represented the sea, he said: 'You've caught it exactly. But it's better in the painting, because there you can count the waves.'†

Irony could also begin in such a preference, if Enriquet were capable of moving from physics to metaphysics.

Irony, as I have said, is nakedness; it is the gymnast who hides behind the pain of Saint Sebastian. And it is also this pain, because it can be recounted.‡

Patience

There is a patience in Enriquet's rowing which is a wise form of inaction; but there is also a patience which is a form of passion, the humble patience in the maturation of the paintings of Vermeer of Delft, which is the same patience as that of the ripening of fruit trees.

And there is yet another form: a form between inaction and passion, between Enriquet's rowing and Van der Meer's painting, which is a form of elegance. I am referring to the patience and the exquisite death-throes of Saint Sebastian.

Description of the Figure of Saint Sebastian

I realized that I was in Italy because of the black and white marble flagstones of the flight of stairs. I climbed these. At the end was Saint Sebastian, tied to an old cherry-tree trunk. His feet rested on a broken capital. The more I observed his face, the odder it appeared. None the less I had the impression that I had known him all my life, and the aseptic light of the morning revealed the smallest details with such clarity and purity that it was impossible for me to be disturbed.

The saint's head was divided into two parts: one, formed of a matter similar to that of a jellyfish and sustained by an extremely delicate circle of nickel; the other occupied by half a face which reminded me of someone very well known; from the latter circle there emerged a support of very white plaster which seemed to be the dorsal column of the figure. All the arrows bore an indication of their temperature and a little inscription engraved on steel which read: *Invitation to the Coagulation of the Blood*. In certain parts of the body the veins appeared on the surface with

---

* Alberto Savinio, ' "Anadiomenon". Principi di valutazione dell'Arte contemporanea', *Valori Plastici*, Roma, I, nos. 4–5, 1919

† The reference is almost certainly to the work *Girl at the Window* (1925), today in Madrid's Museum of Contemporary Art.

‡ In Catalan, as in Spanish, *contar* means both count and recount.

their deep, Patinir-storm blue, and effected curves of a painful voluptuousness on the pink coral of the skin.

When they arrived against the shoulders of the saint, the movements of the breeze were imprinted as if on a sensitive plate.

Trade-Winds and Counter-Trade-Winds

On touching his knees, the tenuous breezes stopped short. The martyr's halo was as though made of rock crystal, and in his hardened whisky there flowered a rough and bleeding starfish.

On the sand covered with shells and mica, precise instruments belonging to an unknown physics projected their explicative shadows, and offered their crystals and aluminiums to the disinfected light.* A few letters drawn by Giorgio Morandi indicated: *Distilled Devices.*

The Sea Breeze

Every minute there came the smell of the sea, constructed and anatomical like the bits of a crab.

I breathed in. Nothing was mysterious any longer. The pain of Saint Sebastian was a mere pretext for an aesthetic of objectivity. I breathed in again, and this time I shut my eyes, not out of mysticism, not in order to see more clearly my inner I – as we might say, platonically – but for the simple sensuality of the physiology of my eyelids.

Later I read slowly the names of the devices, and the terse indications thereon; each annotation was the point of departure for a whole series of intellectual delectations, and a new scale of precisions for hitherto unknown normalities.

With no previous explanations I understood intuitively the use of each of them and the joy of each of their sufficient exactitudes.

Heliometer for the Deaf-and-Dumb

One of the devices was entitled *Heliometer for the Deaf-and-Dumb.* The name was already an indication of its connection with astronomy, but it was above all its constitution that evidenced this. It was an instrument of high physical poetry formed by distances and by the relationships between these distances; these relationships were expressed geometrically in some of the parts, and arithmetically in others; in the centre, a simple indicating mechanism served to measure the saint's death-throes. This mechanism was composed of a small dial of graduated plaster, in the middle of which a red blood-clot, pressed between two crystals, acted as a sensitive barometer for each new wound.

In the upper part of the heliometer was Saint Sebastian's magnifying glass. This was at once concave, convex and flat. Engraved on the platinum frame of its clean, precise crystals could be read *Invitation to Astronomy;* and beneath, in letters standing out as if in relief: *Saint Objectivity.* On a numbered crystal rod one could read further: *Measurement of the Apparent Distances between Pure Aesthetic Values,* and, to one side, on a highly fragile test-tube, this subtle announcement:

* This beach has obvious affinities, as Lorca would have realized, with that of the painting *Honey is Sweeter than Blood.*

Apparent Distances and Arithmetical Measurements between Pure Sensual Values.
This test-tube was half full of sea water.

Saint Sebastian's heliometer had neither music nor voice and, in some parts, was blind. These blind spots of the device were those corresponding to its sensitive algebra and those intended to make concrete that which is most insubstantial and miraculous.

Invitations to Astronomy

I put my eye to the lens, the product of a slow distillation both numerical and intuitive.

Each drop of water, a number. Each drop of blood, a geometry.

I began to look. In the first place, the caress of my eyelids against the wise surface. Then I saw a succession of clear sights, perceived in such a necessary arrangement of measurements and proportions that each detail was shown to me like a simple and eurhythmic architectural organism.

On the deck of a white packet-boat a girl with no breasts was teaching the south-wind-imbued sailors to dance the *black bottom*. Aboard other liners, the *charleston* and *blues* dancers saw Venus each morning in the bottom of their *gin cocktails*, at the time for their pre-aperitifs.

All this was the exact opposite of vagueness, everything could be seen clearly, with a magnifying glass's clarity. When I fixed my eyes on any detail, this detail grew bigger like a close-up in the cinema, and acquired its sharpest plastic quality.

I see the girl playing polo in the nickel headlamp of the *Isotta Fraschini*. I direct my curiosity solely to her eye, and this occupies the maximum visual area. This one eye, suddenly enlarged and now the sole spectacle, is the whole depths and the whole surface of an ocean, in which all poetic suggestions navigate and all plastic possibilities are stabilized; the oily and sweet *mascara* forms, in its microscopic increase, precise spheres through which can be seen the Virgin of Lourdes or Giorgio de Chirico's painting *Evangelical Still-Life* (1926).

When I read the tender letters of the biscuit

> *Supérieur*
> *Petit Beurre*
> *Biscuit*

my eyes filled with tears.

An indicating arrow, and beneath: *Address Chirico; Towards the Limit of a Metaphysics*.

The thin line of blood is a dumb and ample plan of the underground. I don't want to continue until I see the life of the radiant *leucocyte*, and the red ramifications turn into a little stain, passing speedily through all the stages of their decrease. Once again the eye is seen in its primitive dimension in the depths of the concave mirror of the headlamp, like a singular organism in which swim the reflections' precise fish in their watery, lachrymal medium.

Before continuing to watch, I paused again to study the details of the saint. Saint Sebastian, free of symbolisms, was a *fact* in his unique and simple presence. Only with such objectivity is it possible to observe with calm a stellar system. I renewed my heliometric viewing. I was perfectly aware that I was moving within the anti-artistic and astronomical orbit of *Movietone Fox*.

The spectacles succeed one another, simple facts giving rise to new lyrical states.

The girl in the bar plays 'Dinah' on her little gramophone, while she prepares gin for the motorists: inventors of subtle mixtures of games of chance and black superstition in the mathematics of their engines.

At Portland autodrome, the blue Bugatti race, seen from the aeroplane, acquires the dreamlike movement of hydroids which descend spiralling to the bottom of the aquarium, with their parachutes open.

The rhythm of Josephine Baker in slow motion coincides with the purest and slowest growth of a flower produced by the cinematographic accelerator.

Cinematographic breeze again. White gloves and black notes of *Tom Mix*, pure as the last amorous embraces of fish; crystals and stars of *Marcoussis*.

Adolphe Menjou, in an anti-transcendental atmosphere, provides us with a new dimension of the *dinner-jacket* and of ingenuity (now only acceptable with cynicism).

Buster Keaton – here's true Pure Poetry, Paul Valéry! –, post-machine-age avenues, Florida, Le Corbusier, Los Angeles. The Pulchritude and eurhythmics of the standardized implement, aseptic, anti-artistic variety shows, concrete, humble, lively, joyous, comforting clarities, to oppose to a sublime, deliquescent, bitter, putrescent art . . .

Laboratory, clinic.

The white clinic falls silent around the pure chromolithography of a lung.

Within the crystals of the glass case the chloroformed scalpel sleeps like a Sleeping Beauty in the wood of nickels and Ripolin enamel, where embraces are impossible.

The American magazines offer to our eyes *Girls, Girls, Girls*, and, under the sun of Antibes, *Man Ray* obtains the clear portrait of a magnolia, more efficacious for our flesh than the tactile creations of the Futurists.

Shoes in a glass case in the Grand Hotel.

Tailors' models. Models quiescent in the electric splendour of the shop windows, with their neutral mechanical sensualities and disturbing articulations. Live models, sweetly stupid, who walk with the alternative and senseless rhythm of hips and shoulders, and carry in their arteries the new, reinvented physiologies of their costumes.

The models' mouths. Saint Sebastian's wounds.

Putrefaction

The other side of Saint Sebastian's magnifying glass corresponded to putrefaction. Everything, seen through it, was anguish, obscurity, and even tenderness – tenderness because of the exquisite absence of spirit and naturalness.

Preceded by I am not sure what lines from Dante, I saw the whole world of the putrescent philistines: the lachrymose and transcendental artists, far removed from all clarity, cultivators of all germs, ignorant of the precision of the double, graduated decimetre; the family who buy *objets d'art* to put on top of the piano; the public-works employee; the associate committee member; the professor of psychology . . . I didn't want to continue. The delicate moustache of a ticket-box clerk moved me. I felt in my heart all its exquisite, Franciscan and intensely delicate poetry. My lips smiled despite my urge to cry. I stretched myself on the sand. The waves approached the shore with the quiet murmur of Henri Rousseau's *Bohémienne endormie*.[50]

In *Saint Sebastian* Dalí wished to express his passionately held aesthetic of Holy Objectivity, of art's duty to abjure sentimentality and to express the spirit of the age. His search at this time for light and clarity (terms that recur in *Saint Sebastian*) had already been praised in Lorca's ode to the painter, and was a frequent theme in Salvador's letters to the poet. The piece has humour too (that subtle, tight-lipped Dalinian humour that his friends at the Residencia so much admired), and the reference to the 'putrescent' professors, 'transcendental artists' and other exemplars of the insensitivity to contemporary values, as Dalí understood them, must have raised a laugh among the painter's admirers.

That there were allusions in *Saint Sebastian* to Lorca the latter can have been in no doubt. As was pointed out earlier, Dalí had told him while he was at work on the piece that he often thought about him. 'We'll see if it turns out that St Sebastian is you!' he had joked.[51] Part of the saint's head is occupied by 'half a face which reminded me of someone very well known'. It seems likely that Dalí had Lorca's in mind, and the hypothesis is supported by the evidence of his drawing of St Sebastian which illustrated the piece in *L'Amic de les Arts*: the painter twice called Lorca a sole (*lenguado*) in his letters, and here he has given the saint the head of a stylized flatfish.[52]

It had been a fabulous summer for the poet. Not only had he seen Dalí frequently over two and a half months but he had made many new friends and renewed his acquaintance with others. In particular, his time in Cadaqués was to prove unforgettable. Ana María Dalí has recalled nostalgically the impromptu guitar concerts given at night on the terrace by their mutual friend Regino Sáinz de la Maza, Federico's insistence that she should read Ovid's *Metamorphoses* ('It's all there!' he exclaimed), and the poet's marvellous ability with children, which was reflected in the imaginative games he invented for two little friends of the Dalí household who often came to visit them.[53] One of these games he called 'The Letters from Margarita Petita'. Ana María has remembered:

One afternoon, while we played on the beach, Federico suddenly pretended to catch a piece of paper that came floating down through the air. 'It's a letter from Margarita Petita!' he said. And he read it out: 'Dear Children, I am a white horse with the wind in my mane and I'm looking for a star. Look, now I'm galloping in search of it! But I can't find it. I'm tired, I can do no more, my tiredness is turning me into smoke . . . Look how the shapes are changing!' We all sat looking. And, in effect, the mane seemed to separate from the neck . . . the tail grew impossibly long . . . and the legs became wings . . . Suddenly we saw the evening star appear on the horizon and we shouted: 'The star! The star!'[54]

Another day, one of the children gave Federico a stone to read, and the poet improvised again:

Dear Children, I've been here for many, many years. The happiest were when I was the roof of an ants' nest. They were so certain that I was the sky that I believed it. Now I know that I'm only a stone and this memory is my secret. Don't tell it to anyone.[55]

The many photographs taken by Ana María during the summer, most of them on the villa's terrace overlooking the bay of Cadaqués, reveal a radiantly happy Lorca: we see the poet engaging in thought transmission with Dalí (his head connected to that of the painter by the belt of his white beach-wrap) as they work on a 'manifesto';* 'acting dead' or posing in the role of a pensive Moor on the African coast; swimming bravely one yard from the shore; sporting the fisherman's shirt specially made for him by Ana María; playing with the children; standing proudly beside Dalí in his army uniform (Salvador did not finish his military service until the following February) or sitting with his hand on the painter's knee . . . Federico is a picture of contentment.

Meanwhile, characteristically, the poet's parents were becoming impatient: their elder son had now been away from home for almost three months and they wanted him back in Granada. Shortly before Lorca finally tore himself away from Cadaqués there appeared in the Madrid daily *El Sol* a review of *Songs* which must have greatly pleased Don Federico and Doña Vicenta. The critic, Esteban Salazar Chapela, had heard about Lorca's triple success in Barcelona – as poet, dramatist and artist – and was lavish in his praise of the book. He appreciated in particular its elegance and constraint, and Lorca's ability to be fully alive in the modern world and alert to contemporary trends while, at the same time, working within the tradition of 'popular poetry' – the folksong of the Spanish countryside. Salazar Chapela had no doubt that Lorca was now the finest new Andalusian poet writing, nor that his influence was already 'revolutionary'.[56]

At the end of July the poet took his leave of the Dalís. In Barcelona he saw Sebastià Gasch and the critic Lluís Montanyà briefly, staying, as usual, at the Hotel Condal, in the narrow Calle de la Bouqería, not far from the Cathedral.[57] Before catching the train to Madrid he wrote to Salvador, expressing his love for Cadaqués in terms identical to his friend's (clarity, sharp contours, mineral precision) and emphasizing in particular what a deep impression *Honey is Sweeter Than Blood* had made on him. Only a fragment of this highly imaginative (and virtually untranslatable) letter is known:

Cadaqués has the vitality and permanent neutral beauty of the place where Venus was born, *but where this has been forgotten.*

It aspires to pure beauty. The vines have disappeared and day by day are exalted

---

* The definitive version of the document, entitled in Catalan 'El Manifest groc' ('The Yellow Manifesto') and in Spanish 'El Manifiesto antiartístico' ('The Manifesto Against Art'), was published in March 1928, signed by Dalí, Sebastià Gasch and Lluís Montanyà, but not by Lorca.

the sharp edges which are like waves. One day the moon will move with the elasticity of a damp fish and the tower of the church oscillate like soft rubber over the hard or *sorrowful houses*, of lime or chewed bread. I get excited thinking about the discoveries you're going to make in Cadaqués and I remember Salvador Dalí the neophyte licking the twilight's shell without going in altogether, the pale pink shell of a crab lying on its back. Today you're inside. From here I can hear (ay, my little boy, how sad!) the soft trickle of blood from the Sleeping Beauty of the Wood of Gadgets* and the crackling of two little beasties like the sounds of a pistachio nut cracked between one's fingers. The decapitated woman is the finest imaginable poem on the theme of blood, and has more blood than all that spilt in the European war, which was *hot* blood and had no other purpose than to *irrigate* the earth and appease a symbolic thirst for eroticism and faith. Your pictorial blood and in general the whole tactile concept of your physiological aesthetic has such a concrete, well-balanced air, such a logical and true quality of pure poetry that it attains the category *of that which we need absolutely* in order to live.

One can say: 'I was tired and I sat down in the shade and freshness of that blood', or: 'I came down from the hill and ran all along the beach until I found the melancholy head in the spot where the delicious little crackling beasties, so useful for the digestion, gathered.'†

Now I realize how much I am losing by leaving you. The impression I get in Barcelona is that everyone is playing and sweating in an effort to *forget*. Everything is confused and aggressive like the aesthetic of the flame, everything indecisive and out of joint. In Cadaqués the people feel on the ground all the sinuosities and pores of the soles of their feet. Now I realize how I felt my shoulders in Cadaqués. It's delicious for me to recall the slippery curves of my shoulders when for the first time I felt in them the circulation of my blood in four spongy tubes which trembled with the movements of a wounded swimmer.[58]

At the end of this letter, in a passage unaccountably suppressed when it was published in 1986, the poet apologized for his appalling behaviour towards Salvador, without specifying details. Rafael Santos Torroella believes that the reference was to a second (and presumably very recent) attempt on the part of the poet to have anal intercourse with the painter. The hypothesis is supported, in the critic's view, by the evidence of the canvas entitled *Calavera atmosférica sodomizando a un piano de cola* ('Atmospheric Skull Sodomizing a Grand Piano') (1934), in the background of which figures the fishing cottage bought by Dalí in Port-Lligat from Lydia Cabrera and which became the kernel of his zany and later world-famous house. But the fact is that we are dealing with an hypothesis only, since no other information about the incident for which the poet felt the need to ask forgiveness has yet come to light.[59]

* An obvious reference to the 'Sleeping Beauty in the wood of nickels and Ripolin enamel' of *Saint Sebastian* as well as to the decapitated tailor's dummy in *Honey is Sweeter Than Blood*.

† An allusion, perhaps, to the presence of his own severed head in *Honey is Sweeter Than Blood*.

Summer in Granada

Lorca lingered only briefly in Madrid before returning to Granada, where his arrival was proudly announced on 7 August by *El Defensor*, which recalled on its front page the recent 'great success' of *Mariana Pineda* in the Catalan capital. [60]

During the summer, *Songs* continued to attract the benevolent attentions of the critics, and Lorca must have been especially gratified by an article that appeared on the front page of *El Sol* on 31 July, grandly entitled 'A Generation and its Poet'. The author of the piece was the critic and novelist Ricardo Baeza, who was then enjoying considerable prestige in both capacities. Baeza felt sure that Lorca – now that Antonio Machado and Juan Ramón Jiménez seemed to have fallen silent – was to become the most important contemporary Spanish poet; and believed that, by holding back so much unpublished work, especially *Gypsy Ballads*, he was doing himself a serious disservice. The critic rounded off his review:

Señor García Lorca would act wisely by not delaying too long in bringing out his unpublished work, as copious as it is admirable. Because he procrastinated in publishing this book *Songs*, which today reflects only an earlier, initial facet of his personality as a poet, those who are not *au fait* with his work might think that they can identify in him the influence of other poets of his generation, poets who, in point of fact, proceed in large measure from *his* production, generously and incautiously communicated in private, poets who were wise enough to hurry into print . . . For his poetic 'coronation' to take place, it requires only a decision on the part of Señor García Lorca: let him publish his *Gypsy Ballads* and it will occur automatically.

When Lorca received his copy of *L'Amic de les Arts* later that summer, and reread Dalí's *Saint Sebastian*, he could hardly contain himself. 'How admirable Dalí's *Saint Sebastian* is!' he wrote to Gasch:

It's one of the most intense poems one could possibly read. In that lad, in my opinion, Catalonia the Eternal has found its chief pride. I'm preparing a study on him which, if you want, you can translate into Catalan, and I'll publish it first in that language.[61]

Lorca's young entourage was as enthusiastic as the poet. 'Here in Granada we've translated it and it has caused a tremendous impression, especially on my brother who *wasn't expecting it*, despite what I had told him,' Federico wrote to Ana María Dalí.

What it is, simply, is a new prose form full of unimagined relationships and highly subtle *points of view*. It has taken on for me, down here, a charm and a highly intelligent inner light which doubles my admiration.[62]

Towards the end of the holidays, Lorca found himself possessed of a creative frenzy that compelled him above all to draw. The family were spending a few weeks at Lanjarón at the time (perhaps Doña Vicenta's liver was playing up again), and Federico wrote to Gasch to thank him for the amiable review of his Barcelona exhibition just published in *L'Amic de les Arts,* and to attempt, at the same time, a clarification of his present state of mind:

I'm extremely grateful to you for the kind things you say, because they help me more than you can imagine to draw, and really I'm enjoying myself very much with these drawings. Before I begin, I *propose* themes to myself and then I achieve the same result as when I have nothing particular in mind. Naturally, at the moment I'm in a state of sensitivity that is almost physical in quality, and which transports me to levels where it is difficult to stay on one's feet and one is almost hovering over an abyss. I find it almost impossible to sustain a normal conversation with the people here at the spa, because my eyes and my words are somewhere else – in the vast library which nobody has read, in the fresh breeze, in a country where things dance on one leg.[63]

In another fragment, perhaps from the same letter, the poet tried again to explain the process that had taken hold of him: his hand, he said, seemed to have acquired a sort of autonomy, casting itself out into the depths like a fishing line and bringing back a brilliant, unexpected catch of ideas and metaphors which formed themselves into fascinating shapes and lines on the paper:

Some of them are pure miracles, like *Cleopatra*: I felt myself shudder when there emerged a harmony of lines that I hadn't *planned, imagined* or *wished*. Nor was I *inspired*. I said, 'Cleopatra!' when I saw it, and it's true! Then my brother corroborated it. Those lines were *the exact portrait*, the *pure emotion*, of the Queen of Egypt.[64]

The poet was in a state of hypersensitivity – and aware of the dangers that this implied. Gasch, concerned about what was happening to his friend, quickly wrote again. The letter seems to have gone astray, but from Lorca's reaction to it we can get a fair idea of the Catalan's misgivings.[65] At another point in this incomplete correspondence the poet writes:

In effect, you are quite right in everything you say to me. But my state is *not* that of a 'perpetual dream'. I expressed myself badly. For several days I was close to a dream state, but I didn't fall into it completely and anyway I was held back by my good humour, and sustained by a solid wood scaffolding. I never venture into territory uninhabited by man, because I immediately turn on my tracks and almost always tear up the products of my trip. Whenever I produce something purely abstract this always has (I believe) the safe conduct of good humour and a human sense of balance. . . . My state is always happy, and this dreaming of mine isn't dangerous in my case, because I have defences: it's dangerous only for the person who allows himself to be fascinated by the large, dark mirrors that poetry and madness place in the depths of their canyons. IN ART I KNOW THAT I HAVE FEET OF LEAD. It's in the reality of my life, in love, in daily contact with others that I fear the chasm and the dream world. This, yes, is terrible and fantastic.[66]

The excerpts from Lorca's letters published in 1950 by Gasch are cryptic, and it seems likely that in the complete correspondence with the art critic the poet was more forthcoming about the causes of his state of mind, among which his relationship with a Dalí now increasingly attracted by surrealism was undoubtedly foremost. As a result of Gasch's continued interest in his drawings, Lorca devised the idea of publishing a selection of these with an introduction by his friend. But the project, despite occupying him for several months, came to nothing.[67]

We can be certain that Lorca wrote frequently to Dali during the summer, although only one of his letters (not yet published) has come to light so far. It was sent from Lanjarón shortly after the poet arrived there with his family, and hinges, as perhaps we might expect, on the theme of Saint Sebastian. At the end of the letter Federico is explicit about the extent to which he is missing Salvador. Moreover there is not a single well-shaped calf to be seen in Lanjarón, and even the handsome waiters at the hotel cannot rouse his interest.[68]

Lorca also worked during the summer on his prose piece 'Saint Lucy and Saint Lazarus', which seems to have been a direct product of his deep admiration for Dalí's *Saint Sebastian*. The creation of a stark, dream atmosphere, and the use of short paragraphs and phrases without verbs, recall at once the Dalinian precedent, although Lorca's similes reach a higher imaginative level than those of his friend:

The spring day was like a hand swooning on a cushion.

Their dark voices, like two fleeing moles, stumbled against the walls, unable to find the rectangular exit to the sky.

The gaiety of the city had just abated, and it was like a child who had recently been failed in his examinations.[69]

The solemn novena to the eyes of St Lucy (patroness of the blind) is evoked in terms that immediately bring to mind Dalí's aesthetic of Holy Objectivity as expounded in *Saint Sebastian* and in his letters to the poet:

Praise was offered to the external aspect of things, to the pure and fresh beauty of the skin, to the charm of delicate surfaces, and help was sought against the dark physiologies of the body, against the central fire and the funnels of the night, raising, under the nuggetless dome, a sheet of pure crystal riddled, in every direction, by delicate gold reflectors. The world of grass was struggling against the world of the mineral, the fingernail against the heart. The God of outlines, transparency and surface. With the fear of the accelerated pulse and the horror of the jet of blood, a petition was made for the tranquillity of the agate and the shadowless nude of the jellyfish.[70]

When 'Saint Lucy and Saint Lazarus' was published in the November issue of the *Revista de Occidente*, Dalí's reaction, which we know only in part, was, not surprisingly, highly favourable, and he did not fail to perceive that the piece constituted an indirect homage to his *Saint Sebastian*.[71]

Mariana Pineda in Madrid

With the arrival of autumn Lorca returned to Madrid where, true to her word, Margarita Xirgu was preparing to open her season in the capital with *Mariana Pineda*, which, after its necessarily short run in Barcelona, had been favourably received in San Sebastián.[72] Opening night was 12 October, and that morning Lorca published in the Madrid daily *ABC* a note on his intentions in the play, stressing his effort to create an atmosphere, reminiscent of nineteenth-century prints, that would enable him to draw on Romantic 'topics' while at the same time avoiding any attempt at pastiche of the Romantic drama. The note proved useful, for the reviews appearing the following day showed clearly that the critics had read Lorca's comments and taken them into account as they watched the play.[73]

The night was a great success, and even the few hostile critics could not avoid recording the extreme enthusiasm of the audience: bursts of applause constantly interrupted the performance, and at the end of each act Lorca's appearance on the stage was demanded. Among the many friends present was Rafael Alberti, who recalls in his autobiography the intense excitement pervading the theatre that evening, an excitement not unrelated to the suspicion that the play might be banned at the last moment, or even during the performance, by General Primo de Rivera's censors, always alert to the possible political implications of theatrical works, and who, in the case of *Mariana Pineda*, might fairly be expected to discover numerous allusions to the current régime (even though it was written before Primo de Rivera came to power). But the script had presumably been submitted previously to the authorities and, in the event, the evening passed off without a hitch. During an interval Alberti introduced Lorca to a young Andalusian poet, Vicente Aleixandre, whose work was beginning to appear in the 'little magazines' then flourishing throughout Spain. Aleixandre, who years later received the Nobel Prize for Literature, was to become one of Lorca's closest friends and one of those who best understood the complexities of his personality.[74]

Federico was delighted with the reaction of the critics, who, with few exceptions, responded favourably. None the less, he was perfectly conscious that the play, whatever its merits, no longer reflected his thinking on the theatre and that, had he written it more recently, it would have been utterly different. *Mariana Pineda* ran for ten days and, by the time it came off, Lorca had abundant reason to be pleased with himself. Under the protective wing of Margarita Xirgu he had made an effective debut in the theatre, and, if *Mariana Pineda*, with its obvious flaws, had been a considerable success, what might he not achieve with his more up-to-date work? '*Mariana Pineda* reveals a genuine playwright,' stated the dramatist Carlos Arniches a month later, 'and I don't say *poet* because the latter we all greatly admired already.'[75] Lorca must have been grateful for the remark. Before *Mariana Pineda* ended its run, moreover, the *Heraldo de Madrid* had announced in its widely read theatre page that he had no fewer than three other plays ready: *The Shoemaker's Prodigious Wife*, *The Love of Don Perlimplín for Belisa in His Garden* and a puppet play. Few of those who knew Lorca now doubted that, if he was already being hailed as the finest poet of his generation, he was also going to make a name for himself in the theatre.[76]

On 22 October 1927 the *Gaceta Literaria* held a banquet to celebrate the success of *Mariana Pineda*. More than sixty guests turned up, many of them well known, such as Ramón Gómez de la Serna, Ernesto Giménez Caballero (editor of the magazine), Melchor Fernández Almagro, the historian Américo Castro and Dámaso Alonso. Witty speeches were delivered, particularly by Gómez de la Serna, and amid enthusiastic scenes Lorca recited three of his Gypsy ballads. Several telegrams were read out, among them one from Salvador Dalí, the text of which is unknown.[77]

Lorca had sent a telegram to Salvador immediately after the première to tell him that the play had been a success and that his sets and costumes had been widely acclaimed. 'If Lorca earns money,' Dalí wrote soon afterwards to Gasch, 'the appearance of the ANTIARTISTIC review is guaranteed.'[78] The remark suggests strongly that Lorca had given his word that, if *Mariana Pineda* were even a reasonable box-office hit, he would help to finance the venture. But the play did not reap great financial rewards and the magazine never appeared, the 'antiartistic' zeal of Dalí and his friends finding an outlet in other channels.

Since the two separated that summer, Dalí, who had not yet finished his military service, continued to work on his paintings *Honey is sweeter Than Blood*, *Sterile Efforts* (later *The Birth of Venus* and *Little Ashes*) and *Gadget and Hand*. Coinciding with the production of *Mariana Pineda* in Madrid he exhibited the first two of these works in the Barcelona Autumn Salon, and was chagrined to find that the critics, unlike the public, were incapable of appreciating them. Commenting on this insensitivity in *L'Amic de les Arts*, Dalí asked himself why it was that, where the critics had proved obtuse, ordinary people had responded enthusiastically to the two pictures. 'Because', he concluded, 'they were gripped by their poetry, which moved them at a subconscious level, despite the energetic protestations of their culture and their intelligence.' In the same article Dalí claimed that his concern with 'maximum artistic objectivity' was distancing his work increasingly from surrealism, but this was more a boast than an accurate assessment of his current practice, for, as his remark on the critics and the public showed, he was fully aware of the appeal of these paintings to the subliminal reaches of the mind.[79]

In its 31 October 1927 issue *L'Amic de les Arts* reproduced *Honey is Sweeter Than Blood* and enlarged the fragment of the painting in which Lorca's severed head appears on the beach beside the putrescent donkey and not far from the rotting corpse. Did the poet point out to his friends, even to his family, his presence in this painting which he so much admired? It seems likely, although there is no record of such confidences. Moreover it is probably fair to assume that by this time the poet had received from Dalí the excellent photograph of the painting later found among his papers.[80]

Shortly after the production of *Mariana Pineda* in Madrid Dalí wrote Lorca a letter in which the increasing hold being exerted on him by surrealism was manifest, despite his public utterances to the contrary. After describing enthusiastically the paintings on which he was then working, he expressed particular satisfaction with the invention of some 'lost breasts', not to be confused, he insisted, with those *flying* bosoms which had already appeared in his pictures. Then he adopted a more intimate tone. 'Hola Señor,' he teased the poet,

you must be rich now, if I were with you I'd be your little prostitute to move you and steal your banknotes which I'd then soak (this time in the donkey's water). I'm tempted to send you a bit of my lobster-coloured pyjamas, or rather 'lobster's dream' coloured, to see if you take pity on me from your position of opulence and send me money.

Dalí then proceeded to pour out his venom on Margarita Xirgu, who had so far paid him nothing for his *Mariana Pineda* sets, pointing out that with 500 pesetas they would be in a position to publish the first issue of their *Antiartistic Review*, in which they could launch an all-out attack on the 'putrescent' values they detested, represented, as far as Dalí was concerned, by Juan Ramón Jiménez, the donkey-loving sentimentality of whose book *Platero and I* he particularly despised. (His own rotting donkeys, he emphasized, were the only *realistic* ones.)[81] We do not know how Lorca reacted to this letter, but it may be guessed that Dalí's libidinous bantering served only to heighten the poet's unhappiness at being separated from him. By this time, moreover, Dalí was more intent than ever on getting to Paris, and Lorca must have realized that before long the painter would be off to join Buñuel and the other Spaniards resident in the French capital.

At the end of May, when Lorca and Dalí were in Figueras and Barcelona preparing *Mariana Pineda*, Buñuel had returned to Madrid to lecture on avant-garde cinema at the Residencia de Estudiantes, illustrating his talk with representative excerpts from the work of such directors as Lucien Brull, Jean Renoir and Alberto Cavalcanti, and showing, complete, René Clair's astonishing, twenty-four-minute *Entr'acte* (1924). The occasion had gone off well, and Buñuel liked to recall years later that, after the lecture, the philosopher José Ortega y Gasset had confessed to him, with boyish enthusiasm, that, if he were younger, he would devote himself there and then to the cinema.[82] It is possible that, while he was with Dalí in Catalonia, Lorca read the review of Buñuel's lecture published in the 1 June 1927 issue of *La Gaceta Literaria*. And likely that from his friend Pepín Bello, from Dalí or even from Buñuel himself, he learned that at this time the latter was proclaiming his intention of publishing shortly a book of 'narrations' to be called *Polismos*. The title suggests that Buñuel wished to express the spirit of the many 'isms' then current in Europe, and with which he felt himself increasingly identified. The energetic Aragonese was beginning to see himself, in fact, as one of the principal Spanish representatives of the Parisian avant-garde, a John the Baptist to the uninitiated barbarians south of the Pyrenees, for whom Buñuel was not slow to express his petulant scorn.[83]

From Buñuel's letters to José Bello at this time it is clear that the budding film-maker was becoming increasingly jealous of the intense relationship that now existed between Lorca and Dalí. During the summer the two had written to him from Catalonia. 'I have received a revolting letter from Federico and his acolyte Dalí,' Buñuel told Bello from Brittany on 28 July, without adding any further details. The adjective Buñuel used was *asquerosa* ('revolting', 'disgusting') and a further letter to Bello (5 August) shows that he was amused by the coincidence that the García Lorcas had property in a Granadine village of that name, Asquerosa (the etymology of which has nothing to do with the other word). The jocular tone cannot disguise the venom:

> Dalí is writing me revolting letters.
> He's revolting.
> With Federico that makes two revolting types.
> One because he's from Asquerosa and the other because he's revolting.*

On 5 September Buñuel returned to the charge. After providing Bello with some bawdy gossip and up-to-date information about his film activities, he launched into his most ferocious attack on Lorca and Dalí to date:

> * Dalí me escribe cartas asquerosas.
> Es un asqueroso.
> Y Federico dos asquerosos.
> Uno por ser de Asquerosa y otro porque es un asqueroso.

Federico sticks in my craw incredibly. I thought that the boyfriend [Dalí] was putrescent, but now I see that the other is even worse. It's his awful aestheticism that has distanced him from us. His extreme narcissism was already enough to make a pure friendship with him impossible. It's his look out. The trouble is that his work may suffer as a result.

Dalí is deeply influenced by him. He believes himself to be a genius, thanks to the love Federico professes for him. He's written to me saying: 'Federico is better than ever. He's *the* great man, his drawings have genius. I'm producing amazing work, etc.' And then, of course, his successes in Barcelona are so easily achieved. How I'd love to see him arrive here and renew himself far from the dire influence of García! Because Dalí is a real male and very talented.[84]

When Buñuel read in Paris the witty account of the *Mariana Pineda* banquet published in *La Gaceta Literaria*, he was beside himself with delight, deducing, incorrectly, that both it and the play had been signal failures. 'It's what he [Lorca] deserved and I'm really pleased,' he wrote spitefully to Bello (8 November 1927). 'The play has been a flop . . . But it has made him 12,000 pesetas.'[85] Whence Buñuel derived the last piece of information (now impossible to verify) we cannot know, but certainly not from the account published in *La Gaceta Literaria*. In the same letter he commented that, due to Lorca's influence over Dalí, the latter was now 'old hat' in terms of what was happening in Paris, whatever facile success he might be having in Spain. Buñuel could hardly have been further from the mark, but at this time he was attacking all and sundry – not only Lorca and Dalí – and many of his artistic judgements, as his letters show, were based more on personal bias than anything else. At all events, with both a frustrated literary and a musical vocation Buñuel had reason to be envious of Lorca, whose recent *Songs* was receiving such excellent reviews and whose chances of becoming a successful dramatist now seemed considerable. Lorca's intimate friendship with Dalí was a further thorn in the flesh, and from this moment onwards Buñuel did everything in his power to wean Salvador away from the poet and to encourage him to move to Paris.

Góngora in Seville

In December Lorca was in the Residencia to give his by now celebrated talk on Góngora. Among the audience was the Englishman John B. Trend, who wrote to Manuel de Falla a few weeks later to say that the lecture was 'admirable in every sense of the word'.[86] It had been delivered on the eve of the departure for Seville of an enthusiastic group of young writers invited by the city's Arts Club to participate in a series of readings and lectures in honour of Góngora and comprising Lorca, Rafael Alberti, Gerardo Diego, Dámaso Alonso, Juan Chabás, Jorge Guillén and José Bergamín. On the train south with the 'seven Madrid literati', as *El Sol* termed them, was the celebrated bullfighter Ignacio Sánchez Mejías, at once the begetter of the idea to visit Seville and the Maecenas who financed the operation.[87]

Sánchez Mejías was born in Seville in 1891, the son of a distinguished doctor. Having completed his secondary education, and already sure that he wanted to be a bullfighter, he had escaped to Mexico where, for the first time, he donned the matador's 'suit of lights'. A few years later, successful and much gored, he returned to Spain where he soon achieved fame and fortune and married a sister of Joselito el Gallo, one of the most acclaimed bullfighters of his generation. Ignacio reached the pinnacle of his career between 1919 and 1922, in which year he effected the first of what was to be a series of temporary retirements from the ring, with the intention of devoting himself to flamenco, the theatre and literature, in all of which he was passionately interested. But he could not forget the excitement of the *corrida*. The lure was irresistible and, in 1924, at the age of thirty-three, he returned. 'I was dying of boredom,' he explained to the newspapers. That summer he was gored yet again, as a result of his habitual temerity. (While some *aficionados* had their doubts about Ignacio's art, none questioned his extraordinary courage, which often verged on the foolhardy.) Then, in 1925, he revealed new aspects of his gifted personality, publishing widely read bullfighting chronicles in the Seville press and playing a part in the film *La malquerida*, based on Nobel prizewinner Jacinto Benavente's rural drama of that name.[88] Ignacio had an urge, too, to write plays, and by December 1927, when he organized the visit of the 'seven Madrid literati' to Seville, had completed *Sinrazón* ('Without Reason'), inspired by the theories of Sigmund Freud and set in a lunatic asylum. The play was staged, with moderate success, in Madrid the following year.[89]

Sánchez Mejías, then, was no normal bullfighter. The French writer and hispanist Marcelle Auclair, who met Ignacio in the early 1930s, wrote that the matador – handsome, tall by Spanish standards, athletic, bronzed and an excellent conversationalist – was 'charm personified'.[90] To women, certainly, Ignacio was irresistibly attractive. He had soon separated from his wife and, in 1927, found in Lorca's friend the dancer and singer Encarnación López Júlvez, 'La Argentinita', the great love of his life, which did not prevent him from enjoying flirtations on the side. It came as a shock to many people, including Lorca, that the bullfighter also had a liking for pretty young men.[91] Marcelle Auclair wrote that Federico, whose knowledge of bullfighting was limited, admired in Sánchez Mejías the man 'capable of making of his life a duel, loyal but crazy, with love and with death: a gigantic *fiesta*'. In that duel, death was finally to carry the day.[92]

But not yet. On the night of 16 December 1927 took place the first public performance given by the 'Brilliant Pleyade', as the Seville newspapers termed the group of young writers from Madrid. Once José Bergamín had explained to a packed house the purpose of their visit (the proclamation, under the aegis of Góngora, of the new values in art), Dámaso Alonso rose to argue that, contrary to the commonly held view, Spanish literature is not predominantly 'realistic' or 'popular'. He was followed by Juan Chabás, who essayed a critique of contemporary Spanish prose, referring to, among other writers, Pedro Salinas (unable to be present) and José Bergamín. The evening was rounded off by a joint recital, given by Lorca and Alberti, of a passage from Góngora's great poem the *Primera soledad* ('First Solitude'). Alberti recalls in his memoirs that the reading generated such enthusiasm among the audience that it was frequently interrupted by applause.[93]

The second event, however, which was celebrated the following evening, proved particularly memorable. It began with Gerardo Diego, who entoned an impassioned text entitled 'In Defence of Poetry'. Next Dámaso Alonso read an analysis by Bergamín of contemporary trends in Spanish poetry (Bergamín was unable to read it himself because his energetic oratory of the previous evening had left him voiceless). Then came a free-for-all in which the visiting and local poets recited their work and vied for the plaudits of the large and fervent audience. It was, certainly, a remarkable gathering of talents, for contending with the Madrid group were Sevillian poets of considerable stature, such as Luis Cernuda, Fernando Villalón, Adriano del Valle, Rafael Laffón and Joaquín Romero Murube. Alberti has recalled that, though the audience greeted Guillén's difficult *décimas* (highly concentrated ten-lined poems) with enthusiastic 'olés!', the excitement reached its pitch when Lorca rose and recited some of his Gypsy ballads. Handkerchiefs were waved and Adriano del Valle, Lorca's friend from nine years earlier, when *Impressions and Landscapes* appeared, worked himself into such a state that, jumping on to his chair, he tossed jacket, collar and tie at the poet as if the latter had just performed a brilliant pass in the bull ring.[94]

In Seville, Lorca renewed old friendships – with José Bello, for example, who had been living there since the previous year – and initiated some new ones, in particular with Fernando Villalón and Luis Cernuda.

Fernando Villalón-Daoiz y Halcón, to give him his full name, was a forty-six-year-old nobleman – his title proclaimed him Count of Miraflores de los Angeles – who bred bulls with great success and was interested in poetry and spiritualism. Ignacio Sánchez Mejías habitually introduced him as 'the best poet in all Andalusia',[95] and it is a fact that Villalón, who had only recently begun to write verse, was considerably gifted as a poet, having published the previous year two collections, *Andalucía la baja* ('Lowland Andalusia') and *Romances del 800* ('Nineteenth-Century Ballads'). Rafael

Alberti (whose memoirs contain a riveting account of this historic visit to Seville) has described Lorca's terrified expression as Villalón drove them at a preposterous speed through the narrow streets in a 'crazy little motor car', quite unruffled as pedestrians hurled themselves out of the way, and reciting stanzas from his as yet unfinished poem 'The Chaos'. Villalón's interest in the occult could not fail to fascinate Lorca, himself sensitive to parapsychological matters, and the aristocrat had good accounts to give of the many seances in which he had taken part, with numerous ghost stories to boot. Lorca was no doubt intrigued, too, by Villalón's determination to be the first man to breed a bull with green eyes, a project in which he invested, and lost, a considerable fortune.[96]

Luis Cernuda was a younger man than Villalón and, like Salvador Dalí, had been born in 1904. The meeting between him and Lorca was to prove important for both poets, and led, after Lorca's return from New York and Cuba in 1930, to a close friendship – in so far, that is, as the highly introverted Cernuda was capable of such a relationship. Slim and always immaculately dressed, Cernuda, when Lorca met him, was as shy as a gazelle and likely to take himself off at the slightest indication of a threat to his privacy. He recalled in 1938, shortly before the end of the Civil War, that on this first encounter with Lorca he had been struck by the seeming contradiction between, on the one hand, Federico's voice and large, eloquent, melancholy eyes, and, on the other, his 'thickset Granadine peasant's body'. The older poet had waxed enthusiastic over some exquisite dish he had eaten or was going to eat, and Cernuda had suddenly sensed that, in the profusion of detail with which Lorca conjured up the delicacy in question, there spoke an older, ancestral voice springing from the Oriental past of Andalusia, as if from a collective memory. Cernuda had found Lorca surrounded, like a successful bullfighter, by a cohort of admirers and hangers-on, and thought that he noticed in Federico's bearing something of the pride of the matador. He also became aware of another aspect of the poet. 'Something that I hardly understood or that I did not wish to recognize began to unite us despite the rather theatrical manner of our introduction,' Cernuda recalled. 'He took me by the arm and we left the others. . .' Cernuda was to write some of the frankest – and finest – poetry ever produced in Spain on the theme of homosexual love and its frustrations, and, while we know disappointingly little about the nature of his friendship with Lorca, it is probably safe to assume that, in the 1930s, their shared homosexuality was the source of mutual confidences and appreciation.[97]

On the outskirts of Seville Ignacio Sánchez Mejías owned a charming estate called Pino Montano, where he organized an appropriately lavish party for the young writers from the capital. The guests were constrained to dress as Moors, Ignacio dispensing to each a heavy Moroccan *chilaba*. In this garb it has been recorded that José Bergamín looked the oddest, and Juan Chabás the most handsome. Animated by copious libations, the happy band passed the night reciting poems and telling stories. Dámaso Alonso performed the almost impossible feat of reciting from memory the 1,091 lines of Góngora's *Primera soledad*. Lorca was moved to entertain the gathering with one of his many party pieces – improvised sketches and mime – while Villalón, who like Luis Buñuel was an amateur hypnotist, practised on Rafael Alberti, who proved an excellent subject. The fiesta reached its climax in the early hours of the morning with the arrival of the great Gypsy *cantaor* Manuel Torre (whom Lorca had met in 1922 during the *cante jondo* festival in Granada) and the guitarist Manuel Huelva, bosom friends of the host. Torre sang that night with powerful, spine-chilling *duende*. 'He was like a hoarse, wounded animal, a deep well of anguish,' Alberti recalled. When the guests began to discuss the mystery of this primitive music, the Gypsy produced an expression that caught the imagination of those present. 'In *cante jondo*', he pronounced, 'what we have to search for constantly, until we find it, is the black trunk of the Pharaoh.' In other words, a means of connecting with a tradition that, according to Gypsy lore, stretches back to the days when the tribes roamed Egypt.[98]

The visit of the 'Brilliant Pleyade' to Seville ended officially with the poetic 'coronation' – a fresh olive-sprig cut by Ignacio Sánchez Mejías was employed – of Dámaso Alonso, the acknowledged authority on Góngora among these young admirers of the Cordovan poet and of the 'objectivity' of contemporary art.[99] It was the culminating act in a year of Góngora celebrations, and from this point onwards the cult of 'pure poetry', of 'aseptic art', would begin to lose its hold on Lorca and his generation. The experience had been valuable and the battle against sentimentality largely won. Now the stage seemed set for the return to a more human art, an art less concerned to play down emotion and to avoid social issues.

Among the many anecdotes generated by the visit to Seville, one stands out: 'the heroic and nocturnal crossing of the Guadalquivir in flood', as the event was termed by Gerardo Diego.[100] Dámaso Alonso has given us a vivid account of what happened. The poets – 'almost the nucleus of a generation' – had embarked, in pitch dark, in the small boat that, guided by a rope, in those days ferried people across the 'Great River' (*Guadalquivir* is an Arabic word meaning exactly this). No sooner afloat, it became clear that the crossing was going to be unpleasant, for the tidal river, like an 'immense, dark bull', seemed to be shouldering the boat, as if trying to force it downstream towards the sea. The friends' laughter and jokes gradually subsided. Halfway across no one was quipping. Lorca alone refused, or was unable, to hide his terror. So insistent were his lamentations that Dámaso thought at first that he was fooling. But no: this was authentic panic. Looking back years later Alonso found in that crossing of the Guadalquivir a series of significances not apparent at the time. The boat, he decided, represented the links binding together in friendship the members of a generation; the rope was the cord of destiny – a cord that would snap for Lorca, tragically, before it did for his companions – or, perhaps, the guiding hand of God. But whence Lorca's terrible dread, witnessed that night, perhaps for the first time, by Dámaso Alonso and the others, and that Salvador Dalí knew so well? Might it have been a presentiment of his death nine years later? Dámaso Alonso wisely refrains from answering his own question. Only one thing, he concludes, is certain: Lorca's work, in its persistently oneiric imagery, reflects on every page the poet's obsession with death.[101]

The Madrid literati had been put up, as befitted such luminaries, at one of Seville's best hotels, the Paris. But once the official events were over there could be no question of their staying on in such luxurious accommodation. The party was over. Dámaso Alonso and Lorca decided, however, to finance out of their own pockets a few more days in Seville, and consequently moved into cheaper rooms at the top of the building.[102] A few days later, on 23 December, *El Defensor de Granada* announced that Lorca had returned home,[103] and shortly afterwards Alonso, accompanied by his mother, arrived from Malaga to spend a fortnight in the town. Dámaso had never been in Granada, and could have had no better guide to the place than Lorca, who initiated him, as he had done Juan Ramón Jiménez three years earlier, into the delights of the Alhambra, the Generalife and the Albaicín, and the contemplation of Granada's constantly changing light and colours. One night Lorca took his friend out to dinner. He had prepared a surprise. When the waiter came to take their order, Federico asked for 'The "Primera Soledad"'! To Alonso's amazement (he imagined this to be some rare local dish), the waiter launched into a word-perfect recital of Góngora's syntactically convoluted poem, which Dámaso himself knew by heart, as he had so recently demonstrated in Seville. Federico was delighted with the success of his little game. The waiter (in fact the owner) was a friend, and this was not the first time that he had performed for the poet's unsuspecting guests.[104]

Over Christmas Lorca heard from Sebastià Gasch, who informed him that Dalí was greatly taken with the recently published 'Saint Lucy and Saint Lazarus', having written to him enthusiastically on the subject.[105] The letter (which almost certainly Lorca never saw) shows that the painter immediately perceived the importance of the piece: Federico's 'marvellous text', he had written to Gasch, illustrated to perfection his tenet that art should be 'objective'; and it showed, moreover, what a seminal influence his *Saint Sebastian* had exerted on the Granadine poet. 'Lorca seems to be coinciding with me in a lot of things – oh paradox!' Dalí exclaimed, adding that 'Saint Lucy and Saint Lazarus' was 'eloquent in this respect' (as indeed it was). Dalí felt, finally, that the 'intellectual phase' through which Federico seemed then to be passing would be short-lived. It was a shrewd observation, which further confirms the extent to which Dalí knew his man.[106]

Lorca was making little attempt at this time to hide from Gasch the intensity of his feelings for Salvador, although in the excerpts from the poet's letters to the Catalan critic it seems undeniable that some too personal observations were diplomatically expurgated by the editors. One passage deserves to be quoted:

Every day I am more convinced of Dalí's talent. He seems unique to me, and has a serenity and *clarity* of judgement in his thinking which is deeply moving. He gets things wrong and it doesn't matter. He's *alive*. His extreme intelligence is fused with a disconcerting infantility, in a mixture as unusual as it is absolutely original and attractive. What moves me most about him at the moment is his constructivist (that is to say, creative) *delirium*, in which he's seeking to create out of a vacuum, struggling and engaging in bursts of activity with such faith and intensity that it's incredible. Nothing could be more dramatic than this objectivity and search for happiness for the simple sake of happiness. He hasn't forgotten that this was always the Mediterranean law – 'I believe in the resurrection of the flesh,' says Rome. Dalí is the man who takes on ghosts with an axe of gold. 'Don't talk to me about the supernatural,' says Falla. What *I* say is:

> O straight line!
> Pure lance without horseman!
> How my tortuous path
> dreams of your light!

But Dalí won't allow himself to be driven. He needs to be at the wheel himself and, moreover, [there is] his faith in astral geometry. He moves me deeply. Dalí gives me the same pure feeling (may God our Father forgive me!) that I get from the baby Jesus abandoned in his crib, with the seed of the crucifixion already there under the straw of his cradle.[107]

The cryptic lines quoted, whose relevance Gasch must have been at a loss to understand, come from Lorca's poem 'Spiral', written in November 1922:

> Espiral
>
> Mi tiempo
> avanza en espiral.
>
> La espiral
> limita mi paisaje,
> deja en tinieblas lo pasado

y me hace caminar
lleno de incertidumbre.

¡ Oh línea recta! Pura
lanza sin caballero,
¡ cómo suena tu luz
mi senda salomónica!* [108]

From his earliest writings onwards Lorca left a record of the tortuous nature of his path through life. 'His is a spiral path,' Eutimio Martín has written in a commentary on this poem,

oscillating from right to left, from left to right, from a mystical pole to an erotic one, his soul torn between an irresistible tendency both towards the most diaphanous spirituality and towards carnal appetites as irrepressible as they were heterodox. Under the burden of this 'spiral'† anguish Lorca entered 1928. [109]

This puts it aptly. Lorca was never able fully to resolve the conflict that raged in his psyche between God and Dionysus: all he could do was to attempt to come to terms with it, to seek for survival through its expression in his art. But at different moments in his life not even that art sufficed to shield him from deep, almost suicidal depression. At the end of 1927 – a year rich in diverse achievements and new friendships – Federico's spirits were in part sustained by the conviction that soon he would see Dalí again. But he was mistaken, and, in the event, painter and poet were not to meet again for seven years.

* Spiral

My time
advances in a spiral.

The spiral
limits my landscape,
leaves the past in shadows,
and makes me travel
full of uncertainty.

O straight line! Pure
lance without horseman,
how my spiral path
dreams of your light!

† The adjective *salomónico*, rendered 'spiral' in the above version of Lorca's lines, is the usual term to designate the twisted or 'corkscrew' column (*columna salomónica*).

13

1928

gallo

Lorca began 1928 confidently enough, despite his many problems, and his friends were soon being informed that *The Shoemaker's Prodigious Wife* was finished, an *Ode to the Holy Sacrament* and lecture on Spanish cradle songs in the pipeline – and publication of *Gypsy Ballads* imminent (as indeed it was). Moreover the poet had not abandoned the idea of bringing out a book of drawings, and was now announcing the collaboration of Dalí as well of Gasch.[1]

But what was especially occupying Lorca's mind, time and energy at this moment was the review *gallo*, about to appear at long last. Life and soul of the group of young Granadine writers who for years had been trying to get this project off the ground, Lorca, despite his urge to return to Madrid, stayed in the town until the end of April or early May in order to see to the final details.[2] It had been the poet's hope that, with *gallo*, he could remain more or less in the background, giving advice where this was needed, certainly, but letting the other, mostly younger, enthusiasts get on with the job themselves. This was a vain dream, however, and Federico's active participation proved necessary at every level.

By the end of February the first issue of *gallo* had been put together, and, on 8 March, the eve of publication, Lorca and his friends organized a banquet to celebrate their achievement. The evening passed off uproariously. Various speakers held forth on the aims of the new publication and the symbolism of its title. *Gallo*, they affirmed, signified the beginning of a new era, the death knell of Romanticism in the town, 'the serenity and beauty of the present moment', and expressed the 'desire for renewal' felt by all those associated with the project. Federico, in a state of considerable euphoria, stressed in his speech the unity of criteria binding together the members of the group who, if their love of Granada could not be gainsaid, had their eyes firmly fixed on Europe. Although written and published in Granada, *gallo* was going to be an anti-provincial review for the outside world, stimulating local renovation by reflecting contemporary trends. Hopefully, he mused, it would generate a reaction against those tight-fisted *granadinos* who consistently failed to appreciate – much less to support – the arts. Lorca was calling, in fact, for the implementation of Angel Ganivet's little-heeded programme of thirty years earlier for the forging of a 'universal' Granada.[3]

The following day *gallo* went on sale. It was handsomely printed in 24 by 23 cm. format, with twenty-two pages of text and fourteen advertisements, which, in their insistence on the ultra-modernity of the products and services offered, quaintly underlined the provincialism of a city once the capital of a kingdom: the very provincialism lamented and combatted by *gallo*.

The first issue of the review contained Lorca's 'History of This Cockerel', a finely ironic send-up of the Granadine temperament; a poem by Jorge Guillén; aphorisms on the symbolism of cockerels by José Bergamín; thoughts on the spiritual 'reconstruction' of Granada from Melchor Fernández Almagro; Dalí's *Saint Sebastian*, translated into Spanish from the original Catalan; avant-garde prose from Manuel López Banús and Enrique Gómez Arboleya, two young *granadinos* making their literary début; and five small drawings by Salvador Dalí (who had also contributed stylized cockerels for the title and back page), one of them representing a charming *putrefacto*.

Lorca's 'History of This Cockerel', written a year earlier, captured to perfection the spirit of Granada, and nobody doubted that his Don Alhambro was partly inspired by Luis Seco de Lucena, founder–owner of *El Defensor de Granada* and indefatigable compiler of guides to the town. Lorca's Don Alhambro had been in exile in England until 1830 and, inspired by British progress, had returned to Granada determined to shake the city out of its lethargy. But how? He had decided finally that the only hope was to found a magazine, to be called, naturally, *Gallo* (but with a capital – this was not yet twentieth-century, avant-garde Andalusia). The great project failed, Granada being Granada, and Don Alhambro gave up the ghost without achieving his aim:

It was a shame. But in Granada the day is reduced to one immensely long hour – and this hour is used for drinking water, gyrating on the point of one's stick and contemplating the landscape. He simply did not have the time.[4]

Lorca and his companions had done better than Don Alhambro, although they had no illusions about the reception the magazine would receive from their fellow *granadinos*, as philistine in 1928 as they had been in 1830. Federico wrote delightedly to Sebastià Gasch to tell him about the scandal produced by the review's appearance. In two days the copies had been sold out (it is not known how many were printed, but presumably not many), and these were now exchanging hands at double the price. 'In the University there was a great fight yesterday between *gallistas* and *no gallistas*,' the poet exaggerated breathlessly, 'and in cafés, groups of people and homes there is no other topic of conversation.'[5]

Gasch, once a copy of *gallo* was safely in his possession, commented on the uniformity of style characterizing the review. This was true. The influence on Lorca's friends of 'Saint Lucy and Saint Lazarus' was plain to see, as was that of Dalí's *Saint Sebastian* (which the *gallistas* had first read in the summer of 1927 when it appeared in *L'Amic de les Arts*), and the magazine contained an abundance of allusions to the paraphernalia of modern life (Kodaks, the charleston, tennis, American films, motor cars, aerodromes, summer beaches populated by exuberantly erotic cosmopolitan girls of athletic inclination), expressed in a lithe, ironic prose enlivened by metaphors as daring as the writers could make them.

The *gallistas* had set out conscientiously to irritate the Granadine bourgeoisie, and they succeeded admirably. The second issue of the magazine was to contain a chronicle of the hostility and indignation aroused in that sector, contrasting them with the favourable reception in more enlightened circles. It would also comment on Dalí's reaction, which, surprisingly, was adverse. The painter had informed the at first incredulous and then amused company that he found the magazine 'intolerably putrescent' and his own *Saint Sebastian* quite horrible. But Lorca, knowing Dalí as he did, was no doubt prepared for a sally which Gasch, for his part, found inexplicable.[6]

Meanwhile the *gallistas* had prepared a surprise. On 18 March 1928 there appeared in Granada the first issue of another, more modest, literary magazine. Styling itself appropriately *Pavo* ('Turkey'), it claimed to be a 'rearguard' rejoinder to the avant-garde publication that had so recently provoked the irritation of all right-thinking *granadinos*. *Pavo*, of course, was a product of the ingenuity of Lorca and his friends. Here were rules for the composition of a 'putrescent' poem, with a fragment of 'great traditional Spanish poetry', replete with the stock elements of the worst pseudo-Romantic Granadine verse, which, it was hoped, would serve as an example of what could be done in the genre; here was a parody of José Bergamín's aphorisms and another, highly witty, of Dalí's *Saint Sebastian*; here an article in praise of the 'potent architectural revival' taking place, *Pavo* assured its readers, in Granada; here the fervently expressed desire to 'paint, sculpt and speak like our fathers before us', the determination 'never to leave Granada for a single minute' and the promise to await death serenely 'amidst the sound of the fountains and the murmur of the Alhambra woods'.

Not surprisingly, a telegram of support had been received, at the banquet allegedly celebrated by *Turkey* in response to that held by *cockerel*, from Isidoro Capdepón Fernández, the apocryphal poet invented by the *Rinconcillo*. The prank was much appreciated by Lorca's friends in Madrid and Barcelona, and Ernesto Giménez Caballero's *La Gaceta Literaria* stated that, if *gallo* seemed to it of 'exceptional' quality, *Pavo* constituted a 'harsh and definitive joke at the expense of the provincial Philistines, a witty episode indeed in the literary life of Granada'.[7]

Lorca was particularly grateful for the warm response that *gallo* elicited from Gasch and his other friends on *L'Amic de les Arts*. The Sitges group had decided to publish a special issue dedicated to contemporary Andalusian art, and Lorca promised to do everything he could from his end to make the venture a success. 'As you can see,' he wrote to Gasch,

Catalonia and Andalusia are growing closer every day, thanks to us. This is very important although no one realizes it yet. They will later on. Falla hasn't yet returned but he's due any minute now, and he'll be as enthusiastic as we are about the idea. He loves Catalonia and will collaborate faithfully. The issue could well cause an uproar.[8]

At the beginning of April, when the *gallo* and *Pavo* merry-go-round was in full swing, Mildred Adams, a journalist on the *New York Times* then touring Spain, arrived in town, duly armed with letters of introduction to Antonio Gallego Burín and other local notables. During her brief stay she got to know Lorca, four years younger than herself – and was entranced. Sitting at the battered, out-of-tune upright piano in the Washington Irving Hotel, just below the Alhambra, the poet sang for the visitor his ballads on the arrest and death of the Gypsy Antoñito el Camborio. 'In gesture, tone of voice, expression of face and body, Lorca himself was the ballad,' Mildred Adams recalled fifty years later in her book on the poet.[9] Federico introduced Mildred to the other members of his entourage, and one Sunday afternoon took her up the hill to meet Manuel de Falla at his box-scented *carmen* looking out over the Vega. The American observed that, in the house, Lorca was accepted not only as a dear friend and 'disciple' of the famous composer, but as one of the family.[10] Mildred Adams left Granada with copies of *gallo* under her arm – the perfect souvenir of an unforgettable experience – and a year later, when the poet visited New York, was to return his hospitality.

The second issue of *gallo* appeared at the beginning of May. As well as Lorca's 'The Maiden, the Sailor and the Student' and 'Buster Keaton's Stroll', it contained an illustrated article on Picasso by Sebastià Gasch; an excerpt from an avant-garde novel by Francisco García Lorca (never finished), about which Federico enthused to his friends; poems by Manuel

López Banús, Francisco Cirre and Enrique Gómez Arboleya; prose from Francisco Ayala (later a distinguished sociologist, essayist and member of the Royal Spanish Academy); the first translation into Spanish of the Catalan *Manifesto Against Art* issued that March by Gasch, Dalí and Lluís Montanyà; and several notes of lesser interest.

The publication in *gallo* of the Catalan manifesto was a considerable scoop. While Lorca had worked with Dalí in 1927 on a primitive draft of the document, he had played no part in the final elaboration of a text that, directed principally against the Catalan intellectual and artistic establishment, was both original and provocative. The *Manifesto* rejected all imitation of earlier art and insisted on the primacy of the 'new age' of machines – a fast-moving age, free of sentimentalism, symbolized by the aeroplane, the cinema, jazz, the gramophone, transatlantic steamers and the like. At the end of the document the three iconoclasts had appended a list of the artists under whose aegis they now placed themselves: Pablo Picasso, Juan Gris, Amédée Ozenfant, Giorgio de Chirico, Joan Miró, Jacques Lipchitz, Constantin Brancusi, Hans Arp, Le Corbusier, Pierre Reverdy, Tristan Tzara, Paul Eluard, Louis Aragon, Robert Desnos, Jacques Maritain, Maurice Raynal, Christian Zervos, André Breton and, his name figuring between those of Jean Cocteau and Igor Stravinsky, Federico García Lorca. The poet must have felt highly flattered, but he saw to it that in the *gallo* translation of the *Manifesto* his name was silently suppressed.[11]

Emilio Aladrén

Gallo, which, in its own way, had sought to apply the principles expressed in the *Manifesto*, was not destined to appear again. Once he had seen to the publication of the second issue Lorca returned to Madrid, after an absence of four months. There he soon forgot about the magazine, receiving towards the end of May a frantic SOS from his brother (technically the editor): if Federico did not help immediately, Francisco warned, *gallo* was doomed to extinction.[12] But the poet had other matters on his mind – his own work, and, particularly, steering *Gypsy Ballads*, which had been accepted by the *Revista de Occidente* in Madrid, through the press – and did not heed the call for help. He had given up many months of his time, willingly, to *gallo*, but more urgent affairs were now demanding his attention. No doubt he felt that, once *Gypsy Ballads* was published that summer, he would be able to devote himself again to the magazine.

Moreover, despite his intense feelings for Dalí, the poet had now got himself deeply involved with a young sculptor called Emilio Aladrén Perojo, who had entered the School of Fine Arts in 1922, the same year as Salvador.

Eight years younger than Lorca, Emilio had been born in Madrid in 1906, the son of a military officer from Saragossa, Angel Aladrén y Guedes, and Carmen Perojo Tomachevsky, a native of Vienna whose mother was a Russian from Saint Petersburg. The lad was splendidly handsome, with jet-black hair, fine features, large, somewhat oblique eyes – he had a slightly Oriental look – and a passionate, Dionysian temperament. Federico had already met him by 1925, but it seems that they became close friends only in 1927.[13]

The painter Maruja Mallo, a student at the School of Fine Arts and close friend of the young writers of the day, was for a time Aladrén's girl friend. She has recalled that he was like 'a Greek ephebe' and that Lorca, completely won over by his beauty, charm and 'Russian temperament' (as the poet termed it), was responsible for the collapse of their relationship, 'stealing' Emilio for himself.[14]

Aladrén, like Dalí, was a born rebel and constantly in trouble at the School of Fine Arts, where the authorities strongly disapproved of his disreputable behaviour and almost complete lack of discipline.[15] Most of Lorca's other friends, including Dalí, had developed a strong dislike for him, both as an artist and as a person, and felt that his influence over the poet was highly detrimental. Lorca, however, was undaunted, and enjoyed showing him off at parties, introducing him as 'one of Spain's most promising young sculptors'. According to José María García Carrillo, Federico's outrageously uninhibited homosexual ally in Granada, Lorca's relationship with Aladrén provoked considerable jealousy among some of his other friends, leading at times to violent scenes. On one occasion García Carrillo lied to Lorca in an attempt to wean him away from the sculptor, convincing him that he had been to bed with Aladrén. Lorca was deeply upset at the revelation. Some months later García Carrillo found himself hoist with his own petard when he, Emilio and Lorca coincided in a Madrid café. 'Since you two already know each other I needn't introduce you,' sneered the poet. 'I don't think we know each other,' said Aladrén. 'Of course we don't, you bastard!' burst out García Carrillo, unable to contain himself any longer; 'I'm glad to say that I've never known such a shit as you!' A punch-up was imminent and Lorca, terrified, did his best to placate his antagonistic admirers, pleading that if they didn't desist they might all end up in gaol.[16] José María García Carrillo knew Lorca very well indeed. They corresponded frequently (only fragments of the letters have come to light), and whenever the poet was in Granada got together to swap stories and accounts of their activities, sexual and otherwise. It is fair to assume, therefore, that García Carrillo's recollections of Aladrén are substantially true. 'The sculptor was Federico's great love,' he once confided. 'He was the reason why Lorca wanted to get away from Spain, to escape . . . He was the cause of everything.'[17]

Among Lorca's intimate friends the only one who has provided any information at all about Federico's relationship with Aladrén is Rafael Martínez Nadal, who first met the poet in 1923.[18] Martínez Nadal has recalled that Lorca took Aladrén everywhere, introduced him to everybody and found in him, for several years, 'a source of joy'.[19] A scene evoked by Nadal, which he places in the summer of 1928, conjures up the festive nature of the relationship that united poet and sculptor. One night Martínez Nadal was returning home at two or three in the morning after having been with a group of sports addicts in the famous café La Granja del Henar, in the Calle de Alcalá. As he made his way along the street he came face to face with Ignacio Sánchez Mejías and his lover Encarnación López Júlvez. The couple decided to accompany Martínez Nadal homewards and, as the three entered the Plaza de la Independencia, with its handsome triumphal arch erected by Charles III at the end of the eighteenth century, along came Aladrén and Lorca, laughing and singing. There were hugs and kisses – and then occurred one of those improvised 'happenings' for which Lorca was famous:

'Have you seen the new circus? Emilio,' shouted Federico, 'take off your mackintosh and roll on the ground!' It had been raining and the plaza had that greasy coating that sudden summer cloudbursts leave. Emilio handed his raincoat to Lorca. He was wearing a good pearl-grey suit. Without hesitation he threw himself down and, imitating the roars of a lion, rolled on the ground. After he had turned over three or four times, Federico shouted: 'On your feet, Emilio!' He helped him to put on his raincoat and the two of them, effecting a comical circus salute, went off together arm in arm, delighted, killing themselves laughing, with the gin bottle sticking out of the pocket of Emilio's mackintosh.[20]

Gin, as Martínez Nadal explains at another point in his narrative, was the favourite drink of the extravagant 'part-Tahitian, part-Russian' sculptor, as Lorca liked to call him.[21]

Once Lorca invited the poet Jorge Guillén and his wife Germaine to accompany him to Aladrén's studio. The author of Cántico found the young sculptor serious, stiff, ceremonious – but nothing more. It was Germaine who suddenly sensed that there was a love relationship between him and Federico. 'Women sometimes have more of a nose for these things than men,' Guillén commented drily long afterwards.[22]

In the spring of 1928 Aladrén finished a plaster head of Lorca. The poet was proud of it, and did his best to promote his friend as a rising star in the firmament of contemporary sculpture. In this he failed, for Aladrén's was only a minor talent. The head, unfortunately, seems not to have survived, but photographs show that the work was far from incompetent.

Only three of Aladrén's letters to the poet are known, and none at all of the poet's to him. In this correspondence Aladrén reveals the boisterous, childlike, almost manic side to his temperament. There is a tendency to ramble on and on inconsequentially, and at times one suspects that he is modelling his epistolary style on that of Dalí – perhaps Lorca had showed him some of his letters from the painter and Aladrén felt jealous of Dalí's zany originality and of his hold over the poet. But we shall never know the truth of this: the sculptor died on 4 March 1944, shortly after the Civil War, taking his secrets with him, and his family and friends have not cared to add any details about his relationship with Federico.[23]

The Publication of *Gypsy Ballads*

As the summer of 1928 wore on, Lorca's friends eagerly awaited the publication of *Gypsy Ballads*. The book went on sale at the end of July, and was an immediate, all-out success. Writing in *El Sol*, Ricardo Baeza, who had predicted a year earlier, in his review of *Songs*, that the book would lead to the 'enthronement' of Lorca as the finest poet of his generation, stated that Lorca had succeeded in forging 'the most personal and singular instrument of poetic expression in Spanish since the great innovations of Rubén Darío'.[24] No higher praise could have been lavished on the poet than this. In a few weeks, as sales of the book soared, Federico became famous. Nothing like it had ever been known before in Spain. Poetry actually *selling*? It was unheard of.

Lorca was living at the time in the Residencia de Estudiantes, where the annual summer school for foreign students of Spanish, organized by the Centre for Historical Studies, was then in full swing. These courses had become extremely popular, which was hardly surprising in view of the outstanding qualifications of the lecturers participating, among them the philologist Ramón Menéndez Pidal, the historians Américo Castro and Claudio Sánchez Albornoz, and Lorca's friends the poets Pedro Salinas and Dámaso Alonso. An article appearing in *La Gaceta Literaria* that August sent out a witty message to readers in New York, Baltimore, California and London, informing them, male and female, that the delights of the Residencia were waiting: gardens, water, poplars, cool breezes from the Guadarrama mountains and marvellous talks. The reporter had been astonished by the array of pedagogical and literary talent marshalled under the direction of Pedro Salinas, and noted that, walking in the gardens with Dámaso Alonso,

Rafael Alberti and José Moreno Villa, he had seen García Lorca, 'the official poet of the Residencia'.[25]

At the beginning of August Federico was back in Granada where, as usual, his arrival was announced in *El Defensor*.[26] During the summer and autumn numerous reviews of *Gypsy Ballads* reached him, as did the reactions, almost all ecstatic, of his friends. 'I believe that it will be the book of poetry that obtains the greatest popular success of all the work of the new poets,' wrote Juan Guerrero Ruiz from Murcia on 24 August. 'Your ballads, inspired by the tradition of popular poetry, will themselves swell that tradition,' he continued, 'after having first delighted the most delicate palates in the cultured Spain of today. In one fell swoop this book places you on the level of the greatest poets in our language.'[27] The poet Vicente Aleixandre, with whom Lorca was by now on friendly terms, was no less stinting in hiss approval. 'Thank you so much for the magnificent, vehement feast of poetry to which you have invited me,' he wrote (7 September 1928) from his summer quarters in the mountains outside Madrid. 'Only rarely – how rarely! – can one abandon oneself totally, and with absolute contentment, to the enjoyment of such perfect beauty.'[28] Lorca, however, despite his success, was in the depths of depression, as is clear from the letters he wrote during these months to Jorge Zalamea and Sebastià Gasch.

We know disappointingly little about the poet's relationship with Zalamea, an intelligent young Colombian and aspiring writer of fragile appearance, born in Bogotá in 1905, who had a passion for Goethe and a tendency to get noisy and excited when he took one whisky too many.[29] That the relationship was intense there can be no doubt, however, as the correspondence surviving from this summer shows.

Lorca had written to Zalamea soon after arriving back in Granada, hoping for a quick reply. When this did not appear, he wrote again, worried. The second letter reveals that the poet's fast-growing celebrity was beginning to prey on his mind. 'I need my privacy and need it desperately,' he wrote. 'And if I'm frightened of *stupid fame* it's for this very reason.' Lorca was experiencing the quandary of many writers who achieve sudden renown: having one's books well known is one thing but it is quite another being scrutinized publicly oneself. In the same letter the poet, then hard at work on his *Ode to the Holy Sacrament*, informed Zalamea that Dalí was going to visit him that September, and quoted a few lines from a recent letter he had received from the painter (a letter missing among the poet's papers). 'You are a Christian tempest and you need my paganism,' Dalí had said, going on:

During your last stay in Madrid you indulged in something in which you should never have indulged. I'm going to go and see you and give you a sea-cure. It will be winter and we'll light the fire. The poor animals will be frozen with the cold. You'll remember that you're an inventor of marvellous things and we'll live together and take photographs.[30]

To what excesses was Dalí alluding? It seems likely that the painter, informed by Federico himself or by some other person, had in mind Lorca's relationship with Emilio Aladrén, for whom he had little time. The hypothesis is supported by Zalamea's second letter of the summer. (The first is missing.) In this, after alluding to the depression that had gripped him, and revealing the extent to which Lorca's friendship and poetry had become fundamental to his well-being, Zalamea promised that he would never show the poet's letters to anyone ('I love you and myself too much to play at the game of famous manuscripts'), adding, cryptically, 'I haven't seen E— again', before ending: 'Now I'm going to sleep and dream about Granada and about you. Six hours carved like cubes are allotted to me for this dream. Six hours by six sides in each equals 36 pictures of you.' 'E—', in all probability, was Emilio Aladrén, and the fact that Zalamea avoided writing the latter's name in full suggests that he was perfectly *au fait* with the secret – open secret – of the relationship linking Federico and the sculptor.[31]

As for Dalí's promise to visit Lorca in Granada, once again he would fail, or be unable, to keep his word.

Lorca's reply to Zalamea showed the extent to which he was torn by conflicts this summer:

Dear Jorge,
I have received your letter. I thought you were angry with me. With all my poor little heart (unhappy child of mine!), I give thanks that you are as you were before, the first time. You're unhappy, but you shouldn't be. Make a plan of your heart's desire and live in accordance with it, always following a norm of beauty. This is what I do, dear friend. How difficult it is! But I do it. I'm a bit against everybody, but the living beauty I press with my fingers compensates me for all the unpleasantnesses. With deep emotional conflicts, and feeling myself racked with love, with filth, with nastiness, I hold to and follow my norm of happiness at all costs. I don't want to be defeated. *You* mustn't allow yourself to be defeated. I know exactly what's happening to you.

You're at a difficult age, full of doubts, and have an artistic problem which you don't know how to resolve. Don't worry. The problem will resolve itself. One morning you'll begin to see things more clearly. I know. It saddens me that nasty things are happening to you. But you must learn to defeat them at all costs. Anything is preferable to being consumed, broken, crushed by them. I have just *resolved*, using will-power, one of the most painful states in my life. You can't imagine what it's like to spend entire nights at my window looking out at a nocturnal Granada, *empty* for me and without the slightest consolation of any kind.

And then . . . trying constantly to prevent one's feelings from filtering into one's poetry, because that would be to open one's most intimate self to the scrutiny of those who should *never* see it. This is why, with self-discipline, I am now composing these precise *academies,*∗ opening my heart to the symbol of the Sacrament and my eroticism in the 'Ode to Sesostris', which is half written.

I am speaking to you about these things because you asked me to; for myself I would talk only about that which, external to me, hurts me from a distance . . . [32]

The poet included in his letter an extract from the *Ode to the Holy Sacrament,* commenting that the work, now reaching completion, seemed to him of 'great intensity', and was 'perhaps the finest poem' he had written. It is significant that, in the extract which Lorca included with the letter, from the section 'The Devil, Second Enemy of the Soul', the emphasis is on sexuality without love, on the Devil's resplendent beauty 'without nostalgia or dream' (a phrase reminiscent of Dalí), on his concern for present ecstasy, with no personal allegiances or responsibility. 'It seems to me that this Devil is indeed the Devil,' Lorca commented. 'This part of the poem grows increasingly obscure, increasingly metaphysical, until, finally, there erupts the intensely cruel beauty of the enemy, a searing beauty, the enemy of love.'[33] One wonders if Lorca's Devil does not reflect the cynicism with which, according to several of the poet's friends, Emilio Aladrén exploited his beauty.

In the 'Ode to Sesostris', an ambitious project probably never finished (only some forty lines of the poem are known), and no extract from which was published in the poet's lifetime, it was almost certainly Lorca's intention to explore the subject of homosexual love. Out of the experiment came, after Lorca's sojourn in New York, the great *Ode to Walt Whitman.*[34]

Lorca was making strenuous efforts to promote Emilio Aladrén at this time and was particularly keen that a photograph of the sculptor's head of himself should appear in *ABC* – *not,* as he stressed in a begging letter to Cipriano Rivas Cherif, out of any desire to figure himself, but simply in order to please Emilio and his family. Rivas Cherif showed little disposition to intervene with the important newspaper on Lorca's behalf, replying (28 August 1928) that the only people he knew there were out of town, and that, anyway, the whole idea would look to the editorial staff like an attempt to obtain free publicity for an unknown artist. Try somewhere else, he urged.[35] All that Lorca eventually achieved, that summer, was the publication of the photograph in *El Defensor de Granada,* accompanying a review of *Gypsy Ballads* and above the caption, almost certainly written by Federico himself, or at least with his approval: 'The personality of this young sculptor is beginning to stand out amongst the artists of the previous generation as

---

∗ *Academias,* literally 'academies'. Lorca applied the term to a series of poems of sober, 'academic' construction.

one of the most brilliant promises of the present one.' The exaggeration smacks, certainly, of the Aladrén-sponsoring Lorca of these days, so well remembered by his friends.[36]

Dalí continued to prey on Lorca's mind. At the beginning of September the poet received a long, coherent letter in which the painter voiced his dissatisfaction with *Gypsy Ballads*. These, despite containing 'the most fabulous poetic substance that has ever existed', Dalí found in large measure too traditional, too 'local', too anecdotal, too tied to 'the lyrical norms of the past'. Even Lorca's most arresting metaphors Dalí judged stereotyped and conformist. The painter's main gripe, it soon became clear, was that Lorca had not given himself over fully to the claims of the 'irrational'. 'I am convinced', he wrote, 'that effort in poetry today makes sense only in the escape from the ideas which our intelligence has forged artificially, and in the endowment of these ideas with their precise, real meaning.' This led on to a typically Dalinian disquisition on the nature of Reality, which, so far as he was now concerned, consisted in allowing things to be themselves without interpretative interference from the intellect. Thus, the hands of a clock have a right to their own autonomous existence and are not there simply to tell the time of day. Left alone, Dalí insisted, things behave 'in accordance with their real and *consubstantial* manner of being.'

Salvador then proceeded to address himself to Lorca in a more personal tone. In *Gypsy Ballads*, he said, he had perceived the true Federico – the erotic little 'beastie' he knew so well, with his longings and his terror of death, his 'mysterious spirit made up of silly little *enigmas* and of a close horoscopic correspondence, and your thumb in close correspondence with your prick and with the dampness of the lakes of saliva of certain species of hairy planets that exist'. After this extraordinary and authoritative observation (Dalí clearly knew what he was talking about), he continued:

I love you for what your book reveals you to be, which is quite the opposite of the idea the putrid philistines have put out about you, that is, a bronzed gypsy with black hair, childlike heart, etc. etc. . . . . You, little beastie, with your little fingernails, with your body sometimes half possessed by death, or in which death wells up from your nails to your shoulders in the most sterile of efforts! I have drunk death against your shoulder in those moments when you abandoned your great arms, which had become like two crumpled empty sheaths of the insensitive and useless folds of the tapestries ironed at the Residencia. The day you lose your fear, and shit on the Salinases* of the world, give up Rhyme – in short, art as understood by the swine – you'll produce witty, horrifying, intense, poetic things such as no other poet could. Goodbye, I BELIEVE in your inspiration, in your *sweat*, in your astronomical fatality . . . [37]

---

* A reference to the poet Pedro Salinas.

The letter confirms that by September 1928 Dalí was now practically a full-blown surrealist. 'Surrealism is *one* of the means of Escape,' he added in a postscript.

But it is Escape itself that is the important thing. I'm beginning to have my own modes apart from Surrealism, but the latter is something alive. As you can see, I no longer talk about it as I used to, and am delighted to say that my views have changed considerably since last summer. How about that, eh?[38]

Lorca found himself considerably in agreement with Dalí's coolly expressed observations on *Gypsy Ballads*. The day after receiving them he wrote to Sebastià Gasch and told him about the letter, which he said he considered 'intelligent and arbitrary'. It raised, Lorca admitted, 'an interesting poetic issue'. He then went on to say, agreeing with Dalí, that the critics had failed so far to understand his book and that, anyway, the latter now hardly interested him since the poetry he was currently writing seemed to him considerably more acute, more personal.[39]

The arrival of Dalí's letter coincided with the composition of an avant-garde prose poem first entitled 'Technique of the Embrace (Little Homage to a Society Columnist)' and then, with the same bracketed subtitle, 'Little Embraces', the manuscript of which is dated 4 September 1928.[40] In the middle of the month Lorca sent this piece, definitively titled 'Submerged Swimmer' (again with the same subtitle), to Gasch for publication in *L'Amic de les Arts*, accompanying it with another composition in a similar vein, 'Suicide in Alexandria', written at the same time, and various drawings. In a letter to Gasch the poet explained that the two pieces corresponded to his 'new *spiritualist* manner, pure naked emotion, freed from logical control but, mind you, with a tremendous poetic logic', and added, lest he be misunderstood:

It's not surrealism, however – the sharpest consciousness illumines them. They are the first I have done. Naturally they're in prose because verse is a restriction they couldn't admit. In them you'll note, undoubtedly, the tenderness of my feelings these days.[41]

The two pieces, which continued the line initiated a year earlier in 'Saint Lucy and Saint Lazarus', were published in the 30 September 1928 issue of *L'Amic* after a surrealist text by Dalí (in Catalan) entitled 'Fish Pursued by a Bunch of Grapes'. The fact that Dalí and Lorca's efforts appeared together may not have been fortuitous, given the close relationship between both authors and Gasch. Moreover, a typewritten Spanish translation of 'Fish Pursued by a Bunch of Grapes' sent to Lorca by Dalí and preserved among the poet's papers bears the indication: 'Dedicated to a conversation between Federico García Lorca and Lydia', a reference to Lorca's stay at Cadaqués in 1927 when he engaged in numerous discussions with that unusual personage.[42] Between Dalí's piece and the two by Lorca there are several points of contact which suggest strongly that the poet knew Salvador's text before he composed 'Submerged Swimmer' and 'Suicide in Alexandria': beach settings, characters (Baroness X in Dalí, Countess X in 'Submerged Swimmer'), ironic tone, allusions to whisky and motor cars, the tendency or desire of objects to undergo metamorphosis . . . the coincidences are undeniable.[43]

It seems probable, moreover, that in 'Submerged Swimmer' Lorca had his relationship with Dalí to the forefront of his mind. In the first part the narrator, who states that he now knows what it is like to 'say goodbye for ever', addresses Countess X and describes for her his 'last embrace' with his great love, an embrace so perfect that people discreetly put up their shutters:

Countess, that last embrace had three tempos and evolved admirably.

Since then I have given up the old style of writing* which up to that moment I had cultivated with great success.

It's necessary to smash everything in order that the dogmas be purified and the precepts throb with new vigour.

It's necessary that the elephant have partridge's eyes and the partridge unicorn's hoofs.

I know all these things because of an embrace . . .[44]

Of the Indian-ink drawings sent to Gasch with the two texts, the one published alongside 'Submerged Swimmer' in *L'Amic de les Arts* and illustrating the 'last embrace' is particularly remarkable (see opposite).

Can we take the heads of the two lovers fusing in this final kiss to represent those of Dalí and Lorca? The left-hand one, broader than the other, has thick hair and a certain similarity to the poet's self-portraits known to us. The other head is oval, akin to Dalí's, and seems almost devoid of hair, which could perhaps be an allusion to the painter's military service, when he was obliged to wear his hair cropped. The hypothesis presents itself that, in 'Submerged Swimmer', with its accompanying illustration, Lorca was signalling to the painter his decision to abandon his 'old writing', what Dalí had called the 'norms of the old poetry' in his letter on *Gypsy Ballads*, in order to follow more closely the dictates of the new art, that is to say of surrealism. Since we know that 'Submerged Swimmer' was composed, in its first version, on 4 September 1928 and that Dalí's letter reached Lorca before the eighth of the month, it may well be that it was the letter itself that prompted the composition of this piece in what Lorca called his 'new *spiritualist* vein'. 'Submerged Swimmer' and the poignant drawing accompanying it might signify, therefore, the abandonment by Lorca of the

* *la literatura vieja.*

Andalusian world of *Gypsy Ballads* and, perhaps too, show his awareness that he had lost Dalí, whom he was trying in vain to attract to Granada with the pretext of a projected issue of *gallo* dedicated to his work. 'In your letters persuade Dalí that he must come,' he wrote to Gasch. 'Tell him, and it's true, that he needs a visit to this important South.'[45]

But all these efforts were failing. Dalí, unknown to Lorca, was now drawing increasingly close to Luis Buñuel, who had just visited him in Cadaqués and pressed him to escape to Paris as soon as possible. Buñuel, as might have been expected, disliked *Gypsy Ballads* intensely. In a letter to José Bello (14 September 1928) he said that on a recent visit to Madrid he had renewed his intimate acquaintance with Federico (the exact date of the meeting is not known, but it must have been in June or July), and went on to decry the ballads in terms so similar to those employed by Dalí in his letter to the poet that it is impossible not to deduce that he and Salvador had discussed the book together that summer in Cadaqués:

It's a poetry that has the finesse and *apparent* modernity which any poetry needs nowadays in order to please the Andrenios,* Baezas and homosexual, Cernuda-style poets from Seville. But between this and having anything to do with the genuine, exquisite and great poets of today there is a deep gulf. Opening the book at random I read:

> Saint Michael full of lace
> In the boudoir of his tower
> Shows his beautiful thighs
> Enclosed in lights.

(So bloody what!)

After providing some more 'random quotes' (two from 'Preciosa and the Wind', one from 'The Ballad of the Spanish Civil Guard'), Buñuel continued his diatribe:

There's dramatism for those who love this sort of flamenco dramatism; a flavour of the classical ballad for those who want to continue down the centuries with classical ballads; there are even magnificent and really new images, but few and far between and mixed in with a narrative line I find intolerable and which is the sort of thing that keeps Spanish beds full of menstrual blood. Naturally I prefer him to Alberti, who's reaching the limits of lyrical absurdity.

Buñuel's claim that he had opened *Gypsy Ballads* at random can hardly be taken seriously in view of the fact that the first lines quoted are among the most 'camp' in the book (the effeminate statue of the saint in the Church of Saint Michael the High in Granada, evoked in the poem, was much admired by Lorca), and points once again to the future film director's

---

* Andrenio was the pseudonym of the critic Eduardo Gómez de Baquero.

unease about homosexuality. Buñuel went on to list his preferences among contemporary poets writing in Spanish: in pride of place, the Basque Juan Larrea, living in Paris and undoubtedly one of the most original poetic voices of the moment; then Pedro Garfias, the Chilean Vicente Huidobro (who had made such an impact in Madrid in 1918) and Gerardo Diego. That is to say, the avant-garde poets most closely identified with the importation into Spain, from 1918 onwards, of contemporary European trends, and with whom Buñuel had associated in Madrid in the early twenties. Buñuel's detestation of Andalusia (which, like Dalí, he had never visited) was well known among his friends at the Residencia de Estudiantes, and there can be no doubt that such scorn, accurately reflected in this letter to José Bello, would also have told on Dalí, always so impressionable.[46]

During September, while he waited in vain for Dalí's visit, Lorca devoted himself to the preparation of the third issue of *gallo*. Constantino Ruiz Carnero noted on 21 September in *El Defensor de Granada* that, in the Café Alameda, seat of the *Rinconcillo*, frantic nocturnal energy was being expended by the *gallistas* in the effort to get the new issue of the magazine ready for press.[47] But it was not published, despite the fact that printing seems to have begun at the beginning of October. What had happened? We can only assume that the reason was a lack of sufficient advertising income or perhaps a sudden and unexpected rise in costs. As for the contents of the stillborn last number, we know that they included an article by Sebastià Gasch on the painter Manuel Angeles Ortiz, Lorca's 'Chimaera' (a piece similar to 'Buster Keaton's Stroll' and 'The Maiden, the Sailor and the Student'), and a fragment of Gerardo Diego's long poem 'Fable of X and Z'.[48]

Meanwhile Lorca was going through another patch of depression, and told Jorge Zalamea that he had had a terrible summer. 'I need all the happiness that God has given me', he wrote, 'in order not to collapse under the pressure of the many conflicts which have assailed me of late. But God never abandons me.' He had managed to continue working, feverishly. 'After constructing my *odes*, in which I place such hopes,' he went on,

I am now closing this cycle in order to do something different. Now I am writing a *vein-opening* poetry, a poetry of *escape* from reality, in which all my love of things, my tenderness for things, is reflected feelingly. Love of death and scorn for death. Love. My heart, that's it.

'Be happy!' the poet ended his letter to his Colombian friend. 'We must be happy. It's our *duty* to be happy. I'm telling you, as I go through one of the worst and most unpleasant moments in my life.'[49] '*Vein-opening* poetry', 'a poetry of *escape*': it seems clear that Lorca is referring here to 'Submerged

Swimmer' and 'Suicide in Alexandria', which in a letter to Gasch he had already termed 'poems', explaining that, if they were written in prose, it was simply because they resisted any attempt to encapsulate them in verse.[50]

During October Lorca delivered two lectures to the Athenaeum Club in Granada – 'Imagination, Inspiration and Escape in Poetry' and 'Sketch of the New Painting' – which demonstrated further the profound influence of Dalí on his thinking at this time. In the first he explained that, for the modern poet, imagination (in his view always based on reality) was no longer sufficient. Now it was inspiration that counted, inspiration that discovers the 'pure poetic phenomenon' that, although subject to its own laws, eschews all logical control and satisfaction of the demands of conventional reason. Modern poets, Lorca affirmed, seek to free poetry 'not only from the anecdotal, but from the game of trying to unravel metaphors and from the different planes of reality'. Modern poets, in fact, are in search of a *new reality*, which they approach via dreams and the unconscious. And the terms 'beautiful' and 'ugly', Lorca insisted, were no longer of any relevance in the discussion of art. Although the audience had no way of knowing it, these ideas were exactly the ones that Dalí had been developing in his recent letters to the poet.[51]

The second lecture, delivered in the course of an evening on modern art organized by *gallo*, analysed modern painting in the light of these premises, and saw cubism and then surrealism as the great contemporary liberating forces, freeing art from its representational shackles and, where surrealism was concerned, opening to it the possibility of 'expressing the inexpressible'.[52] The lecture was illustrated with slides, and Lorca showed at least one (unidentified) Dalí and two Mirós, including *Insects' Dialogue* (1925). While admitting the primacy of Pablo Picasso as the great innovator of the century, and expressing deep admiration for the Madrid-born Juan Gris, it was the Catalan Miró who particularly elicited the poet's praise on this occasion, no doubt in part due to the contagious enthusiasm of Dalí, who had been much impressed by *Insects' Dialogue*. 'This nocturnal landscape where the insects speak to each other,' said the poet,

and this other panorama, or whatever it is (and I don't care what it is nor do I need to), are on the verge of having never existed. They come from the realm of the dream, from the centre of the soul, where love is white-hot and breezes waft bearing incredible, distant sounds.[53]

It is clear from both lectures that Lorca had resolved that his art, following Dalí's advice, should now be free to express the depths of the unconscious.

About this time the poet sent to the *Revista de Occidente* the first two parts of his *Ode to the Holy Sacrament* – 'Exposition' and 'The World' – dedicated to Manuel de Falla. He had been working on this major poem since the beginning of the year, charting its difficult progress in his letters to Gasch and Zalamea, and announcing in September that it was almost finished.[54]

Writing to Zalamea, Lorca had commented on the extreme difficulty of the ode's composition, adding 'But my faith will do it.'[55] Faith in himself? Or in Christ? It seems fair to assume the latter. In these months, the poet, racked by emotional disturbances, returned, albeit briefly, to the faith of his childhood, which, moreover, he had never entirely lost, despite his rejection of organized religion. In his references to this crisis, whether to Zalamea or to Gasch, Lorca invariably uses the same vocabulary: he is being *knocked around*, *lashed*, *attacked* by *deep emotional conflicts*, by *passions* which he has to *overcome* or *defeat*. He feels that he will *succumb* in the unequal struggle. In his fight against despair, he has recourse to *will-power*. By engaging himself feverishly in work, he tries to forget. And so on.[56] It was little wonder that, at this time in his life, Lorca felt drawn back, irresistibly, to the Christ so ubiquitous in his early work: the loving, crucified Jesus, friend of sinners, the halt and the lame. And also, in the poet's conception, of the sexually tormented.

This is the Christ evoked in the *Ode to the Holy Sacrament*. The poem proposes that, for the helplessness of a sinful, cruel, dehumanized world, where Nature is subjected to systematic mutilation and people live loveless, isolated lives, only the crucified Christ, present in the consecrated host, offers alleviation. In a striking passage, which looks forward to the desolate cityscape of the New York poems, Lorca shows that his imagination was now reaching out far beyond the hills and rivers of his native Granada, out, too, beyond Madrid, still a tiny and friendly capital city, to the horrors of the modern metropolis:

> La gillette descansaba sobre los tocadores
> con su afán impaciente de cuello seccionado.
> En la casa del muerto, los niños perseguían
> una sierpe de arena por el rincón oscuro.
>
> Escribientes dormidos en el piso catorce.
> Ramera con los senos de cristal arañado.
> Cables y media luna con temblores de insecto.
> Bares sin gente. Gritos. Cabezas por el agua.
>
> Para el asesinato del ruiseñor, venían
> tres mil hombres armados de lucientes cuchillos.

Viejas y sacerdotes lloraban resistiendo
una lluvia de lenguas y hormigas voladoras.* [57]

If Lorca's Devil represents sexual exploitation, without love or allegiance, in 'The Flesh', the final part of the poem (not finished until the autumn of 1929, in New York), the poet develops the theme of the dignification of sexuality consequent upon Christ's sacrifice, a sacrifice that, at the same time, opens up the possibility of the resurrection of the flesh, a miraculous rebirth in which it seems the poet never completely lost his faith.

It is not surprising that, given the complexity and hermeticism of the *Ode to the Holy Sacrament*, there should be so much discussion by critics concerning the degree of theological unorthodoxy or otherwise that may be ascribed to the poem. The fact that Lorca dedicated the first two sections to the highly Catholic Manuel de Falla must mean that the poet, at any rate, had no doubts about the issue. But why did he not wait a little longer (the poem was nearly finished, he believed) and, instead of giving an extract, publish the ode complete? It has been suggested that, by bringing out 'Exposition' and 'The World' in the *Revista de Occidente*, Lorca wanted to gauge the reaction of the intellectual establishment. If readers were shocked, he may have argued to himself, they would be much more so by the second half of the poem, certainly less orthodox than the first. [58]

Lorca did not take the precaution of asking for Falla's permission to dedicate the *Revista de Occidente* extract to him. Such a lack of tact would seem to reveal an unaccustomed insensitivity, for how could the poet have imagined that the composer, whatever he might think about the poem's broad orthodoxy, would react favourably to the image of God in the monstrance 'throbbing like the poor little frog's heart / that the doctors put in a glass jar', or to the tension established between the white purity of the host and 'the world of wheels and phalluses'? The mere mention of the male member would in normal circumstances have been sufficient to throw the sin-obsessed Falla into a paroxysm of anxiety and moral outrage. To be

---

* The razorblades lay on the dressing tables
waiting impatiently to sever the heads.
In the dead man's house, the children pursued
a serpent of sand around the dark corner.

Clerks asleep on the fourteenth floor.
Prostitute with breasts of scratched glass.
Cables and half-moon with tremors of insect.
Bars without people. Screams. Heads on the water.

To assassinate the nightingale came
three thousand men armed with shining knives.
Old women and priests wept resisting
a shower of tongues and flying ants.

presented with it in the context of a poem on the Holy Sacrament was profoundly shocking. The composer, who stumbled across the extract only by chance, did not hesitate to write to Federico, then in Madrid. He was, he said (9 February 1929) conscious of the honour the poet had done him by his dedication. But . . . deep differences divided them on the subject of the poem and, if *he* had treated this theme he would have done so with his *spirit on its knees*, and with the aspiration that all humanity should be sanctified by virtue of the Sacrament'. Don Manuel, however, had the good sense to recognize that the poem should be judged as a whole, and said that he placed his hopes in 'the finished work'.[59]

It is not known how Lorca reacted to Falla's letter, which, it may be assumed, given the poet's deep respect for the composer, probably elicited an immediate reply – a reply missing among the composer's meticulously classified papers and perhaps destroyed in order that no record of the disagreement should survive. What can be said is that, if this episode in no way damaged Falla's warm appreciation of Lorca, it does seem to have had the effect of reducing the frequency of the poet's visits to the former's *carmen*. No doubt he felt a bit rueful, perhaps even ashamed, about that undiplomatic dedication.[60]

At the beginning of 1928 Lorca had listed, among the many projects then engaging his attention, a lecture on Spanish lullabies. This was finally delivered on 13 December, at the Residencia de Estudiantes. All Federico's musical and poetic talent had been brought to bear on a subject close to his heart, and in his attempt to explain the deep-rooted melancholy of these songs he had cast his mind back to his childhood in the Granadine Vega – not a difficult task, for that childhood palpitated within him, a perpetual fount of vivid memories – and evoked for his audience the peasant women who, time out of mind, had performed the admirable service of transmitting to the children of the affluent, who would not have come by it any other way, the store of Spanish folk poetry and romance. Without these women, he gave his listeners to understand, he would not have been the poet he was.[61]

Lorca made sure that his lecture contained an allusion to Dalí, so much on his mind at this time. Speaking of the presence of the *coco* (the Spanish bogeyman) in the lullabies, the poet recalled an episode that had occurred, he said, when he visited 'one of the last cubist exhibitions' of his friend. On that occasion, he claimed, a little Catalan girl had worked herself into such a frenzy of excitement over some colourful canvases (which seemed to her to represent *cocos*) that it was almost impossible to get her to leave the gallery.[62] But to which 'cubist' exhibition was the poet alluding? Salvador's last one-man exhibition that could in any way have been considered cubist had been held at Barcelona in 1927, and we know that Lorca did not visit it. Nor had he seen Dalí's 1925 exhibition, held like the 1927 one in the Dalmau Gallery. It seems, then, that the whole episode of the little girl was either an invention in order to boast of his friendship with Salvador or else a rehashing of something the painter had told him. Lorca, we know from many witnesses, was a specialist in the white lie, and matters of historical accuracy worried him as little as they did Dalí.

Two days after the lecture Ernesto Giménez Caballero published in *La Gaceta Literaria* the results of a telephone conversation with Lorca, in the course of which he asked the poet who were his 'habitual friends' in Madrid: 'Dalí, Buñuel, Sánchez Ventura, Vicéns, Pepín Bello, Prados and many others,' Lorca was reported as having answered.[63] It was a revealing reply because, by this time, all these friends had moved away from Madrid: Dalí was in Figueras or Cadaqués; Buñuel, Rafael Sánchez Ventura and Juan Vicéns – all Aragonese – had established themselves in Paris; Pepín Bello, also from Aragon, was in Seville; and Emilio Prados in his native Malaga. The 'heroic days' of the group at the Residencia de Estudiantes had been over for some years, in truth, a fact the poet, no doubt, was all too loath to recognize. Giménez Caballero prompted him to recount the most amusing of the many anecdotes relating to his time at the 'Resi', and once again Dalí's name came to the fore. It was the 'Cabin in the Desert', said Lorca:

One day Dalí and I were totally broke. Like so many other days. We made a 'desert' in our room in the Residencia, with a cabin and a marvellous angel (camera tripod, angelic head and wings made from starched collars). We opened the window and asked for help from the passers-by, lost as we were in the desert. We went two days without shaving, without leaving the room. Half Madrid filed through our cabin.[64]

It seems certain that Federico and Dalí shared a room in the Residencia for only a short time (we cannot say when, because the records were lost during the Civil War), so that, by circulating anecdotes such as this, and talking of 'our room' as though this had been a permanent arrangement, Lorca was clearly intent on emphasizing the closeness of his friendship with the painter. As for Dalí, he too recalled this incident in a conversation with the writer Max Aub in 1969.[65]

Lorca told Giménez Caballero that he was preparing for publication several titles: *Odes; Las tres degollaciones* ('The Three Beheadings'); a volume of theatre including 'The Love of Don Perlimplín for Belisa in His Garden' and *Los títeres de Cachiporra* ('The Andalusian Puppets'); a *Book of Drawings* ('from my Barcelona exhibition'); and other unspecified works.[66] That the poet had in mind to bring out a book of odes was confirmed by the note accompanying the extracts from the *Ode to the Holy*

Sacrament that appeared in the December issue of the *Revista de Occidente*: 'from a forthcoming book of odes to be illustrated with photographs'.[67] There can be no doubt either that he had had an offer to publish a book of plays: the volume was announced a few months later by the Compañía Ibero-Americana de Publicaciones as part of a collection entitled 'New Literature', which included Rafael Alberti's *Sobre los ángeles* ('Concerning the Angels').[68] But, with the exception of two short 'Beheadings' published in magazines, none of the titles announced appeared in the poet's lifetime.

Giménez Caballero asked Lorca to define his current aesthetics. In his reply the poet confirmed that, for him, the period of poetic 'asepticism' was now over. 'A return to inspiration,' he said. 'Inspiration, pure instinct, is the only *raison d'être* of the poet. Logical poetry I now find insufferable. We've had enough of Góngora. For the moment, instinct and passion, that's me.'[69] It was what the poet had said in his two lectures in Granada a few months earlier.

Like Lorca, the other poets of his generation, especially Alberti, were also feeling the pull of the irrational as 1928 drew to its close. Liberated from their obsession with formal perfection, these poets were about to produce some of their finest work.

14

Escape

Crisis

On 15 January 1929, Lorca, Dalí and Buñuel appeared together in *La Gaceta Literaria*, which published, on its front page, the poet's piece 'The Beheading of the Innocents', illustrated by a suitably spine-chilling drawing by Dalí – who since at least 1926 shared with Federico a compulsive interest in severed heads and limbs – and, on its second, a poem and prose text by Buñuel, both of surrealist inspiration. Ironically, for no one could have suspected it, this was the last time that the three friends were to be 'seen' together.

Buñuel, although not yet officially a member of André Breton's group, believed that he was now in possession of surrealist truth, and was pontificating on the subject in letters to José Bello, initiating his fellow Aragonese into the mysteries and techniques of automatic writing. With his characteristic vehemence, Buñuel was ready to attack – verbally, at least – anyone who dared to oppose his views. Lorca's surrealist experiments Buñuel adjudged lamentable, the product of intelligence rather than of instinct. 'The Beheading of the Innocents' he held to be as falsely 'artistic' as the *Ode to the Holy Sacrament* – 'a fetid ode,' he wrote to Pepín, 'which will provoke the erection of Falla's weak member as it will that of so many artists'. None the less, Buñuel conceded, Federico was the best of a bad bunch of *traditional* practitioners.[1]

It seems certain that Buñuel, whose relationship with Dalí continued to grow closer, had been redoubling towards the end of 1928 his attacks on Lorca, designed to undermine Dalí's affection and admiration for the poet. In January he spent a fortnight with Dalí in Figueras. There they worked together, with great seriousness, on the script of the film that, after various hesitations about the title – one suggestion was the facetious *Il est dangéreux de se pencher en dedans* – would be called *Un Chien andalou* ('An Andalusian

Dog'). On 1 February *La Gaceta Literaria* provided details of Dalí's and Buñuel's joint project, explaining that the script was 'the result of a series of subconscious states, expressible only in the cinema', and predicting international interest in the experiment.[2] As for the film's definitive title, it appears that, in the Residencia de Estudiantes, Dalí, Buñuel, José Bello and others used often to refer jocularly to their companions from southern Spain, of whom there were many, as 'Andalusian dogs' (*perros andaluces*).[3] Of these dogs Lorca was undoubtedly the leader, and it may well be that, in conceiving and elaborating the character of the protagonist of the film (designated, simply, 'The Personage'), Buñuel and Dalí had Lorca partially in mind. Certainly the poet seems to have been convinced that this was so for, in 1930, Angel del Río told Buñuel in New York that Lorca had said to him during his sojourn at Columbia University: 'Buñuel has made a tiny little shit of a film called *An Andalusian Dog* – and I'm the Dog.'[4]

Buñuel always denied that the film contained any allusion to Lorca, but the disclaimer cannot be taken altogether seriously and it remains quite possible that the heterosexual impotence of 'The Personage', played by Pierre Batcheff, was an allusion to Lorca's homosexuality ('Lorca was impotent', Buñuel insisted in an interview).[5] At all events, whatever the truth of the matter, the poet undoubtedly believed that in the film Salvador and Luis were holding up to public scrutiny the private side of his personality. The idea that his friends could betray him in such a manner must have come as a painful shock.

Meanwhile, in the autumn of 1928, thanks to the patronage of a wealthy businessman, Lorca's friend Cipriano Rivas Cherif had succeeded in launching an experimental company called Caracol ('Snail'), aimed at providing Madrid with a much needed small auditorium for 'intimate theatre', lectures and chamber music. Rivas was by this time probably the Spanish producer best informed about contemporary trends in European theatre, and explicitly acknowledged his debt to Edward Gordon Craig. In a lecture given in April 1929 in Granada he argued that the essence of the theatre was the marionette, recommended a return to the conventions of Greek tragedy, including the chorus, and pointed out that in modern plays there was a marked tendency to blur the boundaries between stage and audience (as in the case of Evreinoff's *The Comedy of Happiness*, which had been performed in Madrid in February 1928).[6] There is no record of Lorca's conversations about theatre with Rivas Cherif, but there seems little doubt that he listened to the older man attentively and that his own practice as a playwright was influenced by him from this time on.

Caracol's home was a basement in the Calle Mayor (number 8), and from the outset Rivas Cherif was able to count on the support of a select group of actors, writers, artists and intellectuals.[7] Among the company's first successes was the production of Cocteau's *Orphée*, in December 1928.[8] This was followed by Rivas Cherif's *A Sleep of Reason* (after Goya's etching *The Sleep of Reason Produces Monsters*), a play on the then extraordinarily daring subject of female homosexuality.[9] Then, during January, Caracol began to rehearse, under Lorca's personal supervision, a 'chamber version' of *The Love of Don Perlimplín for Belisa in His Garden*, whose première was scheduled for 5 February.

But the curtain never went up on *Perlimplín*. Perhaps for technical reasons, the première was delayed until 6 February. But that morning King Alfonso XIII's mother, María Cristina, died. The event paralysed the life of the capital for several days and the theatres, as a mark of respect, were obliged to close. Behind closed doors, however, Rivas Cherif's company continued to rehearse. Somebody sneaked to the police, and the authorities presented themselves in the theatre with an order closing down the production. The company, Rivas Cherif was informed, had failed to observe mourning for the Queen Mother as decreed by the government, and must take the consequences. The real reason for the ban, however, was almost certainly the subject matter of the play and, in particular, the scene in which Perlimplín appears in bed wearing two outlandish cuckold's horns. Matters had not been helped, either, by the fact that Perlimplín was to be played by a retired army officer, Eusebio de Gorbea. According to Lorca's later account, when the head of the police, Martínez Anido, discovered that Gorbea actually *wore horns* in the play, he almost exploded: 'This is a mockery, an outrage to the army!' he roared.[10]

The débâcle had the effect of intensifying Lorca's already vehement dislike of the Primo de Rivera regime. A few months later he and twenty-four other young writers put their names to a rather naïve document in which they expressed their dissatisfaction with the political situation, determination to search for fresh solutions to the country's problems under the guidance of the philosopher José Ortega y Gasset, and conviction that a new and freer Spain lay just around the corner. The manifesto gave rise to a lively discussion in the press, and was a further indication, if that were needed, of the degree to which Primo de Rivera had alienated the country's intellectuals.[11]

On 16 February 1929, shortly after *Don Perlimplín* was prohibited, Lorca delivered, at Madrid's Lyceum Club, his lecture 'Imagination, Inspiration and Escape', given the previous October in Granada.[12] During the same month the *Revista de Occidente* brought out the second edition of *Songs* and the poet met Carlos Morla Lynch, a Chilean diplomat who had just taken up his appointment at the embassy. Carlos and his wife Bebé, manic entertainers, were to be among Federico's closest friends in the capital.[13]

Lorca's parents were aware that their eldest son was passing through a period of depression. One day, probably in February 1929, when we know that the poet's father was in Madrid,[14] the latter called on Federico's friend Rafael Martínez Nadal to ask him 'what was wrong' with his son and whether, in his view, a change of air would do him good. Martínez Nadal did not reveal all he knew about Federico's problems, but said that a trip outside Spain would undoubtedly be beneficial to the poet. Not long afterwards Lorca began to tell people that soon he was going to travel to New York with his old ally and professor Fernando de los Ríos, who was leaving in June to lecture at Columbia University.[15]

What Nadal hid from Lorca's father, then almost seventy, was that the poet's depression derived, in part at least, from his relationship with Emilio Aladrén, who, according to the same source, was beginning to get involved at this time with the girl who was to become his wife. 'Although they might have wished otherwise,' comments Nadal, 'there was taking place the inevitable distancing between sculptor and poet, giving the latter the sensation of having lost a friendship that had brought him great joy.'[16]

Two years later, in November 1931, Emilio Aladrén married an English girl called Eleanor Dove, from Gosforth in Northumberland, who had been sent to Madrid as the representative of the cosmetics firm of Elizabeth Arden. Was this the girl referred to by Martínez Nadal? Possibly. All we know for sure is that Aladrén, with or without Eleanor Dove, was a born womanizer, just the sort of person to cause misery to a sensitive homosexual admirer. And it seems beyond any doubt that at this time he was having exactly such an effect on Lorca.[17]

Another factor contributing to Federico's depression was almost certainly the absence of Dalí. During March the poet had a very special reason for remembering his friend because, in the exhibition of paintings and sculptures by Spaniards resident in Paris held that month in Madrid, two Dalís were on show – and two Dalís with Lorca associations: *Sterile Efforts* (as we have seen, first called *The Birth of Venus* and, later, *Little Ashes*) and *Honey is Sweeter than Blood*. It is difficult to believe that the poet did not visit the exhibition, in which several of his other friends, among them Manuel Angeles Ortiz and Ismael González de la Serna, were represented. And, on contemplating the Dalís, and seeing his own head among the strange objects littering the eerie beach of *Honey is Sweeter than Blood*, he must have recalled vividly his stay in Cadaqués in the summer of 1927 and his happiness during those weeks at Salvador's side.[18]

The fact that Dalí participated in this exhibition at all must also have hurt, for the artist had not yet moved to Paris. It was as though the inclusion of the paintings heralded his immediate departure for the French capital. Lorca knew only too well that Dalí was obsessed with the conquest of Paris, and the fact that the painter did not deign to visit the Madrid exhibition only rubbed salt into the wound. At the beginning of April Dalí went to Paris to help Buñuel shoot *Un Chien andalou*. During his two months there he was introduced by his fellow Catalan Joan Miró to some of the Surrealists, among them Paul Eluard and Robert Desnos (but not yet André Breton), and sent to a Barcelona newspaper a series of rapturous articles under the general heading of 'Documental–Paris–1929' in which he aligned himself explicitly with surrealism. A few months later, in Cadaqués, he began his all-exclusive relationship with Eluard's captivating wife, the Russian-born Gala – a beginning witnessed by Buñuel, who took an immediate and violent dislike to the seductive and highly experienced 'Sybil of the Steppes', as Patrick Waldberg was to term her.[19]

It seems fair, then, to assume that by the spring of 1929 Federico felt that he had been abandoned by both Aladrén and Dalí. As regards the latter, matters were probably not helped when Lorca discovered that the March, 'antiartistic' issue of *L'Amic de les Arts*, put together almost exclusively by the painter, not only did not include the 'excerpt' from a letter by himself that had been announced in *La Gaceta Literaria* but gave a great deal of prominence to Buñuel, hailed by *L'Amic* as 'a director from whom the European cinema can expect much'. Lorca could have been forgiven for concluding that Dalí was rejecting him in favour of the Aragonese, who moreover had the advantage of living in Salvador's longed-for Paris.[20]

That Lorca was in a disturbed state of mind that March there is no doubt, and this probably lay behind an unusual episode that occurred towards the end of the month.

The people of Granada profess intense devotion to the Virgin of the Sorrows, patroness of the city. In this, Lorca, with his Catholic upbringing, was no exception, and in the period leading up to Holy Week 1929 he felt the urge to draw close to the Virgin, perhaps to ask for protection in days of extreme unhappiness. The Guild of Saint Mary of the Alhambra, little active before 1929, had decided to organize this year its first Holy Week procession, explaining in the local press that its aim in so doing was to link even more firmly Granada's two great sources of pride – the Virgin of the Sorrows and the Alhambra. The procession was to leave the Church of Saint Mary of the Alhambra shortly after midnight on Holy Wednesday (27 March) and, after descending through the woods of the Alhambra, to make its way around the town centre. The expectation aroused in Granada by this announcement was enormous, and Lorca must have been aware of it.[21]

Shortly before the procession began a problem arose. A person had arrived in the church imploring permission to march with the members of the Guild.

He had, he said, promised the Virgin to accompany her on this her first outing, and had come to Granada with that sole purpose. It was Federico García Lorca. The request posed problems, given the strict rules of the Guild and the fact that no spare penitent's habit was available. But Lorca was Lorca and finally a solution was found: it was decided that the poet should take the place of one of the standard-bearers, men not in fact members of the Guild although they too wore the penitent's habit and conical, Ku-Klax-Klan style hat. Federico, deeply grateful, was soon dressed in his identity-cloaking garb, and proceeded to kneel before the image of the Virgin – if we can trust the one eye-witness to the event – in an attitude of prayer. According to the same account Lorca walked at the head of the procession, barefoot, carrying one of the Guild's three heavy crosses, 'which he did not rest once upon the ground during the four hours that the event lasted' (an exaggeration, surely?).[22]

The occasion proved a huge success. The Alhambra Wood, lit by hundreds of coloured flares, took on the appearance of a sacred grove, while, high above, the bell of the Vela Tower tolled out over the town. The following day *El Defensor* reported that the procession's progress through the wood had been something 'beyond the wildest imagination'.[23] At the end of the proceedings Lorca had disappeared as silently as he had come. Affixed to the cross there was a note. 'May God reward you', it said, simply.[24] Having fulfilled his vow to the Virgin the poet returned to Madrid. No mention of his visit appeared in the local press, and almost forty years were to pass before his connection with the Guild of Saint Mary of the Alhambra was discovered.

There is a brief postscript. On 20 May 1929, a few months after the procession, Lorca applied formally to be admitted to the Guild. Heated discussions took place among the members, some of them considering that the request was sincere, others that it was another instance of the poet's 'snobbery' – whatever they may have meant by that. Finally he was accepted, although there seems to be no record of any future participation by him in the Guild's activities.[25]

Cinema

When his visits to Madrid coincided with sessions of the Cine Club (founded by the indefatigable Ernesto Giménez Caballero in October 1928), Lorca used to make a point of attending; and by 1929 he was perfectly familiar with contemporary trends in the cinema. The Cine Club had no premises of its own, and sessions took place in different cinemas hired for the occasion. Buñuel was the Club's man in Paris, responsible both for obtaining suitable films and for supplying *La Gaceta Literaria* with reviews of the new releases appearing in the French capital. In the inaugural season of the Club (six sessions between December 1928 and May 1929), twenty-seven films were shown, thirteen of them documentaries. Among them were Murnau's *Tartuffe* (with Emil Jannings in the lead role), Flaherty's *Moana*, Man Ray's and Robert Desnos's *L'Étoile de mer*, Marcel l'Herbier's *Feu Mathias Pascal* and René Clair's stunning *Entr'acte*.[26]

The latter, which Buñuel had shown at the Residencia de Estudiantes in 1927, was screened on 17 February 1929 and provoked wild enthusiasm among the Club's members.[27] There is no proof that Lorca was present, but it seems highly likely in view of the fame of the film. Shot in 1924, with a scenario by the Cuban-born French painter Francis Picabia and contributions from Erik Satie, Man Ray, Marcel Duchamp and other avant-garde Parisian personalities, *Entr'acte* is a vertiginous succession of disturbing and, at times, hilarious sequences achieved by a virtuoso assemblage of gags, metamorphoses, superimpositions and scenes shot in slow motion (the bullet leaving the mouth of a cannon, for instance). But if we can only guess at the poet's attendance that evening, we know for a fact that he was present at the fifth session of the Club, held at the beginning of April 1929 and dedicated to the theme of 'Orient and Occident'. The East was represented, in the first part of the programme, by two Chinese films – the first to be shown in Spain – *The Dying Rose* and *Pu-Chui's Rose*. A string quartet introduced these with a performance of suitably 'Oriental' music. Then, to bridge the gap between East and West, Lorca rose to recite his *Ode to Salvador Dalí* which he followed with the ballad 'Thamar and Amnon'. Why Lorca? Because, *La Gaceta Literaria* explained, he was from Granada. And Granada, as the poet was fond of reminding people, is a synthesis of East and West. The recital was so 'magnificent and fitting', the *Gaceta* reported, that the poet received a prolonged ovation. It was significant that, out of all the possible poems he could have read on this occasion, Lorca chose his major ode to Dalí. It was another indication of the degree to which he felt himself united to the painter and of the pride he felt in their friendship.[28]

The second part of the programme, for which we may assume that Lorca stayed on, was introduced by gramophone records of jazz and English songs. Then two examples of contemporary Western cinema were screened: Eugène Deslaw's *La Marche des machines* ('The dehumanization of Man. The machine. Its arms, its appetites, its muscles, its charm,' wrote the *Gaceta*) and a film called *Crystallizations*, which evoked the poetry of the chemical world, with its myriad geometrical patterns that, under the microscope, are revealed in all their staggering and complex beauty.[29] Only a few months later, in New York, Lorca may well have remembered Deslaw's film. For where, if not in Manhattan, had the machine age advanced with such awesome velocity? Where else had the process of dehumanization, of Man separated from Nature, reached such limits?

Goodbye to Granada

After a quick dash to Bilbao, to deliver, for the third time, his Dalí-inspired lecture 'Inspiration, Imagination and Escape' and give a poetry recital, Lorca returned to Granada to be present on 29 April at the opening night of *Mariana Pineda*, which Margarita Xirgu and her company were to perform as part of their season in the Teatro Cervantes.[30] The première, inevitably, was a resounding success, given the Granadine theme of the play, the excellence of Margarita Xirgu and her supporting cast and, not least, the fact that Lorca, the local boy made good, was now the most famous young poet in Spain. The theatre was packed, and the audience insisted that Federico take a bow at the end of each act.[31]

On 5 May a banquet in honour of the poet and Margarita Xirgu was held in the Alhambra Palace Hotel. There is a magnificent photograph of the occasion (see illustration 16). Around Lorca and Margarita some forty-five friends and admirers are gathered. In the front row, on the right of the actress, sits Federico, with his hands on his knees, wearing a dark suit, white shirt and spotted bow-tie, and looking oddly serious. Falla, on Margarita's left, bald as an egg, is smiling angelically (Lorca's dedication of the *Ode to the Holy Sacrament* no doubt forgiven). Further along the row we find Federico García Rodríguez, the poet's by now venerable father: an imposing, solid figure, with white hair and shaggy moustache. On the edge of his chair rests a large, powerful right hand – the hand of a countryman who has spent most of his life in the fields. Behind Margarita Xirgu and Falla stands Fernando de los Ríos, the very picture of elegant self-confidence, at a time, moreover, when he is being constantly harassed for his progressive views by the Primo de Rivera regime. Among the other faces we recognize that of Lorca's friend Constantino Ruiz Carnero, editor of *El Defensor de Granada*, who pronounced the speech of welcome at the banquet, praising the art of Margarita Xirgu, 'our greatest actress', and that of Lorca, 'the most brilliant of Spain's young poets'. The speaker was applauded when he said:

García Lorca is a poet of universal horizons, but profoundly Granadine, who in a very short time has conquered the highest position in contemporary Spanish poetry. This ought to be proclaimed out loud, without fear that there may be someone ungenerous enough not to recognize it.

Moreover, we want to destroy the stupid, traditional belief that it is always people from outside who discover what is good in Granada. It was we *granadinos* who discovered García Lorca, the renovator of Spanish lyrical poetry, and it was we who told Madrid and the rest of Spain: 'We're sending you a poet born in Granada, and who expresses all the splendour of this prodigious land that is Andalusia.'[32]

In reply, Federico recalled, without bitterness, the long struggle it had taken to get *Mariana Pineda* produced, two years earlier, and expressed his deep admiration for, and gratitude to, Margarita Xirgu. As for the play, although *Mariana Pineda* no longer reflected his thinking on the theatre, he felt that he had 'done his duty by opposing a lively, Christian and resplendently heroic Mariana' to the cold one that stood, dressed like some freethinking foreigner, on her pedestal in the plaza bearing her name, just outside the theatre. Lorca went on to express unease at finding himself well known in the one part of world where he needed, he said, to be left severely in peace. 'It is as if they had wrenched my childhood from me,' he explained, 'and I found myself burdened with a sense of responsibility in the very place where I never want to feel responsible, where I want only to live quietly in my house, resting and preparing new work.' 'If God continues to help me and one day I become really famous,' he added, 'half that fame will belong to Granada, which made and fashioned this creature that is me – a poet from birth and unable to help it.' He ended his speech by alluding, in that vein at once candid and hermetic of which he was a master, to the difficulties that currently beset him:

Now, more than ever, I need the silence and the spiritual density of Granada to encourage me to keep fighting the duel to the death in which I am engaged with my heart and with poetry.

With my heart, to free it from the impossible passion which destroys and from the treacherous phantom of the world, which fills it with sterile sun;* and with poetry, to construct – despite her efforts to protect herself, like a virgin – the truly alive, wideawake poem, where beauty and horror and the ineffable and the repugnant exist side by side and knock against each other in the midst of the most candescent gaiety.[33]

What was this dangerous passion – so destructive, so *impossible* – that the poet felt obliged to oppose so vigorously? The vocabulary used is not dissimilar to that employed in the previous summer's letters to Jorge Zalamea; and it is difficult to avoid seeing here both a veiled reference to the poet's homosexuality and an allusion to his unhappiness at a time when he believed that he had lost not only Dalí but also Emilio Aladrén. The reference to the new poetry he feels he must write, moreover, also suggests Dalí's aesthetic at this time, recalling not only his letter of the previous

---

* The poet may have said salt (*sal*) not sun (*sol*), the printer's imp seeing to the change of the vowel.

September on *Gypsy Ballads* but the many theoretical musings contained in the rest of his correspondence with the poet.

A fortnight later Lorca returned to the Alhambra Palace Hotel to give a poetry reading (a comprehensive selection from the three books published to date – *Book of Poems, Songs* and *Gypsy Ballads*),[34] and then, on 19 May 1929, the Fuente Vaqueros municipal council held a banquet in honour of its poet, inviting him at the same time to launch officially the council's plans to open a public library.

It was a great occasion, that Sunday, out in the village. Around the table with Federico were his father, his sister Concha and her fiancé, Dr Manuel Fernández-Montesinos, the mayor and local authorities, a numerous selection of the poet's Fuente Vaqueros relatives and, from Granada, Fernando de los Ríos, Constantino Ruiz Carnero, Joaquín Amigo and other friends associated with *gallo* and the *Rinconcillo*. In his speech replying to the words of congratulation pronounced by the mayor, Lorca lavished praise on the village's communal fountain, which, in his view, epitomized the place and its inhabitants, serving as a focus of dialogue, understanding and conviviality.[35]

The poet's departure for New York was drawing near. One of Fernando de los Ríos's nieces, Rita María Troyano de los Ríos, was to spend that summer in England, teaching Spanish to some children in Herefordshire, and, since in those days it would have been unheard of for a young girl to undertake such a long journey alone, the family arranged that her uncle and Federico would see her safely to her hosts before continuing on their way to America. The visit to England would have the advantage, moreover, of enabling the professor and poet to see something of London. Travel agencies and timetables were consulted and a date fixed: Lorca and his mentor would embark at Southampton on 19 June.[36]

On 6 June Federico wrote to Carlos Morla Lynch. He was excited, he told the Chilean diplomat, about his forthcoming trip – but surprised that he had actually decided to leave. He saw clearly that it was vital for him to get away from Spain, and had no doubt that the experience would prove highly beneficial, calculating that he would spend six or seven months in America and then visit Paris for the rest of his year abroad. As for New York, 'I think it's a dreadful place and that's why I'm going,' he stated bluntly, adding that he believed he would have a very good time there. That good time would be guaranteed by Don Federico García Rodríguez's purse ('Papa is going to give me all the money I need and is pleased about my decision') and by Fernando de los Ríos's promise to smooth out whatever initial difficulties might arise. But behind the enthusiasm, somewhat forced, we sense the anxiety. Lorca had never set foot outside Spain. Might he not be chronically homesick? Dreadfully lonely? These are the questions he must have asked himself over and over again.[37]

The following day, 7 June, the poet's friends in Granada gave him a send-off dinner on the eve of his departure for Madrid. It was an emotive occasion. Commenting briefly, *El Defensor* reported that Lorca would be in America for a 'protracted period', after which he would travel to Cuba to give various lectures and recitals.[38] The last snippet of information shows that Federico knew before leaving Spain (although he does not seem to have told Morla Lynch) that he was to visit Cuba, and this may have been an important factor in his initial optimism about the trip across the Atlantic. (One of the members of the *Rinconcillo*, Francisco Campos Aravaca, was Spanish consul in Cienfuegos, moreover, and it may have been he who had suggested the trip to the Caribbean.) If New York depressed him intolerably, Lorca perhaps thought to himself, he could always slip away to Cuba sooner than originally intended. To a Cuba that, since his childhood in Fuente Vaqueros, had always fascinated him.

Lorca arrived in Madrid on 9 June. There he saw Morla Lynch, who recorded in his diary that the poet was leaving Spain 'moved by an impulse that he cannot define and that he says he cannot understand'.[39] Perhaps Morla, whom Lorca had known for only four months, was not yet aware of the poet's homosexuality or of the difficult times he had been going through recently. On 11 June Fernando de los Ríos arrived from Granada, and that day *La Gaceta Literaria* held a farewell banquet for Lorca at which the distinguished professor was also present, alongside Ernesto Giménez Caballero, Melchor Fernández Almagro, Rafael Alberti, Pedro Salinas, Vicente Aleixandre, Adolfo Salazar and other friends of the poet.[40]

Lorca, Fernando de los Ríos and Rita María boarded their train to Paris on the morning of 12 June, and were seen off at the Estación del Norte by a numerous group of well-wishers that included the poets Pedro Salinas and Jorge Guillén and Federico's great friend from the days of the Residencia de Estudiantes, José ('Pepín') Bello. [41] With them on the train was a young nature-loving American student and poet from Vermont, Philip Cummings, who had first met Lorca at the Residencia de Estudiantes the previous year. This summer he had renewed his acquaintance with the poet and briefly visited Granada, where Federico had introduced him to his parents and taken him to see the sights, including the Gypsy caves of the Sacromonte. Cummings, delighted by the Sierra Nevada, had insisted that, when Federico got to New York, he must spend some time with him in Vermont, where he would be shown what America could do in the way of mountains and lakes.[42] During the journey Cummings and Lorca chatted endlessly. The

New Englander later wrote an account of his friendship with the poet in which he recalled these conversations. Federico, he recorded,

talked for hours to the rhythmic click of the wheels over the rails, of what life was for and that man was always playing hide-and-seek with death. I asked him what the meaning of life really was to him. His reply was simple. 'Felipe, life is laughter amid a rosary of deaths; it is to look beyond the braying man to the love in the heart of the people. It is being the wind and ruffling the waters of the brook. It is coming from nowhere and going to nowhere and being everywhere with many fears around you'.[43]

According to Victor Pritchett, who visited Madrid in the twenties and met Lorca at the Residencia de Estudiantes, at that time it took thirteen hours for the train to reach the frontier at Hendaye.[44]

The travellers talked and dozed fitfully during the night, arriving the following morning in Paris, where Cummings took his leave of the group. There was time for only one day in the French capital. Don Fernando and his charges visited the Louvre, where, according to Rita María, Federico made her agree that they would pass the *Mona Lisa* without looking at it ('She's a bourgeois,' the poet laughed), and met up with the French hispanist Mathilde Pomès, who had known – and been much impressed by – the poet in Madrid. In Paris, however, she found him silent, not at all the ebullient presence she remembered. Federico recovered his gaiety for a moment, then withdrew once more into himself. Mathilde Pomès felt sure that Lorca was not as enthusiastic about leaving Spain as he would have had them believe.[45]

Federico must surely have heard in Paris about the sensational première of *Un Chien andalou* on 6 June, in a double bill at the Studio des Ursulines with Man Ray's *Les Mystères du Château du Dé*. The private viewing had been widely covered in the press. Moreover, Mathilde Pomès was in close contact with the Spanish artistic community in Paris and knew that Buñuel and Dalí were intimate friends of the poet. Although it seems that she was not herself at the première, it is likely that she heard about it from other friends. While Federico could not but have felt extreme curiosity about *Un Chien andalou*, there is no possibility that he saw it during his only day in Paris since the film was not shown again (this time publicly) until the following November.[46] Nor, it seems certain, did he meet up with Buñuel. As for Dalí, he had already returned to Spain.

The crossing from Calais to Dover on the night of 14 June was rough, but Federico, who had never been to sea before, succeeded manfully in not being sick.[47] The visitors spent two nights in London, staying at a cheap hotel in the centre, and Don Fernando insisted that they visit the British Museum and the Zoo. In the latter Federico was put seriously out of countenance by the Reptile House, which he had entered only in order to prove himself.

'When he came out he was ashen,' Rita María has recalled. 'Don't go in! Don't go in! It's a nightmare!' the poet exclaimed before collapsing on to a bench. Don Fernando was astonished at this further evidence of his former pupil's hypersensitivity, although, as an Andalusian himself, he knew that Federico, like every true man of the South, had an absolute horror of snakes.[48]

On 17 June the little band caught the train to Hereford, bound for Lucton School near Ludlow, where Rita María was to stay with the headmaster and his family. Lorca, noticing the omnipresent Bovril advertisements that accompanied them across England, wondered why every railway station in England had the same name, and admired the rolling landscape. At the school he played the piano and they visited the stables. Before leaving, the poet autographed a copy of *Gypsy Ballads* to Rita María in memory of their 'unforgettable trip through England'.[49]

Fernando des los Ríos had decided that, before he and Lorca caught their boat at Southampton, they should pay a lightning visit to Oxford, with the purpose not only of seeing the city but, principally, of greeting Salvador de Madariaga, the famous Professor of Spanish at the University. A telegram was duly despatched warning him of their imminent arrival. Madariaga was out of town when they got there, however, and it fell to his Scottish wife, Constance, to meet Don Fernando and the poet at the station. She invited them, naturally, to a cup of tea, and then escorted them on a tour of the sights. Federico bought some shirts and gaily coloured ties that caught his fancy, and was deeply moved when he suddenly found himself standing in front of a statue of Shelley. Mrs Madariaga then conducted the visitors home to her charming house in Church Street, Headington, where they sat down in the garden – a genuine English garden, complete with lawn and roses – to await the return of their celebrated compatriot, who arrived back later that evening.[50]

A witness to Lorca's brief visit to Oxford was Helen Grant, a student of Spanish and French at Somerville College and later distinguished hispanist. Some months earlier Helen had spent a few weeks in Granada with Fernando de los Ríos's family, and had been introduced to Lorca at Manuel de Falla's *carmen*. Fernando de los Ríos, who had greatly liked the girl, now told Constance Madariaga that he would be delighted if he could see her again. Helen was duly invited around. Later she wrote an account of the evening:

I may be wrong but I have always believed that we ate our dinner in the garden, though I suppose it could be that we had dinner inside and spent the rest of that lovely June evening drinking our coffee and wine in the garden. It was really the first time that I had had a chance to talk to Federico, but either I was overwhelmed by the occasion or most of the conversation was monopolised by Don Salvador, who was a great talker, but I can remember very little that was said. What I do remember is that Federico paid me a compliment (a *piropo* with Andalusian gallantry) and I rather awkwardly replied that I had put on too much weight since I last saw him in Granada. (I had had an attack of jaundice in Madrid and was on a very strict diet in Granada, and had lost a lot of weight, putting it on rapidly when I returned to Oxford.) Federico said he did not think so, women were nicer plump than skinny. He gave me a penetrating look that has always remained in my mind for I was as entranced by his personality as I had been by his poems. While the others were talking, mainly about politics, I think, I watched Federico closely. On the surface he seemed lively, even gay, but what struck me most was the sad look in his eyes, the kind of sadness that one sees in the eyes of an animal, not because they are hurt or suffering from anything in particular but a kind of elemental sorrow for the nature of things.[51]

At one in the morning on 19 June 1929 the Madariagas saw Fernando de los Ríos and Federico off at the station, and ten hours later the SS *Olympic*, of the White Star Lines, drew away from the quayside at Southampton with the two Andalusians safely on board. That same day the Spanish newspapers reported that an intense heatwave was currently hitting New York, where ten deaths had already been registered.[52]

BOOK TWO

From New York to the Fountain of Tears
1929–1936

I

New York

First Steps in the 'Sénégal with Machines'

The crossing from Southampton to New York was made in perfect conditions. The huge liner, sister ship of the *Titanic*, hardly swayed as it cut through the glassy water; the sun shone in a clear sky and the poet, delighted with the boat and in the excellent company of Fernando de los Ríos (whom many passengers mistook for his father), appears to have forgotten all about his fear of drowning.[1] He felt far from happy, however, and in a note to Carlos Morla Lynch said that he was depressed and homesick and missing deeply his visits to his friend's house. 'I don't know why I left, and ask myself a hundred times a day,' he wrote; 'I look at myself in the mirror of the narrow cabin and seem another Federico.'[2]

To his parents Lorca told a different story. In his first letter (29 June 1929) he announced that the voyage had been 'delicious', 'six days in a sanatorium', and that he was now sunburnt the way he liked to be, 'Angolan-Negro-style'. Federico claimed that he was 'bursting with happiness' and that all he needed to make his satisfaction complete was to hear from the family.

On board he had become great friends with a little Hungarian travelling to New York to join his father, who had left Europe before he was born. Federico and the boy had wept when they parted. 'This is the theme of my first poem,' the poet reported home. 'A child I'm never going to meet again, a Hungarian rose entering the belly of New York in search of a life which may be tragic or happy, and for whom I'll be only a vague memory fused with the rhythm of the immense liner and the ocean.' But the poem, so far as we know, was never written.[3]

Could Lorca have heard about John Dos Passos's *Manhattan Transfer*, or even begun to read it, before leaving Spain? The novel had been published some months earlier in Madrid, in an excellent translation, and was praised by the poet's close friend Adolfo Salazar in *El Sol* just a few days after

Federico left for New York.[4] Salazar may well have given him his impressions of the book and, in view of Lorca's forthcoming stay in the metropolis, have urged him to take a copy with him to America. Certainly there is a striking resemblance between Dos Passos's description of Jimmy Herf, who at the beginning of the novel arrives in New York, where he will now meet his father for the first time, and the account Lorca gave to his parents of his encounter with the little Hungarian. At all events, we know that, once in New York, Lorca read the novel, whose view of the city is strikingly close to that which we find in his American poems.[5]

As he crossed the Atlantic Lorca may have recalled the splendid poem 'To Roosevelt' by Rubén Darío, the poet who had most influenced him during his adolescence. There Darío establishes a stark comparison between the two Americas. In the United States, Hercules and Mammon are the gods; in Spanish America, spiritual values have still not been lost and Catholicism mixes not uneasily with Aztec and other reminiscences of the ancient, indigenous creeds. Darío is in no doubt about which America he prefers, although he respects the technological genius and pragmatism of the aggressive North. Lorca's view will be not dissimilar.[6]

Sunbathing on the deck of the *Olympic*, Federico may also have remembered Juan Ramón Jiménez. In 1917 Juan Ramón had published his *Diary of a Recently Married Poet*, where he evoked his trip of a year earlier to the United States to wed Zenobia Camprubí. Jiménez had travelled towards the New World in the sure knowledge that happiness awaited him; Lorca approached the same shores depressed and feeling rejected, and perhaps hoping to find in New York a new love relationship. Maybe the poet pondered on the contrast between the two situations. Moreover, Juan Ramón's view of New York was not unlike Dos Passos's. The aeroplanes, the underground and elevated railways, the taxis, trams, motor cars and human masses that thronged the streets, the incessant din of the fire alarms, the breakneck pace of the metropolis, the mortal struggle between nature and concrete, the incredible panoply of luminous advertisements – all of these the hypersensitive Juan Ramón had captured, impressionistically, in the pages of his 'diary', a diary that Lorca must surely have known.[7]

By 1929 the cinema had made New York's silhouette the most famous symbol of modern city life in the world. Fritz Lang's *Metropolis*, clearly inspired by Manhattan, was admired by millions when it appeared in 1927. The film, called by Buñuel 'the most amazing book of images ever composed', reached Madrid in January 1928, and was shown in Granada that February.[8] It is almost certain that Lorca saw it, and that he was deeply impressed by its vision of the dehumanized, robot-controlled society of the future. Many other films of the day and age were also set in New York – and Lorca was an avid cinema-goer. Jazz, Prohibition, crime organized on a scale inconceivable in Spain, with Al Capone as its supreme artificer, Charlie Chaplin, Buster Keaton, Harold Lloyd, the Black revues, faster and faster motor cars, bigger and bigger aircraft: these were the emblems of America, and America was epitomized by New York. At the very moment that Lorca arrived in the States, the French travel writer and novelist Paul Morand, then at the height of his fame, was finishing his book on New York, soon to become an international bestseller. Lorca later tried to make out that Morand's vision of the city was different from his, but in fact the two coincide closely. The Spanish translation[9] of the book was published in Madrid shortly after the poet's return home and seems to have conditioned in part his retrospective impression of New York.

As for Walt Whitman, Lorca must have known the admiring sonnet dedicated to the bard by Rubén Darío, and had read him, perhaps superficially, in the anthology published in a competent Spanish translation by Armand Vasseur in 1912.[10] Whitman had been one of the poets most lionized in the Madrid of the early 1920s by Guillermo de Torre and the *ultraístas*, and something of this enthusiasm may have rubbed off on Lorca. The fact of Whitman's homosexuality, allied to his passionate championship of personal freedom, cannot have failed to interest the Spaniard, and in the self-affirmative lines of the author of *Leaves of Grass* Lorca may have found encouragement in his attempts, often accompanied by depression, to accept his own 'deviation' from the 'norm' of heterosexual love.

Fernando de los Ríos, without whose friendly concern Lorca would not have crossed the Atlantic, must have told the poet about his experiences in the United States, which he had already visited twice, and what he might expect to find in New York. The famous socialist professor, considered by the Primo de Rivera regime one of its most dangerous enemies, had stayed at Columbia, whose size made Madrid's Central University look like a village school, and knew Harlem and the problems of its Black population. Like all good Andalusians, Don Fernando loved the *cante jondo* of his native South, and as a result was appreciative of the Black music he had heard in Cuba and New York, which seemed to him to have affinities with it. We may assume that he and Lorca discussed these matters and that, before he landed in New York, the Granadine poet was already eager to visit Harlem for himself.[11]

Lorca knew that he would not be alone in New York and that several Spaniards were impatiently awaiting his arrival, among them two men particularly well suited to ease him into his new way of life: Federico de Onís and Angel del Río.

Onís – a descendant of the Onís who sold Florida to the United States –

was born in the countryside near Salamanca in 1885. He had collaborated with Alberto Jiménez Fraud in the early days of the Residencia de Estudiantes in Madrid and, after a period at Puerto Rico University, now held the Chair of Spanish at Columbia. Distinguished philologist, author of numerous scholarly works, expert on Spanish folk music and poetry, founder and editor of various hispanist journals, a gruff man who liked people to stand up to him, Onís was undoubtedly one of the leading lights of the Spanish cultural scene in New York at the time. Lorca had perhaps already met him briefly in Spain, but at all events they were to get to know each other well in America and Federico would be godfather to the Onís's first child.[12]

Angel del Río was a younger man than Onís – he was born in Soria in 1901 – and had first met Lorca in Madrid when the latter moved into the Residencia de Estudiantes in 1919. When the poet arrived in New York del Río had been there for only a short time, having recently transferred from the University of Puerto Rico to Columbia's Spanish Department at the bidding of Onís. Since his Madrid days he had followed Lorca's career closely and in 1935 was to publish the first full-length study of his friend, still valuable today despite its many gaps and silences. Del Río and his wife Amelia, like Onís and his, were to go out of their way during Lorca's first months in New York to mitigate the poet's homesickness and sense of strangeness, introducing him to their friends and generally making him welcome.[13]

Both Onís and Del Río were waiting at the dockside when, on 25 June 1929, the *Olympic* edged to its moorings. With them were the Spanish poet León Felipe – then teaching at Cornell University – various journalists, among them José Camprubí, brother-in-law of Juan Ramón Jiménez and editor of the Spanish-language New York newspaper *La Prensa*, and, to Federico's surprise, the painter Gabriel García Maroto who, in 1921, had published Lorca's first book of poems in Madrid. Maroto had recently arrived from Mexico, and was making good money as a portrait artist and designer on various fashionable magazines. The re-encounter of painter and poet was noisy and effusive.[14]

Onís took it upon himself to solve the accommodation problem, helping Lorca to enroll as a student of English at Columbia and finding him a room on the campus in Furnald Hall. He was adamant that the poet should under no circumstances consider staying at the celebrated International House down the road in Riverside Drive, knowing that in such a cosmopolitan setting Federico would never learn a word of English.[15] Once he had settled into his room – it was number 617 – the poet wrote an enthusiastic letter to his parents, bothering little about the strict accuracy of his account:

The University is prodigious. It's situated on the edge of the Hudson River in the centre of the city, on Manhattan Island, which is the best area, very close to the main avenues. Despite this it's deliciously quiet. My room is on the ninth floor and looks over the huge sports field, with its green grass and statues.

On one side – and you can see it from the windows of the rooms opposite mine – runs the immense Broadway, the avenue which crosses the whole of New York.

It would be ridiculous for me to try and describe the huge size of the skyscrapers and the volume of traffic. Anything I could say would be insignificant by comparison. In three of those buildings the whole of Granada would fit. Tiny little houses they are with only about 30,000 people living in each![16]

The poet claimed that he had already put his name down for an English Language and Literature course, but the records show that this was a statement of intent rather than of historical fact, since the enrolment did not take place until 5 July.[17] Clearly he wanted to create a good impression since, as he hastened to say, he would never be able to express adequately his gratitude to his parents for giving him this opportunity, adding that he would do everything in his power to repay them with a work and a life to make them proud. It requires an effort to realize that when he wrote this letter the poet had just turned thirty-one.[18]

Lorca had discovered, not without surprise, that given the layout and numerical nomenclature of New York's streets he could find his way around quite easily, and went on to tell his parents that he already felt 'acclimatized'. 'New York is incredibly lively and welcoming,' he wrote. 'The people are naïve and charming. I feel good here. Better than in Paris, which I found a bit decayed and old.'[19] The previous night he had visited downtown Broadway with García Maroto, León Felipe and the Puerto Rican writer Angel Flores. The spectacle impressed him deeply, as it had Juan Ramón Jiménez some years earlier, above all the skyscrapers resplendent from top to toe with neon advertisements, the crowds flowing up and down the streets, six deep each way, the cars and the aeroplanes. New York, he was already convinced, was 'the most daring and modern city in the world'.[20]

During the evening one of 'Federico's things' had happened. As they walked along Broadway the poet had suddenly heard someone shouting his name and saw a young man in a red jersey jumping from a ground-floor window and hurrying towards him. It was Campbell Hackforth-Jones, an Englishman he had met some years earlier in Spain and to whom he had dedicated one of the poems in *Songs*. 'I was delighted', Federico went on in the same letter, 'because as you must be aware, the odds against meeting someone in New York are extremely great, as great as against two fishes meeting in the open sea. Maroto was stupefied and said: "Yeah, yeah, we know, these things only happen to you." '[21]

What Lorca did not tell his parents was that, when passing through

London, he had sent a telegram to Campbell, hoping to see him there. But the bird had flown, and the lad's parents forwarded the message to New York. Hackforth-Jones, apprised of the poet's imminent arrival, was therefore on the look-out for his friend. But for all that it had certainly been a rare coincidence.[22] Campbell lived in a rented flat near 70th Street and for several weeks Lorca visited him there, drinking his contraband gin and chatting to him and his sister Phyllis. The poet enthusiastically told his parents that his friend was going to give him English classes, but no such arrangement ensued.[23]

Hackforth-Jones's father was a stockbroker and had sent his son to New York to gain experience in the office of one of his Wall Street associates.[24] Federico could have found no better guide to show him around the Stock Exchange and, like Paul Morand some months earlier, he was staggered by what he saw. He wrote home:

It's the spectacle of the world's money in all its splendour, its mad abandon and its cruelty. There'd be no use in my trying to express in words the immense tumult of voices, cries, people dashing hither and thither, lifts, all engaged in the poignant, Dionysian exaltation of money. Here you see the typist with fabulous legs that we have seen in so many films, the cheery bell-boy winking and chewing gum, and your pale individual with his collar up to the throat timidly holding out his hand and begging for five cents. This is where I have got a clear idea of what a huge mass of people fighting to make money is really like. The truth is that it's an international war with just a thin veneer of courtesy.

We ate breakfast on a thirty-second floor with the head of a bank, a charming person with a cold and feline side quite English. People came in there after being paid. They were all counting dollars. Their hands all had the characteristic tremble that holding money gives them. Through the windows we could see the panorama of New York capped with great trees of smoke. Colin* had five dollars in his purse and I three. Despite this, he said to me: 'We're surrounded by millions and yet the only two decent people here are you and I'.[25]

Angel del Río had not seen Federico for several years. He found him not much changed: the same mixture of strength and weakness, the same self-confidence (perhaps even slightly more than before), the same look in the eye although this was now maybe a little more profound, a little sadder. Not that Federico was not as expansive as ever, but, at least during those first months, such moments were less frequent than they had been in the Madrid days. As for his dress, Federico now had a sporting air in accordance with the approved style of the age: thick-knotted, brilliantly coloured ties, natty Oxford shirts, and yellow, white or black sweaters.[26] Angel del Río's account of Lorca's stay in New York, written some time after the event, makes no allusion to the poet's homosexuality or his personal relationships in Spain

---

* Hackforth-Jones's Christian name was Campbell, but he was known familiarly as Colin.

before arriving in New York. It is therefore, while useful, a very incomplete evocation. Was Del Río aware of the poet's intense friendship with Dalí and Aladrén? We have no means of knowing, although there are numerous indications that Del Río kept back much private information in his account.

In his first letter home Lorca told his parents about his meeting with Philip Cummings on the train to Paris, and that his friend had invited him to spend some time with his family during the summer. Cummings had rented a cabin on the shores of Lake Eden, in Vermont, and the invitation was genuine. Soon after Federico arrived in New York he wrote to Philip and told him that he was in despair and needed to see him.[27] Cummings replied at once, enclosing the rail fare for the trip. But by then the poet had enrolled on his English course, and decided that first he must see this through. In six weeks, he promised Philip, he would make his way north. 'I hope that you will reply to me,' the letter ended, 'and that you won't forget the poet lost in this Babylonic, cruel and violent city, full, on the other hand, of a great modern beauty.'[28]

Lorca approached his English course with an unwonted seriousness and, though he did not sit the examination, held in the middle of August, attended class regularly.[29] It was something of a miracle, and suggests that he had come to see that a knowledge of English, no matter how rudimentary, would be useful to his career. If he worked at the language this would also have the advantage, of course, of keeping his parents happy, and he was keenly aware of that necessity. Other people tried to help him – one of Onís's pupils from Puerto Rico, Sofia Megwinoff, for example[30] – but his concentration soon collapsed. Despite his initially good intentions the command of English acquired by the poet during his nine months in New York was minimal, although, if we can believe Adolfo Salazar (himself a competent linguist), he did eventually pick up a considerable number of words, pronounced appallingly.[31]

At Columbia was based, as well as the flourishing Spanish Department run by Federico de Onís, the organization known in Spanish as the Instituto de las Españas en los Estados Unidos and, in English, the Spanish Institute in the United States. The Spanish-language designation was more apt, making explicit the fact that the organization was concerned with Latin America as well as with Spain. The Instituto aimed, among other things, at providing information about educational opportunities in Spain, Spanish America and the United States; to encourage the exchange of teachers and students between the different countries involved; to arrange lectures by eminent hispanists; to hold literary and musical evenings at which people interested in things Spanish could meet; and, generally, to promote in the United States the culture of the Spanish-speaking (and, to a lesser degree,

Portuguese-speaking) world. All of this made Columbia an extremely important centre of Hispanic studies and cultural activities in America. The 'Casa Hispánica' was frequented by hundreds of students, had a good library and a piano, and soon became one of the centres of Lorca's activities in New York, a friendly place where he could speak Spanish to his heart's content, play and sing folk songs to an admiring audience, browse among the books and relax in an atmosphere akin to that of the Residencia de Estudiantes back in Madrid.[32]

Another of the poet's centres was the Hispano and American Alliance, founded by an American millionaire with the object of promoting cultural relations between the United States and the Spanish-speaking world. Through León Felipe, Gabriel García Maroto and Angel Flores, Lorca soon became an habitué of the Alliance, whose premises were at 1 East 42nd Street, on the corner of Fifth Avenue. *Alhambra*, the journal of the association, was edited by Flores, and that August published English versions of two of Lorca's ballads. These were accompanied by an article by Daniel Solana about the Andalusian poet who had just descended on New York and by five photographs supplied by the poet, four of which, significantly, reflected his rapturous stay in Cadaqués with Dalí in 1927. 'The students at Columbia University, the Black elevator attendants of Furnald Hall, the telephone operator downstairs,' wrote Solana,

all are familiar with the deep bows, the peculiar walk, the pirouettes, the exaggerations and the charm of Federico García Lorca. Because, of course, the poet of the *Romancero gitano* neither writes nor speaks any other language but Andalusian Spanish; and he possesses at present no other instrument of expressing himself to his astonished and eager American friends than the music of his songs, his laughs and his ridiculous speech of a precocious child, spoiled by mad fairies.[33]

Federico de Onís, almost as deeply interested in Spanish folk music and poetry as Lorca, decided to make full use of the poet's aptitudes in that direction, asking him to take charge of the students' choir that was to perform an evening of Spanish songs later in the summer. Lorca agreed. Appointed 'Director of the Mixed Choirs of the Instituto de las Españas in the United States', he took his work seriously and trained up the students to a considerable degree of proficiency. The concert was given on 7 August, and the poet's conducting and accompaniment at the piano were much praised.[34]

Philip Cummings was not Lorca's only North American friend. The poet had been exquisitely attentive to the journalist Mildred Adams when the latter visited Granada in the spring of 1928, as we have seen, while she, for her part, had hugely enjoyed Federico and his companions, who were then busily engaged in launching *gallo*. When she heard that Lorca was in town she could hardly wait to see him again. The meeting took place in early July at the house of some mutual Mexican friends, and during the following weeks the two saw each other several times. On 7 August, after the concert at the Instituto de las Españas, Mildred organized a party for Lorca at her parents' luxurious flat. The poet wrote home:

If I didn't have the friends I do in New York, my separation from you would be extemely painful, but the truth is that I'm being extremely well looked after. Maroto, who always argues with everyone, says: 'Wherever you go you're the spoilt child and the centre of attention. Wherever you are there's no room for anyone else. It simply isn't fair.' And it's true that I have marvellous friends who are making my life really exciting. Last night there was a party at Miss Adams's house (she belongs to one of the best families in NY), a party specially given for me, to introduce me to her friends. A lot of really nice people went. Quite a good pianist played music by Albéniz and Falla and the girls wore Spanish shawls. In the dining room, oh bliss!, there were bottles of sherry and Fundador brandy. In short, a delightful time. Naturally I had to do my song bit, and sang *soleares* accompanying myself on the guitar. It was a great success.[35]

Lorca had no gift for languages but, as this and his other letters home show, he did not need one: his musical abilities opened all doors and were the principal key to his success in New York. His friend the poet Dámaso Alonso, who arrived in the city several months later, witnessed a typical scene at a wild party thrown by some millionaire:

People were scattered throughout the spacious salons in small gesticulating groups, where the drinks were beginning to produce their effect. Suddenly, the excited and dispersed mass moved as of one accord in the direction of the piano. What had happened? Simply that Federico had begun to play and sing Spanish songs. The people there didn't know Spanish or have any notion of Spain. But such was the power of his expressivity that their minds were penetrated by a never-seen light and their hearts gnawed by an unknown, sweet bitterness.[36]

Thanks to Mildred Adams, Lorca soon met a couple who were to increase the pleasantness of his stay in New York: Henry Herschel Brickell and his wife Norma. Brickell, nine years older than the poet, was a literary critic on the *New York Herald* and, since 1928, had been manager of the publishers Henry Holt and Company. A keen student of things Spanish, he knew the language and literature well and had visited Granada, where, too shy or respectful to approach Manuel de Falla directly, he had paced up and down in front of the master's *carmen*, hoping for a glimpse of the great man. In Spain people had told him about Lorca, and he was aware of the fame of *Gypsy Ballads*. All was ready, therefore, for the meeting.[37] On 18 July, the poet's saint's day, Brickell arranged a party for him at his flat, situated in a charming redbrick building on the corner of Park Avenue and 56th Street. All went even better than expected. Federico reported to his parents that there was a full house and that the guests had *loved* his inevitable stint at the piano. Modesty was no more Lorca's line than it was Dalí's.[38]

Brickell was dazzled by Federico's gifts, and was to write immediately after the poet's death that in all his experience he had never met such a magic personality.[39] His wife, a cultured and musical woman, was similarly impressed and, despite knowing no Spanish, was soon getting on swimmingly with the poet. During July and the first half of August Federico visited the Brickells frequently, and his friendship with the couple grew when he returned to Manhattan that autumn after the holidays.

Lorca always vibrated at high speed, and soon adapted himself to the vertiginous pace of New York, living his first weeks there with great intensity, as his letters home (the only ones we have) demonstrate. The variety of races and religions flourishing on all sides fascinated him as much as they had done Paul Morand and, perhaps not surprisingly, he felt himself not only profoundly Spanish but profoundly Catholic as he strolled down the canyons of New York, between the skyscrapers. A visit to a Nonconformist Protestant service convinced him of the utter banality of this alternative version of Christianity. 'I can't imagine', he told his parents, 'how anyone could be a Protestant. It's the most ridiculous and odious thing in the world.' And he went on to describe the proceedings: at the head of the church, right in the middle, there was an organ instead of a high altar; in front of this, in a frock coat, stood the minister, who delivered a sermon; the congregation sang some hymns – and then the worshippers emptied out into the street! 'Everything human, everything consoling, everything beautiful is suppressed,' recounted the horrified poet. Moreover, he had discovered that Catholicism in America was vitiated by its contact with Protestant coldness. From his new vantage point in New York the poet now appreciated as never before what he saw as the warmth, dignity and cordiality of Spanish Catholicism, with its fervent cult of the Virgin.[40]

It may well be that the church visited was Wesleyan. In other letters to his parents the poet blamed 'the odious Methodist Church' for the horrors of Prohibition,[41] and came to the conclusion that for him 'the word Protestant is a synonym for *absolute idiot*'.[42] The vehemence of the poet's reaction against Protestantism, and his corresponding exaltation of Spanish Catholicism, can be put down, perhaps, to his need in this strange city to find something spiritually familiar. Another indication of such a need may be found in the fact that during his first months in America Lorca finished the *Ode to the Holy Sacrament*, begun a few years earlier.

As for the Sephardic Jews of New York, that was another matter, and in the synagogue of Shearith Israel (on the corner of Central Park West and 70th Street), with its impressive music and liturgy, the poet saw faces that reminded him strongly, and pleasantly, of various acquaintances back in Granada, where Semitic traits are not uncommon. The service was moving and dignified, but none the less the poet left the building, he told his parents, with the conviction that the figure of Christ was too 'strong to be denied'.[43]

Lorca had lost no time in starting to penetrate the world of the New York Blacks. Shortly after his arrival he met Nella Larsen, the daughter of a Black father and Danish mother, who had just published her second novel, *Passing*.[44] This likeable woman had taken the Spaniard under her wing and together they had visited Harlem. Federico had written home ecstatically on 14 July:

This writer is an exquisite woman, full of kindness and with the deep, moving melancholy of the Blacks.

She had a party at her house and there were only Negroes. It's the second time I've been with her, because it interests me very much.

At the party I was the only White. She lives on 2nd Avenue, and from her windows you could see the whole of New York lit up. It was night and the sky was criss-crossed with searchlights. The Blacks sang and danced.

What marvellous songs! Only our Andalusian *cante jondo* could be compared to them.

There was a boy who sang religious songs. I sat down at the piano and also sang. And I don't need to tell you how much they enjoyed my songs . . . The Blacks are great people. When I took my leave, they all hugged me and the writer gave me copies of her books, effusively signed, something that the others considered a special favour since she doesn't usually do it for them.

At the party there was a black woman who, without exaggeration, is the most beautiful woman I have ever seen. There just couldn't be greater perfection of features or a more perfect body. She danced by herself a sort of rumba accompanied by the tom-tom (an African drum), and seeing her dance was such a pure, such a tender, sight, that it could only be compared to the moon coming out over the sea or something simple and eternal in Nature. As you can imagine I was thrilled with the party. With the same writer I went to a Black night-club, and I remembered Mother, because it was a place like the ones you see in the cinema and which frighten her so much.[45]

Within a few weeks of arriving in New York, then, Lorca had not only begun to make friends among the Blacks but felt able to ratify Fernando de los Ríos's perception about the affinity between their music and the *cante jondo* of Andalusia. Perhaps remembering De los Ríos's account of his visit to a Harlem church, the poet quickly made a point of attending a service in the Black quarter, accompanied by Sofía Megwinoff,[46] and maybe by then had begun to frequent Small's Paradise – this was Scott Fitzgerald's Jazz Age – one of Harlem's leading clubs, with the Mexican graphics designer Emilio Amero and Gabriel García Maroto.[47] The urge to express poetically the predicament of the American Black, as Lorca understood it, soon made itself felt, and he told his mother and father on 8 August that he had begun to write. 'They are typically North American poems,' he explained, 'and almost all of them have a Black theme.' He added, perhaps to impress his parents, that he hoped to take back to Spain 'at least' two books.[48]

'The King of Harlem' was one of these early compositions, although perhaps not the first, and is dated 5 August 1929. The manuscript of the great poem is a labyrinth of crossings out and emendations, and gives the impression of high-speed composition under the impact of intense inspiration.[49] The poem suggests that Lorca had perceived a connection, not only between Black music and *cante jondo*, but between the predicament of the Blacks, condemned to third-class citizenship in a situation of virtual apartheid – they were not even allowed into the Cotton Club, despite the fact that its best performers were Black – and the Gypsies of Andalusia, harassed by an intolerant society. It seems possible, moreover, that in his invention of the mythical King of Harlem Lorca may have had at the back of his mind the 'King of the Gypsies', Chorrojumo, who as an old man could still be seen around the Alhambra when the poet was a child. If the Gypsies, in Lorca's view, were the victims of a harsh, insensitive society, was this not even more true of the American Blacks trying to survive in a dehumanized, machine-dominated world? Suddenly the poet must have grasped that he had his subject, a subject thematically related to his earlier work but which would allow him greater freedom of movement and a more revolutionary treatment.

'The King of Harlem', written little more than a month after Lorca arrived in New York, constitutes a ferocious attack on the materialistic values of contemporary capitalist society and an impassioned plea on behalf of the Blacks. In its anger and denunciation of oppression it goes further than any of the poet's previous work. Back in Spain Lorca was to say that he believed that being from Granada gave him 'deep fellow feeling for all those who suffer. The Gypsy, the Black, the Jew . . . the converted Moor, that we all carry inside.'[50] This fellow feeling pervades 'The King of Harlem' and gives it its power. And when Lorca foresees the day in which the Blacks will rise up against their oppressors and Nature reassert her claims to the land usurped by the city we feel that he is talking not just about the liberation of the Blacks, but about that of all oppressed minorities, including his own homosexual one:

> ¡Ay, Harlem! ¡Ay, Harlem! ¡Ay, Harlem!
> No hay angustia comparable a tus rojos oprimidos,
> a tu sangre estremecida dentro del eclipse oscuro,

a tu violencia granate sordo-muda en la penumbra,
a tu gran Rey prisionero con un traje de conserje.*⁵¹

In the poem '1910 (Interlude)', dated August 1929, New York, we see how, separated for the first time from Spain, like the Blacks from Africa, Lorca was assailed by memories of his lost childhood paradise in Granada. The date of the title is no accident, corresponding to the time (in fact 1909) when Federico García Rodríguez moved his family from the Vega to the capital to see to the boys' education. There seems to be no doubt that for Lorca, who always tended to knock two years off his age, claiming that he had been born in 1900, the date 1910 stood for the end of his childhood, his severance from life in the countryside and the transition to a new and harsh world of duties and obligations as well as to the trials of adolescence. The poem is undoubtedly of great autobiographical interest, revealing the true nature of Lorca's feelings at this moment, which he was careful not to transmit to his parents:

Aquellos ojos míos de mil novecientos diez
no vieron enterrar a los muertos.
Ni la feria de ceniza del que llora por la madrugada,
ni el corazón que tiembla arrinconado como un caballito de mar.

Aquellos ojos míos de mil novecientos diez
vieron la blanca pared donde orinaban las niñas,
el hocico del toro, la seta venenosa
y una luna incomprensible que iluminaba por los rincones
los pedazos de limón seco bajo el negro duro de las botellas.

Aquellos ojos míos en el cuello de la jaca,
en el seno traspasado de Santa Rosa† dormida,
en el desván de la fantasía con bailarinas y manchas de aceite,
en un jardín donde los gatos se comían a las ranas.

Desván dondo el polvo viejo congrega estatuas y musgos.
Cajas que guardan silencios de cangrejos devorados.
En el sitio donde el sueño tropezaba con su realidad.
Allí mis pequeños ojos.

No preguntarme nada. He visto que las cosas
cuando buscan su pulso encuentran su vacío.

---

*   Oh Harlem! Oh Harlem! Oh Harlem!
      There is no anguish comparable to your oppressed reds,
      to your blood trembling within the dark eclipse,
      to your vermilion violence deaf-mute in the shadows,
      to your great King, prisoner in a janitor's suit.

† Saint Rosa (1568–1617) is patron saint of Lima. It seems likely that Lorca is recalling a print of the saint, in mystical transport, contemplated when he was a child.

Hay un dolor de huecos por el aire sin gente
y en mis ojos criaturas vestidas ¡sin desnudo!*⁵²

The wistful poem contains all the principal elements that we find in the New York cycle: the dehumanization of contemporary industrial society; the terror and loneliness of modern man, cut off from Nature; the absence of imagination. The symbol of the empty suits is reminiscent of Eliot's 'The Hollow Men' – and perhaps not by coincidence. Both Leop´n Felipe and Angel Flores admired Eliot, and Flores brought out in 1930 an excellent Spanish translation of *The Waste Land* which he showed to Lorca, who was deeply moved by the poem.⁵³ Indeed the influence of *The Waste Land* on Lorca's vision of New York seems beyond doubt. 'Nobody can get a clear idea of what a New York throng is like,' he said in 1932, immediately correcting himself: 'Well, Walt Whitman, who searched for solitude in it, knew, and T. S. Eliot also knows, T. S. Eliot who squeezes it like a lemon, to extract from it wounded rats, wet hats and river shadows.'⁵⁴ It may well be that, when he wrote these words, Lorca was remembering not only the lines from *The Waste Land* in which Eliot evokes the crowd flowing over London Bridge (not dissimilar, after all, to that flowing up and down Broadway) but those which conjure up the banks of the Thames after the summer trippers have left:

> The river bears no empty bottles, sandwich papers,
> Silk handkerchiefs, cardboard boxes, cigarette ends

> *   Those eyes of mine in nineteen ten
> did not see the burial of the dead.
> Nor the ash-filled funfair of the man weeping before dawn,
> nor the heart cowering in fear like a seahorse.
>
> Those eyes of mine in nineteen ten
> saw the white wall where the little girls peed,
> the snout of the bull, the poisonous toadstool
> and an incomprehensible moon that lit up in the corners
> the pieces of dried lemon under the hard black of the bottles.
>
> Those eyes of mine saw the neck of the mare,
> the pierced breast of slumbering Saint Rosa,
> fantasy's attic with ballerinas and stains of oil,
> a garden where the cats ate the frogs.
>
> An attic where the dust gathers statues and mosses.
> Boxes which preserve a silence of devoured crabs.
> Where the dream stumbled over its reality.
> That's what my young eyes saw.
>
> Don't ask me anything. I've seen that things
> when they search for their pulse find only their emptiness.
> There's an anguish of holes in the air without people
> and in my eyes, clothed creatures with no bodies!

Or other testimony of summer nights. The nymphs are departed.
And their friends, the loitering heirs of city directors –
Departed, have left no addresses.

It is possible, too, that the central image of Eliot's poem, accurately rendered
by Flores as *tierra baldía* may have made its mark on Lorca, who was already
thinking about the play eventually entitled *Yerma*, a word close in meaning
to 'wasteland'.[55]

'1910 (Interlude)' was written before Lorca left the city to visit Philip
Cummings in Vermont. It gives us a sharp insight, therefore, into the feelings
that dominated the poet during those first weeks in which he was trying to
adapt to a new, stimulating and in some ways terrifying world. It is
interesting, moreover, that in a revised version of the poem Lorca modified
the line referring to 'fantasy's attic'. In the recast line the poet's eyes in 1910
are fixed 'on the rooftops of love, with moans and fresh hands' 'en los
tejados del amor, con gemidos y frescas manos': the ballerinas and oil stains
have disappeared and the new image evokes a tender, loving presence now
only a broken memory among the others belonging to that secure, pristine
geography.[56]

Lake Eden, Bushnellsville and Newburgh

On 16 August 1929 the Columbia term ended, and next day Lorca
boarded a train for Vermont, arriving at Montpelier Junction the following
morning.[57] Philip Cummings and his father were there to meet him in the
family's Model-T Ford, a personable vehicle whose maximum speed of 45
m.p.h. made it ideal for landscape viewing. And what a landscape! After the
heat and noise of New York, Lorca was exultant as the car wound its way
northwards through the foothills of the Green Mountains in the direction
of Eden Mills and the Canadian border. Federico talked non-stop, as might
have been expected in the circumstances, recounting (or inventing) his
experiences in New York, questioning the two about the history of Vermont
and the names of the towns they were passing through – Waterbury, Stowe,
Hyde Park, with their English associations – and expressing his joy at finding
himself in such a lush, forest-clad countryside after his six weeks in the
cement jungle of the metropolis.[58]

The cabin rented by Philip for August stood on the very edge of Lake
Eden, flanked and backed by woods and surrounded by a deep silence
punctuated only by the tapping of woodpeckers, the song of countless small
birds and the rushing of the nearby millrace. The leaves were beginning to
turn – autumn comes early in Vermont – and there was already a nip in the
air. There had been a touch of frost, it rained frequently, and each evening

a mist descended on the lake, from whose depths at night came the forlorn call of the loon which, according to Cummings, affected Lorca deeply 'because he was feeling lonely about many things'.[59] Within a month the first fall of snow was expected and it was hardly surprising, given the poet's frame of mind at the time, that, after the initial pleasure of being in the countryside had subsided, the place soon depressed him.

Lorca took immediately to Philip's mother, Addie Cummings, an elegant and robust Vermonter with white hair and a kindly expression. She had been a teacher for fifteen years, was a Congregationalist by persuasion (Lorca had misled his parents by saying that she was a 'fervent Catholic')[60] and had a profound love of Nature, which she had transmitted to her only son. While neither spoke the other's language, communication seems to have been perfect between her and the poet. Lorca, whose sweet tooth was proverbial, enjoyed watching Addie Cummings as she stood at the oven making doughnuts (which he would then consume greedily) and was grateful for her gentleness at a time when probably he was missing his own mother.[61]

The ten days the poet spent with Philip affected him deeply. The two friends roamed the dense woods that surround the lake, followed the trails leading up the slopes of Mount Belvedere, where they visited the asbestos mine (then the largest in the country), worked on an English translation of *Songs* and talked their heads off.[62] That September, after Lorca had left, Cummings organized, with a view to publication, the diary he had kept fitfully during the month. It is a delicate, moving document, couched in a rather quaint English, and reveals a love of the earth akin to the poet's. One passage reads:

I went walking through the woodland this morning with the Spanish poet who has just come. He found many delightful thoughts in the woods. As we crossed the road to the shore he noticed all the little rolled-up bits of dust and said, 'Each is a little world, with its own shadow.' Then when we [were] going through the thickets of dogwood he said that these were the protestations of the woodland that its virginity be unviolated by we trespassers. One decaying stump was for him the ruin of a citadel of Babylon, another became a castle. It was soft nearly in powder and the poet, great child that he and all poets are, knelt and shaped of the white punk material a castle. He covered it with moss and there it stood – first a mere rotten birch stump, now a historic castle of the plains of La Mancha in faraway Spain. He watched me push over a few rotted trees and he said I was a Cyclops intent on destroying the weak and unfit. In other words what had always been a lovely woodland to me had become for him something symbolic.[63]

On another page we find Cummings noting:

The poet of Spain has been comparing things today, especially as to his environment of Andalusia and our hill-embraced lake. Our hills are lower and greener. They are not the mystic snow-capped elegance, that of the Sierra back of Granada, but they give another sentiment, a feeling of infinite comfort. His vega or plain of olive trees* has here given way to the rolling hayfields and the knolls dotted with apple trees and boulders. The oranges, lemons and limes are here apples and currants. He is delighted, the dreamer of all that is ancient Granada, to find here the *zarzamora* of Andalusia, that is, the blackberry. Then we have the raspberries and blueberries which he is less acquainted with. He sees a bush, a familiar tree and the momentary homesickness which we are all prey to takes him and he looks with saddened eyes far far beyond the thicket.[64]

Philip Cummings knew, although he does not go into details in his diary, that Lorca was suffering. And it is likely that the poet told him part, at least, of the background story to his unhappiness. Years later Cummings revealed that during his stay Lorca had confided to him a sealed packet containing private papers and asked him to keep them safely. In 1961 Cummings opened it and found inside fifty-three handwritten sheets containing what in 1974 he described as

a bitter and harsh denunciation of people who were trying to destroy him, to destroy his poetry and to prevent him from becoming famous. He attacked in a more or less confused way people in whom he had placed his confidence and who didn't deserve it. I have the impression that he felt physically and emotionally betrayed.[65]

The only name the Vermonter claimed to recognize among those whom the poet maintained were attacking him was that of Salvador Dalí. At the end of the manuscript Cummings found that Lorca had scrawled a request: 'Philip, if I don't ask you for these papers back in ten years and if something should happen to me, I beg you for God's sake to destroy them.' Carried away by a feeling of loyalty towards the dead poet, Cummings did his bidding and burnt them the following day, an action which he later came to regret.[66]

It is a tragedy that these papers have disappeared, for clearly they contained vital information about the poet's relationships prior to his departure for New York. But at least we know, thanks to Cummings's comments on the documents, that Lorca felt betrayed when he arrived in the United States, irrespective of whether such feelings were justified; and the mention of Dalí perhaps confirms that he believed that in their film *Un Chien andalou* the painter and Buñuel had set out to satirize him.

Cummings has stated that Lorca wrote numerous letters during his brief stay in Eden Mills,[67] but, of these, only two are known: a note to his sisters written under Philip's guidance on a strip of papyrus-like birch bark,[68] and an urgent message to Angel del Río, whom it had been planned he would

---

* In point of fact there are no olive groves in Granada's lush Vega. They begin in the drier land at its edge. Nor are there oranges, lemons and limes.

visit immediately after his stay with Cummings. In the latter the poet explained that, while the family were charming and doing everything possible to make his visit enjoyable, he could not wait to get away. It was raining constantly; he found the landscape beautiful but infinitely sad, and the woods and lake were plunging him into 'a state of almost unbearable poetic despair'; he was pursued by memories of his childhood; in the lake not a frog sang; he was writing all day and feeling exhausted by nightfall. Moreover, there was no alcohol available in Eden Mills, and the poet desperately yearned for the brandy that he knew awaited him at his Spanish friend's summer retreat.[69]

Meanwhile Lorca was introduced by Cummings to Elizabeth and Dorothea Tyler, two little, old and far from well-off retired schoolmistresses, relatives of the former President of the United States John Tyler, who had come from the west and bought an abandoned hilltop farm nearby which they were busily trying to regenerate – against all the odds. Federico was delighted with them. They gave him tea in exquisite porcelain cups, showed him their photographs, and even appeared to understand his terrible French. In his lecture on New York, first given two years later, the poet would allow himself a certain poetic licence in his evocation of the sisters, maintaining that they had a spinet on which he played 'exclusively' for them. But according to Cummings, no such instrument existed.[70] There was, however, an old upright piano in Eden Mills's one restaurant, the modest hostelry run by the Ruggles family. There one evening Lorca played and sang Spanish songs to the villagers who, when he had finished, crowded around to shake his hand. Both the poet and Philip were radiant.[71]

Lorca wrote at least three poems during his stay with the Cummings: 'Poema doble del lago Eden' ('Double Poem of Lake Eden'), 'Cielo vivo' ('Live Sky') and 'Tierra y luna' ('Earth and Moon'). Of these the first is undoubtedly the most revealing as to the poet's state of mind at this time, and confirms the comments in his letter to Angel del Río. As in '1910 (Interlude)' the mood is of despair while, in the midst of persistent memories of childhood happiness and voices from the past, the poet reflects on his painful recent experience:

> Quiero llorar porque me da la gana
> como lloran los niños del último banco
> porque yo no soy un poeta, ni un hombre, ni una hoja
> pero sí un pulso herido que ronda las cosas del otro lado.
>
> Quiero llorar diciendo mi nombre,
> Federico García Lorca, a la orilla de este lago,

para decir mi verdad de hombre de sangre
matando en mí la burla y la sugestión del vocablo.

Aquí, frente al agua en extremo desnuda
busco mi libertad, mi amor humano,
no el vuelo que tendré, luz o cal viva,
mi presente al acecho sobre la bola del aire alucinado.*72

A few verses later there is further allusion that suggests the extent to which the poet feels that he has been cheated by society. Addressing the 'little man with the crest', presumably a figure from the fairy tales of his childhood, Lorca denies that he is searching for the happiness of his first experience of love. Rather, he wants society to return to him his sense of worth, which he feels it has robbed:

Aquí me quedo solo, hombrecillo de la cresta,
con la voz que es mi hijo. Esperando
no la vuelta al rubor y al primer gusto de la alcoba
pero sí mi moneda de sangre que entre todos me habéis quitado.†73

Why did Lorca call his poem 'double'? In view of the accumulation of references to love it seems fair to deduce that the title hints at the discrepancy between the poet's current anguish, when he feels overwhelmed by conflicts, and the security of his childhood before he became aware of being 'different'. There are several allusions in the poem that relate the poet's suffering to that of Christ and remind us of his early work where such a process of identification is constant. The Granadine poet Luis Rosales has said that in his opinion when Lorca left for New York he was close to suicide, and Rafael Alberti has stated that he was 'lost and shattered': certainly this poem reveals a despair almost suicidal in its intensity.[74]

Such was the poet's inner mood on the shores of Lake Eden, and we may

---

* I want to weep because I feel like it,
as the children weep on the dunces' bench,
because I'm not a poet, nor a man, nor a leaf,
but a wounded pulse that probes the things on the other side.

I want to weep pronouncing my name,
Federico García Lorca, on the shore of this lake;
to affirm my true self as a man of blood
refusing mockery and the insinuation of words.

Here, beside the naked water
I'm searching for my freedom, my human love;
not for the flight I may have, light or searing lime,
but my present moment lying in wait on the sphere of the crazed breeze.

† I'll stay alone here, little man with the crest,
with the voice that is my child. Awaiting
not the return of the blush and the first excitement of the bedroom,
but my coin of blood that between all of you you have stolen from me.

imagine his relief when on 29 August 1929 Philip's father drove him to Burlington and put him on board a train for New York.[75] Nothing is known about the trip back to the city, nor about how the poet managed to get on the right train for Kingston. Angel del Río wrote in 1955:

Knowing his incapacity for coping with all practical matters, I wrote him detailed instructions: he must wire me the time of arrival in Kingston; in case I were not there, he must take a bus to Shandaken. The day we were waiting for him no telegram came and there was no sign of Lorca. We began to be worried lest he might be lost, when at nightfall we saw a taxi chugging along the dirt road of the farm. The driver wore an expression of resigned ferocity, and Federico, half out of the window, on seeing me, began to shout in a mixture of terror and amusement. What had happened, of course, was that Lorca, finding himself alone in Kingston, had decided to take a taxi without being able to give the right directions to the driver. They had been going around mountain roads until a kindly neighbour had given them our address. The fare was $15. As Lorca had spent all his money, I had to pay the driver and placate his fury. Federico's terror was the outcome of his conviction that he was lost, without money enough to take care of the bill. Immediately he gave the incident a fantastic twist and said that the driver, whom he could not understand, had tried to rob and kill him in a dark corner of the woods.[76]

The poet spent twenty days with Angel and Amelia del Río in their rented cabin at Bushnellsville, near Shandaken, days which he described to his parents as 'delicious'.[77] No doubt he was happy to be back, safe and sound, with Spanish friends — and the brandy must have helped too. Lorca wrote in a frenzy, played with Stanton and Mary Hogan, the farm owner's children, and went for walks in the woods with Angel. Several photographs from this summer suggest, however, that despite his surface gaiety Federico's depression had not lifted (see illustration 19), and the poems he wrote at Shandaken confirm this. But there is no hint of the poet's gloom in the account of the stay written later by Del Río.

The poet's friendship with Stanton and Mary Hogan, merging with other memories, gave rise to two poems, 'El niño Stanton' ('The Boy Stanton') and 'Niña ahogada en un pozo' ('Little Girl Drowned in a Well'), which have provoked much critical comment and considerable confusion. Stanton Hogan confirmed in 1975 that, as the first poem states, he did indeed possess a Jew's harp and a dog, and recalled that his family had a blind horse, although not the several ascribed to them by Lorca; and went on to say that, while he never suffered from the cancer attributed to him by Lorca, his father did.[78] Writing to his parents from New York the poet told them, correctly, that Stanton was twelve.[79] But in the poem he makes him ten. The change is significant, for, as we already know, ten was for Lorca the critical age at which he was forced to abandon his childhood paradise. In this poem, in fact, there is such a close identification between the poet and Stanton that we sense that Lorca is talking more about himself than about the farmer's son:

> Cuando me quedo solo
> me quedan todavía tus diez años,
> los tres caballos ciegos,
> tus quince rostros con el rostro de la pedrada
> y las fiebres pequeñas, heladas sobre las hojas del maíz.
> Stanton, hijo mío. Stanton.
> A las doce de la noche el cáncer salía por los pasillos
> y hablaba con los caracoles de los documentos,
> el vivísimo cáncer lleno de nubes y termómetros
> con su casto afán de manzana para que lo piquen los ruiseñores.* [80]

As for the second poem, 'Little Girl Drowned in a Well', with its insistent refrain, 'water with no way out' ('agua que no desemboca'), we have Angel del Río's comments on its composition. 'Near the farm,' he wrote in 1955,

where everything seemed abandoned, there were several great pits that had once been quarries. The place, with its bleeding earth and skeletal rocks, had a desolate grandeur. It was, Federico used to say, like a lunar landscape. The water in the pits could not be seen; but one could hear its murmuring crash at the bottom. [81]

Both Angel del Río and Stanton Hogan were adamant that no little girl was drowned that summer in a well at Bushnellsville, and least of all Stanton's sister Mary. The poem was the product, according to Del Río, of the 'contrast between the spontaneous gaiety of the farmer's children and the sadness of the atmosphere'. [82]

But there is more to it than that. While the first title of the poem was 'Little Girl Drowned in a Well', Lorca later added the subtitle, in brackets, 'Granada and Newburgh'. In Granada such accidents were relatively frequent, especially in the steep-streeted quarter of the Albaicín, where there are many wells, and Lorca had actually witnessed one such mishap (but not in the Albaicín), which was probably that reported in *El Defensor de Granada* on 27 March 1928. A ten-year-old girl had lost her ball in a well and, looking over the edge, had fallen in and was drowned. [83] As for the reference to Newburgh, it seems that, when in retrospect he added the subtitle, Lorca

---

> * When I am alone
> I still remember your ten years,
> the three blind horses,
> your fifteen faces with the face battered by the stones
> and the little fevers, frozen on the leaves of the maize.
> Stanton, my son. Stanton.
> At midnight the cancer came out down the passages
> and spoke to the snails of the documents,
> the passionate cancer full of clouds and thermometers
> with its pure desire to be nibbled, like an apple, by the nightingales.

confused this locality, where he went to stay with Federico de Onís immediately after visiting the Del Ríos, with Bushnellsville. It was a simple slip of the memory. In his 1932 New York lecture Lorca embroiled matters still further, alleging that it was in Eden Mills that he had met Stanton and Mary ('Stanton's father has four blind horses that he bought at the Eden Mills market'), and that, after the drowning, he was so depressed that he had to leave Vermont.[84] Such were the licences that Lorca frequently allowed himself when referring publicly to the events of his personal life.

The poem 'Landscape with Two Tombs and an Assyrian Dog' ('Paisaje con dos tumbas y un perro asirio'), written at Shandaken that summer, was the product of a similar process. 'On the farm was an enormous dog, old and half blind,' recalls Angel del Río, 'which frequently slept in the corridor outside the door of Lorca's room. The terror this produced in him and his obsession with the disease of the farmer – a cancerous sore – appear unconsciously transformed into oneiric images.'[85] Thirteen years earlier Lorca had evoked, in *Impressions and Landscapes*, the eerie howling of dogs under the moon at the Benedictine monastery of Santo Domingo de Silos, in Old Castile.[86] Now it is another dog and another moon, but the horror of death is the same:

> Amigo:
> Levántate para que oigas aullar
> al perro asirio.
> Las tres ninfas del cáncer han estado bailando,
> hijo mío.
> Trajeron unas montañas de lacre rojo
> y unas sábanas duras donde estaba el cáncer dormido.
> El caballo tenía un ojo en el cuello
> y la luna estaba en un cielo tan frío
> que tuvo que desgarrarse su monte de Venus
> y ahogar en sangre y ceniza los cementerios antiguos.*[87]

Angel del Río has told us that Lorca spent most of his time with them that summer writing and that, as well as letting them hear his new poems, he

---

> * Friend,
> wake up and listen!
> The Assyrian dog's howling!
> The three cancer-nymphs have been dancing,
> lad.
> They brought some mounds of red lacquer
> and some rough sheets where the cancer lay sleeping.
> The horse had an eye in its neck
> and the moon was in such a cold sky
> that it had to rip open its maidenhead
> and flood the ancient cemeteries with blood and ash.

1   Fuente Vaqueros today from the air.

2   A spruce two-year-old Federico in straw hat
pays a visit to the village school. He is in the
middle of the front row.

3 Federico aged eighteen.

4   With Manuel de Falla, Francisco García Lorca, Angel Barrios and Adolfo
     Salazar beneath the Alhambra (by courtesy of Doña Maribel Falla).

5   Lorca with Manuel Angeles Ortiz in the Alhambra.

6   The Residencia de Estudiantes.

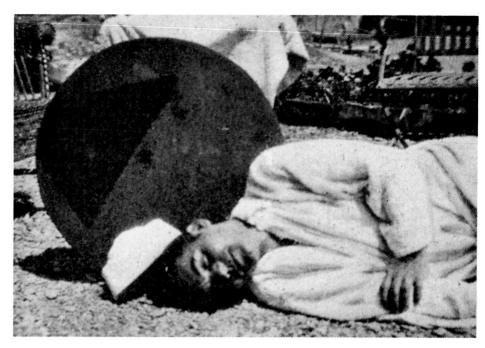

7   Lorca pretending to be dead at Cadaqués, 1927.

8   Dalí's *Invitation to Dream* (1926), featuring Lorca
(location unknown).

9 Lorca's Saint Sebastian postcard to Dalí (by courtesy of
Doña Ana María Dalí).

10 Lorca with Dalí in Cadaqués, 1927 (by courtesy of
Doña Ana María Dalí).

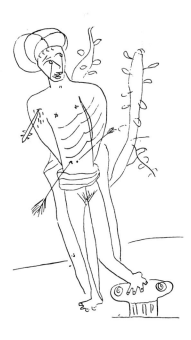

11 Mantegna's *Saint Sebastian* in Vienna.

12 One of Lorca's drawings of Saint Sebastian.

13 Dalí's *Honey is Sweeter than Blood* (location unknown).

14 Close-up of Lorca's head in *Honey is Sweeter than Blood*.

15   The Huerta de San Vicente.

16   The *Mariana Pineda* banquet in Granada,
1929.

17   Lorca with Emilio Aladrén (by courtesy of the Fundación
Federico García Lorca, Madrid).

18   With Philip Cummings at Lake Eden, Vermont, 1929
(by courtesy of Philip Cummings).

19   In sombre mood at Bushnellsville, 1929.

20   With Stanton and Mary Hogan, Bushnellsville, 1929.

21 With some young friends in Cuba, 1930.

22 Self-portrait of the poet in New York.

23 With Mathilde Pomès, Luis Cernuda, José Bergamín, Gerardo
Diego and other friends in Madrid, 1931.

24   Lorca playing The Shadow in Calderón's *Life is a Dream* (by courtesy of Don Gonzalo Menéndez Pidal).

25   The poet arrives in Buenos Aires, 1933.

26   Lorca working his magic in a Buenos Aires theatre.

27   A radio broadcast in Buenos Aires.

28 **With Margarita Xirgu and Cipriano Rivas Cherif.**

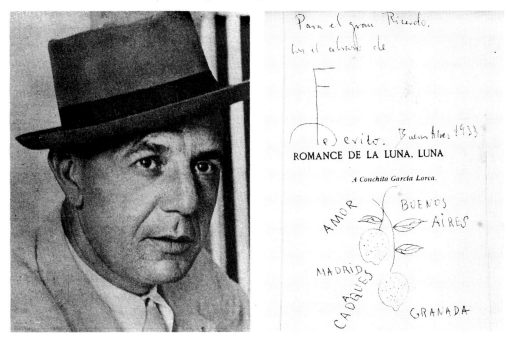

ROMANCE DE LA LUNA, LUNA

29 Ignacio Sánchez Mejías.

30 Ricardo Molinari's inscribed copy of *Gypsy Ballads* in which
the poet identified the places where he had 'loved most deeply'
(by courtesy of Don Ricardo Molinari).

31 With Rafael Rodríguez Rapún in the gardens of the Hotel
Reina Cristina, Algeciras (by courtesy of Don Gonzalo Menéndez
Pidal).

32   A portrait of Lorca in April 1936 by the
       famous photographer Alfonso.

33   Ramón Ruiz Alonso, the ex-deputy who
       arrested Lorca.

34 La Colonia at Víznar, where Lorca spent his last hours. The building was demolished some years ago.

35 Fuente Grande in 1965.

read them fragments of *The Shoemaker's Prodigious Wife*, *Don Perlimplín* (which it seems Federico had revised in New York, perhaps from memory), *The Public* and *Así que pasen cinco años* ('When Five Years Pass').[88] In regard to these last two plays, however, it seems that Angel del Ríos's memory betrayed him, although there is no doubt that by the end of September or beginning of October the poet was already at work on an unspecified play, as a letter to Carlos Morla Lynch shows,[89] nor that the play was avant-garde in character. 'I have begun to write something for the theatre which could be interesting,' Lorca told his parents on 21 October. 'It's necessary to think about the theatre of the future. All the theatre in Spain is dead. Either the theatre changes radically or it's finished for ever. There's no other solution.'[90]

After Lorca had spent almost three weeks with Angel del Río, Federico de Onís arrived by car to bear him away to his country house at Newburgh, fifty miles to the south, where they arrived on 18 September.[91] There Lorca stayed for only three days before returning to Columbia. Onís was working at this time on his monumental anthology of Spanish and Spanish-American poetry, published in 1934, and Lorca told his parents that he had helped his host with the selection of poems by Juan Ramón Jiménez, Salvador Rueda, Jose Asunción Silva and others.[92] Perhaps during this brief visit Federico coincided with León Felipe, who was a frequent guest at Onís's house and also collaborated on the anthology. Lorca appreciated León Felipe's friendliness, and it may well be that the older poet's passion for Whitman fanned Federico's own admiration for the great poet. Felipe had been six years in New York when Lorca arrived, had a good knowledge of contemporary North American literature and was disappointed to find that few Americans had assimilated Whitman's message or even knew his work. Years later he told his biographer Luis Rius that, in Newburgh — although it may not have been on this occasion — he had discussed Whitman with Lorca. Moreover, from his hesitant allusions to the subject of Federico's homosexuality it is clear that Felipe knew considerably more about this aspect of the Granadine poet's stay in New York than he was prepared to divulge, at least in print.[93]

Return to the Metropolis

On 21 September 1929 Lorca moved into room 1,231 at John Jay Hall, in the centre of the Columbia campus, where he would remain until the following January.[94] Eight days later he was formally invited by the Institución Hispano Cubana to visit Havana in early 1930, and as a result his forthcoming escape to the Caribbean must never have been very far from his thoughts during his last six months in the city.[95]

They were months of intense literary activity, and the poems written from October onwards suggest that, whatever the appearances to the contrary, Lorca's depression never lifted entirely. Especially revealing in this respect is 'Infancia y muerte' ('Childhood and Death'), dated 7 October, which the poet sent to Rafael Martínez Nadal at the end of the month with the comment: 'so that you can see my state of mind'. Some years later, when Lorca was revising his New York poetry for publication in book form, Martínez Nadal reminded him of the existence of this poem and showed it to him. On beginning to read it Federico became deeply upset, and, without finishing, threw the paper on the table exclaiming 'Keep it and never show it to me again!'[96] The poem reveals an agonized 'state of mind' quite different from that projected by the poet's letters home:

Infancia y muerte

Para buscar mi infancia, ¡Dios mío!,
comí naranjas podridas, papeles viejos, palomares vacíos
y encontré mi cuerpecito comido por las ratas
en el fondo del aljibe con las cabelleras de los locos.
Mi traje de marinero
no estaba empapado con el aceite de las ballenas
pero tenía la eternidad vulnerable de las fotografías.
Ahogado, sí, bien ahogado, duerme, hijito mío, duerme.
Niño vencido en el colegio y en el vals de la rosa herida
asombrado con el alba oscura del vello sobre los muslos
asombrado con su propio hombre que masticaba tabaco en su costado siniestro.
Oigo un río seco lleno de latas de conserva
donde cantan las alcantarillas y arrojan las camisas llenas de sangre.
Un río de gatos podridos que fingen corolas y anémonas
para engañar a la luna y que se apoye dulcemente en ellos.
Aquí solo con mi ahogado.
Aquí solo con la brisa de musgos fríos y tapaderas de hojalata.
Aquí solo veo que me han cerrado la puerta.
Me han cerrado la puerta y hay un grupo de muertos
que busca por la cocina las cáscaras de melón,
y un solitario, azul, inexplicable muerto
que me busca por las escaleras, que mete las manos en el aljibe
mientras los astros llenan de ceniza las cerraduras de las catedrales
y las gentes se quedan de pronto con todos los trajes pequeños.
Para buscar mi infancia, ¡Dios mío!,
comí limones estrujados, establos, periódicos marchitos,
pero mi infancia era una rata que huía por un jardín oscurísimo,
una rata satisfecha mojada por el agua simple
una rata para el asalto de los grandes almacenes

y que llevaba un anda* de oro entre sus dientes diminutos
en una tienda de pianos asaltada violentamente por la luna.†⁹⁷

The poem is closely linked in theme to 'Double Poem of Lake Eden' and
'1910 (Interlude)', written some months earlier, and it is evident that neither
Lorca's obsession with his lost childhood nor his sexual misery had abated.
The manuscript reveals that, in the lines where he recalled his schooldays,
the poet first wrote 'Federico', then weakly erased his name, leaving it legible,
and continued with the more impersonal 'The boy defeated at school and
in the waltz of the wounded rose'. The young Federico *defeated* at school
and in the waltz, it seems legitimate to infer, of heterosexual love! Perhaps
the pain of his early years in Granada returned as he cast his eye over the
page that day with Martínez Nadal. Maybe he remembered how his

---

* It is not absolutely clear which of several possible meanings Lorca is giving here to the
word *anda*. I have followed that convincingly suggested by the philosopher María
Zambrano.⁹⁸

† Childhood and Death

> To recapture my childhood, dear God!
> I ate rotten oranges, old pieces of paper, empty dovecotes
> and found my little body eaten by the rats
> in the bottom of the well with the lunatics' hair.
> My little sailor's suit
> wasn't soaked in whales' oil
> but it had the vulnerable eternity of old photographs.
> Drowned, yes, drowned good and proper, sleep, my child, sleep.
> Child defeated in school and in the waltz of the wounded rose
> amazed by the dark dawn of the hair on his thighs
> amazed by his own grown-up self chewing tobacco in his left side.
> I can hear a dry river full of tins
> where the sewers sing and they pitch the blood-soaked shirts.
> A river of rotten cats who pretend to be corollas and anemones
> to deceive the moon and persuade it to rest on them softly.
> Here, alone with my drowned self.
> Here, alone with the breeze filled with cold mosses and tinplate lids.
> Here, alone, I see that they've closed the door on me.
> They've closed the door on me and there's a group of dead men
> looking for melon skins in the kitchen,
> and a solitary, blue, inexplicable one
> searching for me on the stairs and putting his hand in the wwell
> while the stars fill the locks of the cathedrals with ash
> and the people suddenly find that all their clothes are too small.
> To recapture my childhood, my God!
> I ate squeezed lemons, stables, faded newspapers,
> but my childhood was a rat that fled down a pitch-dark garden,
> a satisfied rat wet by the simple water
> a rat for the assault of the big stores
> and which carried a golden coffin-ribbon between its diminutive teeth
> in a piano shop assaulted violently by the moon.

companions had jeered at him, calling him 'Federica'.* The sense of shame attendant upon social exclusion pervades the poem, as does that of a bitter self-loathing, and the drowning motif reminds us immediately of 'Little Girl Drowned in a Well'. As for the rat of the last lines, now 'satisfied', it may not be too fanciful to hazard the guess that it represents the poet's attempts to come to terms with the anguished sexuality which, originating in his childhood, is threatening to destroy him.

In John Jay Hall Lorca had become friends by this time with a young American student, John Crow, who lived on the same floor. In 1945 Crow published a book on the poet which, if often naïve, has the virtue of giving us some undoubtedly accurate glimpses into Lorca's everyday life in New York. Crow often accompanied Federico on his excursions into the city, went with him to cinemas and Harlem jazz clubs, noted his tendency to dramatize 'the slightest circumstances of his daily experience' and witnessed the Andalusian's skill on the piano and guitar. He was surprised to find that Lorca never used bad language; and observed that he particularly liked talking about 'violent death, about idiots or any grotesque or abnormal person, about artists, Gypsies and Negroes'. Crow was shocked at first by the poet's tendency to sing his own praises and by his apparently boundless faith in his literary genius, but came to see that this was not mere boasting for boasting's sake: Federico seemed genuinely amazed at his own abilities.[99]

Crow was sometimes taken in by Lorca's exaggerations, however, and believed him when he insisted that the ballad 'The Faithless Wife', with its passionate river-bed copulation, reflected his own lived experience. 'My room-mate and I remarked on the realism and suggested that he seemed to know what he was talking about,' Crow recalled. 'Lorca smiled proudly and came out with a rotund "¡Claro!" Then he spoke of the incident in question in some detail; he was quite puffed up about it, in fact.'[100] The American seems never to have become aware of the poet's homosexuality, and, disagreeing with José Bergamín's comments on Lorca's New York poems, that they reflect the poet's 'mortal anguish' at the time, makes some inconsistent comments which deserve to be quoted:

I came in intimate contact with Lorca day after day while he was working on the *Poeta en Nueva York*, and if he was experiencing any 'mortal anguish', I am a monkey's uncle. At times he must have felt very lonely, but at other times he drank, necked, and caroused like many another young masculine animal, and seemed to have a rather hilarious time doing it. When he settled down to write poetry in the early morning hours of New York after midnight, it was with the strained voice, the high key, the midnight fervours of nostalgia burning deep in the darkness. And the picture was no salutary sight.[101]

* See p. 39.

Lorca necking and carousing in New York 'like many another young masculine animal'! Here, surely, Crow is getting carried away; while, if the spectacle of Lorca's late-night lucubrations was 'no salutary sight', we must assume that it was precisely because of his anguish. Moreover the account of the poet's attentions to the ladies does not tally with Crow's recollection at another moment in his narrative, when we are told that, while Federico admired the beauty of American girls, he thought them too free, and was profoundly shocked to see young couples kissing and petting in public.[102] Given Crow's failure to perceive that Lorca was a troubled homosexual, his observations on the poet's character must be treated with some scepticism.

Did Lorca have any contact with the gay scene in New York? It appears so. One day Angel Flores, the editor of *Alhambra*, who was two years younger than Federico, took him to Brooklyn to meet Hart Crane, then putting the finishing touches to *The Bridge*. A party was in full swing, and they found the American poet surrounded by drunken sailors. Crane was interested in things Spanish but did not speak the language, and after Flores had introduced him to Federico and translated the opening phrases of their salutations, it seems the two poets switched to an insufficient French. Flores realized at once that Crane and Lorca had a lot in common, starting with a shared interest in sailors, and withdrew discreetly. As he left he looked back. Crane was joking in the middle of one group, and Lorca was holding forth in the centre of another.[103]

Lorca, like many homosexuals – the Genet of *Querelle de Brest* comes to mind – was fascinated by the archetype of the sailor, and it is impossible not to relate the seamen who appear so frequently in his American poems and drawings, associated with sex and alcohol, to the scene evoked by Flores. We do not know, however, if Lorca and Crane met again.

As for Lorca's poetic exposition of his homosexuality, several of the American poems previous to the *Ode to Walt Whitman* allude to the matter. In the sonnet 'Adam', for example, dated 1 December 1929, the poet evokes the birth of Eve from Adam's side and the First Man's vision of his future progeny. The last tercet makes an unexpected revelation:

> Pero otro Adán oscuro está soñando
> neutra luna de piedra sin semilla
> donde el niño de luz se irá quemando.*[104]

The use of the adjective *oscuro* in this context looks forward to the group of later sonnets known as the *Sonetos del amor oscuro* ('Sonnets of Dark

---

*   But another, dark Adam is dreaming
  a neuter stone moon without seed
  where the child of light will be burnt.

Love'), over which so much speculation raged until their eventual publication in 1984, and leaves us in no doubt that the 'other Adam' is homosexual: from *his* loins no issue can be expected.

Unlike the rather imperceptive John Crow, Lorca's Spanish friend José Antonio Rubio Sacristán, who arrived at the end of October, was alert to the poet's anguish in New York, an anguish perfectly compatible, moreover, with his surface gaiety. Lorca had spoken to Rubio in 1928 about his problems,[105] and the latter was not only well aware of his homosexuality but knew about his tormented relationship with Emilio Aladrén. A brilliant student, Rubio had just completed his History of Law doctorate in Germany and been appointed a Professor back home in Spain, and had decided that, before taking up his Chair, he would spend a period studying economics at Columbia. He arrived on board the Blue-Riband-winning *Bremen* just in time to see the great Wall Street Crash, and during his time in the city met Lorca often. Probably none of the poet's friends in New York was better fitted than Rubio Sacristán to sense Lorca's true state of mind during these months.[106]

Federico excitedly recounted to his parents what he had seen when the Crash brutally shattered the euphoria of the Wall Street Boom. For more than seven hours, he said, he had joined the crowd outside the Stock Exchange: it had been a hell of shrieking men and women, exhausted officials slumped to the ground, faintings, the sirens of ambulances and, of course, the suicides, one of which Lorca claimed to have seen with his own eyes, just after the man leapt to his death from a hotel window.[107] The poet soon converted what he had witnessed into the stuff not only of several poems but of his habitual exaggerations, and the one suicide became six.[108] Undoubtedly the spectacle greatly affected him and served to intensify the anti-capitalism which had already appeared in his early work. In 'Danza de la muerte' ('Dance of Death'), for example, apparently written shortly after the Crash, in which the poet imagines the arrival of a spine-chilling masked African dancer in Wall Street (seen as a giant columbarium whose funereal niches are the countless windows of the skyscrapers) the denunciation of materialism is made explicit:

> El mascarón bailará entre columnas de sangre y de numeros,
> entre huracanes de oro y gemidos de obreros parados
> que aullarán noche oscura por tu tiempo sin luces,
> ¡oh salvaje Norteamérica! ¡oh impúdica! ¡oh salvaje,
> tendida en la frontera de la nieve!* [109]

* The mask will dance between columns of blood and numbers,
  hurricanes of gold and the moans of the out-of-work
  who will howl in the dark night of your unlighted time,
  oh savage North America! Shameless! Savage,
  stretched along the frontier of snow!

It was the same voice that eleven years earlier, in *Impressions and Landscapes*, had hurled abuse at the municipal authorities of Santiago de Compostela for their failure to provide decently for the children abandoned in the ruined hospice. But now the denunciation is directed not so much against individuals as against the ethos of a whole society, an ethos, moreover, from which a corrupt Catholic Church complacently refuses to disengage itself, as Lorca insists in his great poem 'Grito hacia Roma' ('A Cry in the Direction of Rome'). In New York, as he grappled with the problem of his own self-acceptance, the poet saw human suffering on a scale hitherto unimagined, and began to move closer to a Marxist analysis of the human condition, influenced too, no doubt, by Fernando de los Ríos, who by this time was one of Spain's leading socialist thinkers.

During these months Lorca saw a lot of Herschell and Norma Brickell and at one of their parties met the music critic of the *New York Times*, Olin Downes. A few months earlier Downes had been in Madrid, where he lectured at the Residencia de Estudiantes and was introduced to Federico's close friend Adolfo Salazar.[110] The critic liked to be with writers but not musicians, and had stipulated that, while he would be delighted to meet the poet, he would attend the party only if there were no music. When Lorca began to play and sing Spanish folk songs, however, Downes had to confess himself fascinated, and later that evening Brickell found the two of them in the kitchen discussing musical matters with great seriousness in execrable French.[111]

Lorca joined the Brickells on Christmas Eve after dinner at the house of Federico and Harriet de Onís. There he found, as well as the traditional tree, that the Brickells had built a shrine for an alabaster Virgin from Spain, with a candle for each of their guests to light, one by one, while they made a wish. The poet was deeply touched and, according to Mildred Adams, who had also been invited, reciprocated by reading them *Don Perlimplín*. 'So enthusiastic were we', recalled Mildred, 'that Federico insisted on giving me the script to translate into English. I did, but . . .' No doubt the task proved superior to the young journalist's knowledge of the language.[112] At midnight the Brickells and their party, all Protestants, took Lorca to hear midnight mass at the Catholic church of Saint Paul the Apostle, on the corner of Columbus Avenue and 60th Street. It was an exquisite gesture. Lorca was impressed by the beauty of the service and by the ethnic variety of those taking communion. None the less he could not help remembering the incomparable Christmas Eves back home, in Granada and in Asquerosa.[113]

Despite the kindness with which his Spanish and American friends entertained him during the festive season, the poet probably felt intensely his separation from his family at this time. On 27 February 1930 he wrote a poem, 'Navidad' ('Christmas'), in which he expressed his anguish at the bitter solitude of contemporary man, cut off from God and Nature and condemned to live in a harsh, materialistic society. Once again the theme of the sailor appears – the sailor, here, as symbol of rootlessness and vulnerability:

> He pasado toda la noche en los andamios de los arrabales
> dejándome la sangre por la escayola de los proyectos,
> ayudando a los marineros a recoger las velas desgarradas
> y estoy con las manos vacías en el rumor de la desembocadura.
> No importa que cada minuto
> un niño nuevo agite sus ramitos de venas
> ni que el parto de la víbora desatado bajo las ramas
> calme la sed de sangre de los que miran los desnudos.
> Lo que importa es esto: Hueco. Mundo solo. Desembocadura.* [114]

Given the evidence of poems such as this, written on the eve of Lorca's departure for Cuba, it is difficult indeed to accept the view, so often expressed by scholars, that in America Lorca achieved a new emotional equilibrium. Whatever experience he may have gained in the metropolis, whatever fresh insights he may have obtained into the complexities of his make-up, the pain remained.

Cinema and Theatre

These were the days of the first 'talkies', and Lorca had written home enthusiastically in October to say that he was now an addict of the new cinema. In Spain the first sound picture had been shown in Barcelona on 19 September 1929,[115] but it would be some time before the revolution reached Granada. 'It's astonishing what can be done,' Federico told his parents.

> I'd love to try my hand at sound films and I'm going to look into it. It's in the spoken cinema that I learn most English. Last night I saw a Harold Lloyd film, in sound, and it was delightful. In sound films you hear the sighs, the breeze, all the noises, no matter how small, perfectly reproduced.[116]

The film in question was *Welcome Danger*, Lloyd's first essay in the new

---

*   I have spent the whole night among the scaffolds of the outskirts,
leaving my blood on the plaster of the projects,
helping the sailors to pick up the torn sails,
and I find myself empty-handed amidst the murmurs of the estuary.
It doesn't matter that every minute
a new baby waves the little branches of its veins
nor that the viper's parturition, unleashed under the branches,
calms the blood-lust of those who ogle nude bodies.
What matters is this: Emptiness. Solitary world. Estuary.

medium.[117] With this exception it is not known which sound films Lorca saw during his stay, but we can be sure that he went assiduously to the cinema. Moreover several Spanish-language 'talkies' were screened in New York at this time and it is likely that he saw at least some of these as well.[118]

So far as we know, Lorca did not begin work in New York on a sound-film project. His screenplay *Trip to the Moon* was conceived for the silent cinema, but this does not necessarily mean that it was written before he had seen his first 'talkie'. The scant information we possess about the genesis of the script proceeds from the Mexican artist Emilio Amero, to whom Lorca had been introduced by a young, beautiful and impassioned Mexican woman interested in the arts, María Antonieta Rivas Mercado, lover of the Mexican politician and writer José Vasconcelos and, according to the poet, a 'millionaire'. Amero was a cinema fan, and had just made a short film, *777*, about calculating machines, which he showed Lorca one evening. The poet was impressed, and brought up the subject of *Un Chien andalou*, which he could not yet have seen but about which he was by now well informed. He must have read Eugenio Montes's rave review of the film in the Madrid *La Gaceta Literaria*, for example – the magazine was required reading in New York's hispanist circles – and, given his close relationship with Dalí and Buñuel, it is not impossible that either they or someone else may have sent him a copy of the script of the film which, anyway, had been published in various European journals by the end of the year.[119] The poet, already much attracted by surrealism, cannot fail to have been impressed by the fact that his two friends, whatever hurtful allusions they might have made to him in the film, had forced themselves on the attention of the contemporary world by their daring innovations. And no doubt, when he set out to see what he could do in the same line, he felt the urge to emulate their achievement, just as he had done in his prose pieces inspired by Dalí's *Saint Sebastian*. Amero recalled:

Lorca saw the possibilities of doing a filmscript on the order of my film, with the direct use of motion. He worked at my place one afternoon putting it together. When he would get an idea he'd reach for a piece of paper and jot it down, making annotations on the spur of the moment; that's the way he used to write. The next day he came back and added scenes he'd thought about overnight, finished it up and said, 'Go ahead, see what you can do with this, maybe something will come out of it.' . . . It was something written by a dreamer, a visionary, which is what Lorca essentially was. It had the high quality of all of his writing . . . The film was completely plastic, completely visual, and in it Lorca tried to describe parts of New York life as he saw it. He left most of the scenes for me to visualize, but he did make sketches to show how some of the more difficult ones should be done.[120]

If Lorca's filmscript, as Amero claims, was influenced by his *777*, the direct connection with *Un Chien andalou* seems undeniable. Unlike Méliès's *Voyage à la lune* (1902), Lorca's surrealist script does not concern a trip to the real moon but, rather, a psychical journey towards the moon as symbol of death, in search of a love which proves impossible. From the 'white bed against a grey wall' of the first sequence, where the numbers 13 and 22 emerge from the sheets in pairs until they cover the bed like ants, to the moon and wind-blown trees of the last, the connection with Dalí's and Buñuel's film is evident, although in his use of erotic imagery Lorca has gone further than his former companions, including a close-up of a female genital organ (with the words 'Help! Help! Help!' superimposed) and even what looks like an allusion to fellatio.

Read against the New York poems, *Trip to the Moon* can be interpreted as a narrative of Lorca's own progress in the direction of sexual annihilation. Particularly eloquent in this respect is sequence 36: 'Double exposure of iron bars passing over a drawing, *The Death of Saint Radegunda*'.[121] This is the theme of at least two Lorca drawings from this period. In both of them the face of the dying personage resembles that of the poet himself, and in both the body lies on a table.* In that dated 'New York, 1929', and entitled, as in the filmscript, *The Death of Saint Radegunda*, the body is vomiting, seems to have four wounds in its chest, and bleeds from its genitals.[122] In the second, undated drawing, there is no vomiting but the figure also bleeds from its genitals and is accompanied by a strange, lion-like beast that appears in other of the New York drawings, by a flying angel bearing a lyre – presumably to be explained by the instrument's traditional acceptance as a symbol of poetry – and by another personage who carries a lighted candle. The fact that both figures have bleeding genitals can be only, surely, an allusion to castration – the sense of mutilated sexuality that pervades *Trip to the Moon*.[123]

It should be pointed out that in the filmscript the name Elena is highlighted in a context of violence and horror (sequences 32 and 64). Why Elena? Apart from the obvious allusion to the Greek Helen as Archetypal Woman, we cannot reject the possibility that Lorca now knew about Dalí's relationship with Gala, whose real name was Helena Dimitrievna Diakonava, nor that towards her he felt a bitter resentment and jealousy. Moreover, might there not also be a veiled reference to Eleanor Dove, Emilio Aladrén's English fiancée? True, Eleanor gives Leonora in Spanish, but the English name *sounds* not dissimilar to Elena. The latter reappears, at all events, and with a similar significance, in *The Public*, which Lorca perhaps began in New

---

* St Radegunda – not, as Lorca spells her name, Rodegunda – was a Merovingian princess (520–587), friend of St Gregory of Tours. She died a natural death, and it is not clear why she should have interested the poet.

York although the bulk of the play was written immediately afterwards in Havana.

Soon after his arrival in New York Lorca had started to intimate discreetly, in his letters home, that his monthly allowance was hardly sufficient to enable him to go to the theatre. That he had quickly perceived the relevance of contemporary American plays to his own future as a dramatist there can be no doubt. 'The theatre here is magnificent and I hope to derive great benefit from it for my own things,' he told his parents that August.[124] The complaints about money continued, usually linked to his desire to see theatre, and on 21 October he wrote:

Really, student life is the cheapest in the United States and with 100 dollars anywhere else I couldn't make do, but here I can. We'll see if my budget allows me to go to the theatre, which is what most interests me. I've started a play which I think can be interesting.[125]

As has already been pointed out, nothing is known about the play in question, which may never have been begun, and there is no evidence at all that it was the embryo of *The Public*.

At the end of October 1929 Federico told his parents that some of his rich New York lady friends wanted to sponsor the production of one of his plays, either *Don Perlimplín* or a puppet play, probably *The Tragicomedy of Don Cristóbal and Doña Rosita*.[126] One of these ladies may have been María Antonieta Rivas Mercado, who had introduced Lorca to Emilio Amero. Herschel Brickell never forgot something that this woman, who was then passing through a period of mental disorder, said to him about Lorca: 'I am sure you think of Federico as a poet, but he will be much better known as a playwright. I have read some of his plays and they far surpass in quality even his best poems.' María Antonieta was not destined to witness Lorca's success in the theatre, for she committed suicide – spectacularly – in the cathedral of Notre Dame in 1931. [127]

When Lorca told his parents about the 'new theatre' existing in New York, it seems that he was thinking not so much of the great commercial successes of the day as of the off-Broadway fringe theatres such as the Neighborhood Playhouse, the Theater Guild and the Civic Repertory, all of which were thriving at the time and putting on interesting modern plays.[128] It is probable that Lorca got to know the two remarkable sisters who had founded the Neighborhood Playhouse in 1915, Irene and Alice Lewisohn, and who would produce an English-language version of *Blood Wedding* in 1933. During Lorca's stay in New York the Playhouse staged some lively musicals which he may well have seen: Charles Martin Loefler's *A Pagan*

Poem, Henri Rabaud's *The Nocturnal Procession* and Werner Jansen's *New Year's Eve in New York*.[129]

As for the Theater Guild, founded in 1925, this flourishing club had its own theatre and 26,000 members, no less, and staged works by Tolstoy, Strindberg, Ibsen, Andreyev, Claudel, O'Neill, Molnar, George Bernard Shaw and other leading contemporary playwrights. There is no record of Lorca's attendance, but it is difficult to imagine that he was unaware of the Guild's adventurous work.[130]

The Civic Repertory Theater, whose director was Eva Le Gallienne, opened in 1926 and, like the Theater Guild, put on foreign plays. While Lorca was in New York the theatre produced various works by Chekhov (*Three Sisters*, *The Seagull* and *The Cherry Orchard*), and, where Spain was concerned, Gregorio Martínez Sierra's *Canción de cuna* ('Cradle Song'), a sentimental work with an all-female cast which Lorca loathed.[131]

If these were the days of the Jazz Age, they were also those of the Black musical, which the poet told his parents was 'one of the most beautiful and sensitive spectacles imaginable'.[132] Three Harlem theatres – just down the road from Columbia – were famous at this time for their Black revues: the Lafayette, the Lincoln and (this must have amused Lorca) the Alhambra. The Whites who frequented these theatres were impressed by the sheer vitality of both the actors and the audiences, which they found highly contagious. Lorca and the theatre critics coincided in noticing how, at these shows, the Whites laughed with an uninhibited spontaneity unknown on Broadway.[133]

The poet, poorly equipped linguistically to assess the level of contemporary American culture, tended to overestimate the importance of Black art in the United States, and when he got back to Spain made statements which only those utterly ignorant of America could have taken too seriously. While, as we have noted, the poet read a Spanish translation of *Manhattan Transfer* and of Eliot's *The Waste Land* during his New York sojourn, and met Hart Crane and the Black-Swedish novelist Nella Larsen, there is no evidence that he had any inkling of Scott Fitzgerald (*The Great Gatsby* was published in 1926), Hemingway (*Fiesta* came out in 1927, *Farewell to Arms* in September 1929), Sinclair Lewis, Faulkner or any other contemporary American novelists or poets. Nor, indeed, is there any indication that he showed the slightest interest in knowing more. The experience of New York in itself was clearly sufficiently demanding and inspirational.

Lorca also saw some Chinese theatre in New York. It seems likely that in August 1929 he was present at a performance by the Sun Sai Gai company, which was playing in Grand Street, in Chinatown, Lower Manhattan;[134] while shortly before he left the city he may have been to see the famous actor

Mei Lan-Fang, of the Peking Theatre, whose art stunned the New York public and theatre critics alike. The latter underlined the Chinese theatre's traditional lack of scenery, its sobriety, its extraordinary skill for mime, for suggesting by means of the slightest gesture and without words the most complex states of mind.[135] All of this impressed Lorca, as he stated later, and probably influenced his development as a playwright, reinforcing his determination to escape from the shackles of the traditional theatre and to invent a new dramatic language capable of expressing the most recondite emotions.[136]

Last Days in New York

In the last letter that Lorca is known to have sent to his parents before leaving New York, written in January 1930, the poet announced that in March he would be setting off for Cuba, where he would give 'eight or ten lectures'.[137] We can probably assume that Lorca was well informed about what was going on in the island, for the Spanish-language New York newspaper *La Prensa* kept a close eye on Cuban culture and politics. Moreover, in New York the poet met various Cubans, among them the composer Nilo Meléndez, with whom he coincided at a dinner held in Barnard College on 13 January in honour of the Spanish conductor Enrique Fernández Arbós.[138]

Lorca had been productive over the Christmas and New Year period. Following 'Christmas' (27 December 1929) he wrote 'Paisaje de la multitud que vomita' ('Landscape of the Vomiting Crowd') (29 December); 'Luna y panorama de los insectos' ('Moon and Panorama of the Insects') (4 January 1930); 'Stanton' (5 January); 'Pequeño poema infinito' ('Little Poem of Infinity') (10 January), and 'Sepulcro judío' ('Jewish Tomb') (18 January). They are poems redolent of death, disgust, horror and pity, set in a nocturnal landscape of cemeteries, vomit, hospitals and wharfs where moribund patients and drunken sailors reel under the moon and brusque shifts of tense express the emotional dislocation that inspired them. Perhaps of particular biographical interest is 'Little Poem of Infinity', where the poet states bluntly that to 'take the wrong road is to arrive at Woman', and rejects the view that heterosexual love, with its reproductive nature and alleged harmonization of opposites, constitutes a necessarily desirable aim.[139]

In the middle of January Andrés Segovia arrived in New York to give a series of recitals in the Town Hall Theater, which specialized in Spanish productions. Segovia and Lorca met at several Manhattan speakeasies and saw each other at parties.[140] At about this time the poet left his room in John Jay Hall, where he had been living since September. It has been said that he moved into the flat rented by his friend José Antonio Rubio Sacristán at 542 West 112th Street, on the corner of Broadway, although Rubio has denied this, stating that the poet 'disappeared' with an unidentified friend.[141] Whatever the truth of the matter it does seem that, shortly before leaving for Cuba, Lorca lived briefly at the famous International House, where the future art critic Josep Gudiol met him and heard numerous anecdotes about the poet.[142]

On 21 January 1930 Lorca delivered his first lecture in America, at Vassar College: a touched-up version of his talk about cradle songs, first given in 1928 at the Residencia de Estudiantes.[143]

In November the great Spanish dancer Antonia Mercé, had opened in New York and, at a function organized in her honour on 16 December by the Instituto de las Españas, Lorca had read poems published a year later in his book *Poem of Cante Jondo*.[144] Antonia Mercé's season was an enormous success, and to celebrate its conclusion the Cosmopolitan Club put on a luncheon for the dancer on 5 February. Lorca was among the guests and rose to praise – in Spanish, of course – his famous compatriot.[145]

Then, on 10 February, the Instituto de las Españas honoured Lorca himself on the eve of his departure for Cuba. The function included a lecture by the poet, who this time produced a revised version of 'Imagination, Inspiration and Escape in Poetry', first delivered, like the talk on cradle songs, in 1928, and now entitled 'Three Modes of Poetry'. It was a fitting choice, for if the original lecture had shown Lorca's new interest in surrealist theory and practice, now he could draw on the direct experience of having written many poems (and a filmscript) of more-or-less surrealist orientation during his stay in New York. The brief account of the talk published in *La Prensa* shows that on this occasion the poet spoke with renewed fervour about what he liked to call the *hecho poético* or 'pure poetic phenomenon', liberated, in accordance with surrealist tenets, from logical control, an independent 'fact' in itself. 'Today there are no barriers, no limits, no explicable laws. Admirable Liberty!' he exclaimed, going on to affirm (no doubt with Dalí in mind) that in *Gypsy Ballads*, despite the collection's traditional form, there were numerous moments that reflected contemporary aesthetic notions.[146]

Meanwhile, on 6 February, Ignacio Sánchez Mejías and his lover, the dancer Encarnación López Júlvez, had arrived in New York.[147] The latter gave several highly praised concerts and Lorca saw her frequently, working with her on the harmonizations of Spanish popular songs, which, when they were back in Spain, they would record for His Master's Voice.[148] On 20 February Ignacio gave a lecture on bullfighting introduced by Lorca. According to the correspondent of a Cuban newspaper present that evening in the Instituto de las Españas the poet did his job so successfully that Ignacio protested, with mock indignation, that instead of preparing the bull for him he had made the animal impossible to play.[149]

The political situation in Spain changed spectacularly at this juncture with the fall, on 28 January, after almost seven years in power, of the dictator Miguel Primo de Rivera, and his replacement by the more moderate General Dámaso Berenguer, who promised general elections. Lorca must have been delighted on hearing the news, for he had long disliked Primo de Rivera and all he stood for, not least because of the way in which his regime had closed down the rehearsals of *Don Perlimplín* in 1929. On 14 February *La Prensa* reproduced a statement by Fernando de los Ríos which the poet may have seen. In it the socialist professor and politician expressed his conviction that the new Spain of which he had long dreamed was about to be born. A few days later the same newspaper reported that after so many years of proscription, Don Fernando had just begun teaching again at Granada University.[150]

Federico's days in New York had come to an end, and *La Prensa* informed its readers that the poet was awaited eagerly in Cuba.[151] Lorca had decided not to travel by boat, as would have been more usual, because, as he told José Antonio Rubio Sacristán, he wanted the crossing from the United States to be as short as possible – his fear of the sea was still with him.[152] On 4 March 1930 he boarded a train for Tampa, some 1,300 miles away. It is not known who, if anyone, accompanied him to the station, nor if he was given a send-off by his friends. Surprisingly, his last hours in New York have not been chronicled.[153]

Lorca arrived in Tampa on 6 March and embarked immediately on the American steamer *Cuba*, which arrived the following afternoon in Havana.[154]

The New York correspondent of *Diario de la Marina*, Havana's most important newspaper, commenting at the time on Lorca's stay in America, wrote that the poet was leaving Manhattan more Spanish, more Andalusian, more Granadine, than ever.[155] No doubt it was true. In his reaction against the metropolis, in his struggle for emotional survival in an environment initially so hostile to everything he had known previously, the poet had come to appreciate, far from home, how passionately he loved his native land.

2

Cuba

Havana – Fuente Vaqueros – Cadiz

Cuba! Ever since Lorca was a child in the Vega of Granada it had been a magic name. He had listened with precocious delight to the languid *habaneras* sung by his Aunt Isabel and other members of that musical family and, as he was to explain to his new friends in Havana, some of his earliest impressions of the island derived from the exotic labels inside the boxes of cigars his father received directly from Cuba: there he had contemplated Romeo and Juliet embracing amidst a flurry of roses and gold medals, admired the leonine head of the tobacco magnate Fonseca and imagined himself sailing past the Morro, the famous lighthouse situated at the entrance to Havana harbour, or sauntering through forests of palm trees under a turquoise sky.[1] Later, in Granada, when he discovered Debussy, the poet must have been intrigued by the fact that the composer's works of Granadine theme consistently drew on the rhythm of the *habanera*. The Cuban poet José Chacón y Calvo, whom Lorca met for the first time during the 1922 Holy Week celebrations in Seville, had become a friend during the following years, and had talked to him enthusiastically about the island. Chacón y Calvo was there now, awaiting Federico's arrival, as were many other admirers who did not yet know the poet personally. Before setting foot in Cuba, then, Lorca must have felt sure that he was going to enjoy himself hugely.

In his lecture and recital on New York and Cuba, first given in 1932, the poet did not mention his long train trip from Manhattan to Miami, giving his audience to understand that he had travelled by boat. Doubtless it was more picturesque to leave New York as he had come, by sea.[2] The description of his arrival (on the morning of 7 March 1930) left nothing to the imagination:

But what's this? Spain again? Universal Andalusia again?

It's the yellow of Cadiz, a bit stronger, the pink of Seville just turning carmine and the green of Granada with a slight, fish-like phosphorescence.

Havana emerges among bamboo groves and the sound of maracas, Chinese horns and marimbas.* And in the harbour, who comes to meet me? The dusky Trinidad of my childhood, the one who 'went walking one morning along the quayside in Havana, down the quayside in Havana one morning went walking'.†

And here come the Blacks with their rhythms, which I suddenly realize derive from our great Andalusia – friendly Blacks, with no anguish, who show the whites of their eyes and say: 'We are Latins . . .'⁴

The Havana newspapers, several of which followed closely what was happening in Spain, had been announcing for days the arrival of the Andalusian poet. So well known was *Gypsy Ballads* in Cuba, in fact, that there was a widespread belief that the poet himself was a Gypsy. Particularly famous was the poem 'The Faithless Wife' which, with its earthy eroticism, had offended the capital's staid Catholic bourgeoisie and delighted the progressives, who saw in Lorca the most representative voice of a new generation of Spanish poets. It seemed clear that the presence of the young *granadino* in Cuba was going to have the effect of provoking a lively debate between the upholders of modern art and those who wished to maintain more traditional values. And indeed Lorca's three-month stay was to have just such an effect.⁵

When the *Cuba* moored that morning in Havana, not only dusky Trinidad was awaiting the poet. On the quayside, in flesh and blood, were representatives of the Hispano-Cuban Institution which had invited him, among them the familiar figure of José María Chacón y Calvo, the young writer Juan Marinello, and the journalist Rafael Suárez Solís.⁶ The latter had a regular column on Spanish affairs in the *Diario de la Marina* – and that morning had informed his readers of the arrival of a truly revolutionary Spanish poet.⁷ Suárez Solís soon became one of Lorca's closest friends in Havana.

Lorca, as was usually the case with guests of the Hispano-Cuban Institution, stayed at the Hotel La Unión, situated on the corner of Calle de Cuba and Calle de la Amargura, across the road from the Franciscan Church and in the middle of a labyrinth of narrow streets strongly Andalusian in character. Shortly after his arrival the poet said that Havana seemed to him like 'a big Cadiz, very hot and where the people speak very loudly'.⁸ In point of fact the *habaneros* speak much more softly than Spaniards, so Lorca was

---

* Both instruments are of African origin. The *maraca* is a rattle consisting of a dried, hollowed-out gourd with beans, beads or lead-shot inside.

† Trinidad was the protagonist of one of the *habaneras* Federico had learnt as a child and from which these lines are taken. His friend the poet Rafael Alberti, being from Cadiz, also knew the song well, for Cadiz is the Spanish port most closely associated with Cuba.³

probably thinking of the contrast with New York, where, except perhaps in the Stock Exchange, he must have found that talking noisily was not normal behaviour. Federico would come to feel increasingly during his stay that Andalusia and Cuba were linked by subtle filaments of temperament and culture, and his intuitions about the Andalusian influence on Cuban music would be fully confirmed as he got to know several authorities on the subject, among them Fernando Ortiz. As for the mulatto youths, with their chocolate-coloured skin and breathtaking bodies, Lorca was by all accounts almost speechless with admiration; and if we can believe the few indications it is now possible to glean about his private life in Cuba, he soon began to pursue them.

One of the first things the poet did on arriving was to contact Antonio Quevedo and María Muñoz, a Spanish couple who had been living in Havana for several years and were well known as lovers of the arts, particularly music. María, an excellent pianist, had been a pupil of Manuel de Falla in Madrid, and in Havana founded with her husband the Bach Music Conservatory, the review *Musicalia* and the Society of Contemporary Music. The Quevedos' house in Calle de la Lealtad was a leading centre of culture in the capital, and Spaniards arriving in Cuba to lecture were made welcome there.[9] A few weeks before Lorca disembarked, the Quevedos had received a letter from Falla in which the composer asked them to look after the poet, speaking with deep appreciation of Federico's abilities. 'If I tell you that this poet and musician is one of my best friends in Granada, that is only half the truth,' he wrote, 'for he is also, for many reasons, one of my followers whom I most admire from all points of view, and moreover, in the matter of Spanish folk tradition, he is a splendid collaborator.' Falla had continued:

When God decides that an artist of such quality should be born, capable not only of assimilating the technique necessary for his work but of going beyond what in technique is merely mechanical (and this is the case with García Lorca in his arrangements of Spanish folk songs), we realize the enormous difference between that which is the product of teaching and that which wells up of its own personal, creative accord, stimulated by that teaching.

I don't want to say anything more about our Federico, but simply to entrust him to you and your friends and pupils. He deserves whatever you can do for him, both as a person and as an artist. I would like you to see in Federico an extension, as it were, of myself.[10]

The poet did not disappoint those who had been impatiently awaiting his arrival. The Cubans were as impressed by Lorca's personality as he was by the beauty of the island and the vitality, style and musicality of its inhabitants. The five lectures given in the capital, at the Principal de la Comedia Theatre, were enormously successful. They were, on 9 March, 'The Mechanics of

Poetry' (a new version of 'Imagination, Inspiration and Escape in Poetry', first delivered in 1928 and, more recently, at Vassar College); on 12 March, 'A Paradise Closed to Many, Gardens Open to Few. A Gongorist Poet of the Seventeenth Century' (this was the lecture on Pedro Soto de Rojas, first given in 1926 and then again in 1928); on 16 March, 'Spanish Cradle Songs' (the talk dated from 1928); on the 19th, 'The Poetic Image in Don Luis de Góngora' (first given in 1926 and then on several other occasions); and, finally, on 6 April, 'The Architecture of *Cante Jondo*', a revised version of the lecture on the same subject given at Granada in 1922.[11] The Havana newspapers provided widespread coverage of the five lectures, the last of which was delivered to a packed house during a torrential rainstorm. People queued to buy tickets, which were sold out the moment they went on sale, and in a few weeks Federico was the talk of the town. It was a triumph that perhaps the poet had foreseen, for if in New York he had had ample opportunity to witness the effect of his performances on Black, White, Spanish and Spanish-American audiences, surely, he may have felt, Cuba would receive him with open arms.

Not all the reactions were positive, however, and when the critic Francisco Ichaso, in the course of introducing the first lecture, read some excerpts from the *Ode to the Holy Sacrament*, some people were shocked.[12]

The only letter written by Lorca to his parents from Cuba that seems to have been preserved, dated 4 April 1930, expressed the poet's jubilation at the success of his lectures and at the generous hospitality he was receiving in the island. He promised to send them a copious selection of newspaper cuttings to prove it. He had lectured in Sagua and Caibarién, being introduced to the public in the latter town by Chacón y Calvo, who was proving a marvellous host; he had taken part in a crocodile hunt – characteristically without firing a shot – in the marshes of Zapata; at a ladies' club function given in his honour he had seen the most beautiful women in the world – nothing could match that mixture of Spanish and Black blood; he was being continually invited out. 'This island is a paradise,' he concluded. 'If ever I get lost, they should look for me either in Andalusia or Cuba.'[13]

In his introductury words at Caibarién – the lecture took place on 30 March – Chacón y Calvo had demonstrated his deep understanding of Lorca's poetry, pointing out that his friend was at once ancient and modern and, where the transmission of his work was concerned, a *jongleur* who relied above all on direct contact with a live audience.[14]

If Chacón y Calvo introduced Lorca in Caibarién, it was the turn of the poet's old Granadine friend and one-time *rinconcillista* Francisco Campos Aravaca to do the honours on the two occasions (7 April and 5 June) on which Federico visited Cienfuegos, where Campos was Spanish consul.[15]

On 8 May, back home in Spain, *El Defensor de Granada*, which stated that it had been following with great interest Lorca's successes in America, quoted from a Cienfuegos newspaper where, after praising the poet, the writer glossed Campos's speech on one of those occasions, terming it 'a masterly evocation of immortal Granada'. It seems that it was the only time during Lorca's absence that the Granada press referred to his achievements on the other side of the Atlantic, and it may be that the clipping from the obscure Cuban newspaper had been sent by Federico to his family, who then made it available to the poet's great friend Constantino Ruiz Carnero, editor of *El Defensor*.[16]

A Misleading Account of Lorca's Stay in Cuba

In 1961 Antonio Quevedo published in Havana a *plaquette* on Lorca's visit to Cuba which has been the starting point of almost everything written on the subject since that date. The image Quevedo projects of the poet is almost exactly that explicitly rejected by Vicente Aleixandre – that of the happy, extrovert poet–minstrel who, free of any shadow of anxiety, passes triumphantly through life, always successful, always admired. Literary gatherings, especially connected with the reviews *Carteles, Social* and *Revista de Avance*; visits with José María Chacón y Calvo to the exclusive Yacht Club of Havana, with Quevedo himself to the magnificent beaches of Varadero and to the Valley of Yumurí, in Matanzas, or with tobacco-planting friends to the even lusher Valley of Viñuales, which to Federico seemed 'a sort of telluric drama'; a brief contact with the composer Sergei Prokofiev, whose two concerts were not appreciated by the *habaneros*; the massive consumption of ice-cream; drawings in autograph albums; a poetry recital in the University of Havana, which provoked the admiration of students, among them the young poet José Lezama Lima; folklore sessions around the Quevedos' piano; dinner parties; nocturnal ramblings through Old Havana . . . It is all a bit disappointing. We are told nothing about the poet's amorous adventures, which are still talked about in Cuba, although Quevedo just manages to hint that during his stay Federico effected several unexplained 'disappearances' which baffled his friends. And we learn very little about the Lorca who wrote *The Public* during his stay in Havana. Quevedo whets our appetite but does not satisfy it.[17]

There is an episode that indicates the degree to which Antonio Quevedo and María Muñoz were unable to keep tabs on Lorca, despite an obvious desire on their part to monopolize him. This concerns the poet's visit to Santiago de Cuba. Lorca had promised to give a lecture in the city – at the other end of the island, more than 600 miles away – on 5 April. But due to the success of his lectures in Havana this became impossible, and in the event he did not travel to Santiago until the end of the month. Antonio Quevedo could never be convinced that Lorca really went there, claiming that, had he done so, the poet would certainly have informed him and his wife.[18] But the fact is that Federico told hardly anyone about the visit, slipping away, as he often did when the party was in full swing, without saying a word. The Quevedos were the unwitting victims of the poet's ability to make everyone feel that he or she was his only friend at the time – a two-edged ability that could lead on occasions to ugly, jealous scenes.

His forthcoming trip to Santiago inspired the only poem Lorca is known to have composed in Cuba. Federico was as excited by the Afro-Cuban music he heard in Havana as he had been by the jazz of Harlem, and showed particular interest in the variety known as the *son*, then all the rage, a highly sensual dance, similar to the rumba, with a mixture of African and Spanish elements. Federico was soon an addict. He made friends with the best *soneros*, trying their instruments of African origin and quickly picking up the complicated rhythm; and his nights in Havana habitually ended in the *fritas* of the district of Marianao, famous for its music. Suddenly out of all this came inspiration, and when Lorca set off for Santiago at the end of April he had the manuscript of his poem 'Son' in his pocket:

> Cuando llegue la luna llena
> iré a Santiago de Cuba,
> iré a Santiago,
> en un coche de agua negra.
> Iré a Santiago.
> Cantarán los techos de palmera.
> Iré a Santiago.
> Cuando la palma quiere ser cigüeña.
> Iré a Santiago . . .*[19]

Lorca explained to Juan Marinello about the cigar boxes he had seen in Fuente Vaqueros as a child, recalled now in the images of the poem, with its allusions to Romeo and Juliet and Fonseca and the 'paper sea and silver money' of the inner labels.[20] The poem is peppered with references to the real Cuba that Lorca saw all around him – to the *bohíos*, for example,

*   When the full moon comes
      I'll go to Santiago de Cuba,
      I'll go to Santiago,
      in a coach of black water.
      I'll go to Santiago.
      The roofs of palm will sing.
      I'll go to Santiago.
      When the palm tree wants to be a stork.
      I'll go to Santiago . . .

traditional houses made of wood, branches and palm-leaf fibre, and to the instruments of African origin used by the *son* players.[21] As for the 'coach of black water', no one seems quite sure. It has been suggested that Lorca is imagining a journey to Santiago in a paddle-steamer.[22] Others hold that he has in mind the Central Havana–Santiago railway and the smoke-belching engine that, in reality, will convey him across the island – but that hardly explains the 'black water'.[23]

One of the most notable gaps in Quevedo's narrative concerns Lorca's friendship with the Loynaz family, famous in Havana for their eccentricity, who do not receive even a single mention. These were four brothers and sisters – Flor, Enrique, Carlos Manuel and Dulce María – whose father had been a famous general in the War of Independence against the Spaniards, and who lived in decadent splendour in a large mansion surrounded by a tropical garden in the quarter of Vedado on the outskirts of the city. All the Loynazes were artistic, and before arriving in Cuba Lorca had read some poems published in Spanish reviews by Enrique and Dulce María. It seems, too, that he may have corresponded with Enrique, although no letters appear to have survived.[24]

The poet could hardly have imagined the colourful world he was about to enter. The Loynaz family had inherited money and could afford to indulge its whims. The house was palatial and rambling, filled with Chinese and Sèvres porcelain, sculptures, French eighteenth-century furniture, pictures and other art treasures mixed in with a huge quantity of bric-à-brac gleaned on numerous trips abroad. And if Lorca loved the house – 'The Enchanted House' he termed it – he was wildly enthusiastic about the overgrown garden, which contained several almost unbelievable white peacocks, perhaps unique in Cuba, and a pair of flamingos. For two months the poet was a daily visitor, virtually making the house his base in Havana and becoming an especially close friend of Carlos Manuel and Flor, who was a vegetarian and brave opponent of Gerardo Machado, the dictator of the moment. With Dulce María (years later, under Fidel Castro, President of the Cuban Academy), things were more difficult. She was serious, did not share the Bohemian tendencies of the rest of the family, and to make matters worse had composed a clever parody of one of Lorca's ballads. 'It's the best poem you've written!' he retaliated, although probably not amused. As for Enrique, he too seems to have been of a more introverted and serious nature than Flor and Carlos Manuel.[25] With the latter the poet's night-time explorations of Havana grew more frenzied, and in Flor's car they wandered further afield, often ending up at haunts in outlying places like Guanabacoa, Guanajay or Santa María del Rosario. But wherever they went, Flor recalled in 1980, Federico was never back in his hotel before dawn.[26]

In the 'Enchanted House' Lorca was almost as much at home as in the Huerta de San Vicente, back in Granada. There he wrote, played the piano, told stories, drank whisky and soda, read, recited. Sometimes he even stayed there by himself, quite content, while the others went out. Part of the time he worked on his play *The Public*, and it seems that, when the poet read them the work, the Loynaz family found it utterly incomprehensible. None the less, before he left Cuba Federico gave Carlos Manuel a present of a draft, or part of a draft, of the revolutionary play.[27]

Dulce María Loynaz has recalled that, as well as *The Public*, Lorca read them some scenes from *Yerma*, a work that was to occupy him for several years on and off and whose origin reached back to the poet's childhood, when he first became aware of the annual pilgrimage to the village of Moclín, in the hills some eight miles to the north of the Vega.[28]

The almost inexpugnable castle of Moclín, built by the Arabs on a steep hill at the head of a long valley running down to the Vega, played an important role in the war leading to the fall of Islamic Granada, and was finally captured by the Catholic Monarchs in 1486. Ferdinand and Isabella spent protracted periods there with their Court until Granada succumbed six years later, and expressed their affection for the place by donating to the newly erected church a standard of Christ that had been carried throughout the campaign against the infidel. During the sixteenth century miraculous powers began to be attributed to the picture, and at the end of the seventeenth the cult was officially recognized by the Archbishop of Granada, 5 October being fixed as the date for honouring the Christ of the Cloth, as the work had come to be called. Little by little the notoriety of the annual festivity increased, and by the eighteenth century a pilgrimage famous throughout Andalusia made its way to the village at the beginning of each October. No one seems to know quite why the Christ of the Cloth concerned himself with impotence and infecundity in general and female infertility in particular, but so it was – and the afflicted travelled every autumn to the hermitage of Moclín in search of alleviation.[29]

As a child in Fuente Vaqueros and later Asquerosa Federico must have seen the strings of men and women passing through the Vega on their way to Moclín, and Francisco García Lorca has stated, moreover, that a crude lithograph of the 'Most Holy Christ of the Cloth' presided over his and his brother's bedroom.[30] By the early twentieth century the pilgrimage had acquired a markedly orgiastic quality, and if many pregnancies ensued from the annual celebration it was more a result of human than of divine intervention, hundreds of men from the surrounding villages participating in the fun. 'Cuckolds! Cuckolds!' the locals would shout as the processions passed, alluding to the erotic sport which, in the interests of obtaining progeny, the unfortunate husbands were expected to tolerate during the expedition.[31]

It is not known for sure if Lorca ever visited Moclín during the pilgrimage, or, indeed, at any time. His brother states that neither he nor Federico ever set foot in the village,[32] although Marcelle Auclair, in her biography of the poet, reported a comment by Lorca on the painting that suggested that he had indeed been to the church: 'If you look at it well you can see, under the thin coating that covers it, the hoofs and thick hair of a faun.'[33]

Lorca talked about Moclín to his friends in Madrid, one of whom, the composer Gustavo Pittaluga, decided to write a ballet on the theme, based on a plot devised by Federico and Cipriano Rivas Cherif. It is not known when Pittaluga began *La romería de los cornudos* ('The Cuckolds' Pilgrimage'), but it was finished by 1927, in which year the composer attempted, without success, to produce it in the Residencia de Estudiantes, with a backdrop by the sculptor and painter Alberto Sánchez.[34] The work was first performed orchestrally in Madrid in 1930,[35] but was not destined to have its première as a ballet until November 1933, when Encarnación López Júlvez and her company produced it in the capital.[36]

The plot of *The Cuckolds' Pilgrimage* is trivial and the tone festive: neither has much to do with *Yerma* (the hitherto sterile wife, Sierra, is luckier than Lorca's character, and will get her baby), and from the fact that for the few performances of the ballet Rivas Cherif was paid more than the poet it is probably safe to deduce that the latter simply provided the general idea of the work while Rivas Cherif wrote the brief scenario.[37] What is important, at all events, is that from at least 1927, and perhaps earlier, Lorca had collaborated on a ballet inspired by the Moclín pilgrimage, and it may well be that he got the first idea of writing a play on the theme of a married woman's sterility while Gustavo Pittaluga was busily composing the music for that venture. When he began to work on *Yerma* we do not know, but Dulce María Loynaz's recollections suggest that it may have been fairly advanced when the poet arrived in Cuba.

It seems that by this time Lorca was also working on *Doña Rosita the Spinster*, the idea for which had come perhaps ten years earlier, for Dulce María Loynaz has recalled that the poet sang at their piano some of the songs that appear in the first act of the play.[38]

The Loynazes were irritated when it was discovered that Lorca had set off for Santiago without announcing his departure. One day, when he did not turn up as usual at their house, they drove to the hotel and were informed that the poet had just caught a train for the distant city. This struck the family as extremely odd, and Carlos Manuel was particularly piqued, maintaining that if he had known what was afoot he would have driven

Federico to Santiago in his own car. Taking this evidence together with that of Antonio Quevedo, it does seem that the poet felt the need, suddenly, to get away from Havana for a few days by himself. If there was anything more to it than that we shall probably never know, and no one has ever come up with any information suggesting that Federico was accompanied on his trip by some other friend, although this cannot be completely ruled out. When Lorca returned he refused to offer any excuse or explanation for his action. For Flor he brought a medallion from the sanctuary of Our Lady of Copper – the patroness of Cuba, to whom Hemingway would later offer his Nobel Prize insignia – giving it to her with the words: 'From one Cuban virgin to another'.[39]

By this time Lorca had become a friend of the great expert on Afro-Cuban culture Fernando Ortiz (1881–1969), President of the Hispano-Cuban Institution, who must have informed him about the many rites of African origin still surviving on the island. In Madrid, three years earlier, at the house of José María Chacón y Calvo, the poet had met Lidia Cabrera, Ortiz's sister-in-law, later to become an international authority on Cuban folklore, and had dedicated to her and her Black servant in Havana, Carmela Bejarana, the ballad 'The Faithless Wife' (the one that so offended the Catholic bourgeoisie of the city). Lidia was now back in Cuba, and one day contrived to take Federico to a *ñañigo* ceremony, by what means we do not know, since normally women are not allowed to be present at these gatherings (the *ñañigos* are a predominantly Black secret society previously much feared for their magic-working). According to her account, when the poet was approached by the *diablillo* ('little devil'), with his painted face and weird dance, he was so terrified that he almost fainted.[40] Given Lorca's obsession with death and his interest in the occult, it was inevitable that the magic rites still prevalent in Cuba (more so than among the Black community of Harlem) should have enthralled him. But his interest went beyond the magical, and Dulce María Loynaz has recalled that during his stay he took a lively interest in everything Black, and not least the Black society columns in the Havana newspapers which, in imitation of those devoted to 'White' Cubans, gave colourful accounts of weddings, baptisms, balls and other festive occasions. The poet asked the Loynaz family to send him cuttings of these columns to Spain, but if they did so they never received any acknowledgement. Once Lorca left Cuba none of the family ever heard from him directly again, although some years later the poet decided that Flor should have the manuscript of *Yerma*, arranging that Adolfo Salazar take it to her in Cuba.[41]

The Theatre Alhambra

Lorca coincided in Cuba with a young, twenty-six-year-old Guatemalan poet called Luis Cardoza y Aragón, who had just been appointed his country's consul in the island. The meeting took place in the offices of the literary journal *Revista de Avance*, and before long the two were friends.[42]

Cardoza y Aragón had been recommended by the Cuban novelist Alejo Carpentier, whom he had met recently in Paris, to visit the famous Theatre Alhambra in Havana. The theatre, of which Lorca became an assiduous fan, specialized in a brand of ebullient satire directed against the corruption and injustice that at this time, under the dictatorship of Machado, were rife throughout the island. In Havana, specifically, poverty was reducing the thousands of immigrants pouring in from the countryside to near starvation, prostitution in all its varieties flourished, and casinos for the rich and for American tourists pullulated. Of all this the poet, always sensitive to the suffering and exploitation of others, must have become fully aware during his stay, despite his euphoria at the time.[43]

The Alhambra was a strictly men-only establishment (nobody remotely respectable ever set foot there), and along with the satire it did a line in pornographic playlets and lascivious dancing girls. 'It was total theatre,' recalls Cardoza y Aragón. 'The delirious audience took part with the delirious actors who, in turn, joined the delirious audience.' The shows derived to some extent from the tradition of the Italian *commedia dell'arte*. There were stock characters – the Galician, the Black, the Mulatto Girl, the Policeman, the Homosexual and so on – and a great deal of improvisation. Federico was delighted.[44]

Cardoza took Lorca to see one of Havana's most opulent brothels where, apparently, the poet expressed surprise that only girls were on offer. Lorca's homosexuality was obvious to the Guatemalan, although the latter records that the poet's gestures were not at all effeminate. This tallies with what most of Federico's friends have said and explains why many people who knew Lorca have found it difficult to believe that he was homosexual. 'According to the division established by Gide in his *Diary* while he was writing *Corydon*,' Cardoza goes on, 'I don't know if he was a pederast, a sodomite or an invert. I would say that his appetite included all three categories.'[45]

During their frequent conversations Lorca talked often, and fervently, about Salvador Dalí. Cardoza was full of Paris and wildly enthusiastic about surrealism, which seemed to him the new religion of Personal Liberation. For this reason he could not fail to be fascinated by the fact that Lorca knew Dalí well, although it is not clear how much the poet told him about their relationship. Lorca confided his projects to Cardoza. He was going to write a play more daring than anyone had had the courage to attempt before him – by comparison, he said, Oscar Wilde (whom Lorca undoubtedly admired) would appear an out-of-date, fat and pusillanimous old queen. From the brief description Cardoza provides of the scenes from one of the projected works Lorca described for him, it is clear that this was to be *The Destruction of Sodom*, of which the poet later wrote at least one act (only the first page seems to have survived). The theme: the pleasures of the homosexual confraternity, who have made such a contribution to world culture.[46]

If we can believe Cardoza's account – and in so far as it can be checked it seems trustworthy enough – he and Lorca planned to write together an *Adaptation of Genesis for Music-hall*, which was to be a sort of farce constructed of grotesque and blasphemous elements. But nothing more is known of the work.[47]

One day Cardoza went to see Lorca in the clinic where he had had some moles removed from his shoulders, fearing that they might become cancerous – among the poet's numerous obsessions that of developing cancer was one of the most tenacious, as the Loynaz family, who also visited him in the clinic, became aware.[48] The Guatemalan found the poet propped up happily in bed, surrounded by a group of admiring Blacks and singing *sones* with a *maraca* and a huge red celluloid fish at his feet.[49] Remembering this scene in 1936, numbed by the terrible news of the poet's assassination, Cardoza y Aragón referred to Lorca's extraordinary charisma, his unremitting fear of death and his method of working – the complete abandonment to the creative impulse when this made itself felt, which could produce in him a sort of frenzy. Lorca wrote, according to Cardoza y Aragón, only when he could no longer bear the strain of not expressing what he was feeling.[50] The practice of poetry, by this token, was absolutely necessary to Federico's survival as a person, and the observation has been confirmed by other friends of the poet.

Cardoza y Aragón, while coming close to telling us something interesting about Lorca's homosexuality, provides no solid information about the poet's amorous activity in Cuba. Many anecdotes still circulate in Havana about this. According to one, Lorca stole the boyfriend (a Scandinavian sailor) of the Colombian poet Porfirio Barba Jacob, whom he had met at the office of the *Revista de Avance*.[51] Another has it that on one occasion he spent a night in gaol, accused of some petty homosexual offence, and had to be rescued by his friends. But in Cuba as in Andalusia rumour and gossip are the order of the day and it has been impossible to substantiate this particular episode.[52] It is certain, however, that the poet had a relationship with a handsome and vigorous twenty-year-old Mulatto called Lamadrid.[53]

Over another good-looking *habanero*, Juan Ernesto Pérez de la Riva, slightly younger than himself, Lorca got into hot water. Pérez de la Riva was the son of well-off parents who, when they discovered that the Granadine poet was homosexual, informed Federico that his visits to the house were no longer welcome. Despite such a harsh rebuke the friendship continued, and it seems that with 'Juanito' Pérez de la Riva (later a distinguished engineer and geographer) Lorca spent some of his happiest moments in Havana.[54]

The Public and Ode to Walt Whitman

While, as we have seen, Lorca may perhaps have begun to think about *The Public* in New York, and even jotted down ideas, no documents have come to light to prove that he began to write the play there. The first pages of the only known manuscript, criss-crossed with emendations, are written on notepaper with the heading of the Hotel La Unión in Havana, and have all the appearance of belonging to the original draft; we know that Lorca worked on the play at the Loynaz family's house and read passages to them; and it seems certain that the bulk of the work was written in Cuba (the final page is dated 22 August 1930, a few months after the poet returned home).[55]

It has been said that *The Public* is the first Spanish dramatic work to explore the theme of homosexual love,[56] but, as was said earlier, Lorca's friend Cipriano Rivas Cherif had produced in January 1929, at the Caracol Theatre Club in Madrid, his play *A Sleep of Reason*, whose theme was precisely such love – in this case the love of two women. The work, immensely daring for its day, had been well received by the critics, who considered Rivas's treatment of the theme dignified and humane.[57] It is difficult to believe that Lorca did not see the play – produced when Rivas Cherif was preparing the première of *Don Perlimplín* in the same theatre – and, given his close friendship with Rivas, he may even have read it, as did other friends of the author. There was, at all events, a recent forerunner for *The Public*, although Lorca's play was to go far beyond his friend's in theme and treatment.*

Jean Cocteau's *Orphée*, successfully produced by Rivas Cherif in the same theatre club in December 1928, also undoubtedly impressed Lorca, and it is not difficult to find similarities with *The Public*. Cocteau's mysterious white horse with a man's legs, for example – the oracular link between Orpheus and the world beyond the veil which, repelled by modern society, he desires so desperately to penetrate – may have suggested Lorca's horses,

---

* *A Sleep of Reason* was never published and, according to Rivas Cherif's family, the manuscript is missing.[58]

while Death's accomplices, represented as surgeons (with white gowns, masks and rubber gloves), prefigure the poet's sinister Male Nurse. Lorca's Elena, too, seems to owe something to Cocteau's Death, who is represented as a woman 'with large blue eyes painted on a black mask' (Elena has 'blue eyebrows' and the coldness of Death, while masks are everywhere in *The Public*), and, indeed, the atmosphere of mystery and death that pervades *Orphée* is very akin to that generated in Lorca's play. Then, in both there are moments when the barrier between stage and auditorium is deliberately blurred, although this may be due to the influence of Pirandello on each. It can be added that, if Orpheus–Cocteau is a revolutionary poet at loggerheads with contemporary society, whose aesthetic norms he rejects, in *The Public* Lorca defends the 'theatre under the sand' – authentic theatre, inaugurated by the horses 'in order that the truth of the tomb be made known' – as opposed to the 'open-air theatre', a conventional, *superficial* theatre that rejects the exploration of the depths of human experience. At the same time, Lorca makes an impassioned plea for the right of the individual to love according to his nature and needs.

As for other contemporary influences on *The Public*, apart from the obvious one of Pirandello (whose *Six Characters in Search of an Author* had been played in Spain and Lorca must have known) and the possible one of Evreinoff's *The Comedy of Happiness* (so admired by Rivas Cherif), the poet was probably vaguely aware of the dadaist and then surrealist theatrical experiments that had been taking place in Paris where, between 1920 and 1930, some thirty avant-garde plays were staged.[59] Lorca, highly sensitive to what was going on around him, must have picked up the waves emanating from the French capital, and perhaps first-hand information about the fringe theatre there came his way from Cardoza y Aragón and other friends.

Lorca's debt to Shakespeare is made explicit in *The Public*, which follows the precedent of *A Midsummer Night's Dream* and *Hamlet* by the insertion of a play within a play – in this case *Romeo and Juliet*, performed offstage – and in which there is a discussion on the significance of the love philtre administered by Puck. Lorca deeply admired *A Midsummer Night's Dream*, as we said earlier (p. 97), finding in it a vindication of all expressions of love, including homosexual, and in *The Public* the Conjuror's observations to the Producer at the end of the performance of *Romeo and Juliet* undoubtedly reflect Lorca's own views on the subject:

If love is pure chance and Titania, Queen of the Fairies, falls in love with an ass, it would hardly be surprising if, by the same procedure, Gonzalo drank in the music-hall with a boy dressed in white on his knee.[60]

And hardly surprising if other peoples' eroticism were tinged, for example, with sado-masochism – one of love's cross-currents of which Lorca was much aware, as can be seen in the *Ode to Walt Whitman*.[61] *The Public* contains many references to the subject: the whip becomes almost a character in the play; there is a clear allusion to the floral flagellation of Hieronymous Bosch's *The Garden of Earthly Delights* (which Lorca must often have admired in the Prado) and the Third Man even wears wristlets (those perennial s/m standbys) with gold studs.[62]

If in *The Public* Lorca is not just upholding the rights of homosexual love but of love in all its varieties, the weight of the argument comes down in support of the former. The only character in the play who stands free of hypocrisy, without a mask, is the First Man, Gonzalo, whom it seems plausible to identify with Lorca as well as with Christ.[63] Throughout the play Gonzalo denounces the duplicity that prevents people from being themselves and living their particular sexuality. 'My struggle had been against the mask until I finally saw you naked,' he tells Enrique, the Producer, adding a few moments later: 'I love you openly in front of the others because I hate the mask and because I've managed to tear it off you.'[64] The words are reminiscent of the poem 'Your Childhood in Menton', probably inspired by Aladrén or Dalí and perhaps written after Lorca's return to Spain (it was first published in 1932). In it, too, the poet accuses the beloved of self-deceit and claims to have broken his mask. Enrique, then, may contain elements of both friends.[65] Gonzalo's last words before dying on the cross can also be related to the poem in question, where the poet refers to 'The train and the woman who fills the sky'. Utterly alone, Gonzalo exclaims, apostrophizing the beloved Enrique:

Agony. Loneliness of the man in his dream full of lifts and trains where you travel at speeds I can't apprehend. Loneliness of the buildings, of the corners, of the beaches, where you will never be seen again.[66]

It is difficult not to sense in *The Public*, as in several of the New York poems, a reflection of the anguish that took hold of the poet when his relationships with Dalí and Aladrén foundered; and, in general, not to find in the play an attempt to come to terms with his homosexuality and the problem of having to live in large part a double life. In the harsh recriminations that the characters hurl at each other, in the jealousy that torments them, in their bursts of venomous spite – in all of this we may be justified in feeling that Lorca is expressing his own experience. Moreover, the scorn with which the Centurion refers to homosexuals mirrors only too accurately the attitudes with which Lorca was familiar in Spain.[67] As for the choice of the name Elena for the far-from-satisfied companion of Enrique, one wonders if, as was said earlier in discussing the filmscript *Trip to the Moon*, this might not be an allusion, as well as to the classical Helen, to Dalí's Gala, Helena Dimitrievna Diakonava, and to Aladrén's fiancée, Eleanor Dove. For neither woman could Federico have been expected to entertain warm sentiments.

To what extent did Lorca's stay in Havana condition the writing of *The Public*? It seems possible that the circus-like, irreverent atmosphere of the play, and even some of its characters, owe something to the atmosphere and style of the Alhambra Theatre, so often frequented by Lorca. But there are only one or two direct allusions, of no great importance, to Cuba. Lorca himself never explained, publicly, the sources of the play nor, so far as we know, wrote an account of his intentions in it, and, as so often, we have little to go on apart from the text of the work in question.

Dulce María Loynaz did not enjoy the scatological and erotic passages of *The Public*, and was bemused by the series of metamorphoses enunciated by the lovers in the scene entitled 'Roman Ruin', perhaps inspired by *A Midsummer Night's Dream* ('If I changed myself into a turd?' 'I would change myself into a fly', etc.).[68]

The Public is a revolutionary play from many points of view. Both a reflection on the contemporary theatre and itself a highly original dramatic work, it was far in advance of its time both in its proclamation of erotic liberty and its treatment of this theme. (Genet did not arrive on the scene for twenty years.) If the work owes an obvious debt to surrealist theory and practice, it cannot be considered strictly surrealist, for at no time, despite the starkly oneiric atmosphere of the play, had Lorca abandoned himself completely to the dictates of the unconscious. It is, above all, an angry and even bitter work, in which we sense the anguish of a writer condemned by an unjust society to mask his true self.

This anguish found further expression in the *Ode to Walt Whitman*, one of the least understood of Lorca's poems. At the end of what was almost certainly the first draft of the ode the poet wrote 'June 15'.[69] It seems likely that the unspecified year in question was 1930, and, if this hypothesis is correct, the first draft of the poem was finished at sea two days after Lorca left Cuba. Whether it was begun on the island or in New York we do not know, although the latter possibility seems more plausible.

Lorca's Whitman, as well as being the lover of Nature, sincerity and simplicity, symbolizes a homosexuality free equally of shame and promiscuity, and has an almost religious seriousness. This Walt does not drink alcohol, and if he loves male bodies he is careful not to frequent the sordid world of male prostitution, with its exploitation of the young and, often, its sado-masochistic undertones. Whitman here is an archetypal male with no womanish traits and, above all, the poet of friendship. (Lorca knows that one of his key words is 'comrade'.) The diatribe – for much of the poem is that – is directed not against homosexuals as such, but against the effeminate variety and those who 'corrupt' others, all of it from the point of view of a hypothetically 'pure' homosexuality free of blemish.

The ode suggests strongly that, despite his efforts, Lorca had not yet come to terms with his sexuality. The cruel use made in the poem of the word *marica* ('effeminate gay'), the evocation of such individuals in terms of rats, mud and cloaca, seem out of all proportion to the implied shortcomings of the group, and one is bound to wonder if the poet has not fallen prey to some sort of defence mechanism whereby he deprecates in others what he fears in himself. There is some external evidence to support this view. The Granadine poet Luis Rosales, for example, has stated that Lorca told him that he was terrified that people would think he was a *marica*,[70] and Cipriano Rivas Cherif, himself homosexual according to many of Lorca's friends, recorded some relevant words reputedly spoken to him by Federico in 1935:

I've only been with men; and you know that the invert, the *marica*, makes me laugh with his womanish urge to wash, iron and sew, to wear skirts, to speak with feminine gestures and manners. I don't like it.[71]

The discussion between the two homosexuals on just this subject in the second scene of *The Public* comes immediately to mind: what is important is to be manly. It seems quite clear, on the face of it, that this was one of Lorca's great hang-ups.

The ode was not published until 1934, and then only in Mexico, in a limited, non-commercial edition of fifty copies which the poet distributed among his closest friends.[72] It never appeared in Spain in his lifetime and he did not refer to it in his lecture on New York. Clearly, in this instance, Lorca felt that discretion was the better part of valour.

Last Days

One of the most interesting eye-witness accounts of Lorca's visit to Cuba is that published in Havana, during the poet's stay, by the historian Emilio Roig de Leuchsenring, a frequent contributor to the review *Carteles*. Roig admired Lorca's work but had decided that he did not want to meet him because, according to his information, the poet was apolitical and had not participated in the struggle against the Spanish dictator Miguel Primo de Rivera. (As we have seen this was not strictly true.) Such a posture he found untenable, given Primo de Rivera's persecution of intellectuals; and his feelings were intensified by the fact that, in Cuba, Gerardo Machado was exerting a similar tyranny. No, Roig was sure that Lorca was a brilliant, ivory-tower poet unconcerned about politics. But he soon found that he was wrong. To be sure, the Andalusian was extroverted, always ready to have a drink and a chat, to slip away at the least provocation to hear Cuban popular music. Indeed he seemed completely adapted to the Cuban way of life and gave the impression of knowing more about Havana than the *habaneros* themselves. But there was more to it than that and Roig discovered to his surprise that Lorca was deeply concerned about injustice, not only in Cuba but also in Spain and elsewhere. For example, the poet had gone to congratulate, spontaneously, a certain Dr Cosme de la Torriente, who had just won a case in Havana upholding the rights of the individual against the power of the State. Roig also discovered that Lorca had sided with the Blacks in a nasty apartheid issue that had blown up in the snobbish Havana Yacht Club. The poet expressed himself violently opposed to all dictatorships (Gerardo Machado's regime included by implication) and voiced his enthusiastic support for the Cuban opposition politicians. There was no question, therefore, of Lorca's being apolitical, and Roig was happy to acknowledge his mistake.[73] The poet may have told him, moreover, that in the Havana papers, always well informed about Spanish politics, he was following closely developments back home. On the reverse of a photograph sent at this time to his parents, he scribbled (referring no doubt to the rising clamour for elections and to the general unrest in the country): 'Every day I read with intense interest about the situation in Spain. It's a volcano.'[74]

Meanwhile, on 16 May, one of Lorca's best friends in Madrid, the musicologist Adolfo Salazar, arrived in Havana to give a series of lectures.[75] 'The Lorca–Salazar tandem was memorable for those of us who shared their friendship during those months,' wrote Antonio Quevedo (who assumed, wrongly, that Salazar had disembarked earlier than he did.)[76] In fact, it was more a trio than a duo, for the painter Gabriel García Maroto, who had arrived in the island on 28 April, was almost always with Lorca and Salazar in the month leading up to the departure of Federico and Adolfo together in June, and the three appear side by side in numerous photographs.[77]

Salazar's account of those days, published in 1938, makes good reading. But he does not tell all. As a homosexual himself (and, unlike Lorca, an 'obvious' one), he knew more about the real Federico than almost any of the poet's other innumerable friends, and it is a tragedy that Lorca's many letters to him seem to have disappeared.[78] When he arrived in Havana one of the first things he did was to make his way to Lorca's hotel. The poet was in bed, wrapped in a yellow dressing-gown, and reading to a group of enthusiastic youths his poem 'The Boy Stanton' which, according to Salazar, he had written the night before under the impact of his recent minor operation for the removal of the moles on his shoulders. Salazar found him obsessed by the fear of cancer, and this might explain why he was reciting precisely the Stanton poem (composed not the night before but in New York), given the sinister role played there by the same disease.[79]

Recalling Lorca's happiness in Cuba, Salazar wrote: 'I never knew him so Andalusian as in Havana.'[80] Juan Marinello, who was not in a position to make such a judgement since he had only just met Lorca for the first time, was astonished by the extent to which the poet became immediately attuned to Cuban life. Cuba

was for his thirst like a noisy, turbulent Andalusia, like his childhood found again at last. Cuba stimulated his powers and he took pleasure in extracting the utmost from her. The Gypsy rhythms of his blood fused with the rush of Black blood. *Cante Jondo* – his great passion – was soothed in the swaying rhythms of the Afro-Cuban *son*.[81]

Shortly before Lorca, Salazar and Luis Cardoza y Aragón left Cuba their friends on the journal *Revista de Avance* held a lunch in their honour at the Hotel Bristol. There were speeches, and the painter Jorge Mañach expressed the company's sadness at the imminent departure of the three writers, whose presence in Havana had been such a tremendous stimulus.[82]

Almost inevitably, there are conflicting accounts of Lorca's last hours in Havana, although about the date of his departure there can be no doubt: it was 12 June 1930.[83]

According to Flor Loynaz, Federico and Salazar lunched that day with her in a dingy restaurant in the basement of the modest hotel, probably the Detroit, where Lorca had gone to live after finishing his cycle of lectures. Flor stated (in 1980) that Salazar was nervous because he thought that Federico, who still had not packed and seemed interested only in reciting his poems, would make him miss the boat. Taking charge of the situation she had dashed upstairs to Lorca's room and thrown the few things she found there (the poet always travelled light and tended to give away almost all his acquisitions) into one small case. Her powerful Fiat was waiting at the door and, with characteristic panache, the enemy of the dictator Machado had driven the vehicle at breakneck speed to the harbour, where they arrived just in time.[84]

Antonio Quevedo, for his part, would have us believe that Lorca and Salazar spent their last hours in Havana with him and his wife. After a long conversation came the sad moment:

Salazar looked at his watch: 3 p.m. The four of us, as if moved by a sole impulse, got up and merged in an embrace. Federico said: 'They need me in Spain.'

Afterwards, in the old house, which had heard so much laughter during those three months, there remained only loneliness, shared by the others living there. Time has not been able to erase so many images. The house is still there, but what a spiritual ruin! We had to abandon it soon afterwards, because, when he left, Federico took with him his *duende* and his grace and the house became enclosed and dark, the widow of García Lorca.[85]

Perhaps it is unnecessary to try and make the two accounts tally. People often thought that they were Lorca's only friend, and this circumstance, added to the lack of contemporary accounts, frequently makes it impossible to get at the truth. It seems, however, that Flor's account is substantially accurate, for it has been confirmed by the independent-minded Dulce María Loynaz in all its essentials.

María Muñoz de Quevedo had written to Federico's mother on 6 May to inform her of the 'double success' her son was enjoying in Cuba: that of his personality and that of his talent,[86] and shortly before embarking the poet told various friends that on the island he had just spent the happiest days of his life.[87] Certainly he had been in his element. 'My son speaks with such enthusiasm about Cuba', Vicenta Lorca replied on 2 September, 'that I think he likes it even more than his own country.'[88]

There is a footnote to Lorca's stay in Cuba. On the morning of 18 June 1930 the *Manuel Arnús* docked in New York.[89] The poet could not go ashore because his visa had run out, but Salazar hurried to see Olin Downes, the music critic, whom he had met in Madrid the previous summer. Lorca, ship-bound, dashed off a telegram to Federico de Onís, asking him to visit him on board with José Antonio Rubio Sacristán. He also contacted Herschel Brickell and other friends. When Salazar returned, accompanied by Downes, he found the saloon crowded and a party in full swing. Among those present were a group of girls to whom Lorca had taught Spanish songs while at Columbia. Seated at the piano, the poet (who according to Brickell had put on a lot of weight in Cuba), was playing one of his favourites, 'The Three Muleteers', which all were singing at the tops of their voices.[90] The following day Norma Brickell gave Mildred Adams some disturbing news. 'It's just as well you couldn't come,' she confided sadly. 'He's not our Federico any more, but a very different person. Wholly male, and very vulgar.' Mildred Adams comments: 'This sea change was Cuba's gift.'[91]

A wholly male and very vulgar Lorca? The picture tends to confirm the recollections of various friends of the poet, including Buñuel, who found that, after his year away from Spain, Lorca had become more openly homosexual.[92] This, presumably, was the 'gift' Cuba had made to Federico – a gift for which, it may be imagined, Lorca had reason to be grateful, even though some of his friends regretted it.

'An unforgettable episode,' Adolfo Salazar termed their Atlantic crossing. Federico's talents unfolded 'like the wings of the praying mantis', and nobody was allowed to escape. Along with the rest of his inexhaustible repertoire the poet sang Spanish and Cuban songs, with and without the complicity of the ship's piano, and hardly a passenger or member of the crew failed to join in. Discipline began to be so affected that, when the *Manuel Arnús* reached Cadiz, on 30 June, the captain allegedly swore that if the voyage had lasted another two days he would have thrown himself overboard in despair.[93]

There at the quayside to meet the poet were his brother Francisco and sister Isabel, who had driven down from Granada. The reunion was an emotional occasion, and the trip home, according to Isabel, a riot of laughter and excited talk.[94]

3

The Coming of the Republic

Summer in Granada and Malaga

On 1 July 1930 Lorca was once more in Granada, where his arrival was duly registered by the local press, both the *Noticiero Granadino* and *El Defensor de Granada* expressing their pride in the poet's achievements on the other side of the Atlantic and pointing out that, if Lorca had gained by his visit, so too had the prestige of Spanish literature in those parts.[1]

While we have little information about Lorca's activity in Granada during that summer, we can be sure that the situation prevailing in Spain after Primo de Rivera's exile and death was the subject of constant discussion in the poet's home and among his friends. These were moments of great uncertainty, and King Alfonso XIII was steadily losing the support of his subjects, even of his Monarchist subjects. The Republicans were convinced that their moment was at hand – the government headed by General Berenguer had promised general elections, although the date for these had not yet been announced – and, where Granada was concerned, *El Defensor* continued to voice local opposition to the status quo.

And Fernando de los Ríos? The great socialist thinker and politician, back at Granada University since the fall of Primo de Rivera, now occupied a key position among the opponents of the monarchy, who were busily preparing for the coming of democracy. By dint of both their friendship with Don Fernando and their own liberal inclinations, the García Lorcas must have followed the course of events closely during the summer, and become aware of the terms of the agreement reached on 17 August, in the so-called 'San Sebastián Pact', between the various political groups pledged to work for the downfall of the regime.[2]

Four days after the signing of the pact, Lorca wrote on the last page of the manuscript of *The Public*, after the stage direction 'Slow Curtain', the date 'Saturday 22 August 1930' (in fact, the 22nd was Friday, and we may perhaps assume that the work was finished in the early hours of the following morning). Whether the poet told any of his friends in Granada about the play, or read it to them, we do not know; certainly no reference to it appeared in *El Defensor de Granada*, which suggests that for the moment he preferred not to broadcast the fact that he had written a revolutionary work.

Meanwhile Emilio Aladrén had heard that Federico was back in Granada, and wrote him a mock-formal note from Madrid on 30 August. 'Emilio Aladrén Perojo', it ran, 'kisses the hand of Federico García Lorca, is delighted about his return to Spain, and takes the opportunity to inform him that he cannot imagine with what pleasure he would hear from him.'³ Had the two corresponded during Lorca's absence in New York and Cuba? Once again we are unable to say. Nor do we know if Lorca replied to this communication. It is certain that he renewed his friendship with the sculptor that autumn in Madrid, however, although perhaps not on the same passionate basis as before.

One of the only accounts we have of Lorca's return to Granada comes from a famous local character: the dissident left-wing priest Luis Dóriga Meseguer, later a Radical Socialist Party Member of Parliament, who was loathed by the Catholic establishment in the town, not least for the virulent attacks on the Spanish Church he published in *El Defensor*. Dóriga, who went into exile at the end of the Civil War, told Fernando Vázquez Ocaña, one of the poet's first biographers, that Federico had returned to Granada from Cuba exultant. The priest knew Lorca and his poetry well, and was concerned that his experiences on the other side of the Atlantic might have altered him, made him harder. But he need not have worried. The poet assured him that not only had he not changed but that he now felt even more compassion for the halt, the weak and the lame. In New York, he said, he had felt obliged to express his feelings in a poetry in which love 'penetrated like a drill'.⁴

Towards the end of the summer the García Lorcas, following their usual pattern, spent some weeks in Malaga, the city that Federico repeatedly claimed was his favourite. There he must have heard, from Emilio Prados and other friends, numerous anecdotes about Dalí's and Gala's stay at Torremolinos (then a tiny village) that April and May, an episode later recalled in some detail in the painter's *Secret Life*. Gala had recently undergone a serious bout of pleurisy and Salvador, beside himself with anxiety, hoped that, by taking up an invitation to stay by the sea at Malaga, her convalescence might be hastened. It proved to be their 'honeymoon of fire', Dalí wrote in his autobiography: his initiation into the delights of love-making with a highly experienced woman as guide. After a few weeks the couple had acquired a tan of African intensity. Gala wandered round the village with her breasts bare, hardly eliciting any surprise among the fisherfolk, who seem themselves to have been quite free of false modesty, while Salvador worked at his painting *The Invisible Man*, begun in France, and wrote the definitive version of his essay 'The Invisible Woman', dedicated to Gala. Sometimes the 'Malaga Surrealists', as Dalí termed them, dropped in to visit the two in their cottage by the sea.[5]

One of these, Dario Carmona, later recalled his amazement on witnessing the terror that grasshoppers produced in Salvador – a terror chronicled in the *Secret Life* and reflected in many of Dalí's paintings. If one of the panic-inspiring creatures crossed his path on the way to the beach, Salvador would turn back indefectibly. Carmona also remembered an occasion on which Dalí and Gala went shopping in Malaga. The painter was now so dark-skinned, and dressed in such Bohemian fashion (bare chest, long hair, a string of green beads around his neck), that children came up to him shouting 'Muhammad, one penny, Muhammad, one penny', because they had got it into their heads that he was an 'English Arab'. Emilio Prados and his friends could not help noticing how totally immersed Dalí and Gala were in each other. 'Look, how strange,' Salvador quipped one day, 'a surrealist actually holding hands with his woman!'[6]

That summer in Malaga Lorca must have listened to countless stories about the Catalan, from whom, so far as we know, he had not heard since 1928 (although there could well be missing letters). And once again he must have wondered what manner of woman it was who could satisfy the needs of a person as complex, perverse and unremittingly anal as Salvador Dalí.

Madrid Again

At the beginning of October Lorca was back in Madrid, after an absence of fifteen months. There he was interviewed about his American experience for the *Heraldo de Madrid* by his friend Miguel Pérez Ferrero. He announced that he had three books ready for press: *Odes, Tierra y luna* ('Earth and Moon') – the latter was written, he said, in the New England countryside – and *New York*, a 'poetic interpretation' of the American metropolis. Half of the last book, the poet assured Pérez Ferrero, no doubt indulging in his usual tendency to exaggerate, was devoted to the Blacks. As it turned out, none of these titles was published in the poet's lifetime.

Pérez Ferrero had heard rumours about a sensational drama that the poet had brought back from America. Lorca now revealed, so far as we know for the first time to the press, that it was called *The Public*. 'It comprises six acts and an assassination,' he explained, going on to express his doubts as to whether the work could ever be performed, since the main characters were horses.[7] Soon afterwards Lorca began to read the play to carefully selected friends, and the general view was that, whatever the merits of the strange work, there was no chance whatsoever that it could be staged at the moment.[8]

But what about Lorca's other plays? The poet spoke to Cipriano Rivas Cherif, who at this time was planning to revive his experimental company Caracol which, since the Primo de Rivera authorities closed down *Don Perlimplín* in 1929, had given no sign of life. Rivas probably advised Lorca that it was better for the moment not to try again with *Don Perlimplín* (the Berenguer regime was somewhat more liberal than the previous one, but there was still censorship), and undertook to produce *The Shoemaker's Prodigious Wife* – a perfectly safe bet. Rivas was literary adviser to Margarita Xirgu who, on 16 September, had opened a season at Madrid's municipal theatre, the Teatro Español. Between the three it was agreed that Caracol would produce the play that Christmas with Margarita in the lead role.

Meanwhile, on 6 December, accompanied by Emilio Aladrén, Lorca travelled up to San Sebastián, where he gave his lecture 'The Architecture of *Cante Jondo*'. Among the audience was a young student, later to become a distinguished authority on Spanish painting, Rafael Santos Torroella, who met the poet afterwards. Santos has recalled that someone whispered in his ear that the sculptor, who hardly spoke a word, was the poet's boyfriend. It is the only indication we have that Lorca was now seeing Aladrén again.[9]

These were turbulent days. In the early hours of 12 December a group of rebel Republican officers involved in a plot against the monarchist regime, which was growing daily more unpopular, jumped the gun and staged a premature rising in the town of Jaca, in Aragon. The results for the conspiracy were disastrous. The insurrection was immediately crushed and after a summary court-martial the officers principally responsible, Captains Galán Rodríguez and García Hernández, were shot. The executions took place in the early hours of Sunday, 14 December, almost before the country had time to realize what was happening. That morning Lorca was in the mining town of Gijón, on the Asturias coast in north Spain, to give his lecture 'The Architecture of *Cante Jondo*' to the Workers' Club. He did so, but no reports appeared in the local newspapers owing to the general strike that had been declared.[10]

The following day, 15 December 1930, it was the turn of the Madrid rebels to launch their rising. But the authorities, warned by what had happened in Jaca, were ready, and the insurrection was quickly put down, many anti-Monarchist officers, left-wing party members and politicians being arrested. Among the latter were the socialist leader Francisco Largo Caballero, Fernando de los Ríos and the future President of the Republic,

Niceto Alcalá-Zamora. While the rising had failed, however, it was clear to almost everyone that the regime was tottering.[11]

On 24 December the curtain of the Teatro Español went up on *The Shoemaker's Prodigious Wife*. That morning the poet explained in a newspaper interview his intentions in the play, stressing the function therein of the chorus (the neighbours who comment on the action), which, he said, now seemed to him an essential element of the theatre.[12] The observation suggests that Lorca had been reading ancient Greek drama as well as listening to Rivas Cherif, for whom the return of the chorus was a matter of vital importance,[13] and in this respect the play can be seen to look forward to *Blood Wedding* and *Yerma*, where the device is given a much fuller treatment. Lorca was careful to stress that *The Shoemaker's Prodigious Wife*, whose first version he had begun several years earlier, did not represent his current theatrical practice. 'No,' he said in the same interview,

it isn't my *real work*. My real work will come later . . . I've already got something . . . something. What's coming later will be my *real work*. Do you know what I've called it? *The Public*. That's it . . . that's it . . . powerfully, powerfully dramatic.[14]

It was an arresting statement. Over the next few years Lorca would try in vain to have *The Public* produced, and it seems legitimate to assume that it was on account of this failure that, desperate to achieve financial independence, he decided to draw again on the Andalusian tradition he knew so well, a tradition already tapped in *The Shoemaker's Prodigious Wife* and the earlier puppet plays.

The première was a success. Lorca himself read the witty prologue to the play ('he could be a splendid actor if he decided to,' commented one paper),[15] decked out in a resplendent star-spangled cape, and the audience loved Margarita Xirgu's vivacious *Zapatera*. Next day Enrique Díez-Canedo, perhaps the most distinguished drama critic in the country, noted the influence of the Andalusian puppet tradition on the work, and praised Salvador Bartolozzi's sets and costumes, which were based on drawings by the poet, themselves in turn influenced by Picasso's for Falla's *Three-Cornered Hat*.[16] In general the other critics were indulgent, although Juan Olmedilla, of the *Heraldo de Madrid*, was disappointed that after a year in America Lorca had not put on something more modern.[17]

All in all *The Shoemaker's Prodigious Wife* did remarkably well, running for some thirty performances before it came off in April.[18] One of the most positive results was that the relationship between Margarita Xirgu and Lorca was greatly strengthened, a factor that may well have encouraged the poet to continue writing for the theatre.

Before returning to Granada for Christmas and New Year Lorca was interviewed for *La Gaceta Literaria*, very intelligently, by the writer Rodolfo Gil Benumeya. If, a few months earlier, Federico had told Miguel Pérez Ferrero that three books were ready to be handed over to the publishers, he now claimed to have four. He expatiated on the supremacy of Black art in America, showing no awareness of the outstanding non-Black artists and writers of the day, and spoke of the enormous contribution the Blacks were making to contemporary theatre, the poet's 'principal concern', he underlined, at the moment.

Gil Benumeya asked about *Gypsy Ballads*, which Lorca hastened to point out belonged to the past. The poet felt that his visit to New York had helped him to see the book more clearly. On returning home he had discovered not only that the collection had become astonishingly famous but that he himself was now considered by many people to be a Gypsy. (Perhaps Lorca remembered at this point what Dalí had said to him in his letter about the ballads, that the *putrefactos* considered him 'a bronzed Gypsy with black hair and a childlike heart.')[19] The poet confessed himself sick of the whole thing, and wished that people would grasp that the collection had in fact very little indeed to do with Gypsies.[20]

If what really interested Lorca at the time was the health of the Spanish theatre, he can have had little cause for elation when he returned to Madrid that January. It is true that, in the Fontalba, the Argentinian actress Lola Membrives was performing *Anna Christie*, the first play by Eugene O'Neill seen in Spain.[21] But apart from that the situation was depressing. Nothing new could now be expected from the veteran Nobel Prize-winner Jacinto Benavente, nor was Eduardo Marquina (whose verse dramas are today forgotten) likely suddenly to change direction and come up with a work more attuned to the times. And there was little new talent. Moreover, competition from the film industry was growing stiffer all the time. Madrid's cinemas were booming, and in January 1931 there were queues to see Buster Keaton in *The College Boy*, Rudolph Valentino in *The Eagle* and Victor McLachlan in *All Quiet on the Western Front*.[22]

Since the failed *coup* of December, the political temperature of the country had been rising steadily. On 8 February General Berenguer announced that the promised elections would be held soon. He and his Cabinet resigned six days later. On 18 February King Alfonso XIII invited Admiral Juan Bautista Aznar to form a new government, and the latter stated that he would honour the decision of the previous Cabinet to go to the country. Before long, however, it began to be bruited that the elections would be municipal, not general. This was confirmed on 14 March, when the date of the consultation was finally made public. Polling day was to be Sunday, 12 April 1931.

In the midst of it all, on 26 February, Lorca's friend the poet Rafael Alberti staged in Madrid a play called *The Uninhabited Man*. Termed by the author a 'mystery play without the sacrament',[23] the little piece expressed a profound disillusionment. Masks, somnambulistic tailor's dummies, empty suits, treachery lurking behind false appearances, a criminal, murderous Creator who surrounds the Man with temptations only to condemn him to hell – it was the same, identity-obsessed, disgusted, iconoclastic Alberti who had surprised readers of his book of poems, *Concerning the Angels*, published just before Lorca left for New York in 1929.

The première was something of a scandal and Alberti, when the final curtain fell, jumped on to the stage and shouted: 'Long live extermination, death to the filthy contemporary Spanish theatre!'[24] According to him, the audience then divided into two warring factions, and Jacinto Benavente and the Alvarez Quintero brothers (the latter had written innumerable pseudo-Andalusian comedies) left amid boos.[25] A fortnight later the Friends of the New Universal Theatre, of which Lorca was a member, organized a function in honour of the leading actress María Teresa Montoya, which took place after a special performance of the play. Given Alberti's militant republicanism, the provocative quality of the play itself and the situation prevailing in the country, the evening could not fail to be strongly political in flavour. Messages were read out, and those from Niceto Alcalá-Zamora, Francisco Largo Caballero and Fernando de los Ríos, all three still in prison as a result of the events of the previous December, were greeted with cheers and foot-stamping. When a telegram arrived from Miguel de Unamuno, the *enfant terrible* of the Primo de Rivera regime, the theatre went almost wild with enthusiasm.[26]

Meanwhile, Lola Membrives continued her season at the Fontalba. The actress was as famous in Spain as Margarita Xirgu and, back home in Buenos Aires, had done more than anybody else for the Spanish theatre in that city. We do not know when Lorca first met her, although by the end of March 1931 they were certainly on friendly terms for, according to a report appearing in the press at that time, the poet, Rafael Alberti and their bullfighter friend, Ignacio Sánchez Mejías, had just been seen in her room at the theatre, where their ebullient arrival had secured the 'elegant withdrawal' of the Alvarez Quintero brothers, for whose work Lorca had no time.[27] Before the actress returned to Argentina that spring it seems likely that Lorca had already come to admire her art deeply, and it may well be that she stimulated in him a desire to see his work performed in Buenos Aires, then one of the great theatre capitals of the world.

Another facet of Federico's rich personality came to the fore at this time, when His Master's Voice released the first of a series of records of Spanish folk songs harmonized by the poet and sung to his piano accompaniment by Encarnación López Júlvez, 'La Argentinita'. On 13 March 1931 Adolfo Salazar reviewed the first record in *El Sol*. The critic was enthusiastic, his only misgiving being that HMV had not planned to publish with the records an explanatory study by Lorca.[28] Over the following months the four remaining records were issued and the series had a considerable success, both in Spain and in South America. These are the only recordings of Lorca playing known to exist (none of his voice has been found), and they leave no doubt as to his ability at the keyboard, nor as to the astringency of his interpretations of the folk songs he loved so much.

On 10 April 1931, on the eve of the municipal elections and with Republican fervour running high throughout the country, the French hispanist Mathilde Pomès arrived in Madrid. She had not seen Federico since that day in Paris, in June 1929, when she had noticed that the poet was not as pleased as he maintained about the trip to New York, and she was excited at the prospect of meeting him again. Accordingly, on the morning following her arrival, she made her way to the studio flat occupied by the poet and his brother at 60 (later 72) Calle de Ayala.

It is not clear when Lorca and his brother Francisco first took this studio, situated at the top of the house overlooking a convent school, but it was almost certainly soon after the poet returned to Spain from Cuba. Francisco at that time was busy preparing for his entry into the Diplomatic Corps, achieved shortly after the establishment of the Republic, and no doubt the brothers felt that they would have more freedom with a flat of their own than staying at the Residencia de Estudiantes. Moreover the company was good, for other friends had studios in the same building (which is no longer standing): the guitarist Regino Sáinz de la Maza, Encarnación López Júlvez, José Jiménez Rosado and, according to the latter, Emilio Aladrén.[29]

It was eleven thirty when Mathilde Pomès arrived at Federico's flat, and the poet, characteristically (he was a confirmed night bird) was only just waking up. Unconcerned, he sat down at the piano in his dressing-gown and played for his visitor some songs he had learned in Havana. Then he turned to his Spanish repertoire: Asturian, Castilian, Leonese, Andalusian . . . Two hours passed in a flash. When the poet finally retired to dress, Mathilde jotted down in her notebook a punctilious inventory of the contents of the room. First, of the books piled on the table: these were the Bible; Dante's *Divine Comedy*, in an Italian edition; a complete English Shakespeare in one volume (publisher unspecified); the *Chinese Poems*, translated by Arthur Waley; two volumes, in French, from the 'Ars Una' collection (*France* and *Angleterre*); volume XXXII (*Líricos españoles*) of the famous Biblioteca Rivadeneyra collection of the Spanish classics; works by the nineteenth-century poet José Zorrilla, the playwrights Lope de Rueda and Tirso de Molina; and, finally, Fernando de Rojas's great *La Celestina*. Clearly the poet was reading widely.

Among the books lay a large box of coloured pencils. On one wall was pinned a drawing by the poet of a group of three sailors surrounding an effeminate cabin-boy in front of a quayside bar. Beside this hung a painting by Dalí, probably *Bottle of Rum with a Syphon* (1924), which the painter had given to Federico during the days of their friendship in the Residencia de Estudiantes. On top of the piano was the score of Mozart's *Don Giovanni* and a volume of Pedrell's *Cancionero popular español* ('Collection of Spanish Folk Songs'), one of the poet's constant companions. Some old copper pots and two tapestries from the valley of the Alpujarras in Granada – violet, black and red on a white background – complete Mathilde Pomès's invaluable list.

Before she and Lorca left the studio on their way to the restaurant, where a group of writer friends had been waiting for over an hour, Federico presented her with an unpublished *suite*, 'The Poem of the Fair'; a self-portrait belonging to the New York series in which he tries to shield himself from one of the lion-like animals so frequent in the drawings of those days; and, to cap it all, the drawing of the sailors pinned to the wall.[30]

In view of the photographs taken that afternoon in the garden of the restaurant (the Buenavista, in what were then the upper reaches of the Calle de Alcalá), it is not difficult to understand Mathilde Pomès's uneasiness about arriving excessively late, for the friends in question were a distinguished group and included some of the best poets of the day: Vicente Aleixandre, the Mexican Jaime Torres Bodet, José Bergamín, Pedro Salinas, Luis Cernuda and Gerardo Diego (see illustration 23).

During lunch we can be sure that there was an animated discussion about the municipal elections to be held the following day, although Mathilde Pomès, writing twenty years later, does not mention this. Given the possibility that the Second Republic was just around the corner, it is hard to imagine that the conversation that afternoon was limited to literature.

The End of the Nightmare

Sunday, 12 April 1931 was a fine day throughout almost the whole of Spain as the people flocked to the polling stations.

That morning Carlos Morla Lynch bumped into Lorca in the Puerta del Sol and they sat down together in a café. The square was rapidly filling with a gesticulating and noisy crowd shouting against the regime, and there was panic when the police suddenly charged.[31] Later in the day the poet experienced in his own flesh what it was like to be at the receiving end of a mounted charge by the Civil Guard. He was sitting with Rafael Martínez Nadal on the terrace of the Café Granja del Henar, in the Calle de Alcalá, not far from the Bank of Spain, when a Republican demonstration came towards them from the Puerta del Sol, heading down the street in the direction of the Plaza de la Cibeles. Nadal suggested that they join the crowd, and was surprised when Federico agreed. As they entered the Paseo de Recoletos, with Lorca and Nadal in the front row, a Civil Guard detachment suddenly appeared, blocking the way. There were shots and the marchers fled in panic, Nadal among them. When he looked back he saw the poet trying to escape as fast as his congenitally stiff gait would allow him (even fear could not galvanize him into running), his white suit making him a perfect target for the guards.[32]

Francisco Vega Díaz, later a distinguished heart surgeon, took part in the demonstration, and with Martínez Nadal witnessed the poet's arrival back at the Granja del Henar – ashen-faced, dusty, his shirt unbuttoned, and wiping the sweat that poured from his forehead with a handkerchief lightly stained with blood (he had fallen and scraped a finger). Vega Díaz has recalled:

He began to tell us in a loud voice what had happened, with a verbal exuberance, precise details, a vocabulary and a mimicry that were absolutely fantastic. He expressed his terror in words that gushed from his mouth, and such was the emotion he generated in the café that someone made him get up on one of the marble tables so that eveyone present could hear the account he had begun. I can honestly say that in all the work of García Lorca I have found nothing that could equal what, in a seemingly inextinguishable flood of words, he said in only a few minutes, turning from one side to the other.[33]

That night the election result was known the length and breadth of the country: the Republicans had won. In the face of such an outcome, and perhaps hoping thereby to prevent civil war, King Alfonso XIII decided to leave the country immediately. Two days later, without a single life being lost, the Second Republic was proclaimed. The monarchy had fallen like a rotten apple, and, almost unbelievably, the possibility of a new democratic Spain was suddenly no longer a dream but a reality.

4

Early Days in the New Spain

The Cultural Battle

Lorca knew that the Republic's greatest battle was going to be fought in the field of primary and secondary education, which for centuries had been controlled by the Church. The men of the new Spain were determined to destroy this monopoly and create a state system capable of meeting the huge challenge posed by widespread illiteracy – in 1931, out of a population of 25 million, 32.4 per cent were illiterate and the Republicans estimated that 27,150 new schools were needed. The Provisional Government immediately drew up a five-year plan to meet this requirement, aiming to build 7,000 schools in the first year and 5,000 over the following four. As things turned out they succeeded in meeting their target for the first year: in 1932 they built 2,580 schools; and in 1933, before the Right came to power in November, 3,990. It was an amazing achievement. In thirty years of Monarchy only 11,128 schools had been built; the Republic, in two and half, had created 13,570.[1]

As well as building schools the Republicans were determined to raise the status of the teaching profession, traditionally very badly paid, and especially to improve the lot of primary schoolteachers. Salaries were raised by 50 per cent and 5,000 new posts created.[2] But the reforming zeal of the Republicans was not limited to education, and among other controversial measures it was also proposed to legalize divorce, expedite agrarian reform, secularize the cemeteries and hospitals and reduce the number of religious orders.[3]

The reaction of the Church was predictably hostile – and instantaneous. On 7 May 1931, hardly three weeks after the proclamation of the Republic, Cardinal Segura, Archbishop of Toledo and Primate of Spain, attacked the reforms in his pastoral letter. He referred to the dangerous threat posed to the 'rights' of the Catholic Church by the Republic's projects, and asked the women of Spain to organize a crusade of prayers to counteract such nefarious designs. He recalled what had happened in Bavaria in 1919 when the Catholics intervened to 'save' the country from a brief Bolshevik occupation, hinting thereby that the recently inaugurated Spanish Republic was virtually communist. (Nothing could have been further from the truth.) It was clear that, by proposing to separate Church and State, the Republicans had outraged the Catholic hierarchy, entrenched in its hitherto unchallenged privileges.[4]

Four days later, on 11 May, six convents and a Jesuit building were set on fire in Madrid. It was never discovered who was behind the working-class incendiaries, and the intervention of right-wing *agents provocateurs* cannot be ruled out. At all events the result was the same, particularly in view of the fact that the police had not been deployed against the mob: the Right now had a hefty stick with which to beat the 'anti-clerical' Republicans, and Catholic opposition to the new regime hardened.[5]

These events coincided with the long overdue publication of Lorca's *Poem of Cante Jondo*, which appeared at the end of May. Rafael Martínez Nadal had been instrumental in persuading Federico to cede the manuscripts to the young Madrid publishing house Editorial Ulises, and had helped the poet to organize the poems, most of them composed in 1921 and 1922 when Lorca was in Granada helping Falla with the preparations for the *Cante Jondo* Festival. *Poem of Cante Jondo* attracted many reviews, one distinguished critic, Eugenio Montes, seeing Lorca as a sort of poetic Heinrich Schliemann who had succeeded in digging down to the very bedrock of 'eternal Andalusia'.[6] Federico was perhaps surprised by the reaction of the Catalan Sebastià Gasch, with whom he had almost lost contact. Gasch, who previously had praised the poet's surrealist vein, now maintained that his 'flirtation with a pseudo-surrealism more avant-garde than surrealist', inspired by Salvador Dalí, had led him down a false path, and that in *Poem of Cante Jondo* Lorca was at his most 'intense and pungent'. Federico must have wondered what had happened to his former friend. What had happened, in fact, was that Gasch had developed a dislike of all things surrealist and, first and foremost, of Salvador Dalí.[7]

When Five Years Pass

Back in Granada, Lorca worked with the energy he habitually mustered during his summer holidays in the Huerta de San Vicente. On 19 August he finished a new play, *Así que pasen cinco años* ('When Five Years Pass'), writing excitedly to his friend the guitarist Regino Sáinz de la Maza to tell him that he was 'to a certain extent satisfied' with the work and that he had half finished another – almost certainly *Blood Wedding* – for Margarita

Xirgu. Moreover he had written a book of poetry, *Poems for the Dead*, which he considered the most intense he had produced to date. 'I've been like a fountain,' he told Regino, 'writing morning, noon and night. Sometimes I've been feverish, like the old Romantics, but without losing the immense conscious joy that creation gives.'[8] Lorca never published a book with the title *Poems for the Dead*, and it is impossible to be sure to which compositions, out of those known today, he was referring, although the best candidate seems to be *Diwan of the Tamarit*.

We possess very little information about the gestation of *When Five Years Pass*, and only the vaguest indications as to the poet's intentions in the play. On one of the rare occasions on which it appears he talked about these, he was reported as saying: 'It's a mystery play with the characteristics of this genre, a mystery play about time, written in prose and verse.'[9]

Procrastination in love is always, for Lorca, a crime against Nature, as is the masking of true feeling, and it inevitably brings death in its train. The echoes of Lorca's first poems, with their obsessive allusions to lost love, can be heard in all the poet's later work, but perhaps nowhere as insistently as in this modern mystery play, this 'legend about time', as it is subtitled. *When Five Years Pass*, where the traditional and the ultra-modern in Lorca fuse more completely than in any of his other plays, expresses with supreme artistry the poet's anguish about the future, the certainty of death and the impossibility of sexual fulfilment.

Of all Lorca's characters, the Young Man embodies most poignantly the consequences of love deferred, just as does the Fiancée the furious desire to live fully in the here and now. The dialogue that takes place between the two after the Young Man returns from his five-year trip is vintage Lorca:

FIANCÉE: But weren't you taller?
YOUNG MAN: No, no.
FIANCÉE: Didn't you have a violent smile that made me think of a heron in flight?
YOUNG MAN: No.
FIANCÉE: And didn't you play rugby?
YOUNG MAN: Never.
FIANCÉE: (*Passionately*) And didn't you pull a horse by its mane and kill three thousand pheasants in one day?
YOUNG MAN: Never.
FIANCÉE: In that case . . . why have you come for me?[10]

There are other numerous allusions in the text to the sexual impotence of the Young Man, not least the comments made to him (in verse) by the Tailor's Dummy, poignantly clothed in the wedding dress bought by the youth for the Fiancée he has lost:

Tú tienes la culpa.
Pudiste ser para mí
potro de plomo y espuma,
el aire roto en el freno
y el mar atado en la grupa.
Pudiste ser un relincho
y eres dormida laguna
con hojas secas y musgo
donde este traje se pudra.*[11]

The Young Man, in fact, is an Old Man, and it can be no accident that he is accompanied in the play by a character with this name, clearly his *alter ego*. Gather ye rosebuds while ye may! Perhaps nowhere in Lorca does the message come through so loud and clear.

Our suspicion that there is much of the poet himself in the Young Man is confirmed by the fact that passages in *When Five Years Pass* echo lines written ten years earlier. The anxious dialogue that takes place in the wood between the Young Man and the Typist (Act III, scene 1), for example, draws on the poem 'Aire de nocturno' ('Nocturne Breeze'), dated 1919, whose theme, once again, is that of love lost or unattainable:

¿Qué es eso que suena
Muy lejos?
Amor. El viento en las vidrieras.
¡Amor mío!†[12]

In the scene in question the Young Man, who five years earlier, obsessed by the Fiancée, had rejected the Typist – failing in his blindness to perceive that she was the one for him – tries to convince her to take him back. But it is too late. Glossing 'Nocturne Breeze', the two characters entone the dirge of impossible love:

TYPIST: What's that noise far away?
YOUNG MAN: Love,
    the day returning.
    My love![13]

*   You are to blame.
    You could have been for me
    a stallion of lead and spume,
    the air parted by his bridle
    and the sea tied to his rump.
    You could have been a whinny
    and you're a sleeping lake
    with dry leaves and moss
    where this dress will moulder.

†   What's that noise
    Far away?
    Love. The wind in the shutters.
    My love!

Other echoes of earlier works strengthen the identification between Lorca and the Young Man. For example, the song recalled by the Second Friend in the first act – and which he claims to have heard from the lips of a little nymph (*mujercilla del agua*) seen in a drop of water when he was a child – is reminiscent of 'Suite of the Return', mentioned earlier, which was finished on 6 August 1921, almost exactly ten years before the poet dated the final page of *When Five Years Pass*:

> Yo vuelvo por mis alas,
> dejadme volver.
> Quiero morirme siendo amanecer,
> Quiero morirme siendo
> ayer.
> Yo vuelvo por mis alas,
> dejadme volver.
> Quiero morirme siendo manantial.
> Quiero morirme fuera de la mar.* 14

When the Young Man refuses to address his sweetheart as Fiancée, preferring as terms of endearment *niña* or *muchachita* ('little girl'), and talks to the Typist in a similarly childish way,15 we are reminded not only of the *suite* just mentioned, where the girl is also called *niña*, but of another poem from the same period, 'Moments of Song', dated 10 July 1921, in which the poet evokes the lost *muchachita de la fuente* ('little girl of the fountain'), arguably the same personage.16 Both *When Five Years Pass* and these poems from ten years earlier conjure up a pre-adolescent, almost infantile setting, and suggest once again that in the Young Man Lorca was expressing his own sense of heterosexual failure.

Complementing the frustration that racks both the Young Man and the Typist is their shared obsession with sterility, which looks forward to *Yerma* (already in the poet's mind when he visited Cuba) and back to *Book of Poems* and *Suites*. As for Lorca's ever-present concern with death, in none of his plays is it as insistent as here. And how can we fail to be impressed by the fact that Lorca was killed exactly five years after the day on which he finished a play with this title, and in a manner not dissimilar to that of the Young Man – the victim of a bullet rather than an arrow?

> * I've returned for my wings,
> let me return.
> I want to die being the dawn.
> I want to die being
> yesterday.
> I've returned for my wings,
> let me return.
> I want to die being a spring.
> I want to die away from the sea.

At the end of the summer Federico attempted to get away from Granada to visit Regino Sáinz de la Maza in Santander. He was very fond of his family, he told the guitarist, but, as usual, his parents wanted to keep him with them. Could Regino arrange a lecture for him in Santander? It would be a perfect excuse. But nothing came of the plan.[17] Instead the poet made a brief visit to Fuente Vaqueros, whose annual fair he always tried not to miss. This year there was a special reason for being present: the Republican Town Council had invited him to inaugurate the public library whose creation he had recommended two years earlier just before leaving for New York. Moreover, the Calle de la Iglesia, where the poet was born, had now been renamed Calle de Federico García Lorca in his honour. It was more than enough reason to return to the village.

After effusively praising La Fuente, the poet spoke on the topic of books – their origin and development and the vital role they play in forming free men and women. It was a passionate speech, very much in tune with the Republican fervour wafting at these moments through the land. Lorca expressed agreement with the great philologist Ramón Menéndez Pidal, who had said that the Republic should mean, above all, Culture, and explained to the audience, taking Voltaire as his authority, that the civilized world has been governed by a handful of great books: the Bible, the Koran, the works of Confucius and Zoroaster. He argued that true wisdom lies in the contrasting of ideas, and hoped that the Fuente Vaqueros public library would be eclectic in its acquisitions. There should be room for both the mystics and the revolutionaries: for St John of the Cross and Tolstoy; side by side the shelves should hold Augustine, Nietzsche and Marx, for these writers 'coincide in their love of humanity and the elevation of the spirit, and, when all is said and done, they are akin in their high idealism'.

At the end of his speech Lorca gave his listeners to understand that he not only believed that the classless society was at hand, but that he approved of this evolution. In order that such a society should become a reality, culture was vital – and culture, he insisted, requires sacrifice and abnegation. The villagers of Fuente Vaqueros could have been in no doubt that afternoon that their poet was firmly aligned with the Republic, nor that he held strongly anti-capitalist views. What most of them cannot have realized, however, was that these views, whose roots lay deep in Federico's childhood, had become more tenacious during his stay in New York, where he had seen human suffering on a scale hitherto unimaginable. Lorca, like Fernando de los Ríos, undoubtedly believed that the Republic could and should be the beginning of a marvellous new adventure in the history of Spain, and his speech showed that he felt he had a part to play in the enterprise.[18]

The Barraca

On 29 May 1931 the Provisional Government of the Republic, pressing ahead with its educational and cultural reforms, had created an organization that was to have a profound effect on Spanish life during these years, the *Misiones Pedagógicas* ('Teaching Missions'), presided over by Manuel Bartolomé Cossío, a collaborator of Francisco Giner de los Ríos in the Free Teaching Institution and author of an important book on El Greco. The aim of the Missions was to take the message of the new democratic Spain out to the underprivileged people of the country's lonely, isolated and often appallingly poor villages, putting on plays, performing concerts, helping the local teachers, organizing art exhibitions and talks, setting up public libraries, showing films and in general striving to bring hope to folk who in many cases still lived almost in the Stone Age.[19]

These were days of intense democratic enthusiasm and the Missions immediately fired the imagination of the country's best writers and artists, among them Lorca. The poet was interested in what was going on in the new Parliament. On 8 October he was there to hear a speech by Fernando de los Ríos, now Minister of Justice, on the religious issue, which promised to be unforgettable – and was. De los Ríos, directing himself explicitly to the Catholics present in the house, spelled out the liberal attitude towards a Church that, in his opinion, had been throttling the life of the country for more than five centuries, and recalled the abuses of the Inquisition. 'We are the descendants of the Erasmists,' he affirmed authoritatively, 'the descendants of those whose dissident conscience was stifled for hundreds of years.' The Church had persecuted, burned, maimed; it had expelled the Jews; merged with an oppressive monarchy and the financial establishment, it had stood for the suppression of freedom, the putting down of all heterodoxy. It had misrepresented the views of those who disagreed with it. How could the Church now expect that Spaniards would not assert their right to live as they pleased, to educate their children as they pleased, to marry as they pleased and be buried as they pleased? He was not calling for revenge, simply for justice. The Republic must not repay the Church in its own coin of intolerance. But it must be firm in the assertion of its rights.

What De los Ríos wanted was some form of compromise which would permit the construction of a democratic society without excessive acrimony and, certainly, without violence. But it was not to be. Those to his Left were impatient with what they saw as half-measures (De los Ríos and his friends were not revolutionaries), while the Right rejected absolutely his analysis of the role of the Church in Spanish history. If Don Fernando obtained a huge ovation from the Republicans when he finished his long speech, the Right was equally delighted with the performance on this occasion of José María Gil Robles, a brilliant young lawyer from Salamanca, who in his reply to the Minister of Justice set out the conservative attitude to the Church and to the Republic. It was becoming increasingly clear that in backward Spain compromise was going to be difficult if not impossible. And, in fact, things were to grow progressively worse during the brief life of the Republic.[20]

On 16 October 1931 Manuel Azaña became Prime Minister. Small, fat and ugly, with a moon-like face spattered with moles, Azaña had a piercing mind, was a devastating orator and distinguished writer and soon became, with Fernando de los Ríos, one of the Republican politicians most hated by the Right. Azaña was an intimate friend of the Catalan actress Margarita Xirgu, and had been present when Lorca read *Mariana Pineda* to her and her company in 1927. Moreover he was the brother-in-law of Lorca's friend Cipriano Rivas Cherif, and in his review *La Pluma* had published some of the first poems by Federico to have appeared in the capital in the early twenties. Such contacts – and Lorca knew other Republican politicians – sharpened the poet's awareness of the issues at stake in the country and strengthened his determination to participate in the shaping of the New Spain.

Soon a splendid opportunity to do something useful was presented to him. Late on the night of 2 or 3 November 1931 Lorca burst into Carlos Morla Lynch's apartment in a state of feverish excitement and told the assembled company about a great project in which he was going to become involved: the creation of a university travelling theatre which, following the lines already laid down by the Teaching Missions, would perform classical works – Cervantes, Lope de Vega, Calderón de la Barca – in the villages and marketplaces of rural Spain, so bereft of culture.[21]

The original idea was not, it seems, Lorca's, but had appeared, as if by spontaneous combustion, among the students of Madrid University. No one seems to remember exactly how the first contacts were forged between the students and Lorca, although it is almost certain that they took place at the Residencia de Estudiantes. What is certain is that the poet immediately identified himself fully with the project, expressing his willingness to act as Artistic Director of the company if the nomination were ratified by the Students' Union (whose official support was absolutely necessary for the enterprise to be successful). The preliminary contacts were soon under way and Lorca explained the project to Fernando de los Ríos, who guaranteed government support.[22]

The Students' Union, whose President, Arturo Sáenz de la Calzada, was a close friend of Lorca, at once adopted the project as its own, elected the poet Artistic Director of the University Theatre and set up a committee, composed of members of both the Philosophy and Letters and Architecture Faculties, to plan and run the operation. It was proposed not only to construct a mobile theatre, which the students would take to the provinces during their vacations, but to establish in Madrid a permanent *barraca* or barn in which to perform plays throughout the year. The latter venture did not get off the ground – but the name, soon to become famous, stuck to the project as a whole, which became known as La Barraca.[23]

Lorca's enthusiasm that night in Morla Lynch's apartment was understandable. His plans to take a puppet theatre to the Alpujarras in Granada with Manuel de Falla had come to nothing, but now he was being offered a concrete project along similar lines with the possibility of making a real contribution to the Republic. It seemed too good to be true. To help him with the running of the theatre the students called upon a likeable but unambitious young playwright, Eduardo Ugarte, whose father had been one of Primo de Rivera's Ministers. Ugarte was proud of having a Basque mother, wore inordinately thick glasses, had a stout hairy body and yellow teeth, was already balding, asked so many questions that his fellow *barracos* soon nicknamed him 'Ugarte-qué' ('Ugarte-what?') and had recently returned from Hollywood, where he had gained some experience in the film world and met Chaplin and other stars of the moment.[24]

Ugarte was to be the poet's faithful right-hand man during the entire life of the Barraca. Intensely modest, it seems that he never once as much as took a bow. But behind the scenes he was stage-manager, stage-hand, critic, guide, comrade, prompter, stand-in make-up artist – whatever had to be done, Ugarte was the man. Lorca and Ugarte complemented each other perfectly, and the poet lost no opportunity to insist that the Barraca owed its success every bit as much to Ugarte as to him. 'I do everything the way I feel it,' he said once. 'He watches it all and tells me as we go along if I'm doing it correctly or not, and I always follow his advice because I know he's right. He's the critic that every artist needs to have with him.'[25]

In an interview published in *El Sol* on 2 December, Lorca explained that the fundamental aim of the new University Theatre was to help to educate people who for centuries had been deprived of seeing plays. He expressed his gratitude to the Minister of Education, Marcelino Domingo, who was supporting the venture, and to Fernando de los Ríos for his 'exquisite and paternal' sponsorship, and voiced the hope that the activities of the Barraca could be dovetailed into the existing structure of the Teaching Missions.[26] (This would prove to be impossible.) When, a few days later, De los Ríos replaced Domingo as Minister of Education, the viability of the enterprise was assured. Don Fernando, who soon became known as the 'father' of the

University Theatre, brought the strength of his personality to bear on his colleagues in the Cabinet, and a substantial government grant (100,000 pesetas annually) was made available to the students for the purchase of equipment and vans, the construction of a portable stage and to meet whatever other costs might arise. Suddenly, the Barraca was taking shape.[27]

If the Republicans were excited by the prospect of a students' theatre travelling up and down the country, the proto-fascists of the extreme Right soon began to take issue with the state-subsidized venture, which they considered as little more than a cover for the dissemination of Marxist propaganda inspired by the 'Jewish atheist' Fernando de los Ríos, whom they now nicknamed 'Minister for Lay Education'.[28] The Right made a special point of attacking the government subsidy awarded to the Barraca. On 24 March 1932 De los Ríos patiently explained in Parliament the reasons why, in his view, the Students' Union deserved this support. Under the Primo de Rivera regime, when the country was subjected to an ignoble despotism, was it not the students who had made a stand for decency? Had they not demonstrated extraordinary bravery? They deserved more, much more, than the grant that had been awarded. Moreover, who could object to their proposal to take theatre to the villages and marketplaces of Spain, motivated only by the urge to contribute to the betterment of the country?[29]

Meanwhile, Lorca and his colleagues were hard at work making preparations for the company's first tour. When auditions were held, the would-be actors were found to be products, in the most part, of the Instituto-Escuela, a liberal secondary school, inspired by the Free Teaching Institution, which had close connections with the Residencia de Estudiantes. The audition procedure was straightforward: the poet opened, more or less at random, a volume of Spanish classics and asked the candidate to read a few passages, in prose and verse, while he jotted down succinct observations on his or her diction, physical characteristics and so forth. Often those students who did not quite make the grade as actors found that they could be extremely useful to the theatre in other ways – as electricians, carpenters, make-up artists or drivers. As for the general functioning of the Barraca, it was decided from the beginning that there were to be no 'stars'. Anonymity was to be the rule. Moreover it was clear that there would be a considerable turnover in actors, given the fact that almost all of them were students subject to examination and other pressures.[30]

Lorca was able to count on the help of many painter friends, such as Benjamín Palencia, who designed the emblem of the Barraca (an actor's mask in the centre of a wheel against a blue background), Alfonso Ponce de León, Ramón Gaya and Santiago Ontañón, later to be joined later by José Caballero and Alberto Sánchez. The scenery designed by these artists was simple, modern and, of necessity, strictly functional: a stage measuring only eight yards by eight, which had to be erected and dismantled at speed, could not have a cumbersome or excessively ornate décor. On the contrary, it had to be pared down to the very essentials.

In accordance with the spirit of the first clause of the new Constitution, which stated emphatically that Spain was now a 'democratic Republic of workers of all kinds', the official 'uniform' of the men of the Barraca was a blue boilersuit, while the girls wore a simple blue and white dress. A Barcelona critic who met Lorca during one of the Barraca's performances commented that he looked more like a mechanic than a poet.[31] Naturally the uniform provoked sneers from the Right, particularly in view of the fact that many of the student actors were from well-off families.

Since the purpose of the Barraca was to educate while entertaining, in accordance with the Horatian precept, and to do this by performing Spanish classical theatre, it was not surprising that Lorca's instinct drew him first to Cervantes's *entremeses*, short plays or interludes. Three were selected: *The Cave in Salamanca*, *The Watchful Guard* and *The Two Talkers*, the last of which Lorca had produced in his puppet theatre in Granada eight years before. (In 1932 the play was still considered to have been written by Cervantes, an ascription today rejected by scholars.) As for the poet's decision to include in the repertoire Calderón de la Barca's miracle play *Life Is a Dream*, this gave rise to severe misgivings both from the Right and the Left – the former wondering how a 'Marxist' group could dare to put on a 'sacred' play, and the latter asking what a Republican company with a government subsidy was doing producing a 'Catholic' work. Lorca was above such petty considerations, and in the speech with which he used to introduce performances of the offending play he habitually explained that, as he saw it, Cervantes and Calderón represent the two sides to the Spanish temperament: the earthy, human side is the terrain of the author of *Don Quixote*, the spiritual that of Calderón. Between these two 'antagonistic poles', Federico claimed, the Spanish theatre always oscillates, and *Life Is a Dream* should not be seen simply as a dramatization of Catholic dogma.[32]

That explained the inclusion of Calderón in the repertoire, but why had the poet opted specifically for *Life Is a Dream*? One reason was that, apart from the intrinsic merits of the work, the miracle plays of Calderón's day had been produced in the public squares, exactly what the Barraca had in mind. Then the fact that Calderón's play had musical illustrations and lent itself to an almost balletic interpretation appealed greatly to the poet, with his interest in 'total theatre'. But it seems almost certain that there was another, more personal, reason, and that Lorca chose *Life Is a Dream* because he himself wanted to play the part of the Shadow (*Sombra*) – that is, of death. This at least is the view of some of the *barracos* who acted in the play. Certainly his Shadow was impressive, and a few seconds of film that survived the ravages of the Civil War have preserved for posterity (unfortunately without sound) something of the effectiveness of Lorca's performance as, swathed in Benjamín Palencia's black veils and capped by a strange, two-horned headpiece that almost hides his face, he moves like a ghost across the stage. Each time the sinister personage appeared he was pinpointed by a cold, metallic beam, suggestive of moonlight, and it is difficult to avoid the suspicion that in insisting on playing this part Lorca was indulging in a confrontation with his fear of death not dissimilar to that which Dalí and other friends had witnessed, a few years earlier, in the Residencia de Estudiantes, when the poet used to enjoy enacting his own demise and decomposition.[33]

Lorca was determined that the Barraca should take art, not 'literature', out into the countryside of Spain, putting on productions of the classics that would fire the imagination of the peasants and village folk by dint of both their simplicity and their modernity. The poet felt sure that, given the essentially Spanish quality of the works to be performed, the ordinary people they were going to meet on their tours would follow the plays with interest. He was to be proved right.

As for the training of the actors, many of the *barracos* have recalled that the poet insisted on imposing his criteria on their movements and gestures as well as on their diction, which had to be crystal clear.[34] Such attention to detail was of course vital given the total lack of experience on the part of most of the students who surmounted the hurdle of the auditions. It could even be said that that very lack of experience was an advantage, allowing Lorca to mould his young, eager and unprejudiced actors exactly according to his wishes. Little by little during the first six months of 1932, as rehearsals proceeded and the date of the first outing approached, the Barraca developed a unique style quite unlike that of any professional company then performing in Spain.

Lectures and Galicia

Between March and May 1932, while preparations were steaming ahead for the Barraca's inaugural tour, Lorca gave a series of lectures around the country, mainly under the auspices of the newly formed Committees for Intellectual Co-operation, an organization, strongly Republican in character, whose principal aim was to stimulate intellectual life in the provinces by inviting important speakers. Lorca gave five talks for the Committees during the first half of the year: in Valladolid ('The Architecture of *Cante Jondo*', 27 March), Seville (the same lecture, 30 March), the Galician towns of Vigo (the same lecture, 6 May), Santiago de Compostela (readings from the New York poems with commentaries, 7 May) and La Coruña ('The Architecture of *Cante Jondo*', 8 May) and, finally, Salamanca (the same lecture, 29 May). During this period, invited by other bodies, he gave his New York recital in Madrid (16 March) and San Sebastián (8 April).[35]

The poet's visits to the provinces always followed the same pattern. In the morning he would arrive in the town, where a group of young intellectuals and artists awaited him. After some preliminary sightseeing there would be an animated lunch. Then he would withdraw to his hotel, issuing forth a few hours later to see a bit more of the town before giving his lecture to what was almost always a full house. Afterwards, accompanied by a horde of admirers, he would initiate one of his famous nocturnal perambulations, dazzling everyone with his conversation, pointing out architectural details that no one else had seen, commenting on the other peculiarities he kept noticing, reciting poems, telling stories – and, if anyone could find him a piano, regaling the company with one of his impromptu folk-song sessions. Late at night the group would eat, still talking excitedly, in some friendly hostelry, and finally in the early hours of the morning the poet would tumble into bed. The following day, after perhaps reading the accounts of his lecture in the local press, he would be off, leaving behind him new friends, a poem or two, a drawing . . . and a feeling of awe among those who had just come into contact for the first time with his charismatic personality.

Lorca was delighted to have returned to Galicia. Since his first visit to these parts in 1916 with Martín Domínguez Berrueta, the green landscape of the north-east, with its mists, superstitions and sad music, had continued to fire his imagination, and he had added numerous Galician songs to his repertoire, culled both from the medieval Galician–Portuguese *Cancioneiros*, or songbooks, of the twelfth, thirteenth and fourteenth centuries,* and from his Galician friends in Madrid – people such as the young musician Jesús Bal y Gay, who lived at the Residencia de Estudiantes, the poet Eugenio Montes, another 'resident' (who had written a rave review of Buñuel's and Dalí's *Un Chien andalou* in *La Gaceta Literaria* when it was first shown in Paris and, more recently, of Lorca's *Poem of Cante Jondo*), Serafín Ferro, also a poet, and Ernesto Pérez Guerra.

Pérez Guerra had been born at El Ferrol, near La Coruña, in 1911, the son of a doctor and a schoolteacher. Tall, slim and handsome, he spoke Galician fluently and was a passionate nationalist. When in 1922, after his

---

* The *Cancionero da Vaticana*, the *Cancionero Colocci-Brancuti* and the *Cancioneiro de Ajuda*.

father's early death, the family moved to Madrid, that nationalism was exacerbated by the lad's intense nostalgia for his native landscape and the scorn which many Madrileños expressed for Galicia and its culture. Ernesto developed at school a hatred of Castile and Castilian centralism that was to remain with him throughout his life.[36]

Lorca and he met in 1931, when Federico was thirty-three and Ernesto twenty, and the poet was fascinated by the tall youth's looks, virulent espousal of the Galician cause and knowledge of the folksong of the region. By 1932 they knew each other well, and when Lorca returned to Galicia that year for the first time since 1916 he did so with all that Pérez Guerra had told him about those parts to the forefront of his mind.[37]

The poet's enthusiasm for the city of Santiago de Compostela knew no bounds. There was a thriving galaxy of young writers and artists in the town and, after the lecture, Federico was escorted by them on a late-night tour of the sights. In the group was a young student from La Coruña called Carlos Martínez Barbeito, who was as dazzled by the poet's charisma as was Lorca by the Galician's rare good looks. Fifteen years later Martínez Barbeito recalled that he and his friends had been deeply impressed, even a bit shocked, by the poet's clothes and shoes on that occasion, which were stridently American in style. Barbeito also noticed Lorca's stiff, swaying gait, and wondered about its causes. As they made their way through the narrow streets, conjuring up in their minds the pilgrims who had come here during the Middle Ages from every corner of the Christian world, Federico talked with what was even for him undue fluency. 'As we walked around the Cathedral,' wrote Martínez Barbeito, 'his astonishment was limitless at the sight of the huge Baroque squares flanked with noble buildings shrouded in a night-mist that made them seem even more phantasmagorical.' The poet's admiration reached its height when they entered the Plaza de la Quintana, with its famous flight of stairs running the whole width of one side of the square. 'It's like the stalls of a theatre!' exclaimed the poet.[38] He did not forget this first impression of the Quintana, and when the Barraca visited Santiago some months later he saw to it that the stage was erected there, in the square. He was also intrigued to discover that in the Middle Ages the plaza had been a cemetery, and in his poem 'Dance of the Moon in Santiago', composed some time later, with the help of Pérez Guerra, he made the moon sway, as if on her home territory, across the 'Quintana of the dead'.

Federico was so moved by Santiago that he soon felt the urge to express his feelings in a poem dedicated to the city, references to the projected composition appearing in the local press during his stay.[39] Before leaving he gave Carlos Martínez Barbeito a copy of a poem he had just written, which may have been the one alluded to in the newspapers. Martínez subsequently mislaid the manuscript (Lorca's original does not seem to have survived either), recalling in 1945 that the poem evoked, in a mood of deep melancholy, the landscape, damp and sea of Galicia.[40] It seems quite clear that there was no intention in Lorca's mind while in Santiago of writing a poem in Galician, however, a Romance language that, like any literary Spaniard, he could read with relative ease but which, naturally, he could not speak or write. Back in Madrid he read Pérez Guerra the poem he had written in Santiago. It was only then, or perhaps a little later, that the idea suddenly arose of their collaborating on a composition of similar theme in Galician.[41] Thus was written, that summer, 'Madrigal to the City of Santiago', in which the poet sought to express his impression of the city in the rain – the persistent rain of Galicia – and, at the same time, a vague amorous nostalgia:

> Chove en Santiago
> meu doce amor.
> Camelia branca do ar
> brila entebrecido o sol . . .*[42]

Lorca committed the poem to memory, and when he returned that autumn to Galicia with the Barraca he not only recited it frequently but handed it over for publication. The myth of the Andalusian poet capable of writing poems in Galician was born – when the truth was that without Pérez Guerra's collaboration the feat would have been impossible. If we can trust the latter's memory, the 'Madrigal' was the only poem in Galician written by Lorca that summer, the other five compositions of the collection *Seis poemas galegos* ('Six Galician Poems') being composed a few years later.[43]

At the end of May Lorca was in Salamanca. The poet had not been in the old university town since his visit with Martín Domínguez Berrueta in 1916, and the crowd of students and teachers who accompanied him through the streets on the night of his arrival were amazed at his ability to recall exactly his impressions of sixteen years earlier. Among the students was Berrueta's son Luis Domínguez Guilarte, who had not seen the poet since the friendly relations between Federico and his father had been so brutally severed in 1918, two years before the Professor's death. Lorca swore to Luis that he would never forgive himself for his treatment of his father, nor José Mora Guarnido for his part in the miserable affair.[44]

Before returning to Madrid, Lorca, Martínez Nadal and Morla Lynch

> *   It's raining in Santiago
> my sweet love.
> The sun, white camellia in the air,
> shines behind the clouds . . .

called on Miguel de Unamuno, whom the poet had first met in 1916 during the Berrueta visit. Unamuno, exiled by the Primo de Rivera regime, had now recovered his Mastership of the University and at the same time was an Independent Member of Parliament for Salamanca. He was one of the outstanding men in Spain, and it would have been unthinkable for Lorca and his friends to leave the city without paying their compliments. Unamuno, a supreme egoist, specialized in a very personal brand of monologue which made it difficult for others to get a word in edgeways. After insisting on reading one of his forthcoming newspaper articles to the visitors, he invited them to join him on a stroll through the town. In the open air the monologue continued, Unamuno interrupting it only to shake hands with the many passers-by who recognized him, or to wave at someone. Lorca was becoming impatient and decided to provoke a little incident. 'When you are in Madrid, Don Miguel, where do you take your walk?' he asked innocently, guessing at the reply. 'Along the Manzanares,' answered the philosopher, adding that in his view Madrid's tiny river had been grossly maligned by the poets. 'There I disagree, Don Miguel,' exclaimed Federico. 'Lope de Vega said something fabulous in *Santiago the Green*.' Unamuno had no option but to ask what it was, since he could not remember any allusion to the river in that play. The poet obliged:

> Manzanares claro,
> río pequeño,
> por faltarle el agua
> corre con fuego.*

Unamuno, impressed, took out his notebook. A few days later an article by the philosopher appeared in *El Sol*. It was entitled 'On the Banks of the Manzanares', and in it Don Miguel quoted, without mentioning Lorca, a 'pearl' by Lope de Vega – the little couplet Federico had recited in Salamanca.[45]

One of the focal points of Lorca's social life in Madrid at this time was Manuel Altolaguirre's flat in the Calle de Viriato. Altolaguirre, who had collaborated with Emilio Prados on *Litoral*, the Malaga review, was not only a fine poet but a compulsive printer, and had installed a press in his small flat on which he was now laboriously producing a new poetry magazine, *Héroe*, the first two numbers of which had appeared at the beginning of 1932. With the poet Concha Méndez, whom he married that June, Altolaguirre kept open house, and their flat became one of the favourite

---

> *   Clear Manzanares,
> tiny stream,
> because it has no water
> it flows with fire.

haunts of the fine group of young poets then writing in Madrid, and which included, as well as Lorca, Guillén, Alberti, Diego, Aleixandre, Salinas and Cernuda.[46] Six poems by Lorca appeared in the magazine, among them the sonnet 'Adam' and 'Ribera de 1910' ('Shore of 1910'), whose title was later changed to 'Your Childhood in Menton'. It was an act of some daring to publish 'Adam', given its overtly homosexual content; while, for those in the know, 'Shore of 1910' alluded very closely (if in suitably recondite language) to the poet's frustrated love life, with possible references to Dalí and Aladrén.

Lorca had become close friends at this time with a young Andalusian painter, José Caballero, who later designed sets for the Barraca, and been persuaded by him to take part in an exhibition of modern art to open in the painter's home town of Huelva on 26 June. Federico, no doubt remembering his 1927 exhibition in Barcelona exactly five years earlier, was pleased at this new opportunity to show his work, and sent eight drawings of surrealist tendency, including *The Death of Saint Radegunda*, which had reflected his anguished state of mind during his New York stay and was mentioned in the filmscript *Trip to the Moon*. Immersed as he was in the frantic preparations to get the Barraca on the road, Lorca was not able to be present at the exhibition, which ran for a week, and was vaguely amused to hear that the reaction of public and critics had been largely hostile.[47]

5

The Barraca and *Blood Wedding*

The Barraca Takes to the Road

On the morning of 10 July 1932 the Barraca set out amid great excitement for the old town of El Burgo de Osma, in the province of Soria, a hundred miles away. The caravan was made up of several vehicles – the Chevrolet lorry, bought with the government grant, which carried the portable stage, the scenery, props and other paraphernalia; two prison vans provided by the Police Department, drivers included, for the transport of the student actors (the bars on the windows had been removed); and several private cars.[1]

The vehicles travelled north on the Burgos road, crossed the Guadarrama mountains via the high pass of Somosierra and then, leaving the main highway, turned right in the direction of Riaza, arriving at five in the afternoon at their destination, where they were awaited by the local authorities. After refreshments the students began the laborious business of erecting the stage in the town's handsome main square, built in the seventeenth century. All went smoothly – it was the first time the stage had been assembled in public – and a few hours later the Barraca was ready to make its début.[2]

At ten o'clock the square was packed. Lorca came on to explain the aims of the University Theatre and to thank the people of El Burgo de Osma, who were about to be the first audience to see them perform. When he finished there was a loud burst of applause and then the first Cervantes 'interlude', *The Cave in Salamanca*, got under way, followed by *The Two Talkers* and *The Watchful Guard*. The evening, according to both the local and the Madrid press, was a great success: the audience loved the sets, the colours, the humour, the movements and gestures of the actors. Lorca was delighted and spoke enthusiastically with the reporters, explaining how the theatre was run and indicating the Barraca's itinerary over the following days.[3]

The next stop was San Leonardo, where bad weather forced the students to perform indoors,[4] and on 12 July they were in Vinuesa, a small town surrounded by dense pine forests made famous by Antonio Machado's long ballad 'La tierra de Alvargonzález' ('Alvargonzález's Land'). When the *barracos* arrived they met an unexpectedly hostile reaction from the inhabitants, many of whom were wealthy *indianos*, that is, people who had returned from America after making their fortunes. 'Imagine a little Castilian village, clustered around its church,' the Madrid Republican daily *Luz* asked its readers:

Suddenly two buses and a van arrive from which emerge dishevelled youths aged between eighteen and twenty wearing overalls. The Communists! people shouted. Suspicion, hostility, silence. Some shops refused to serve them food. But finally the suspicions receded.[5]

On 13 July the Barraca reached Soria itself, where it had been announced that the students would perform twice in the main square. But the weather got worse and through no fault of the *barracos* the management of the Principal Theatre, where the students were constrained to perform that evening, insisted on charging for tickets. The Barraca's right-wing enemies, always looking for an opportunity to discredit the company, moved in to the attack. How could the University Theatre, which received a substantial government grant, justify taking money for a performance, making it impossible at the same time for ordinary people to attend? It was a scandal![6] The students, denying that they had received a single peseta, announced that next day a free performance of the three interludes would take place in the main square. But the following morning another storm threatened and they decided that it was too much of a risk to erect the stage in the open air, opting instead to perform in the apse of the ruined Romanesque church of San Juan, on the banks of the nearby river Duero. As things would have it the expected storm did not break and the afternoon was delightful. But it was too late. The people of Soria were becoming impatient, and their pique increased when the special bus service to take them to San Juan was organized with great inefficiency.[7]

With so many factors against them the students were hardly in the right frame of mind to give their first public performance of *Life Is a Dream*, a difficult enough undertaking at the best of times. Moreover, their enemies were waiting for them among the audience. How did the trouble start? The accounts vary. In perhaps the earliest to be published, María del Carmen García Lasgoity, who played the Earth, said that soon after the performance began there were murmurs of protest and that Lorca twice ordered the lights on and asked for silence. Then, at the point where, as the Shadow, the poet had to ask Sin not to cut him short, that he would tell him what he wanted to know, a group of hecklers, no doubt waiting for this moment, shouted in unison, 'No, no, don't tell him!' and there was a hullaballoo. Finally it seems that the electricity failed, perhaps due to sabotage, plunging the already irate audience into darkness and bringing the show to a disastrous end amid jeers and a hail of stones fired by invisible hands. The police had to be called in to escort the students safely to their vehicles, which were in danger of being turned over. The wreckers, it seems certain, were Monarchist students who had travelled from Madrid with the express aim of ensuring that the Barraca's first performance in a provincial capital be a resounding failure. Events played into their hands, and they exploited their opportunity to the full.[8]

The success of the *barracos* in the nearby town of Almazán made up in large part for what had happened in Soria. Shortly after the performance started it began to rain, but the audience, mainly composed of peasants, was entranced and stayed on, even refusing to put up their umbrellas so as not to block the vision of the people behind. Accompanying the students were Fernando de los Ríos, the poet Dámaso Alonso and, among other well-wishers and relatives, a friend of Lorca's from Granada, the engraver Hermenegildo Lanz. Also present was a reporter from Madrid, who observed the audience closely during the performance. 'The people of the town of Almazán ranged behind us looked as if they were dreaming with their eyes open,' he wrote. 'Row upon row of peasant faces, smiling, in ecstasy, above all expectant, fearing and desiring what was going to happen next on the stage. And suddenly the expectation was relieved in a burst of laughter and applause.'[9] Two years later, while visiting Santander, on the northern coast, with the students, Lorca recalled that performance of *Life Is a Dream* in Almazán. 'It began to rain,' he said. 'All one could hear was the rain falling on the stage, Calderón's lines and the music accompanying them, with the peasants listening, deeply moved.'[10]

On the way back to Madrid there occurred the only accident to happen to the Barraca throughout its career, when, near the town of Medinaceli, a hundred miles from their destination, one of the police vans overturned on a corner. Several students were injured by broken glass, and there were fractured arms and a serious case of concussion. Federico, with Eduardo Ugarte in another vehicle, was horrified. Luckily there happened to be several doctors with the group, quite by chance, and they took charge of the situation. After the wounds had been cleaned and dressed, the now dejected caravan started off again for Madrid.[11]

The Barraca rounded off its first tour by giving a performance in the Residencia de Estudiantes of *The Two Talkers, The Watchful Guard* and the first part of *Life Is a Dream*. In the audience were not only those 'residents' who had not yet left for the holidays, but students attending the summer school held annually on the premises and one exceptional friend of the house: Miguel de Unamuno. The evening went off splendidly and Lorca was delighted – not least, it can be supposed, because the Barraca was in large part a product of the spirit of service to Spain that animated the university hostel so admirably run by Alberto Jiménez Fraud.[12]

The news of what had happened in Soria soon reached Madrid, where the right-wing press twisted the incident of the tickets in an obvious attempt to discredit not only the Barraca but Fernando de los Ríos and all those associated in any way with the newly founded University Theatre, particularly Lorca. *Gracia y Justicia*, the ultra right-wing satirical magazine, went further and, as well as accusing the *barracos* of swindling the public, made blatant insinuations about Lorca's homosexuality.[13] Another article in the same review sank so low as to accuse the *barracos* of taking work away from professional actors when, on the contrary, one of the consequences of the students' efforts was an increased demand for theatre in the provinces.[14] As for the Liberal and Republican commentators, they were sure that one of the reasons for the right-wing aggression in Soria was the fact that the Barraca, sponsored by a lay government, had 'dared' to stage what the traditionalists understood to be an exclusively 'Catholic' work. The analysis was probably largely correct.[15] Certainly what had happened in San Juan de Duero was an indication of how already, a year after the coming of the Republic, conservative opposition was becoming even more hostile. From this moment Lorca can have been in no doubt concerning the extent to which the Barraca, and he as its Artistic Director, were now considered enemies of the 'true Spain', the Spain of sword and mitre, the inquisitorial Spain that was busily plotting the downfall of the fledgling democracy that threatened its privileges.

The Barraca's enemies also got a good run for their money on the question of the University Theatre student actresses. At a time when in the mind of the Right to be an actress was almost tantamount to being a prostitute, the young ladies of the University Theatre naturally attracted sneers and insinuations of promiscuity. To think that five or six girls actually went on tour with twenty boys! What can they have got up to after the show? Despite the fact that the student actresses were accompanied by a *dueña*, and sleeping quarters were rigidly separated, the rumours of immorality continued to be spread, as were others concerning the vast amounts of choice food and drink reputedly consumed by the *barracos*. In fact expenditure was kept to an absolute minimum, in accordance with the seriousness of the enterprise, and accounts were faithfully rendered to the Students' Union.[16]

Despite all the nastiness, Lorca was satisfied with the outcome of the Barraca's first tour, and particularly elated by the reaction of the audiences in the small towns, which he felt proved that he and his friends had been right in believing that the theatre of the seventeenth century, Spain's 'Golden Age', could get through to ordinary people, even to illiterate peasants, when it was produced in a modern, lively, uncomplicated style. 'Cervantes and Calderón aren't archaeological relics,' the poet told the reporters emphatically, insisting that the simple village folk of Soria had positively enjoyed the plays.[17]

It all looked good, then, for the future of the Barraca. The poet talked excitedly about plans for the second outing and what they would do the following academic year in Madrid, when they hoped to perform modern European plays in premises lent by the Residencia de Estudiantes. There were also projects to launch a magazine, create a Society of Friends of the University Theatre, found a students' theatre club . . . Most of this came to nothing but there could be no doubt that the Barraca was already firmly on the way to becoming one of the most exciting cultural experiments of the day.[18]

At the end of July or beginning of August Lorca returned to his beloved Huerta de San Vicente in Granada with the express purpose of finishing *Bodas de sangre* ('Blood Wedding'), begun, almost certainly, the previous summer. There, while he listened over and over to gramophone records of the great *cante jondo* singer Tomás Pavón and of a Bach cantata, probably *Wachtet auf, ruft uns die Stimme* (BWV 140) – the music almost drove the rest of the household beserk – he completed the play in a few weeks, working feverishly day and night.[19] A year and a half later, in Buenos Aires, the poet explained that he could write only while listening to music, and that the third act of *Blood Wedding*, 'the bit with the moon and the wood, with death prowling,' was all in the Bach cantata he had listened to obsessively that summer.[20]

Lorca's stay at the Huerta coincided with an event that shook out of their complacency those who believed that the Republic was now fully consolidated, just over a year after its inauguration. On 10 August 1932 the Monarchist general José Sanjurjo staged a military *coup* against the Government in Seville. While the insurrection failed, it was suddenly plain for all to see that there was a right-wing conspiracy against the Republic. Sanjurjo's abortive *coup* was front-page news for several days in *El Defensor de Granada* while the poet worked on *Blood Wedding*, and when he left his desk the poet must have discussed the disturbing situation with his family.

Blood Wedding

It was four years since the day on which Lorca's eye had been caught by a short account appearing in the Madrid daily *ABC* about a mysterious assassination that had just been perpetrated before a wedding near the Andalusian town of Níjar, in the province of Almería. Although Lorca was no Zola he was in the habit of proclaiming that his work derived from real events, and where *Blood Wedding* is concerned we know that he followed the Níjar case closely in the reports that appeared during the week in the Madrid press. In these it was finally revealed that the dead man, Curro Montes Cañadas, was a previous lover of the bride who, after stealing the lady the night before the wedding, had been killed by the groom's outraged cousin. In particular, it is almost certain that Lorca read the detailed accounts of the crime and the legal investigation following it which appeared for six consecutive days in one of his favourite newspapers, the *Heraldo de Madrid*. The coincidences between the reports sent from the *Heraldo* correspondent in Almería and *Blood Wedding* make such a conclusion almost inevitable.[21]

Consider, first, the case of Francisca Cañadas Morales, the model for Lorca's Bride, who was about twenty when the tragedy occurred. Francisca, who lived on an estate near Níjar with her father – her mother, like the Bride's, had died some years ago – was no Helen. Lame and squint-eyed, with prominent teeth, she had none the less quite a pleasing face, was of independent character and possessed a certain charm which was appreciated by the local gallants who, no doubt, coveted even more the substantial dowry which it was known her father would settle on her when she married. For several years Francisca had been unofficially engaged to a modest labourer, Casimiro Pérez Pino, an uninspiring man who, pressured by his ambitious brother and sister-in-law, saw in his marriage with the lame heiress his best chance of moving up in the world.[22] In *Blood Wedding*, drawing on the newspaper reports, Lorca developed this theme – the avarice of people desperate to acquire property of their own and obsessed by the wealth of their neighbours.

If Francisca had agreed to marry Casimiro, however, it was for a very different reason: because her cousin Curro Montes Cañadas, whom she loved passionately, was showing no interest in accompanying her to the altar. Curro, the model for Lorca's Leonardo, was, unlike Casimiro, handsome and dashing (as befitted a young man with a name worthy of an Andalusian bandit or bullfighter), and much admired by the ladies. Lorca no doubt took good note of revelations such as the following, published by the *Heraldo*:

335

Francisca had had a love relationship with her cousin and kidnapper when she was almost a child, a relationship which was broken off when her parents discovered what was going on. Curro Montes, moreover, was a great womanizer and had a girlfriend on every estate. This factor was largely responsible for the opposition of Francisca's family.[23]

The theme of love lost, of the love that could or should have been, but which is thwarted, is fundamental in all Lorca's work and, as we know, reflects his own early experience. In the Níjar tragedy the poet found a powerful metaphor, it seems fair to assume, for that experience, and in *Blood Wedding* exploited it to the full. Leonardo and the Bride, like their real-life prototypes, have experienced a passionate adolescent love which lasted for three years, a love frustrated by economic considerations and almost forgotten by their neighbours. Nature had 'made' the two for each other, but society frustrated her designs. Tragedy is the inevitable outcome.

Lorca must have read with fascination the account of the dramatic conversation that took place between Francisca and Curro in the farmhouse kitchen a few hours before the wedding party set out at dawn for the church (a traditional practice in the parched Almerian plain in order to avoid the worst of the pitiless summer heat). Curro, one of the first guests to arrive – another detail lifted from the newspapers – overheard a violent altercation taking place between Francisca and her fiancé and suddenly, realizing that the girl was marrying Casimiro only out of spite and that she still loved him, Curro, had decided to run away with her. When the bridegroom withdrew, apparently indisposed, Curro persuaded his cousin to flee with him to the church, where they would try to convince the priest to marry them before the guests found out what was happening. Francisca told the judge:

Since I liked my cousin more than my fiancé, and since what he offered me was better than the life I would have had with Casimiro, I thought about it alone in my room while I was putting on my wedding dress, and when my cousin, going round to the back of the house, came to my room, I said: 'It's now or never. Take me away with you before Casimiro wakes up and my brother-in-law arrives.' And we escaped on Curro Montes's horse.[24]

In *Blood Wedding*, following this account, Lorca makes the Bride take the initiative, go down the stairs first, put new reins on the horse and fix on Leonardo's spurs.

Not only Leonardo's temerity but his skill as a horseman derives from his model, Curro. Given the fact that the horse is a potent sexual symbol throughout Lorca's work, it is not surprising that the poet took note of this detail, stressed in the newspaper accounts, making the relationship between Leonardo and his steed a leitmotif of the play. The horse takes Leonardo to the Bride's cave-dwelling almost against its owner's wishes, as if possessed of a superior will of its own; and the animal is the disquieting protagonist of the lullaby Leonardo's mother-in-law sings to the child. Once again Lorca, with his myth-making capacity, has developed the journalistic detail.

If Lorca drew on the newspaper reports for his characterization of Leonardo, he also took careful note of what they had to say about the groom, Casimiro Pérez Pino, who was not only introspective but so bashful that a few hours before his wedding he had still not yet kissed his bride-to-be, Francisca, and was completely under her thumb – and that of her widowed father.[25] Again *Blood Wedding* stays close to its source for, in the play, the Mother insists that her son is a virgin and that he has never tasted wine; while he promises her that he will always do what she tells him. This dominating mother reminds us of Don Perlimplín's (already dead when the play begins, but the references to her make it quite evident that she was of the stifling variety) and she may at a deeper level reflect Lorca's own domestic experience as a child, for Doña Vicenta Lorca was, by all accounts, a formidable figure in her own way. At all events the Bride, like the character with the same name in *When Five Years Pass*, explains to the Mother with brutal clarity, after the deaths, the difference between Leonardo and the Bridegroom, perhaps implying that the latter's lack of virility was not unrelated to maternal overprotectiveness:

I was a woman scorched and full of sores inside and out, and your son was a little drop of water from which I hoped for children, land, health; but the other was a dark river, full of branches, who brought me the whisper of rushes and a song between his teeth. I ran along with your son, who was like a little child of water, but the other sent hundreds of birds to trip me up wherever I walked and which placed their frost on my poor thwarted woman's wounds, on the wounds of a girl courted by fire! I didn't want to, you must believe me; I didn't want to! Your son was my desire and I didn't deceive him, but the other swept me away like a tidal wave, like a butt from a mule's head, and would always have swept me away, always, always, always, though I were an old woman and all your son's children held me back by the hair![26]

Pondering on the Níjar crime, Lorca must surely have remembered his childhood months in Almería and excursions through the arid surroundings of the town with Antonio Rodríguez Espinosa. The *Heraldo de Madrid* correspondent underlined the terrible dryness of the terrain in his reports on the tragedy, noting that he had found 'fields full of stones and calcinated by the sun with scarcely a tree as far as the eye could stretch.'[27] The landscape of *Blood Wedding*, where 'it doesn't get cooler even at dawn' – a landscape that symbolizes the erotic thirst of Leonardo and the Bride – was undoubtedly inspired by that of Almería (although there is no explicit reference to the

337

locality in the play) and conjures up the barren ochre desert lying between the Sierra Alhamilla and Sierra de Gata where rain is almost unknown and, until the recent drip system of watering under plastic was developed, only cactus, esparto grass and the occasional palm tree could survive. But while this was the landscape that inspired the play, Lorca decided to set the action more inland than Níjar, which, in fact, is only some twelve miles from the sea. The wood of the third act, moreover, with its 'great humid trunks' and its river, is pure invention – Almería's plain has nothing to offer in this line – and was already prefigured in *When Five Years Pass*, with its debt to *A Midsummer Night's Dream*. Perhaps, too, as he sat in the Huerta de San Vicente that summer working frantically at the play, Lorca remembered his childhood adventures in the damp poplar groves of the Vega along the banks of the Genil and the Cubillas, as dark and mysterious as any imaginative child, or poet, could wish.

Lorca also made a highly significant change when he substituted a cave for El Fraile, the farm where Francisca Cañadas lived with her father, presumably thinking not only of the Gypsy caves of Granada's Sacromonte but of those at Purullena, near Guadix, which he had visited with Manuel de Falla, and which Gerald Brenan was to describe later in *South from Granada*.[28] Doubtless the change was made for reasons of symbolism, and one critic has observed with insight that the cave situates the action 'in the most telluric landscape of Andalusia', on the boundary between observable reality and prehistory.[29]

As for the wedding itself, Lorca seems to have noted the details provided by the *Heraldo* correspondent concerning the lavish preparations for the wedding celebrations, which were to have lasted into the early hours of the following morning. Feasting, music, dancing, drinking – the farmhouse at El Fraile had been decked out in fine style and guests were invited from all over the dry and dusty plain.[30] But there was no marriage and no feast. Lorca, as *Blood Wedding* began to take shape, probably realized that, given the musical, choreographic and stage-design potential of the play, his lovers' flight simply had to take place *after* the ceremony, in the midst of the merry-making back at the Bride's cave: in this way he would be able to use music to the fullest effect and to orchestrate a colourful scene while, at the same time, both heightening the dramatic impact of the discovery of the elopement and drawing on the traditional Spanish obsession with honour. (There is a difference, after all, between running away with someone before or after a marriage ceremony.)

As for the death of Curro Montes, clarified when José Pérez Pino, the groom's brother, admitted that he was responsible for the shooting, Lorca realized that in the play he would have to depart from the real events. Pérez

Pino, as he made his way on horseback towards El Fraile, had come face to face with the fleeing lovers before those at the farmhouse had even noticed that they were missing. There was no question, therefore, as in *Blood Wedding*, of the 'two bands' setting out in pursuit of the fugitives – and no question of the outraged groom having participated in the death of Curro Montes, as he does in that of Leonardo in *Blood Wedding*.[31] Having decided that for his purposes both men must die, each at the hands of the other, it was in character for Lorca to substitute two sacrificial knives for the banal revolver with which Curro Montes was killed. The knife, which appears at the beginning of the play in an obviously premonitory role, is present throughout the action and, fittingly, *Blood Wedding* ends with a ritual hymn to the instrument sung alternately by the Mother and the Bride. It could be said that the knife is the protagonist of the work.

But where Lorca perhaps departs most radically from his source material is in his delineation of Leonardo as the victim of ineluctable fate, the youngest in the line of a family of killers who have already reduced the Bride's family to its last male. There is no indication in the newspaper accounts that in Curro Montes's background there was any history of violence (although we may be permitted to wonder what the groom's brother, José Pérez Pino, was doing riding to a wedding with a loaded revolver in his pocket). Lorca, conscious of working within the tragic tradition, had to ensure that Leonardo was the victim of fate, and chose to do so by making him almost biologically incapable of resisting the temptation to abscond with the bride.

We need insist no further in trying to separate out what Lorca took from the events, as reported in the press, and what he made up. While his debt to such accounts is beyond question, the result transcends the rural tragedy that had first fired his imagination in 1928 – an imagination that in the third act of the play reaches one of its finest flowerings when, in the wood scene, everyday reality is transformed as the moon comes to preside over the sacrificial deaths of lover and groom.

Lorca must have been conscious as he completed *Blood Wedding* that he had succeeded in writing a play of Andalusian inspiration quite unlike the pseudo-Andalusian works made popular at this time by the Alvarez Quintero brothers, works all fun, clever talk and inconsequence. In *Blood Wedding* there are no concessions to southern speech (with its tendency to drop intervocalic consonants and final 's's), and local colour is reduced to an absolute minimum. Clearly Lorca had set himself the task of writing a timeless tragedy in the Mediterranean tradition, ironing out the picturesque and the superficial. For this he could find no model in the contemporary Spanish drama – but he could and did in the Anglo-Irish. In, to be precise, J. M. Synge's *Riders to the Sea*.

Lorca had probably read the play in the translation published in 1920 by Juan Ramón Jiménez and Zenobia Camprubí, and we also know that his friend Miguel Cerón read it to him, translating from the original English, at around the same time. The primitive world reflected in Synge's play has many points of contact with Lorca's Andalusia, despite the differences of climate and customs, and Cerón remembered the poet's great enthusiasm for the Irishman's achievement.[32] Perhaps, pondering on *Riders to the Sea*, Lorca realized that in order to write a modern tragedy it was not necessary to attempt a futile pastiche of those of ancient Greece and that, in certain rural communities, such as still existed in Andalusia or the west of Ireland, it was still possible to recapture the flavour of life lived in close contact with the soil and the seasons.

To be more specific, it is difficult not to see in the mother of *Riders to the Sea* a clear forerunner of Lorca's in *Blood Wedding*. Maurya lives only for her last son and knows in her bones that he too is going to be lost to her. Which is precisely the case with the Mother in *Blood Wedding*. When the dreaded death finally occurs, both mothers try to find consolation in the fact that now, at last, they will be able to sleep peacefully, for there is no further cause for anguish. Maurya murmurs on hearing that Bartley has been pitched by his horse into the sea:

They're all gone now, and there isn't anything more the sea can do to me . . . I'll have no call now to be up crying and praying when the wind breaks from the south, and you can hear the surf is in the east, and the surf is in the west, making a great stir with the two noises, and they hitting one on the other. I'll have no call now to be going down and getting Holy Water in the dark nights after Samhain, and I won't care what way the sea is when the other women will be keening.[33]

These words seem to have made a deep impression on Lorca. After the death of her son, the Mother of *Blood Wedding* rejects a kindly invitation to move in temporarily with a neighbour:

I want to be here. At peace. They're all dead now. This midnight I'll sleep, without being terrified of guns or knives. Other mothers will be up leaning out of the window, lashed by the rain, looking for their sons' faces. Not me. I'll turn my dreams into a cold ivory dove to carry frosty camellias to the cemetery. No, not cemetery. Not cemetery: earthen bed, a cradle to hide them and rock them in the sky.[34]

There was, however, one striking difference between Synge and Lorca: while the former's work was the result of a conscious attempt to assimilate the language and modes of feeling of the people of the west of Ireland (an attempt not always successful), Lorca's sprang from an early and total immersion in the folk poetry, music and speech of rural Andalusia. What in

Synge required application and study, to Lorca came naturally.[35] It was his own life-blood, as he once explained:

I'm more interested in the people who inhabit the landscape than in the landscape itself. I can look at a mountain for a quarter of an hour; but then I immediately run and talk to the shepherd or woodcutter who lives on the mountain. Afterwards, when I'm writing, I recall these dialogues and up comes the authentic Andalusian expression. I've a huge storehouse of childhood recollections in which I can hear the people speaking. It's poetic memory and I trust it implicitly.[36]

As for the theme of *Blood Wedding*, it is formulated unforgettably by the mysterious Woodcutters, who comment, chorus-like, on the lover's flight:

SECOND WOODCUTTER: One must follow one's heart's desire; they did right in fleeing.
FIRST WOODCUTTER: They were deceiving each other and finally the blood had its way.
THIRD WOODCUTTER: The blood!
FIRST WOODCUTTER: One must follow the way of the blood.
SECOND WOODCUTTER: But the blood that escapes is drunk by the earth.
FIRST WOODCUTTER: And so? It's better to be dead without blood than alive with it gone bad.[37]

Lorca, always obsessed by the subject of erotic frustration, knew that there can hardly be a worse loneliness than that of an unhappy marriage in a situation allowing of no escape, no second chance, and developed the theme in *Yerma*. If Leonardo and the Bride had followed at the right time the call of instinct instead of yielding to socio-economic pressures, the tragedy would not have occurred. Yerma and Doña Rosita have a similar fate. A fate against which Lorca's last tragic heroine, Adela, rebels furiously and vainly in the *The House of Bernarda Alba*.

Lorca said once that the only hope for happiness lies in 'living one's instinctual life to the full'.[38] *Blood Wedding* can be understood as a gloss on that belief. In it the poet succeeded in creating a medium that allowed him to express the deepest elements in his personality while at the same time to deploy his multiple talents; and, as he packed his bags for Madrid, he may have sensed that at last, after so many frustrating experiences in the theatre, he had produced a work capable of reaching a mass audience. And of making money.

The Barraca and More Lectures

On 21 August 1932 the Barraca set off for Galicia and Asturias, performing without hitch in La Coruña, Santiago de Compostela, Vigo, Pontevedra, Villagarcía de Arosa, Ribadeo, Grado, Avilés, Oviedo and Cangas de Onís.[39]

Back in Madrid that September Lorca read *Blood Wedding* to various friends and began to think about who might be the best actress to play the Mother. He opted eventually for the Argentinian Lola Membrives (whose parents were from Cadiz), then at the height of her fame. Lola loved the play but explained that she could not possibly produce it that season owing to her many previous commitments.[40] Disappointed, the poet turned to another famous actress, Josefina Díaz de Artigas, who on the death of her husband in 1931 had withdrawn from the theatre but now wanted to return – and if possible with a smash hit. When the poet, accompanied by Ignacio Sánchez Mejías, read her the play she was ecstatic: it was just what she had been waiting for and, backed by her artistic adviser, the dramatist Eduardo Marquina, to whom Lorca owed so much, she immediately agreed to produce it the following spring.[41]

At the beginning of October the Barraca travelled south to take part in the University of Granada's fourth centenary celebrations. Federico's excitement was intense – he was returning home to show 'his' theatre to his family, friends and fellow citizens – and this showed in the words with which he introduced the performance of *Life Is a Dream*. He was deeply moved, he said, to be with the Barraca in the very theatre (the Isabel la Católica) in which, as a child, he had seen his first performances of Spanish classics.[42]

The following day the students performed their three Cervantes interludes in the patio of the ex-Artillery Barracks of Santo Domingo, to an audience composed mainly of workers and schoolchildren. Lorca gave pride of place in the front row to Dolores Cuesta, the family's old servant from whom he had learned so much and who, years earlier, had been one of the principal participants in his dressing-up games.[43]

During their few days in Granada Federico made a point of introducing his student friends to the delights of the town, taking them to a Gypsy *zambra* in the Sacromonte and, of course, up to the Alhambra, where they were entertained in the famous tavern *El Polinario* by the guitarist Angel Barrios and his Iberia Quartet.[44] One of the *barracos*, Arturo Sáenz de la Calzada, has recalled an incident that deserves to be mentioned. They had been accompanied to Granada by the young millionaire Luis Villalba, a great admirer of Lorca and of the Barraca, and Federico, piqued because the local bourgeoisie was giving the student theatre the cold shoulder, decided to make a subtle protest. Villalba had come down in a magnificent open car, and Lorca persuaded him to drive him up and down the streets of central Granada, as visibly as possible, hoping to irritate the burghers by the display of such opulence and to demonstrate at the same time that it was possible for a Republican to have rich friends. Whether the performance had the required effect has not been recorded.[45]

After Granada it was the turn of Madrid to put the Barraca through its paces. On 25 and 26 October the students played in the Central University, and passed the test with flying colours. One critic, Miguel Pérez Ferrero, was astonished by Lorca's performance in *Life Is a Dream*, and found himself in a dilemma. Was Federico better as a poet, a producer or an actor? It was difficult to say, for with Lorca the surprises never ended.[46]

As preparations went ahead for the production of *Blood Wedding*, Federico started lecturing again. His first stop was Pontevedra, in Galicia, where on 20 November he talked about the Spanish artist María Blanchard, who had just died in Paris. In Pontevedra there was an enthusiastic group of young painters and writers who had launched a modest review, *Cristal*, the fifth issue of which was circulating when Lorca arrived in the town. The sixth included a sonnet supplied during his visit by the poet, who perhaps did not reveal that it had already appeared in Cuba in 1930.[47]

From there Lorca made his way to Lugo where, on 22 November, he repeated his María Blanchard talk. Here he made the great revelation (withheld in Pontevedra) that he had composed a poem in Galician, although he almost certainly omitted to point out that without the help of Ernesto Pérez Guerra the task would have been unthinkable. Before leaving for Madrid he left a copy of the 'Madrigal' with his friends, who published it in the December issue of their review *Yunque*, whence it was taken by other Galician periodicals and even by *El Sol* in Madrid, which expressed some astonishment at the poet's latest achievement.[48]

Then, on 16 December, Lorca was in Barcelona to give his New York recital (for the fourth time). The event took place in the luxurious setting of the Hotel Ritz – and began late, the poet turning up considerably after the appointed time, accompanied by one of his latest acquisitions, according to the Catalan poet J. V. Foix: an unidentified and somewhat effeminate-looking youth with red shoes.[49] Despite the initial setback – the Catalans are the most formal people in Spain and this was a distinguished gathering – the evening went off excellently. Among the audience were many friends the poet had made during his visit to Barcelona in 1927 but not, it seems, Sebastià Gasch. Probably the critic deemed it more diplomatic to stay away after his review of *Poem of Cante Jondo*, in which, as we saw, he had deprecated Lorca's 'surrealist vein' with an insensitivity that must have surprised Federico. As against Gasch's view of Lorca's New York poetry, the opinion of the young critic Guillermo Díaz-Plaja is worth mentioning. Díaz-Plaja was in the audience that evening and listened to Lorca's recital with near awe. In an article published shortly afterwards he wrote that the most interesting aspect of the poet's new mode was the persistence of the primitive elements that had appeared in his earlier work – the sun and the moon, rivers and the sea – but now 'applied to a new imagery, naturally more complex and audacious'. Where others saw only 'surrealism', Díaz-Plaja rightly perceived a highly personal idiom, influenced undoubtedly by surrealism but with its own implacable poetic logic.[50]

Lorca returned immediately to Madrid where, on 19 December, in the Teatro Español, the Barraca performed *Life Is a Dream* and the three interludes to an audience that included the President of the Republic, Niceto Alcalá-Zamora; the Prime Minister, Manuel Azaña; the President of the Parliament, Julián Besteiro; Fernando de los Ríos and many other Ministers, Deputies and public figures. The evening was triumphant and practically all the Madrid newspapers published glowing critiques. As might have been expected, those appearing in the conservative press were less enthusiastic.[51] The Right felt convinced that the Barraca was not simply a Republican organization whose function was to take plays to the people, but a propaganda machine serving the interests of 'Marxist', 'Jewish' and 'Communist' agitators determined to bring the Red Revolution to Spain. Such charges were, of course, ludicrous.

The Barraca spent the last few days of December in Murcia and Elche, and on New Year's Eve performed *Life Is a Dream* to an enthusiastic audience in Alicante. Over these days Lorca renewed his friendship with the poet Pedro Salinas and with Juan Guerrero Ruiz, editor a few years earlier of the excellent Murcian review *Verso y prosa*. Guerrero was a good amateur photographer and took several pictures of Federico on the beach at Alicante: with his back to the sea and wearing his Barraca boilersuit, the poet would look just like a machine operator if it were not for his impeccably polished leather shoes, quite as shiny as those of his more conventionally dressed companions.[52]

In Murcia Lorca met a dark-skinned, highly gifted and pitifully poor young shepherd–poet from the town of Orihuela, Miguel Hernández, who was correcting the proofs of his first book, *Perito en lunas* ('The Moon Specialist'). Federico warmed to the lad, then only twenty, expressed his admiration for the poems he had read to him and promised to do all he could to promote him in Madrid. But when the book was published a few weeks later amid a deafening silence Lorca failed to review it himself, as Hernández had begged him to, and received a series of disconsolate letters from Orihuela asking desperately for help.[53] Federico did his best to console the young poet, telling him (it was not strictly true) that his own first book of poems had been similarly ignored. He advised him to keep working, fighting and struggling and, above all, not to succumb to the temptation of vanity. 'Your book is powerful,' he wrote. 'It has lots of interesting things and reveals, to those who know, a *virile passion*, but it doesn't have more *balls*, to use your expression, than the books by the established poets. You must calm down a bit . . .'[54]

The year had ended brilliantly for the Barraca, which in the six months since it first set out had more than justified the hopes placed in it by the Government. Over the next three years Lorca's life was to be inextricably bound up with the University Theatre in whose creation he had played such a vital role. At times, it is true, his involvement with the Barraca deflected his attention from his own work, but in general he benefited hugely from the experience, which taught him not only a great deal about the theatre, but about people and the reality of contemporary Spain.

6

1933

Breakthrough with *Blood Wedding*

Two events, one national and one international, dominated the Spanish newspapers at the beginning of 1933: the Casas Viejas massacre and the rise to power of Adolf Hitler.

Casas Viejas, today renamed Benalup de Sidonia, was a village in Cadiz belonging to the Duke of Medina Sidonia where, on 11 January 1933, some 500 anarchist labourers, sick of living in almost sub-human conditions, proclaimed the Libertarian Communist Revolution. They surrounded the barracks of the hated Civil Guard and in the ensuing fray a sergeant and a guard were killed. The orders from Madrid were uncompromising: the rebellion must be put down immediately. On 12 January a strong contingent of Civil Guard and Assault Guard (the new Republican constabulary) arrived in the village under the command of Captain Manuel Rojas Feigespán. A group of anarchists had shut themselves into a cottage and, when they refused to surrender, Rojas ordered that the house be set on fire. Only two escaped the flames – and they were mown down by a hail of bullets. The next day Rojas executed a further twelve men on the mere suspicion that they had been involved in the attack on the Civil Guard barracks.[1]

The massacre immediately became the political issue of the day. Was it true that the Prime Minister, Manuel Azaña, had given the order to 'shoot them in the belly'? On the face of it it seemed impossible, but the rumour, fanned by right-wing malevolence, soon acquired the status of historical fact. During the following weeks what had happened in Casas Viejas was clarified with a politically suicidal lethargy. Finally it turned out that Azaña had been misled by the police authorities. A full inquiry was ordered and, on 7 March, the Prime Minister admitted in the House that there had been illegal executions. The head of the police was prosecuted and Captain Rojas, who claimed that he had simply obeyed the latter's orders, sentenced to twenty-one years in prison.[2]

As a result of the Casas Viejas affair the Government lost credibility, despite its determination that those responsible should be brought to trial, and over the next months the Right lost no opportunity to use the unfortunate episode as a weapon against Azaña.

Meanwhile, on 30 January, Hitler had been named Chancellor of Germany, and the Spanish press was following closely the course of events in that country. The burning of the Reichstag on 27 February, the dissolution of the political parties in March and the accordance of full powers to Hitler, the Concordat with Rome, the growing persecution of Jews and intellectuals . . . all of this received wide coverage in Spain. The Republican and left-wing newspapers, as they contemplated the vertiginous growth of fascism in Germany, with the National Socialist Party now in sole control, had no illusions about what was happening behind the scenes in Spain where the Right, encouraged by the downfall of the Weimar Republic (on whose constitution that of the Spanish Republic was based), was busily plotting the collapse of democracy south of the Pyrenees.

Preparations for the première of *Blood Wedding*, with sets and costumes by Santiago Ontañón and Manuel Fontanals, were well advanced by the beginning of March. Lorca himself directed the rehearsals, taking particular care over the play's subtle shifts from prose to poetry, prohibiting any over-emphasis on the part of the actors and controlling the rhythm of each scene as if he were conducting a symphony. His brother Francisco recalled that the poet needed all his skill, experience and patience to get the actors, unused to such total theatre, to do what he wanted. 'Particularly difficult', he writes, 'was the scene in which the Bride leaves for the church, a scene fragmented into numerous entries by different characters from different and carefully graduated levels, with the alternating play of female and male voices speaking lines of extreme rhythmic complexity.' 'It has to be mathematically precise!' the poet would exclaim, interrupting the actors again and again until he produced the desired result.[3]

The latter were astonished at Lorca's knowledge of stagecraft, much of which had been acquired through his work with the Barraca, and were grateful for his absolutely clear notion of what he wanted to achieve. The young actress Amelia de la Torre, who played the part of Death, never forgot Federico's roar of disapproval when she appeared in the first rehearsal as an old woman with her face painted white and wearing no lipstick. 'Death is young and beautiful!' Lorca had insisted, perhaps remembering Cipriano Rivas Cherif's production of Cocteau's *Orphée* a few years earlier.[4]

Lorca, although by this time undoubtedly the most famous young poet in

Spain, had still not had a major success in the theatre. Was he going to achieve it now? The veteran critic of the *Heraldo de Madrid*, Juan González Olmedilla, asked himself this question in his column on 8 March, the morning of the première. He had seen part of the dress rehearsal and felt sure *Blood Wedding* was the 'great work' he and others had been waiting for from the poet. Moreover, said Olmedilla, the play had something for everyone – for the intellectuals and for the ordinary theatre-going public. It had to be a success.[5]

He was right, and *Blood Wedding* scored an all-out hit. Madrid's leading intellectuals, writers and artists were there in strength, with a liberal sprinkling of society people and politicians, and there was not a spare seat in the house. The Nobel Prize playwright Jacinto Benavente, now in his late sixties and quite out of touch with contemporary dramatic trends, attended; so did Miguel de Unamuno and Fernando de los Ríos, who was no doubt delighted with his former pupil; while representing Lorca's generation could be seen the poets Vicente Aleixandre, Luis Cernuda, Jorge Guillén, Pedro Salinas and Manuel Altolaguirre, sitting among students from the Barraca.[6]

After the first scene, the audience, if we can believe the right-wing daily *La Nación*, was somewhat indecisive in its response, but from the second onwards there was constant applause. At the end of each scene the curtain rose and fell several times, and the performance even had to be interrupted twice to allow Lorca to take a bow. When the final curtain fell the audience went wild and Federico, Ontañón and Fontanals joined Josefina Díaz de Artigas (who had played the Bride, not, as Lorca originally intended, the Mother) and the other actors on the stage amidst scenes of great emotion and joy.[7]

Next day the reviews were almost wholly favourable, although some critics were a bit unhappy about the appearance of the moon on stage. Clearly Lorca had touched a nerve, or several nerves, common to all Spaniards. At least three critics pointed out the vital connection between *Blood Wedding* and *Gypsy Ballads*, which seemed to them to spring from a common inspiration, Lorca's close friend Melchor Fernández Almagro concentrating on the mythical aspect of the poet's Andalusia. *Blood Wedding* had to do 'not with the Andalusians of east or west, the mountains or the coast', wrote Melchor, 'but with the Andalusians in their deepest historical and psychological projection . . . Arabs, Romans, Greeks, the offspring of God knows what classical myths: the Sun and the Moon'. As for the latter, Melchor had no doubt that she is the divinity who presides over the poet's poetic universe, 'the most expressive cypher or emblem of his world'. Just in case there should be any confusion about the matter Fernández Almagro added:

And of course this is not a Moon that has anything to do with the literary moon of the Romantics and Symbolists – Musset, Laforgue – but the real and mythical moon of the Celtiberians, who offered up to her their hymns, bonfires, dances and songs. The full moon of Turdetania.*[8]

Melchor had proved, once again, that he was Lorca's most perceptive (as well as best-informed) contemporary critic.

Blood Wedding ran for thirty-eight performances before Josefina Díaz de Artigas ended her season at the Beatriz on 8 April, and constituted Lorca's first box-office success. From this moment on the poet began to achieve the financial independence which for so many years had obsessed and eluded him.[9]

Meanwhile Spanish fascism, stimulated by the progress of the German and Italian regimes, was on the move. On 16 March 1933 the first issue of a new periodical, *El Fascio*, appeared in Madrid. The publisher was Manuel Delgado Barreto, editor of the satirical review *Gracia y Justicia*, among whose favourite targets were Lorca and the Barraca. One of Barreto's close collaborators was José Antonio Primo de Rivera, son of the dictator, who at this moment was in the process of forming a Fascist Party, which would crystallize a few months later as the Falange Española or Spanish Phalanx.[10] Lorca's position on what was happening in Germany, and on fascism in general, became public knowledge at this time. At the beginning of April he joined the recently formed Association of Friends of the Soviet Union (the list of founder members was published in the press), and ratified this gesture on 1 May when he was the first signatory to a protest against the 'fascist barbarism' being perpetrated by Hitler, a barbarism that was becoming increasingly known in Spain, due partly to the arrival of Jews fleeing from the dictatorship.[11]

During the spring a significant change in the poet's life-style occurred when his parents arrived to live in Madrid and he moved with them into the enormous top-floor flat they had rented in Calle de Alcalá, 102 (today 96, just where the street crosses Goya).[12] In view of this new situation it seems that the poet gave up the studio flat at Calle de Ayala, 72, which he and his brother Francisco had been renting for several years. What are we to make of such a decision? It is understandable that the attraction of home comforts was strong (with mother and servants to wait on the poet), but to relinquish his own private den at the same time sounds like a sort of emotional suicide. Probably Lorca felt that it was his duty to live with his parents; perhaps, even, they asked that he be with them. At all events Federico was surrounded by friends at his new address. Adolfo Salazar lived just across the road, José

---

* An ancient name for part of pre-Roman Andalusia.

Caballero, Regino Sáinz de la Maza and Rafael Martínez Nadal around the corner. 'It was a little world within a little world,' Caballero recalled nostalgically in 1980.[13]

At this time Lorca had become involved in the amateur Club Teatral de Cultura, later known as Anfistora, which had been founded by an extraordinary woman from northern Spain, Pura Maórtua de Ucelay, with the aim of promoting modern theatre. Lorca had met Pura Maórtua the previous year and promised that, if she managed to rescue from Madrid's Police Headquarters the copies of *Don Perlimplín* confiscated in 1929, he would produce for her not only that play but a new version of *The Shoemaker's Prodigious Wife*. She was successful in her mission and, true to his word, the poet spent several months rehearsing the two plays, which were performed (once only, as was the club's policy) in the Teatro Español on 5 April. *Blood Wedding* was still running at the Beatriz.[14]

While the audience greatly enjoyed *The Shoemaker's Prodigious Wife*, interest was centred, naturally, on the première of *Don Perlimplín*, whose eponymous protagonist was played with huge gusto by Lorca's friend the painter and set designer Santiago Ontañón. The complex little work made a deep impression on those present, as the press reviews show. Among the critics, Fernández Almagro proved once again to be the best informed and most acute. He pointed out the chronological discrepancy that often existed in Lorca between composition and production or publication, in this case a discrepancy of eight years, and suggested that *Don Perlimplín* had influenced the poet's subsequent work in ways that few people were in a position to appreciate, given the fact that its performance had been banned in 1929. It was a sensible observation.[15]

It was at about this time that Lorca met a person who was to play a role of some importance in his life, the Galician journalist and writer Eduardo Blanco-Amor, who for some months had been pestering the poet's friend Ernesto Pérez Guerra for an introduction. Although like Lorca he used to claim that he was born in 1900, the truth was that Blanco-Amor had come into the world in 1897, at Orense, where he had lived until he emigrated to Buenos Aires at the age of nineteen. As passionately Galician as Pérez Guerra, Blanco-Amor missed his native parts intensely and, as was the case with so many of his fellow exiles in Argentina, dreamt of returning home; not surprisingly, the first poems he wrote in Buenos Aires were imbued with that nostalgia and sadness characteristic of Galician verse. In the Argentinian capital, which had a flourishing and varied culture in the 1920s, Blanco-Amor acquired a cosmopolitan outlook and appearance that never left him. 'In my time there,' he wrote, a young man could see Pavlova and Nijinsky dance, Siegfried Wagner conduct his father's work, visit exhibitions of the French Impressionists, hear lectures by Clemenceau and Ortega y Gasset (still in his thirties), go to the theatre in five languages, among them Yiddish, with fabulous actors, and read the latest books almost at the same time as in London, Paris or Rome.[16]

Blanco-Amor frequented many important writers then living in Buenos Aires, among them the Mexican Alfonso Reyes (whom Lorca met in Madrid and greatly admired), Jorge Luis Borges, Leopoldo Lugones and Horacio Quiroga,[17] and devoted himself energetically to the propagation of Galician culture in a city that contained more Galicians than any in Spain.[18] In 1926 he began to contribute to the great newspaper *La Nación*, whose literary supplement was probably the most influential in the whole of South America and which regularly published original pieces by Spanish writers such as Ortega y Gasset, Unamuno, Gregorio Marañón, Américo Castro, Enrique Díez-Canedo, Ramón Gómez de la Serna and others, as well as providing information about current literary and artistic trends in the 'Mother Country'.

In September 1928 Blanco-Amor published in Buenos Aires a small collection of poems in Galician entitled *Romances galegos* ('Galician Ballads'), some of which had already appeared in 1927 in the Madrid review *La Gaceta Literaria*;[19] and when he was sent by *La Nación* to Spain at the end of the year to write a series of articles on Galicia he distributed copies of the little book among friends and critics. One of the latter was Enrique Díez-Canedo, who had reviewed Lorca's *Gypsy Ballads* in *La Nación* a few months earlier and, as Blanco-Amor may have discovered, was a close friend of the Granada poet.[20] That Blanco-Amor knew about Lorca by then there can be no doubt whatsoever, although it is almost certain that he did not meet him before returning to Buenos Aires in 1929.[21]

Blanco-Amor was in Spain again in April 1933 and, once he had been introduced to Lorca, did everything in his power to make himself attractive to the poet. His homosexuality, unlike Lorca's, was flamboyant, and many of Federico's friends were offended by what they considered his brash and even vulgar manners.[22] Lorca shrugged aside such hostile comments, however, and seems to have found the sensual Galician amusing and stimulating; Blanco-Amor was a welcome addition to his inner circle of gay writers and painters (that included, for example, Luis Cernuda and Emilio Prados), and they saw each other frequently. Many years after the poet's death the Galician would come nearer than almost any of the poet's contemporaries to saying something coherent about Lorca's homosexuality; and there are indications that, had he lived just a little longer (he died in 1985), he might have told all he knew. But he left it too late.

After the performance of *Don Perlimplín* and *The Shoemaker's Prodigious Wife* by Pura Maórtua de Ucelay's theatre club, Lorca set off with the Barraca for a Holy Week tour that took them to Valladolid, Zamora and Salamanca. Like all the theatre's sorties this one left its crop of memories and anecdotes, and the art critic Rafael Santos Torroella has recalled that on the banks of the river Pisuerga in Valladolid the poet read the *Ode to Walt Whitman* to him and some friends, providing them with what was to prove one of the most deeply moving experiences of their lives.[23]

Meanwhile Lola Membrives, who was about to return to Argentina, had expressed the desire to produce *Blood Wedding* in Buenos Aires. On 25 April Lorca was in San Sebastián to repeat his lecture on María Blanchard, and took advantage of the fact that Lola was playing in the town to renew his contact with her. The next day he followed her to Vitoria, and read *Blood Wedding* to the assembled company. Everyone was delighted with the play and Lorca and the actress quickly reached agreement on the terms of the contract. Two days later, on 5 May, the company sailed from Barcelona for Buenos Aires.[24]

Music, Falla, Rodríguez Rapún

Since the flop of *The Butterfly's Evil Spell* in 1920 Lorca had never lost touch with the dancer and singer Encarnación López Júlvez, 'La Argentinita'. The five records of folk songs they made together for HMV in 1931 had ensured that their names were linked in the minds of many people, and the connection was reinforced from 1932 onwards by the concerts given by 'La Argentinita' throughout Spain and South America, which often included songs arranged by the poet. On 6 May 1933 Rafael Alberti was to deliver a lecture in the Teatro Español on the influence of folk elements in Spanish poetry. Encarnación López agreed to 'illustrate' the talk with songs and dances, Lorca to accompany at the piano and Santiago Ontañón and Salvador Bartolozzi to design the sets. The newspapers stirred up considerable public expectation about the one-off event, and that night Madrid's leading theatre was packed with friends and admirers of the highly talented trio. Half-way through his lecture Alberti broke off and invited Federico to leave the piano and recite one of his own poems of folk inspiration. He did so and the audience responded with great enthusiasm. Among those present were several members of the Barraca, one of whom, Modesto Higueras, retained years later a vivid memory of the concert. How could anyone have such a varied range of gifts as Federico, he had wondered during the performance? It was a question asked by all those who came into contact with the poet.[25]

On 31 May Josefina Díaz de Artigas opened her Barcelona season with *Blood Wedding*.[26] Lorca had not travelled to the Catalan capital, perhaps because he did not want to miss the dress rehearsal of Encarnación López's production of Falla's *Love the Magician*, in the Teatro Español.[27] The première of the ballet was not held in this theatre, however, but, as a gesture to Falla, in the latter's home town of Cadiz, on 10 June. Lorca went south for the occasion, accompanied by Santiago Ontañón, Manuel Fontanals, Eduardo Ugarte and other friends. The evening was an immense success, and Federico dashed off an enthusiastic telegram to Falla, who was then in Palma de Mallorca working on *La Atlántida*, the opera he never finished.[28] Two days later 'La Argentinita' was back in the capital with her company to play *Love the Magician*, which received rave reviews, Adolfo Salazar claiming that Encarnación López had 'revealed' Falla for the first time to a Madrid audience.[29]

Towards the end of June the dancer gave a special performance of *Love the Magician* in the Residencia de Estudiantes. Among the audience was a handsome young engineering student, Rafael Rodríguez Rapún, who was to become the great love of Lorca's last two years. Born in Madrid in 1912, Rapún was of athletic build, a good footballer and passionate socialist. He had joined the Barraca a few months earlier and was now its secretary, a position in which he quickly gained everyone's respect for his efficiency and scrupulous rendering of accounts.[30] Carlos Morla Lynch, present that evening in the Residencia, had met Rapún a month earlier at the première of *Don Perlimplín* and found him 'charming, open-faced, both insolent and polite, and full of personality'. That impression was now confirmed.[31] It seems that Rapun may have accompanied Federico to Cadiz for the première of *Love the Magician* , and that the photograph of him and Lorca in the gardens of the Reina Cristina Hotel in Algeciras may be from this trip (illustration 31). Luis Sáenz de la Calzada, who had also joined the Barraca recently, and became one of Rapún's best friends, has left a moving description of him at this time, a description all the more valuable in view of the fact that it is the only one committed to print by a member of the University Theatre or, for that matter, by any of Rapún's other friends:

Rafael was at a crossroads: on the one hand there was the difficulty of the mathematical problems which he had to solve daily in order to complete his course in Mining Engineering; on the other, the constant pressure of being surrounded day in and day out by the members of the Generation of 1927,* scientific rigour versus poetry, poetry versus scientific rigour; I believe that, deep down, Rafael preferred a line of poetry to the angles of a dodecahedron, but both things were part of him, not

---

* The habitual label attached to the poets of Lorca's generation, who had visited Seville for the Góngora tercentenary celebrations held that year.

without what at times was a manifest antagonism: that was why he often became so furious and why he had those tragedies which he could not avoid and which prevented him from sleeping.

He had a big, brachycephalic head, curly hair, a not very broad forehead furrowed by a deep transversal line; a regular nose emerging almost from the forehead, which gave him almost the profile of a Greek statue; a generous mouth with brilliantly white teeth that overlapped slightly, making him lift one corner of his mouth while dropping the other when he laughed. An energetic chin, a strong body with relaxed muscles . . . He normally wore black, a colour that made his smile more luminous. He had a firm, decided manner of walking . . . I've said that he had his tragedies – that, at least, is what he called certain things that happened to him and which I never knew about; the ones I found out about didn't seem tragedies to me, but he was violent and elemental, elemental at least in certain things: for example, the orgasm which used to happen automatically when our van overtook another car on the road. This wasn't normal, but it wasn't his fault if the acceleration our excellent Eduardo applied when our van was about to overtake was to a certain extent like making love to a woman.[32]

Rafael Rodríguez Rapún, who did not survive the Spanish Civil War to tell his own story, was not homosexual but, according to his close friend Modesto Higueras, eventually succumbed so totally to the magic of Lorca's personality that there was no escape. 'Rafael was crazy about women,' Higueras recalled,

but he got caught in the net, no, not caught, *immersed* in Federico. Just as I was immersed in Federico, but without going so far, he became immersed in the whole affair without realizing what was happening. Later he tried to get away but he couldn't . . . It was tremendous.[33]

When Rodríguez Rapún joined the Barraca rehearsals were in full swing for Lope de Vega's *Fuente Ovejuna*. The play, with its theme of the exploitation of the peasants by a corrupt and brutal oligarchy, was ideal for the socially committed Barraca, and this was beyond doubt the company's most 'Republican' and politically 'engaged' production. Lorca took liberties. To make the play's message more relevant to contemporary rural society, which in many ways had hardly changed since the seventeenth century when Lope was writing, he eliminated the references to the so-called Catholic monarchs, Ferdinand and Isabella, and dressed his peasants in the clothes they wore habitually in the 1930s.[34] Lorca entrusted the backdrop, sets and costumes to Alberto Sánchez, a sculptor from Toledo, and he himself arranged the songs. To the production he applied all the experience he had accumulated with *The Shoemaker's Prodigious Wife* and *Blood Wedding*, as well as with the previous four works staged by the Barraca, and the result was stunning. *Fuente Ovejuna*, with its mixture of action, songs, dances and social message, elicited of all the Barraca's expanding repertoire the most vibrant responses up and down the country. The première took place in Valencia on 31 May and the audience, composed mainly of workers, immediately grasped that the play was as relevant to the Spain of 1933 as it had been to Lope's. At the point where the heroine Laurencia accuses the men of the village (Fuente Ovejuna is in Cordova) of being a bunch of cowardly homosexuals (*maricones*), the theatre exploded.[35] For in those days, as Luis Sáenz de la Calzada has recalled, a woman would not allow herself to pronounce the terrible word even under torture – and to hear an actress do it in a theatre was unheard of.[36]

The Barraca's *Fuente Ovejuna* was greatly disliked by the Right, not least for the suppression of all reference to Ferdinand and Isabella, revered by the 'forces of law and order' as the champions of Catholicism, artificers of Spanish unity and promoters of the discovery of the New World. The reaction against Lorca's production of the play began in the town of Albacete that summer, where it was attacked in the local press, and grew more vehement in the following years.[37]

In Albacete Lorca was interviewed by a young journalist, José S. Serna, and talked about his plans to publish his work, 'slowly but surely'. Poetry? *The Poet in New York, Earth and Moon, Odes* and a volume to be called *Because I Love Only You* (of which no trace seems to survive) were ready. Theatre? He had, he said, 'eight or nine works' at the disposal of the printer. *Mariana Pineda*, to start with, was going to appear in a new, exquisite edition (but never did). And for the first time he was going to publish *The Shoemaker's Prodigious Wife, Don Perlimplín, Blood Wedding, When Five Years Pass* and *The Public*. Of the list, the only play to be published in his lifetime was *Blood Wedding*, and that not the following October, as the poet promised, but in 1936. As for *The Public*, he assured the journalist: 'It has not yet been produced and never will be, because, quite simply, it *cannot* be.'[38] Lorca offered no reason for this conviction, although anyone who had read carefully the two scenes of the work that had just appeared in the new Madrid magazine *Los Cuatro Vientos* would have had little difficulty in suspecting why: they were the first (entitled 'Roman Ruin') and the fifth, both of them of a very pronounced homosexual character.[39]

The poet told Serna that *Blood Wedding* was the first in 'a dramatic trilogy of the Spanish earth', adding that he was currently at work on the second. The latter did not yet have a title, but its theme concerned female sterility. As for the third, entitled *The Destruction of Sodom* – a project Lorca had mentioned in Cuba to Luis Cardoza y Aragón – it seems that the poet never got beyond the first act.[40] Lorca had news too about *When Five Years Pass* which, he said, would be produced by Pura Maórtua de Ucelay in her theatre club.[41] It was true that the project existed but, like so many others, it failed to become a reality before the Civil War intervened.

The drama about female sterility had no title when Lorca talked to Serna in Albacete, but a few weeks later it was common knowledge that the poet was working on a new play on this topic. A play called *Yerma*.[42]

Yerma

If the point of departure for *Blood Wedding* had been a real-life incident that occurred in Almería in 1928, the origin of *Yerma*, as we have seen, was much earlier, and reached back to the poet's childhood, when he first became aware of the annual 'cuckold's pilgrimage' to the village of Moclín.

It is not known to what extent, if any, Lorca had continued work on the play after returning from Cuba, where he had read a few scenes to the Loynaz family, in 1930. Nor is there any documentary evidence about how much he achieved this summer of 1933, although it seems that by October he had finished the first two acts.

Was the protagonist of *Yerma* based on a real person? It would not be surprising to learn that the poet had someone, or various people, in mind. One possible candidate was his father's first wife, Matilde Palacios, who had died childless, although we do not know whether her infertility caused her a despair akin to Yerma's. As early as 1918 Lorca had evoked in the poem 'Elegy', as we saw, the plight of a Granada spinster known to the *Rinconcillo* and whom he imagined to be waiting in vain not only for a husband but for the day when she would be a mother; and, where his theatre was concerned, he had already touched on the theme of maternal frustration in *When Five Years Pass*. Moreover, on a personal level, Lorca was poignantly aware of his own 'sterility' as a homosexual, as can be seen from some of the *suites*, poems in *Songs* and the sonnet 'Adam', written in New York and already mentioned. It was almost inevitable, therefore, that sooner or later he should have written a play exclusively devoted to the theme of infecundity; and the Moclín pilgrimage gave him a ready-made framework within which to develop it.

Gynaecological considerations apart, *Yerma* can be seen to be another variation on the theme that if lovers meet but do not follow their 'inclination' (as one of the woodcutters in *Blood Wedding* recommends), their amorous journey has ended, but not in the felicitous sense indicated by Shakespeare. That this is so is shown not only by Yerma's references to the way in which shame prevented her from giving herself to the shepherd Víctor when the opportunity arose – she was fourteen then[43] – but in her psychosomatic reaction every time he appears in her presence now. In Nature's eyes Yerma is meant for Víctor. Lorca himself underlined this in 1935:

When my protagonist is alone with Víctor, she exclaims, after a silence: 'Can't you hear a child crying?' What this means is that the longing embedded in her adolescent memories is coming up to the surface from the subconscious echo which she carries inside.[44]

Shame and then her materialistic father saw to it that Yerma married Juan and not Víctor – and neither society-induced modesty nor financial considerations have anything to do with love in Lorca's primitive world, where lack of desire and infecundity are virtually synonymous.

In the same interview Lorca explained that Yerma is a victim of the Spanish code of honour which is almost part of her blood and bone, and which, once she has made the fatal mistake of marrying a man for whom she does not feel passion, prevents her from opting out and looking for a suitable partner. Implicit in *Yerma* is the rejection of the rigidities of Spanish Catholicism, as the Right was quick to see when the play was produced in December 1934. And the rejection, too, of *machismo*, which relegates women to the category of second-rate citizens, of penned-up sheep.

Argentina Calling

At the end of July Lorca heard that Lola Membrives's production of *Blood Wedding* in Buenos Aires, which had just opened, was a huge hit. The telegram and then letters from the actress's husband–manager Juan Reforzo were ecstatic. On 4 August the latter assured Federico that the play had conquered Buenos Aires in a few hours and had already earned him the equivalent of some 3,500 pesetas (a sum corresponding to the annual salary of the highest-paid miner or metal worker in Spain at the time). The company was about to set off for a tour of the provinces, and Reforzo calculated that they would be back in Buenos Aires by the middle of September, when they would give *Blood Wedding* its second run, he hoped in the presence of the author.[45] Lorca, acutely aware of the vital importance of Buenos Aires, with its highly demanding audiences, for the launching of Spanish plays in South America, must have been exhilarated by the news, which confirmed the success of the work in Madrid and showed that at last he had hit on a money-spinning dramatic formula.

Blood Wedding had twenty consecutive performances before Lola Membrives's season at the Teatro Maipo came to its scheduled end on 7 August, and the company set off on their tour. No doubt if the actress had staged the work earlier the success would have been tremendous.[46]

Lola Membrives and Juan Reforzo continued over the following days and weeks to press Lorca to make the trip to Buenos Aires, and became increasingly uneasy as the poet failed to commit himself. In despair the couple wrote to his friend Santiago Ontañón and asked him to intervene. The message went back that the poet would take a decision once he had talked to his parents, no doubt about the financial aspects of the visit[47] – a further indication of Federico's dependence on his family. He had been invited to give a series of lectures in the Argentinian capital under the auspices of the Friends of Art Club, but perhaps felt that the terms were not satisfactory.[48] In view of the financial success of *Blood Wedding* in Madrid, the money he had already earned in Buenos Aires and that which would undoubtedly accrue when the play was put on again there in September, his lecture contract and Lola Membrives's interest in producing *The Shoemaker's Prodigious Wife*,[49] such hesitation might seem strange: but Lorca was obsessed with achieving full economic independence and no doubt wanted to make absolutely sure, before embarking, that the conditions could not be bettered. Moreover, he had the Barraca to think about. On 10 August, making it more difficult for Lola Membrives and her husband to contact him, he set off once again with the students, this time on an ambitious four-week trip that took them north to León, Mieres, Santander, Pamplona, Jaca, Ayerbe, Huesca, Tudela, Estella, Logroño and Burgos.[50]

In León the poet was interviewed by two young journalists, whose questions he answered with startling frankness, blasting off, first, against politically inspired poetry such as that now being written by Rafael Alberti, who had 'just returned a Communist' from Russia. Lorca was certain that there was no room in poetry for political propaganda:

The artist, and particularly the poet, is always an anarchist, and can only listen to the voices that rise up from within his own being, three imperious voices: the voice of Death, with all its presentiments; the voice of Love and the voice of Art.

Then came acerbic comments on other contemporary writers: Ramón del Valle-Inclán was in the main 'detestable', and his Galicia as false as the Andalusia of the Alvarez Quintero brothers, the *bêtes noires*, in the poet's view, of the Spanish theatre. As for Azorín, whose books on Castile Lorca had admired as an adolescent, he 'deserved to be hanged for his volubility'. The journalists, awed by the tone of these replies, hesitated before asking Federico's opinion of modern Spanish theatre in general. But finally they did so. The answer, as they expected, was uncompromising. 'It's theatre by and for swine,' the poet assured them. 'Exactly that, a theatre written by swine for swine.' Changing the subject, the interviewers then asked Lorca about *Blood Wedding*. Exaggerating, the poet said that the following season the play would be performed in various theatres abroad: New York, London,

Paris, Berlin and Warsaw. (Negotiations were under way, it was true, for a New York production.) Clearly the success of *Blood Wedding* was going to his head or, at least, giving him a new confidence in his future as a dramatist. 'If I continue working,' he ended, 'I hope to influence the European theatre.'[51]

The most important stop-off on the Barraca's tour was on the coast at Santander, where the first session of the International University Summer Course, set up by the Government, was in full swing in the Magdalena Palace, a splendid property belonging to the Spanish Royal Family and overlooking the sea. Given the Barraca's debt to the Government, and particularly to Fernando de los Ríos, it was only natural that the company should have decided to perform this summer in Santander, where it was awaited by a discriminating audience of professors, foreign students and visiting lecturers. Over several days the Barraca put on its full repertoire, which now included another interlude by Cervantes and dramatized excerpts from Antonio Machado's long ballad *The Land of Alvargonzález*, recited by Lorca. Among the teachers present were Federico's friends the poets Pedro Salinas, Dámaso Alonso, Jorge Guillén and Gerardo Diego, the French writer Marcelle Auclair – his future biographer, who was then translating *Blood Wedding* with her husband Jean Prévost – the guitarist Regino Sáinz de la Maza, the historian Américo Castro, the Law Professor José Antonio Rubio Sacristán (with whom Lorca had coincided in New York and who was Secretary of the Summer School), the German Hispanist Karl Vossler and – to Lorca's delight – the American literary critic Herschel Brickell, who had entertained him so generously at his home in New York.[52]

In the town of Somo, on the coast not far from Santander, Carlos and Bebé Morla Lynch were spending the summer. There Federico visited them one afternoon, with Rafael Rodríguez Rapún and some other members of the University Theatre.[53] The *barracos* also dropped in on José María de Cossío, the great expert on bullfighting, at his house in the hill town of Tudanca. Federico liked and admired Cossío and now named him honorary member of the Barraca, a designation ratified by all the members of the group.[54]

Back in Madrid Lorca made arrangements for his trip to Buenos Aires and then hurried down to Granada, where he arrived on 24 September, to take his leave of his family.[55] On 2 October the Buenos Aires daily *La Nación* announced that Lola Membrives had just received a telegram from the poet in which he told her that he would reach the city on 13 October on board the Italian steamer *Conte Grande*. The newspaper went on to point out how important the visit by such an outstanding poet and dramatist was to be for the cultural life of the capital, and confirmed that Lorca would give four lectures during his stay as well as attend the performances of *Blood Wedding*.

What neither *La Nación* nor anyone could have foreseen was the incredible impact that Federico's personality as well as his work would make in Buenos Aires.[56]

The poet left Madrid for Barcelona on 28 September, and was accompanied in the taxi that took him to Atocha station by Rodríguez Rapún, with whom his relationship had grown increasingly close over the previous months. To see the poet off were Carlos Morla Lynch and, according to the latter, 'the complete group of the Barraca'.[57]

The following day Lorca embarked on the *Conte Grande* with the Catalan stage designer Manuel Fontanals, who had also been summoned to Buenos Aires by Lola Membrives. Before boarding ship the poet paid a lightning visit to Margarita Xirgu, who was then playing in Barcelona. Sixteen years later the actress recalled the conversation that had taken place in her dressing room: Lorca wanted to read to her there and then the first two acts of *Yerma*, insisting that he was writing the play with her in mind. But Margarita had refused, convinced as she was that Federico was going to have an enormous success in Buenos Aires and that they would ask him for *Yerma*. She did not want him to feel committed to her. Far better to wait and see what happened.[58]

Before the *Conte Grande* left Barcelona Federico sent a postcard to Rodríguez Rapún. From the latter's reply (12 October 1933) we know that the poet's departure affected him deeply. Rapún had just heard that he had been exempted from military service – a blessed deliverance for which he thought an *ad hoc* spell intoned by Federico in the taxi on the way to the station might have been responsible. The Barraca was hard at work rehearsing Tirso de Molina's *El burlador de Sevilla*,* Rapún assured Lorca. He himself had been allotted the part of the fisherman Coridón, which he felt he was playing reasonably well – although, he added, 'according to Ugarte I am a "Coridón" in the good sense of the word.' Given the fame of André Gide's *Corydon*, first published in Spanish translation in 1929 and now in its third impression, there can be little doubt that the allusion was to the 'love that dare not speak its name'. Rapún went on:

I remember you constantly. Not to be able to see a person with whom you have been every hour of the day for months is too much to be forgotten. Especially if towards the person in question you feel yourself drawn as strongly as I do towards you. But since you're going to return I console myself with the thought that these hours will be repeated. And there's another consolation: to know that you have gone on a mission. This consolation is reserved for those of us who have a sense of duty – and we're fewer all the time [. . .] Since at least I've written something to you, although

---

* 'The Seducer of Seville', by Tirso de Molina, pseudonym of Gabriel Téllez (1571–1641) was the first play on the theme of Don Juan.

you deserve more, I'm going to stop here. I'll write to you often. A big hug from your friend who never forgets you.[59]

This is the only letter exchanged between Lorca and Rodríguez Rapún that has come to light, although we may assume that the two wrote to each other frequently. The disappearance of the letters is just one more maddening gap in the story of Lorca's private life – a story that many circumstances, and not least the poet's own discretion, have contrived to make at times almost impenetrable.

7

Argentina

Buenos Aires Welcomes a Spanish Poet

Before agreeing to travel to Buenos Aires, Lorca, whose terror of drowning was well known to his friends, insisted that the boat should be as large as possible.[1] The *Conte Grande*, one of the most modern transatlantic liners in the world, met the stipulation to perfection. Moreover the weather was good and the sea as tranquil as it had been when the poet sailed to New York in 1929 on board the *Olympic*. So all went well. Federico worked on a new lecture, 'Play and Theory of the *Duende*', polished the others and took part in the usual celebrations when the ship crossed the Equator. A few hours before the *Conte Grande* arrived at Rio de Janeiro on 9 October some small white butterflies appeared on board. Flying fish broke the surface on all sides. The poet, who was then writing to his parents, felt again, as he had done three years earlier when he neared Cuba, the excitement of arriving in '*our* America', 'Spanish America'.[2]

Waiting for Lorca and Fontanals in Rio was the Mexican writer Alfonso Reyes, whom Federico had got to know in Madrid and who was now his country's ambassador in Brazil. Reyes gave the poet the first copies of the *Ode to Walt Whitman*, which thanks to his good offices had just been published in a limited edition in Mexico, and took the two friends on a brief tour of the city.[3]

On 11 October the *Conte Grande* arrived at Santos, and early the following morning stopped in for a few hours in Montevideo. *Blood Wedding* had been an enormous success in the Uruguayan capital during Lola Membrives's season some months earlier, and the poet was awaited there with intense curiosity. Journalists, photographers and friends hurried aboard. Among them was Pablo Suero, one of Buenos Aires's most distinguished theatre critics, who had been following Lorca's career with interest since the appearance of *Gypsy Ballads*. He took to the poet immediately and would soon become one of his closest acquaintances in Argentina.

Suero found Lorca chatting animatedly to Enrique Díez-Canedo, currently Spanish ambassador in Uruguay and one of whose sons was a member of the Barraca. Also with the poet were Lola Membrives's husband Juan Reforzo, José Mora Guarnido – his friend from the early days of the *Rinconcillo* in Granada, now established in Montevideo – and the Spanish actress Rosita Rodrigo.[4] Suero and Reforzo crossed the river Plate with Lorca to Buenos Aires, where a few days later the critic published two brilliant articles on his meeting with the Spaniard. It had not taken him long to realize just what a remarkable personality was about to disembark in the Argentinian capital. Lorca's vitality amazed him, as did his capacity for switching rapidly from one topic, and one mood, to another. Federico appeared to him old and modern, grave and merry, the very incarnation of the 'genius' of his race. Suero was particularly interested to hear the poet affirm that his 'real' theatre was not *Blood Wedding* but two avant-garde works called *The Public* and *When Five Years Pass*. Even before he set foot in Buenos Aires, therefore, Lorca was already making it quite clear that he aspired to much more than being the author of a successful rural tragedy.[5]

Since the beginning of October the newspapers of the capital had been announcing Lorca's imminent arrival, alleging that he was the greatest contemporary renovator oof poetry and theatre in the Spanish language on both sides of the Atlantic. Lectures and readings by the poet, a new run of *Blood Wedding* and the South American première of *The Shoemaker's Prodigious Wife* – the stage was set for Federico to take Buenos Aires by storm. And he did.[6]

At the dockside to meet Lorca and Fontanals were a crowd of journalists and photographers, representatives of various cultural organizations and even a few old friends, among them Gregorio Martínez Sierra. Especially intense emotion was generated when some erstwhile neighbours of the García Lorca family in Fuente Vaqueros, Francisco Coca and his wife María Montero, pressed through the throng with their eighteen-year-old niece to embrace the poet. The couple had emigrated to Argentina in 1922 and could hardly contain themselves. 'He's from our village, from our village, from La Fuente!' they shouted. 'I can tell you that I couldn't help weeping,' Lorca wrote to his parents.[7]

The poet was installed in the Hotel Castelar, one of the best in Buenos Aires, situated in the Avenida de Mayo in the very heart of the city. From the window of room 704 – 'It's so small that it's like a cabin,' wrote one visitor[8] – he could look down on the crowds passing up and down this elegant street which has always been the one most closely associated with the capital's Spanish community, being known familiarly as 'Spanish Avenue'. Between 1920 and 1930 some 300,000 Europeans had arrived in Argentina, mainly Spaniards and Italians.[9] Among the former, as Lorca was well aware before he set foot in the country, those from Galicia predominated; and in his poem 'Cántiga do neno da tenda' ('Song of the Shop-Boy'), written in Galician on his return to Spain (with the help of Ernesto Pérez Guerra), he was to express the intense nostalgia felt by these exiles for their native land. Moreover, if the Buenos Aires Spanish community at large welcomed Lorca with open arms, it was the Galicians who expressed most enthusiasm at Federico's presence. Word had got around that the poet had published a poem in *gallego* – the 'Madrigal to the City of Santiago' – and it was rumoured that he had others in progress. The Galician community had its own newspaper in Buenos Aires, and in an interview the poet spoke of his love for the north-west corner of Spain, with its melancholy music and green valleys. The 'Madrigal' was reprinted on the front page of the newspaper in question – but the rumours about other Lorca poems in the vernacular proved to be false.[10]

Shortly after he settled in at the Hotel Castelar Federico was visited by María Molino Montero, the young niece of Francisco and María Coca, who was surprised to find that the poet had pinned to the wall a large photograph of himself standing in the middle of a field in his Barraca uniform, his arms outstretched in imitation of Christ on the cross. Every time she returned to the room the sombre photograph intrigued her more. She could not decipher its significance but felt intuitively that it had to do with a 'secret' aspect of the poet.[11] The Castelar was to be Federico's base for most of his stay in Buenos Aires. A mere hundred yards away, on the same side of the street, stood the Avenida Theatre, where on 25 October Lola Membrives was to reopen with *Blood Wedding*, while in the basement of the hotel, as well as a confectionery shop much patronized by the poet, were the recently inaugurated studios of Radio Stentor, where he would participate in various broadcasts.

The night of his arrival in Buenos Aires Lorca attended the première of Ferdinand Bruckner's *The Sickness of Youth*, in a Spanish version by his new friend Pablo Suero. He was struck by this starkly realistic portrayal of the disillusionment of post-war German youth, sunk in vice and sexual promiscuity, and told reporters that in Madrid it would be impossible at the moment to stage such a daring play.[12]

From the day he landed in Buenos Aires, Federico's presence in the city's newspapers and magazines was constant. His success was more resounding than that of any Spanish writer who had visited the Argentinian capital before him – the Chilean poet Pablo Neruda spoke of 'the greatest triumph ever achieved by a writer of our race'[13] – and for months it was impossible to open a periodical without reading something about the Andalusian prodigy who had descended on the city. Lorca lecturing; Lorca walking down Corrientes or Florida surrounded by a crowd of admirers, or officiating in the Café Tortoni; Lorca with Lola Membrives; Lorca with another famous actress, Eva Franco; Lorca talking enthusiastically about tangos (he met the singer Carlos Gardel, then at the pinnacle of his fame, and the two apparently got on swimmingly); Lorca at such and such a banquet or reception; Lorca playing the piano; Lorca reciting; Lorca eating in La Costanera, one of his favourite haunts on the shore of the river Plate . . . Within a few weeks he was the talk of the town and his photograph was appearing on all sides. He told his parents that he was rarely in the hotel, that he was being constantly invited out, that he had hardly a moment to himself, that he had had no option but to take on a young man as his secretary and typist and to keep people away from the door. 'Buenos Aires has three million inhabitants,' he explained, 'but so many photographs of me have appeared in the press that they recognize me in the street. I don't like it but it's very important because it shows that I've conquered a huge public for my theatre.'[14]

Lorca had told Pablo Suero as they crossed the river Plate that *The Public* and *When Five Years Pass* constituted his real theatre. In an interview with *La Nación* the poet enlarged on the observation a few days later. He revealed that he had brought *When Five Years Pass* with him, although he had no illusions about seeing it performed during his stay. As for *The Public*, he did not think it would ever be produced. Why not?

Because it's the mirror of the audience. It stages the personal drama being enacted in each member of the audience's mind while he is following the play, often without his fully realizing what's happening. And since the inner drama of each of us is often very poignant and usually not very edifying, the members of the audience would get up at once in indignation and prevent the performance from continuing. Yes, my play is not for performing. It is, as I once defined it, 'a poem for booing'.[15]

The poet was as careful as he had been in Spain not to be explicit about the theme of *The Public*, and at no point during his stay in Buenos Aires does he seem to have hinted (at least in public) at its homosexual content. Wisely, because for all its cosmopolitan air Buenos Aires was almost as strait-laced about homosexuality as was Madrid.

The Lorca who arrived that October in the Argentinian capital was the apostle of a new theatre radically concerned with the problems of contemporary society. All his commentaries were along these lines. 'Personally I would rip out the boxes and stalls and bring the gods downstairs,' he said to one journalist. 'We've got to get ordinary working people into the

theatre. "Are you wearing a nice silk dress, Madam? Yes? Then, get out."
An audience dressed in hemp shirts watching *Hamlet*, the works of Aeschylus
and all the other great plays, that's it.' Having transcribed the poet's
vehement observations, the reporter commented: 'García Lorca jumps from
one topic to another. Always, however, some flash of insight about the
theatre illumines the conversation.'[16]

Soon after disembarking Lorca said that he would probably be in
Argentina for only a month and a half, because he had promised to rejoin
his family for Christmas;[17] and in one of his first letters home he reiterated
his pledge to return to Spain after he had delivered the four lectures that had
been contracted by the Friends of Art Club.[18] But as had happened in Cuba
three years earlier, it was to prove impossible for him to keep his word.
Buenos Aires made so much of him that the month and a half became two,
three and finally almost six. But Spain was never far from his thoughts.
'Here among us,' the poet José González Carbalho recalled, 'living days of
unforgettable successes, he was very often nostalgic for his father's house
and for Granada. At every moment he wanted to leave.'[19] The young critic
Alfredo de la Guardia, who in Buenos Aires renewed a friendship with the
poet initiated in Madrid thirteen years earlier, remembered that Vicenta
Lorca, about whom Federico spoke with 'such devotion', was constantly
calling her son back (by letter or telegram, presumably, since the telephone
service between the two countries was then very primitive),[20] while other
Argentinian friends remembered how Lorca's small room at the Hotel
Castelar was soon bursting at the seams with the presents he accumulated
for his mother.[21]

As for the poet's correspondence at this period, the situation is disheart-
ening. We have his letters to his family, to be sure (although perhaps not all
of them), but not those he received from home; none of the letters exchanged
between him and Rafael Rodríguez Rapún is known; and it seems that
during his stay he wrote to hardly anyone else.

By the time Lorca arrived in Buenos Aires on 13 October 1933 the election
campaign in Spain was hotting up. On 29 October José Antonio Primo de
Rivera held the inaugural meeting of his Falange Española, a fascist party
more Italian than German in inspiration, while the various conservative
groups merged in an electoral coalition, the CEDA (Confederación Española
de Derechas Autónomas or Spanish Confederation of Autonomous Right-
Wing Groups), headed by the Salamanca lawyer José María Gil Robles,
leader of the Catholic Party. Widespread differences between the Republican
and left-wing parties were making a democratic coalition impossible; the
anarchists, with their rejection of the State, announced their intention to
abstain; and given the provisions of the new Electoral Law, which favoured

large groupings, the Right's victory in the polls, which had been set for 19
November, seemed not only feasible but probable. The Buenos Aires
newspapers gave extensive daily coverage to the campaign and the Spanish
community in the city became increasingly divided into two antagonistic
camps as the weeks passed: the pro-republicans on the one hand and the
monarchists and conservatives on the other. Lorca, constantly questioned
by the journalists about the situation in Spain, did not hesitate to give his
views, expressing his intense dislike of the monarchy and recalling his
satisfaction when King Alfonso XIII had left the country in 1931.[22] The poet
was well informed about what was going on back home. 'I read about
unpleasant things in Spain. These elections are going to be terrible. We'll
see what happens!' he wrote. 'I'm really worried about all these political
upheavals.'[23] Lorca made it clear in his statements to the press that the
Spanish Right did not like his work, and said on one occasion that in
Granada the clergy had a low opinion of his poetry.[24]

Friends and Lectures

The day after landing in Buenos Aires, Lorca and Fontanals had paid a call
on the writer Pablo Rojas Paz and his wife Sara Tornú. There they found,
among others, Pablo Neruda, the painter Jorge Larco, who had designed
the sets for Blood Wedding, the writers Oliverio Girondo and Conrado Nalé
Roxlo and the poets Raúl González Tuñón, Norah Lange, José González
Carbalho and Amado Villar. The latter had met Lorca in Madrid some years
earlier, and in the months leading up to the poet's arrival in Argentina had
been his most fervent apostle. Federico always rose to this sort of occasion,
and did not fail his hosts that night.[25]

A week later, on 20 October, Lorca gave his first lecture to the members
of the Friends of Art Club, which was run by a woman of great sensitivity,
Bebé Sansinena de Elizalde, and enjoyed enormous prestige in the city. Lorca
got to like Bebé and her husband so much that he was heard to claim that
theirs was the only house at which he had ever turned up on time.[26] The
lecture, 'Play and Theory of the Duende', was ideally suited to the audience,
and showed the poet at his most profoundly Andalusian. Few people present
can have doubted that, in his exploration of the duende, that mysterious,
Dionysian inspiration, Lorca was really talking about himself and his own
poetic world. The atmosphere in the crowded room was electric, and
according to a journalist Lorca conquered in one evening the heart of Buenos
Aires.[27]

Then, on 25 October, Lola Membrives reopened with Blood Wedding in
the Avenida Theatre. Before the curtain went up the poet, resplendent in

dinner-jacket, walked on to speak a few words to the packed house. A voice shouted, 'On your feet!' and the entire audience stood up and gave him an ovation that lasted, he told his parents, for five minutes.[28] Once the applause died down Lorca expressed his gratitude for the wonderful welcome he was receiving in Argentina and for the encouragement this meant to him at a time when he was 'beginning' his career as a dramatist.[29]

The evening passed off triumphantly. Jorge Larco's sets, too restricted in the smaller Maipo Theatre during the first run, were immensely effective in the vast Avenida and greatly impressed the audience, who applauded wildly after each scene and provided another standing ovation at the end of the play, persuading Lorca to speak again.[30] The poet told reporters that it was the first time in his life that a work of his had been afforded such a reception; he was particularly pleased, he said, that it had appealed to people from all levels of society, to intellectuals and non-intellectuals alike.[31] As for Lola Membrives's performance, Lorca's admiration was boundless and he told his parents that, at the point in the play where the Mother encourages the 'two bands' to set off in pursuit of the lovers, Lola had sent shivers down the audience's spine.[32]

Blood Wedding played for several months and made a huge amount of money for the poet, to whom Lola Membrives and her husband had agreed to pay 10 per cent of the takings.[33] Lorca's letters home showed to what an extent such success was boosting his ego. As more and more pesos flowed in his comments became increasingly presumptuous. 'Whatever they put on by me in the theatre will pack them in,' he wrote in November while *Blood Wedding* continued to draw the crowds to the Avenida, a theatre that Federico claimed was about ten times the size of the Teatro Español in Madrid – a considerable exaggeration.[34] Again and again he returned to the subject of his earnings and to the fabulous remittances his parents could expect once restrictions on the export of Argentinian currency were removed. Finally he sent his father, now seventy-four years old, a cheque for an astronomical sum to convince him once and for all of his viability as a self-supporting writer; to show him, as he told Enrique Díez-Canedo, that by writing poetry it was possible to make more money than by selling land and grain. Lorca asked María Molino Montero at the same time to write to his father and tell him how well his son was doing in Buenos Aires.[35]

The day after the opening of *Blood Wedding* Lorca delivered his second lecture, 'How a City Sings from November to November', which provided him with the opportunity to demonstrate his musical ability. It was the first time he had given this performance – Granada's seasons as expressed in folk song, with the poet accompanying himself at the piano – and the audience was stunned. Lorca, they discovered, was not only a poet and dramatist but an excellent pianist who also sang, in an expressive if not professional voice. Federico the complete minstrel was living up to his reputation. Following this success he gave, on 31 October, his New York recital and finally, on 8 November, 'Primitive Andalusian Song', a reworked version of the lecture first delivered in Granada in 1922.[36]

The talks had been attended exclusively by the members of the fashionable club presided over by Bebé Sansinena, and as a result of the wide coverage afforded by the newspapers the poet was increasingly pressed to repeat one of them for the general public. Accordingly, on 14 November, he gave 'Play and Theory of the *Duende*' in the Avenida Theatre. There was not a spare seat. The lecture, according to one newspaper, appealed especially to the women in the audience,[37] an observation that finds some confirmation in a *billet doux* preserved among the poet's papers. 'The best *duende* of all is you,' wrote Ana and Celia, appending their address.[38] Shortly after his arrival in the city Federico had told his parents that every day he was receiving amorous notes from the ladies, which he would let them read;[39] and two years later he confided to a friend in the Barraca that one night, on returning to the hotel, he had found a girl waiting for him in his room with evidently lascivious intentions. He had thrown her out.[40]

In Buenos Aires Lorca renewed contact with Victoria Ocampo, a beautiful, rich and Francophile writer he had met in Madrid in 1931 and who edited the literary journal *Sur*, perhaps the most important in South America. In view of the fact that not a single book by Lorca was available in the city, Victoria Ocampo offered to publish a special Argentinian edition of *Gypsy Ballads*. The poet agreed, and the book appeared at the end of the year, selling out almost overnight.[41]

Neruda

During his months in Buenos Aires Lorca saw a lot of Pablo Neruda and they became good friends. Neruda, six years younger than Lorca, had a father who did not approve of Bohemians and arty people and who, like Lorca's, was dismayed to find that he had engendered a son who was interested in, of all things, poetry. But while Federico had been able to count as a child on the support of his mother, Neruda had been granted no such consolation, for his had died bringing him into the world. Things had gone from bad to worse and finally, desperate to escape from his tyrannical father, Pablo had joined the Chilean Diplomatic Corps. In 1927 he was appointed consul in Rangoon, visiting on the way to his destination Buenos Aires, Rio de Janeiro, Lisbon, Madrid, Paris, Port Said, Djibouti, Colombo, Singapore, Bangkok, Shanghai and Tokyo. After Rangoon he was moved to Ceylon

(Sri Lanka), Java and Singapore, returning to Chile in 1932 and being sent to Buenos Aires in August 1933, two months before Lorca's arrival. Neruda was tall and pale, with a slow voice and wide-open eyes that, like Picasso's, seemed to devour everything and everybody on which they rested. When Lorca met him he had just published the first edition of his book of poems *Residencia en la tierra* ('Residence on Earth') and was becoming well known in Buenos Aires literary circles. But his marriage (to a Dutch woman he had met in Java, Maruja Agenaar) was not working out, and his current poetry expressed a profound sense of the futility of things.[42]

In his memoirs, *I Confess That I Have Lived*, Neruda recalled one of the adventures he shared with Lorca in Buenos Aires when they coincided at a riotous party thrown by the Citizen Kane of Argentina, Natalio Botana, proprietor of the newspaper *Crítica*, at his splendid house on the outskirts of the capital. During dinner Neruda became aware that a poetess across the table was giving him the glad eye. Afterwards he, Lorca and the lady climbed a tower overlooking the swimming pool, where it soon became evident to Neruda that the poetess meant business. Federico, who up to then had suspected nothing, was despatched to keep guard below, but was so bemused by what was happening that he tripped and fell, bruising a leg in the process. Whether the offering to Venus could be satisfactorily effected in such circumstances Neruda does not make clear. The story seems not to have been an invention by the Chilean poet, certainly, for on one of her visits to the Hotel Castelar María Molino Montero found Federico propped up in bed with his leg in bandages. He had had an accident at a party, he said sheepishly.[43]

On 20 November Lorca and Neruda staged an unexpected happening at a luncheon given in their honour by the Buenos Aires branch of the PEN Club. Both deeply admired Rubén Darío, the Nicaraguan who had renovated Spanish poetry at the end of the nineteenth century and had been one of the great influences on Lorca's early poetic development. Darío had lived in Buenos Aires and had written a long poem in praise of Argentina, but he was now apparently largely forgotten in the city, and this seemed to the two friends unjust. They decided, therefore, not simply to talk about Darío but to come up with something special. In bullfighting there is a pass, rarely seen, in which two matadors play the animal together, each holding one corner of the cape. With this in mind Lorca and Neruda devised a speech whose sentences they would deliver alternately from different ends of the table. They told nobody beforehand, and, when they rose simultaneously to speak, the guests thought that there had been a mistake. Once the point of the joint discourse had been explained – it had to be, since there is no bullfighting in Argentina – the poets brought to the attention of the company the lack of a monument to Darío in Buenos Aires, the lack of a flower shop, street or square with his name. How could this be? It was an outrage! Some of Darío's work was excessively exuberant – this the Spaniard and the Chilean were prepared to concede; but they were equally sure that Rubén at his best was a very great poet indeed.[44] Few if any of those listening can have realized to what an extent Lorca's early contact with Darío's poetry had been fundamental in shaping his own vocation. Lorca was somewhat evasive about his literary debts. But that he revered Darío no one in Buenos Aires could doubt, for on several other occasions he spoke of the *maestro* with reverence.[45]

Neruda's memoirs tell us disappointingly little about his friendship with Lorca in Buenos Aires, and there are no diaries or letters to flesh out the account. We have, though, the evidence of their collaboration on a very special gift for their friend Sara Tornú, the wife of Pablo Rojas Paz, at whose house they had first met. This consisted of a beautifully bound typescript of a little book of poems by Neruda, *Paloma por dentro, o sea La mano de vidrio* ('Inner Dove, or The Hand of Glass'), illustrated by a series of ten spine-chilling Indian ink drawings by Lorca. The poems, in accordance with Neruda's mood at the time, expressed a deep weariness, a profound sexual disillusionment, an obsession with death and an angry rejection of bourgeois values. Lorca's drawings matched the mood suitably and were in the mould laid down in New York: severed hands, drops of blood, skeletons, sailors with empty eye-sockets, the poet's head converted into a skull (this drawing clearly echoed the Dalí of eight years earlier), the decapitated heads of Lorca and Neruda observed by the eye of a waxing moon (or perhaps waning, depending on whether Federico took into account the change of hemisphere) . . . The poems and drawings are so akin in feeling that we must conclude that the two poets had come to a perfect understanding during these months.[46]

Neruda mentions in his memoirs that both he and Lorca had their detractors in Buenos Aires, although he supplies no names.[47] One of these was the writer Arturo Cambours Ocampo, who later described his intense disappointment on meeting the famous author of *Gypsy Ballads* and *Blood Wedding*, works he admired. That day Lorca talked non-stop about himself. Spanish poetry began and ended with him; so too did the Spanish theatre; *Yerma* (not yet finished) was the resurrection of Greek tragedy. 'We had never seen such pedantry and pride; such immodesty and vanity together,' Cambours wrote. 'We were in the company of a stupid puffed-up fool, a fat and petulant little charlatan.' We do not have the poet's side to the story but, whatever really happened, Cambours's account shows once again that you either had to love or hate Lorca: no half-measures were possible.[48]

Another enemy was Jorge Luis Borges, then thirty-four. Lorca had probably met Borges in Madrid in the early 1920s, when the Argentinian was one of the leading lights of the *ultraísta* movement. In Buenos Aires he appears to have seen Federico only briefly. 'He gave me the impression of a man acting a part,' he recalled. 'You know, playing a role. I mean, he was a professional Andalusian.' Lorca talked at length on that occasion about a well-known personality who, he said, expressed all the tragedy of the United States. Intrigued, Borges asked who it was. 'Mickey Mouse,' replied the poet. The Argentinian, offended, had left in a huff.[49] Maybe by the facetious sally it had been Lorca's purpose to irritate the writer, or to see his reaction. Perhaps he knew that Borges considered him a 'professional Andalusian'. What is clear, at any rate, is that he and Borges were incompatible, not least because both wanted the stage exclusively for themselves.

Elections in Spain and Earnings in Argentina

While *Blood Wedding* continued its triumphant run at the Teatro Avenida and Lola Membrives rehearsed *The Shoemaker's Prodigious Wife*, the electoral campaign in Spain reached its climax in an atmosphere of increasing tension and, in the face of the Republican disarray, the Right carried the day, emerging with a large majority in the new Parliament. Suddenly the situation had changed radically and, from the democratic point of view, for the worse.[50]

A letter to Lorca from Eduardo Ugarte (28 November 1933) reflected the anxiety felt by the poet's liberally minded Spanish friends at this time. Ugarte informed him that he was utterly sick of politics and that as result of the conservative win the Barraca was already having difficulty in collecting its government grant. None the less rehearsals of Tirso de Molina's *The Seducer of Seville* were going ahead. The *barracos* were delighted about Lorca's success in Buenos Aires, but Ugarte urged the poet to return as soon as possible to Madrid, where he was badly needed.[51] Lorca now found himself in a dilemma. He had promised to be home for Christmas, true. But Rafael Rodríguez Rapún had told him that he was on a 'mission', and if he left Buenos Aires too soon he might fail to carry this out adequately and to extract the maximum benefits from his stay. Moreover he might lose money. As usual the poet allowed events to take their course and kept putting off a decision.

On 1 December, shortly after *Blood Wedding* had its hundredth performance, the curtain of the Teatro Avenida went up on Lola Membrives's production of *The Shoemaker's Prodigious Wife*, with sets and costumes by Manuel Fontanals. It was a fuller version than the one staged by Margarita

Xirgu in 1930, and in his statements to the press the poet explained that the Buenos Aires public was about to see the play's 'authentic première'.[52] Lorca had collaborated closely with Lola Membrives, supervising the music and songs and bringing all his experience with the Barraca to bear on the movements of the actors, which had an almost balletic character and precision. The première was another huge success and initiated a run of more than fifty performances.[53] From 15 December the poet added a tailpiece to the play in the form of three dramatized folk songs, with sets and costumes by Fontanals. Two of them – 'The Pilgrims' and 'The Four Muleteers' – were already famous, thanks to the records made by Lorca and 'La Argentinita' for HMV, and once again the audiences were enchanted. Lorca expressed his admiration for Lola Membrives and her company, whose versatility and enthusiasm made him feel that he was on tour with the Barraca.[54] And, of course, he was equally pleased with the new ingress of pesos that the play generated. 'Lola Membrives is thrilled with me,' he boasted in a letter home. 'Naturally! I'm a lottery she's just won!' Federico now hoped that he would be able to return to Spain in January, taking with him 'plenty of cash' which he expected to be able to export with the help of the Spanish Ambassador, Alfonso Dánvila.[55]

It seems that *The Shoemaker's Prodigious Wife* gave rise to only one adverse reaction – from a Jewish woman who had been offended by what she considered the anti-Semitism of some of the protagonist's highly colourful expressions of contempt for her neighbours (none of them Jews). Lorca apologized in the Jewish review *Sulem* for any offence that might have been caused to the large Hebrew community in Buenos Aires, explaining that such turns of speech, common in Spain, had long since lost their anti-Semitic intention. While arguing that, given the Jewish blood that flowed in his own veins, he was incapable of feeling hostility towards that race, he none the less made the gesture of replacing the offensive words.[56]

On the morning of the première of *The Shoemaker's Prodigious Wife* the Mexican writer Salvador Novo, who had just arrived in Buenos Aires, met Lorca, and that evening, surrounded by friends of the poet, including Pablo Neruda, was in the Avenida to see the play. In his book *Continente vacío* ('Empty Continent'), published in Madrid in 1935, Novo recounted a conversation with Lorca a few days later in one of Federico's favourite restaurants on the banks of the river Plate. The poet talked about his visit to New York three years earlier (Novo had just read the Mexican edition of the *Ode to Walt Whitman*), and recalled a *ñañigo* ceremony he had seen in Cuba. He wanted news of Mexico, a country that had long fascinated him and which he hoped to visit, and remembered his friendship in New York with the artist Emilio Amero and María Antonieta Rivas. Was it true that the latter's lover José Vasconcelos, the Mexican politician, had been responsible for her suicide in Paris in 1931? If so he would tell him what he thought of his behaviour![57]

Shortly after arriving in Buenos Aires Lorca had got to know the poet Ricardo Molinari, who was the same age as himself and a good friend of Novo. Molinari had written to him in 1927, asking for a copy of *Songs*, and now produced a first edition of *Gypsy Ballads* in which the poet executed a drawing with, for him, an unusually explicit autobiographical theme. Around the motif of a pair of lemons hanging from a branch, which recurs in many of his signed copies, Federico placed an inscription in capital letters reading: LOVE BUENOS AIRES GRANADA CADAQUES MADRID (see illustration 30). When Molinari inquired as to the significance of the place-names mentioned the poet replied: 'They're where I have loved most.'[58]

If the reference to Cadaqués confirms the extraordinary importance of Dalí in Lorca's life – it was now five years since the poet and painter had last seen each other – the inclusion of Buenos Aires raises questions. What affair or affairs did Lorca have in the Argentinian capital? Fifty years later it is almost impossible to know. The only identity that can be established convincingly is that of a young communist tram-driver and amateur actor, Maximino Espasande, born in Asturias in 1911, who it seems may have been an extra in *Blood Wedding*. According to Espasande's family Lorca fell passionately in love with Maximino, pursuing him energetically until he agreed to accompany him on his jaunts through the city. The idyll appears to have been short lived: when the lad realized that the poet wanted to have a physical relationship with him he opted out. Espasande fought in and survived the Spanish Civil War; and, on his death, his family destroyed the evidence of Lorca's inscribed copies and even, it appears, a manuscript poem.[59]

As for the other young men who were the object of Federico's attentions in Buenos Aires, no detailed information is forthcoming, although various names are often shuffled in Argentinian literary circles. That the poet loved deeply in the city there seems little doubt from Molinari's drawing, and it may be that by his inclusion there of Buenos Aires Lorca was alluding to several separate experiences.

Through the good offices of Molinari, Salvador Novo succeeded in persuading Lorca to illustrate a *plaquette* of his poems, entitled, in English, *Seamen Rhymes*. The poet agreed, and Novo's little book appeared in Buenos Aires at the beginning of 1934 before Federico set off on his journey home. Lorca also illustrated two slim volumes of verse by Molinari himself published during the same year. The thematic content of the drawings in the three collections is similar to that of the poet's illustrations to Neruda's

Inner Dove: drowned sailors, severed and bleeding hands and heads, spectral forms, disembodied nervous systems, mortiferous flowers – emblems, all of them, of the poet's relentless obsession with death.[60]

Mariana Pineda, Yerma and Montevideo

News of Lorca's successes in the capital quickly spread to the Spanish communities scattered throughout this gigantic country (where Buenos Aires province alone is larger than the whole of Spain) and invitations to lecture flowed in. It seems, however, that the only one he took up was to the city of Rosario where, on 22 December, accompanied by Pablo Suero, he gave his talk on *duende*.[61] The visit was memorable for another reason: in Rosario the poet met and was able to help a relative from Asquerosa, Máximo Delgado García, the destitute ex-fiancé of one of his favourite cousins, Clotilde García Picossi. A year later Federico introduced into *Doña Rosita the Spinster* an allusion to Máximo, when Rosita's fiancé leaves for Tucumán – even further away than Rosario – and never returns.[62]

Meanwhile *Blood Wedding* and *The Shoemaker's Prodigious Wife* were doing so well that Lola Membrives had decided that she wanted to put on something else by the money-spinning Spanish wizard. But what? Lorca had taken *When Five Years Pass* with him to Buenos Aires, but it seems that he had not yet read it to the actress. There are indications that he also had *Don Perlimplín* in his bag, but none that there was ever a question of its being performed in the city.[63] As for *Yerma*, the poet had not yet got around to tackling the third act. The only possibility open to Lola Membrives was, therefore, *Mariana Pineda*, and she decided to go ahead. Lorca, understandably, was uneasy about the play's chances and feared that, coming after the success of the other two productions, it might be a flop. He confided his doubts to the theatre critic Alfredo de la Guardia, who was almost certainly the only person in Buenos Aires who had been present at the disastrous première of *The Butterfly's Evil Spell* in Madrid in 1920. De la Guardia had read *Mariana Pineda* and was therefore in a good position to give an informed opinion. He understood Lorca's misgivings and suggested that, in view of the fact that historical plays did not usually go down well in Buenos Aires, the poet should preclude any possible difficulties by giving a brief talk from the stage, before the curtain went up, about the Granadine heroine. In this way the audience would be prepared for what was coming.[64] The idea struck Lorca as sensible but, in the event, he opted instead to give a broadcast talk about the play and to publish some observations on it in the papers. He insisted that *Mariana Pineda* was one of his earliest works if not the first, which was true, and said that he was only twenty when he wrote it, which was not.[65] Once again he was lavish in praise of Lola Membrives who, a fortnight before opening night on 12 January, was already 'becoming' Mariana.[66]

A few moments before the première a huge basket of flowers bedecked with the intertwined Spanish and Argentinian flags was delivered to Lola Membrives in her dressing room. The card bore the names of Federico García Rodríguez and Vicenta Lorca. The poet told reporters that he had received a telegram from his parents in which they asked him to send the flowers to the actress, and that, knowing them as he did, he had bought the biggest basket he could find. 'I think I interpreted their wishes correctly,' he added. Had Federico really received such a telegram? A letter home suggests not. The flowers, almost certainly, were intended by the poet as a double tribute to Lola Membrives and to his mother and father.[67]

Mariana Pineda, despite Lorca's explanations, Fontanals's sets and costumes and the excellence of Lola Membrives and her company, was far from being a hit. One newspaper in particular, the influential *La Prensa*, felt that it had been a mistake, after *Blood Wedding* and *The Shoemaker's Prodigious Wife*, to produce this early work in which the critic could find no hint of the 'future creator'.[68] Lorca's persuasive and broad-girthed friend Pablo Suero did his best to defend the play, but even he could convince no one. *Mariana Pineda* was a mere 'curiosity' and failed to interest the demanding Buenos Aires audiences.[69]

In this situation, not surprisingly, Lola Membrives tried to get Lorca to finish *Yerma*. On 18 January he read her the first two acts of the play, and the following day the press announced that when the work was finished the actress would produce it in the Teatro Avenida.[70] The matter, however, was more complicated. In a letter to his parents, written just before the première of *Mariana Pineda*, Federico reported that Lola's idea was that she and Margarita Xirgu should stage *Yerma* simultaneously in Buenos Aires and Madrid. It looked like a reasonable compromise, but in the event Federico failed to complete the play before returning to Spain.[71]

Lola Membrives's season in the Avenida, which should have continued until 4 February, was brusquely cut short on 20 January when the actress, exhausted, fell ill and was advised by her doctors to rest. It was hoped that she would be able to resume her performances on 1 March.[72] Meanwhile the poet, who for weeks had been announcing that he would leave for Spain on 6 February, decided to prolong his stay yet again and to spend the month taking things easy and finishing *Yerma*.[73]

Lorca, Lola and her husband Juan Reforzo agreed to spend the first fortnight of February across the river Plate in Montevideo, where the poet arrived on 30 January. Waiting at the quayside were his friend Enrique Díez-

Canedo (the Spanish Ambassador), the novelist Enrique Amorim, whom he had met in Buenos Aires, José Mora Guarnido and various Uruguayan writers.[74] If Lola Membrives thought that Lorca was going to shut himself in to finish *Yerma* in Montevideo, however, she was soon proved wrong. During his stay the poet was almost literally besieged by the Uruguayan press and by society people desperate to have him at their parties and tables. It was high summer, the Carnival was in full swing . . . and Lorca's brilliant successes in Buenos Aires had been fully reported in the papers. No one was prepared to leave him in peace. Moreover when he received an invitation to give a public and highly paid lecture in the 18 July Theatre, where Lola had performed *Blood Wedding* the previous August, the poet found it impossible to refuse. He chose 'Play and Theory of the *Duende*', which had been such a hit in Buenos Aires, and it went down so well, on 9 March, that he was persuaded to give two further talks – 'How a City Sings from November to November' and 'A Poet in New York'. The money flowed in, the journalists milled round, the impromptu folk-song sessions and the parties continued . . . and the third act of *Yerma* receded further and further into the distance.[75]

Probably Lorca used it all as an excuse not to finish the play, for there are indications in the poet's letters home that he was growing tired of Lola Membrives's insistence that he get *Yerma* to her as soon as possible. 'She sees in the play all her business hopes for next season,' he wrote.[76] Díez-Canedo, with whom Lorca almost certainly discussed the problem, later recalled that the famous and domineering actress had done her best to put the poet under lock and key at his hotel, the Carrasco, virtually forcing him to finish a tragedy which 'he had promised to another actress, the one who had first believed in him'. That is, Margarita Xirgu.[77] It is not certain that Lorca had yet promised the play exclusively to Margarita, who may have written to him during his stay in Buenos Aires, although probably deep down he felt that, after all the Catalan actress had done for him, it would be a betrayal to give it to Lola Membrives. It seems, moreover, that Margarita Xirgu's friend, adviser and manager Cipriano Rivas Cherif may have intervened through Enrique Díez-Canedo to persuade Lorca not to give the play to Lola Membrives,[78] who was undeniably the first actress to have earned him a great deal of money, an achievement for which he was extremely grateful, as his letters to his parents show. But whatever the truth of the matter, Lorca did not finish the third act of *Yerma* before sailing for Spain.

One of the excuses the poet may have given for failing to finish the play, moreover, was that at this time he was working on an adaptation of Lope de Vega's *La dama boba* ('The Simple-Minded Lady') for another famous

Argentinian actress, Eva Franco, and reworking his *Don Cristóbal's Puppet Show*, begun in about 1931, but not yet performed, which he wanted to put on at a special function for his friends before he left Buenos Aires.

Federico lived for part of his fortnight in Montevideo at Díez-Canedo's official residence, in a whirl of receptions, recitals and parties. He helped the daughters of the family to prepare their carnival masks, walked around the town in his Barraca uniform, no doubt with the express intention of scandalizing the local philistines, and generally provided people with what they wanted of him – that is, frequent performances of the famous Lorca 'one-man show'.[79] On 9 February Díez-Canedo's wife, Teresa Manteca Ortiz, wrote to the poet's mother to tell her about his success in Montevideo, enclosing newspaper cuttings and referring to the tenderness with which he constantly talked about her. At a society luncheon held a few days earlier he had been asked if he planned to marry. 'My brother and sisters, yes, they can marry,' Federico said, 'but I belong to my mother.'[80] The reply contained a deeper psychological truth than most of those present can have realized, including, perhaps, the Ambassador's wife, and may be placed beside the words the poet wrote on a photograph of himself sitting with his mother in the Huerta de San Vicente and inscribed to Eduardo Blanco-Amor: 'For Eduardo, with the person I love most in the world'.

One perceptive journalist, who had noticed that all Lorca's protagonists in the works known to date were female, put a blunt question. Why women and not men? Lorca looked surprised. 'It wasn't a conscious decision,' he replied, and then, 'as if returning from a dream', added:

It's because women are more passionate, they rationalize less, they're more human, more vegetal; moreover an author would find himself in great difficulties if his heroes were men. There's an appalling lack of actors, of good actors, you understand.

The journalist did not comment on the reply, which must surely have struck him as pretty unconvincing (assuming that these were the poet's actual words). Rarely had Lorca been asked such a difficult question in an interview, and what he said demonstrated his capacity for quick thinking if nothing else. He could not, of course, give an honest answer to the reporter. Neither in *The Public* nor *When Five Years Pass* are the protagonists female, and he had just told the interviewer, as he had others before him, that the former was 'a play not to be performed, a poem for booing', without any indication as to why. Lorca was a master at hinting but not explaining. Again and again in his comments to the press we find him making veiled allusions to his homosexuality, to his 'struggle', to his desire to strip away the masks people wear to protect themselves. But rarely, if ever, is he put on the spot by a journalist and asked to explain what he means, what he *really* means.

For this reason the approach of the Uruguayan reporter comes as a positive relief.[81]

Before leaving Montevideo, Lorca went to the Buceo cemetery to visit the tomb of his friend the Uruguayan painter Rafael Pérez Barradas, whom he had first met in Madrid in the early 1920s and saw again in Barcelona in 1927. Barradas had returned to Montevideo not long afterwards and died there of tuberculosis in 1929, as poorly off as ever. José Mora Guarnido, who with other writers and artists accompanied the poet to the cemetery, wrote later that it was a wet, grey day, 'as if expressly chosen for the occasion'. The group stood around the tomb and Lorca threw flowers, one by one, on the grave. Perhaps as he did so he reflected on the courage and dignity with which Barradas had fought his particular fight against adversity, never free from the threat of poverty – a threat that he, Lorca, had never experienced.[82]

On 16 February the poet caught the ferry back to Buenos Aires, where Eva Franco was waiting impatiently for his version of *La dama boba*. The following day he wrote home to tell the family about his great success in Montevideo, where his lectures had earned him a fabulous amount of money. The letter reveals again Lorca's compulsive need to prove to his parents that he was capable of being financially viable. He had already sent them 15,000 pesetas and 8,000 were still to follow. 'This money is for you to use, naturally, because it's *yours*, and Mamma and Pappa can spend it all if they want,' he wrote, adding that now it was *his* turn to lay out funds on *them* in return for all those that they had invested in his career. As for the adaptation of *La dama boba*, Lorca felt sure that this, too, would make profits. He had already booked his ticket for the boat, which was scheduled to leave Buenos Aires on 6 March, and said that he felt a mixture of sadness and happiness on leaving Argentina – sadness because everything had gone so splendidly, happiness at the thought that soon he would see his family again. 'In Buenos Aires and Montevideo I see my financial future,' he wrote. 'Here I can earn money that would be impossible in Spain.'[83] After years of dependence on his father and the resultant humiliation, it was now the son's turn to affirm himself. The comparison with Dalí jumps to mind – with a Dalí who at this time was devoting ferocious energy to killing his father symbolically and who one day was to draw up in front of the paternal house in Figueras, from which he had been banished in 1930, in a huge and luxurious Cadillac shipped back from America, proof of his validity as a person and of the uselessless of his father's 'rebellion' against his genius.[84]

Last Days in Buenos Aires

Shortly after arriving back in the Argentinian capital Lorca read his pruned-down version of Lope's *La dama boba* to Eva Franco and her company, and over the following fortnight the press occupied itself extensively with the actress's determination to give new life to this almost forgotten classic. Manuel Fontanals had converted the Teatro de la Comedia into a daring imitation of a seventeenth-century theatre, and Lorca, who maintained that his task had consisted solely in making some judicious cuts, occupied himself with the musical aspects of the production, introducing various dances and songs.[85] The play, which opened on 4 March, was a hit, and Pablo Suero pointed out that the production owed much to Federico's experience with the Barraca – in its rhythm, in the intentionally puppet-like movements of the actors, in its grace. Years later Irma Córdoba, whose Clara was much praised by the critics, confirmed one of Suero's observations: Lorca had imposed on the actors a rigid timing to which they were quite unaccustomed.[86]

Meanwhile Lola Membrives, recovered from her exhaustion, had re-opened in the Avenida on 1 March with an attractive programme in honour of Lorca: the first act of *The Shoemaker's Prodigious Wife*, the final scene of *Blood Wedding*, the third act of *Mariana Pineda* and a recital by the poet of two scenes from *Yerma*. Before the reading Lorca promised the audience that Lola would produce *Yerma* that April in the same theatre, and that he particularly wanted the première to take place in Buenos Aires, as a mark of his gratitude for the welcome he had received there. It is hard to credit that Lorca believed that the play could be staged in April, given the fact that he had not yet finished it and that he was about to leave for Spain, but at any rate his gesture had the desired effect on the audience, who applauded delightedly and then listened with rapt attention to the reading. When this was over Lorca added that, before he caught his boat, he would discuss with Lola Membrives the details of the more difficult scenes of the play so that the production could go ahead without a hitch, although he himself would not be there to supervise.[87] Reading between the lines it seems that the poet had not yet communicated to Lola his determination to give the play exclusively to Margarita Xirgu. He must have done so shortly afterwards, however, for on 10 March the newspapers announced that, being unable to finish *Yerma* before leaving, the poet had just read *When Five Years Pass* to the actress and had offered it to her instead. Lola, according to one report, had greatly liked the play.[88] At about the same time Lorca read it to Pablo Suero, who wrote in his famous theatre column that it was the poet's finest and most revolutionary work. But would Lola Membrives be capable of producing it without the author's assistance? Suero doubted it – and was soon proved right.[89]

On 10 March 1934 the newspaper *Crítica* published an interview with the poet on the eve of his departure. Perhaps because of the imminence of this, as well as of the journalist's skilful questions, Lorca came closer than at any other moment during his stay in Argentina to providing some real insights into the sources of his work. The interview got off to a cracking start when Lorca commented on the discrepancy between the image people try to project of themselves, and the inner, grey, frightened and often tortured reality they attempt to hide 'as if it were an ugly sin'. It was an observation he had made before in referring to *The Public* – and he would make it again back in Spain. As Lorca talked he fixed his dark eyes on the journalist, José R. Luna, who suddenly realized that the poet was alluding obliquely to something in himself. Thus apprised, Luna tried throughout the interview tactfully to explore the depths of the poet's 'hidden', private side and was soon convinced that there was very much more to Lorca than the surface gaiety of the talented *jongleur*. When the conversation turned to death, Luna noticed an instantaneous change in the poet's expression, which was 'transfigured'. All Lorca's close friends, and not least Dalí and Buñuel, knew of these sudden metamorphoses, when Federico's gaze turned inwards and he seemed to sink into himself, but they were not usually apparent to the casual observer. Lorca explained, probably not exaggerating, that he was unable to stretch out on a bed with his shoes on because he was reminded unfailingly of the corpses he had seen as a child in Fuente Vaqueros, always laid out dressed in their Sunday best and wearing new shoes. 'Shoes and feet, when they are still, have an obsessively death-like appearance,' he insisted, perhaps thinking of Magritte.

Before the interview ended Luna extracted an important confession from the poet, who explained that his growing fame was making him feel more and more vulnerable and that he could not bear to see his name written up in big letters. 'It's as if inside me there were a second person, my enemy, mocking me for my timidity from all the posters,' he said.[90] He had made a similar revelation to Eva Franco. The actress was surprised to find that the poet, despite his great confidence in his art, never risked speaking from the stage without a text, despite his amazing verbal brilliance, spontaneity and charm. One day Lorca confided to her that he felt ashamed in public and always felt that people were scrutinizing him.[91] He was repeating something almost identical he had said in Granada seven years earlier, when Margarita Xirgu staged *Mariana Pineda;** and there is no evidence that he ever fully

* See p. 236.

resolved the conflict, born presumably of the simultaneous need to exhibit and the fear of being 'found out'.

As for Lorca's care always to have a text with him when he had to speak in public, Luis Sáenz de la Calzada has recalled an occasion on which the poet walked on to the Barraca's stage in León. Federico began his speech (there was a huge audience) and then found to his horror that he had forgotten his 'paper'. As he fumbled in his pockets his panic mounted and, after clumsily improvising some words, he retired in defeat, red with shame. He, of all people, had muffed his lines! The *barracos* were secretly pleased at the poet's discomfiture. Lorca, the beguiler, the magician, the spoilt child of the Muses, had failed for once like any mortal. It made him human.[92]

Federico had postponed his departure for Spain once again, until 27 March. It was to be the last change in his plans. On 15 March Eva Franco put on a special performance of Lorca's version of *La dama boba* for the city's actors, and in one of the intervals Federico made an impassioned plea for a contemporary theatre, free from sordid commercial interests, which would reflect the realities of modern society.[93] Then, at two in the morning on 26 March, he organized a private performance in the Avenida of his new version of *Don Cristóbal's Puppet Show*, in which there were several burlesque allusions to his friends in Buenos Aires. The event passed off hilariously.[94]

María Molino Montero visited the poet in the Avenida shortly before he left for Spain. In one of the passages was exhibited the mountain of presents that had been given to Federico, including many silver objects. María had never seen anything like it: it was a tangible expression of the extent to which Lorca had conquered Buenos Aires during his six months' stay. Federico was elated, imagining his mother's surprise when the hoard reached home.[95]

Lorca always hated goodbyes – and it was particularly difficult for him to take his leave of Argentina. On his last night he begged his friends to pretend the following day that they were only seeing him off to the resort of Tigre, further up the river Plate, and that they would meet again soon. Otherwise he would be unable to put a brave face on things.[96] When the moment came, and the poet, Fontanals and the latter's daughter Rosa María were driven to the *Conte Biancamano*, a huge crowd was at the quayside to see Lorca off.[97] Before the final parting the poet made a typical gesture, handing his friends a packet with the injunction that they were 'to continue the party'. When Pablo Neruda and the poet Amado Villar opened it after the boat had sailed, expecting to find sweets or something like that, they were confronted by a thick wad of banknotes. It was the final proof, as if any were ever needed, of the poet's generosity. He wanted to earn money, certainly, but he was always prepared to let other people spend it.[98]

Two days later the Buenos Aires press announced that Lorca had left a copy of *When Five Years Pass* with Lola Membrives. The actress stated that, while at first she had not felt competent to produce the play without the author's help, she now thought that she was up to the exacting task. The following day, however, the newspapers reported that she had changed her mind, alleging that there was not enough time for rehearsals before the season ended in May.[99] It was no doubt a wise decision, given the intrinsic difficulty of a work never performed in the poet's lifetime.

In all, including her tour of the provinces and Montevideo the previous year, Lola Membrives, before returning to Spain the following autumn, was to perform *Blood Wedding* approximately 150 times; *The Shoemaker's Prodigious Wife* about 70; and *Mariana Pineda* fewer, only some 20. As for Lorca's version of *La dama boba*, Eva Franco would put it on almost 200 times before the year ended. That the poet's visit to Buenos Aires had been an enormous success in every way no one could doubt.[100]

On 30 March 1934 the *Conte Biancamano* docked in Rio de Janeiro, where the poet saw Alfonso Reyes again and the Mexican presented him with a glass case of tropical butterflies, soon to be proudly displayed in the family flat in Madrid.[101] As the great liner crossed the Atlantic Lorca, elated by his recent triumphs, must surely have wondered what awaited him back in Spain, where the political situation had changed so dramatically since he left the previous October.

8

1934

The Spanish Ambassador Returns Home

The *Conte Biancamano* reached Barcelona on 11 April and Lorca returned at once to Madrid, where he was interviewed for the *Heraldo* by his friend Miguel Pérez Ferrero, who found the poet sorting out a stack of newspaper cuttings that he had brought back from Buenos Aires. When Pérez Ferrero left the flat in the Calle de Alcalá he had no doubt that Federico was one of the most efficient ambassadors that Spain had ever sent to South America.[1]

The students of the Barraca, who had recently been performing in Spanish North Africa, playing in Tetuán, Ceuta and Tangiers, were jubilant that their director was back at last. The rehearsals of Tirso de Molina's *The Seducer of Seville*, which had slackened off during the poet's absence, now became more dynamic, and the *barracos* had the feeling that a new period in the life of the company was about to begin.[2]

Lorca must quickly have taken in the changed socio-political situation in the country. The Right had just reinstated the death penalty, a gesture that disgusted the progressives; and during April General Sanjurjo, who had engineered the abortive rising against the Republic in 1932, was pardoned by the Government, as was José Calvo Sotelo, Primo de Rivera's Finance Minister, who had been familiarizing himself during his exile in Paris with the corporativist ideas of Charles Maurras and who, soon after his return, would found an ultra-right-wing monarchist group. Gil Robles's Catholic Party was growing more militant and had a vociferous quasi-fascist youth movement. As for José Antonio Primo de Rivera's Falange Española, this was resorting increasingly to bully-boy tactics of Hitlerian inspiration. The advanced legislation of the early years of the Republic was being whittled away, and, as the brutalities of the Nazi regime became increasingly known, Spain polarized more and more between the democrats and the antidemocrats. Sensitive souls were already frightened that such Manichaeism might lead to civil war.[3]

The poet travelled down to Granada for Holy Week. There he discovered that the town was rent by political dissension and that the conservative council, which had replaced the representatives elected in 1931, was behaving with a high-handed disdain for the working class. Significantly, while Lorca's return and his triumphant visit to America were glossed in the Republican *El Defensor de Granada* (which had published in March an account of his stay in Buenos Aires sent by a correspondent in the Argentinian capital), the Catholic daily *Ideal* did not deign to mention the presence of the famous poet and dramatist: it can hardly have been an oversight.[4]

One day Lorca met an old acquaintance from the days of the *Rinconcillo*, the Arabist José Navarro Pardo, now a member of the right-wing town council. Lorca told him that such had been his success in Buenos Aires that he had no option but to believe in God.[5] In the Avenida Theatre something incredible had happened:

After leaving the stage, with the house coming down with applause, I wanted to offer thanks to God. In the dressing room there was a crucifix. There I saw the face of a Spaniard, unknown to me, who was living in Buenos Aires and in terrible financial trouble. I was stupefied, because I was earning money hand over fist . . . When I left the theatre I began to look for him everywhere. His face was etched on my mind. After looking and looking finally he appeared. It was true, the man was in great financial hardship and I resolved the problem. I gave him half of what I had earned . . . God is too good to me.[6]

A typical Lorca exaggeration, one of those famous white lies? Games played by Navarro Pardo's memory? It is impossible to know the truth of the matter, although there are other indications that the poet had parapsychological aptitudes. An account proceeding from the poet's Colombian friend Jorge Zalamea deserves to be mentioned in this regard. One summer's day (Zalamea places it in 1932) Lorca was invited to lunch at the country house of some acquaintances in the village of Canillejas outside Madrid, where Zalamea and his wife were spending their holidays. The table had been laid out in the patio, and the company sat down merrily to consume the gigantic paella prepared by the hostess. All at once the poet turned pale, began to sweat profusely and left the table. Zalamea followed him into the orchard. What was wrong? Federico replied that he had suddenly had the feeling that they were surrounded by the dead. He sensed bones, skulls. There could be no question of his going back. That afternoon, compelled by his intuition, the poet inquired in the village about the house and its garden. What had been there before? No one seemed to know. Finally a very old man informed him that the building stood on the site of a convent pulled down in the nineteenth century – and that beneath the patio lay the nuns' cemetery. Lorca, according to Zalamea, found in the old man's account absolute proof that his hunch had been correct. The Colombian's version of this episode, published more than thirty years after the alleged event, may not be accurate in every respect – any more than Navarro Pardo's. But the fact remains that Zalamea, to whom Lorca had confided his troubles in 1928 and who seems to have known the poet very well indeed, had no doubt that he was little short of a medium.[7]

Lorca was visited this spring in the Huerta de San Vicente by Eduardo Blanco-Amor, who wanted to hear about his stay in Argentina. It was the first time that Eduardo had seen the poet in his Granada setting, and the experience was a revelation. He had not grasped to what an extent Federico was a man of the Vega; and when the poet's father took him out to Fuente Vaqueros and showed him around the village he realized just how much Lorca's work was rooted in the landscape and speech habits of his childhood. In the Huerta, surrounded by the presents he had brought from South America, the poet talked excitedly about his experiences in Buenos Aires, and that night, assisted by Federico's great friend José García Carrillo, who had been with them in the Huerta, Blanco-Amor wrote down some of the most arresting things Lorca had said. Probably, given the fact that both García Carrillo and Blanco-Amor were uninhibited homosexuals, the poet also told them something of his amorous adventures in Buenos Aires. But of this nothing has come down to us.[8]

Before Blanco-Amor left for Madrid Lorca gave him copies of various poems from his unpublished collection *Diwan of the Tamarit*, compositions in honour of the old Arab poets of Granada, whose title was inspired by the nearby Huerta del Tamarit, which belonged to the father of one of his favourite cousins, Clotilde García Picossi. The word Tamarit means 'abundant in dates' in Arabic, and the poet used to say that he loved Clotilde's *huerta*, with its wonderful views of the Sierra Nevada and the poplar groves of the Vega, even more than that of San Vicente. 'My uncle has the most attractive address in the world,' he once said. 'Huerta del Tamarit, Término de Fargüi, Granada.'[9]

After his sojourn in Granada, Lorca returned to Madrid to direct the Club Anfistora's production of Ferenc Molnar's *Lilion*, which was performed to critical acclaim on 12 June in the Teatro Español,[10] and to help with preparations for the Barraca's summer tour to the north. During the rehearsals for *Lilion* the poet renewed his friendship with Ernesto Pérez Guerra, and together they began to compose some more poems in Galician.[11] Lorca was also trying to finish *Yerma*.[12]

Meanwhile the attacks on the Barraca continued. During Lorca's absence in Argentina one particularly virulent extreme-right-wing periodical had complained that State money was being squandered on a troupe of homo-sexual university students.[13] Now, in July, the Falangist organ *FE* accused the *barracos* of perverting the peasants with their display of 'corrupt, foreign-inspired customs', their 'shameful promiscuity', their squandering of public money and their obedience to the dictates of 'Jewish Marxism'. Free love and communism! The article gave a good idea of the hatreds and suspicions now rending Spain and, although there is no record of Lorca's reaction to the offensive piece, or to the earlier slander, this can be imagined.[14]

The poet was soon back in Granada again to spend St Frederick's Day (18 July) with his family in the Huerta de San Vicente and, according to *El Defensor de Granada*, to 'finish a new play to be produced in Madrid next season'.[15] This was *Yerma*, which the poet did indeed manage to complete over the next month, reading it one day to an enthusiastic group of friends on the terrace in front of the house.[16] It is not difficult to understand Federico's affection for this delightful, shady retreat on the outskirts of Granada: here he could always count on being able to work in peace, far from the madding crowd of the capital. It had not been possible to dispatch *Yerma* in Buenos Aires, Montevideo or Madrid, but at the Huerta, listening to the servants from the Vega chatter in their rich, metaphorical speech, redolent of the earth, it seems that the last act of the play caused him few problems.

The Death of a Bullfighter

This summer two famous bullfighters, both of them a bit long in the tooth and both from Seville, had emerged from their retirement and donned again the 'suit of lights': the classical Juan Belmonte, aged forty-one, and the daring, unconventional Ignacio Sánchez Mejías, a year older. The two were closely linked to the world of literature and the arts. In Belmonte's group were the painter Ignacio Zuloaga, the novelist Ramón Pérez de Ayala and the politician, writer and outstanding medical man Dr Gregorio Marañón; while Sánchez Mejías continued to be frequented by some of the poets and writers whom he had invited to Seville in 1927 – Lorca, Bergamín (a passionate taurophile) and, especially, Rafael Alberti – and was often accompanied by people connected with the world of flamenco.

Sánchez Mejías's clique was worried by his decision to return to the ring. Fifteen kilos overweight, he had subjected himself for months to a rigid diet and had partially recovered his former dimensions, but his age showed and he had lost much of his agility. It seemed like madness. Why take the risk? Probably he not only badly needed the money but missed the danger and excitement of the *corrida* as well: Ignacio always felt obliged to prove himself, to show that he was not frightened of death, and he had acquired the reputation of being the bravest man in the business.[17]

His first fight took place in Cadiz, on 15 July. On 22 July he was in San Sebastián; on 5 August in Santander; on 6 August in La Coruña and on 10 August in Huesca. He was scheduled to appear next on 12 August, in Pontevedra where, almost seven years earlier to the day, he had announced his retirement.[18] In Santander the *corrida* was witnessed by Marcelle Auclair, the attractive and vivacious young French writer married to Jean Prévost. She had met Lorca, Ignacio and their friends in Carlos Morla Lynch's elegant salon in Madrid, and the bullfighter had immediately taken a tremendous fancy to her. After the fight Sánchez Mejías told Marcelle that his appearance in Pontevedra would be his last. He had had enough and was going to retire definitively.[19]

The drama began in the bull ring at La Coruña on 6 August, where the line-up also included Juan Belmonte and another famous matador, Domingo Ortega. When Belmonte went to kill his first bull the sword flew from his hand, sailed across the barrier and mortally wounded a young spectator. Then the news came that Domingo Ortega's brother had died. After the *corrida* was over, Ortega started off by car for Madrid. There was an accident: the vehicle swerved off the road and fell down a gully, killing the driver and injuring the bullfighter. Ortega was to have fought on 11 August in Manzanares, a small town south of Madrid. Now that was impossible, and he asked Sánchez Mejías to stand in for him. Ignacio agreed, but no sooner had he given his word than he began to have his doubts.[20]

Afterwards the newspapers were to insist on the elements of fatality that seemed to have presided over Ignacio's last hours. First, the car in which he was being driven from Huesca to Manzanares broke down, near Saragossa, and he had to continue by train to Madrid. There he was told that he would not have Ortega's team, as promised, but another. Once in Manzanares he asked to be allowed to fight first so as to be able to leave for Pontevedra as soon as possible, but they did not let him have his way. At this point he decided to pull out, but was persuaded by the only man he had been able to take with him that such a defection would be interpreted as cowardice. Obsessed by the death of his brother-in-law Joselito in 1920, who in his view had not been adequately attended to in the clinic at Talavera de la Reina after being gored, Ignacio inspected the medical facilities at the ring in Manzanares. He thought them so terrible that he insisted that, in the case of an accident, he should be taken to Madrid. A fatal decision, as it turned out.[21]

The *corrida* began late – not, as Lorca's elegy would have us believe, at the traditional 'five o'clock sharp'. Ignacio was wearing a navy blue 'suit of lights'. With him on the bill were the Portuguese Simão da Veiga, who fought on horseback, the Mexican Armillita and the young Spaniard Alfredo Corrochano. Among the spectators were José Bergamín and another friend, Antonio Garrigues, who had come from Madrid specially to see him fight. Garrigues thought that Ignacio looked absolutely exhausted.[22]

When lots had been cast for the bulls earlier in the day, the first name on Ignacio's piece of paper was 'Granadino'. The *torero* had not liked the look of the animal in the pen, and he liked it even less when it emerged now into the brilliant afternoon light. 'This one's out to get me,' he observed laconically, turning to his friends.[23]

Ignacio specialized in a pass that consists in playing the bull while sitting on the wooden ledge running around the ring at the base of the barrier – an extremely dangerous position because it allows the bullfighter little manoeuvrability and no escape if things go wrong. After playing the bull conventionally in the first part of the fight, and letting someone else place the *banderillas* or barbed darts in the second, Ignacio sat down on the ledge. There was a hush in the crowd. All went well with the first charge. On the second, 'Granadino' came so close that he slashed the bullfighter's trousers. Ignacio tried to get to his feet but the animal turned suddenly and sank a horn deep into his thigh, tossed him to the ground and gored him furiously. When they managed to get the bull away, Sánchez Mejías was lying in a pool of blood, and, as he was carried to the infirmary, he left a thick red trail across the sand. It was the blood that in his elegy Lorca would refuse to see, begging the moon to come and cover it with its white, cool light. 'I think I'm done for,' Ignacio muttered to Alfredo Corrochano.[24]

The bullfighter remained coldly lucid, and demanded, in view of the deficiencies of the infirmary, that he be taken by ambulance to Madrid, allowing the doctors only to effect the necessary cleansing of the huge gash in his thigh. But there was no local ambulance and the one summoned from Madrid broke down and did not arrive until after midnight – by which time it was almost too late.[25] José Bergamín never moved from Ignacio's side during the long hours of waiting for the ambulance, and accompanied him during the terrible drive to Madrid (100 miles away over a deficient, bumpy road), which they finally reached at seven in the morning – thirteen hours after the goring.[26] The operation began immediately but little could be done, for gangrene had already set in and these were the days before penicillin. It was desperately hot in the clinic and Ignacio asked constantly for water. He spent a dreadful night, fighting the death he knew was fast approaching and falling gradually into a delirium, raving about bulls and olive trees.[27] Sánchez Mejías had told Marcelle Auclair and Lorca that, as a boy, he had practised bullfighting illegally by moonlight at an estate in Seville. There were no spectators and, when he executed a good pass, he used to pretend that the olives, swaying in the breeze, were applauding him.[28] Perhaps these were the trees that Ignacio now recalled in his death throes – and that Lorca was to immortalize in the last alexandrines of his great elegy:

> Tardará mucho tiempo en nacer, si es que nace,
> un andaluz tan claro, tan rico de aventura.
> Yo canto su elegancia con palabras que gimen,
> y recuerdo una brisa triste por los olivos.*[29]

In his agony Ignacio shook the bed with such violence that it moved around the room. Lorca heard of this, perhaps from José Bergamín, and in his poem called the bed 'a coffin with wheels'.[30]

Federico, so terrified of death, did not have the courage to visit Sánchez Mejías in the clinic. On the afternoon of 11 August, when he heard about the goring, he immediately telephoned Jorge Guillén in Santander (where the Barraca had now arrived to begin their new season) to tell him the appalling news, and from that moment on kept his friends there informed hourly of the situation, deciding himself to stay in Madrid until the outcome was known, for good or for bad.[31] At eight on the morning of 13 August the doctors realized that there was nothing more to be done: the gangrene that Lorca personifies in his poem had spread dramatically. 'It's all over; Ignacio died at nine forty-five,' Lorca announced shortly after 10 a.m. in his last telephone call to Guillén; 'I'm leaving for Santander. I don't want to see him.'[32]

When he reached the northern city later that day Lorca shut himself up with his friends and explained to them that Ignacio had tried desperately to avoid having to fight in Manzanares. The poet had followed the matador's last hours minute by minute, both in the press and on the radio and, it seems fair to assume, by questioning friends who went to the clinic. He was convinced, and the conviction grew stronger with passing time, that Ignacio was fated to die that afternoon. It even appeared that, in the hotel at Manzanares, the bullfighter had been allotted a room with the number 13 in which to dress for the *corrida*. 'Poets are mediums,' Lorca said, 'and Ignacio, who was a poet, did everything he could to escape from his death, but everything he did only helped to tighten the strings of the net.'[33]

In the first part of his *Lament* Lorca insists on the elements of fatality that had conspired against Ignacio that afternoon in Manzanares (everything is

---

*   It will be a long time before there's born again, if ever,
     an Andalusian so noble, so full of adventure.
     I sing his elegance with words that moan,
     and remember a sad breeze among the olives.

'ready' for the enactment of his death to begin at an exact point in time), and apparently told Marcelle Auclair, shortly after the tragedy, that he had felt sure from the moment Ignacio announced his return to the ring that his fate was sealed. 'Ignacio's death is like mine, the trial run for mine,' he explained to the young French writer. 'I feel a tranquillity that amazes me. Perhaps because I had a premonition about what was to happen?'[34]

Federico was apparently not the only one to have sensed that Ignacio was fated to be killed. Immediately after the death of Sánchez Mejías the rumour spread that for months there had hung about him a perceptible (to the initiated) odour of doom. Hemingway remembers this in *For Whom the Bell Tolls*, where Pilar insists that the smell (which she tries to define) was so strong that many people refused to sit with the matador in the cafés of Madrid. It is hard to believe that Lorca, with his nose for the occult, could have been unaware of what people were saying.

As for Sánchez Mejías's lover Encarnación López, 'La Argentinita', her grief can be imagined. According to some oral sources the bullfighter's family refused to allow her to see the dying man, although her younger sister Pilar has denied this, alleging that she did not attempt to visit the clinic. 'Encarna', as she was always known to her friends, died eleven years later in New York and apparently left no written account of her relationship with Ignacio, Lorca or any other member of the group.[35]

During the last two years of his life Federico never forgot Ignacio or the circumstances of his death, as many of the friends of both have testified. Sánchez Mejías had died nobly, sacrificing his life in an ancient ceremony which, as Lorca once explained to Giovanni Papini, has nothing to do with sport but is a 'religious mystery', the 'public and solemn enactment of the victory of human virtue over the lower instincts . . . the superiority of spirit over matter, of intelligence over instinct, of the smiling hero over the frothing monster'.[36] This mythical view of the *corrida* was to find astonishing expression in Lorca's *Lament for Ignacio Sánchez Mejías*, begun shortly afterwards, a threnody from which the poet was careful to exclude the name of the animal appointed by fate as agent of the death of his friend. What a terrible irony that the bull should have been called 'Granadino'! It may have suggested to the superstitious Lorca that in death, even as in life, his and Ignacio's destinies were inseparably linked – as indeed would prove to be the case two summers later.

Autumn without Ignacio

In these circumstances the Barraca's performances took place at the International Summer School in Santander, which the company had visited for the first time the previous year. When they were over the students continued their tour, travelling south and arriving at Palencia on 25 August, where they played *The Seducer of Seville* to an attentive audience that included Miguel de Unamuno, who had already seen the production in Santander and liked it so much that he had come again specially. It appears that it was in Palencia that there occurred a scene that Modesto Higueras, perhaps the best actor in the Barraca, liked to relate. While the students were eating in a restaurant they were surprised by the arrival of José Antonio Primo de Rivera, accompanied by some friends. Lorca became visibly edgy and more so when, during the meal, the handsome aristocrat sent him a note scribbled on a napkin, which the poet glanced at and then hurriedly stuffed into his pocket. Higueras used to claim that he had managed to see the napkin later on without Lorca's realizing it. The note read: 'Federico, don't you think that with your blue overalls and our blue shirts we could between us forge a better Spain?' Given the attacks to which the Barraca had been subjected in the Falangist press as well as his strong dislike of fascism, Lorca's reaction to the presence of Primo de Rivera – and to the note – was understandable. The mentalities represented by the Falange and the democratically orientated Barraca respectively were incompatible.[37]

The tour over, Lorca spent a few days in Madrid before returning to Granada to join his parents, who had moved south to their summer quarters in the Huerta de San Vicente some weeks earlier. In the Residencia de Estudiantes he was interviewed by Juan Chabás (one of the writers who had travelled to Seville in 1927), expressing his satisfaction with the Barraca's performances in Santander, which had been warmly praised by Jean Prévost and the celebrated Italian theatre critic Ezio Levi. As for his own work, Lorca assured Chabás that he had finished *Yerma* and was now writing a new play, *La bestia hermosa* ('The Beautiful Animal') – a project about which nothing more is known.[38]

So delighted had Levi been with Lorca and the Barraca that, once back in Italy, he invited the poet to the Rome Theatre Congress, planned for that October, to talk about his experience with the student company. Lorca replied that he wanted to accept but could not do so until he knew when the rehearsals were to begin for *Yerma*, whose première was scheduled for November. Lorca's wife had also been invited to the Congress, and Federico, no doubt amused, asked Levi if, in view of the fact that he was unmarried, he might take with him the secretary of the Barraca, who was now his also? A free holiday in Rome with Rafael Rodríguez Rapún must have been a stimulating prospect but, in the event, the trip never came off and Levi's reply to the poet (if he replied, that is) is not known.[39] The fact that Lorca had now made Rodríguez Rapún his personal secretary suggests that recently they had grown even closer, although we possess no documentary or even oral evidence about their relationship at this time.

Early in September Lorca was back in Granada,[40] where at the end of the month a large group of friends and admirers gave him a dinner. Among them was the writer Nicolás María López, a contemporary of Angel Ganivet now in his sixty-ninth year. Unfortunately López's speech on this occasion was not published: an occasion that, as *El Defensor de Granada* pointed out, brought together two epochs and two tendencies ('tradition and revolution'), symbolized respectively by the older writer and by Lorca.[41]

Also present at the dinner was Emilio García Gómez, head of Granada's School of Arab Studies, set up by the Government in 1932. García Gómez, who was born in Madrid in 1905, had sprung to prominence in 1930 when he published a fascinating volume of translations of Andalusian Arabic poetry, and was by now a familiar figure in Granada. Lorca could not fail to be interested in the young man and his work, and must have devoured his translations when he returned from New York.

In his book of memoirs *Silla del moro* – the title is taken from an Arab building behind the Generalife palace known as 'The Moor's Seat' – García Gomez recalls how, after a reading of *Yerma* that summer, Lorca had told him about his collection of poems *Diwan of the Tamarit*, whose title contained an obvious allusion to Islamic Granada. García Gómez was impressed by the compositions the poet showed him, and when the University of Granada, in the person of Antonio Gallego Burín, offered to publish the little book, the Arabist undertook to prepare the twenty-one poems for the press and to write an introduction.[42] But the volume never appeared, despite the fact that it was at proof stage by that winter and that Lorca said in an interview published on 15 December that it would be out shortly.[43] Some time later, apparently exasperated by the University of Granada's procrastinations, the poet ordered a young friend, Eduardo Rodríguez Valdivieso, to recover the original manuscript from Antonio Gallego Burín, which he duly did, posting it back to Lorca in Madrid.[44]

In his introduction García Gomez observed that, while there were few formal connections between Lorca's *casidas* and *gacelas* and the Arab genres from which he had borrowed these terms, the 'delirious Granadinism' exhaled by several of the poems did link Federico, in his opinion, to the tradition of the Islamic poetry of Andalusia. In particular, García Gomez had been struck by Lorca's fascination with water – a fascination felt by all true sons of Granada, as Angel Ganivet had pointed out, and easy to understand for anyone who has visited the Alhambra hill.[45] In the poems of the *Diwan* Lorca expressed, as well as his 'delirious Granadinism', and in an intensely concentrated language, the themes that had always obsessed him and that were inseparable from his vision of the town: the terror of death, the fugacity of love, the inexorable passing of time.[46]

Before the poet returned to Madrid there occurred events that shook the country. On 1 October 1934 the Conservative Government fell, deprived of the backing of the largest right-wing group in the country, Gil Robles's coalition the CEDA (Confederación Española de Derechas Autónomas), which for ten months had supported it without itself having any Cabinet representation. Gil Robles now demanded this, and the President of the nation, Alcalá-Zamora, who mistrusted him for his lack of explicit allegiance to the Republic, had virtually no option this time but to give in. In the new Government Gil Robles's party obtained three vital Ministries: Agriculture, Labour and Justice. The reaction of the workers and of liberally minded people generally was unanimous: the presence of CEDA Ministers in the Government might well spell the beginning of a fascist takeover along the lines that had brought Hitler to power in Germany. Something had to be done.[47] For 4 October the trade unions called a revolutionary general strike which was supported unevenly throughout the country, but massively in the Basque provinces, Catalonia and, particularly, Asturias, where the coal miners seized control of the valleys and the capital, Oviedo, and prepared themselves to fight to the end. In fact they resisted fiercely until 15 October, when they were finally crushed by the units of the Spanish Army in Africa which, Moorish soldiers included, were landed on the northern coast. The repression was brutal, with numerous executions and thousands of prisoners taken, and left unforgettable memories among the populace. Owing to the strict censorship imposed by the Government the full truth about what was taking place could not be published in the newspapers but, where the García Lorcas were concerned, Fernando de los Ríos, who was on the parliamentary commission that investigated what had happened, could have kept them informed.[48]

In Barcelona the 'Catalan Republic within the Spanish Federal Republic' had been proclaimed by President Companys on 6 October. The adventure lasted for only ten hours. Manuel Azaña, who happened quite by chance to be in the Catalan capital at the time, was arrested and accused of complicity in the rebellion – nothing could have been further from the truth – and his innocence would not be established until 6 April 1935. In November almost 100 intellectuals, including Lorca, protested in an open letter to the Government against the intolerable treatment being meted out to the former Prime Minister. But the censorship prevented the document from appearing in the newspapers.[49]

The events of October, and particularly the Catalan separatist bid, played straight into the hands of the Right. On 7 October, coinciding with the initiation of the general strike, José Antonio Primo de Rivera, now the undisputed head of the fascist movement, had participated in a mass demonstration outside the Ministry of the Interior in Madrid's Puerta del Sol. For him the issue was clear: Spain's 'sacred unity' was being threatened by a sinister, Marxist–Jewish conspiracy organized from (naturally) Moscow, and it was the duty of every true Spaniard to prepare himself to resist these nefarious designs. As for the Falange, Primo de Rivera was happy about the part played by his organization in helping to put down the rebellion. In Oviedo and Gijón, Falangists had fought side by side with the Army and lost five men, five 'martyrs' to the Nationalist cause.[50]

Someone asked Lorca at this time why the Barraca was not putting on any plays. 'How could we be expected to perform when there are so many widows in Spain?' he replied. The main reason, however, was that the Barraca's government grant had recently been cut to half and it was becoming increasingly difficult to finance the company's tours.[51]

Meanwhile the poet was composing, in almost a frenzy, the elegy for Ignacio Sánchez Mejías which had begun to form in his mind shortly after the tragic event. Towards the end of October the poem was almost complete, and on 4 November Federico gave what was perhaps the first reading of the work to a group of friends at Carlos Morla Lynch's flat. Morla had no doubt about the quality of the four-part elegy: it was in his view 'a masterpiece'.[52]

At some point during the summer, when finishing *Yerma*, Lorca must have been in touch with Margarita Xirgu, to whom he had now promised the play, about the première. The Catalan actress's season at the Teatro Español opened at the end of October, and four weeks later rehearsals for *Yerma* were in full swing.[53] On 15 December, a fortnight before opening night, Lorca was interviewed by a well-known journalist on *El Sol*, Alardo Prats. The poet revealed that he was at work on a new play, *Doña Rosita the Spinster*, which he defined as a 'reveille for families divided into four gardens':

It will be a piece full of gentle ironies and touches of tender caricature; a comedy of middle-class manners, soft-toned, imbued with the charm and delicacy of past moments and periods. I think that people will be surprised by this evocation of time past, when the nightingales really sang and the gardens and flowers were topics for novels. That wonderful period when our parents were young. First, the days of the hooped skirt; then, bell-shaped skirts and the hobble: 1890, 1900, 1910.

Lorca does not seem to have said so on this occasion, but in *Doña Rosita the Spinster* he was exploring his own specific time past as well as the spirit of the Granada that had made him the poet he was. The interview confirmed how much he now felt himself to be involved in a personal struggle to renew the contemporary Spanish theatre, so pusillanimous about confronting real human and social issues. Millions of people were deprived of theatre, the poet insisted, and, drawing on his experience with the Barraca, he expressed again his conviction that good, well-produced plays always get through to 'ordinary' people, even though these may not grasp all the subtleties. Lashing out against the commercial theatre, concerned only with profits, the poet left no doubts about his commitment to society at a time when only a few months earlier the Asturias rising had been put down so brutally, and there were tens of thousands of political prisoners. 'In this world I am and always will be on the side of the poor,' he insisted.[54]

Lorca told Alardo Prats that he was planning to complete the trilogy that he had begun with *Blood Wedding* and continued with *Yerma*. The final work, he said, was to be entitled *The Drama of Lot's Daughters*. This was almost certainly the projected play he had talked about in Cuba in 1930 to Luis Cardoza y Aragón and later, back in Spain, to Rafael Martínez Nadal, and which was then called *The Destruction of Sodom*.[55] At least one act of the play was written, although the manuscript has been lost except for the first page, and dating is impossible. Lorca read it to Rodríguez Rapún and Luis Sáenz de la Calzada in the Residencia de Estudiantes, and according to the latter it recounted, in a setting reminiscent of Piero della Francesca and Giotto, the arrival of the angels in the city, and how, when the inhabitants want to sodomize them, Lot, appalled, offers his daughters instead and himself commits incest with one of them. Thus, by trying to avoid sodomy the wayward citizens sin even more heinously.[56] Lorca had told Cardoza y Aragón in Cuba that, compared to this play, Oscar Wilde would look out of date and cowardly. With *The Drama of Lot's Daughters*, clearly, Federico intended to shock, and shock deeply.

Yerma scandalizes the Right

At this time Lorca was frequenting one of Madrid's most colourful cafés, the Ballena Alegre or 'Merry Whale', situated in the basement of the Café Lyon, opposite the Post Office in the Calle de Alcalá. There one night he was discovered shortly before the première of *Yerma* by the journalist Alfredo Muñiz, who described the scene in the *Heraldo de Madrid*. The poet, as always, was surrounded by friends and admirers: Pablo Neruda (who had arrived in Madrid that summer and in whose flat Lorca had composed much of the elegy to Sánchez Mejías), the painter Isaías Cabezón, the Chilean musician Acario Cotapos, the architect Luis Lacasa, Eduardo Ugarte, Rodríguez Rapún and other Barraca companions, and José Amorós, who, since the death of Ignacio, had become the bullfighter of the group.[57] Lorca used to make his way from the Ballena Alegre to the Teatro Español to attend the rehearsals of *Yerma*, often accompanied by Eduardo Ugarte, Rodríguez Rapún and the painter José Caballero. To the latter the poet had entrusted the design of the poster for the play, and the handsome young artist from Huelva was also at work on the illustrations for the *Lament for Ignacio Sánchez Mejías*. At the rehearsals Caballero was struck, as he had been in Josefina Díaz de Artigas's production of *Blood Wedding*, by the poet's insistence on the split-second timing of the actors' movements.[58]

The dress rehearsal of *Yerma*, on 28 December, aroused tremendous expectation and was attended by many notables, including Ramón del Valle-Inclán and Unamuno. Lorca, one malicious journalist reported, came and went smoking a pipe surrounded by 'pale young men' reminiscent of those who always accompanied José González Marín, a professional reciter well known in Madrid for his homosexuality.[59] Profoundly irritated by the article, Cipriano Rivas Cherif, Margarita Xirgu's artistic director (widely believed himself to be homosexual and to be involved in an amorous relationship with, of all people, his brother-in-law Manuel Azaña), prohibited the journalist further access to the theatre.[60]

The première took place the following night. Unamuno attended again, a gesture whose significance was not lost on the journalists, and when the curtain went up there was not a seat left in the house.[61] Lorca and his friends had perhaps heard the rumour that extreme-right-wing elements were preparing trouble for the first night of the play, not only because of its by Spanish standards daring contents, but on account of the poet's known Republican sympathies and, particularly, Margarita Xirgu's close friendship with Manuel Azaña, who had just been freed from prison on bail. The fact that Cipriano Rivas Cherif was Azaña's brother-in-law cannot have helped either. That the rumours were true became apparent immediately the play began, when insults were hurled from the upper gallery at Margarita Xirgu and the ex-Prime Minister. According to one witness, shouts of 'Lesbian!' and 'Queer!' were also directed at the actress and Lorca respectively.[62] The rest of the audience reacted indignantly and, after a scuffle, the hecklers were ejected. The identity of those responsible for the episode – according to Carlos Morla Lynch 'a group of youths' – was never established, although Eduardo Blanco-Amor, also present, claimed that they were Falangists.[63] Oddly enough Luis Buñuel, who was in a box, does not mention the noisy incident in his memoirs – perhaps the agonizing bout of sciatica he was suffering from that night blotted out the memory and might also account in part for his adverse reaction to the play, which he considered banal by surrealist standards.[64] Once calm was restored the performance continued, amid scenes of rising enthusiasm, not only on account of the quality of the work in itself but of the excellence of the acting and sets. Lorca had to come on stage frequently, and when the final curtain fell the applause was deafening. The poet had known triumphant success in Buenos Aires but never in Spain: he was overwhelmed, as was Margarita Xirgu, whose Yerma had deeply moved the audience.[65]

But if all the liberal, Republican and left-wing press came up with rave reviews, the right-wing newspapers were unanimous in their condemnation of what they considered an immoral, anti-Spanish, irreligious and odious play. They were offended both by the theme of the work, which they considered more fit for textbooks on gynaecology than for dramatic exploration, and by what they saw as its implicit rejection of Catholic values. The Old Pagan Woman was found repellent, and the moment when she asserts that she does not believe in God, and recommends Yerma not to do so either, was picked out as especially reprehensible. Obloquy fell, too, on the Bacchanalian scene in the final act, based on the annual pilgrimage to the village of Moclín. These critiques, more like pastoral letters than theatre reviews, read as if they had been dictated by the Primate of All Spain in person.[66]

The satirical press of the extreme Right went further. *Gracia y Justicia*, so ready to denigrate the Barraca and Lorca, at whose homosexuality it had begun to sneer back in 1932, not only attacked the play, but alluded snidely to Lorca's group of 'hangers-on', as it pleased to see them. In the same issue there was a commentary on Lorca's and Neruda's joint speech on Rubén Darío, given in Buenos Aires and recently reproduced in two Madrid newspapers. *Gracia y Justicia* could not resist pointing out that it was Neruda who started off the proceedings by saying 'Ladies', Lorca adding the 'and Gentlemen', and that this order was maintained throughout. It had struck the writer as odd at first. But then, he explained, 'I realized that it was the most normal thing in the world, or rather, in García Lorca.'[67] There were even more scurrilous innuendoes and allusions in at least one other extreme-right-wing periodical.[68]

The intense and widespread dislike of Lorca felt by many conservative Catholics dated from the première of *Yerma*. As for Granada, an indication of this can be found in the fact that, while the Republican *El Defensor* reported enthusiastically on the first night, neither the increasingly conservative *Noticiero Granadino* nor the Catholic *Ideal* even mentioned it.[69] Lorca was now seen as an enemy of the Church, and this impression would be confirmed when Margarita Xirgu produced the play in Barcelona some months later. From the point of view of democratically minded people, however, *Yerma* had brought a breath of fresh air to the Spanish theatre at a time when, with a strongly conservative Government in power, a repressive Church was once again enjoying, and abusing, its centuries-old position of privilege. As one critic wrote, 'This healthily realistic work, with its limpidity, sincerity and dignified revaluation of the functions of the human body, marks a decisive step towards our liberation from the medieval backwardness that still oppresses us.'[70]

9

1935

Success in the Theatre

Lorca was at work at this time on *Lot's Daughters*, which according to some comments published by the poet in *El Sol* had now reverted to its original title *The Destruction of Sodom* and was 'almost finished' (this last claim is impossible to verify since, as has already been pointed out, only the first page of the manuscript is known). He was also busy with *Doña Rosita the Spinster*, whose theme, he now explained – amplifying an earlier statement to the journalists – was 'the tragic aspect of our social life: all those Spanish women who never found a husband.'[1]

During January and February crowds flocked to see *Yerma*, while in New York, on 11 February, *Blood Wedding*, translated by José Weissberger with the title *Bitter Oleander* and produced by Irene Lewisohn, opened at the Neighborhood Playhouse. The virtual impossibility of rendering Lorca's Andalusian idiom into viable English meant that the play had little chance of success, despite the fact that the poet had collaborated closely with the theatre, sending music and suggestions since 1933. The audience response was far from adverse, however, and, although most of the critics were bemused, some made encouraging noises. When the play came off on 2 March Lorca at least had the satisfaction of knowing that his name was beginning to be mentioned in the city that had affected him so deeply six years earlier.[2]

On 18 February an extremely important interview with the poet appeared in the Madrid evening newspaper *La Voz*. The reporter, Angel Lázaro, had met Lorca's father late on the morning of the interview at the entrance to the block of flats in the Calle de Alcalá, and Don Federico had told him wryly that his son had only just got out of bed, adding that it was his habit to write well into the night. Thus apprised Lázaro made his way upstairs. He found the poet modest, despite his recent successes and the money he was now earning. Insisting that above all he loved simplicity, Federico recalled his early days in Fuente Vaqueros, when he had been part and parcel of the life, speech and rhythms of the countryside, and Lázaro noted that, as he spoke, his 'childlike face' lit up with enthusiasm. It was the look of the Lorca who, in Buenos Aires, had said that he suffered from what the psychoanalysts would call an 'agrarian complex'.[3] But Lázaro found that Federico did not just want to talk about his childhood. His theatre and his desire to write revolutionary plays capable of making people think – this is what was mainly on his mind. A few weeks earlier he had told an audience of actors and theatre people that poets and dramatists should be daring enough to express 'the despair of the soldiers who are against war';[4] now he claimed that he had accepted his own challenge and was planning an anti-war play. Of this project nothing remains but the title: *A Drama against War*.[5] As for the publication of his work, Lorca told Lázaro that he was about to bring out *Lament for Ignacio Sánchez Mejías* – the elegy, published by José Bergamín, appeared in May, with illustrations by José Caballero – and *Introduction to Death*, which he said contained 'some three hundred poems'. Doubtless this was yet another Andalusian exaggeration. No book with this title ever appeared and it can only be assumed that the poet had in mind his New York cycle.[6]

On 28 February, while *Yerma* continued its run in the Teatro Español, Lola Membrives, who had just arrived back in Spain, opened in the Madrid Coliseum with the production of *Blood Wedding* that had been such a smash hit in Buenos Aires. The critics were enthusiastic and one of them, remembering the original, Josefina Díaz de Artigas production of the play two years earlier, wrote that the Membrives version was a 'revelation'.[7] The play ran until the end of the month. It was then normal practice for companies to perform twice each evening, and on 18 March Lola Membrives gave *Blood Wedding* at the early performance and, at the second, her version of *The Shoemaker's Prodigious Wife*. The critics were impressed by the latter production, and that day Lorca could boast that he had three plays on in Madrid – a feat perhaps unequalled in the annals of the Spanish theatre.[8] Not long afterwards Lola Membrives added a musical tailpiece to *The Shoemaker's Prodigious Wife*, based on the one devised by Lorca in Buenos Aires. The play had 20 performances in all before coming off at the end of the month, and *Blood Wedding* 30. As for *Yerma*, it had more than 130 before ending its run in the Teatro Español on 21 April.[9] All of this meant money as well as prestige, and Lorca, now one of the most financially successful dramatists in Spain, could face the future confidently. This showed increasingly in his statements to the press.

Federico spent Holy Week in Seville as the guest of the poet Joaquín

Romero Murube, whom he had first met during his visit to the city in December 1927. Romero Murube was keeper of the marvellous Arab palace of the Alcázar, so reminiscent of the Generalife in Granada, and was determined to entertain Federico in the grand style. Lorca had three old friends in Seville whom he saw frequently during his stay: José Bello, who had been living there since 1927, the poet Jorge Guillén and José Antonio Rubio Sacristán, with whom he had coincided in New York and who was now Professor of Law at the University. Romero Murube installed a grand piano in the gardens near the house: there the poet played Spanish folk songs, the music mingling with the murmur of the fountains and the singing of the birds. 'We were like caliphs,' Rubio Sacristán recalled.[10] For his part Guillén remembered Lorca's wonderful recitation, in the same gardens, of the *Lament for Ignacio Sánchez Mejías* – a recitation all the more poignant because Ignacio was a *sevillano* through and through and rarely missed a Holy Week in his home town.[11]

Lorca, who from his childhood had a passionate love of pageantry, lived his visit to Seville with characteristic intensity, boasting a few months later in Barcelona that not only had Romero Murube got him the best seats for the processions but that he had been fêted by the local Gypsies as if he were one of their own. The poet claimed that he had read his elegy to Sánchez Mejías before an improvised Gypsy altar, and slept in a giant, apple-scented bed prepared specially for him by the great flamenco dancer 'La Malena'.[12] How much of this was true no one will ever know. As the poet's brother Francisco once said, Federico could never be relied on to tell the truth about himself.[13]

Lorca was back in Madrid at the beginning of May and soon afterwards finished *Doña Rosita the Spinster*, stimulated, it seems, by his conversations with Romero Murube's aunts, expert horticulturalists, and the gardeners of the Alcázar, all of whom he had questioned closely on botanical matters relevant to the play.[14]

For months the Republicans had been fearing that a right-wing *coup* might occur at any moment, and these fears grew when, on 6 May, José María Gil Robles, the leader of the conservative coalition, became Minister of War. Gil Robles, one of whose obsessions was to strengthen the Army in preparation for taking on a possible Marxist revolution, appointed the young General Francisco Franco as head of his general staff, a move deplored by the progressives in view of the officer's reputation as an enemy of democracy. Other appointments by Gil Robles seemed equally suspicious. In the following months the Ministry of War carried out an implacable purge of known liberal and left-wing elements in the Army, all of which added fuel to the fire. Years later Gil Robles denied that he had ever been in favour of a *coup d'état*. But, while this may have been so, few republicans had any doubt that the Minister of War could not be trusted, and it was widely felt that he supported the restoration of the monarchy within the framework of one form or another of fascist-style corporative state.[15]

What seemed to be Gil Robles's irresistible ascent coincided with the Madrid Book Fair, celebrated annually in the Paseo de Recoletos. The fifth impression of *Gypsy Ballads*, which had just been published, sold out immediately, and soon it was announced that the sixth had gone to press.[16] The *Lament for Ignacio Sánchez Mejías* had appeared recently, with perfect timing, and was also selling well; Lorca's *Don Cristóbal's Puppet Show* was performed in the Paseo, close to the stands;[17] and, to cap it all, the *Heraldo de Madrid* reported that Angel del Río had just published, in the New York *Revista Hispánica Moderna*, the first comprehensive study of the poet's work. Lorca's reaction to his friend's long article is not known, although he must surely have read it by this time, probably in the copy sent to him from Alicante on 3 March 1935 by Juan Guerrero, one of the editors.[18] Del Río was well equipped for the task of assessing Lorca's work to date, both as a sensitive critic and as a close friend of the poet, first in Madrid in the early twenties and later in New York. He had come to believe that Lorca tended 'towards the interpretation of the mystery of life and of man at their deepest levels' and that, if the promise of his production so far were realized, he would be not only the finest 'popular poet' of his generation (that is, a poet working within a tradition nurtured by folk art) but one of the great poets of the age.[19]

During these months Federico's friendship with Pablo Neruda had deepened. Each day they and their numerous friends met in the Cervecería de Correos, just across the Calle de Alcalá from the Post Office. If Federico was the star turn of the group, Neruda more than held his own. Often the band moved on to the Chilean's flat, known familiarly as 'The House of Flowers', in Calle de Rodríguez San Pedro, on the west side of Madrid looking towards the mountains. Nearby was the Argüelles market where Neruda, a voracious eater, bought the fruit, vegetables and hot peppers he relished. In his flat the parties went on sometimes for days on end, and people could be found asleep in every nook and cranny. Sometimes the group would sally forth to indulge in one of their favourite activities, 'inaugurating monuments', a proclivity perhaps not unrelated to a hilarious scene in Buñuel's *L'Age d'or*. These occasions provided ample opportunity for the deployment of verbal wit, and the speeches improvised at the 'inauguration' of the nearby memorial to the novelist Emilia Pardo Bazán were, it is said, particularly riotous.[20]

In June Neruda published an 'Ode to Federico García Lorca' which must have moved the Spaniard deeply. The poem, drawing on memories of the months when the two coincided in Buenos Aires as well as on their shared experience in Madrid, shows to what an extent Neruda was aware of the dark, death-obsessed side to Federico. In it he imagines the arrival at Lorca's house of an interminable succession of presences, human and non-human, who crave the consolation of talking to the Andalusian poet. 'The summer with its broken lips' turns up; so do 'many people in dying dress', 'broken ploughs and poppies' and 'a rose of hate and needles'; they are followed by Neruda and an assortment of his and Federico's friends in the Argentinian capital and Madrid.[21] Almost forty years later Neruda remembered with intense nostalgia those pre-war months in Madrid. 'They were the great days of my life,' he said on French television. 'It was such a splendid and generous rebirth of Spanish creative life that I never again saw anything that could approach it.'[22]

Doña Rosita the Spinster, or the Spirit of Granada

Lorca had said in December 1934, shortly before the première of *Yerma*, that the acts of his new play *Doña Rosita the Spinster* were set respectively in 1890, 1900 and 1910 and that the work evoked 'the marvellous time when our parents were young.'[23] In January he had been a little more explicit, saying that in the play was expressed 'all the tragedy of Spanish provincial pseudo-refinement, something that will make our newer generations laugh but which is profoundly dramatic socially since it reflects what the middle class was like then'.[24] If the poet seemed in these first observations to be suggesting that *Doña Rosita the Spinster* explored a social tragedy set in the past, he was shortly to correct any misunderstanding on that point by insisting that the play was perfectly relevant to contemporary Spain:

It would be better to say the drama of Spanish pseudo-refinement, of Spanish hypocrisy, of the desire for sensual pleasure that women have to repress forcibly in the deepest recess of their fevered flesh. For how much longer will all the Doña Rositas of Spain have to carry on like this?[25]

It was some time before the poet publicized the fact that *Doña Rosita the Spinster* was not only set in Granada but, more specifically, in a typical *carmen* of the hilly Albaicín quarter, one of those delightful villas with enclosed gardens that look across the valley of the Darro to the Alhambra and, beyond, to the slopes of the Sierra Nevada, and which Lorca felt expressed exactly the introverted spirit of the town.* The Albaicín and its *cármenes* held few secrets for Lorca, and in 1924 he had written to Melchor

---

* For earlier comments on *cármenes*, see p. 36.

Fernández Almagro: 'I love Granada but only to live there on another plane, in a *carmen*. The rest is nonsense. In a *carmen*, close to what one loves and feels. Whitewash, myrtle and fountain.'[26] Lorca knew that to share a *carmen* with the beloved would be bliss – paradise on earth – but that to be there alone and without love could be a form of death, given the incomparable beauty of the surroundings and shut-in, almost conventual, architecture of the houses. The definitive subtitle of the play, 'A Granadine Nineteenth-century Poem', underlined the poet's intention: *Doña Rosita the Spinster* is the dramatization, with Romantic tints and subtle distancing, of the *pena negra* or 'black anguish' of *Gypsy Ballads*, which Lorca identified on several occasions with the spirit of Granada.

The 'poem' is also a meditation on the poet's childhood and youth and on the inner history of his family. No other work of his contains so many allusions to his background. The dates apportioned to the three acts are highly significant in this respect. Rosita is twenty in 1890, when the play begins, which means that, like Lorca's mother, she was born in 1870; she is an orphan (the circumstances are not explained), and we are reminded that Vicenta Lorca's father died before she was born. The poet's mother had known penury, and the family had to move frequently, once from a villa not dissimilar to a *carmen;* and when, at the end of the play, after the dead uncle's ruinous expenditure on his botanical experiments has been discovered, the mortgaged *carmen* must perforce be relinquished, Lorca may perhaps be remembering this episode. Rosita, on another level, is a sort of failed Vicenta Lorca. The latter, from a poor family, became a teacher by sheer grit; Rosita, from a middle-class background, has no such opportunity and cannot go out into the outside world. Only marriage to the man she loves could free her – and he leaves for Tucumán.

Lorca places the second act of the play in 1900, the year he consistently claimed, even in his passports, to be that of his own birth, for reasons not entirely clear but perhaps to distance himself from the débâcle of 1898, when Spain had to abandon Cuba, Puerto Rico and the Philippines, and, at the same time, to identify himself resolutely as a man of the twentieth century.[27] As for the last act, set in 1910, this is the date habitually assigned by the poet to the loss of his childhood happiness, to his great and unspecified amorous failure and to his entry into the sordid world of examinations and social pressures. The abandonment of the *carmen*, with the wind rattling the shutters (intimations of Chekhov), and the descent from the Albaicín to the centre of town, may reflect, for the poet, his family's departure from Asquerosa in 1909 and its arrival in Granada. There is more to it than that, of course. The poet said that the last act of the play contains a presentiment of the First World War, and perhaps too we can find a premonition of the collapse of the Republic.[28]

As for Rosita herself, she embodies elements not only of Vicenta Lorca and of the poet's cousin Clotilde García Picossi, whose broken-down ex-fiancé Federico had helped in Rosario, but of Maravillas Pareja, who inspired the poem 'Elegy' (1918), of various other spinsters known to the family and perhaps also of his friend Emilia Llanos who, as the years passed, became more and more like the protagonist of Lorca's play. As for the other characters, Don Martín, as was seen earlier, is a compendium of Lorca's music teacher, Antonio Segura Mesa, and the journalist and teacher at the Institute, Martín Scheroff y Aví; the ridiculous Professor of Economics, 'Mr X', is based on the real-life Ramón Guixé y Mexía; the teacher Consuegra really existed with this same name; while the marvellous Housekeeper derives from the many servants, particularly Dolores Cuesta, who had attended to the García Lorca children's every whim both in the Vega and later in Granada.

The Housekeeper deserves more than a passing word. When Lorca's cousin Mercedes Delgado García, another of his favourites, saw *Doña Rosita the Spinster*, she immediately recognized that this character's manner of expressing herself derives from the speech of Asquerosa.[29] In the stagnant world of the Granada petty bourgeoisie represented by Rosita and her aunt and uncle, where maintaining appearances is a full-time occupation, the Housekeeper stands for the natural life that Lorca always proposes as the only possible salvation for human beings. The Housekeeper speaks the most agonizing words in the play when Rosita's fate is sealed and the red rose has turned spectral white:

I'm not calm enough to stand these things without my heart going mad inside me like a dog being chased. When I buried my husband I was very sad, but deep down I felt happy, no, not exactly happy – tremendous relief more like – at not being dead myself. When I buried my daughter it was as if they'd stamped on my guts, but the dead are dead – they're dead, that's all, you cry, you shut the door and try to keep on living! But what's happening to Rosita is the worst of all. It's loving and not finding another body; it's weeping without knowing for whom, it's sighing over someone who doesn't deserve the sighs. It's an open wound with a constant trickle of blood, and there's nobody, nobody in the whole wide world, to bring cottonwool, bandages or a little cool ice.[30]

Many other details in the play can be shown to derive from the Granada Lorca knew as a child and adolescent, or heard about from his mother, who must have been an inexhaustible fund of information concerning life in the town in the years before his birth. The Ayola girls' father, for example, really was 'Photographer to His Majesty the King',[31] while the Ponce de Leóns and Pérez de Herrastis were well-known local gentry. As for the three *manolas* evoked in the song, who go together to the Alhambra in search of love, it appears that Lorca was not only drawing on a folk song but alluding to three inseparable girls who lived in the Cuesta de Gomérez (the hill leading up to the Alhambra Wood) and were later, according to the poet's friend and biographer José Mora Guarnido, scattered far and wide by a 'lamentable fate'.[32]

As regards the 'language of flowers', from which the poet extracts such subtle play in *Doña Rosita*, illustrated guides to the topic were popular throughout Europe until the First World War did away with such senti-mentality, and Lorca's brother Francisco recalled that the flower ballad was taken from a little book that also contained the language of stamps, fans, dreams and so forth. A book, perhaps, that had belonged to Vicenta Lorca.[33]

Doña Rosita the Spinster is the work that expresses most subtly Lorca's complex relationship with Granada, a town he both loved and feared – feared on account of its intense introspection, its resistance to change, its lack of vitality and its intolerance. Shortly before the work was first performed later in the year, the poet said that he had written it in order to relax after the tragedies *Yerma* and *Blood Wedding*, thinking that it would turn out to be a 'simple and pleasant comedy'. But in fact, he added, it contained more tears than his two previous plays.[34] Given the poet's view of Granada and the work's theme it could hardly have been otherwise, and if ever Lorca came close to identifying with one of his protagonists it was with Rosita.

Goodbye to the Barraca

The long summer holidays were approaching and, with them, the dispersion of the ebullient group that frequented the Cervecería de Correos. It may have been at this time that Jorge Guillén had a conversation with Lorca's father, now seventy-six. The old countryman was proud of his son's success in the theatre – a pride not unrelated to the volume of the poet's earnings – and, remembering former setbacks, exclaimed, 'Yes, this time he's got there!' It was true. Lorca was now telling his friends about his plans to put his domestic life on a more independent footing and to invest the money he was earning in building a villa of his own on the Mediterranean. Probably he felt that the time had come at last to abandon the family nest.[35]

For Corpus Christi Federico returned to Granada, where, on 28 and 29 June, Margarita Xirgu performed Lope de Vega's *Fuente Ovejuna* and *El Alcalde de Zalamea* ('The Mayor of Zalamea') in the open-air Palace of Charles V on the Alhambra Hill. Lorca now had an extremely close friendship with Margarita, who had just announced that that autumn, after a brief season in Barcelona, she would be touring with her company in Mexico and other Latin American countries. 'I want a little rest from Spain,' she told journalists, 'and I want Spain to have a little rest from me.'[36] As things turned out, however, she did not leave the country until the following January.

At the beginning of July a nasty incident took place in Granada when the President of the local branch of the Catholic Party, irritated by an article that had appeared in *El Defensor de Granada*, took it upon himself to assault the newspaper's editor, Constantino Ruiz Carnero, in the latter's own home. It so happened that Eduardo Blanco-Amor had just arrived in Granada on his second visit to Lorca and witnessed the scene. In an article published in *El Defensor* a few days later, the Galician journalist called his readers' attention to the increase in violence that the 'big-stick parties' were now provoking all around Spain. The attack on Ruiz Carnero was but another symptom of a deeply disturbing national situation.[37]

In the Huerta de San Vicente Blanco-Amor took some excellent photographs of the poet, and up at the Alhambra one afternoon was witness to a Lorca 'happening' when Federico suddenly jumped on to a rampart looking out over the immense sweep of the Vega, and began to declaim the *Ode to Walt Whitman* at the top of his voice and as if down below there were a 'Biblical multitude' receiving his words. 'He was utterly changed, transfigured, in a trance,' Blanco-Amor recalled years later.[38] Lorca took his friend to the Casino so that he could observe at his ease the cream of Granada's 'putrid philistines'. Blanco-Amor did not like what he saw, and suspected that many of the members were jealous of the money Federico had brought back from Buenos Aires. 'They say that you poets are all queers,' one of them ventured.[39] The Arabist and landowner José Navarro Pardo noted down in his diary a similar scene which occurred, probably at about this time, in the Café Hollywood (a well-known establishment mentioned by Malcolm Lowry in *Under the Volcano*). One day he was sitting with some friends when Lorca came in. He got up to greet the poet, had a chat and then rejoined his table. 'How could you have anything to do with that queer?' his companions objected.[40] Lorca was commonly known among the local bourgeoisie as 'The Queer with the Bow-Tie' (*el maricón de la pajarita*).[41] Such was the mentality of the Granada Right in the months leading up to the electoral victory of the Popular Front. After that victory it would grow even more vicious.

In Granada Blanco-Amor renewed his acquaintance with Lorca's confidant José María García Carrillo, as unashamedly homosexual as always and extraordinarily witty and inventive, and was introduced by Federico to his young friend Eduardo Rodríguez Valdivieso, whom the poet had first met at a carnival masquerade in the Alhambra Palace Hotel a few years earlier. Rodríguez Valdivieso has recalled that Lorca was very reserved about his private life and about sex but that, none the less, he heard him make an unambiguous statement one of those days: the male organ, Lorca insisted, was infinitely superior, in its erect, thrusting dynamism, to the abject female affair.[42] Another young *granadino*, the poet Luis Rosales – whose first book of verse, *Abril*, was published that July – heard Lorca say something similar. One day, after praising women's thighs, hair and breasts, Federico exclaimed: 'But their genitals, Luis, their genitals!'[43] While Salvador Dalí, for his part, always said that the poet was as horrified as himself by the female genitals (a horror expressed in several of Lorca's drawings); he refused, in an interview in 1986, to accept that Federico could ever in seriousness have praised the mammary glands, at least the well-developed variety. 'Lorca really hated them!' he asserted forcefully.[44]

Federico returned to Madrid around 10 July and read *Doña Rosita the Spinster* to Margarita Xirgu, her husband–manager Miguel Ortín and Cipriano Rivas Cherif at the *parador*, or state-run hotel, in the Gredos mountains outside the city where the actress was taking a quick holiday. According to an interview with Ortín published on 16 July, Margarita planned to begin her season in Barcelona on 10 September with *Yerma*, and hoped to be able to produce *Doña Rosita* before her brief run ended on 15 October. After that the company would spend a few days in Italy and sail for Mexico at the start of November. More details of the trip to Italy were announced shortly afterwards.[45] Fourteen years later Margarita recalled that, the day after the revelation of *Doña Rosita the Spinster* in Gredos, Lorca read them the first act of a startling avant-garde play, as yet without a title.[46] If the actress had read *The Public*, which it is clear she had not, she would have perceived that the new play, only the first act of which is known and which Lorca was to call, some months later, *The Dream of Life*, was both technically and thematically the child of the former work: theatre within the theatre (here the offstage performance of *A Midsummer Night's Dream*), the blurring of actors and audience, a revolution taking place in the street outside and the theme of the love that dare not speak its name. When the Author, who identifies himself explicitly with 'the people', explains to the audience that his purpose is to move them by revealing the simple truths they do not want to acknowledge, we are reminded immediately of the Producer's words in the closing moments of *The Public*;[47] while in the play's affirmation of the individual's right to love freely according to his or her needs we also recall the earlier work written in Havana in 1930.

Commenting on *A Midsummer Night's Dream*, the Author in *The Dream of Life* says:

Everything in the play tends to prove that love, of whatever kind, is merely fortuitous and in no way depends on us. The people go off to sleep, along comes Puck the sprite and makes them sniff the flower* and, when they wake up, they fall in love with the first person they see even though they were in love with someone else before they went to sleep. Thus the Queen of the Fairies, Titania, falls in love with a peasant with an ass's head![48]

They are words that echo precisely the Conjuror's observations at the end of *The Public:*

If love is pure chance and Titania, Queen of the Fairies, falls in love with an ass, it would hardly be surprising if, by the same procedure, Gonzalo drank in the music-hall with a boy dressed in white on his knee.[49]

That both the Conjuror and the Author are expressing Lorca's own view is confirmed by the poet's friend Rafael Martínez Nadal, who has remembered a conversation with the dramatist in 1936 about the scene between Titania and the ass. 'What Shakespeare is telling us', Lorca said more or less, 'is that love, which does not depend on the free will of the individual, is to be found at all levels with equal intensity.'[50]

In the Second Member of the Audience Lorca has embodied the mentality of those opposed both to freedom in love and to the liberation of the working class. That he had the Spanish extreme Right in mind seems obvious. This character believes all the stories about atrocities committed by the workers, himself kills one of them in the theatre ('Good shooting! God will repay me. Blessed be He in His holy vengeance'),[51] and is an archetypal *macho* for whom women are mere objects. It is the mentality that in August 1936 would be responsible for the poet's death. Lorca knew only too well who were his enemies.

Margarita was fascinated by what she had heard, and on another occasion that summer Lorca read the act for her again, this time in one of his favourite Madrid haunts, the restaurant Casa Pascual (16 Calle de la Luna), famous for its roast kid and house wine.[52]

At this time Lorca at last got around to assembling his New York poems so that a typewritten copy could be prepared for the publishers. Begging a friend to return to him the manuscript of one of the compositions, the poet announced proudly (August 1935) that he had never before dictated a letter, adding that it was being taken down by his private secretary.[53] About Lorca and Rafael Rodríguez Rapún's relationship at this time, it is almost

---

* The Author has got it slightly wrong, forgetting that Puck administers a phial to the eyes, not a perfume to the nostrils.

impossible to obtain any information: no correspondence has come to light; there are no diaries, and oral information on the subject is as scant as it is unhelpful. All we can surmise is that, given their professional as well as affective relationship, the two must have been together virtually every day.

On 19 August the Barraca's performances began at the International Summer School in Santander, where a distinguished Italian drama critic and Professor of the History of Theatre at Rome University, Silvio D'Amico, met Lorca and was duly impressed. D'Amico wanted to know how the Barraca was financed, and Lorca explained that, if they had started in 1932 with an annual government grant of 100,000 pesetas, this had later been cut to half (when the Right came to power) and that very summer, finally, altogether. How was the company going to survive in such unfavourable circumstances? Federico insisted that they would continue to perform, no matter what happened. Somewhere the money would be found.[54]

In Santander Lorca was interviewed by his old friend Miguel Pérez Ferrero, who in the columns of the *Heraldo de Madrid* had been following his career with interest for several years. Federico was full of praise for Margarita Xirgu, and excited about her forthcoming trip to Italy, where Pirandello, one of the sponsors of the company's visit, had expressed his impatience to see her perform *Yerma*. As for the suppression of the Barraca's grant, which was being heatedly discussed on the pro-Republican campus of the International University, Lorca was forthright: they would continue to perform, even if there were no costumes and they had to do so in their boilersuits. If the Right tried to prevent them from erecting their stage, they would act on foot in the village streets and squares of the villages. If necessary, they would put on clandestine theatre in caves! Anything rather than give in.[55]

Lorca left Santander before the Barraca's performances finished because he had promised to be with Margarita Xirgu in the town of Fuenteovejuna, in Cordova, on 25 August, where the actress was to perform Lope de Vega's famous play of that name. These were the days of the tercentenary celebrations in honour of the great Madrid playwright; the papers carried articles on the 'Phoenix', new editions of his works were appearing, many of his plays were being staged up and down the country and Lorca's version of Lope's *La dama boba* was about to be given by Margarita Xirgu in the Teatro Español – another reason for getting back quickly to Madrid. The *barracos* could not help feeling that they had been abandoned by their progenitor, and it was, in fact, the beginning of the end. From this summer onwards Lorca, increasingly engrossed in his own work, began to distance himself from the organization that he more than anyone else had helped to shape; and the process was completed when, that winter, the Students'

Union elected new representatives to the committee that ran the University Theatre and Rafael Rodríguez Rapún lost his position as secretary.[56]

Margarita Xirgu's performance of *Fuente Ovejuna* could not fail to be a success in the Andalusian town where the tumultuous events remembered in the play had occurred 300 years earlier, and even less so at a time when the peasants were suffering the results of the Right's determination to clamp down on their legitimate demands. The square was thronged.[57] The following day the poet visited Cordova, a city for which he felt something approaching veneration. There he met Fernando Vázquez Ocaña, editor of the newspaper *El Sur* and a socialist Member of Parliament. Vázquez Ocaña, who was to be one of Lorca's first biographers, recalled that during their over-lunch conversation, just before the poet caught the train back to Madrid, someone asked him why he had such a manifest obsession with death. 'I can't help it,' Lorca had replied. 'I'm like a little glow-worm in the grass, terrified that someone is going to step on me.'[58]

On 8 September, after performing *La dama boba* and *Fuente Ovejuna* in Madrid, Margarita Xirgu took her leave of the Teatro Español, where for five years she had reigned supreme, and left for Barcelona with Federico.[59] The newspapers announced that it might be some time before she returned – in Latin America she was awaited eagerly – but probably no one, not even Lorca with his uncanny presentiments, could have suspected that the actress was never again to set foot in the Spanish capital.

10

Barcelona

Re-encounter with Dalí

Margarita Xirgu began her month's season in the Teatro Barcelona on 10 September with Lorca's version of Lope de Vega's *La dama boba*, which was such a success that the opening of *Yerma* was delayed for a week.[1] Given the strongly hostile reaction of the right-wing press in Madrid when *Yerma* was staged the previous December, the adulation the Catalans felt for Margarita Xirgu and the much discussed merits of the play itself, the expectation in Barcelona in the week leading up to the première was tremendous.[2] The evening passed off triumphantly, and such was the emotion generated that many members of the audience wept openly. Predictably, the press response was similar to that in Madrid: the liberal, Republican and left-wing papers all praised the work (one critic found in it 'a poetic interpretation of the most profound Spanish reality', an observation that must have pleased Lorca),[3] while the others expressed themselves disgusted by its 'immorality', its vulgarity, its blasphemies, its lack of verisimilitude, its 'gynaecological experimentation' and its lasciviousness.[4]

Yerma played to full houses for the rest of Margarita Xirgu's run in the Teatro Barcelona and had 29 performances in all, interspersed with 25 of *La dama boba*.[5]

Lorca was interviewed at this time by a reporter on the weekly paper *L'Hora*, the organ of the POUM (Partido Obrero de Unificación Marxista), the small anti-Stalinist communist party whose tribulations George Orwell was later to chronicle in *Homage to Catalonia*. The poet gave vent to his loathing of fascism and spoke of his deep admiration for Russia, its art and its struggle to achieve a humane society. He repeated, as he had done so frequently over the last two years, that the theatre had a social mission, its true purpose being 'to educate the masses', and expressed his admiration for the 'revolutionary' work of the German playwright Erwin Piscator. Then he recalled his experience in New York during the Crash – the desperate efforts of the laid-off men to sell apples in the street – and announced that soon he would publish a book in which he protested against the injustices of contemporary society. Which book? The interviewer did not record its title, but presumably Lorca was referring to his New York cycle and later poems of similar theme.[6]

At the end of September Lorca and Dalí met again, after seven years without seeing each other. In April 1934 Salvador, who now had an international reputation, had written to the poet from Cadaqués on discovering that he had just passed through Barcelona on his return from Argentina. In his postcard he said that he was sure they would enjoy being together again, and suggested that Lorca collaborate with him on an opera he was planning in which would appear Leopold Sacher-Masoch and Ludwig II, Duke of Bavaria, notorious, the two of them, for their deviant eroticism. 'I think that we could do something *together*,' wrote Dalí. 'If you came we would be able to reach an agreement this time on a lot of things. Gala is dying to meet you.' The card, signed 'Your Buddha, Salvador Dalí', is the only communication known to have been exchanged between the painter and poet since 1928,[7] although there may have been others and anyway, via their mutual friends, they must surely have followed each other's progress. (Buñuel, for example, may have informed Dalí about the première of *Yerma*.) Lorca had been astonished, certainly, on returning to Spain from the United States, to learn of Dalí's total obsession with Gala, and told Rafael Alberti that he could not conceive how any woman would be able sexually to satisfy his friend, who hated breasts and vulvas, was terrified of venereal disease, had problems about impotence and a tremendous anal obsession.[8] If Gala was excited about meeting him, Federico's curiosity to know the woman who had 'saved' Salvador must have been intense by 1935.

The momentous re-encounter took place on 28 September, and provoked a minor scandal. That night Lorca was to have attended a concert in his honour. But to the consternation of the organizers the poet failed to appear. The hall was full; the orchestra ready; the choir lined up – but there was no sign of Lorca. Finally Cipriano Rivas Cherif announced that the poet had just met Salvador Dalí, whom he had not seen for years, and had gone off with him to the town of Tarragona, fifty miles south of Barcelona.[9]

Lorca was exhilarated to be with Dalí again and made no attempt to hide it. The young journalist Josep Palau i Fabre noticed that the poet never missed an opportunity to chatter on about his friend, proclaiming that he was going to write something in collaboration with the painter and that they would design the sets together. Perhaps it was the opera that Dalí had suggested the previous year. 'We are twin spirits,' Lorca told Palau. 'Here's the proof: seven years without seeing each other and yet we agree on everything as if we'd never stopped talking since then. Salvador Dalí is a genius, a genius.'[10] The poet's observation that he and Dalí were twin spirits reminds us of the drawing the poet had done of Salvador in 1927, of which the painter said: 'Lorca saw me as the incarnation of life, with a hat like one of the Dioscuri.' Like, that is, one of the twins Castor and Pollux.[11]

Palau had heard the rumour that Lorca belonged to the fraternity of odd creatures called 'homosexuals'. Not prepared to accept this on mere hearsay, he determined to test the truth of the matter for himself. Ratification came when he asked Lorca why *Don Perlimplín* was never performed. Lorca assured him that the reason was that no Spanish actor wanted to wear horns, even on stage! 'How ridiculous,' the poet added, 'when all men are cuckolded by someone, by a woman – or by a boyfriend!' Palau observed that, when Lorca said 'boyfriend', he looked at him sideways to see his reaction. When they parted the journalist was convinced that the rumours were true.[12]

There is no record of the conversations that took place between Dalí and Lorca during their few days together in Barcelona. It is difficult to believe, however, that Federico did not question Salvador closely about *Un Chien andalou* and the painter's and Buñuel's possible intention therein to satirize him. Certainly, for their friendship to have been renewed so triumphantly, the poet must have already forgiven that suspected assault on his intimacy. In his *Secret Life*, Dalí, surprisingly, does not mention this meeting in Barcelona. He did so for what seems to have been the first time in an interview published in 1954. There, believing that the re-encounter had occurred two months before the outbreak of the Civil War in 1936 (Dalí was always chaotic on dates), he declared that Gala had been delighted with Federico and the poet absolutely intrigued with her, to the extent of talking about her non-stop for three days. Lorca's fascination was understandable: here at last was the woman capable of satisfying Dalí, a Dalí whose secret desires Federico probably knew better than anyone in the world, Gala excepted.[13]

Dalí and Gala were accompanied these days by the poet and art collector Edward James, the immensely rich English aristocrat said to be the illegitimate son of King Edward VII. James liked to wear a kilt, an eccentricity always calculated to amaze Spaniards, and was to put together one of the finest collections of Dalís in the world. Salvador remembered that Lorca was charmed with the Englishman, who appeared to him 'a humming-bird dressed like a soldier from the time of Swift'. According to Dalí, James was equally impressed by Lorca. Despite this there is no reference to him in

Swans Reflecting Elephants, the very incomplete memoirs the aristocrat dictated to George Melly; and no reference either to this stay in Barcelona.[14]

Dalí and Gala were about to leave for Italy, where James owned a splendid house, the Villa Cimbrone, in Amalfi. They invited Lorca to go with them but, given the pressure of work and his other plans, he was unable to accept. After the poet's death Dalí, forgetting that the meeting had occurred nine months before the beginning of the war, blamed himself for not having insisted sufficiently that Federico accompany them to Italy, believing that had he done so the tragedy would have been avoided.[15]

A witness to the impassioned discussions that took place during these days between Dalí and Lorca, usually in a café next door to the Teatro Barcelona, was the young actress Amelia de la Torre, one of the new stars of Margarita Xirgu's company. Amelia was astonished by Dalí's ties, which were fashioned out of newspapers, and by the rapt attention with which Federico listened to his friend.[16] In 1986 Salvador recalled with deep nostalgia his last meeting with the poet, which was celebrated in the Canari de la Garriga, the famous restaurant opposite the Hotel Ritz, much frequented by artists and writers, which Lorca had first visited in 1927.[17]

Federico's presence was much required at literary gatherings and banquets in Barcelona. He recited his poetry to small and large groups, gave interviews, told stories, continued to make his Repubican sentiments clear ... and whatever he did or said appeared in the newspapers. Once again Lorca was the talk of the town, just as he had been in Havana and, later, Buenos Aires.

Meanwhile, producing world-wide consternation, Mussolini had invaded Abyssinia, and the course of the war was being followed closely in the Spanish press, despite the habitual censorship imposed by the Government. In view of what had happened, the vehemently Republican Margarita Xirgu immediately decided that she had no option but to cancel her trip to Italy – a gesture much in character that was greatly appreciated by her admirers. Margarita now announced that, after a brief tour of the Catalan provinces and a visit to Valencia, she would return to Barcelona to perform *Blood Wedding* and *Doña Rosita the Spinster*.[18]

During a quick dash to Madrid at the beginning of October Lorca took part in a broadcast to Buenos Aires. (He had already made two.) For the occasion he prepared a 'self-interview', the manuscript of which has been preserved and which gives us a useful insight into his thinking at this time. That Lorca was deeply concerned about the state of the contemporary theatre, none of those who knew him then could have doubted, and in the broadcast he reiterated his well-publicized position: the theatre was desperately in need of rejuvenation. As for his own work, the poet expressed himself dissatisfied with what he had achieved to date and said that *Don Perlimplín* was the play he most liked. He was writing new things. 'Human beings are afraid to see themselves reflected in the theatre,' he said, repeating a notion that now formed the kernel of many of his reflections, and added:

I aspire to express the social drama of the period in which we're living and my aim is that audiences learn not to be frightened of situations and symbols. I want audiences to come to terms with those fantasies and ideas without which I cannot advance a step in the theatre.[19]

No doubt the poet had in mind here not only *The Public* but its successor, whose first act he had read during the summer to Margarita Xirgu and Rivas Cherif.

On 14 October Margarita finished her season at the Teatro Barcelona and the next day Lorca read *Doña Rosita the Spinster* to the company. A photograph of the occasion survives. Listening attentively to the poet are Rivas Cherif, the writer Max Aub – who was then passing through Barcelona – and the theatre critic Ernest Guasp.[20]

On 23 October Margarita Xirgu's Barcelona admirers flocked to a special performance of *Fuente Ovejuna* organized in her honour in the huge Teatro Olympia Circo, the proceeds of which were to be distributed among the political prisoners still thronging the gaols as a consequence of the revolutionary events of the previous year. Eight thousand people filled the gigantic auditorium. The President of the Catalan Government, Lluis Companys, imprisoned in the maximum security gaol in Puerto de Santa María, near Cadiz, sent a garland of flowers; telegrams arrived from all over the country and there was a special message from Manuel Azaña. When the performance ended the audience threw hundreds of red flowers on to the stage. Margarita was in tears, and Lorca, deeply moved by this display of Catalan fervour, was heard to exclaim, 'What a people!'[21]

Shortly afterwards the poet returned again to Madrid, where the Radical Party, which shared power with Gil Robles's CEDA, was now implicated in a tremendous scandal over the government licence awarded to a fraudulent variant on the roulette wheel, known as the *straperlo*, which, it was claimed, allowed for an element of skill and was to be introduced into Spanish cafés. When the seedy business was uncovered several heads fell, among them that of Prime Minister Alejandro Lerroux, one of whose nephews was apparently involved in the confidence trick. The word *straperlo* quickly became a synonym for 'black market' and shady political deals in general.[22] The CEDA sought to use the discomfiture of its government partners to its own ends, no doubt hoping to gain full control of the Cabinet, and in such a fraught situation, with the internal dissensions of the Right hung out for all to see, the possibility of a general election was soon in the air. At this time Lorca put his name, alongside those of the poet Antonio Machado, Fernando de los Ríos and various distinguished lawyers and politicians, to a manifesto protesting against Mussolini's invasion of Abyssinia. The document, dated 6 November 1935, appeared immediately in only one of the capital's many newspapers, the *Diario de Madrid*, no doubt due to the fear of reprisals from the censors.[23]

Valencia and the *Sonnets of Dark Love*

On 26 October Margarita Xirgu had opened a short season at the Teatro Principal in Valencia where, on 5 November, she gave the first of several performances of *Yerma*. Lorca's presence in the city had been announced for that date, but the poet failed to turn up, due, according to the local newspapers, to an indisposition. It was now hoped that he would be in Valencia for the last performance of the tragedy, with which Margarita was to take her leave of the city.[24] Lorca kept his word, and if we can believe a report appearing in one of the Valencian papers on 10 November, arrived from Madrid by air. If this really was the case, it is the only instance on record of the poet having entrusted himself to an aircraft – a means of transport that, given his terror of death and his almost pathological avoidance of physical danger in all its varieties, must have been a harrowing experience.[25]

In the absence of letters and diaries, Lorca's press interviews are often our only way of coming at all close to his thinking at a given time. Luckily, during the last two years of his life, such interviews were fairly frequent. In Valencia, an intelligent journalist on *El Mercantil Valenciano*, Ricardo G. Luengo, asked him a series of perceptive questions which the poet answered with unwonted vehemence. Luengo raised the subject of the 'vulgarity' of *Yerma*, which had offended certain people. Lorca rejected the imputation, while admitting that he wanted to shake his audiences. 'One of my aims in the theatre is precisely to scandalize and horrify a little,' he explained. 'I want to and know how to. I want to provoke a strong reaction, to see if the sickness of the contemporary theatre can be vomited up once and for all.' As for the people who had been shocked by *Yerma*, that was nothing compared to what was coming, because he intended to write plays with 'terrible themes'. For example, one called *Blood Has No Voice*, whose subject was incest, and beside whose crudity and violent passions the language of *Yerma* would be 'archangelic'. The poet stated emphatically that in the theatre only two topics now had any hope of interesting people:

social problems and sex. Given so little choice, personally he preferred to write about the latter.[26]

According to Cipriano Rivas Cherif, the idea for *Blood Has No Voice* had come in Barcelona (presumably during the previous month) when the poet found out about a case of incest in a friend's family, a case not unlike that of the biblical brother and sister Amnon and Thamar which had inspired one of Federico's 'Gypsy' ballads.[27] Another source, however, indicates that the relationship the poet had discovered concerned a mother and daughter, not a brother and sister.[28] Lorca continued to talk about this project over the following months but, so far as we know, never began the play, whose title changed at some point to *The Taste of Blood*, with the subtitle *A Drama of Desire*.[29]

Mauricio Torra-Balari, a young acquaintance of Lorca's in Barcelona, who had met the poet for the first time in Carlos Morla Lynch's apartment in 1929, travelled down to Valencia to see *Yerma* and found Federico impatiently awaiting the arrival from Madrid of an 'intimate friend', who to his chagrin did not turn up at the expected time.[30] The friend in question was almost certainly Rodríguez Rapún, who joined him a few days later in Barcelona. There are indications that Lorca was anxious at this time about his relationship with Rapún, and the unhappiness expressed in two sonnets composed in Valencia may well reflect this situation. These are 'The Sonnet of the Letter' and 'The Poet Tells the Truth', which the poet scribbled on sheets of notepaper bearing the heading of the Hotel Victoria, where he stayed during his visit, and belong to the series known as the *Sonetos del amor oscuro* ('Sonnets of Dark Love').[31]

About the poem entitled 'Soneto gongorino' ('A Gongoristic Sonnet'), also written at this time in Valencia, we have more information. When the Barraca visited the city in 1933 Lorca had met briefly a young and exquisitely elegant poet from the nearby town of Alcoy, Juan Gil-Albert, whose father was a rich industrialist. Now he saw him again. Gil-Albert, who was about to publish a book of sonnets in which he made no effort to disguise his homosexuality, listened entranced one afternoon while Federico read *Doña Rosita the Spinster* to Margarita Xirgu and her company; and it may have been the following day that he had the idea of sending Lorca the present of a dove in a cage, which he had just brought at the local market. Gil-Albert knew nothing of Rodríguez Rapún, or indeed of Lorca's private life in general, and was surprised to discover the following spring in Madrid that Federico had written a sonnet in the style of Góngora in which the poet delivers a pigeon in a cage to his beloved.[32]

No document has been found in which Lorca himself ever referred to his amorous sonnets under the generic title of *Sonnets of Dark Love*. The principal source for the title, which he heard from the poet himself, was Vicente Aleixandre who, in 1937, recalled a private reading of the poems a few months before Lorca's death. When Federico finished, Aleixandre exclaimed, 'What a heart! How much it must have loved! What it must have suffered!'[33] Forty-five years later, shortly before the eleven sonnets of the series were finally published together,[34] Aleixandre stated that, while the poems were undoubtedly inspired by a particular male friend – he was not prepared to say whom – in his view the expression 'dark love' did not have for Lorca an exclusively homosexual connotation. In these sonnets, according to Aleixandre, love is 'dark' because it is tormented, difficult, unrequited, not understood, and so forth, and not simply because it is homosexual.[35] Despite such scruples, however, it seems undeniable that, if in the poems there is a clear allusion to St John of the Cross's 'dark night of the soul' – Federico deeply admired St John's poetry, which Dalí often heard him recite[36] – the adjective *oscuro*, as applied by Lorca to love, had a manifestly homosexual sense already registered in the sonnet 'Adam', written in New York and mentioned earlier. At all events, the *persecution* and *spying* to which the lovers in the Hotel Victoria sonnets are subject point inescapably to the forbidden nature of their passion.[37]

Blood Wedding and *Doña Rosita* in Barcelona

After Valencia Margarita Xirgu and Federico returned to Barcelona to prepare for the opening of *Blood Wedding* in the Principal Palace Theatre, which was scheduled for 22 November. Were it not for a series of articles on Lorca published in Mexico by Cipriano Rivas Cherif twenty years after the poet's death, we might never have known that Rodríguez Rapún was with Federico in Barcelona at this time. Rivas recalled that one day the poet failed to turn up for a rehearsal and that he found him sitting alone, deeply depressed, in a café, his head in his hands. It transpired that the previous night, after a binge in a downtown flamenco joint, Rapún had left with a Gypsy girl and failed to return to the hotel where he was staying with Lorca. Federico was in despair, believing that Rapún had abandoned him; and, according to Rivas Cherif, pulled a wad of Rafael's letters out of his pocket to prove the passionate nature of their relationship. If we are to credit Rivas Cherif's reconstruction of that conversation, Lorca went on to relate his homosexuality to his early experience, saying that he had never recovered when, before he was seven, his best friend in Fuente Vaqueros school, slightly younger than himself, was taken away by his parents to another village. The poet also asserted that his close relationship with his mother made it impossible for him to feel heterosexual passion – a claim that Rivas dismissed as cheap Freudianism but that none the less the poet had made publicly in Montevideo two years earlier, when he said that while his brothers and sisters were free to marry, he belonged to his mother.*38

On another, probably subsequent, occasion Lorca told Rivas Cherif about a daring play he was going to write called *La bola negra* ('The Black Ball'), in the first scene of which a son reveals to his conventional father that he has been refused membership of, that is, been 'black-balled' by, the local casino – because he is a homosexual. 'How about that for an opening?' the poet had laughed.39 Only four pages of the manuscript of this play, which is wittily subtitled 'A Drama of Contemporary Customs', are known to exist. The first two contain a list of characters; the second two, the opening moments of the play, in which the protagonist, Carlos, is questioned by his sister.40 Later, in a list of projects, Lorca changed the title of the play, now subtitled 'Drama epéntico', to *La piedra oscura* ('The Dark Stone').41 The word *epéntico* was invented by the poet (perhaps without having epenthesis consciously in mind), who said that it meant someone who 'could create but not procreate'.42 Given the sense in which Lorca used the adjective *oscuro* in his love sonnets, the modified title and subtitle of the play underlined its homosexual theme, the reference to the stone suggesting both sterility and society's desire to 'stone' sexual deviants to death. But, apart from the four pages of the manuscript, nothing more is known of this work.

Lorca was delighted with Margarita Xirgu's Mother in *Blood Wedding* and told journalists that he could not have dreamt of finding a better actress for the part. José Caballero's sets seemed to him magnificent, while he himself had seen to the musical aspects and would accompany at the piano, during his stay in the city, the poignant lullaby of the horse that refuses to drink. He felt certain that Margarita's production was going to be a hit and constitute its 'real première'. Given Lola Membrives's great success with *Blood Wedding* in Buenos Aires and her recent performances of the work in Madrid, which had received critical acclaim, it is hard to see how Barcelona was about to enjoy its 'real première'. Perhaps the poet was carried away by the euphoria of the moment and the warmth of his feelings for the great actress.43

Blood Wedding was a hit, certainly, and the critics were almost unanimous in their praise both of the play and of the production. Lorca, however, was principally concerned at this time with the forthcoming première of *Doña Rosita the Spinster*, directed, like *Blood Wedding*, by Cipriano Rivas Cherif. As rehearsals proceeded and the date for the opening night, 12 December, approached, the excitement grew. One newspaper wrote that no première

* See p. 378.

had ever aroused such expectation in Barcelona and that during these days there were only two topics of conversation in the city: *Doña Rosita* and the political situation. The latter was chaotic, for the Government had fallen at the beginning of the month and two distinguished conservatives, Miguel Maura and Joaquín Chapaprieta, had declined the President's offer to form a new Cabinet. (Finally, on 13 December, the moderate Manuel Portela Valladares would undertake to head a caretaker Government at a time when a General Election was inevitable.) Lorca, the same newspaper reported, was now as famous as Maura, Chapaprieta and Portela Valladares together. The leading Madrid theatre critics had arrived by air for the première, invited by the management of the Principal Palace, and were inspiring among their Barcelona colleagues 'a certain mythical admiration'; while, on the great night, there was 'a sepulchral silence' in the flamenco establishments off the Ramblas because the proprietors, all friends of the poet, were in the theatre.[44]

Doña Rosita the Spinster staggered the audience that packed the Principal Palace that 12 December, and the critics did not fail to see (that was impossible) that, far from being a comedy, the play was essentially a tragedy not dissimilar in theme from *Blood Wedding* and *Yerma*, although conceived in a different register. A comment by María Luz Morales, perhaps the only female professional theatre critic in Spain, put it succinctly: the play 'induced the lips to smile and the heart to grieve'.[45] Domènec Guansé perceived the influence of *The Cherry Orchard* on the last act and felt that, like the Russian, Lorca had mastered the art of expressing the inexpressible.[46] Juan G. Olmedilla believed, with María Luz Morales, that Lorca had achieved a miracle by making people laugh and cry at the same time,[47] while Eduardo Haro went further: Lorca had demonstrated with *Blood Wedding, Yerma* and now with *Doña Rosita the Spinster* that in Spain it was possible to write excellent theatre for mass audiences, a theatre that combined high art with a genuine concern for social problems.[48]

On hearing about the immense success of the première, José Moreno Villa, remembering the day eleven years earlier when he had told Lorca about his discovery of the *rosa mutabilis*, sent him a telegram from Madrid. It read laconically: 'Warmest congratulations from the grandfather of Doña Rosita.'[49]

Lorca, who had never met María Luz Morales, was touched by her review and paid her an unannounced visit to express his gratitude. He told her about two new works he wanted to write: a tragedy called *The Soldiers Who Don't Want to Go to War* (almost certainly the project he had first begun to mention at the beginning of 1935) and a play about St Teresa of Avila.[50] Nothing more is known concerning the latter.

On 19 December, while *Doña Rosita* played to packed houses, Lorca gave his lecture with musical illustrations about Granada, 'How a City Sings from November to November', rounding this off with the first public reading of *Diwan of the Tamarit*. The members of the Chamber Music Society who organized the event were as enthusiastic about Lorca's performance as had been those of the Friends of Art Club in Buenos Aires where the poet first delivered it in October 1933. Afterwards Federico joked that he was going to send a copy of his lecture, and the reviews, to the Mayor of Granada, to show him which of them was the *real* Mayor of the City of the Alhambra. The journalist Luis Góngora, who knew Lorca well, realized that the poet was not being altogether flippant, and asked him if he felt he was appreciated back home. Federico gave him to understand that he did not.[51]

Dinners, back-slapping, articles in the papers, a special performance of *Doña Rosita* for the flower sellers of the Ramblas, which Lorca called 'the most lively street in the world';[52] late-night excursions with his friends through the medieval quarter; and, to cap it all, a multitudinous banquet in the Majestic Inglaterra Hotel on 23 December attended by the cream of Catalonia's artists and intellectuals – probably never, not even in Buenos Aires, had the poet known such lionizing and such euphoria as during these last days in Barcelona before he returned home for Christmas.[53]

Meanwhile, against the background of the Abyssinian war and the increasing belligerence of Hitler's Germany, the fear of a new conflagration was spreading across Europe. In Spain, where the political situation was growing daily more fraught, the sessions of Parliament had been suspended until 1 January 1936, and the presidential decree dissolving the House and setting a date for General Elections was expected at any moment. It came on 7 January, when it was announced that polling would take place on 16 February.[54]

With the calling of elections came the end of press censorship and, for the first time since the events of October 1934, detailed accounts appeared in the newspapers of what had happened in Asturias, Catalonia and the Basque country. There were still many thousands of political prisoners, and the clamour for their release grew day by day. Rumours were circulating about the formation of an electoral Popular Front, along the lines of the French one, to combat the Right at the polls, while the conservatives, monarchists and fascists now widened their contacts with a view to creating an enlarged and coherent National Front. The left-wing newspapers talked at this time of 'the recuperation of the Republic', and the term 'black biennium' was soon being applied to the two years of right-wing rule the country had just undergone.[55]

Margarita Xirgu told journalists at this time that Lorca would accompany her to Mexico, and the poet himself confirmed this before he left Barcelona, adding that he would not stay away from Spain for long, however, since he had to see to the staging of his puppet play *Los títeres de cachiporra* ('The Andalusian Puppets'), which the Philippine composer Federico Elizalde had set to music.[56] But things were more complicated than that, and we know from Rivas Cherif that Margarita realized perfectly that, unless some excuse could be found for taking Rodríguez Rapún along too, Lorca would not easily leave for America. Rapún, however, was busily preparing for examinations and, for the moment, nothing could be done.[57]

Lorca left for Madrid on 24 December with Rivas Cherif, having promised Margarita that he would join her in Bilbao at the end of January before she embarked for Cuba, the first stop of her overseas tour.[58] On 6 January 1936 Margarita ended her brilliant season in the Catalan capital. Since opening the previous September she had performed Lorca's versions of *La dama boba* 23 times; *Yerma*, 37; *Blood Wedding*, 35; and *Doña Rosita* 47. This without counting her performances of his works in the Catalan provinces and in Valencia.[59] They had been three marvellous months for poet and actress – months that, after Federico's assassination, Margarita would find it impossible to forget.

Last Months in Madrid

Margarita Xirgu Leaves Spain

By failing to form a broad-based coalition the progressives had lost the November 1933 general elections, with disastrous results. Now, two years later, with a new poll looming on 16 February, it was evident to almost everyone on the Left that this time the same mistake must be avoided. In the summer of 1935 the Communist International had opted for a policy of collaboration with the democratic parties and, following this lead, the main progressive alignments in Spain, with the exception of the Anarchists, now signed, on 15 January 1936, an agreement creating a Popular Front based on a minimum programme: the return to the religious, educational and regional policies of the first two years of the Republic; efficient and rapid agrarian reform; and an immediate amnesty for the 30,000 political prisoners still in gaol as a result of the events of 1934.[1]

The five weeks of the electoral campaign were extraordinarily tense. José María Gil Robles was presented by the Right as a sort of Spanish Mussolini, who, given the necessary mandate, would save the country from the threat of the Red Revolution. As for the Falangists, they had already begun to prepare themselves for the civil war which they were certain was imminent. Violent clashes were registered as Spain divided increasingly into two seemingly irreconcilable camps with less and less room for the moderates in between.

Lorca, who during the two years of right-wing rule had grown steadily more radical in his views, threw in his lot immediately with the Popular Front, as his friend the portly and affable Argentinian journalist Pablo Suero discovered when he arrived in Madrid at the beginning of February to take the pulse of contemporary Spain and to cover the elections. One day Federico took Suero to meet his family, and the journalist, himself a liberal Catholic, was delighted with what he found. 'Federico's parents are rich landowners from the Vega of Granada,' he wrote. 'None the less they are on the side of the ordinary people of Spain, whose poverty angers them, and want to see the arrival of a Christian socialism.' The García Lorcas were fervent admirers of Azaña and Fernando de los Ríos, and Doña Vicenta, whose strong personality did not escape Suero, expressed her anxiety about the outcome of the polls. 'If we don't win we can say goodbye to Spain,' she exclaimed. 'They'll throw us out – if they don't kill us, that is!' Suero got on well with Doña Vicenta. *Blood Wedding* had just been brought out by José Bergamín in an elegant volume, and the poet's mother raised the subject of her son's unwillingness to publish his work, confiding to the Argentinian that the play would never have appeared had it not been for the insistence of José Fernández-Montesinos, the poet's friend from the days of the *Rinconcillo* in Granada (and, since 1929, brother-in-law). Doña Vicenta agreed with Suero: they must all try to persuade Federico to publish.[2]

Actually – and apparently Suero was not aware of it – two new titles had been issued recently. On 27 December 1935 the printing of the *Six Galician Poems*, edited by Eduardo Blanco-Amor (who had just returned to Buenos Aires) was completed in Santiago de Compostela. In his prologue to the handsomely produced slim volume the editor deliberately omitted all reference to the part played by Ernesto Pérez Guerra in the elaboration of the poems, and even went so far as to suppress Lorca's dedication of the 'Cántiga do neno da tenda' ('Song of the Shop-Boy') to his young friend.[3] The poet must have been angered by these arbitrary omissions, and even more so by the fact that his own 'epilogue' (also in Galician) had been omitted too – an epilogue in which, it may be presumed, he explained how the poems had been composed.[4] Then, on 28 January, Manuel Altolaguirre had finished the printing of *Primeras canciones* ('First Songs'), a minuscule volume containing a selection of *suites* culled from the huge mass of Lorca's unpublished verse written between 1920 and 1924.

In January Federico told another journalist, Antonio Otero Seco, that ready to go to press he had not only *Poet in New York* but no fewer than five other books of poems: *Earth and Sky, Diwan of the Tamarit, Odes, Prose Poems* and *Suites*. The publishers were asking too for *Yerma* and his other plays, he said, and as for his current projects for the theatre he was finishing a 'social drama', so far without a title, in which the audience intervenes and a revolutionary crowd takes the theatre by storm. From Otero's description there can be no doubt this was the play whose first act the poet had read to Margarita Xirgu the previous summer. Lorca was also at work on an Andalusian comedy, set in the Vega of Granada – almost certainly *The Dreams of My Cousin Aurelia* – and *Blood Has No Voice*, the play on the theme of incest he had begun several months earlier. Clearly he was busy.[5]

Before keeping his word to join Margarita, Lorca made a brief visit to Saragossa to see the actress Carmen Díaz, a vivacious brunette from Seville, whom he had decided would be the best person to produce the revised version of *The Andalusian Puppets*, which, as has been said, the composer Federico Elizalde had recently set to music. Carmen Díaz was delighted with the offer, and undertook to put on the work during her summer season in Madrid. When Pura Maórtua de Ucelay, director of the Anfistora theatre club, heard that Lorca had given the piece to Carmen Díaz she was horrified, convinced as she was that the Sevillian actress projected a pseudo-Andalusia utterly different from the poet's conception of the south.[6] Whether she voiced this opinion to the poet we do not know, although given their close friendship it would not have been surprising. At all events disagreements soon arose between Lorca and Carmen Díaz, and the poet withdrew the play, promising it instead to Encarnación López Júlvez, 'La Argentinita', then on tour in South America. But it was too late: Encarnación did not return until July and a few weeks later the Civil War broke out. Elizalde's version of the play has never been produced.[7]

At the end of the month Lorca was with Margarita Xirgu in Bilbao where, on 26 January, they gave a joint recital. Two days later the actress took her leave of the Basque city with a performance of *Blood Wedding* attended by the poet.[8] On 30 January Lorca was to have delivered his *duende* lecture to the local Athenaeum Club, but that morning the newspapers announced that owing to 'unforeseen circumstances' the poet had returned suddenly to Madrid.[9] What had happened? Margarita said thirteen years later that Federico had not wanted to continue with her to Santander, where she and the company were to embark for America, because the farewell would have been so painful.[10] Perhaps, after she left Bilbao, the poet was too upset to go through with the lecture. On 31 January Margarita sailed on the *Orinoco*, bound for Havana.[11] She never saw Lorca again. Over the following months she would try desperately to persuade him to join her in Mexico, but to no avail. The poet was immersed in so many projects that it was almost impossible for him to think of moving away from Madrid. It is likely, too, that the idea of leaving Rodríguez Rapún behind was intolerable to him.

After Federico's assassination Margarita was haunted by the memory of their leave-taking in Bilbao, and can have found little consolation in the deeply affectionate lines the poet had once dedicated to her:

> Si me voy, te quiero más,
> si me quedo, igual te quiero.
> Tu corazón es mi casa

y mi corazón tu huerto.
Yo tengo cuatro palomas,
cuatro palomitas tengo.
Mi corazón es tu casa
¡y tu corazón mi huerto!*¹²

The Poet and the Popular Front

Politics and the arts had by now become inextricably mixed, and political significance was given to the least word or most apparently trivial action on the part of writers, painters and thinkers. Keenly aware of the threat of fascism to Europe, and of the danger of a right-wing *coup* in Spain, many of these men and women now openly voiced their support for the Popular Front, and used their influence as public figures to warn the electorate of the dire consequences of another conservative victory.

Among the young intellectuals militating in favour of the Popular Front were Rafael Alberti and his wife María Teresa León, who had just returned to Madrid after a long visit to South America and Russia. On 9 February, the last Sunday before polling, friends of the couple held a well-attended lunch in their honour at the Café Nacional, just behind the Plaza Mayor in the Calle de Toledo. During the meal Lorca read for the gathering's approval a draft statement in support of the coalition, which was published in the leading communist daily *Mundo Obrero* the day before the elections with his own name at the head of more than 300 signatures. The document, entitled 'The Intellectuals and the Popular Front', appealed to the common sense of voters and expressed the signatories' conviction that only through a united effort on the part of all the progressive forces in Spain could the country recover the dynamism and idealism of the first years of the Republic. It was vital to support the Popular Front candidates.¹³

There could now be no doubt about Lorca's commitment to the cause of democracy, and during the following months this was reaffirmed over and over again and received widespread publicity in the press.

Lorca continued to work on the revolutionary play whose first act he had read to Margarita Xirgu the previous summer and whose second, according to the *Heraldo de Madrid*, he was now finishing. The work, which Lorca

---

* If I leave, I love you more,
    if I stay, I love you the same.
    Your heart is my home
    and my heart your orchard.
    I have four doves,
    four little doves.
    My heart is your home . . .
    and your heart my orchard!

had mentioned to Antonio Otero Seco in January, was, according to the well-informed theatre page of the *Heraldo*, 'ultra-modern', and had recourse to the most 'audacious theatrical procedures and systems'. The poet had stated that he would have liked to be able to call it *Life Is a Dream*, but that, unfortunately, Calderón had pre-empted him. None the less, he had given people to understand, the title would be something similar.[14] And it was: a few months later he announced that he had decided to call the play *The Dream of Life*.[15] When the poet read the first act to Pablo Suero, the Argentinian was astounded. In his view, the work was far in advance of the efforts of the expressionist German dramatists Georg Kaiser and Ernst Toller. 'I told Federico that with this play he was situating us in a new theatrical world, where the boundaries between stage, audience and street are broken down,' Suero wrote later that year.[16]

On 14 February, two days before the elections, the tireless Rafael Alberti and María Teresa León organized a Popular Front function in Madrid's Zarzuela Theatre in honour of the playwright and novelist Ramón del Valle-Inclán, who had died on 5 January. Lorca was there with his friends, and participated in the programme by reading an extract from the prologue to one of Valle-Inclán's plays and two sonnets by Rubén Darío dedicated to the great writer. Then Valle's violently anti-militaristic farce *The Horns of Don Friolera* was staged for the first time in public. At a moment when rumours of a *coup d'état* were in the air and nobody in the theatre could be sure that the Popular Front would win the elections, the play riveted the attention of the audience.[17] Among those present was the Catalan journalist Ignacio Agustí, who had frequented Lorca a few months earlier in Barcelona. Agustí, a friend of Margarita Xirgu, wanted to know when Federico was going to join the actress in Latin America. The poet replied that for the moment there could be no question of his leaving Spain – although he did not give his reasons.[18]

Margarita Xirgu opened her Havana season the following evening and the next day staged *Yerma*. The Cubans, who had not forgotten Lorca's visit in 1930, were wildly enthusiastic, and from this moment the actress began to bombard the poet with telegrams begging him to keep his word and join her in Mexico.[19]

On Sunday 16 February Spain went to the polls. The final results gave the Popular Front a narrow victory, although, because of the provisions of the Electoral Law, which automatically awarded the victorious side a much increased parliamentary representation, the left-wing and Republican coalition obtained 267 seats in the new Cortes and the Right only 132 (an exact reversal of what had happened in 1933, when the Conservative coalition swept the board). The Republicans were euphoric, and the first decision by the new Government, in accordance with the Popular Front electoral programme, was to free the political prisoners. The scenes outside the gaols were jubilant.[20]

The failure of Gil Robles to win the election had a shattering effect on his followers, many of whom now shifted their allegiance to José Antonio Primo de Rivera's Falangist Party, which saw a marked increase in its membership throughout the country. The Popular Front's success had terrified the moneyed classes, who imagined that a Marxist revolution was just around the corner, and the urge to throw in their lot with the hard-liners was felt by many people who previously had resisted the temptation. From February onwards, with almost daily provocations, assassinations and retaliations, the picture was to grow increasingly grim until, finally, came civil war.[21]

In this process the fascist Falange played a dominant role, mounting a direct-action campaign with the specific object of creating chaos and making a right-wing *coup* inevitable in the name of 'law and order'. Things quickly got to such a pitch that on 14 March several Falangist leaders, including José Antonio Primo de Rivera, were arrested. Four days later the organization was outlawed.[22] Such a move by the Government of the Popular Front only made matters worse, however, as did the imposition of the State of Emergency, which gave the police special powers and was renewed month by month until the war began in July. What price democratic freedom, the Right could now jeer. Behind the scenes the military conspiracy against the Republic took on a new lease of life. More and more the issue was coming to be seen in terms of a crude opposition between fascism and communism, and while young right-wing militants thought about joining the Falange, the communist and socialist youth organizations fused on 1 April 1936.[23]

In the midst of it all Lorca continued to make his left-wing position clear, reading his poems at a mass meeting in the Madrid Worker's Club (including the provocative 'Ballad of the Spanish Civil Guard,' from *Gypsy Ballads*),[24] joining the recently formed Association of Friends of South America, dedicated to combating the dictatorships of Miguel Gómez in Cuba and Getulio Vargas in Brazil,[25] and the Friends of Portugal, founded with the aim of informing the Spanish public about the fascist regime of Oliveira Salazar.[26]

On 5 April Lorca gave a short radio talk about the hidden, melancholy Granada whose Holy Week, in his childhood days, was silent, solemn and utterly unlike the 'Baroque tumult of universal Seville'. The poet expressed himself in disagreement with recent innovations, which had made the occasion more noisy and brash, and begged his fellow *granadinos* to restore Easter as it was before, in accordance with the inner, contemplative nature of the town. He went on to say that in his opinion Granada was still divided into two incompatible halves, symbolized by the stark contrast between the Moorish Alhambra and the neighbouring Renaissance palace of the Emperor Charles V. Spoken only a few months before the beginning of a civil war that would cause the deaths of thousands of *granadinos*, his own included, these words acquire an almost prophetic tone.[27]

Two days later the Madrid newspaper *La Voz* published an important interview with Lorca in which he referred yet again to his current obsession with the theatre, which, in his view, now had an absolute duty to immerse itself in the problems assailing humanity – there could no longer be any question of art for art's sake. Referring to *When Five Years Pass*, which Pura Maórtua de Ucelay's Anfistora Club was rehearsing, Lorca made it clear that his 'true intention' lay in his 'impossible' and 'unplayable' theatre and that, if in the meanwhile he had written other more conventional things, this was to prove that he had personality and to gain people's respect. He might have added that it was also to earn the money that would allow him to write what he wanted.[28]

As for *When Five Years Pass*, Lorca was frightened that it might be a failure, no matter how well performed; and, although he did not say so in public, he had prevailed on Pura Maórtua de Ucelay not to put it on until after the Madrid production of *Doña Rosita the Spinster*, scheduled for the autumn when, it now seemed certain, Margarita Xirgu would return to Spain, cutting short her tour of Latin America.[29] The poet was determined to see *Doña Rosita* produced the following season in Madrid – understandably so in view of its huge success in Barcelona – and it may be that he had brought pressure to bear on Margarita to come back earlier, not wishing, if he could help it, to give the play to anyone else. Probably he felt that with *Doña Rosita* running to full houses in Madrid (an almost inevitable outcome), *When Five Years Pass* would do better.

Referring to his work in progress, Lorca told *La Voz* that he was writing a new play with a religious and socio-economic theme:

As long as there is economic injustice in the world, the world will be unable to think clearly. That's the way I see it. Two men are walking along a river bank. One of them is rich, the other poor. One has a full belly and the other fouls the air with his yawns. And the rich man says: 'What a lovely little boat out on the water! Look at that lily blooming on the bank!' And the poor man wails: 'I'm hungry, so hungry!' Of course. The day when hunger is eradicated there is going to be the greatest spiritual explosion the world has ever seen. We'll never be able to imagine the joy that will erupt when the Great Revolution comes. I'm talking like a real socialist, aren't I?[30]

It is not clear if the poet was alluding here to *The Dream of Life* or to some new play he was writing or going to write, but at all events his social commitment was evident. In terms of the political situation at the time, Lorca was indeed talking like 'a real socialist', despite his lack of formal membership of the Socialist Party, and his sympathies could be seen to lie squarely with the proletariat. From a Spanish right-wing point of view, Federico García Lorca, by April 1936, was little short of a communist.

As for his publishing plans, Lorca told *La Voz* that soon he would bring out his 'drama without a title' – almost certainly *The Dream of Life* – his New York poems and, surprisingly, a book of sonnets, a verse form in which there was a new interest among the younger poets of the day such as Juan Gil-Albert, Miguel Hernández, Germán Bleiberg and Luis Rosales. And his plan to join Margarita Xirgu? Lorca maintained that he was waiting for a telegram from the actress and, probably exaggerating, told the interviewer, Felipe Morales, that he hoped to embark later that month for New York, where he would briefly visit some old friends – 'Yankees who are supporters of Spain' – before continuing to Mexico to see Margarita perform his plays and to give a lecture on the great sixteenth-century writer Quevedo, whose work he admired deeply.[31]

On 18 April Margarita opened her season at the Bellas Artes Theatre in Mexico, triumphantly, with *Yerma*, following this success with *Doña Rosita the Spinster*, *The Shoemaker's Prodigious Wife* and *Blood Wedding*.[32] Over the following weeks Lorca was intensely conscious that his theatre was conquering new audiences in a country that fascinated him. He must have received many communications from Margarita Xirgu, and probably knew that the Mexican press was already announcing his imminent arrival in the capital.[33]

On 20 April Lorca participated in a launching party for Luis Cernuda's new book of poems *La realidad y el deseo* ('Reality and Desire'), which brought together a remarkable group of poets that included Manuel Altolaguirre, Pablo Neruda, Rafael Alberti, José Bergamín (publisher of the book), Pedro Salinas and Vicente Aleixandre. In his speech Lorca referred to the poems' 'amorous anguish', and, between the lines, showed how deeply impressed he was by the courage with which Cernuda had given poetic form to his predicament as a homosexual in an intolerant and uncomprehending society.[34] It is possible that, before meeting Rodríguez Rapún, Lorca had been briefly involved sexually with Cernuda, whom he had first met in Seville in 1927.[35] What is certain is that, when Cernuda arrived in Madrid in 1930, the two became close friends and greatly admired each other's poetry, although it is perhaps safe to assume that Lorca cannot have found himself in sympathy with the bitter resentment against society and the family that so often erupts in Cernuda's work – and which is absent in his own.

Meanwhile the Barraca had been in Barcelona, to take part in the celebrations commemorating the coming of the Republic in April 1931,[36] celebrations that in Madrid had been marred by violence and killings. Lorca was not with the students (presumably now receiving their government grant again) having distanced himself definitively from the University Theatre. The original *barracos* were disheartened by Lorca's defection, but there was nothing they could do. As things turned out, the performances in Barcelona were to be the last before the war began a few months later.[37]

If it had not been for his estrangement from the Barraca, Lorca would probably have been delighted to have an excuse to travel to Barcelona, for he had just received an affable postcard from Salvador Dalí in Cadaqués. The painter regretted that Federico had not visited him in Paris (it seems he had invited him the previous autumn when they met in Barcelona); said that he had seen and approved of *Yerma* – perhaps one of Margarita Xirgu's last performances before she left Barcelona in January – which (unlike Buñuel) he had found 'full of highly obscure and surrealist things'; and suggested again that they collaborate. 'We will always be glad to see you arrive at our house,' the card ended. 'Gala sends you her love and I embrace you.'[38] It is not known if Federico replied, although after the poet's death Salvador always insisted that he and Lorca had agreed to work together. Given the perfect understanding re-established between the two the previous October, after their long separation, it seems quite likely, in fact, that they might have embarked on a joint venture, picking up from where they had left off with *Mariana Pineda* in 1927.[39]

On 1 May the United Socialist Youth Movement was out in strength, a month after the socialist–communist fusion, to show the fascists what they were up against. By this time the Socialist Party was split down the middle between the supporters of the moderate Indalecio Prieto and the quasi-revolutionary Francisco Largo Caballero. Despite having supported the Popular Front electoral coalition, the Party had refused, as had the Anarchists, to participate in the new Government, a fatal error, and was wasting its energies in what was practically a civil war within its own ranks. All of this while the conspirators were perfecting their plans. Lorca, who never joined the Party, continued to side with the workers in their legitimate demands for better conditions. His May Day message, published in a communist magazine, was straightforward: 'My greetings to all the workers of Spain, united this First of May by the desire for a more just and more fraternal society.'[40] It seems, moreover, that he watched the May Day parade, waving with a red tie from a window in the Ministry of Communications (today the General Post Office), in the Plaza de la Cibeles.[41]

Violence was increasing throughout the country. On 7 May the extreme Right assassinated a Republican officer, Captain Faraudo, known to be one of the instructors of the socialist militia.[42] The following day an attempt was made on the life of the ex-Minister Alvarez Mendizábal, who had made some insulting remarks about the Army.[43] Faraudo's funeral on 10 May turned into an angry political demonstration. There were demands for revenge, insults, clenched fists.[44] This same 10 May saw the elections for President of the Republic, made necessary by the new Parliament's dismissal of Niceto Alcalá-Zamora, accused by the Popular Front of having supported right-wing policies during the two years of conservative government and with the excuse that he had dissolved Parliament twice during his term in office, an action that according to the provisions of the Constitution entailed almost automatic removal. Manuel Azaña was appointed in his place, and asked the moderate and charismatic socialist Indalecio Prieto to form a government. Prieto was willing, but the Party refused to give its assent. This was a tragedy because Prieto, a newspaperman with friends in all the right places, was perhaps the only person in the country capable of taking charge of a situation that demanded firmness, tact and pragmatism. By opting out of government the Socialist Party virtually ensured that whatever new cabinet took office would be unviable. Thwarted in his plans, Azaña appointed Santiago Casares Quiroga, from his own Republican Left Party, Prime Minister. Casares was not the right man for that extremely difficult job: sick, stubborn, arrogant and aggressive in debate, he would refuse consistently to listen to advice or take seriously the information he received daily about the military conspiracy. And when the rebellion began he collapsed.[45]

The Dreams of My Cousin Aurelia and The House of Bernarda Alba

On 29 May 1936 the *Heraldo de Madrid*, which for years had been following Lorca's career with interest, published in its theatre page the 'rumour' that in eight days the poet expected to finish a new play, *La Casa de Bernarda Alba* ('The House of Bernarda Alba'); that *The Dream of Life* was well advanced; and that the production of *When Five Years Pass* by Pura Maórtua de Ucelay's Club Anfistora had been postponed until October, when it would be directed personally by the author. Moreover, the column added, Lorca had just been to see the actress María Fernanda Ladrón de Guevara to offer her a new play called *The Dreams of My Cousin Aurelia*.[46] The anonymous writer (perhaps Lorca's friend Miguel Pérez Ferrero) was probably unaware that the title referred to a real person. Aurelia González García, the daughter of Federico's aunt Francisca, as we have said, was one of the poet's favourite cousins in Fuente Vaqueros and knew that he was writing about her, telling the painter Gregorio Prieto twenty years later that 'she' was to have been played by María Fernanda Ladrón de Guevara.[47]

It is significant that the first act of *The Dreams of My Cousin Aurelia* – the only act surviving and perhaps the only one written – is set, like *Doña Rosita the Spinster*, in 1910, the date that recurs obsessively in the poet's work in connection with the irreparable loss of love and security. The young boy appearing in the play is called Federico García Lorca, just in case we were in any doubts about his identity, and the love he feels for his cousin (twenty-three in the play and in reality some thirteen years older than the poet) reflects that which Federico really felt for the 'theatrical' Aurelia, who fainted during thunderstorms, was a passionate reader of novels, played the guitar with characteristic García flair and spoke an arrestingly metaphorical Spanish. Throughout this first act we have the feeling that in the relationship between the Child and Aurelia the poet has concentrated that nostalgia for lost or impossible love which pervades the early poems and never disappears altogether from his work ('If I were grown up I would be your boyfriend, wouldn't I?', the Child asks his cousin). Aurelia married in 1909 (the year of the departure of the García Lorcas for Granada) and it may well be that the eleven-year-old Federico felt then that he had lost her for ever. In the event, Aurelia often visited the family in Granada and, according to her daughter, always kept a photograph of Federico close by her in later years.[48]

Lorca finished *The House of Bernarda Alba* on 19 June, as the date at the end of the manuscript testifies.[49] Was it he who told the *Heraldo* that the play was a 'drama of Andalusian sexuality'? Perhaps. At all events no statement directly attributed to the poet seems to have appeared about the play in the few weeks leading up to the outbreak of the war. Manuel Altolaguirre recalled in 1937 Lorca's insistence that in *The House of Bernarda Alba* he had aimed at total simplicity and sobriety, cutting out all unnecessary details.[50] 'No literature, pure theatre,' the poet told Guillermo de Torre,[51] while Adolfo Salazar, who lived just across the street from Federico in Madrid, witnessed Lorca's euphoria while he worked on the play that summer. 'Each time he finished a scene he would come running, hot with excitement. "There's not a drop of poetry!" he would exclaim. "Reality! Pure realism!" ' Such was the poet's enthusiasm that he was prepared to read the play to anyone who would listen. Salazar had never seen Federico so pleased with anything he had written: he was like a child.[52]

At the foot of his list of *dramatis personae*, the poet wrote that the three acts of the play 'were intended to be like a photographic documentary'.[53] Carlos Morla Lynch, who was present at a reading of the work on 24 June, thought it 'an austere and gloomy etching of dramatic Castile',[54] although in fact it was inspired not by central Spain but by the village of Asquerosa where the poet had lived for one or two years after his family left Fuente Vaqueros and where, after settling in Granada, they habitually returned for a few months each summer. Although the definitive subtitle of the play was 'A Drama of Women in the Villages of Spain', Lorca's first intention was to locate the action in 'an Andalusian village on arid land'[55] – a designation that exactly fits Asquerosa, situated as it is on the dry edge of the lush Vega.

Bernarda Alba is based on Frasquita Alba Sierra, who lived with her family across the street from Don Federico García's first house in Asquerosa and next door to Federico's cousins the Delgado Garcías. Frasquita was born in 1858 and by her first marriage had a son and two daughters.[56] When her husband died she married, in 1893, one Alejandro Rodríguez Capilla, seven years older than herself, and produced four more children: three daughters and a son. The latter, Alejandro, was the same age as Lorca and for a time his classmate in the village. Frasquita died in 1924 and her husband in 1925.[57] While in Asquerosa she was remembered as a woman of domineering temperament, she could at no time have ruled as a widow over the children of both marriages, as the dates show. Bernarda Alba's widowhood tyranny, that is, was invented by the poet.

Lorca was fascinated as a child by the gossip about the Albas transmitted to him by Mercedes Delgado García, another of his favourite older cousins. The Albas and Delgado Garcías shared a well at the back of their houses which was divided in half by the corral wall. Through the gap everything said on the other side could be clearly heard, and it seems that as a result Mercedes and her brothers and sisters were always fully informed about what was going on next door.[58] The discussions overheard by the eavesdroppers may have hinged at times on questions of inheritance similar to those that cause such jealousy among the daughters of Bernarda, but this is speculation.

One of the daughters of the first marriage, Amelia, had married José Benavides, from the village of Romilla or Roma la Chica on the other side of the Genil, whose inhabitants are known as *romanos*. When Amelia died, Benavides, known familiarly in Asquerosa as 'Pepico el de Roma', married her sister Consuelo. This was the seed from which Lorca developed the pervasive role of Pepe el Romano in *The House of Bernarda Alba* although, again, there is no evidence that Frasquita's remaining daughters were passionately in love with him.[59] As for other characters appearing in the play, the servant La Poncia is based on a real person, although she never worked for Frasquita;[60] Bernarda's crazed grandmother María Josefa derives from an old García relative suffering from erotic hallucinations, whom Federico and his brother Francisco visited as children in Fuente

Vaqueros;[61] while Enrique Humanes (the rejected suitor) and Maximiliano (whose wife gets carried off to the olive grove) also existed in flesh and blood.[62] As for Adela's green dress, Lorca took the idea, as was said earlier, from the one that had belonged to another of his favourite cousins, Clotilde García Picossi, who because of mourning in the family could flaunt it only to the hens in the back corral.[63] As well as these borrowings, *The House of Bernarda Alba* evokes the speech of the inhabitants of Asquerosa, lively despite the rather introspective character of the village compared to Fuente Vaqueros; the incredibly long periods of mourning which it was then customary to observe, hardly exaggerated in the play; the eyes spying behind the curtains; the curiosity about sexual scandal (reflected when the dead baby is discovered); the arrival of the reapers each summer from the hills around the Vega, an annual event much looked forward to by the village girls; and the pitiless heat that beats down in summer.

As in all Lorca's work, however, the 'facts' serve simply as a starting point. Bernarda Alba is a grotesque magnification of Frasquita Alba, who died over eleven years before the work was written, and it is not surprising that the poet's mother should have begged him to change her surname in order not to offend the family.[64] Had he lived to see the play performed, perhaps Lorca would have accepted this maternal advice, although the loss would have been considerable, given the symbolic connotations of the name (a learned adjective for 'white') which the poet develops throughout the tragedy.

It cannot have been by chance that Lorca wrote a play on the theme of despotism at a time when everyone with any sense knew that there was a very real possibility of a right-wing *coup* in Spain. Bernarda, with her hypocrisy, her inquisitorial Catholicism and her determination to suppress other people's freedom, represents a mentality known only too well to the poet. Reading the play against the context in which it was written it is impossible not to think of *El Debate*, Spain's leading Catholic newspaper, which had attacked the Barraca and *Yerma* and, during the 1936 election campaign, presented Gil Robles as a Spanish equivalent of Mussolini. In calling the play *The House of Bernarda Alba* and not simply *Bernarda Alba*, moreover, Lorca put the emphasis on the environment within which the tyrant moves and has her being, making such an intention explicit in the subtitle 'A Drama of Women in the Villages of Spain'. When he termed the play 'a photographic documentary' the poet was indicating that it constituted a sort of report, with black-and-white illustrations, on the intolerant Spain always ready to crush the vital impulses of the people, represented here not only by Bernarda's daughters but by the servants. 'The poor are like animals,' Bernarda pronounces. 'They seem to be made of different materials from the rest of us.'[65] Writing out of his own experience of conditions in the Spanish countryside, Lorca must have been bitterly aware of the failure of the agrarian reform promised by the Republic – a reform initiated during the first two years of democratic rule, paralysed when the Right came to power in 1933 and still to be implemented in June 1936 when he finished the work.

It is likely that Lorca had his father in mind as he wrote the play. Federico García Rodríguez was probably the only powerful landowner in Asquerosa who professed democratic and Republican ideas. He had had several brushes over the years with his peers, and was disliked because he paid his men better than they did and had even gone to the extent of building houses for them. Such generosity was unheard of in the area and explains why in Asquerosa there is a street named after the benevolent patriarch. Don Federico was the 'good landowner' of the village, while Bernarda Alba is precisely the opposite. The play, on one level, is an oblique homage to the poet's father.

Adela, who at the end of the play breaks Bernarda's stick, her symbol of office, is undoubtedly the most revolutionary of all Lorca's womenfolk, rejecting a code of honour based on keeping up appearances at all costs and on the belief that men are superior to women. Adela affirms her absolute right to her own sexuality ('I do with my own body what I feel like!'), and not surprisingly perhaps, in view of the identification with the suffering Christ fundamental in Lorca's early development and present throughout his work, she sees her determination to be her authentic self in terms of Christian sacrifice. When the family discovers that she not only loves Pepe el Romano but that the relationship has been consummated, her exclamation contains a clear allusion to the crucifixion:

After tasting his mouth I can't stand the horror of these ceilings any longer. I'll be whatever he wants. With the whole village against me, pointing at me with their burning fingers, persecuted by people who claim to be decent – in full view of all of them I'll put on the crown of thorns worn by the mistresses of married men.[66]

Adela's programme for her personal fulfilment is that recommended by the poet throughout his brief life, both to himself and to the people he cared about. 'The day we stop resisting our instincts, we'll have learnt how to live,' he had said emphatically in 1933.[67] The play begins and ends with Bernarda's shouted injunction 'Silence!' – the first time to stifle the public expression of grief, the second to impose a lie. Two months after he finished *The House of Bernarda Alba* Lorca was killed by people with a mentality akin to that of his tyrant. And for forty years the Franco regime would efficiently silence the manner of his death.

On 10 June, while he was putting the finishing touches to *The House of Bernarda Alba*, Federico was interviewed for *El Sol* by Luis Bagaría, one of the finest political cartoonists of the day. The poet, who took the precaution of answering the questions in writing, began by insisting, as he had done so often of late, on the social mission of the theatre in modern society:

The idea of art for art's sake is something that would be cruel if it weren't, fortunately, so ridiculous. No decent person believes any longer in all that nonsense about pure art, art for art's sake.

At this dramatic moment in time, the artist should laugh and cry with his people. We must put down the bouquet of lilies and bury ourselves up to the waist in mud to help those who are *looking* for lilies. For myself, I have a genuine need to communicate with others. That's why I knocked at the door of the theatre and why I now devote all my talents to it.

Lorca was then asked about his opinion of the fall of Moorish Granada to Ferdinand and Isabella in 1492. He came out with a statement as carefully weighed as it was provocative:

It was a disastrous event, even though they may say the opposite in the schools. An admirable civilization, and a poetry, architecture and sensitivity unique in the world – all were lost, to give way to an impoverished, cowed city, a 'miser's paradise' where the worst middle class in Spain today is busy stirring things up.*

In his allusion to the Granada middle class the poet presumably had in mind the constant provocations of the extreme Right in the town since the victory of the Popular Front candidates, after the annulment of the Granada results, in the reconvened election of May. *El Sol* was the most widely read liberal newspaper in Spain, and Lorca's harsh comments quickly became known in the town, where they infuriated many people.[68] Having made his position on Granada clear and attacked the myth, dear to the heart of the traditionalists, that the fall of the Moorish kingdom was a great Christian victory over paganism, paving the way to national unification and the conquest of the New World, the poet went on to talk about what it meant to him to be Spanish. Here too he trod on not a few conservative toes:

I am totally Spanish, and it would be impossible for me to live outside my geographical boundaries. At the same time I hate anyone who is Spanish just because he was born a Spaniard. I am a brother to all men, and I detest the person who sacrifices himself for an abstract, nationalist ideal just because he loves his country with a blindfold over his eyes. A good Chinaman is closer to me than a bad Spaniard. I express Spain in my work and feel her in the very marrow of my bones; but first and foremost I'm cosmopolitan and a brother to all.[69]

Having handed over his answers to Bagaría, Lorca became uneasy, and

---

* 'Una "tierra del chavico" donde se agita actualmente la peor burguesía de España.'

left a note for his friend Adolfo Salazar at *El Sol*, asking him discreetly to remove, without Bagaría's finding out, his answer to a question by the latter about fascism and communism. 'It seems indiscreet to me at this moment,' the poet tried to explain, 'and, moreover, I had already answered the question earlier.'[70] Salazar did as he was told and the offending part of the interview did not appear. Why the caution? Various witnesses have stated that Lorca was then being constantly pressed by different friends, particularly by Rafael Alberti and María Teresa León, to join the Communist Party or at least to identify himself more closely with it, and that there came a point when he had had enough.[71] Perhaps he feared that his answer to Bagaría's question would lead to further pressures. Lorca had gone out of his way over the previous months to make his position clear on fascism. But to do so on communism was more tricky, and it seems that, prudently, he decided simply to avoid the issue. In support of this hypothesis it can be added that, shortly before the Civil War erupted, the young poet José Luis Cano was present when Lorca refused to sign a Communist manifesto. Federico told him that he felt under no obligation to support the Party publicly. Vicente Aleixandre later informed Cano that Lorca had said to him that he was tired of having his arm twisted by his communist friends. He was not anti-communist but nor was he a fellow-traveller.[72]

In the same letter to Salazar Lorca told his friend that he was just off by motor car to Granada for two days to 'say goodbye' to his family. Since his parents were still in Madrid, he can have been alluding only to his sister and brother-in-law, Manuel Fernández-Montesinos, and their children; and if he wanted to say goodbye to them it must have been because he had finally taken the decision to join Margarita Xirgu in Mexico. There is other evidence for this deduction, not least that from Francisco García Lorca, who stated that when the war began Federico had the tickets for Mexico in his pocket.[73] The poet did not return to Granada for those two days, however – perhaps his unidentified driver let him down – and when he eventually travelled south it was too late to escape.

Another indication of the poet's increasing irritation with the pressuring of his communist friends can be found in the fact that he failed to turn up at a function in memory of Maxim Gorky, who had just died, organized by the Alliance of Intellectuals for the Defence of Culture, to whose Spanish branch he belonged. With other intellectuals Federico had signed a telegram of condolence to the Soviet Government and people, and the newspapers announced his participation in the programme along with 'La Pasionaria' – Dolores Ibárruri – and other well-known political figures of the Left. But he stayed away.[74]

Two nights earlier, Lorca had enjoyed a relaxed evening out with a group of intimate friends that included Rodríguez Rapún, José Caballero, Adolfo Salazar, Eduardo Ugarte and José Amorós, the young bullfighter from Salamanca, who was recovering from a serious goring he had received that May in Saragossa. In a photograph of the occasion, taken late that night at a downtown studio, a radiantly happy Lorca is fondling Rapún's forehead. It is the last known photograph in which the two appear together.[75]

The poet continued to read *The House of Bernarda Alba* to all and sundry, more and more enthusiastic about what he had achieved in the play, and was already preparing drawings of the sets, which he showed to José Caballero.[76] Among those who heard him read the work was the German writer Hans Gebser, well known in his country as a translator of contemporary Spanish poetry. With Federico's help Gebser was working on a version, in Spanish this time, of Wedekind's *Spring Awakening* which, he hoped, the poet would produce for him in the Teatro Español. Lorca gave Gebser a present of thirteen drawings of surrealist inspiration which the German published in 1949 with a psychoanalytically orientated commentary.[77]

One night, perhaps on 9 July, the poet dined at the house of Carlos Morla Lynch. Fernando de los Ríos was there, looking 'visibly disturbed'. 'The Popular Front is falling apart and fascism is growing fast,' said the ex-Minister of Education. 'We mustn't deceive ourselves. The situation is extremely grave.' As a Member of Parliament Don Fernando must have been well aware of the rumours that were circulating at the time concerning the military conspiracy against the Republic, and probably knew that the Prime Minister, Santiago Casares Quiroga, was refusing to take them seriously, believing that if there were a rising it would be put down as easily as that headed by General Sanjurjo in 1932.[78] Lorca arrived late, and despite bringing the good news that his brother Francisco, Secretary of the Spanish Legation in Cairo, was well – the newspapers had wrongly reported him injured by an assassin's bullet – he was depressed and hardly talked all evening.[79]

One of the reasons for Lorca's sombre mood that night may have been his anxiety about the increasing violence and chaos that was gripping the capital. On 2 June the anarchist National Confederation of Workers (CNT) and socialist General Union of Workers (UGT) had brought out the builders, electricians and lift-repairers on a strike that was still continuing, and that indeed was not settled until two weeks after the beginning of the war. Between the rival anarchist, socialist and communist unions there was constant skirmishing, while the Falangists were adding their own fuel to the fire. Shots were becoming more and more frequent, and one day Lorca showed José Caballero where a stray bullet had come through the window of his family's flat in the Calle de Alcalá. 'It could have killed me,' he said, trembling.[80]

On 11 July the poet and some other friends, among them the Socialist Member of Parliament Fulgencio Díez Pastor, dined at Pablo Neruda's flat. That afternoon a group of Falangists had jumped the gun and seized Radio Valencia, announcing the imminence of the Fascist Revolution.[81] Madrid was buzzing with rumours and gossip and Díez Pastor, like Fernando de los Ríos, was extremely worried about the political situation. Lorca, guessing that his friend knew more than he was prepared to admit, assailed him with question after question. What was going to happen? Was there going to be a military *coup*? What should he do? Finally the poet burst out, 'I'm going to Granada!' 'Don't do it,' replied Díez Pastor. 'You'll be safer in Madrid than anywhere else.'[82] It seems that the Falangist writer Agustín de Foxá proffered similar advice: 'If you want to leave Madrid, don't go to Granada. Go to Biarritz.' 'What would I do in Biarritz?' the poet is said to have exclaimed. 'In Granada at least I can work.'[83] Luis Buñuel recalls in his memoirs that he too advised Federico to stay in the capital. 'Dreadful things are going to happen,' he claims to have told him. 'Stay here. You'll be much safer in Madrid.'[84]

On the evening of Sunday, 12 June, the situation in the city became explosive when a group of gunmen assassinated Lieutenant José Castillo of the Assault Guard, the constabulary founded a few years earlier for the explicit defence of the Republic. Castillo, a militant anti-fascist, had been a marked man for months, receiving numerous anonymous threats. In the early hours of the following morning his friends carried out an appalling reprisal, kidnapping and assassinating José Calvo Sotelo, leader of the extreme-right-wing opposition in the Parliament, and dumping his body in the municipal cemetery, where it was not identified until several hours later. Calvo Sotelo was the martyr the rebels needed, and his death fitted the bill all the more neatly because, thanks to the participation in it of uniformed men, it could be presented as a *crime d'état*. Many Army officers who had hesitated to join the conspirators now threw caution to the winds. Calvo Sotelo's murder was used later to justify the rebellion, although, in fact, plans for it were well advanced before his brutal death.[85]

It was almost certainly on the fateful night of 12 July that, perhaps unaware of the killing of Lieutenant Castillo, Lorca gave his last reading of *The House of Bernarda Alba*. Among those present were the poets Jorge Guillén, Dámaso Alonso and Pedro Salinas and the critic Guillermo de Torre. Dámaso Alonso recalled in 1948 that, as they were leaving the flat, a lively discussion was taking place about a certain writer, probably Rafael Alberti, who had become deeply involved in politics. 'He'll never write anything worthwhile now,' Lorca commented according to Alonso, adding, 'As for me, I'll never be political. I'm a revolutionary, because all true poets are revolutionaries – don't you agree? – but political, never!'[86] It may be presumed that what Lorca meant was that he would be incapable of joining a political party, not that he did not have political allegiances. Years after publishing the conversation, Dámaso Alonso, by then an old man, came up with another detail, remembering that among his list of revolutionary poets Lorca had included Jesus Christ.[87]

The double assassination of Castillo and Calvo Sotelo threw Lorca into a mood of black anguish. 'When I saw him for the last time in Madrid,' wrote the poet Juan Gil-Albert, 'he was literally terrified. Calvo Sotelo's death seemed to suggest to him that the end was near. "What's going to happen?" he said to me, like someone who by intuition expected the worst of his fellow countrymen.'[88]

Lorca, whose parents had left for Granada a few weeks earlier, decided to join them there without delay.[89] That 13 July, as more facts about Calvo Sotelo's assassination became known, he lunched with Rafael Martínez Nadal, who had recently returned to Madrid from Stockholm, where he had lectured on the poet's work. After the meal the two took a taxi out to the Puerta de Hierro, on the outskirts of the city, to have a quiet brandy and to discuss the situation. Lorca was intensely agitated and asked repeatedly what he should do. Finally he took a decision. 'Rafael, these fields are going to be strewn with corpses!' he exclaimed, and stubbing out his cigarette jumped up. 'My mind is made up,' he went on. 'I'm going to Granada, come what may.' According to Martínez Nadal they then drove to the Gran Vía, where the poet bought copies of his books for friends in Scandinavia, proceeding afterwards to Thomas Cook's to reserve a *couchette* on that night's train to Granada. In the García Lorcas' flat Martinez Nadal helped the poet to pack. As they were leaving, Federico turned back, opened a drawer in his desk and extracted a package. 'Take this and keep it for me,' he said to Martínez Nadal. 'If anything happens to me, destroy it all. If not, you can return it to me when we next meet.' The package, which Martínez Nadal opened later that night, contained the manuscript of *The Public* and 'personal papers'. 'I took it that his request to destroy the whole package could not possibly apply to that manuscript,' Martínez Nadal wrote later.*

Before going with Martínez Nadal to the station, Lorca took his leave of his friend's family. And, although the visit is not mentioned in Martínez Nadal's account, also dropped in on his sister Isabel and the latter's great friend Laura de los Ríos, both of whom were then staying at the Residencia

---

* And the 'personal papers'? Were they destroyed? As far as we know, Señor Martínez Nadal has never clarified this point.

de Señoritas in 8 Calle Miguel Angel.[90] At Atocha station Martínez Nadal helped to install Federico in his sleeping-car. And then something unexpected happened:

> Someone went by down the corridor of the sleeping-car. Federico turned away quickly, stuck the forefinger and little finger of each hand in the air, to ward off the evil eye, and chanted: '*Lagarto, lagarto, lagarto.*' ['Lizard, lizard, lizard.']
> I asked him who the man was.
> 'A Member of Parliament for Granada. The evil eye. Real poison.'
> Federico stood up, obviously unnerved and upset.
> 'Look, Rafael, you go now. Don't wait on the platform. I'm going to pull the blinds down and get into bed. I don't want that creature to see me or talk to me.'
> We gave each other a quick hug and for the first time in my life I left Federico on a train without waiting for its departure, and without laughing and joking until the last moment.[91]

As regards the identity of the sinister Member of Parliament whose presence on the train so disturbed the poet, we are completely in the dark. And at all events he was probably an ex-Member, since on 31 March all the opposition Deputies had lost their seats when the Granada election results were annulled by the Parliament, and none were re-elected in May. It does not seem likely, that is, that Lorca would have felt so strongly about any of the Republican or left-wing Members for Granada, many of whom, starting with Fernando de los Ríos, were personal friends of the poet – although, of course, this possibility cannot be entirely ruled out.

Martínez Nadal's account of Lorca's last hours in Madrid, published twenty-seven years later,[92] cannot be considered an absolutely trustworthy document in every detail. Not only does the author get the date wrong – Lorca left Madrid on the night of 13 July, not the 16th – but there are important omissions, while the reconstructed snatches of dialogue are too word-perfect to be convincing. One wonders in particular at the lack of all reference to Rodríguez Rapún. Did Lorca not see him before he left Madrid? It would seem impossible on the face of it that he could consider suddenly hurrying off to Granada without first taking leave of his lover. About the last months of his friendship with Rapún information is almost completely lacking. But we do know that, if Federico had not already gone to Mexico by this time, he had delayed principally because he felt he could not manage without his friend – without a Rapún who by now was deeply involved in the united Socialist and Communist Youth Movement.[93]

That night Lorca was expected by Carlos Morla Lynch. Luis Cernuda was in the company, and recalled in 1938 that the elegant salon was rife with speculation about the assassination of Calvo Sotelo. Lorca did not turn up, to the surprise of Morla, and finally someone came in and announced that he had just seen the poet off at the station. The someone, presumably, was Rafael Martínez Nadal.[94]

Next morning, 14 July 1936, Lorca was with his parents in the Huerta de San Vicente; and the following day Doña Vicenta wrote to her daughter Isabel, who had just obtained an appointment as a secondary-school teacher, to say how delighted they were that Federico had joined them.[95]

12

The Death of a Poet

Terror in Granada

The city to which Lorca returned on the morning of 14 July 1936 had been the scene since the February elections of constant disturbances, provocations and strikes. Although the Right had won in Granada, the results were hotly debated in the new Cortes, where the Popular Front members considered that serious infringements had been committed on polling day. The Parliament had finally annulled the Granada results and a fresh election was called for early May. This time the campaign took place in a climate very different from that of February. With the Popular Front in power, right-wing electoral bullying was almost impossible, and aggressive heckling made havoc of the opposition's meetings. The outcome was inevitable: 'the forces of law and order', as they liked to call themselves, abstained massively and the Popular Front won an overwhelming victory, not a single right-wing candidate being returned. Deprived of parliamentary representation the Granada middle class swung even further to the Right, and support grew for the anti-Republican conspirators who were now completing their plans for the downfall of the hated regime.[1]

In Granada the small but determined Falangist party took on a new lease of life after the electoral failure of José María Gil Robles's coalition in February, and grew even stronger when the Granada results were abrogated. The Falangists lived in the belief that the days of the Republic were numbered and that, within a few months, the Popular Front Government would be overthrown by the joint action of the Army and themselves, and some form of corporativist state instituted. The Falange now devoted itself to the nationwide propagation of street violence and the preparation of civil war. Assassinations became more frequent with the consequent reprisals, and, where Granada was concerned, angry confrontations between the trade unions and the Falangists made life in the city increasingly tense. The

446

workers' reaction to the Falange's provocations was, naturally, energetic. In March, after a massive left-wing demonstration, two churches were gutted, the premises of the Catholic daily *Ideal* wrecked, the offices of rightist organizations pillaged and even the Isabella the Catholic Theatre destroyed – no doubt because its owner was right-wing. Certainly, it would be unfair to ascribe to the Falange a monopoly of the violence: among the left-wing organizations – socialist, communist, anarchist – there was no shortage of individuals prepared to take up the gun.[2]

During these months the Granada Falange worked in close liaison with the rebels in the Army garrison, whose chief conspirator, Commandant José Valdés Guzmán, a fanatical enemy of the Republic, was one of their members. Born in Logroño – capital of the wine-growing district of La Rioja, in northern Spain – Valdés had been in Granada for seven years and knew intimately the workings of the city, as well as the mind of the officers.[3]

Three days before Lorca returned to Granada, a new Military Governor had arrived in the town. This was General Miguel Campíns Aura, a man with a distinguished record in the field – the African field – and known to be a friend of General Franco. It immediately became apparent to Valdés and his accomplices, however, that Campíns was a staunch Republican and that they could not count on his support for the rising.[4]

The Civil Governor of the province, like Campíns, was at a grave disadvantage in these moments of extreme tension. César Torres Martínez, a lawyer from Galicia, had come to Granada only a month before to take charge of a difficult situation in both the capital and the province. Young, affable, conciliatory, he immediately proved his ability as a negotiator, helping to solve a strike of long standing. But Torres knew few people well in Granada; several men who could have helped him to understand what was happening were out of town; like the Prime Minister, Casares Quiroga, he seemed more disturbed about the possibility of anarchy than of fascism; and, when the moment struck, he would prove unable to act with the necessary determination and imagination.[5]

On his arrival at the Huerta de San Vicente Lorca was delighted to find that a telephone had just been installed. He immediately called his old friend Constantino Ruiz Carnero, editor of *El Defensor de Granada*, who announced on the front page of the following day's issue that the great poet had just arrived in the city to spend a 'brief period' with his family. It seems fair to assume, in view of this detail, that Lorca had told Ruiz Carnero of his plan to join Margarita Xirgu in Mexico during the summer.[6] Lorca's return was also mentioned in the town's other two leading newspapers, the Catholic *Ideal* and the conservative *Noticiero Granadino*.[7] The conspirators must have been aware, therefore, that the poet was among them. Lorca did not remain in the seclusion of the Huerta, moreover, but, sociable as ever and no doubt enjoying the impact of his presence on his fellow citizens, was often seen in the town. One day he ran into Miguel Cerón, whose flat he had frequented fifteen years earlier, when he was beginning his literary career. As they talked a group of girls collecting funds for the communist Red Aid organization came up and asked for a contribution. Lorca acquiesced. 'Why don't we go to Russia together, Miguel!' he quipped. Cerón never saw him again.[8]

Glad to be back with his friends, Lorca read *The House of Bernarda Alba* to a group who gathered in Fernando Vílchez's beautiful *carmen* in the Albaicín.[9] Did any of these comment on his interview with Luis Bagaría, published a month earlier in *El Sol*? It is hard to believe that nobody referred, during the week leading up to the rising, to Lorca's scathing allusion on that occasion to the Granada middle class, which he had qualified as the 'worst in Spain', stating that it was deliberately provoking trouble in the town. The interview had caused a considerable stir in Granada, and did nothing to enhance the poet's reputation among those who at this very moment were finalizing their plans for the assault on democracy.[10]

Every 18 July, St Frederick's Day, the García Lorcas held open house at the Huerta de San Vicente in honour of the father and eldest son of the family. Friends and relatives would arrive, bearing gifts, from the town and the Vega, and the revelry would continue well into the night. But this year things were different. The previous evening the feared anti-Republican revolt had begun in Spanish Morocco, and this morning General Franco had broadcast a message from the Canary Islands announcing the beginning of the National Movement. So Franco had thrown in his lot with the rebels! No informed observer of the Spanish scene could fail to recognize the seriousness of what was happening – and the García Lorcas were certainly in that category. While, in Madrid, the Prime Minister, Casares Quiroga, doubted, prevaricated and finally broke down emotionally, and government bulletins insisted that the Republic was in control of the situation, General Queipo de Llano – one of the blue-eyed boys of the regime, now turned traitor – succeeded that afternoon in usurping the command of the Seville garrison, the most important in Andalusia. By nightfall Queipo had taken the centre of the city and was preparing his assault on the working-class quarters. Seville Radio was one of the most potent transmitters in Spain and, from the moment the city fell, the charismatic Queipo used it to full effect. The General's nightly harangues (an astonishing mixture of lies, threats, wishful thinking and bloodthirstiness) quickly became famous and were listened to throughout Spain, by both sides, with bated breath.[11]

In Granada, the Civil Governor, César Torres, obeying strict orders from

Prime Minister Casares, refused stubbornly to accede to the demands of the left-wing organizations that arms be distributed at once to the people. Convinced by General Campíns that the officers were loyal to the Government, Torres continued to stand firm. That night Casares resigned and, while the moderate Republican Diego Martínez Barrio tried desperately to form a new government, which would seek to negotiate a truce with the rebels, the order to distribute arms to the masses was still withheld. The Republicans, understandably, wanted above all to combat the rising by strictly legal means. Once the left-wing organizations were armed, they felt, absolute anarchy might ensue and democracy collapse. First, every effort must be made to reach some sort of compromise with the rebels. But the insurgents wanted none of this. And, as Franco himself would say a few days later, if it was necessary to destroy half the population in order to win what was now a civil war, he was prepared to do so.[12]

Faced by the refusal of the socialists to co-operate, Martínez Barrio's efforts to put together a coalition government foundered, and the Cabinet that emerged at 5 a.m. on 19 July was stillborn. (There was no communist or anarchist representation either.) That morning, panic, fear and rage, fanned by the news that further garrisons had fallen to the rebels, seized the Madrid working class, who rejected to a man the Martínez Barrio Government, which kept refusing to make arms available. A few hours later the Prime Minister realized that he had no option but to resign. A new Government under José Giral was formed with, this time, full left-wing representation and the explicit undertaking to arm the people at once.[13]

But the order to distribute weapons was not transmitted immediately to Granada, where confusion reigned at every level. Campíns and Torres Martínez continued to believe that the garrison would remain loyal, and despite constant demands from left-wing delegations not a single gun was made available to the workers. When the reversal of government policy became known, it was already too late.[14]

The Mayor of Granada – elected only eight days earlier – was the young socialist doctor Manuel Fernández-Montesinos, husband of Lorca's sister Concha. There can be little doubt that he kept the family informed of what was happening in the city, telephoning them at the Huerta de San Vicente. But of those conversations no record remains.

On the afternoon of 20 July the Granada garrison finally rose. An incredulous General Campíns was arrested at gun-point by the officers in whom he had so unwisely trusted, and was forced to sign the proclamation of war. At 5 p.m. the troops left their barracks and without opposition took the principal official buildings in the town. Torres Martínez, as incredulous as Campíns, was apprehended in his office; so too was Manuel Fernández-

Montesinos. Within an hour most of the Republican authorities had been rounded up and imprisoned, and the whole town centre occupied. Only in the steep working-class quarter of the Albaicín was there any resistance. There trenches were hurriedly dug to prevent the access of vehicles, and makeshift barricades thrown up blocking the entrances to the narrow pedestrian streets. It took the rebels three days to reduce the Albaicín – not much of an achievement given the fact that the workers were virtually without arms or ammunition, while the garrison had mortars, hand grenades, cannons and even three or four aeroplanes, which machine-gunned the quarter.[15]

By 23 July the whole of Granada was in the hands of the insurgents. They knew, however, that their position was far from secure. The town was almost completely surrounded by Republican territory and a counter-attack might, theoretically, be launched at any moment. It was essential, therefore, that they should immediately consolidate their supremacy by strengthening Granada's defences and eliminating all possibility of renewed resistance from within. To the latter end a reign of terror was now established in the city, which, over the following months, led to the deaths of many hundreds of innocent men and women. Not only were there daily executions of left-wing prisoners against the walls of the cemetery, behind the Alhambra, but, on a less official level, assassination squads operated with impunity, butchering and torturing and reducing the population to a state of absolute panic.[16]

All this the García Lorcas, sick with anxiety about the fate of Manuel Fernández-Montesinos, knew only too well. According to one of the family's neighbours, Federico had naïvely taken a basket of food to the gaol for his brother-in-law on the first day of the rising, when the Republicans still held the Albaicín, returning home in tears and taking to his bed. He had been unable to hand over the provisions and had probably witnessed harrowing scenes.[17] Soon the family themselves had first-hand experience of fascist violence. On 6 August, a Falangist squad, commanded by Captain Manuel Rojas Feigespán – the man responsible for the massacre of anarchists in Casas Viejas in 1934 and whom the rebels had freed from prison – arrived at the Huerta and searched the premises. Looking for what? There was a rumour at this time, no doubt put about by the poet's enemies, that Federico had a clandestine radio in the house with which he was in touch with 'the Russians', no less. Perhaps the group was searching for this improbable transmitter. But we know no more about the visit: no member of the family, it seems, kept a record of these events.[18]

The following day Alfredo Rodríguez Orgaz, a young friend of the poet who until recently had been city architect of Granada, appeared at the

Huerta. He had been in hiding since the beginning of the rising but, realizing that he was in extreme danger, had decided that he must try to escape. Federico's father promised that that night some peasant friends of his would take him across country to the Republican zone, only a few miles away. Federico told Rodríguez that he had been listening to the Madrid radio, with its regular government bulletins, and was convinced that the 'war' would be over in no time. There could therefore be no question of his going with him. Just then someone gave the alarm. A car was approaching down the lane. Perhaps they were after Rodríguez! Alfredo bid a hasty farewell and dashed behind the house, where he hid under some bushes. The visitors were indeed pursuing Rodríguez. But on finding no trace of the fugitive – the García Lorcas, it seems, coolly denied having seen him – they left, apparently without threatening the family. That night the architect crossed the Republican lines to safety.[19]

Then, on 9 August, things took a decided turn for the worse, when a group arrived at the Huerta looking for the brothers of the caretaker, Gabriel Perea, wrongly accused of having killed two people in Asquerosa on the day the rising began in Granada. Most of the men were from the village and the nearby town of Pinos Puente, and among them were two brothers, the landowners Miguel and Horacio Roldán Quesada, enemies of Federico's father, supporters of Gil Robles, and known for their conservativism.[20] The group searched Perea's house, adjoining the Huerta, and then proceeded to pitch his mother down the stairs. Where were her other sons, the assassins? Where were they hiding? When the poor woman insisted that she did not know, they hauled her and the rest of the family out on to the terrace in front of the building. There they tied the terrified Gabriel to a cherry tree and someone began to beat him with a whip. The poet, who was witnessing this scene with his parents and sister, could stand it no longer and rushed forward to protest Gabriel's innocence. He was thrown to the ground and kicked. The group immediately recognized him and one of the men snarled, 'Ah, the little queer friend of Fernando de los Ríos!' Lorca protested that he was the friend not just of the socialist professor, but of many people of different persuasions. What names he may have given has not been recorded. There was no doubt that the thugs knew exactly where the poet's political sympathies lay. Nor that they despised him.[21] It seems that, before the men left, taking Gabriel with them for interrogation (he was later released), they warned Lorca that he was under house arrest and that he must on no account leave the premises.[22]

The poet was now frightened. The next time they might come for him. Where could he seek refuge? To whom could he turn for protection? Then he thought of his friend the young poet Luis Rosales, who had returned to

451

Granada, like himself, just before the trouble began in July, and two of whose brothers, José and Antonio, were among the town's leading Falangists. Of course! Was it not a fact that Luis considered Federico, twelve years his senior, his poetic 'master'? Lorca had seen a lot of Rosales recently in Madrid and their friendship had grown stronger. Of course Luis would help! Federico immediately telephoned the Rosales's house and was fortunate in being able to contact Luis straightaway. He explained briefly what had happened, and Rosales promised to go at once to the Huerta. He arrived shortly afterwards, accompanied by his younger brother Gerardo. What took place then is best told in Rosales's own words:

Federico explained to me that some individuals had been there twice* during the day, roughing him up and going through his private papers . . . In view of this I promised to help in any way they thought I could. I am the only surviving witness of the discussion – Federico's parents and sister Concha have all died. Well, Federico discussed the various possibilities open to him and I put myself at his disposal. The possibility of getting Federico into the Republican zone was discussed. I could have done this fairly easily and had already done it with other people – and had brought people back from the Republican zone. But Federico refused. He was terrified by the thought of being all alone in a no-man's-land between the two zones. Nor would he consider going to seek refuge in Manuel de Falla's *carmen* . . . He said that he would prefer to come to my house. And that's what we decided. He came that day.[23]

Before Rosales left he warned the family that on no account must they reveal Federico's whereabouts. That night the poet was driven to the Rosales's house at 1 Calle de Angulo, in the taxi owned by Don Federico's driver Francisco Murillo.[24] The building was a mere 300 yards from the Civil Government, where Commandant Valdés Guzmán was now busy organizing the repression. Seen in retrospect, and given the poet's reputation among the town's right-wing sectors, to have moved so close to that hub of violence and hatred, seething with gossip and denunciations, might seem suicidal. But presumably to Lorca the Rosales's spacious house appeared a haven of security. We know nothing of the brief journey from the Huerta, potentially fraught with danger, but it is not difficult to imagine that, once the door of 1 Calle de Angulo closed behind him, the poet felt an overwhelming sense of relief.

With the Rosales Family

The Rosales's father, Miguel Rosales Vallecillos, had built up a thriving haberdashery and hardware shop just off the Plaza de Bibarrambla, where

---

* Whether there was in fact a second visit that day to the Huerta it is now impossible to determine.

jousts used to be held in Moorish times. He was one of the best-known merchants in the town, respected for his kindness and probity. A 'liberal conservative' in politics, according to Luis, he had little time for the Falangists. His wife, Esperanza Camacho, on the other hand, approved of the Falangist fervour of her sons José and Antonio.[25]

The fine house has been altered almost beyond recognition since 1936, and is now an hotel. It was of typical local design, comprising an entrance hall with numerous rooms built around an ample patio, where the family lived in summer, and, upstairs, two floors and a rooftop terrace. On the second floor, which was virtually independent – the flat had its own staircase to the street as well as a connecting door to the floor below – lived Señora Rosales's sister, Aunt Luisa Camacho. It was decided by common consent that Federico should stay there.[26]

Little by little, thanks to the attentions of the women of the house – Señora Rosales, her daughter Esperanza, Aunt Luisa Camacho and a female servant – the poet regained a modicum of tranquillity, spending hours talking about his experiences in New York, Buenos Aires and Cuba, or playing folk songs on the piano, which the family installed specially in his room. As for the Rosales menfolk, Federico saw little of them: the father was occupied most of the time with his shop; Miguel and José were married and had their own flats; while Gerardo, Luis and Antonio hardly slept at home during these days.[27]

In no way engaged in politics before the war, the twenty-six-year-old Luis Rosales, like his father a liberal conservative, had found himself in a difficult situation when the rising began, and finally decided that he had no option but to don the blue Falangist shirt. His efficiency impressed his superiors, and before long he was promoted to positions of some importance. By the time Lorca moved to the Rosales's house Luis was obliged to spend most of the day out of town. When he returned in the evening he would talk to Federico, but this was not possible every day and, since the poet spent only a week with the family, it is safe to deduce that the two saw each other infrequently.[28]

It ought to be stressed that, in agreeing to shelter the poet, Don Miguel Rosales behaved with considerable bravery and magnanimity. These were dangerous days and it was strictly forbidden to protect a 'Red', whatever extenuating circumstances might be adduced – indeed, infringement could mean death. The Rosales family helped many people, among them a young communist, Manuel López Banús, one of the contributors to Lorca's magazine gallo eight years earlier, who saw Federico briefly at 1 Calle de Angulo while Luis arranged for him to join the Falange.[29] As events turned out, Miguel Rosales had to pay, literally, for the privilege of having done his best to protect the poet from his enemies: a hefty fine disguised as a contribution to the war effort.[30]

Lorca could not possibly write under such conditions, and spent much of his time perusing *Ideal*, which Esperanza took up to him each morning, and, above all, listening to the radio, both Republican and rebel.[31] He also made good use of Luis's well-stocked library, rediscovering the medieval monk–poet Gonzalo de Berceo, whose lines he read enthusiastically to Gerardo and Aunt Luisa Camacho.[32] As for his projects, Lorca spoke about the book of sonnets he was going to publish and of his intention of finally getting down to an epic poem entitled *Adam*, along the lines of *Paradise Lost*, which he had been thinking about for several years.[33]

It was frequently alleged by Franco propagandists that, during his stay with the Rosales, Lorca and Luis worked together on the composition of a hymn in honour of the Falange. This was untrue, and Rosales has stated emphatically that the plan, never implemented, was to compose a joint elegy to all those who had already died in the Civil War.[34]

How much can Lorca have known about the ruthless repression then being imposed by Valdés and his accomplices? While he cannot have been aware of the full horror of what was happening, it is impossible to doubt that he knew about the executions taking place daily in the cemetery, for these were sometimes mentioned prominently in *Ideal*. He must have been deeply worried about his brother-in-law, too, since random executions were being carried out in alleged reprisal for the feeble bombings Republican aeroplanes were inflicting these days on the town, and probably begged the Rosales family to do everything in their power to intervene on Montesinos's behalf.

According to Esperanza Rosales, Federico occasionally talked to his family by telephone. But of these conversations, doubtless very brief and to the point given the danger of being overheard, no record remains.[35]

The poet's time was running out. Shortly before sunrise on Sunday, 16 August, Manuel Fernández-Montesinos was shot in the cemetery along with twenty-nine other prisoners. At his request the execution was witnessed by a priest of his acquaintance, who now had the unenviable task of informing Concha García Lorca of her husband's death. The terrible news immediately reached Federico, probably by telephone. Esperanza Rosales was at his side: Lorca was shattered,[36] and we can conjecture that from this moment he must have lost whatever peace of mind he may have recovered during the week. If the rebels were capable of shooting people as innocent as Montesinos, simply because he held a political post, how could a 'Red' poet hope to escape? Had he not made numerous anti-fascist statements to the press? Had he not criticized the Granada middle class in *El Sol* that June?

Was he not a close friend of Fernando de los Ríos? Had the Catholic press not greatly disliked *Yerma*, considering it immoral and an attack on traditional values? Was he not a homosexual and loathed as such by many people in Granada? And, perhaps above all, was he not famous and therefore the victim of envy – the Spanish Vice, as Unamuno calls it? Moreover, it is possible that Federico knew from his parents that his enemies were on his track, for the previous day, 15 August, another group had arrived at the Huerta, this time with a warrant for his arrest. On discovering that Lorca was no longer there the men had combed the house and even dismantled the baby grand piano in search of incriminating papers – or perhaps the phantom radio. Finally the leader of the group had threatened the family that, if they did not reveal the whereabouts of the poet, he would take his father away instead. Terrified, Concha blurted out that Federico had not escaped but was staying in the house of a Falangist friend, like him a poet. Perhaps she even supplied Rosales's name. Either way it made little difference. By 15 August Lorca's pursuers knew where he was hiding.[37]

The Rosales family was also becoming uneasy and beginning to feel that Federico would be safer somewhere else. But where? If we can trust the accuracy of Esperanza Rosales's memory twenty years after the event, Lorca suggested his friend Emilia Llanos's flat. The Rosales thought that Manuel de Falla's *carmen* would be preferable. Who would dare to violate the house of the internationally renowned, intensely Catholic Falla, who, moreover, deeply admired Lorca? If, at the first threats a week earlier, the poet had seemed unwilling to disturb the composer, now, surely, he could see the logic of seeking refuge with him?[38]

But the enemy moved faster than the Rosales family. They looked for him first at the house of Luis's brother, Miguel, and realizing their mistake soon located him at 1 Calle de Angulo.[39] On the afternoon of 16 August Federico was arrested and taken away. It was a large-scale operation mounted by the Civil Government: the block was cordoned off, police and guards surrounded it and armed men were even stationed on the rooftops to prevent the poet from escaping that way.[40]

The person who arrived at the Rosales's house to detain Lorca was well known in Granada: the ex-Member of Parliament Ramón Ruiz Alonso, who belonged to Gil Robles's right-wing Coalition Party.

Ruiz Alonso was born at the turn of the century in the village of Villaflores, in the province of Salamanca, where his parents were comfortably off landowners. Like Gil Robles he was educated by the Salesian brothers in Salamanca, and, before the coming of the Republic in 1931, had worked as a draughtsman for the Aerial Photogrammetry Company in Madrid. At this period his life was prosperous. Under the Republic, however, he found himself converted into a menial bricklayer. How this came about is not clear, although he himself wrote that he was persecuted for his anti-Marxist ideas, and that his dismissal was secured from six jobs because he refused to join the ranks of the left-wing trade unionists. The genuine proletariat surrounding Ruiz Alonso evidently took an immense dislike to the violently anti-Republican *nouveau pauvre* who refused to participate in their class struggle, and who was clearly bent on regaining his former status. In these days fascism was gathering momentum, and it was natural that a man of Ruiz Alonso's temperament should have joined, in 1933, the newly formed Juntas de Ofensiva Nacional-Sindicalista ('National-Syndicalist Action Groups'), the first coherent fascist organization in Spain, which later merged with José Antonio Primo de Rivera's Falange Española. Soon afterwards Ruiz was given a job as a typographer on the Jesuit daily *El Debate*, Spain's leading Catholic newspaper and virtual mouthpiece of Gil Robles. The latter must have become aware at this time of the services Ruiz Alonso could lend to the party, and it was probably due to his influence that he was transferred to Granada to work on the newspaper *Ideal*, which, like *El Debate*, was controlled by Editorial Católica, the Jesuit publishing company.

Things were now looking up for Ruiz Alonso and his satisfaction knew no bounds when, included on Gil Robles's list of candidates for Granada in the November 1933 General Election, as representative of Acción Obrera (the Catholic Workers' Party), he suddenly found that he was a Member of Parliament.

The 'domesticated worker' (*obrero amaestrado*), as he soon came to be nicknamed, immediately earned the scorn and dislike of the Left, and not only in Granada. Pompous, noisy, pugnacious – to have this man from a bourgeois background taking upon himself the task of redeeming the Spanish working class was more than most Republicans could stomach. During his first year in the Cortes he failed to distinguish himself on behalf of the Catholic Workers' Party, over whose Central Committee he now presided. In 1934 he resigned from the Party but did not relinquish his seat, and for the next two years, until the victory of the Popular Front, allied himself more closely with mainstream elements within the coalition.

Ruiz Alonso loathed Fernando de los Ríos, and there are indications that for Lorca (widely considered the latter's protégé) he felt a mixture of scorn and envy. During the electoral campaign of January and February 1936, the 'domesticated worker' held a meeting in Fuente Vaqueros in the course of which he referred disparagingly both to De los Ríos and to Lorca, terming the latter *el poeta de la cabeza gorda* ('the poet with the big fat head'). There can be little doubt about his opinion of the author of *Blood Wedding*.[41]

The Right's candidates were victorious in Granada in the February 1936 elections but, as has been said, the results were declared null and void by Parliament and a new poll was held in May. This time, when the Popular Front prevailed, Ruiz Alonso and his colleagues all lost their seats. Ruiz's fury was gleefully reported in *El Defensor de Granada*, and his hatred of the Granada Left, who had never ceased to bait him in the columns of that newspaper, grew apace. His book *Corporativism*, an orthodox fascist manual published in 1937, shows that from then on he became fully involved in the conspiracy against the Republic, establishing contact with the Falangists and, no doubt, other groups.[42]

On 10 July Ruiz Alonso had left Madrid by car for Granada, almost certainly in the knowledge that within a few days the rising would break out, and with the purpose of participating in events in the town. But his journey was unexpectedly cut short when, outside Madridejos, in the province of Toledo, he crashed into a lorry. He was driving, in character, at high speed, and was lucky to escape with little more than some nasty bruises. Taken by political colleagues to Granada in another car, he was ordered by his doctor to bed – but did not stay there long. When the garrison took control of Granada on 20 July, Ruiz Alonso was soon operative and played a significant role in the early days of the repression.[43]

It seems that Ruiz Alonso was a friend of Horacio Roldán Quesada, the Asquerosa landowner who had had brushes with Lorca's father and who, with his brother Miguel, had participated in the visit to the Huerta de San Vicente during which Gabriel Perea had been beaten. It is possible, therefore, that Ruiz knew what had happened that day and that his arrival at the Rosales's house was not unconnected with those events, nor with the Roldáns' dislike of the García Lorca family.

When Ruiz Alonso knocked on the door of 1 Calle de Angulo, on the afternoon of 16 August, he was accompanied by two political friends: Juan Luis Trescastro – a well-known local landowner and playboy in the purest *machista* tradition – and Luis García Alix, the Secretary of Gil Robles's Party in Granada.[44]

None of the Rosales menfolk were at home at the time. Luis and José had gone to one of the fronts; Antonio, Gerardo and their father were in different parts of the town; and Miguel was on duty at Falange HQ. Señora Rosales stood up bravely to Ruiz Alonso and refused point-blank to allow him to take the poet away. How dare he come to their house, a Falangist house, on such a mission? Ruiz Alonso probably insisted at this point that he was acting on orders from the Civil Government but, at all events, Señora Rosales stood firm. Why did they want to question Lorca anyway? According to Esperanza Rosales, who listened horrified to the conversation between her mother and Ruiz Alonso, the latter stated categorically that the poet was in trouble because of what he had written. Probably, Ruiz Alonzo felt, this was what the authorities wanted to talk to Lorca about.[45]

Señora Rosales now tried to contact her sons by telephone, eventually locating Miguel at Falangist HQ and telling him what was happening. It was agreed that Ruiz Alonso should drive over immediately to consult with him about what should be done. Soon afterwards the ex-Member of Parliament returned with Miguel. Rosales was amazed when they entered the street to see that the area had been cordoned off and was thick with police and militia. In the car Ruiz Alonso had told him that Lorca was a 'Russian spy' and that 'he had done more damage with his pen than others with their guns'. As for him, he was merely carrying out orders to escort the poet to the Civil Government for questioning. The car was driven by its owner, Trescastro, and Ruiz Alonso was accompanied by García Alix and two other men unknown to Miguel.[46]

Upstairs on the second floor Lorca must have realized from the outset that something serious was taking place. Given Ruiz Alonso's vehement personality and loud voice, it is difficult to believe that, from one of the interior windows giving on to the well, the poet did not follow the conversation taking place below. And from the window of his bedroom he must surely have seen the armed men in the narrow street outside. Moreover, Esperanza Rosales has said that shortly after Ruiz Alonso's arrival she slipped upstairs to tell Federico what was afoot. He must have felt that the end had come. No worse inquisitor could have appeared to torment him.[47]

When Ruiz Alonso returned with Miguel Rosales, the poet was ready to leave. Miguel explained to his mother that, in the circumstances, he had no option but to allow Ruiz Alonso to take Federico to the Civil Government building. He would personally accompany them and find out what the problem was. Nothing would happen to the poet. Probably all they wanted was to ask him some questions. He would sort the whole thing out with the Governor. Esperanza went to fetch Lorca. On top of the piano there was an image of the Sacred Heart of Jesus to which Aunt Luisa Camacho was devoted. Before Federico went downstairs the three of them said a prayer at Aunt Luisa's suggestion, in front of the image. 'Now everything will be all right,' she assured the poet.[48]

In 1956 Luis Rosales told the Spanish-born American researcher Agustín Penón that Lorca in these moments was in a state of almost complete collapse, trembling and weeping.[49] Luis must have learnt this when he returned home that evening. As he took his leave of Esperanza, whom he had nicknamed his 'Divine Gaoler', Federico murmured, 'I'm not going to shake hands with you, because I don't want to think we're never going to meet again.'[50]

Then, with Miguel and Ruiz Alonso, he went out into the street.

The Poet in the Hands of his Enemies

Opposite the Rosales's house lived the owner of Los Pirineos, a bar situated on the corner of the nearby Plaza de la Trinidad. One of the children, then twelve years old, who had been told by the police to get indoors, peeped through his window and saw the poet step out from the doorway. He was wearing dark grey trousers, a white shirt with a loose tie, and had his jacket over his arm. The group walked round the corner into the Plaza de la Trinidad and disappeared from view.[51] It was there, it seems, that the men had parked the car waiting to drive Lorca the short distance to the Civil Government building.

In the car Federico, terrified, implored Miguel to intervene at once on his behalf with the authorities and, above all, to get hold of his brother José, who he knew was one of the most important Falangists in Granada.[52]

When they reached the building a minute later Miguel discovered that Valdés, the Governor, was not there. In charge was a retired Lieutenant-Colonel of the Civil Guard, Nicolás Velasco, who explained that Valdés was visiting positions in the Alpujarras and was not expected until that evening. Meanwhile he would take charge of Lorca. Miguel tried to calm the poet, promising him that he would return as soon as possible with José, and assuring him that nothing would happen to him. But, although he did not say so, Rosales was extremely worried, fearing especially that Federico might fall into the hands of one of Valdés's brutal accomplices who, in these moments of panic and hatred, were not above torturing their victims.[53]

After being searched, Lorca was locked in one of the rooms on the first floor of the building.[54]

Miguel hurried back to Falangist HQ and tried desperately to contact José by telephone. To no avail. His brother was apparently inspecting some outposts in the Vega and would not be back till later. Nor could Miguel locate Luis or Antonio, both of whom were at the front. As for Gerardo, the youngest, he had apparently gone to the cinema.[55]

When Luis and José Rosales arrived in Granada that evening they were outraged to learn what had happened. They decided to confront Valdés immediately, and accompanied by another leading Falangist friend, Cecilio Cirre, hurried to the Civil Government building. There Velasco insisted that Valdés had not yet returned from his visit to the Alpujarras (it seems almost certain that this was true), and suggested that Luis should immediately make a formal statement concerning the matter. Luis Rosales has said:

There must have been a hundred people in the room. It was packed. Among them was Ramón Ruiz Alonso, whom I didn't know by sight. I knew no one there. I said, with violent hatred: 'Who is this Ruiz Alonso who went to our house to remove without either a verbal or written warrant* someone staying under the roof of his superiors?' I stressed the 'this Ruiz Alonso', and repeated the question a couple of times. Then – I was speaking with passion, with hatred in my voice – one of the individuals present stepped forward. 'I am *this* Ruiz Alonso,' he announced. I asked him before the whole gathering (there were a hundred people there who could confirm the accuracy of this) how he had dared to go to my house without a warrant and arrest my guest. He replied that he had acted on his own initiative. I said to him: 'You don't know what you're saying. Repeat it!' I was aware of the poignancy of the moment and wanted to be sure that both I and those present remembered the exact words spoken. So I repeated the question three times and each time he replied: 'I acted on my own initiative.' Then I said to him: 'Salute and get out!' 'Who, *me?*' he replied. Cecilio Cirre was great, and got hold of Ruiz Alonso and shook him. To avoid more trouble Cirre said to him: 'You're speaking to a superior! Now salute and get out!' Finally, since nobody else there intervened on his behalf, Ruiz Alonso left.[56]

Ruiz Alonso denied in 1966 that he was present during the scene described by Luis Rosales, alleging that, after leaving Lorca in the Civil Government building, he returned home.[57] None the less, Rosales's account was confirmed independently by Cecilio Cirre, and there seems no reason to disbelieve it.[58]

As for Luis Rosales's formal statement to Velasco, this has never come to light. 'I said that Lorca had been threatened in his own house, on the outskirts of Granada,' Rosales has explained, 'that he had requested my help, that he was politically harmless and that, as a poet and as a man, I could not refuse to help a person who was being unjustly persecuted. I said that I would do the same thing again.'[59]

Later that night José Rosales returned to the Civil Government building and, forcing his way into Valdés's room, began a violent discussion with the Governor. Two days before his death in 1978 Rosales recalled that scene, claiming that, on his desk, Valdés had a typewritten accusation against the poet, two or three pages long, drawn up and signed by Ramón Ruiz Alonso. The document, if we can believe Rosales, stated that Lorca, a subversive writer, had a clandestine radio in the Huerta de San Vicente with which he was in contact with the Russians; that he was a homosexual; that he had been the secretary of Fernando de los Ríos (which was not the case); that, moreover, the Rosales brothers were betraying the movement by sheltering a notorious Red . . . Valdés, waving it in Rosales's face, had exclaimed: 'Look, José, if it weren't for this I'd let you take him away right now. But I can't because look what it says!' According to Rosales, Valdés told him that,

---

* Luis Rosales has never accepted that there was a warrant. Miguel, on the other hand, always insisted that Ruiz Alonso showed it to him.

if he wanted to, he could kill Ruiz Alonso there and then, but that, as regards Lorca, it was his duty as Governor first to check on the truth or otherwise of the charges. Meanwhile he promised that nothing would happen to the poet.[60]

Seven years earlier, in 1971, José Rosales swore in the presence of a lawyer that Valdés was accompanied on that occasion by the brothers José and Manuel Jiménez de Parga, well-known members of the Granada middle class, the police chief Julio Romero Funes and the lawyer Jose Díaz Pla, local head of the Granada Falange.[61]

When he left Valdés, José Rosales saw Lorca briefly and gave him his word that the following morning he would come and take him away.[62] Luis, on the other hand, never saw the poet again. After the scene in the Civil Government office, José Díaz Pla, who was a close friend of the Rosales brothers, helped him to draw up a carefully worded exculpatory statement, in which he gave his reasons for protecting Lorca and incorporated some inside information concerning the visits to the Huerta. Both men hoped that such a procedure would help not only the poet but the Rosales family as well. Luis then delivered copies of the document to the various rebel authorities in the town.[63] These disappeared as if into thin air, and for over forty years Rosales would try in vain to trace them. Finally, in 1983, the Granada journalist Eduardo Molina Fajardo found and published the copy sent by Rosales to the Provincial Chief of the Falange. This vital document enables us to date with precision the visits of the different groups to the Huerta, to establish the composition of these and to know the names of various other people who participated in the events surrounding the last week of Lorca's life.[64]

When Ruiz Alonso took Lorca away, Señora Rosales immediately telephoned the poet's family who, the previous day, after the violent scene that had taken place in the Huerta, had moved into their daughter Concha's flat near the Puerta Real. She also contacted her husband, who went straightaway to see the García Lorcas. Accompanied by Don Federico, Rosales set off in search of the lawyer Manuel Pérez Serrabona, with a view to engaging him to defend the poet. 'We thought that there might be some sort of a trial,' Esperanza Rosales has said, 'and that there would be the possibility of a legal defence.' But no such defence was feasible.[65]

The following morning José Rosales obtained from the Military Command an order for Lorca's release, hurrying with it to the Civil Government building. There Valdés, livid, told him that it was too late, that Lorca had already been taken away and that he should now see what he could do to save his brother Luis's skin for his involvement in the affair. We do not know how José reacted, but it seems certain that he believed Valdés when the latter said that Lorca was no longer in the building. Rosales died persisting in that belief. None the less, there can be no question whatsoever that Lorca had still not been taken away.[66]

Our main witness in this respect is Angelina Cordobilla, the nanny of Concha García Lorca's three children, who was with the family at the Huerta when the rising began and had now moved with them into their town flat. Angelina remembered perfectly in 1955, when she was interviewed by Agustín Penón, her experiences during those terrible days twenty years earlier. For a month she had made her way each day across Granada from the Huerta to the gaol to take food and clean clothing to Manuel Fernández-Montesinos. Then, on the morning of 16 August, they had told her that he had just been shot. She returned home with the undelivered basket. That afternoon the news came that the poet had been arrested. 'How could I ever forget it?' Angelina exclaimed in 1966. 'Don Manuel that dawn and the poet in the afternoon!'[67]

Angelina insisted that she went on three successive mornings, terrified, to the Civil Government building with food, coffee and other things for Lorca. After squabbling among themselves, the guards on duty at the entrance had allowed her on each occasion to go up to the first floor where the poet was imprisoned. There was no bed in the bare room: only a table with an inkwell, a pen and some paper. The first time – it must have been 17 August, at ten or eleven in the morning – there were men at the door to the cell. They had their guns at the ready and searched the basket. The following day Angelina found that Federico had eaten nothing. The third, as she left the flat in Calle de San Antón, a stranger stopped her. 'The person you are going to see is no longer there,' he said. But Angelina continued on her way to the Civil Government building. At the entrance the guards told her that the poet had left, and allowed her to go up to the room to collect the things. There she found only an empty thermos and a napkin. Thinking that Lorca had perhaps been transferred to the gaol, the distressed servant now made her way across town, handing in the basket at the door. But no, the poet was not there, and the basket was given back. Almost collapsing, she returned to Calle de San Antón.[68]

Why did Valdés lie to José Rosales on the morning of 17 August, alleging that Lorca was no longer in the building? It seems that the rebel Governor, aware of the poet's celebrity, hesitated before giving the order to shoot him. Much as he must have disliked Lorca and what he stood for, Valdés was probably apprehensive about the consequences that the poet's death might have for the Nationalist cause. On the other hand, he was not the sort of man to worry too much about such niceties and, by the time Lorca fell into his clutches, he had already agreed to many assassinations. Valdés was implacable in his persecution of 'Reds', and, if he thought twice in the case of Lorca, the only reason can have been his concern about adverse reaction to the killing. There is good circumstantial evidence to suggest that, before the fatal decision was taken, Valdés got in touch with General Queipo de Llano – the supreme commander of the Nationalists in Andalusia – to ask for his advice. And, according to a reliable source, the General's reply was that the poet should be given 'coffee, plenty of coffee' – his formula when recommending an execution.[69] But whether Queipo de Llano was consulted or not, Valdés must still be considered the person most responsible for the poet's death. Despite the accusations of Ramón Ruiz Alonso and others, despite even a ruling from Queipo, Valdés could have reprieved Lorca if he had so wished. But he did not wish. From Valdés's point of view Lorca was a repellent Red. His work was subversive, his private life disgusting. He had attacked the Granada Catholic middle class, the very people who were now supporting the rebellion. Why should he be spared?

We do not know if there was a confrontation between Lorca and Valdés before the fatal order was given – and almost certainly never shall. Valdés took his secrets with him to the tomb on 5 March 1939, a victim of cancer and of a wound received in action after he was removed from his post in Granada in 1937.[70].

Lorca left the Civil Government building handcuffed to another victim: a primary school-master called Dióscoro Galindo González, from Valladolid. Between 1929 and 1934 Galindo had taught in the province of Seville, being transferred to the village of Pulianas, not far from Granada, in September of the latter year. A staunch Republican, he was much loved by his pupils but fell foul of the secretary of the local municipal corporation who, when the war began, denounced him as a dangerous enemy. He was arrested at his home by a group of Falangists and taken to Granada. His family never saw him again.[71]

That night, a young friend of Lorca, Ricardo Rodríguez Jiménez, happened to see the poet and Galindo González being taken out of the Civil Government building. Rodríguez had an atrophied right hand and, several years earlier, Federico, aware of the boy's musical ability, had bought him a small violin so that he could learn to play an instrument, a gesture that Rodríguez never forgot. He recalled in 1980:

I lived in Horno de Haza Street, near the police station across the road from the Civil Government building, in Duquesa Street. During the first weeks of the Movement a friend and I used to go late each night to the police station to hear Queipo de Llano's last bulletin, which was broadcast at around 3 a.m. We played cards with the guards until the bulletin came on. That night I left the station at 3.15 a.m. and suddenly heard someone call my name. I turned around. 'Federico!' He threw an arm over my

shoulder. His right hand was handcuffed to that of a schoolmaster from La Zubia*
with white hair. 'Where are they taking you?' 'I don't know.' He was coming out of
the Civil Government building, surrounded by guards and Falangists belonging to
the 'Black Squad',† among them one who had been thrown out of the Civil Guard
and who joined the killers. I don't remember his name. Someone stuck a gun in my
chest. I screamed: 'Murderers! You're going to kill a genius! A genius! Murderers!'
I was arrested and taken into the Civil Government building. They locked me up for
two hours and then let me out.[72]

A few seconds after this incident Valdés's thugs pushed Lorca and Galindo
González into the car that was to drive them to their place of execution.

Angelina Cordobilla, the Fernández-Montesinos's nanny, insisted, as we
have seen, that she saw Lorca on two successive mornings in the Civil
Government building, and that when she went there on the third he had
disappeared.[73] If her memory was accurate, the poet must have been taken
away during the night of 18–19 August. However, it is possible that, twenty
years after the event, Angelina was wrong, and that she saw the poet only
once. Information from the family of Dióscoro Galindo González suggests
strongly that the teacher was taken from the Civil Government building in
the early hours of 18 August[74] – and we know that he was handcuffed to
Lorca. The evidence would seem, therefore, to tilt the balance in favour of
the latter date, although the truth is that we cannot be sure of this. No
documentary record of any aspect of Lorca's last hours has come to light.

Fuente Grande

At the foot of the Sierra de Alfacar, to the north-east of Granada, there are
two villages: Alfacar, which gives its name to the mountain, and Víznar.
Alfacar (the name derives from the Arabic for 'potter') is situated several
hundred feet lower than Víznar, from which it is separated by a sloping
valley of olive groves. The village is famous for its excellent bread, but
remarkable for little else. Víznar – here the word descends from the Arabic
version of a still earlier place-name – is an attractive, steep-streeted little
hamlet of dazzlingly white houses, against whose front walls strings of
orange capsicums and pots of geraniums make a brilliant contrast. While
Granada swelters in the heat of summer, Víznar is often fanned by cool
breezes, and it was doubtless for this reason that the rich Archbishop
Moscoso y Peralta built his palace here at the end of the eighteenth century,
when he returned to Spain from Cuzco.

---

*   A village in the foothills of the Sierra Nevada. A small slip on the part of Rodríguez.
†   An assassination squad recruited by Valdés and given virtual *carte blanche* to butcher
    'Reds'. Some of its members were from comfortably off middle-class families.

In July 1936, on the outbreak of the war, Víznar was converted into one of the Granada Nationalists' fortified outposts, it being evident to the rebels that the village would become a position of considerable importance in the struggle to resist Republican incursions from the hills. The Commander of the sector was the young Falangist Captain José María Nestares, who established his HQ in Archbishop Moscoso's spacious palace.

But Víznar was not only a military position. Had it been that alone, it would not be so notorious today in Granada. Víznar is remembered because it was above all a Nationalist execution place, a Calvary for many hundreds of men and women liquidated by the rebels. Nestares was in constant touch with Valdés (only five miles of bumpy road separated the village from the capital) and every night cars would arrive from the Civil Government building and the surrounding countryside with batches of 'undesirables' to be dispatched at dawn. The vehicles from Granada had first to pass in front of the palace and usually they would stop to exchange papers with Falange HQ before setting off up the hill in the direction of Alfacar. The car that brought Lorca and Galindo González from the Civil Government building almost certainly came this way.

Hugging the palace wall, a narrow street leads out of Víznar's little square, climbing as it goes. Above the village the ground levels out. Down below spreads the broad expanse of the Vega, with, at its edge, the stark Sierra de Elvira, whose treeless slopes form a harsh contrast with the lushness of the plain; directly ahead rises the Sierra de Alfacar, with a cross on its highest peak. A watercourse runs beside the road, and, a little further on, the visitor comes upon the ruins of a watermill. In the days of the Republic this was a spacious building, Villa Concha, which served as a summer residence for schoolchildren from Granada and was known to the local inhabitants, accordingly, as 'La Colonia' ('The Colony'). When the Falangists converted Víznar into a military position at the end of July 1936 they turned the 'Colonia' into a makeshift prison, and here the cars came each night with groups of condemned men and women. A building associated with holidays and happiness had suddenly become a house of death.

A party of fourteen freemasons and other 'undesirables' was brought here to dig the victims' unmarked graves. Many of these men were themselves executed later. As for the killers, most were 'Black Squad' volunteers – men who enjoyed the work – but there were also some Assault Guards forced to participate in the shootings as a punishment for their initial lack of support for the Nationalist insurrection.

The victims were locked in a downstairs room at the 'Colonia' until early morning, and the parish priest of Víznar was usually at hand to hear their last confessions, if they so desired. Upstairs were the quarters of the men who took part in the executions. At dawn the prisoners were taken out and shot (although killings often took place during the day as well and sometimes at night), and then the gravediggers would arrive and bury them where they lay. Not infrequently the latter would find themselves staring at the corpse of a friend or relative.[75]

We know from various witnesses that Lorca spent his last hours at the 'Colonia'. Especially important is the testimony of José Jover Tripaldi. This man was twenty-two when the war began, and holidaying in Víznar. In order to avoid being called up he asked Captain Nestares, a friend of the family, to let him work with him in some capacity. Nestares agreed, and arranged for the lad to be given guard duty at the 'Colonia'. He was there the night that Lorca arrived. A fervent Catholic, it was Jover Tripaldi's custom to inform the victims that they would be taken the following morning to work on fortifications, or to repair roads. Then, as the moment for the executions drew nearer, he would tell them the terrible truth. This he saw as charity. If the prisoners wanted, they could then be confessed by the priest and give the guards a last message for their families.

According to Jover Tripaldi, Lorca, when told that he was going to be shot, wanted to take confession. But the priest had already left. The younger man, seeing the poet's deep distress, assured him that, if he asked God's forgiveness sincerely, his sins would be forgiven him. He helped Federico with the prayer beginning 'I, sinner . . .', which the poet only half remembered. 'My mother taught it to me,' he murmured, 'but I've almost completely forgotten it.' According to Jover Tripaldi – and we have only his word for it – the poet seemed more tranquil once he had prayed.[76]

With Lorca and Galindo González were two small-time bullfighters from Granada, Joaquín Arcollas Cabezas and Francisco Galadí Melgar. Both men were militant anarchists and had been among those who most vociferously demanded arms for the people when the rising broke out. Their capture (in the Albaicín) meant summary execution.[77]

From the remains of the 'Colonia' the road winds on around the valley in the direction of Alfacar, accompanied by the watercourse which, a few hundred yards further on, passes over a narrow aqueduct where the road loops sharply. Immediately in front a slope of bluish clay and pebbles, full of tall pine trees, stretches back steeply up the hillside towards the first rocky outcrops of the Sierra de Alfacar. This is the *barranco* or gully of Víznar where lie the bodies of most of the victims of the system operating at the 'Colonia'. Shallow graves were dug all over the slope – there were no trees here then – the bodies were tossed in and a thin covering of stones and soil was thrown over them. When Gerald Brenan visited the site in 1949 he found that the 'entire area was pitted with low hollows and mounds, at the head of each of which had been placed a small stone'.[78] By the early 1950s the evidence afforded by these headstones had been removed and pines had been planted, presumably to mask the outlines of the graves which, none the less, were in some cases still clearly visible ten years later.

In the first days of the war, however, the killings were not carried out here, but in the olive groves that clothe the slopes of this wide valley. Lorca was one of the early victims, and, contrary to what has often been said, is not buried in the *barranco* at Víznar. He and the three other condemned men were taken, before sunrise, further along the road to Alfacar. There was no moon – Federico, lunar poet that he was, did not have even that consolation.[79] The lorry stopped not far from the famous spring known as the Fuente Grande, or 'Big Fountain', which has a fascinating history. The Arabs, intrigued by the bubbles that rise continually to the surface of the pool, called it Ainadamar, 'The Fountain of Tears', and in the eleventh century began the construction of a canal to carry the water to Granada. Almost a millennium later the watercourse still exists, looping around the valley to Víznar, where it used to move the wheel of the 'Colonia' (Lorca must have listened to its rush that last night), dropping down to El Fargue and skirting the hills to the Albaicín, where until quite recently it supplied the whole quarter. Ainadamar was apparently more vigorous in the past, however, for when Richard Ford visited the place between 1831 and 1833 he found 'a vast spring of water which bubbles up in a column several feet high'.[80]

The Arabs admired the loveliness of the pool's surroundings, and a sizeable colony of summer residences soon appeared in the vicinity. No vestiges of the villas remain – perhaps as a result of an earthquake – but there survive several compositions by Arab poets in praise of Ainadamar's beauty, among them one by Abū'l-Barakāt al Balafīqī, who died in AD 1372:

Is it my separation from Ainadamar, stopping the pulsation of my blood, which has dried up the flow of tears from the well of my eyes?

Beside it the birds sing melodies comparable to those of the Mausili,* reminding me of the now distant past into which I entered in my youth, and the moons of the place,† beautiful as Joseph, would make every Muslim abandon his faith for that of love.[81]

It seems appropriate that the Fuente Grande, sung by the Islamic poets of Granada, should continue to bubble up its clear waters close to the last resting place of the greatest poet ever born in this part of Spain. For it was here, just before reaching the pool, that the killers shot their victims, leaving

---

* A reference to Ishāh al-Mausilī (that is, from Mosul), the most famous of all Arab musicians.
† In plain words, the local women.

their bodies beside an olive grove on the right-hand side of the road coming from Víznar.

A few moments later the gravedigger arrived, a young communist called Manuel Castilla Blanco whom Captain Nestares was protecting. The lad immediately recognized the bullfighters, noticed not without surprise that another of the victims had a wooden leg, and observed that the last one wore a loose tie, 'you know, the sort artists wear'. He buried them in a narrow trench, on top of each other, beside an olive tree. When he returned to the 'Colonia' they told him that the man with the wooden leg was a schoolteacher from a nearby village, and that the one with the loose tie was the poet Federico García Lorca.[82]

No fully trustworthy account of Federico's last moments has come down to us: there is no record of his words, if he spoke any; none of any request. Did he perceive the almost uncanny parallel between his fate and that of his heroine Mariana Pineda? Did he think about his mother, about Rafael Rodríguez Rapún, about his projected trip to join Margarita Xirgu in Mexico, or remember the lines (there were so many) in which he had expressed his horror of death? We can never know. According to two independent sources, however, the poet was not killed outright by the fusillade, and had to be finished off by a *coup de grâce*.[83] Among the assassins, almost certainly, was Juan Luis Trescastro, Ruiz Alonso's accomplice, who boasted later that morning in Granada that he had just helped to shoot Lorca, firing, for good measure, 'two bullets into his arse for being a queer'.[84] Such was the mentality of the Granada bourgeoisie criticized by the poet in *El Sol* two months earlier; and the possibility that Lorca was tortured in this way before the squad completed the job cannot be excluded.

Meanwhile someone was trying to intervene on the poet's behalf back in Granada: Manuel de Falla. When the rising started, Don Manuel, appalled and terrified, had shut himself up in his *carmen* below the Alhambra. There he learned of the killings that were taking place in the town; indeed he could hardly fail to hear the sinister firing from the nearby cemetery in the early hours of every morning. Then, one day, they told him that Federico had been arrested and was in mortal danger. Falla, a gentle, timid man, knew that he must try to help his friend, and accordingly set out in search of some young Falangists of his acquaintance with whom he made his way to the Civil Government building. He found the place packed with people and sat down on a bench while one of the Falangists went to make inquiries. When the lad returned his face told the story. It was too late. The poet had been taken away that morning. Shattered, the composer then went to the flat of the recently executed Dr Manuel Fernández-Montesinos in the Calle de San Antón, to which he knew the García Lorcas had moved from the Huerta de

San Vicente. The news of Federico's death had been withheld from his parents, who still believed that he might be saved, and one of the poet's cousins, Isabel Roldán, begged Don Manuel to say nothing.[85]

That same day a member of the 'Black Squad' turned up at the flat with a note scrawled by Federico. It read: 'Father, please give this man a donation of 1000 pesetas for the Army.' Lorca had been persuaded, perhaps forcibly, to write it either before he was removed from the Civil Government building or in Víznar. Don Federico, believing that by paying up he could perhaps save his son, handed the money over to the extortioner. They were almost certainly the last words written by the poet, and his father carried the note in his wallet until he died in voluntary exile, nine years later, in New York.[86]

Before Lorca was shot that morning at least 280 people had already been killed in the cemetery, while the burial records for the three years of the war list 2,000. The true total was undoubtedly much higher. And this is without taking into account the many hundreds of less 'official' assassinations carried out in the villages.[87] Seen in the context of the repression of Granada, the poet's death was no more exceptional than that of the university professors, the town councillors, doctors and teachers, and the thousands of more humble workers and trade unionists who were murdered throughout the province. The rebels were determined to liquidate all their left-wing opponents, and, so far as they were concerned, Lorca was just one more 'Red', albeit a particularly obnoxious one.

The guitarist Angel Barrios, Lorca's friend from the days of the *Rinconcillo*, was spending the summer in Víznar when the war began. Hearing the terrible news of Federico's assassination, he made inquiries and discovered where it had taken place. A few days after the tragedy he visited the spot, and found that lime had been thrown over the grave. The whole area stank of rotting corpses.[88]

It was three weeks before the Republican press picked up the rumour that Lorca had been killed by the fascists. Disbelieved at first, the rumour became a certainty soon afterwards when several people escaped from Granada and told the story of what was happening in the city, with convincing information about the poet's arrest and death.[89] There was consternation throughout the Spanish-speaking world, while the European press also reported on the matter.[90] Almost overnight Lorca became a Republican martyr. Symptomatic of the growing international concern over the poet's fate was the telegram sent to the Granada rebel authorities from England on 13 October 1936. It read: 'H. G. Wells, President of the PEN Club of London, anxiously desires news of his distinguished colleague Federico García Lorca and will greatly appreciate courtesy of reply.' The answer, signed by Colonel Antonio González Espinosa, was laconic. 'From Governor of Granada to

H. G. Wells,' it ran. 'I do not know whereabouts of Don Federico García Lorca.' The reply made it obvious that Lorca had indeed been killed for, by this stage, the Nationalist authorities realized what an appalling blunder had been committed in Granada, and, had the poet been alive, would have stopped at nothing to demonstrate that the rumours were false.[91]

At the end of 1939, nine months after the war finished, Lorca's family started proceedings to have his death officially entered in the Civil Register. Two witnesses produced by the Granada authorities swore that they had seen the body by the roadside between Víznar and Alfacar; and, in 1940, the inscription was duly effected. The document stated that Lorca died 'in the month of August 1936 from war wounds'.[92] It sounded for all the world as if the poet had been the unfortunate victim of a stray bullet.

Afterword

María Teresa León, the militant communist wife of Rafael Alberti, knew Rafael Rodríguez Rapún well and about the relationship that existed between him and Lorca. When Colonel González Espinosa's reply to H. G. Wells was published in the Madrid newspapers that October, and it became clear that the poet had indeed been killed, that the appalling rumour was true, she saw Rapún again. 'Nobody can have suffered the way that quiet lad did on account of his death,' she wrote in her memoirs. 'Finished the nights, the days, the hours. Better to die. And Rapún went off to die in the north. I am convinced that, after firing his rifle furiously, he allowed himself to be killed. It was his way of recovering Federico.'[1] Cipriano Rivas Cherif, who was arrested by the Nazis in France and handed over to Franco, heard a similar version when he was released from prison in 1945. Someone told him that Rapún, who had enlisted voluntarily in the Republican Army once he felt certain that the fascists had killed Federico, jumped out of the trench one day saying that he wanted to die. A few seconds later he was mown down. Rivas Cherif was never able to verify the truth of the account, which he admitted might be merely a legend.[2]

But it was substantially accurate. After taking an artillery course (in, of all places, Lorca, in Murcia) Rapún obtained the rank of lieutenant, and in the summer of 1937 was commanding a battery not far from Reinosa, in the north. One of his men has recalled that he was serious, cultured, and talked little. These were the days of Franco's offensive against Santander, and the fighting in the area was intense. On the morning of 10 August the battery was in action against the rebel air force and, towards midday, faced with a strong enemy advance, Rapún left with two guns to find a new position. They stopped just outside the town of Bárcena de Pie de Concha, where a sudden air attack caught them unprepared. Unlike the other men Rapún did not throw himself to the ground but remained sitting on a parapet. A bomb exploded nearby and he was mortally wounded.[3]

Rapún's death certificate states that he died on 18 August 1937, in the military hospital at Santander, from shrapnel wounds in the back and lumbar region. Lorca – and it seems impossible that Rafael could have been aware of this – had been assassinated a year earlier to the day. No one in the hospital knew the artillery lieutenant's age, place of birth or the names of his parents. No record remains of his last moments, of any death-bed request, of any comments. He was buried in Ciriego Cemetery, beside the Cantabrian sea. Eight days later Santander fell to Franco. Rodríguez Rapún had celebrated his twenty-fifth birthday that June.[4]

References and Occasional Notes

The following abbreviations are used throughout:

AFGL   Fundación Federico García Lorca Archive, Madrid

APP   The Agustín Penón papers, Madrid, kindly put at my disposal by the late Agustín Penón's friend William Layton

E   García Lorca, *Epistolario*. Introducción, edición y notas de Christopher Maurer, 2 vols., Madrid, Alianza, 1983

FGL   Federico García Lorca

FGLNY   *Federico García Lorca escribe a su familia desde Nueva York y La Habana (1929–1930)*, edición de Christopher Maurer, *Poesía. Revista ilustrada de información poética*, Madrid, Ministry of Culture, nos. 23–4, 1983

Gibson I   Gibson, *Federico García Lorca. I. De Fuente Vaqueros a Nueva York (1898–1929)*, Barcelona, Grijalbo, 1985

Gibson II   Gibson, *Federico García Lorca. II. De Nueva York a Fuente Grande (1929–1936)*, Barcelona, Grijalbo, 1987

OC   García Lorca, *Obras completas*, 2 vols., Madrid, Aguilar, 20th ed., 1978

OC (1986)   García Lorca, *Obras completas*, 3 vols., Madrid, Aguilar, 22nd ed., 1986

Notes to Book One

Introduction

1 Brickell, *A Spanish Poet in New York*, p. 386
2 Quoted by Pedemonte, p. 59
3 Aleixandre, 'Federico', p. ix
4 Auclair, p. 101

1 Childhood

1 Pareja López *et al*, I, p. 193
2 Ford (1955), p. 115; Francisco García Lorca, p. 12
3 Francisco García Lorca, p. 12
4 Madoz, XIV (1849), p. 516
5 FGL, 'Mi pueblo', AFGL
6 Pareja López *et al.*, I, p. 193
7 Pérez de Hita, p. 549
8 Ford (1955), pp. 115–17
9 Document in Fuente Vaqueros parish church
10 Ford (1955), pp. 115–17
11 Hammick, p. 407; Madoz, XIV (1849), p. 516
12 Hammick, p. 395
13 Ford (1955), pp. 114, 117
14 Ibid., p. 236, note 1
15 Madoz, VIII (1847), p. 224
16 Ibid.
17 Ibid.
18 Hammick, pp. 8–9
19 Ibid., p. 11
20 Ibid., p. 395
21 Pareja López *et al.*, I, p. 196
22 Hammick, pp. 324–5
23 Seco de Lucena [y Escalada], p. 366
24 Cabrolié, pp. 62–4
25 Francisco García Lorca, p. 30
26 Ibid., pp. 28–9
27 Conversation with Doña Isabel García Lorca, Madrid, 16 March 1983
28 Francisco García Lorca, p. 29
29 Ibid., p. 30

30 Ibid., p. 32
31 Ibid.
32 Ibid., pp. 33–4
33 Author's research in Fuente Vaqueros
34 Francisco García Lorca, p. 36
35 Cabrolié, p. 65
36 Francisco García Lorca, pp. 36–7
37 Conversation with Doña Clotilde García Picossi, Granada, 29 August 1965
38 It has not been possible to locate a copy of Baldomero's book, and all references are from notes and quotations made from a copy by Agustín Penón (APP).
39 Granada Civil Register, Sagrario District, Book 153, folio 253, death certificate number 974
40 Conversation with Doña Clotilde García Picossi, Granada, 1966
41 OC (1986), III, p. 431
42 The documents disagree as to the birthplace of Isabel Rodríguez Mazuecos, one (Cabrolié, p. 62) indicating that she was born in Fuente Vaqueros, another (the poet's birth certificate) that the event took place in Asquerosa.
43 Francisco García Lorca, 45
44 Ibid., p. 47
45 Ibid., p. 49
46 Ibid., pp. 48–9
47 Salobreña (1982), p. 95
48 Watson, II
49 Ibid.
50 Major Eudo Tonson-Rye, in Watson, I, p. 779
51 Francisco García Lorca, p. 55
52 Conversation with Don Federico García Ríos, Madrid, 3 June 1983
53 Francisco García Lorca, p. 68
54 Higuera Rojas (1980), p. 12
55 Mora Guarnido (1958), p. 18; Francisco García Lorca, p. 56; conversation with Doña Isabel García Lorca, Madrid, 16 March 1983; OC (1986), III, p. 496
56 Cabrolié, pp. 35–6
57 Ibid., pp. 37–8, 71
58 Ibid., pp. 99–102
59 OC, II, p. 935
60 Cabrolié, pp. 99–102
61 Seco de Lucena [Paradas], pp. 4–5, 35; conversation with the proprietors of the estate, 1 September 1982
62 Francisco García Lorca, pp. 57–8
63 Molina Fajardo (1983), p. 20
64 Higuera Rojas (1980), pp. 164–5
65 Cabrolié, p. 85
66 Ibid., p. 82
67 Ibid.
68 Bernardo Lorca Alcón's birth certificate is preserved in the Iglesia Arciprestal of Santiago el Mayor, Totana, Murcia.
69 Cabrolié, pp. 76, 77
70 Ibid., p. 77
71 Menasché
72 Cabrolié, p. 81
73 Ibid., p. 77
74 Molina Fajardo (1983), p. 20; Gallego Burín, p. 395
75 Conversation with Doña Isabel García Lorca, Madrid, 10 March 1983

76 Ibid.
77 OC (*1986*), II, p. 1111
78 Molina Fajardo (1983), p. 20; Vicenta Lorca's diploma is preserved in the Huerta de San Vicente, Granada; Cabrolié, p. 83
79 Cabrolié, p. 83
80 Conversation with Doña Isabel Carretero, Madrid, 1 February 1982
81 Laffranque (1957)
82 Gallego Morell (1954)
83 Conversations with Doña Carmen Ramos, Fuente Vaqueros, 1965–6; Couffon's conversations with Doña Carmen Ramos, pp. 17–26; Higuera Rojas's with Doña Carmen Ramos (1980), pp. 163–72
84 Ibid.
85 Martínez Nadal (1942), p. vii.
86 Sáenz de la Calzada, p. 57
87 Conversation with Doña Isabel García Lorca, Madrid, 18 March 1983
88 Molina Fajardo (1983), p. 15; Schonberg, p. 7
89 Conversation with Don Alfredo Anabitarte, Madrid, 21 November 1983
90 Moreno Villa, 'Recuerdo a Federico García Lorca', p. 23; Francisco García Lorca, p. 61; conversation with Don Santiago Ontañón, Toledo, 15 May 1979
91 Conversations with Don José Caballero, Don Santiago Ontañón and Don Rafael Alberti, Madrid, 1978–86
92 Martínez Nadal (1942), p. vii
93 Francisco García Lorca, p. 61
94 Martínez Nadal, in FGL, *Autógrafos. I*, p. xvi, note 4
95 Conversation with Doña Isabel García Lorca, Madrid, 5 July 1982
96 Francisco García Lorca, pp. 60–1
97 Ibid.
98 FGL, 'Mi pueblo', AFGL
99 OC, II, p. 1020
100 Letter to the author from Don Enrique Roldán, son-in-law of Aurelia's daughter, Jaén, 20 November 1987
101 Francisco García Lorca, p. 18
102 Conversation with Doña María García Palacios, Fuente Vaqueros, 1966
103 OC, II, pp. 257, 862–3; conversation with Doña Clotilde García Picossi, Granada, 1966
104 Higuera Rojas (1980), p. 186
105 Letter from FGL to Carlos Martínez Barbeito reproduced partially by Rodrigo (1986); OC, II, p. 934.
106 FGL, 'Mi pueblo', AFGL
107 Couffon, pp. 23–4
108 OC, II, p. 1022
109 For the discoveries at Daragoleja, see Gómez-Moreno
110 Cabrolié, p. 87
111 Ibid., p. 89
112 FGL, *Suites*, pp. 267–8
113 Civil Register, Fuente Vaqueros, Births, Book 21, Vol. 90, folio 48, no. 48
114 Ibid., Book 22, folio 61, no. 61
115 Conversation with Doña Isabel García Lorca, Madrid, 24 June 1982
116 Francisco García Lorca, p. 79
117 Conversation with Doña Isabel García Lorca, Madrid, 24 June 1982
118 Conversation with Don Enrique González García, Granada, 1966
119 Conversation with Don Manuel Torres López, Madrid, 10 March 1981
120 Couffon, p. 24
121 Higuera Rojas (1980), p. 166

122 FGL, 'Mi pueblo', AFGL
123 Conversation with Doña Adoración Arroyo Cobos, granddaughter of 'The Shepherd', Fuente Vaqueros, 11 April 1984
124 Ibid.
125 OC, I, p. 557
126 Ibid., p. 1103
127 Francisco García Lorca, pp. 58–9
128 See note 123
129 González Guzmán
130 Ibid.
131 Francisco García Lorca, pp. 21, 65
132 FGL, 'Mi pueblo', AFGL
133 OC (1986), pp. 420–1
134 OC, II, pp. 1021–2
135 Ibid., pp. 1040–1
136 Emilia Llanos told Agustín Penón in June, 1955 that Lorca frequently used this phrase (note in APP).
137 Cabrolié, p. 99
138 González Guzmán, pp. 206–207
139 Ibid., p. 207
140 Ibid., pp. 213, 216
141 Ibid., pp. 213, 219
142 Letter to the author from Manuel del Aguila Ortega, Almería, 1 August 1982
143 Ibid.
144 Rodríguez Espinosa
145 OC, I, p. 404
146 Francisco García Lorca, p. 67; Brenan (1957), p. 214
147 E, II, p. 30
148 OC, II, p. 935
149 Ibid., I, p. 1167
150 Francisco García Lorca, p. 67
151 Martín Martín, p. 56
152 Lorca's academic records in the General Library of Granada University
153 Ibid.
154 Ibid.

2 Granada

1 Baedeker, pp. 379–80
2 Ibid.
3 OC, I, p. 1157
4 Caro Baroja, passim
5 Maeso, pp. 99–105
6 Mora Guarnido (1958), pp. 35–9
7 There is recent reprint of Azaña's translation of Borrow; see Bibliography.
8 Rodríguez Spiteri
9 OC, II, p. 1085
10 Ibid., p. 939
11 Caro Baroja, pp. 88–9
12 Francisco García Lorca, p. 70
13 Ibid., pp. 71–5
14 Ibid., p. 72; Higuera Rojas (1980), p. 33
15 OC, I, p. 1077

16 Francisco García Lorca, p. 80
17 Hugo, I, pp. 660–3; this quotation, p. 662
18 Pedrell, 'Glinka en Granada'
19 *OC*, I, p. 1011
20 Falla (1972), p. 69
21 Trend (1921), p. 238
22 *OC*, I, pp. 1011–12
23 Mora Guarnido (1958), p. 65
24 Ganivet, II, p. 730
25 G. O. W. *Apperley (1884–1960), passim*
26 Gallego Burín, p. 418
27 *OC (1986)*, III, p. 320
28 Gautier, pp. 219–20
29 Brenan (1957), p. 242
30 Mora Guarnido (1958), pp. 105–7
31 Ford (1845), p. 363
32 *E*, I, p. 98
33 *OC*, I, p. 970
34 Ibid.
35 *OC (1986)*, III, p. 321
36 *OC*, I, p. 973
37 Ibid., p. 970
38 Ibid.
39 *OC (1986)*, III, p. 325
40 *OC*, I, p. 967
41 Seco de Lucena [y Escalada], p. 139
42 Ganivet, I, p. 61
43 *E*, II, p. 56
44 *OC*, II, p. 1075

3 School, Music, University

1 Francisco García Lorca, p. 76
2 Ibid., p. 82
3 Schonberg, p. 13
4 Conversation with Don José Rodríguez Contreras, Granada, 23 August 1978
5 FGL, *Poeta en Nueva York*, ed. Martín, p. 200
6 Ibid., p. 294
7 Francisco García Lorca, p. 85
8 *OC*, II, pp. 814–15
9 Francisco García Lorca, p. 84
10 Mora Guarnido (1958), p. 74
11 *OC*, II, p. 935
12 Lorca's academic records, Granada University
13 *OC*, I, p. 1167
14 Ibid, II, p. 936
15 Ibid.; *La Alhambra*, Granada, 1923, p. 81
16 *OC*, I, p. 1167
17 Mora Guarnido (1958), p. 75
18 Conversation with Doña Isabel García Rodríguez, Fuengirola, 15 July 1966
19 Lorca's academic records, Granada University
20 Cruz Ebro, pp. 226–7; Esperabé de Arteaga, pp. 44–5

21 Martín Domínguez Berrueta's academic records, Granada University; *El Lábaro*, Salamanca, *passim*
22 Domínguez Berrueta (1910)
23 Conversations with various of Berrueta's ex-students, Granada, 1965-6
24 Zapatero, pp. 10-11
25 Ibid., p. 11
26 Ibid., p. 13
27 Ibid., pp. 14-15
28 Ibid., pp. 15-16
29 *Boletín del Centro Artístico*, Granada (April 1915), p. 2; *La Prensa*, New York, 11 October 1937
30 Mora Guarnido (1958), p. 145
31 Ibid., p. 81
32 Lorca's academic records, Granada University
33 Mora Guarnido (1958), pp. 102-3
34 Ruiz Carnero and Mora Guarnido, *El libro de Granada* (see bibliography). Ruiz Carnero's inscription in Lorca's copy is reproduced by Fernández-Montesinos García, p. 97. The book was reviewed in the August 1915 issue of the *Boletín del Centro Artístico*, Granada (second series, no. 5) and, given Lorca's close friendship with both authors, I think we may safely assume that the copy was inscribed immediately on publication.
35 Conversations with Don Ricardo Gómez Ortega, Ibiza, summer 1966
36 For the date of Segura's death the records in Granada cemetery were consulted; information concerning Lorca's plans to study in Paris comes from a conversation with Don Francisco García Carrillo, Granada, 1 January 1966
37 *OC*, I, p. 1167
38 *Lucidarium*, Granada, II (January 1917), pp. 81-94
39 *Noticiero Granadino* (15 June 1916)
40 *Diario de Córdoba*, 12, 13 June 1916; *Diario Liberal*, Cordova, 12 June 1916; *OC*, I, pp. 896, 916, 1103
41 *Lucidarium*, Granada, II (January 1917), p. 83
42 Martínez Fuset's letters to Lorca are in AFGL.
43 Conversations with Don José Rodríguez Contreras, Granada, 1966-7; with Don Antonio Jiménez Blanco, Madrid, 3 March 1984; letters from Martínez Fuset to Lorca in AFGL.
44 Conversations with Don Ricardo Gómez Ortega, Ibiza, summer 1966; *Lucidarium*, Granada, II (January 1917), p. 92
45 *Letras*, Granada, 10 December 1917, p. 3
46 *Diario de Galicia*, Santiago de Compostela, 27 October 1916
47 Conversation with Don Ricardo Gómez Ortega, Ibiza, summer 1966
48 *OC*, I, pp. 952-3
49 Cruz Ebro, pp. 228-9
50 *Noticiero Granadino*, 9 November 1916
51 *OC*, I, pp. 959-61

4 The *Rinconcillo* of the Café Alameda

1 Villaespesa, p. 52
2 Ibid., p. 12
3 Francisco García Lorca, p. 74
4 Constantino Ruiz Carnero in *El Defensor de Granada*, 22, 26 November 1914, 3 December 1914
5 José Mora Guarnido's file in Granada University; *Noticiero Granadino*, 22 December 1914
6 Mora Guarnido (1958), pp. 45-6

7 Ibid., p. 51
8 Mora Guarnido (1958), pp. 55–6; Soriano Lapresa's obituary in *El Defensor de Granada*, 18 July 1934, p. 2; Orozco (1966); Francisco García Lorca, pp. 141–3; Molina Fajardo (1983), p. 206; conversation with Dr José Rodríguez Contreras, Granada, 23 August 1978
9 Auclair, p. 99
10 Francisco García Lorca, p. 146
11 *E*, I, p. 31
12 Fernández Almagro (1962), pp. 170–1
13 Gallego Morell (1968), pp. 22, 24–5, 50, 52
14 Mora Guarnido (1958), p. 177
15 Gallego Morell (1968), p. 31
16 *E*, I, p. 22
17 Mora Guarnido (1958), pp. 58, 116; Gallego Morell, in FGL, *Cartas a sus amigos*, p. 46
18 Pizarro, p. 12; OC, I, pp. 766–7
19 Ruiz Carnero and Mora Guarnido, p. 11
20 Mora Guarnido (1958), *passim*
21 Ibid., pp. 57–8; Silverman
22 Fragments of various undated letters from José María García Carrillo to Lorca in APP; conversations with Don José María García Carrillo, Granada, 1965–6; Orozco (1987)
23 Rodrigo, *Memoria de Granada*, *passim*; conversations with Don Manuel Angeles Ortiz, Granada, summer 1966; Buñuel, *Mon dernier soupir*, p. 147
24 Murciano
25 Mora Guarnido (1958), pp. 56–7; Fernández-Montesinos García, pp. 119, 170–1, for Lorca's annotated copy of *De Profundis*
26 Mora Guarnido (1958), pp. 62–3
27 Ibid., pp. 60–2; conversation with Mr Charles Montague Evans, London, 1968
28 Mora Guarnido (1958), p. 65; *Noticiero Granadino*, 4 July; 6, 19 August; 1, 4, 5 October 1922
29 Mora Guarnido (1958), p. 67; Soria Olmedo

5 Juvenilia

1 For fuller details of this trip, see Gibson I, pp. 162–6.
2 For the trip to Burgos, see Gibson I, pp. 166–74
3 OC, I, pp. 885–6, 889
4 Conversations with Don Ricardo Gómez Ortega, Ibiza, summer 1966; conversation with Don Miguel Carlón Guirao, Vélez-Rubio (Almería), 1965
5 *El Diario de Burgos*, 22 August 1917
6 OC, I, pp. 1145–8
7 Undated letters written during the summer of 1917 by José Fernández Montesinos to Lorca, AFGL
8 Letter from Lorenzo Martínez Fuset to Lorca, 17 September 1917, AFGL
9 Mora Guarnido (1958), pp. 79–89
10 Domínguez Berrueta (1917)
11 Conversations with Don Ricardo Gómez Ortega, Ibiza, summer 1966; OC, I, pp. 856–8
12 'Un tema con variaciones y sin solución', 17 December 1917, AFGL
13 'Mística en que se habla de la eterna mansión', undated, AFGL
14 Untitled draft of play, begun on 6 May 1920, AGFL
15 'Mística. El hombre del traje blanco', undated, AFGL
16 'Consideración amarguísima acerca de la idea en las ciudades y en los campos', 15 October 1917, AFGL
17 'El patriotismo', 27 October 1917, AFGL
18 AFGL

19 Alonso (1966), p. 75
20 OC, I, pp. 839–40; Darío (1967), pp. 665–6
21 Darío, Obras completas, II, p. 295
22 Devoto, 'García Lorca y Darío'
23 AFGL
24 Ibid.
26 OC, I, pp. 19–20
27 AFGL
28 'Beethoven. Elogio', 20 December 1917, AFGL
29 See especially 'Carnaval. Visión interior', 'Los cipreses' and 'Crepúsculo espiritual', all from February 1918, AFGL.
30 OC, I, pp. 39–41
31 Ibid., p 21–3
32 Conversation with Don Andrés Segovia, Madrid, 19 December 1980
33 Eloy Escobar de la Riva, 'Centro Artístico', Noticiero Granadino, 18 March 1918
34 Murciano
35 Aureliano del Castillo, 'Libros. Impresiones y paisajes', El Defensor de Granada, 19 April 1918
36 OC, I, p. 840
37 Arciniegas
38 Conversation with Don Ricardo Gómez Ortega, Ibiza, summer 1966
39 Letter from Berrueta to Lorca (3 May 1918), AFGL. It has been impossible to locate a file of La Publicidad
40 Letter to the author from Berrueta's son, Don Luis Domínguez Guilarte, Salamanca, 12 January 1966
41 Letter from Adriano del Valle to Lorca, dated 'May 1918', AFGL
42 E, I, pp. 16–19
43 AFGL
44 Undated letter, AFGL
45 Conversation with Doña Gloria Ibáñez, Madrid, 21 November 1965
46 Agustín Penón's conversations with Emilia Llanos in the former's diary, APP; the inscription is reproduced by Higuera Rojas (1980), p. 71; Llanos
47 Llanos
48 Auclair, p. 248
49 Lorca's file at Granada University
50 E, I, p. 21
51 Don Ricardo Gómez Ortega told the author (summer 1966) that Lorca always blamed Mora for what had happened; for the poet's references to Berrueta, see E, I, p. 94; OC, II, p. 936; and Diego (1932), p. 297

6 The Residencia de Estudiantes. Martínez Sierra

1 Quoted by García de Valdeavellano, p. 33
2 OC, II, p. 936; the documents relating to Lorca's military service are preserved in Granada Town Hall.
3 García de Valdeavellano, pp. 13–15; Jiménez Fraud (1971), pp. 435–6
4 Jiménez Fraud (1971), pp. 437 ff.
5 Ibid., p. 456
6 Ibid., pp. 457–8
7 García de Valdeavellano, pp. 25 ff.
8 Jiménez (1926)
9 Santiago

10 Crispin, p. 41
11 Ibid., pp. 40–41
12 Trend (1921), p. 36
13 Ibid., pp. 37–8
14 Conversation with Don José Bello, Madrid, 30 October 1987
15 Trend (1921), p. 39
16 Américo Castro, p. 17
17 Jiménez Fraud (1971), pp. 464–5
18 Jiménez Fraud (1957)
19 Mora Guarnido (1958), p. 118
20 Ibid., pp. 118–19; Videla, pp. 1–88, *passim*; Buñuel, *Mon dernier soupir*, pp. 71–2
21 Conversations with Don José Bello, Madrid, 1983–4
22 Buñuel, *Mon dernier soupir*, p. 74
23 Ibid., p. 61
24 Ibid., pp. 62–4
25 Ibid., p. 64
26 Ibid., pp. 71–2
27 Jiménez (1973), p. 105
28 *El Defensor de Granada*, 16 June 1919, p. 1
29 *La Alhambra*, Granada, 15 June 1919, pp. 333–4
30 Reyero Hermosilla, p. 3
31 O'Connor, p. 31; Borrás, p. 10; Reyero Hermosilla, pp. 19–21
32 *La Tribuna*, Madrid, 8 April 1917, pp. 7–8
33 Borrás, pp. 10–16; April, p. 24; Reyero Hermosilla, pp. 8–10, 13–16; Rodrigo (1975), pp. 126–8
34 Mora Guarnido (1958), p. 123
35 Conversation with Don Miguel Cerón, Granada, 17 September 1965
36 Ibid.

7 *The Butterfly's Evil Spell*

1 Molina Fajardo (1963)
2 Ibid.
3 María Martínez Sierra, p. 124
4 Ibid., pp. 134–6
5 *El Defensor de Granada*, 27 June 1916, p. 1
6 Pahissa, pp. 105–7
7 García Matos, pp. 55–9
8 FGL, *La zapatera prodigiosa*, Madrid, Alianza, 1982, pp. 117–18
9 Sopeña (1962), p. 61
10 Letters from Angel Barrios to Falla in the Falla archive, Madrid; letter from Falla (4 September 1919) to Angel Barrios, preserved by the guitarist's daughter, Doña Angela Barrios; the following letter (7 September 1919) is reproduced in Sopeña (1962), p. 62
11 Trend (1921), pp. 237–8
12 Ibid., pp. 240–1
13 Ibid., pp. 243–4
14 Trend, 'A Poet of "Arabia" '
15 Pahissa, p. 126
16 Cossart, *passim*
17 Orozco (1966)
18 Cossart, p. 136
19 Loxa, p. 9
20 Buñuel, *Mon dernier soupir*, pp. 61–93

21 Ibid., pp. 75–6
22 Moreno Villa (1944), p. 107
23 Caffarena, p. 6
24 Prados, p. 26
25 Ibid., pp. 29–30
26 Ibid., p. 13
27 Conversation with Don Manuel Angeles Ortiz, Granada, summer 1965
28 Letter from Gregorio Martínez Sierra in AFGL
29 Mora Guarnido (1958), pp. 126–7
30 Fernández Almagro (1952)
31 '[Yo estaba triste frente a los sembrados]', in AFGL
32 OC (1986), II, p. 664
33 OC, I, pp. 53 and 19–20 respectively
34 Conversation with Don José Bello, Madrid, 12 September 1979; conversation with Don Manuel Angeles Ortiz, Madrid, 25 September 1982
35 Gibson, 'En torno al primer estreno de Lorca (*El maleficio de la mariposa*)', pp. 72–4
36 Francisco García Lorca, p. 266
37 Gibson, 'En torno al primer estreno de Lorca (*El maleficio de la mariposa*)', pp. 72–4
38 Alberti (1945), p. 28
39 OC, II, p. 1043

8 New Directions

1 *E*, I, pp. 21–2
2 Mora Guarnido (1958), p. 82
3 Lorca's academic records in Granada University
4 Francisco García Lorca, p. xii
5 Ibid., pp. 160–6
6 Mora Guarnido (1958), pp. 121–2
7 Ibid.
8 Undated letter from García Maroto to Lorca, AFGL
9 Conversation with Don Francisco García Lorca, Madrid, April 1973
10 Mora Guarnido (1921)
11 Adolfo Salazar (1921)
12 Rivas Cherif (1921); Torre (1921)
13 Letter from Melchor Fernández Almagro to Lorca (August 1922), AFGL; Torre (1925), pp. 80–1
14 AFGL
15 Ibid.
16 *E*, I, pp. 36–7
17 Belamich, Introduction to FGL, *Suites*, p. 19
18 For details, see FGL, *Suites*, in Bibliography.
19 Belamich, Introduction to FGL, *Suites*, p. 22
20 FGL, *Suites*, p. 67
21 Gibson (1969)
22 *E*, I, p. 39
23 FGL, *Suites*, pp. 103–4
24 Ibid., p. 108, note
25 Ibid., pp. 220–1
26 *E*, I, p. 38
27 Conversations with Don Miguel Cerón Rubio, Granada, summer 1965
28 Menéndez Pidal, II, pp. 438–9
29 *E*, I, pp. 38–9

30 AFGL
31 FGL, 'El jardín de las morenas', *Indice*, Madrid, no. 2, 1921
32 Lorca's academic records in Granada University
33 Ibid.
34 Francisco García Lorca, pp. 148–9
35 Mora Guarnido (1958), p. 159
36 OC, I, p. 1167
37 Molina Fajardo (1962), pp. 45–6
38 Ibid., pp. 49–50; conversations with Don Miguel Cerón, Granada, 1965–6
39 E, I, p. 49
40 Conversation with Don Miguel Cerón, Granada, 27 December 1965
41 OC, I, p. 157
42 Ibid., p. 175
43 For details, see Falla (1922; 1972). The drafts of the pamphlet are in the Falla Archive, Madrid.
44 OC, II, p. 1020
45 Ibid., I, pp. 1003–24, *passim*
46 Ibid., pp. 1097–1109, *passim*
47 Molina Fajardo (1962), *passim*
48 Letter from Vicenta Lorca (14 April 1922) to her sons in Seville, AFGL; Chacón y Calvo, p. 101
49 *La Gaceta del Sur*, Granada, 8 June 1922, p. 3; Molina Fajardo (1962), pp. 117–18
50 Trend, 'A Festival in the South of Spain'
51 Legendre, p. 152; García Hidalgo; Mora Guarnido (1958), pp. 162–3; Molina Fajardo (1962), pp. 122–4
52 Molina Fajardo (1962), p. 152
53 Ibid., pp. 151–9

9 1922–3

1 E, I, p. 50
2 Salazar's letters to Falla are in the Falla Archive, Madrid.
3 The dated manuscript of the play is in AFGL
4 E, I, pp. 56–7
5 Undated letter from Lorca to Fernández Almagro, E, I, p. 43
6 OC, II, p. 71
7 E, I, pp. 44–5; letter from Fernández Almagro to Lorca, AFGL
8 Lorca's academic records in Granada University
9 E, I, pp. 58, 60
10 Copy of programme by courtesy of Doña Isabel Carretero
11 Suero, 'Hablando de "La Barraca" con el poeta García Lorca'
12 OC, I, p. 1211
13 Crichton, p. 54
14 Orozco (1968), pp. 145–6; Cossart, pp. 136, 147–50
15 Lorca's academic records in Granada University; Francisco García Lorca, p. 102
16 E, I, pp. 58, 65, 68
17 Dalí's academic records in the Facultad de Bellas Artes, Madrid University
18 Ana María Dalí, pp. 81–4
19 This account follows that given by Dalí in his *Secret Life* and *Confesiones inconfesables*, supplemented by conversations with numerous friends of the painter at this time, such as Don Cristino Mallo, Don José Bello, Don Rafael Sánchez Ventura and Doña María Luisa González; see also Moreno Villa (1944), p. 111, and Ana María Dalí, *passim*.
20 Salvador Dalí (1942), pp. 175–6

21 Ibid., p. 187
22 Ibid., p. 176
23 Ibid., p. 203
24 Buñuel, *Mon dernier soupir*, pp. 85–9
25 María Martínez Sierra, p. 146
26 Mora Guarnido (1958), p. 86
27 *E*, I, pp. 68–9
28 AFGL
29 *E*, I, p. 87
30 Ibid., p. 95
31 Ibid., p. 73
32 AFGL
33 *E*, I, pp. 69–70
34 FGL, *Suites*, pp. 182–3
35 Ibid., p. 13
36 Ibid., pp. 198–9
37 Ibid., pp. 199–200
38 Ibid., pp. 204–6
39 *E*, I, p. 73
40 Postcard from Federico and Francisco García Lorca to Falla from Malaga, mid-August 1923, in Falla Archive, Madrid
41 Undated letter from Lorca to Fernández Almagro (mid-September 1923), AFGL; *OC*, II, pp. 1002, 1008–9; *OC*, I, p. 1169
42 *E*, I, pp. 84–5
43 AFGL; letter reproduced in Rodrigo (1975), pp. 65–6
44 *E*, I, pp. 89–90
45 Mora Guarnido (1958), p. 131
46 Lorca attended a PEN Club meeting in Madrid on 13 November 1923; see *El Sol*, Madrid, 14 November 1923, p. 5.
47 Fernández Almagro (1923)
48 'Sobre unas oposiciones. Una cátedra de pintura al Aire Libre, en la Real Academia de San Fernando', *Heraldo de Madrid*, 18 October 1923, p. 5; for Dalí's account of what happened, see Salvador Dalí (1942), pp. 196–8

10 1924–5

1 Mora Guarnido (1958), p. 158
2 Introduction by Gutiérrez Padial to Jiménez (1969), p. 14
3 Jiménez (1969), pp. 65–6
4 FGL, *Autógrafos. I*, pp. 138–41, for the facsimile manuscript; Mora Guarnido (1958), pp. 209–10
5 FGL, *Autógrafos. I*, pp. 150–5
6 *E*, I, pp. 97–8
7 Ibid., p. 178
8 *OC*, II, p. 940
9 FGL, *Romancero gitano*, Madrid, Alianza, 1981, pp. 142–3
10 *El Defensor de Granada*, 4, 5, 6, 7 November 1919; conversation with Don Manuel Angeles Ortiz, Granada, 27 August 1965; FGL, *Autógrafos. I*, pp. 96–107
11 Jiménez (1962); Salinas (1951), p. 219
12 FGL, *Romancero gitano*, Madrid, Alianza, 1981, pp. 143–4
13 *E*, I, p. 139
14 *OC*, I, pp. 1117–18
15 *E*, I, pp. 81–2

16 Text reproduced by Hernández in his edition of FGL, *La zapatera prodigiosa*, Madrid, Alianza, 1982, p. 24; Francisco García Lorca, pp. 121–2, 307–8
17 Conversation with Don Santiago Ontañón, Madrid, 21 July 1980
18 Conversation with Doña María Molino Montero, Buenos Aires, 18 May 1987
19 *OC*, II, p. 292
20 Higuera Rojas (1980), pp. 80–2
21 Dalí's student card for the 1924–5 session, dated 18 September 1924, is reproduced in Santos Torroella (1987), p. 118
22 *E*, I, pp. 104–5
23 Alberti, *La arboleda perdida*, pp. 173–4; for Lorca's jealousy of Alberti, see Dalí in Aub, p. 549
24 Alberti (1945), pp. 19–20
25 Moreno Villa (1944), p. 113
26 Ibid.
27 Alberti, *La arboleda perdida*, p. 176
28 Santos Torroella (1987), *passim*
29 Moreno Villa (1944), pp. 120–1; *OC*, II, p. 1079
30 I am grateful for this information to my friend M. André Belamich.
31 AFGL
32 *OC*, II, p. 933
33 Ibid., p. 151
34 Ibid., p. 223
35 Private collection
36 Rodrigo (1975), p. 30
37 Rodrigo (1981), p. 39
38 Ana María Dalí, *passim*; *E*, I, p. 122
39 Ana María Dalí, p. 102
40 Rodrigo (1975), pp. 28–9
41 *E*, I, p. 121
42 Salvador Dalí (1942), p. 304
43 Ibid.
44 Ibid.; *E*, I, p. 108
45 Rodrigo (1975), pp. 30–2; *E*, I, p. 108
46 *E*, I, p. 111
47 Ibid., p. 110
48 Salvador Dalí (1942), p. 65
49 *E*, I, p. 122
50 Rodrigo (1975), p. 29
51 Rodrigo (1983)
52 Letter to the author from Don Luis Domínguez Guilarte, Salamanca, 12 February 1966
53 Salvador Dalí (1975), p. 17
54 Private collection
55 Rodrigo (1975), pp. 40–4; Ana María Dalí, pp. 103–4
56 Rodrigo (1981), p. 61
57 *E*, I, p. 133
58 The manifesto is reproduced in Sainz Rodríguez, pp. 345–6
59 Rodrigo (1981), p. 63
60 Ibid., pp. 63–6
61 *E*, I, *passim*
62 Aragon, p. 25
63 Vela
64 Lorca's copy of Torre's *Literaturas europeas de vanguardia* is preserved in the AFGL. The

author's dedication is dated 24 May 1925. See Fernández-Montesinos García, pp. 110–11, and, for the poet's underlinings, ibid., p. 169, note 47.

65 The portrait is reproduced in *400 obras de Salvador Dalí, 1914–1983*, I, p. 53; Buñuel, *Mon dernier soupir*, p. 229

66 *E*, I, p. 118

67 Santos Torroella (1987), p. 19

68 Ibid., pp. 22–4

69 [Salvador Dalí], *La Vie publique de Salvador Dalí*, p. 57

70 Salvador Dalí (1942), p. 332

71 Morris, pp. 134–9

72 *OC*, II, p. 234

73 Ibid., pp. 235–6

74 *Venus and the Sailor* is reproduced in Gómez de Liaño, p. 112, and *400 obras de Salvador Dalí, 1914–1983*, p. 60; a similar painting with the same title, also from 1925, is reproduced in Descharnes (1984), p. 65. The quotations are from *OC*, II, p. 239, and *E*, I, p. 112.

75 *E*, I, pp. 101–2

76 Santos Torroella (1987), p. 19

77 Palencia's reply, undated, is in AFGL; Lorca's letters to Palencia are in the archive of Don Ignacio de Lassaletta y Delclos, Barcelona.

78 See note 77.

79 Santos Torroella (1987), p. 16

80 *E*, I, p. 122

81 AFGL

82 Santos Torroella (1987), p. 24

11 1926

1 Melchor Fernández Almagro, 'El homenaje a Santiago Rusiñol', *La Epoca*, Madrid, 11 January 1926; 'El pulso de Barcelona', *La Epoca*, Madrid, 23 January 1926

2 *E*, I, pp. 132–5

3 The information on Francisco García Lorca's career is mainly from Mario Hernández's introduction to the former's *Federico y su mundo*; Lorca's remark about Francisco's good looks was reported to me by Manuel Angeles Ortiz, who boasted about his and Francisco's philandering in Paris (Granada, 1965–6); for Lorca's letter to Francisco, see *E*, I, pp. 143–4.

4 *E*, I, pp. 135–8

5 *OC*, II, p. 325

6 Ibid., p. 355

7 Ibid., p. 358

8 Ibid., p. 360

9 Santos Torroella (1987), p. 86

10 Buñuel, *Mon dernier soupir*, pp. 122–3; conversation with Don Salvador Dalí, Figueras, 24 October 1980

11 *E*, I, p. 146

12 AFGL

13 Letter to the bookseller León Sánchez Cuesta (10 February 1926) quoted by Sánchez Vidal in his introduction to Buñuel, *Obra literaria*, p. 25

14 *OC*, I, p. 1039

15 Ibid., p. 1116

16 Ortega y Gasset

17 *OC*, I, pp. 771–2

18 Santos Torroella (1987), pp. 16, 20

19 *OC*, I, p. 775

20 Ibid., p. 776

21 Ibid., p. 777
22 Ibid.
23 Ibid., p. 778
24 Conversation with Don Salvador Dalí, Figueras, 24 October 1980
25 Cassou
26 *E*, I, p. 155
27 Santos Torroella (1987), pp. 32, 34, 36
28 On 12 March 1926 the poet attended a lunch held in Granada in honour of the cartoonist Luis Bagaría. See *El Defensor de Granada*, 13 March 1926, p. 1; *Reflejos*, Granada, April 1926.
29 Guillén (1978), p. li
30 Guillermo de Torre (1960), p. 63
31 *El Norte de Castilla*, Valladolid, 11 April 1926, p. 1; *El Defensor de Granada*, 13 April 1926, p. 1
32 Salvador Dalí (1942), pp. 154–6
33 Ibid., p. 206; on the trip, see Ana María Dalí, pp. 120–1
34 Bosquet, p. 52
35 Gibson, 'Con Dalí y Lorca en Figueres'
36 Santos Torroella (1984), pp. 13–43, 206–11
37 *400 obras de Salvador Dalí, 1914–1983*, II, p. 171
38 Salvador Dalí (1942), p. 218
39 *E*, I, p. 156
40 Ibid., p. 157
41 Pedro
42 *E*, I, p. 158
43 Ibid., p. 173
44 Ibid., p. 176
45 Ibid., pp. 159–60
46 Guillén (1959), pp. 95–6
47 *E*, I, pp. 161–2
48 Santos Torroella (1987), p. 44
49 *E*, I, p. 167
50 Santos Torroella (1987), p. 42
51 Ibid., p. 44
52 *L'Amic de les Arts*, Sitges, 26 November 1926, p. 4
53 Reproduced in colour in Gómez de Liaño, no. 30; and in *Salvador Dalí. Rétrospective 1920–1980*, no. 33, p. 47
54 Reproduced in colour in Descharnes (1984), p. 49
55 *OC*, I, pp. 1056–63
56 *E*, I, p. 173
57 Ibid., pp. 174–5
58 Letter in AFGL reproduced in Rodrigo (1975), p. 83
59 *E*, II, p. 22
60 AFGL

12 A Decisive Year

1 Reproduced in black and white in *Salvador Dalí. Rétrospective 1920–1980*, no. 29, p. 46, and in Descharnes (1984), p. 67
2 Santos Torroella (1984), p. 223. The painting is reproduced in colour in Descharnes (1984), p. 69, entitled *Figura cubista*.
3 Santos Torroella (1984), pp. 223–4. The painting is reproduced in colour in Descharnes

(1984), p. 71; in the black-and-white reproduction in Gómez de Liaño, no. 31, the outline of Lorca's head can be appreciated more clearly.

4 The catalogue of Dalí's exhibition is reproduced in Santos Torroella (1987), p. 132.
5 Salvador Dalí (1942), pp. 202–3
6 Santos Torroella (1984), *passim*; see especially the diagrams on pp. 227–8
7 AFGL
8 *E*, II, *passim*
9 Santos Torroella (1987), p. 48
10 Ibid.
11 *E*, II, p. 28; Fernández Almagro's reply, in AFGL, is quoted in Rodrigo (1975), p. 84
12 AFGL
13 *E*, II, p. 33
14 Ibid., pp. 37–8
15 AFGL
16 *E*, II, pp. 38–41
17 Ibid., p. 41
18 *Heraldo de Madrid*, 1 April 1927, p. 5; *E*, I, pp. 83–4; Pedro
19 Santos Torroella (1987), pp. 52, 54
20 *E*, II, p. 60
21 *La Veu de Catalunya*, Barcelona, April–May 1927, for Margarita Xirgu's season
22 Gasch, pp. 7–9
23 Ibid., p. 10
24 Ibid., pp. 10–11
25 Santos Torroella (1987), p. 36
26 Gasch, pp. 10–11
27 *E*, II, p. 71
28 *La Noche*, Barcelona, 23 June 1927, p. 3
29 *E*, II, p. 69
30 *La Veu de Catalunya*, Barcelona, 25–30 June 1927
31 Rodrigo (1975), p. 100
32 *La Vanguardia*, Barcelona, 26 June 1927, p. 15; *El Diluvio*, Barcelona, 26 June 1927, p. 30
33 'La obra de un granadino. El éxito de García Lorca en Barcelona', *El Defensor de Granada* (3 July 1927), p. 1; *La Gaceta Literaria*, Madrid, 1 July 1927, p. 5
34 *E*, II, pp. 66–7
35 Salvador Dalí (1942), p. 205
36 A photograph of the catalogue is reproduced in Rodrigo (1975), p. 115.
37 *El beso* is reproduced in colour in FGL, *Dibujos*, p. 152, no. 112.
38 The comment was made by Dalí to Robert Descharnes (Descharnes (1962), p. 21); the drawing is reproduced in colour in FGL, *Dibujos*, no. 114, p. 153, and in Romero, no. 277, p. 220.
39 *OC*, II, p. 1069
40 *E*, II, p. 72
41 *La Gaceta Literaria*, Madrid, 1 September 1927, p. 2
42 *E*, II, p. 69; Romero, no. 213, p. 172
43 Ibid.
44 Santos Torroella (1984), pp. 224–5
45 Information from Robert Descharnes; see Santos Torroella (1984), p. 86
46 Sánchez Vidal (1988), p. 116.
47 Dalí, interview with Lluís Permanyer, see Bibliography under Salvador Dalí; Salvador Dalí (1942, 1975, 1983), *passim*
48 *Cenicitas* is reproduced in colour and with enlargements of its different parts in Descharnes (1984), pp. 72–3

49 Dalí's foreword to his novel *Hidden Faces* [Salvador Dalí (1944)], p. XI. He ascribes Lorca's augury to 1922 but in fact they did not meet till 1923.

50 Salvador Dalí, 'Sant Sebastià'

51 Santos Torroella (1987), p. 48

52 Ibid., pp. 46, 93

53 Ana María Dalí, pp. 122–32; Rodrigo, *FGL, el amigo de Cataluña*, p. 196

54 Rodrigo (1981), p. 176

55 Ibid.

56 *El Sol*, Madrid, 20 July 1927, p. 2

57 *E*, II, p. 70

58 Fragment reproduced in FGL, *Dibujos*, p. 153

59 Conversations with Don Rafael Santos Torroella, Madrid and Barcelona, 1987

60 'Federico García Lorca', *El Defensor de Granada*, 7 August 1927, p. 1

61 *E*, II, p. 74

62 Ibid., p. 76

63 Ibid., pp. 78–9

64 Ibid., p. 79

65 Ibid., p. 80

66 Ibid.

67 Ibid., p. 86

68 My thanks to Don Rafael Santos Torroella, who transcribed this letter in the 1940s. The whereabouts of the original is unknown.

69 *OC*, I, pp. 977–9

70 Ibid., p. 980

71 Letter from Dalí to Sebastià Gasch in the collection of Gasch's widow, Doña Caritat Gasch, Barcelona

72 *La Voz de Guipúzcoa*, San Sebastián, 11 August 1927, p. 5

73 *OC*, I, pp. 1169–70

74 Alberti, *La arboleda perdida*, pp. 260–1; conversation with Don Vicente Aleixandre, Madrid, 26 April 1982

75 *Heraldo de Madrid*, 10 November 1927, pp. 8–9

76 Ibid., 20 October 1927, p. 5

77 *La Gaceta Literaria*, Madrid, 1 November 1927, p. 5

78 Letter from Dalí to Gasch in the collection of Gasch's widow, Doña Caritat Gasch, Barcelona

79 Dalí, 'Mis cuadros del Salón de Otoño', reproduced in *400 obras de Salvador Dalí, 1914–1983*, I, p. 174, document 8

80 FGL, *Dibujos*, p. 102

81 Santos Torroella (1987), pp. 80–1

82 Miguel Pérez Ferrero, 'Films de vanguardia', *La Gaceta Literaria*, Madrid, 1 July 1927, p. 8; Buñuel, *Mon dernier soupir*, p. 124

83 Sánchez Vidal (1982), p. 25

84 The three letters quoted are reproduced in Sánchez Vidal (1988), pp. 158–62

85 Ibid., pp. 166–7

86 Letter from Trend to Falla (18 January 1928) in the Falla Archive, Madrid

87 Alberti, *La arboleda perdida*, p. 263

88 The information on Sánchez Mejías is taken from the following sources: *Heraldo de Madrid*, 19 June 1924, p. 6, and 28 June 1924, p. 4; 'Uno al sesgo', (pseud.), *passim*; Gallego Morell's prologue to Sánchez Mejías

89 Gallego Morell, prologue to Sánchez Mejías

90 Auclair, p. 15

91 Conversations with Don José Amorós, Madrid, 1986–7

92 Auclair, p. 17

93 Durán Medina, p. 264; Alberti, *La arboleda perdida*, p. 263
94 Durán Medina, pp. 198–9; conversations with Don José Bello, Madrid, 1978–1984; *Carmen*, Santander, no. 5 (1928), not paginated; Alberti, *La arboleda perdida*, p. 264
95 Alberti, *La arboleda perdida*, p. 264
96 Alberti (1945), p. 25
97 Cernuda (1975), pp. 1334–41
98 Alberti, *La arboleda perdida*, pp. 264–6
99 'Coronación de Dámaso Alonso', *Lola, amiga y suplemento de Carmen*, Mardrid, no. 5 (1928), pp. 114–16
100 Ibid.
101 Alonso (1978), pp. 167–8
102 Conversation with Don Dámaso Alonso, Madrid, 6 October 1980
103 'Ecos de sociedad', *El Defensor de Granada*, 23 December 1927, p. 1
104 Conversation with Don Dámaso Alonso, Madrid, 6 October 1980
105 Letter from Gasch to Lorca (26 December 1927) in AFGL
106 The letter is reproduced in full, in the original Catalan, in Gibson, I, p. 667, n. 71
107 *E*, II, p. 92
108 The poem is quoted from Martín (1986), pp. 261–2
109 Ibid., p. 262

13 1928

1 *E*, II, pp. 93–4
2 Ibid., p. 94
3 Ibid; *OC*, I, pp. 1179–82
4 *OC*, I, pp. 1156–7
5 *E*, II, p. 96
6 'Recepción de *gallo*', *gallo*, Granada, no. 2 (April 1928); *E*, II, p. 101
7 The author's copy of the extremely rare *Pavo* is now in the Casa-Museo Federico García Lorca, Fuente Vaqueros, Granada
8 Undated letter in AFGL
9 Adams, p. 78
10 Ibid.
11 The *Manifesto* is reproduced in Fornés, p. 16
12 Postcard in AFGL
13 Aladrén's School of Fine Arts records are preserved in the library of the Faculty of Arts, Universidad Complutense, Madrid; in AFGL there is a card from Aladrén to Lorca (summer 1925), written from El Paular (Madrid), in which he asks the poet to write to him regularly. Whether Lorca did so or not there seems to be no way of knowing.
14 Conversation with Doña Maruja Mallo, Madrid, 26 June 1982
15 In Aladrén's file (see n. 13) there is a document, dated 10 March 1926, in which the head of the establishment warns him of the consequences if he continues to misbehave.
16 Account given by José María García Carrillo to Agustín Penón and transcribed in the latter's diary, 24 June 1955, APP
17 Ibid.
18 Martínez Nadal (1980), p. 13
19 Ibid., p. 29
20 Ibid., pp. 29–30
21 Ibid., pp. 28
22 Conversation with Don Jorge Guillén, Malaga, 8 December 1979
23 Conversation with Don José Jiménez Rosado, Madrid, 13 June 1984. Aladrén died on 4 March 1944, of tuberculosis.
24 Baeza, 'Los *Romances gitanos* de Federico García Lorca'

25 Arconada
26 *El Defensor de Granada*, 3 August 1928, p. 1
27 AFGL
28 AFGL
29 Morla Lynch, p. 210
30 *E*, II, pp. 106–7
31 Undated letter in AFGL
32 *E*, II, pp. 119–21
33 Ibid., p. 121
34 'Oda y burla de Sesostris y Sardanápalo', *OC* (*1986*), I, pp. 972–4
35 *E*, II, p. 62; Rivas Cherif's reply is in AFGL.
36 Conversations with Don José Caballero, Madrid, 1978–86; Martínez Nadal (1980), p. 29
37 Santos Torroella (1987), pp. 88–94; this quote, pp. 93–4
38 Ibid., p. 94
39 *E*, II, p. 113
40 AFGL
41 *E*, II, p. 114
42 Santos Torroella (1987), pp. 76–9
43 *OC*, I, pp. 993–4 and 990–2 respectively
44 Ibid., pp. 993–4
45 *E*, II, p. 111; see also p. 114
46 The letter is quoted in Sánchez Vidal (1988), pp. 178–80
47 *E*, II, pp. 110, 113; *El Defensor de Granada*, 21 September 1928, p. 1
48 Conversation with Don Manuel López Banús, Fuengirola, 28 February 1984
49 *E*, II, pp. 108–9
50 Ibid., p. 114
51 'Imaginación, inspiración, evasión', *OC*, I, pp. 1064–70; Santos Torroella (1987), pp. 82–94
52 'Sketch de la nueva pintura', *OC* (*1986*), III, pp. 272–81; this quotation, p. 278
53 Ibid., p. 280
54 *E*, II, p. 110
55 Ibid., p. 112
56 Ibid., pp. 108, 110, 119
57 *OC*, I, p. 789
58 Martín (1986), pp. 310–13
59 AFGL
60 Conversations with Don Miguel Cerón Rubio, Granada, 1965–6
61 'Las nanas infantiles', *OC*, I, pp. 1073–91; this quotation, p. 1077
62 Ibid., p. 1080
63 Ibid., II, p. 936
64 Ibid., p. 937
65 Aub, p. 550
66 *OC*, II, p. 937
67 *Revista de Occidente*, Madrid, vol. XXII (December 1928), pp. 295–8
68 Flap of the front cover of Alberti, *Sobre los ángeles*, the first book in the new series
69 *OC*, II, p. 937

14 Escape

1 See, for example, Buñuel's letter to Bello (17 February 1929), quoted by Sánchez Vidal in his notes to Buñuel, *Obra literaria*, p. 266; the quotation is from Sánchez Vidal's introduction to the same volume, p. 36.

2 Aranda, p. 83; Rodrigo (1981), pp. 214–15; 'Buñuel y Dalí en el Cineclub', *La Gaceta Literaria*, Madrid, 1 February 1929, p. 6
3 Aranda, p. 65, n. 1
4 Interview by José de la Colina and Tomas P. Turrent with Buñuel (1980) quoted by Sánchez Vidal in his introduction to Buñuel, *Obra literaria*, p. 32; Buñuel repeats the same comment in *Mon dernier soupir*, p. 193.
5 Sánchez Vidal (1982), p. 32, for Buñuel's denial; Aub, p. 105, for Buñuel's remark on Lorca's alleged impotence
6 'En el Centro Artístico. Conferencia de Rivas Cherif', *El Defensor de Granada*, 7 April 1929, p. 3
7 *Heraldo de Madrid*, 5 November 1928, p. 5
8 *El Sol*, Madrid, 20 December 1928, p. 3
9 *Heraldo de Madrid*, 7 January 1929, p. 6
10 Programme for the production in AFGL; *El Sol*, Madrid, 3 February 1929, p. 3; 5 February, p. 3; conversation with Don José Jiménez Rosado, Madrid, 27 February 1984; Rivas Cherif (1957); Ucelay; Lorca's comment is in Río (1941), p. 17, n. 2
11 Gibson, *El asesinato de García Lorca*, pp. 14, 327–31
12 *El Sol*, Madrid, 19 February 1929
13 Morla Lynch, pp. 22–8
14 Letter from Falla to Lorca (9 February 1929) in AFGL
15 Martínez Nadal (1980), pp. 33–4
16 Ibid., pp. 31–2
17 Copy of Aladrén's marriage certificate obtained from Somerset House, London
18 For details of the evolution of the painting's titles, see Santos Torroella (1984), pp. 224–5
19 Santos Torroella (1987), p. 113, for the date of Dalí's departure; Dalí (1942), pp. 207–17; Dalí's six articles were published in *La Publicitat*, Barcelona, between 26 April and 28 June 1929; for Dalí's account of his meeting with Gala, see Salvador Dalí (1942), pp. 226–34; for Buñuel's reaction, *Mon dernier soupir*, pp. 115–16
20 'Un número violento de *L'Amic de les Arts*', *La Gaceta Literaria*, Madrid, 1 February 1929, p. 7; *L'Amic de les Arts*, Sitges, no. 31 (31 March 1929), p. 16, for Dalí's interview with Buñuel
21 *El Defensor de Granada*, 27 March 1929, p. 3
22 Gómez Montero
23 *El Defensor de Granada*, 28 March 1928, p. 3
24 See note 22.
25 See note 22.
26 Details from *La Gaceta Literaria* after each session
27 *La Gaceta Literaria*, Madrid, no. 53, 1 March 1929, p. 1
28 Ibid., no. 56, 15 April 1929, p. 1
29 Ibid.
30 *El Liberal*, Bilbao, 16 April 1929, pp. 1–2; *El Defensor de Granada*, 23 April 1929, p. 1
31 *El Defensor de Granada*, 30 April 1929, p. 1
32 Ibid., 7 May 1929, p. 1
33 OC, I, pp. 1184–5
34 *El Defensor de Granada*, 19 May 1929, p. 1
35 Ibid., 21 May 1929, p. 1
36 Conversation with Doña Rita María Troyano de los Ríos, Madrid, 15 June 1984
37 *E*, II, pp. 126–7
38 *El Defensor de Granada*, 9 June 1929, p. 5
39 Morla Lynch, pp. 42–3
40 For Fernando de los Ríos's departure from Granada, *El Defensor de Granada*, 11 June 1929, p. 1; conversation with Don Vicente Aleixandre, Madrid, 4 April 1984
41 *El Socialista*, Madrid, 13 June 1936, p. 1; *Heraldo de Madrid*, 14 June 1936, p. 2

42 Eisenberg, editor's introduction to FGL, *Songs,* translated by Philip Cummings, pp. 4–5
43 Cummings, 'August in Eden', pp. 178–9
44 Pritchett, p. 121
45 Pomès (1967)
46 For a reproduction of the invitation to the private screening, see García Buñuel, p. 80; for Buñuel's account of the occasion, *Mon dernier soupir*, pp. 126–8
47 García-Posada (1977)
48 Conversation with Doña Rita María Troyano de los Ríos, Madrid, 15 June 1984
49 Ibid.
50 Madariaga (1960), pp. 221–3; Gregorio Prieto, pp. 60–6
51 Letter from Dr Helen Grant to the author, Oxford, 23 April 1979
52 *The Southern Daily Echo*, Southampton, 19 June 1929, p. 2; *Heraldo de Madrid*, 19 June 1929, p. 3

Notes to Book Two

1 New York

1 *FGLNY*, p. 35
2 *E*, II, p. 128
3 *FGLNY*, p. 35
4 Ad. S. [Adolfo Salazar], 'Notas críticas. *Manhattan Transfer* y sus perspectivas'
5 Río, *Poeta en Nueva York*, p. 35
6 Darío (1967), pp. 639–41
7 Jiménez (1970), *passim*
8 *Heraldo de Madrid*, 23 January 1928, p. 6; ibid., 25 January 1928, p. 5; Luis Buñuel, 'Metrópolis', *La Gaceta Literaria*, Madrid, 1 May 1927, p. 6; *El Defensor de Granada*, 5 February 1929, p. 1; ibid., 7 February 1929, p. 1; ibid., 9 February 1929, p. 1
9 Morand
10 Darío (1967), p. 538; Whitman; Martín (1986), p. 91
11 *El Defensor de Granada*, 24 February 1929, p. 1; ibid., 10 March 1929, p. 1
12 On Onís, see Jiménez Fraud (1971), pp. 446–8
13 Eisenberg, *Textos y documentos lorquianos*, p. 22
14 *FGLNY*, p. 36
15 Eisenberg, 'A Chronology of Lorca's Visit to New York and Cuba', p. 235
16 *FGLNY*, p. 36
17 Eisenberg, 'Cuatro pesquisas lorquianas', p. 2
18 *FGLNY*, p. 37
19 Ibid.
20 Ibid.
21 Ibid.; letter to the author from Campbell Hackforth-Jones, 25 June 1982
22 Anderson (1985)
23 Ibid.
24 Ibid.
25 *FGLNY*, pp. 61–2
26 Río (1941), p. 204
27 Eisenberg, Editor's introduction to FGL, *Songs*, p. 5
28 *E*, II, pp. 128–9
29 Eisenberg, 'Lorca en Nueva York', pp. 17–18
30 Eisenberg, 'Cuatro pesquisas lorquianas', pp. 12–19
31 Adolfo Salazar, 'In memoriam. Federico García Lorca en La Habana', p. 30
32 The information concerning the aims of the Instituto de las Españas is taken from a prospectus included at the end of Federico de Onís's essay, 'Disciplina y rebeldía', published by the Instituto in 1929.

33 Bussell Thompson and Walsh, p. 1; Solana
34 *La Prensa*, New York, 9 August 1929, p. 4
35 *FGLNY*, p. 56
36 Alonso (1937), pp. 260–1
37 *FGLNY*, p. 54, note 1; Brickell (1945), pp. 386–7
38 *FGLNY*, pp. 51–2
39 Brickell (1937)
40 *FGLNY*, p. 47
41 Ibid., p. 86
42 Ibid., p. 68
43 Ibid., p. 48
44 Ibid., p. 50, note 7
45 Ibid., pp. 46–7
46 Eisenberg, 'Cuatro pesquisas lorquianas', p. 15
47 Diers, pp. 33–4
48 *FGLNY*, p. 55
49 FGL, *Poeta en Nueva York. Tierra y luna*, pp. 138–51
50 OC, II, p. 939
51 FGL, *Poeta en Nueva York. Tierra y luna*, p. 141
52 Ibid., pp. 115–16
53 Telephone conversation with Don Angel Flores (in Palenville, New York), 3 August 1987
54 OC, II, pp. 1129–30
55 Conversation with Doña Dulce María Loynaz, Havana, 27 April 1987
56 OC, I, p. 448
57 Eisenberg, 'A Chronology of Lorca's Visit to New York and Cuba', p. 237
58 Conversations with Mr Philip Cummings, Woodstock, Vermont, 4, 5, 6 April 1986
59 Ibid.
60 *FGLNY*, p. 58
61 Conversations with Mr Philip Cummings, Woodstock, Vermont, 4, 5, 6 April 1986
62 Ibid.
63 Cummings, 'August in Eden. An Hour of Youth', p. 159
64 Ibid., pp. 162–3
65 Letter from Philip Cummings to Daniel Eisenberg, dated 21 October 1974, published in Eisenberg (1976), p. 181, note 155
66 Ibid.
67 Conversation with Mr Philip Cummings, Woodstock, Vermont, 4 April 1986
68 A colour photograph of this letter is reproduced in *FGLNY*, p. 25
69 *E*, II, pp. 130–31
70 Cummings, 'August in Eden. An Hour of Youth', pp. 155–6; OC, I, p. 1131; visit with Mr Philip Cummings to Lake Eden, Vermont, 5 April 1986
71 Schwartz, p. 51; Eisenberg, Editor's introduction to FGL, *Songs*, p. 11; Adams, pp. 107–8; conversation with Mr Philip Cummings, Lake Eden, 5 April 1986
72 FGL, *Poeta en Nueva York. Tierra y luna*, p. 203
73 Ibid.
74 Conversation with Don Luis Rosales, Madrid, 25 May 1985; Alberti (1985)
75 Eisenberg, 'A Chronology of Lorca's Visit to New York and Cuba', pp. 237–8
76 Río (1955), p. xv
77 *FGLNY*, p. 72
78 Eisenberg, 'Cuatro pesquisas lorquianas', pp. 11–12
79 *FGLNY*, p. 72
80 FGL, *Poeta en Nueva York. Tierra y luna*, p. 182
81 Río (1955), p. xxxvii
82 Ibid.; Eisenberg, 'Cuatro pesquisas lorquianas', p. 12

83 *El Defensor de Granada*, 27 March 1928, p. 1; *OC*, I, p. 1131–2
84 *OC*, I, pp. 1131–2
85 Río (1955), p. xxxvii
86 *OC*, I, pp. 877–8
87 FGL, *Poeta en Nueva York. Tierra y luna*, p. 288
88 Río (1955), p. xvi
89 *E*, II, p. 134
90 *FGLNY*, p. 78
91 Ibid., p. 67; Eisenberg, 'A Chronology of Lorca's Visit to New York and Cuba', p. 238
92 *FGLNY*, p. 67
93 Rius, p. 161
94 Eisenberg, 'Lorca en Nueva York', pp. 21–2
95 Letter in AFGL
96 FGL, *Autógrafos. I*, p. xxxv and note 16
97 Ibid., pp. 242–5
98 Zambrano, p. 189
99 Crow, pp. 3–8, *passim*
100 Ibid., p. 7
101 Ibid., p. 47
102 Ibid., p. 4
103 Bussell Thompson and Walsh, p. 1; Adams, p. 122
104 *OC*, I, p. 264
105 Letter from Lorca to Rubio Sacristán quoted in *FGLNY*, p. 11
106 Conversations with Don José Antonio Rubio Sacristán, Madrid, 19 February 1979, 16 and 20 October 1986
107 *FGLNY*, pp. 81–2
108 *OC*, II, p. 978
109 FGL, *Poeta en Nueva York. Tierra y luna*, p. 159 note
110 García de Valdeavellano, p. 48; Ad. S. [Adolfo Salazar], 'La vida musical. Un crítico norteamericano en Europa'
111 Brickell (1945), pp. 390–1
112 Adams, p. 124; see also Brickell (1945), p. 391, and *FGLNY*, pp. 85–6
113 *FGLNY*, p. 86
114 FGL, *Poeta en Nueva York. Tierra y luna*, p. 212
115 *El Sol*, Madrid, 20 September 1929, p. 8
116 *FGLNY*, p. 80
117 Ibid., note 2
118 Gibson, II, p. 70
119 Diers, pp. 33–4; *FGLNY*, p. 82, note 4; letter to Lorca, 20 December 1929, from María Antonieta Rivas Mercado in Los Angeles, AFGL
120 Diers, p. 34–5
121 *OC (1986)*, II, p. 1143
122 FGL, *Dibujos*, no. 158, p. 167, and commentary by Mario Hernández
123 Ibid., no. 159, p. 168
124 *FGLNY*, p. 59
125 Ibid., p. 78
126 *FGLNY*, p. 79
127 Brickell (1945), p. 392; *FGLNY*, p. 84, note 4
128 Maurer, 'El teatro', pp. 133–41
129 Ibid., pp. 134–6
130 Ibid., p. 136
131 Ibid.; conversation with Don Ernesto Guerra da Cal, Lisbon, 26 July 1986
132 *FGLNY*, p. 80

133 Quoted by Maurer, 'El teatro', p. 137
134 *FGLNY*, p. 60, note 6, and Maurer, 'El teatro', pp. 137–8
135 Maurer, 'El teatro', p. 139
136 'Charlando con García Lorca', *Crítica*, Buenos Aires, 15 November 1933; interview reproduced by Hernández in his edition of FGL, *Bodas de sangre*, Madrid, Alianza, 1984, pp. 212–14
137 *FGLNY*, p. 86
138 *La Prensa*, New York, 14 February 1930, p. 4
139 *OC*, I, pp. 547–8
140 *La Prensa*, New York, 16, 18, 21 January 1930, and 5, 10 February 1930; conversation with Don Andrés Segovia, Madrid, 19 December 1980
141 Eisenberg, 'Lorca en Nueva York', p. 22; conversation with Don José Antonio Rubio Sacristán, Madrid, 21 October 1986
142 Conversation with Don José Gudiol, Barcelona, 5 July 1985
143 Eisenberg, 'Lorca en Nueva York', pp. 23–5; Anderson (1983)
144 *Heraldo de Madrid*, 6 November 1929, p. 7
145 *La Prensa*, New York, 7 February 1930
146 Eisenberg, 'Lorca en Nueva York', pp. 26–9, and 'Dos conferencias lorquianas'
147 Eisenberg, 'A Chronology of Lorca's Visit to New York and Cuba', p. 243
148 Adams, p. 133
149 Elena de la Torre
150 *La Prensa*, New York, 14 February 1930, p. 1; 22 February 1930, p. 5
151 Ibid., 25 February 1930, p. 4; 7 March 1930, p. 4
152 Conversation with Don José Antonio Rubio Sacristán, Madrid, 21 October 1986
153 Eisenberg, 'A Chronology of Lorca's Visit to New York and Cuba', p. 244
154 'Barcos llegados ayer' and 'Los que llegaron en el *Cuba*', *Diario de la Marina*, Havana, 8 March 1930, p. 24
155 Elena de la Torre

2 Cuba

1 Marinello (1965), pp. 18–19
2 *OC*, I, pp. 1133–4
3 Rafael Alberti, 'Encuentro en la Nueva España con Bernal Díaz del Castillo'
4 *OC*, I, p. 1134
5 Rafael Suárez Solís, 'Entre paréntesis. Federico García Lorca', *Diario de la Marina*, Havana, 7 March 1930, p. 68
6 *Diario Español*, Havana, 8 March 1930, p. 2; *Diario de la Marina*, Havana, 8 March 1930, p. 24
7 *Diario de la Marina*, Havana, 7 March 1930, p. 68
8 Quevedo, p. [16]
9 The information about the Quevedos from Dobos (1980), pp. 397–8
10 Quevedo, pp. [17–18]
11 Havana press, *passim*; Eisenberg, 'A Chronology of Lorca's Visit to New York and Cuba', pp. 244–7; Marinello (1930)
12 Quevedo, p. [18]
13 *FGLNY*, pp. 89–90
14 Chacón y Calvo
15 'La conferencia de García Lorca', *Diario de la Marina*, Havana, 9 April 1930, p. 5; Obdulio A. García, 'Sobre la mecánica de la poesía, habló García Lorca en Cienfuegos' *Diario de la Marina*, Havana, 6 June 1930, p. 20; Roque Barreiro
16 'Un poeta granadino. García Lorca triunfa en Norteamérica y en Cuba', *El Defensor de*

Granada, 8 May 1930, p. 1. The article quoted appeared in *La Correspondencia*, Cienfuegos.

17 Quevedo, *passim*
18 Interview with Antonio Quevedo in Dobos (1980), pp. 47–8
19 *Musicalia*, Havana, no. 11 (April–May 1930), pp. 43–4
20 Marinello (1965), pp. 18–19
21 Cabrera Infante, p. 245
22 Auclair, p. 430
23 Sarabia, p. 58
24 Conversation with Doña Dulce María Loynaz, Havana, 27 April 1987
25 Ibid.
26 'El recuerdo de Flor', in Bianchi Ross, p. 30
27 Ibid.
28 Conversation with Doña Dulce María Loynaz, Havana, 27 April 1987
29 Pedregosa and Ferreras; Villegas
30 Francisco García Lorca, p. 357
31 Mora Guarnido (1958), pp. 31–2; Francisco García Lorca, p. 356
32 Francisco García Lorca, p. 356
33 Auclair, p. 323
34 For the date, see *Poesía*, Madrid, nos. 18–19 (1984) (special issue dedicated to the Residencia de Estudiantes), p. 11
35 Pittaluga, p. [4]
36 *Heraldo de Madrid*, 10 November 1933, p. 4; Adolfo Salazar, *El Sol*, 10 November 1933, p. 8
37 Document reproduced in Landeira Yrago, *Viaje al sueño del agua*, p. 65
38 Conversation with Doña Dulce María Loynaz, Havana, 27 April 1987
39 Loynaz, pp. 54–5; conversation with Doña Dulce María Loynaz, Havana, 27 April 1987
40 Telephone conversation with Doña Lydia Cabrera (in Miami), 6 December 1986
41 Loynaz, p. 55
42 Cardoza y Aragón, *El río*, p. 336
43 Conversation with Don Miguel Barnet, Havana, 26 April 1987
44 Cardoza y Aragón, *El río*, p. 328
45 Ibid., p. 351
46 Ibid., pp. 352–3
47 Ibid; see also Gaudry's and Olivares's interview with Cardoza y Aragón, p. 61
48 Conversation with Doña Dulce María Loynaz, Havana, 27 April 1987
49 Cardoza y Aragón (1936)
50 Ibid.
51 Cabrera Infante, pp. 247–8
52 An account repeated to the author several times in Havana, April 1986
53 Ibid.
54 Conversation with Mme Sara Fidelzeit, second wife of Pérez de la Riva, Havana, 25 April 1987
55 FGL, *El público y Comedia sin título*, p. 164
56 Martínez Nadal, in FGL, *El público y Comédia sin título*, p. 175
57 Paulino Masip, '*Caracol* en la Sala Rex. *Un sueño de la razón*, de Cipriano Rivas Cherif', *Heraldo de Madrid*, 7 January 1929, p. 6
58 Letter to the author from Don Enrique de Rivas, son of Cipriano Rivas Cherif, Mexico, 31 March 1987
59 García Pintado, pp. 8–10
60 FGL, *El público y Comedia sin título*, p. 153
61 OC, I, p. 530
62 FGL, *El público y Comedia sin título*, p. 51

63 André Belamich, in his analysis of *El público* to appear in the second volume of his translation of Lorca's *Oeuvres complètes*, Gallimard, Paris

64 FGL, *El público y Comedia sin título*, pp. 105–7

65 García Lorca, *Poeta en Nueva York. Tierra y luna*, pp. 117–19

66 FGL, *El público y Comedia sin título*, p. 145

67 Ibid., p. 69

68 Conversation with Doña Dulce María Loynaz, Havana, 27 April 1987

69 Manuscript of the ode reproduced in facsimile by Martínez Nadal in FGL, *Autógrafos. I*, pp. 204–17

70 Conversation with Don Luis Rosales, Madrid, 24 November 1978

71 Rivas Cherif (27 January 1957), p. 1

72 FGL, *Oda a Walt Whitman*

73 See Roig de Leuchsenring

74 Francisco García Lorca, illustration no. [32]

75 'Del Puerto . . . El Alfonso XIII', *Diario Español*, Havana, 17 May 1930, p. 9

76 Quevedo, p. [23]

77 'Conferencias de García Maroto en la Hispanocubana. Hoy llegará el insigne pintor', *Diario de la Marina*, Havana, 28 April 1930, p. 1

78 Conversation with Doña María Teresa Babín (to whom Salazar showed Lorca's letters in Puerto Rico), Madrid, 8 August 1986. The musicologist Emilio Casares Rodicio, who examined Salazar's papers in Mexico after the latter's death in 1950, has confirmed that there is not a single letter from Lorca in the archive (telephone conversation, 31 January 1987).

79 Adolfo Salazar, 'In memoriam. Federico en La Habana', p. 30

80 Ibid.

81 Marinello (1939), pp. 18–19

82 'Comida de "1930" ', *1930. Revista de Avance*, Havana, 15 June 1930, p. 192

83 *Diario de la Marina*, Havana, 12 June 1930, p. 13

84 'El recuerdo de Flor', in Bianchi Ross (1980), p. 30; Bianchi Ross (1986), p. 60; Flor Loynaz, p. 55; conversation with Doña Dulce Maria Loynaz, Havana, 27 April 1987

85 Quevedo, pp. [38–9]

86 María Muñoz de Quevedo's letter to Vicenta Lorca is in AFGL.

87 Marinello (1965), p. 15

88 Dobos (1978), p. 17

89 'Noticias marítimas', *La Prensa*, New York, 18 June 1930, p. 8; 'Llegada de pasajeros', *La Prensa*, New York, 19 June 1930, p. 8

90 Brickell (1945), pp. 394–5; Adams, p. 137

91 Adams, p. 137

92 Aub, p. 105

93 Adolfo Salazar, '*La casa de Bernarda Alba*'

94 Conversation with Doña Isabel García Lorca, Madrid, 28 June 1987

3 The Coming of the Republic

1 *El Defensor de Granada*, 2 July 1930, p. 1; *Noticiero Granadino*, 4 July 1930, p. 1

2 'Nota biográfica', in Fernando de los Ríos (1976), p. 52; for the 'San Sebastián Pact', see Cabanellas, I, pp. 161–2; Jackson, p. 24, and Indalecio Prieto (1967–9), I, pp. 55–6

3 AFGL

4 Vázquez Ocaña, pp. 269–70

5 Dalí (1942), pp. 274–81

6 Carmona

7 Pérez Ferrero (1930)

8 Martínez Nadal, 'What I Know about *The Public*', p. 19

9 *La Voz de Guipúzcoa*, San Sebastián, 5 December 1930, p. 9; 6 December 1930, p. 2; conversation with Don Rafael Santos Torroella, Madrid, February 1986

10 *El Noroeste*, Gijón, 14 December 1930, p. 2; *Ahora*, Madrid, 16 December 1930, p. 14

11 For a résumé of what happened in Madrid, see Cabanellas, I, pp. 167–8

12 'Antes del estreno. Hablando con Federico García Lorca', *La Libertad*, Madrid, 24 December 1930, p. 9

13 'En el Centro Artístico. Conferencia de Rivas Cherif', *El Defensor de Granada*, 7 April 1929, p. 3

14 'Antes del estreno. Hablando con Federico García Lorca', *La Libertad*, Madrid, 24 December 1930, p. 9

15 *La Libertad*, Madrid, 25 December 1930, p. 4

16 E. D.-C. [Enrique Díez Canedo], in *El Sol*, Madrid, 26 December 1930, p. 4

17 J. G. Olmedilla, in *Heraldo de Madrid*, 25 December 1930, p. 7

18 Theatre page of *Heraldo de Madrid* for these weeks

19 Santos Torroella (1987), p. 93

20 *OC*, II, pp. 938–41

21 E. Díez Canedo, in *El Sol*, Madrid, 21 January 1931, p. 12

22 Cinema advertisements in *Heraldo de Madrid* for these dates

23 Alberti, *La arboleda perdida*, p. 309

24 J. G. Olmedilla, in *Heraldo de Madrid*, 27 February 1931, p. 5; C.S., in *Heraldo de Madrid*, 27 February 1931, p. 5; Alberti, *La arboleda perdida*, p. 309

25 Alberti, *La arboleda perdida*, p. 309

26 Miguel Pérez Ferrero, in *Heraldo de Madrid*, 6 March 1931, p. 5

27 J. G. Olmedilla, in *Heraldo de Madrid*, 28 March 1931, p. 7

28 S. [Adolfo Salazar], 'Discos. La Voz de su Amo. – Un cancionero viviente'.

29 Conversation with Don José Jiménez Rosado, Madrid, 4 November 1985

30 Pomès (1950); for the drawing, see FGL, *Dibujos*, no. 177, p. 180

31 Morla Lynch, p. 54

32 Information given by Martínez Nadal to Marcelle Auclair, Auclair, pp. 261–2

33 Vega Díaz

4 Early Days in the New Spain

1 Pérez Galán, *passim*

2 Ibid.

3 Jackson, p. 30

4 Ibid., pp. 31–2

5 Ibid., pp. 32–4

6 Eugenio Montes, 'Poema del "cante jondo" ', *El Sol*, Madrid, 18 July 1931, p. 2

7 FGL, *Autógrafos*. *I*, p. xiii; Sebastià Gasch, 'Un llibre de García Lorca. "Poema del cante jondo" ', *Mirador*, Barcelona, 20 August 1931, p. 6

8 *E*, II, p. 142

9 *OC*, II, p. 992

10 Ibid., pp. 409–10

11 Ibid., pp. 417–18

12 *OC*, I, pp. 143–4

13 *OC*, II, p. 438

14 Ibid., p. 391

15 Ibid., pp. 369, 438

16 FGL, *Suites*, p. 67

17 *E*, II, p. 143

18 FGL, 'Alocución al pueblo de Fuentevaqueros', *OC (1986)*, III, pp. 420–33

19 'Patronato de Misiones Pedagógicas', *Residencia. Revista de la Residencia de Estudiantes*, Madrid, IV, no. 1 (February 1933), pp. 1–2

20 For Lorca's visit to the Cortes and a full account of De los Ríos's speech, see Vidarte, pp. 192–5

21 Morla Lynch, pp. 127–8

22 Conversations with Don Arturo Sáenz de la Calzada and Don Pedro Miguel González Quijano, Madrid, 1983

23 Ibid.; conversation with Don Emilio Garrigues, Madrid, 1983

24 For Ugarte, see Sáenz de la Calzada, p. 184

25 *OC*, II, p. 1013

26 V. S.

27 *El Liberal*, Madrid, 25 March 1932, p. 11

28 Gibson, II, pp. 164–6

29 'Programa y presupuesto de Instrucción Pública. Magnífico discurso de don Fernando de los Ríos', *El Liberal*, Madrid, 25 March 1932, p. 1

30 Conversation with Doña María del Carmen García Lasgoity, Madrid, 1980

31 *OC*, II, p. 945

32 *OC*, I, p. 1193; Sáenz de la Calzada, facsimile of Lorca's introduction between pp. 124 and 125

33 Conversations with Don Emilio Garrigues and Don Luis Sáenz de la Calzada, Madrid and León respectively, 1986

34 Conversations with Don Pedro Miguel González Quijano, Don Luis Ruiz-Salinas, Don Luis Sáenz de la Calzada, Doña María del Carmen García Lasgoity and other *barracos*, in Madrid, 1983–6

35 For the dates of Lorca's visits to Galicia, see Franco Grande and Landeira Yrago (1974)

36 Details from the biographical note included in Ernesto Guerra da Cal, *Futuro inmemorial (Manual de velhice para principiantes)*, Lisbon, Libraria Sa Da Costa Editora, 1985, and conversations with Don Ernesto Guerra Da Cal, Lisbon, 1985–7

37 Conversations with Don Ernesto Guerra Da Cal, Lisbon, 1985–7

38 Martínez Barbeito

39 Franco Grande and Landeira Yrago, p. 12

40 Martínez Barbeito

41 Conversation with Don Ernesto Guerra Da Cal, Lisbon, 4 January 1986

42 *OC*, I, p. 561

43 As for note 41

44 Letter to the author from Don Luis Domínguez Guilarte, Salamanca, 12 January 1966

45 Martínez Nadal (1965), pp. 43–4

46 Aleixandre (1977)

47 *E*, II, p. 155

5 The Barraca and *Blood Wedding*

1 Conversations with several *barracos*, especially Doña María del Carmen García Lasgoity, Don Modesto Higueras, Don Pedro Miguel González Quijano and Don Arturo Ruiz-Castillo, Madrid, 1978–87

2 ' "La Barraca" inaugura su actuación en Burgo de Osma', *Noticiero de Soria*, 11 July 1932, p. 3; 'La Barraca, en Burgo de Osma. El Teatro Universitario que creara D. Fernando de los Ríos', *Luz*, Madrid, 12 July 1932, p. 7

3 Ibid.

4 Conversation with Doña María del Carmen García Lasgoity, Madrid, 4 December 1980

5 'El ensayo de "La Barraca" estudiantil. En busca del teatro español', *Luz*, Madrid, 25 July 1932, p. 9

6 'Teatro Universitario. "La Barraca" ', *El Porvenir Castellano*, Soria, 14 July 1932, p. 3;

'Teatro Universitario. "La Barraca" ', *Noticiero de Soria*, 14 July 1932, p. 3; 'La Barraca Universitaria en Soria', *La Voz de Soria*, 15 July 1932, p. 2

7   C., 'Muy lamentable. Lo ocurrido ayer', *El Avisador Numantino*, Soria, 16 July 1932, p. 3

8   García Lasgoity, 17 May 1945; conversations, all in Madrid, with Doña María del Carmen García Lasgoity, 4 December 1980, Don Pedro Miguel González Quijano, 11 May 1983, and Don Emilio Garrigues, 12 November 1985

9   'El ensayo de "la Barraca" estudiantil. En busca del teatro español', *Luz*, Madrid, 25 July 1932, p. 9

10 *OC*, II, p. 969

11 Lanz

12 Agraz; Sáenz de La Calzada, p. 166; García de Valdeavellano, p. 48

13 'La silueta de la semana. Federico García Loca [sic] o cualquiera se equivoca', *Gracia y Justicia*, Madrid, 23 July 1932, p. 10. *Loca*, in the feminine, is a common term for 'gay'.

14 'El carro de Tespis', *Gracia y Justicia*, Madrid, 23 July 1932, p. 13

15 See, for example, Cipriano Rivas Cherif, 'Apuntaciones. Por el Teatro Dramático Nacional', *El Sol*, Madrid, 22 July 1932, p. 3

16 Emilio Garrigues y Díaz-Cañabate, p. 107

17 Agraz

18 Ibid.

19 Conversation with Doña Isabel García Lorca, Madrid, 4 October 1978

20 Alfredo Mario Ferreiro, 'García Lorca en Montevideo', article exhumed by Andrew A. Anderson and reprinted in Anderson (1981), pp. 154–61; this quotation, p. 156

21 *Heraldo de Madrid*, 24–8 and 30 July 1928

22 Ibid., 27, 30 July 1928

23 Ibid., 30 July 1928

24 Ibid., 27 July 1928

25 Ibid., 26 July 1928

26 *OC*, II, p. 660

27 *Heraldo de Madrid*, 28 July 1928

28 Brenan (1957), ch. 14

29 Josephs and Caballero, introduction to FGL, *Bodas de sangre*, p. 69

30 *Heraldo de Madrid*, 26 July 1928

31 *El Defensor de Granada*, 25 July 1928

32 Conversations with Don Miguel Cerón Rubio, Granada, 1966

33 Synge, p. 91

34 *OC*, II, p. 658

35 On the influence of Synge in Lorca, see Chica Salas and Sainero Sánchez.

36 *OC*, II, p. 1041

37 Ibid., p. 637

38 *Noticias Gráficas*, Buenos Aires, 14 October 1933

39 For the chronology of this trip see Franco Grande and Landeira Yrago, pp. 16–20, and Benito Argüelles

40 Conversations with Lola Membrives's son, Dr Juan Reforzo Membrives, Buenos Aires, 5 May 1987

41 *OC*, II, pp. 958; conversation with Don Pedro Massa, Buenos Aires, 15 May 1987

42 *El Defensor de Granada*, 8 October 1932, p. 1; *Noticiero Granadino*, 8 October 1932, p. 1; *Ideal*, Granada, 8 October 1932, p. 4

43 *Noticiero Granadino*, 9 October 1932, p. 1; Sáenz de la Calzada, p. 166

44 *Noticiero Granadino*, 8 October 1932, p. 1; conversation with Don Eduardo Rodríguez Valdivieso, Granada, 3 June 1981; *El Defensor de Granada*, 9 October 1932, p. 1

45 Conversation with Don Arturo Sáenz de la Calzada, Madrid, 1 November 1985

46 Pérez Ferrero, 'Teatro hoy antiguo', *Heraldo de Madrid*, 26 October 1932, p. 5

47 For the poet's visit to Pontevedra, see Franco Grande and Landeira Yrago, pp. 2–22, and Landeira Yrago, *Federico García Lorca y Galicia*, pp. 98–103

48 For Lorca's visit to Lugo, see Franco Grande and Landeira Yrago, p. 22; Landeira Yrago, *Viaje al sueño del agua*, pp. 13, 23–4; *El Sol*, Madrid, 10 December 1932, p. 2

49 Conversation with Don Josep V. Foix, Barcelona, 31 October 1986

50 Díaz-Plaja (1932)

51 For full details, see Gibson, II, p. 221 and notes 123 and 124.

52 Sáenz de la Calzada, p. 166

53 On the meeting of Lorca and Hernández, see Ifach; Díez de Revenga (1979), pp. 225–30; Díez de Revenga (1981), pp. 13–14. For Hernández's letters to Lorca (the first is unknown), see Miguel Hernández

54 *E*, II, pp. 156–7

6 1933

1 Cabanellas, I, pp. 236–9; Preston, pp. 140–2; 'Medio siglo de la rebelión anarquista de Casas Viejas. Hambre, pasión y muerte', *Diario–16*, Sunday Supplement, Madrid, no. 69 (9 January 1983)

2 Cabanellas, I, pp. 236–9

3 Francisco García Lorca, p. 335

4 Conversation with Doña Amelia de la Torre, Madrid, 17 March 1987

5 J. G. Olmedilla, in *Heraldo de Madrid*, 8 March 1933, p. 5

6 Morla Lynch, p. 330; *La Voz*, Madrid, 9 March 1933, p. 3

7 Buenaventura L. Vidal in *La Nación*, Madrid, 9 March 1933, p. 7, and other Madrid newspapers for the same day

8 Melchor Fernández Almagro, in *El Sol*, Madrid, 9 March 1933, p. 8

9 The *Heraldo de Madrid* theatre page for these weeks

10 Jackson, pp. 124–5; Gibson (1980), pp. 43–56

11 Gibson, *El asesinato de García Lorca*, pp. 17, 331–6

12 *E*, II, p. 154

13 Conversation with Don José Caballero, Madrid, 27 November 1980

14 Conversation with Doña Margarita Ucelay, daughter of Pura Maórtua de Ucelay, Madrid, May 1984; *OC*, II, pp. 954–7

15 Melchor Fernández Almagro, in *El Sol*, Madrid, 6 April 1933, p. 10

16 Ruiz Silva, p. 10

17 Casares, p. 342

18 Ibid., p. 341

19 *La Gaceta Literaria*, Madrid, no. 3 (1 February 1927), p. 3, and no. 13 (1 July 1927), p. 3

20 Díez-Canedo's inscribed copy of the *Romances galegos* is in the National Library, Madrid, pressmark HA/29183.

21 Blanco-Amor (1930)

22 Telephone conversation with Don Ernesto Guerra Da Cal (in Lisbon), 5 January 1986

23 Santos Torroella (1984), p. 20, n. 9

24 *Voz de Guipúzcoa*, San Sebastián, 23 April 1933, p. 15; 26 April 1933, p. 6; *La Libertad*, Vitoria, 27 April 1933, p. 6; conversation with Dr Juan Reforzo Membrives, Buenos Aires, 5 May 1987

25 M. P. F. [Miguel Pérez Ferrero], in *Heraldo de Madrid*, 5 May 1933, p. 5; Miguel Pérez Ferrero, *Heraldo de Madrid*, 8 May 1933, p. 5; Pérez-Domenech, in *El Imparcial*, Madrid, 7 May 1933, p. 2; conversation with Don Modesto Higueras, Madrid, 31 January 1981

26 Reviews in the Barcelona press. See Gibson, II, p. 527, note 64.

27 Miguel Pérez Ferrero, *Heraldo de Madrid*, 30 May 1933, p. 6

28 *E*, II, p. 157

29 S. [Adolfo Salazar], *El Sol*, Madrid, 16 June 1933, p. 10

30 Conversation with Don Pedro Miguel González Quijano, Madrid, 11 May 1983; conversations with Don Luis Sáenz de la Calzada and other members of the Barraca, 1978–86

31 Morla Lynch, p. 351

32 Sáenz de la Calzada, pp. 187–91

33 Conversation with Don Modesto Higueras, Madrid, 31 January 1981

34 On Lorca's production of *Fuente Ovejuna*, see Byrd (1984)

35 *El Mercantil Valenciano*, 1 July 1933, p. 7

36 Conversation with Don Luis Sáenz de la Calzada, León, 31 July 1986

37 ' "La Barraca" en Albacete. "Fuenteovejuna" y "La guarda cuidadosa" en el teatro Circo', *Vanguardia. Semanario del socialismo y de la U.G.T. de Albacete*, 8 July 1933, p. 4; Luis Escobar, 'La barraquera de un "camarada". "La Barraca" ', *Diario de Albacete*, 20 July 1933, p. 1

38 Interview reproduced in *OC*, II, pp. 960–3

39 *Los Cuatro Vientos*, Madrid, June 1933, pp. 61–78

40 *OC*, II, p. 962

41 Ibid.

42 ' "Yerma" ', in the section 'Mercurio literario', *Heraldo de Madrid*, 3 August 1933, p. 7

48 *OC*, II, p. 683

44 Luengo

45 Letter from Juan Reforzo to Lorca, 4 August 1933, AFGL. For a commentary on this and the other letters sent by Reforzo to Lorca, see Hernández (1984), pp. 44–7.

46 *La Nación*, Buenos Aires, 31 July 1933, p. 10; 2 August 1933, p. 11; 3 August 1933, p. 12; 7 August 1933, p. 10; 9 August 1933, p. 9

47 Hernández (1984), p. 46

48 Letter from Juan Reforzo to Lorca, 4 August 1933, AFGL

49 Ibid.

50 For the newspaper reports of this trip, see Gibson, II, p. 530, note 132

51 *OC*, II, pp. 964–7

52 *El Cantábrico*, Santander, 9, 12, 13, 18, 20 August 1933; Valbuena Morán, pp. 7–19; Morla Lynch, pp. 364–5; Brickell (1945), pp. 395–7

53 Morla Lynch, pp. 366–7

54 Sáenz de la Calzada, pp. 142–3

55 *El Defensor de Granada*, 26 September 1933, p. 1

56 *La Nación*, Buenos Aires, 2 October 1933, p. 16

57 Morla Lynch, pp. 371–2

58 Interview with Margarita Xirgu by Valentín de Pedro in *¡Aquí Está!* Buenos Aires, 26 May 1949, quoted in Rodrigo (1975), pp. 314–15

59 AFGL

7 Argentina

1 Suero, 'Crónica de un día de barco con el autor de *Bodas de sangre*'

2 Letter, 9 October 1933, from Lorca to his parents, AFGL

3 Suero, 'Crónica de un día de barco con el autor de *Bodas de sangre*'

4 Suero, 'El autor de *Bodas de sangre* estuvo hoy en Montevideo', *El Plata*, Montevideo, 13 October 1933, p. 4

5 Suero, 'Crónica de un día de barco con el autor de *Bodas de sangre*'

6 *Noticias Gráficas*, Buenos Aires, 2 October 1933, p. 16; 13 October 1933, p. 18

7 Conversation with Doña María Molino Montero and her husband Don Antonio Alcaraz, Buenos Aires, 18 May 1987. All the leading Buenos Aires newspapers referred to Lorca's arrival.

8 Guardia (1961), p. 93

9 Villarejo, p. 33

10 OC, II, pp. 997–1000; *El Correo de Galicia*, Buenos Aires, 19 November 1933, p. 1
11 Conversation with Doña María Molino Montero, Buenos Aires, 18 May 1986
12 *Noticias Gráficas*, Buenos Aires, 14 October 1933, p. 10; *Crítica*, Buenos Aires, 14 October 1933, p. 12
13 Quoted in Villarejo, p. 69
14 Commentary on the back of a photograph sent by the poet to his parents; transcription by Agustín Penón in APP. The information concerning Lorca's meeting with Gardel from the composer Sam Molar, transmitted by Don Antonio Carrizo, Buenos Aires, May 1987
15 *La Nación*, Buenos Aires, 14 October 1933, p. 9. The interview is reproduced in OC, II, pp. 989–93, but with so many errors that the quotation is taken from the original article.
16 OC *(1986)*, III, pp. 559–60
17 Suero, 'Hablando de "La Barraca" con el poeta García Lorca'
18 Letter dated 18 October 1933, AFGL
19 González Carbalho, p. 33
20 Guardia (1961), p. 93
21 Jascalevich, p. 14
22 Suero, 'Hablando de "La Barraca" con el poeta García Lorca'; González Carbalho, p. 79
23 Undated letter in AFGL
24 *Crítica*, Buenos Aires, 14 October 1933, p. 10
25 González Carbalho, p. 34; for Amado Villar's promotion of Lorca, see *Crítica*, Buenos Aires, 14 October 1933, p. 10; for his meeting with Lorca in Madrid, Jascalevich, p. 14
26 Conversation with Don Federico de Elizalde, the son of Bebé Sansinena de Elizalde, Buenos Aires, 12 May 1987
27 *Correo de Galicia*, Buenos Aires, 22 October 1933, 2nd section, p. 1
28 Undated letter from the poet to his parents, AFGL
29 OC, I, pp. 1197–8
30 *Correo de Galicia*, Buenos Aires, 29 October 1933, p. 18
31 *Crítica*, Buenos Aires, 27 October 1933, p. 16
32 Undated letter from Lorca to his parents, AFGL
33 Conversation with Dr Juan Reforzo Membrives, Madrid, 22 February 1988
34 AFGL
35 Conversation with Doña María Molino Montero, Buenos Aires, 18 May 1986; Mora Guarnido (1958), p. 108
36 *Diario Español*, Buenos Aires, 27 October 1933, p. 2; *La Nación*, Buenos Aires, 1 November 1933, p. 4; *Diario Español*, Buenos Aires, 1 November 1933, p. 1; *La Nación*, Buenos Aires, 9 November 1933, p. 6
37 *Diario Español*, Buenos Aires, 15 November 1933, p. 5
38 AFGL
39 Undated letter from Lorca to his parents, AFGL
40 Conversation with Don Modesto Higueras, Madrid, 31 January 1981
41 For Lorca's meeting with Victoria Ocampo in Madrid, see Morla Lynch, pp. 116–17
42 Chronology in Neruda (1957)
43 Neruda (1974), p. 163; conversation with Doña María Molino Montero, Buenos Aires, 17 May 1987
44 OC, I, pp. 1226–8
45 See, for example, OC, I, pp. 1197–8
46 The drawings are reproduced in FGL, *Dibujos*, pp. 224–7
47 Neruda (1974), p. 157
48 Cambours Ocampo, pp. 136–7
49 Burgin, pp. 112–14
50 Brenan (1960), pp. 265–6
51 AFGL; the letter from Pura Maórtua de Ucelay is dated 23 October 1934.
52 OC, I, p. 1172

53 Theatre pages of the Buenos Aires press for these months
54 OC, II, p. 1007
55 Undated letter, AFGL
56 OC (1986), III, pp. 583–5
57 Novo, pp. 203–4
58 Conversation with Don Ricardo Molinari, Buenos Aires, 18 May 1987
59 Conversations with Maximino Espasande's daughter Lidia, Buenos Aires and Madrid, 1987
60 FGL, Dibujos, pp. 222–3, 228–9
61 For Lorca's projected lecture tour to the provinces, see Crítica, Buenos Aires, 17 November 1933; for the trip to Rosario, see Correas
62 Undated letter from Lorca to his parents, AFGL
63 Edmundo Guibourg, 'Calle Corrientes', Crítica, Buenos Aires, 1 March 1934, p. 11
64 Guardia (1961), pp. 84–6
65 Noticias Gráficas, Buenos Aires, 13 January 1934, p. 14; Crítica, Buenos Aires, 10 January 1934, p. 20
66 OC, II, p. 1011
67 Noticias Gráficas, Buenos Aires, 14 January 1934, p. 15; undated letter from Lorca to his parents, AFGL
68 La Prensa, Buenos Aires, 13 January 1934, p. 15
69 Noticias Gráficas, Buenos Aires, 13 January 1934
70 El Diario Español, Buenos Aires, 19 January 1934, p. 10
71 Undated letter, AFGL
72 La Nación, Buenos Aires, 21 January 1934, p. 12; La Prensa, Buenos Aires, 22 January 1934, p. 15
73 La Nación, Buenos Aires, 22 January 1934, p. 11
74 Anderson, 'García Lorca en Montevideo: una cronología provisional', p. 169
75 Ibid.
76 Undated letter, AFGL
77 Comments reproduced, without an indication of their source, on the flap of Trece de Nieve, Madrid, 2nd series, nos. 1–2, 1976
78 Conversation with Dr Juan Reforzo Membrives, Lola Membrives's son, Buenos Aires, 5 May 1987
79 Anderson, 'García Lorca en Montevideo: una cronología provisional', p. 172; conversations with Doña María Luisa Díez-Canedo de Giner de los Ríos, Nerja, 18 June 1987
80 AFGL
81 La Mañana, Montevideo, 6 February 1934; reproduced in part in García-Posada (1982), pp. 84–6, whence the quotation
82 Mora Guarnido (1958), pp. 212–13
83 AFGL
84 Salvador Dalí, Diario de un genio, pp. 177, 215; Confesiones inconfesables, pp. 40–1
85 La Nación, Buenos Aires, 16 February 1934, p. 9; La Prensa, Buenos Aires, 17 February 1934, p. 15
86 Noticias Gráficas, Buenos Aires, 5 March 1934, p. 12; Irma Córdoba interviewed by Antonio Carrizo, Buenos Aires, May 1987 (tape-recording kindly facilitated by Señor Carrizo)
87 Crítica, Buenos Aires, 2 March 1934, p. 10; La Nación, Buenos Aires, 2 March 1934, p. 13; Correo de Galicia, Buenos Aires, 4 March 1934, p. 2
88 Correo de Galicia, 10 March 1934, p. 8
89 Noticias Gráficas, Buenos Aires, 12 March 1934, p. 12
90 OC, II, pp. 1019–25
91 La Nación, Buenos Aires, 4 March 1934
92 Sáenz de la Calzada, p. 201

93 OC, I, pp. 1206–10
94 *Crítica*, Buenos Aires, 26 March 1934, p. 10
95 Conversation with Doña María Molino Montero, Buenos Aires, 18 May 1987
96 Cruz
97 *Crítica*, Buenos Aires, 27 March 1934, p. 11
98 Jascalevich, p. 85
99 *Crítica*, Buenos Aires, 29 March 1934, p. 16; 30 March 1934, p. 3
100 Theatre page of *La Nación*, Buenos Aires, for the entire period
101 OC, II, pp. 1032

8 1934

1 *La Vanguardia*, Barcelona, 12 April 1934, p. 20; *Diario de Barcelona*, 12 April 1934, p. 26; Miguel Pérez Ferrero (1934)
2 Conversations with Don Luis Sáenz de la Calzada, Madrid, 1986 and 1987
3 Jackson, p. 175; Preston, pp. 184–8
4 *El Defensor de Granada*, 22 April 1934, p. 3; Fernández
5 José Navarro Pardo in an interview with Agustín Penón, APP
6 Moreiro, p. 23
7 Zalamea
8 Eduardo Blanco-Amor, 'Evocación de Federico'; in '¡Juventud, divino tesoro!' *La Nación*, Buenos Aires, 2nd section, 15 July 1934, p. 2, Blanco-Amor referred briefly to his visit to Granada but without alluding to Lorca.
9 Conversations with Doña Clotilde García Picossi, Huerta del Tamarit, Granada, summer 1966; Auclair, p. 349
10 *Heraldo de Madrid*, 14 June 1934, p. 5
11 Conversation with Don Ernesto Guerra da Cal, Lisbon, 27 July 1986
12 OC, II, p. 1027
13 'No hay crisis teatral', *El Duende*, Madrid, 10 February 1934, p. 15
14 'La Barraca', *FE*, Madrid, 5 July 1934, p. 11
15 *El Defensor de Granada*, 22 July 1934, p. 1
16 Conversation with Don Luis Jiménez, Granada, 22 March 1987
17 Cossío, 'Sánchez Mejías', p. 880; 'Breve semblanza de Sánchez Mejías', p. 975
18 *Heraldo de Madrid*, 13 August 1934, p. 6
19 Morla Lynch, p. 400; Auclair, p; 22
20 Santainés, pp. 190–2
21 *Heraldo de Madrid*, 13 August 1934, p. 6; 14 August 1934, pp. 2 and 16
22 *El Pueblo Manchego*, Ciudad Real, 13 August 1934, p. 1; Antonio Garrigues y Díaz-Cañabate, p. 234
23 *Heraldo de Madrid*, 13 August 1934, p. 6
24 Ibid., pp. 6, 16
25 Ibid., 13 August 1934, pp. 4, 16; Bergamín, p. 73
26 *Heraldo de Madrid*, 13 August 1934, p. 16
27 Antonio Garrigues y Díaz-Cañabate, p. 24
28 Auclair, p. 30
29 OC, I, p. 558
30 Auclair, p. 24; OC, I, p. 552
31 Auclair, pp. 22–5
32 Ibid., p. 25
33 Ibid., p. 27
34 Ibid., pp. 28–9
35 Conversations with Doña Pilar López, Madrid, 1986–7
36 Papini, pp. 182–3

37 Conversation with Don Modesto Higueras, Madrid, 31 January 1981
38 OC, II, pp. 1029–31
39 Lorca's letter to Levi is reproduced in E, II, pp. 160–1.
40 'El teatro universitario. García Lorca y "La Barraca" ', El Defensor de Granada, 5 September 1934, p. 1
41 'Comida íntima. En honor de Federico García Lorca', El Defensor de Granada, 28 September 1934, p. 3; 'Retablillo', El Defensor de Granada, 30 September 1934, p. 1
42 García Gómez, pp. 139–40
43 OC, II, p. 1033
44 Conversation with Don Eduardo Rodríguez Valdivieso, Granada, 3 September 1982
45 Emilio García Gómez's introduction is reproduced in García Gómez, pp. 139–45
46 OC, I, pp. 569–98
47 Jackson, pp. 146–8
48 Ibid., pp. 148–68, passim. For the background to the October rising see also Gerald Brenan's comprehensive chapter 'The Bienio Negro' in Brenan (1960), pp. 265–97
49 Jackson, pp. 166–7. The text is reproduced in Gibson, Granada en 1936 y el asesinato de Federico García Lorca, pp. 297–9.
50 Ximénez de Sandoval, pp. 231–4; Payne, p. 67
51 Sáenz de la Calzada, p. 167
52 Morla Lynch, pp. 424–5
53 Rodrigo (1974), p. 203
54 OC, II, pp. 1032–7
55 FGL, Teatro inconcluso, p. 117; extract from a letter from Martínez Nadal to Lorca (August 1931) in Maurer, 'De la correspondencia de García Lorca', p. 76
56 Sáenz de la Calzada, pp. 156–7
57 Heraldo de Madrid, 26 December 1934, p. 4
58 Caballero (1984)
59 Salado
60 Rivas Cherif (13 January 1957), p. 4
61 Heraldo de Madrid, 31 December 1934, p. 4
62 Conversation with Don José Frank, Madrid, 14 January 1988
63 Morla Lynch, pp. 434–5; Blanco-Amor (1978), p. vi
64 Buñuel, Mon dernier soupir, p. 123
65 El Pueblo, Madrid, 31 December 1934, p. 3; Morla Lynch, pp. 434–5
66 For fuller details, see Gibson, II, pp. 336–7, and Mario Hernández (1979)
67 Gracia y Justicia, Madrid, 5 January 1935, p. 14
68 Unidentified cutting reproduced in Gibson, II, p. 338
69 El Defensor de Granada, 30 December 1934, p. 1
70 A. Bazán, in Tiempo Presente, Madrid, no. 1 (March 1935)

9 1935

1 OC, II, p. 1038
2 La Prensa, New York, 13 February 1935, p. 5; 14 February 1935, p.4; 22 February 1935, p. 5; 1 March 1935, p. 1. For the reaction of the rest of the New York press, see Mario Hernández (1984), pp. 56–62
3 OC, II, p. 1022
4 Ibid., I, p. 1214
5 FGL, Teatro inconcluso, p. 157
6 OC, II, pp. 1039–43
7 Arturo Mori in El Liberal, Madrid, 1 March 1935, p. 1
8 El Liberal, Madrid, 19 March 1935, p. 7; El Sol, Madrid, 19 March 1935, p. 2; La Voz, Madrid, 19 March 1935, p. 3

9 The number of performances has been calculated by consulting the theatre pages of *El Sol* and *Heraldo de Madrid* for these weeks.
10 Conversation with Don José Antonio Rubio Sacristán, Madrid, 21 October 1986
11 Guillén (1978), p. l.
12 Ernest Guasp, ' "Yerma" y su autor en la plaza de Cataluña', *El Mercantil Valenciano*, 22 September 1935, p. 9
13 Conversation with Don Francisco García Lorca, Nerja, summer 1966
14 Conversation with Don José Caballero, Madrid, 6 November 1980
15 Preston, pp. 257–66
16 *Ciudad*, Madrid, 3 April 1935, p. [28]; *Heraldo de Madrid*, 12 April 1935, p. 9; 27 June 1935, p. 5
17 *La Libertad*, Madrid, 11 May 1935, p. 6; *Heraldo de Madrid*, 11 May 1935, p. 2
18 Letter from Juan Guerrero Ruiz to Lorca, AFGL
19 *Heraldo de Madrid*, 24 May 1935, p 6
20 Conversations with Don José Caballero, Madrid, 6 November 1980, and Doña Maruja Mallo, Madrid, 3 March 1984
21 Neruda, 'Oda a Federico García Lorca', in *Obras completas*, pp. 223–6
22 Neruda (1971)
23 *OC*, II, pp. 1032–3
24 Ibid., p. 1038
25 Ibid., pp. 1072–3
26 *E*, I, p. 98
27 In the passport obtained for his visit to the United States and Cuba in 1929 the poet is stated to have been born on 5 June 1900 (AFGL); when in 1933 the poet registered at the Spanish Embassy in Buenos Aires he gave his age as thirty-three (document in AFGL).
28 *OC*, II, p. 1072
29 Higuera Rojas (1980), p. 189
30 *OC*, II, p. 812
31 Ortiz de Villajos, p. 130
32 Mora Guarnido (1958), p. 171
33 Francisco García Lorca, introduction to FGL, *Three Tragedies*, Harmondsworth, Penguin, 1961, p. 22
34 *OC*, I, p. 1175
35 Guillén (1959), p. lxx.
36 *Heraldo de Madrid*, 21 June 1935, p. 7
37 Blanco-Amor, 'Apostillas a una barbaridad'
38 Pérez Coterillo, 'En Galicia con E. Blanco-Amor', p. 18
39 Ibid., pp. 17–18
40 The account was kindly transmitted to me by José Navarro Pardo's daughter, Señora de Benito Jaramillo, Madrid, 7 November 1984
41 Conversation with Don Fernando Nestares, Madrid, 12 January 1988
42 Conversation with Don Eduardo Rodríguez Valdivieso, Granada, 30 July 1980
43 Conversation with Don Luis Rosales, Madrid, 16 January 1979
44 Gibson, 'Con Dalí y Lorca en Figueres'
45 'Tópicos', *Heraldo de Madrid*, 16 July 1935, p. 8; 'Margarita Xirgu irá a Italia para rendir un homenaje a Lope de Vega', *Heraldo de Madrid*, 19 July 1935, p. 8
46 Valentín de Pedro, 'El destino mágico de Margarita Xirgu', *¡Aquí Está!*, Buenos Aires, 26 June 1949, quoted in Rodrigo (1975), pp. 358–61
47 *OC (1986)*, II, p. 1069
48 Ibid., p. 1081
49 Ibid., p. 664
50 Martínez Nadal (1974), p. 78
51 *OC (1986)*, II, p. 1093

52 Suero (1943), pp. 181–4
53 Letter from FGL to Miguel Benítez Inglott, *E*, II, pp. 164–5
54 *OC*, II, pp. 1049–53
55 Ibid., p. 1057
56 Sáenz de la Calzada, pp. 157–8; conversations with Don Luis Sáenz de la Calzada, Madrid, 1986–7
57 *Heraldo de Madrid*, 24 August 1935, p. 8; 26 August 1935, p. 8; Rivas Cherif, 'Poesía y drama del gran Federico' (6 January 1957), pp. 1 and 4
58 Vázquez Ocaña, p. 338
59 *Heraldo de Madrid*, 28 August 1935, p. 8; 29 August 1935, p. 9; 1 September 1935, p. 8; *El Sol*, Madrid, 8 September 1935, p. 2; 11 September 1935, p. 2

10 Barcelona

1 *La Publicitat*, Barcelona, 8 September 1935, p. 10; 11 September 1935, p. 6; *La Vanguardia*, Barcelona, 12 September 1935, p. 9
2 *La Publicitat*, Barcelona, 15 September 1935, p. 6; *El Diluvio*, Barcelona, 15 September 1935, p. 10
3 Domènec Guansé, in *La Publicitat*, Barcelona, 19 September 1935, p. 6
4 For a more detailed account of the press reaction to *Yerma* in Barcelona, see Gibson II, pp. 378–80
5 Theatre pages of *La Publicitat* and *La Vanguardia* for this period
6 'Federico García Lorca parla per als obrers catalans', *L'Hora*, Palma de Mallorca, 27 September 1935, p. 1; reprinted in Cobb, pp. 281–6
7 Santos Torroella (1987), p. 96
8 Tape-recorded conversation with Don Rafael Alberti, Madrid, 4 October 1980
9 *La Humanitat*, Barcelona, 1 October 1935, p. 1
10 *OC*, II, pp. 1067–9
11 Santos Torroella (1984), p. 106
12 Don Josep Palau i Fabre was interviewed on my behalf by Samuel Abrams, Barcelona, 7 April 1987. My sincere thanks to both.
13 Salvador Dalí (1954); also included in Salvador Dalí (1964), pp. 81–7
14 Ibid.; James
15 Salvador Dalí (1954)
16 Conversation with Doña Amelia de la Torre, Madrid, 3 April 1987
17 Gibson, 'Con Dalí y Lorca en Figueres'
18 *Heraldo de Madrid*, 5 October 1935, 9; *El Día Gráfico*, Barcelona, 12 October 1935, p. 17
19 *OC* (1986), III, pp. 634–6
20 First published by Rivas Cherif, 'Poesía y drama del gran Federico', 27 January 1957, p. 3; there is another photograph, dedicated by Lorca to Guasp, in Rodrigo (1975), p. 359
21 *La Publicitat*, Barcelona, 24 October 1935, p. 1; *Diario de Madrid*, 24 October 1935, p. 7; *Diario de Tarragona*, 25 October 1935, p. 1
22 Jackson, pp. 176–7
23 The document is reproduced in Gibson, *Granada en 1936 y el asesinato de Federico García Lorca*, pp. 300–301
24 *El Mercantil Valenciano*, 30 October 1935, p. 4; 6 November 1935, p. 7; 9 November 1935, p. 9
25 Ibid., 10 November 1935, p. 4
26 Luengo
27 Rivas Cherif, 'Poesía y drama del gran Federico', 27 January 1957, p. 3
28 Nicolas Barquet, 'Lorca à Barcelone', *Opéra. Le Journal de la vie parisienne*, Paris, 9 January 1952. Not seen. The article is quoted in Rodrigo (1975), pp. 398–9
29 FGL, *Teatro inconcluso*, p. 344

30 Conversation with Don Mauricio Torra-Balari, Barcelona, 22 January 1987
31 The originals of the sonnets are in AFGL.
32 Gil-Albert, pp. 244–51; conversation with Don Juan Gil-Albert, Valencia, 12 July 1987
33 OC, II, p. xi
34 The sonnets were published in ABC, Madrid, 17 March 1984 and subsequently incorporated into OC (1986), I, pp. 937–49
35 Tape-recorded conversation with Don Vicente Aleixandre, Madrid, 26 April 1982
36 Salvador Dalí, Diario de un genio, p. 24
37 OC (1986), I, pp. 942–3; 'Soneto gongorino', p. 946
38 Rivas Cherif, 'Poesía y drama del gran Federico', 13 January 1957, p. 4; 27 January 1957, p. 3
39 Ibid., 27 January 1957, p. 3
40 FGL, Teatro inconcluso, pp. 220–7
41 Ibid., pp. 344–5
42 Sáenz de la Calzada, p. 189
43 OC, II, pp. 1070–1; La Vanguardia, Barcelona, 22 November 1935, p. 4
44 G.T.B. [G. Trillas Blázquez], in Crónica, Madrid, 22 December 1935
45 La Vanguardia, Barcelona, 14 December 1935, p. 9
46 La Publicitat, 14 December 1935, p. 9
47 Heraldo de Madrid, 13 December 1935, p. 8
48 La Libertad, Madrid, 19 December 1935, pp. 1–2
49 Moreno Villa (1944), p. 121
50 Morales
51 Luis Góngora, in La Noche, Barcelona, 21 December 1935, p. 2; see also L'Instant, Barcelona, 20 December 1935, p. 6.
52 OC, I, p. 1218
53 Ibid., II, pp. 1074–5
54 Heraldo de Madrid and El Sol, Madrid, passim, for these weeks
55 Ibid.
56 G.T.B. [G. Trillas Blázquez], 'Hablando con Margarita Xirgu, que se va a América y recuerda su vida', Crónica, Madrid, 22 December 1935; OC, II, p. 1075
57 Rivas Cherif, 'Poesía y pasión del gran Federico', 27 January 1957, p. 3
58 L'Instant, Barcelona, 24 December 1935, p. 6
59 Computation derived from the theatre pages of the Barcelona press for these three months

11 Last Months in Madrid

1 Jackson, pp. 185–7
2 Suero, 'Los últimos días con Federico García Lorca. El hogar del poeta'
3 At the end of Landeira Yrago, Viaje al sueño del agua, is included a facsimile edition of the Seis poemas galegos, with Blanco-Amor's prologue.
4 Fernández del Riego, pp. 106–7; Landeira Yrago, Viaje al sueño del agua, p. 58
5 Otero Seco (1937)
6 Heraldo de Madrid, 15 January 1936, p. 9; El Heraldo de Aragón, Saragossa, 21 January 1936, p. 2; the account of Pura Maórtua's reaction was given to me by her daughter, Doña Margarita Ucelay, Madrid, 4 February 1987
7 Heraldo de Madrid, 17 March 1936, p. 9; 9 July 1936, p. 9
8 El Liberal, Bilbao, 28 January 1936, p. 1; ibid., 29 January 1936, p. 10
9 Ibid., 28 January 1936, p. 10; 30 January 1936, p. 12
10 Valentín de Pedro, ¡Aquí Está!, Buenos Aires, 30 April 1949, quoted in Rodrigo (1974), p. 234
11 El Cantábrico, Santander, 1 February 1936, p. 7
12 OC, I, p. 811

13 Gibson, *Granada en 1936*, pp. 26–8
14 'Sección de rumores', *Heraldo de Madrid*, 12 February 1936, p. 9
15 *Heraldo de Madrid*, 29 May 1936, p. 9
16 Suero, 'Los últimos días con Federico García Lorca. El hogar del poeta'
17 Gibson, *Granada en 1936*, pp. 26–7
18 Agustí, p. 94
19 *Diario de la Marina*, Havana, 16 February 1936, p. 6; 18 February, p. 6; 7 March 1936, p. 3, and throughout March and April
20 Brenan (1960), p. 298; *Heraldo de Madrid* for these days
21 Southworth, p. 9
22 *Heraldo de Madrid*, 14 March 1936, p. 16; 18 March 1936, p. 3
23 Jackson, p. 207
24 Gibson, *Granada en 1936*, pp. 29–30, 305–8
25 Ibid., p. 29
26 Ibid., pp. 32, 310
27 *OC*, I, pp. 971–4
28 Ibid., II, p. 1079
29 *La Voz*, Madrid, 23 June 1936; *Heraldo de Madrid*, 1 July 1936, p. 9
30 *OC*, II, pp. 1079–80
31 Ibid., p. 1080
32 *Excelsior*, Mexico, April–June 1936, *passim*
33 Ibid., 18 May 1936, pp. 5, 8
34 *OC*, I, pp. 1231–3
35 Emilio Garrigues y Díaz-Cañabate, pp. 106–7
36 *La Vanguardia*, Barcelona, 15 April 1936, p. 7
37 Telephone conversation with Don Luis Sáenz de la Calzada (in León), 31 January 1987; conversation with Doña María del Carmen García Lasgoity, Madrid, 1 February 1987
38 Santos Torroella (1987), p. 97
39 See, for example, Salvador Dalí (1944), p. xiii
40 *¡Ayuda!*, Madrid, 1 May 1936, p. 1
41 Information from Carlos Gurméndez, quoted by Santa Cecilia, p. xi
42 *Heraldo de Madrid*, 9 May 1936, p. 16; Ximénez de Sandoval, p. 548; Gibson, *La noche en que mataron a Calvo Sotelo*, pp. 60–1
43 *El Socialista*, Madrid, 9 May 1936
44 *La Libertad*, Madrid, 10 May 1936, pp. 5–6
45 Jackson, pp. 203–6
46 *Heraldo de Madrid*, 29 May 1936, p. 9
47 Gregorio Prieto, p. 29
48 Aurelia González García married José Giménez Fernández in Fuente Vaqueros parish church on 2 April 1909. According to the entry in the Fuente Vaqueros marriage register (kept in the town hall), she was twenty-four, he twenty-eight. I have been unable to trace her birth certificate in Fuente Vaqueros, despite a careful search and the fact that her daughter has assured me that she was born there. It is something of a mystery. Aurelia died in Granada in 1964.
49 AFGL
50 Altolaguirre (1937), p. 36
51 Guillermo de Torre, 'Indicación de fuentes', at the end of his edition of FGL, *La casa de Bernarda Alba*, Buenos Aires, Losada, 4th ed., 1957, p. 182
52 Adolfo Salazar, '*La casa de Bernarda Alba*', p. 30
53 Manuscript of the play, AFGL
54 Morla Lynch, p. 484
55 Manuscript of the play, AFGL
56 The inscription on Francisca Alba's tomb in Valderrubio (Asquerosa) Cemetery states that

she died on 22 July 1924 at the age of sixty-six; information about her children from neighbours in the village and from a letter by a relative of the family, Antonio Rodríguez Roldán, published in *Ideal*, Granada, 4 October 1986, p. 2

57 The marriage is entered in the Pinos Puente municipal register. The inscription on Rodríguez Capilla's tomb in Valderrubio Cemetery states that he died on 23 December 1925 at the age of seventy-four. For the children of this marriage, see note 56 above.

58 See Mercedes Delgado García's account in Higuera Rojas (1980), pp. 187–9; also Ramos Espejo (1981), p. 61

59 Conversation with Don José Arco Arroyo, Valderrubio, 17 August 1986

60 Ramos Espejo (1981), p. 62

61 Francisco García Lorca, pp. 377–8

62 Ramos Espejo (1981), p. 63

63 Rodrigo (1980), p. 4; Ramos Espejo (1981), p. 60

64 Rodrigo (1980), p. 4

65 *OC*, II, p. 843

66 Ibid., pp. 925–6

67 Suero, 'Crónica de un día de barco con el autor de *Bodas de sangre*'

68 Miguel Rosales Camacho, the brother of Luis Rosales, told me in 1966 that he had heard many people expressing an unfavourable opinion of Lorca as a result of the interview.

69 *OC*, II, pp. 1082–7

70 *E*, II, pp. 170–1

71 Conversation with Don Fulgencio Díez Pastor, Madrid, 11 June 1980

72 Conversation with Don José Luis Cano, Madrid, 9 May 1979

73 Letter from the poet Juan Larrea to Mario Hernández, 10 February 1968

74 *Heraldo de Madrid*, 22 June 1936, p. 2; 29 June 1936, p. 9

75 Conversation with Don José Amorós, Madrid, 24 January 1986

76 Conversation with Don José Caballero, Madrid, 15 February 1987

77 'Por primera vez se traduce Novalis al castellano', *Heraldo de Madrid*, 16 July 1936, p. 13; Gebser, pp. 14–16

78 For a particularly hostile view of Casares Quiroga from the point of view of a militant socialist politician, see Largo Caballero, 157–8

79 Morla Lynch, pp. 491–2

80 Jackson, pp. 220–21; account given by José Caballero to Marcelle Auclair, in Auclair, p. 367

81 *La Libertad*, Madrid, 12 July 1936, p. 3; *Heraldo de Madrid*, 13 July 1936, p. 2

82 Account by Fulgencio Díez Pastor in Auclair, pp. 368–9; conversation with Don Fulgencio Díez Pastor, Madrid, 10 October 1978

83 Auclair, p. 369

84 Buñuel, *Mon dernier soupir*, p. 193

85 Gibson, *La noche en que mataron a Calvo Sotelo*, passim

86 Alonso (1978), pp. 160–1

87 Alonso (1982), p. 13

88 Gil-Albert, p. 250

89 Rodríguez Espinosa, p. 110; it has not been possible to confirm the date.

90 Conversations with Doña Isabel García Lorca and Doña Laura de los Ríos, Madrid, September 1978

91 Martínez Nadal, 'Lorca's Last Day in Madrid'

92 Martínez Nadal (1963)

93 Conversation with Don Luis Sáenz de la Calzada, Madrid, 31 January 1987; with Don Arturo del Hoyo, Madrid, 6 Febuary 1987

94 Cernuda (1975), p. 1337

95 Part of the letter, dated 15 July 1936, is reproduced in Marío Hernández, introduction to Francisco García Lorca, p. xxvi

12 The Death of a Poet

1 Gibson, *Granada en 1936*, pp. 57–9
2 Ibid., pp. 56–7
3 Ibid., p. 67
4 Ibid.
5 Ibid., pp. 59–61
6 Conversation with Lorca's cousin Doña Isabel Roldán García, Chinchón (Madrid), 1 February 1982, who remembered distinctly that there was a telephone in the Huerta. The poet's sister has stated that this was installed just before the war (conversation with Doña Isabel García Lorca, Madrid, 23 June 1984).
7 'Carnet mundano', *Ideal*, Granada, 16 July 1936, p. 6; *Noticiero Granadino*, 17 July 1936, p. 1
8 Conversation with Don Miguel Cerón, Granada, 1966
9 Conversation with Don José Fernández Castro, Granada, 11 February 1987
10 Conversation with Don Miguel Rosales, Granada, 1966
11 Gibson, *Granada en 1936*, p. 155; Gibson, *Queipo de Llano, passim*
12 Gibson, *Granada en 1936*, pp. 70–81; Franco's statement was made to Jay Allen and reported by the latter in the *News Chronicle*, London, 29 July 1936; Martínez Barrio, pp. 358–9
13 Martínez Barrio, pp. 360–1
14 Gibson, *Granada en 1936*, pp. 79–80
15 Ibid., pp. 80–95
16 Ibid., pp. 96–118
17 The information about Lorca's visit to the gaol was given to me by Doña Aurora de la Cuesta de Garrido, who lived in the Huerta de la Virgencica, near that of San Vicente, and was a close friend of the family. She received a detailed account of the poet's return home after his shattering experience at the gaol from the García Lorcas' servant, Angelina Cordobilla. Conversation with Doña Aurora de la Cuesta, Granada, 8 August 1987
18 Date and details from Luis Rosales's exculpatory document of 17 August 1987, reproduced by Molina Fajardo (1983), p. 347
19 Conversation with Don Alfredo Rodríguez Orgaz, Madrid, 9 October 1978
20 Gibson, *Granada en 1936*, pp. 158–62; subsequent research by the author in Valderrubio (previously Asquerosa), summer 1986; see, too, Luis Rosales's exculpatory document of 17 August 1936, in Molina Fajardo (1983), p. 347.
21 Gibson, *Granada en 1936*, pp. 158–62; conversation with Doña Carmen Perea, the sister of Gabriel, who witnessed the events at the Huerta, Valderrubio, 22 August 1980
22 Tape-recorded conversation with Don Luis Rosales, Cercedilla (Madrid), 2 September 1966, and subsequent conversations in Madrid
23 Tape-recorded conversation with Don Luis Rosales, Cercedilla (Madrid), 2 September 1966
24 Higuera Rojas, 'Habla el chófer de García Lorca'
25 Gibson, *Granada en 1936*, p. 172
26 Ibid., p. 175
27 Ibid., p. 176
28 Ibid., p. 173
29 Ibid., pp. 177–9; conversation with Don Manuel López Banús, Fuengirola, 8 December 1979
30 Gibson, *Granada en 1936*, pp. 229–30
31 Ibid., p. 180
32 Ibid., p. 179
33 Ibid., p. 181

34 Ibid.
35 Ibid., pp. 112–13
36 Ibid., pp. 179–80
37 The details of this visit are taken from Luis Rosales's exculpatory document, in Molina Fajardo (1983), p. 347.
38 Gibson, *Granada en 1936*, pp. 183–5. Account given by Doña Esperanza Rosales to Agustín Penón, Madrid, 2 July 1956, and transcribed in the latter's diary (APP), confirmed in conversation with Doña Esperanza, Madrid, 7 November 1978
39 Conversation with Don Antonio Jiménez Blanco, a witness to the arrival of the group at Miguel Rosales's house looking for Lorca, Madrid, 24 March 1986; almost exactly the same account had been given to me independently a year earlier by Don José Mercado Ureña, Malaga, 4 June 1985. Miguel Rosales lived at 2 Calle de Lucena, only a few hundred yards away from Calle de Angulo.
40 Gibson, *Granada en 1936*, pp. 183–5
41 Ibid., pp. 132–52; conversation in Fuente Vaqueros (December 1986) with Don José Martín Jiménez, who was present at Ruiz Alonso's meeting in the village
42 Ruiz Alonso, pp. 249–50
43 Gibson, *Granada en 1936*, pp. 151–2
44 Ibid., p. 192
45 Ibid., pp. 191–2; conversation with Doña Esperanza Rosales, Madrid, 7 November 1978
46 Gibson, *Granada en 1936*, p. 192
47 Ibid., pp. 193–4
48 Ibid., p. 194
49 Account given by Luis Rosales to Agustín Penón, Madrid, 30 May 1956 and transcribed by Penón in his diary (APP)
50 Gibson, *Granada en 1936*, p. 194
51 Conversation with the witness, Don Miguel López Escribano, Granada, 29 September 1980
52 Conversations with Don Miguel Rosales, Granada, 1965–6
53 Ibid.
54 Ibid.
55 Ibid.
56 Tape-recorded conversation with Don Luis Rosales, Cercedilla (Madrid), 2 September 1966
57 Tape-recorded conversation with Don Ramón Ruiz Alonso, Madrid, 3 April 1967
58 Conversation with Don Cecilio Cirre, Granada, September 1966
59 Tape-recorded conversation with Don Luis Rosales, Cercedilla (Madrid), 2 September 1966
60 Tape-recorded conversation with Don José Rosales, Granada, 26 August 1978
61 Vila-San-Juan, pp. 190–3
62 Ibid., pp. 150–2
63 Gibson, *Granada en 1936*, pp. 199–200
64 Molina Fajardo (1983), p. 347
65 Conversation with Doña Esperanza Rosales, Madrid, 7 November 1978
66 Vila-San-Juan, p. 152; tape-recorded conversation with Don José Rosales, Granada, 26 August 1978
67 Agustín Penón interviewed Angelina Cordobilla González at El Padul, Granada, in 1956 (diary in APP); the quotation is from my tape-recorded conversations with her that took place in Granada in the summer of 1966, in the presence of her daughter.
68 Conversation with Doña Angelina Cordobilla González, Granada, summer 1966
69 Gibson, *Granada en 1936*, pp. 204–8
70 Ibid., p. 208

71 Conversations with Don Antonio Galindo Monge, son of Dióscoro Galindo González, Madrid, 1977–8; Gibson, *Granada en 1936*, pp. 215–17

72 Tape-recorded interview with Don Ricardo Rodríguez Jiménez, Granada, 28 July 1980

73 Angelina Cordobilla González, interviewed by Agustín Penón, El Padul (Granada), 1956 (diary in APP)

74 Conversations with Don Antonio Galindo Monge, 1977–8; Gibson, *Granada en 1936*, pp. 215–17

75 This account of the functioning of the 'Colonia' derives mainly from many conversations in Granada (1965–6) with a survivor of those days, Don Antonio Mendoza Lafuente, a mason who worked as a gravedigger in Víznar.

76 Agustín Penón interviewed Jover Tripaldi repeatedly in Granada in 1955, as his diary shows (APP); Señor Jover Tripaldi confirmed these details in my conversation with him, Granada, 13 April 1984

77 Gibson, *Granada en 1936*, p. 214

78 Brenan (1950), p. 145

79 Communication from The Royal Observatory, Greenwich, 29 October 1986. My special thanks to Professor Anthony Watson.

80 Richard Ford, *A Handbook for Travellers in Spain*, London, John Murray, 1869, p. 372. (This reference to Aindamar is not contained in earlier editions of the work.)

81 I am most grateful to my friend the Arabist Dr James Dickie for his researches on my behalf concerning Ainadamar. The translation of this poem is his. His renderings of other Arabic texts relating to Ainadamar may be found in Gibson, *The Assassination of Federico García Lorca*, Appendix D, pp. 230–2

82 Conversations with Don Manuel Castilla Blanco, Alfacar and Granada, 1966

83 The first source is Lorca's friend from the *Rinconcillo*, José Navarro Pardo, who left an account (as yet unpublished) of Lorca's death, based on information received from the person who drove the poet to Víznar. According to this, Lorca said that he was a Catholic, asked for a priest, was not killed outright and had to be finished off by a *coup de grâce* (details from Navarro Pardo's daughter, Señora de Benito Jaramillo, Madrid, 7 November 1984); the second source is a Falangist called Cuesta who claimed, shortly after the poet's death, that he had participated in the execution and that, after the salvo, Lorca had given them a 'fright' by getting to his knees crying 'I'm still alive!' They gave him a *coup de grâce* (information from Don Manuel López Banús, who received this account from Cuesta during the war, Fuengirola, 29 January 1988)

84 Gibson, *Granada en 1936*, pp. 239–40

85 Ibid., pp. 223–4

86 Eye-witness account given to the author by Doña Angelina Cordobilla González, Granada, 1966, and confirmed by Lorca's cousin Doña Isabel Roldán García (Chinchón, 22 September 1978). Don Manuel Marín Forero told me that Federico García Rodriguez showed him the note in Granada before the family went into exile in New York (Madrid, 26 September 1978).

87 Gibson, *Granada en 1936*, Appendix 2, pp. 314–17

88 First-hand information from Doña Angela Barrios, the daughter of the guitarist, who accompanied her father on that lugubrious occasion (conversation with Doña Angela Barrios, Madrid, 17 September 1983)

89 Gibson, *Granada en 1936*, pp. 245–55

90 See, for example *The Times*, London, 12, 14, 23 September and 5 October 1936

91 Gibson, *Granada en 1936*, pp. 257–8

92 Thanks to the kindness of my friend William Layton I have been able to consult the photograph of the document preserved among the papers of Agustín Penón (APP). The original has probably been destroyed or lost

Afterword

1 León, p. 214
2 Rivas Cherif, 'Poesía y drama del gran Federico', 27 January 1957, col. 3
3 Details from a written account kindly supplied by Don Paulino García Toraño, who fought at Rapún's side
4 I am grateful to Don Tomás Rodríguez Rapún for a photocopy of his brother's death certificate

Bibliography

Works by Federico García Lorca

Alocuciones argentinas, Madrid, Fundación Federico García Lorca, 1986

Autógrafos. I. Facsímiles de ochenta y siete poemas y tres prosas, Prólogo, transcripción y notas de Rafael Martínez Nadal, Oxford, The Dolphin Book Co. Ltd, 1975

Autógrafos. II. 'El público'. Facsímil del manuscrito, Prólogo, versión depurada y transcripción por Rafael Martínez Nadal, Oxford, The Dolphin Book Co. Ltd, 1976

Autógrafos. III. Facsímil de 'Así que pasen cinco años', Transcripción, notas y estudio por Rafael Martínez Nadal, Oxford, The Dolphin Book Co. Ltd, 1979

Cartas a sus amigos, Prólogo de Sebastián Gasch, Barcelona, Ediciones Cobalto, 1950

Cartas, postales, poemas y dibujos, Edición, introducción y notas por Antonio Gallego Morell, Madrid, Moneda y Crédito, 1968

Conferencias, Introducción, edición y notas de Christopher Maurer, 2 vols., Madrid, Alianza, 1984

Dibujos, catálogo, proyecto y catalogación de Mario Hernández, Madrid, Ministerio de la Cultura, Fundación para el Apoyo a la Cultura, etc., 1986

Epistolario [E]. Introducción, edición y notas de Christopher Maurer, 2 vols., Madrid, Alianza, 1983

Federico García Lorca escribe a su familia desde Nueva York y La Habana [1919–30], [*FGLNY*], Edición de Christopher Maurer, *Poesía. Revista ilustrada de información poética*, Madrid, nos. 23–4, 1986

'Mi pueblo' [1916–17]. Manuscript in Fundación Federico García Lorca, Madrid

Obras completas [OC]. Recopilación, cronología, bibliografía y notas de Arturo del Hoyo, 2 vols., Madrid, Aguilar, 20th ed., 1978

Obras completas [OC (1986)]. Recopilación, cronología, bibliografía y notas de Arturo del Hoyo, 3 vols., Madrid, Aguilar, 22nd ed., ('Edición del cincuentenario'), 1986

Poesía, edición de Miguel García-Posada, 2 vols., Madrid, Akal, 1982

Poeta en Nueva York. Tierra y luna, Edición crítica de Eutimio Martín, Barcelona, Ariel, 1981

El público y Comedia sin título. Dos obras teatrales póstumas, Introducción, transcripción y versión depurada de R. Martínez Nadal y Marie Laffranque, Barcelona, Seix Barral, 1978

Songs, translated by Philip Cummings, with the assistance of Federico García Lorca, edited by Daniel Eisenberg, Pittsburgh, Duquesne University Press, 1976

Suites, edición de André Belamich, Barcelona, Ariel, 1983

Teatro inconcluso. Fragmentos y proyectos inacabados, Estudio y notas de Marie Laffranque, Universidad de Granada, 1987

Trip to the Moon. A Filmscript, translated by Bernice C. Duncan, introductory note by Richard Diers, *New Directions*, Norfolk, Conneticut, vol. 18 (1964), pp. 33–41

Viaje a la luna (guión cinematográfico), edición e introducción de Marie Laffranque, Loubressac, Braad Editions, 1980

Articles, Books and Other References

ABRIL, Manuel, [no title; on the theatre of Martínez Sierra], in Martínez Sierra (1925)

ADAMS, Mildred, *García Lorca: Playwright and Poet*, New York, George Braziller, 1977

AGRAZ, Antonio, 'El Teatro Universitario. La primera salida y lo que hará, según García Lorca, en su próxima campaña. La experiencia de la excursión: Cervantes y Calderón no están anticuados y sus obras son jubilosamente recibidas por todo el público sano', *Heraldo de Madrid*, 25 July 1932, p. 5

AGUSTÍ, Ignacio, *Ganas de hablar*, Barcelona, Planeta, 1974

ALBERTI, Rafael, *Sobre los ángeles*, Madrid, Compañía Ibero-Americana de Publicaciones, 1929

– 'Encuentro en la Nueva España con Bernal Díaz del Castillo', *El Sol*, Madrid, 15 March 1936, p. 5

– *Imagen primera de* . . . Barcelona, Losada, 1945

– *La arboleda perdida. Libros I y II de memorias*, Buenos Aires, Fabril Editora, 1959

– *Teatro*, Buenos Aires, Losada, 3rd ed., 1959

– 'De las hojas que faltan', *El País*, Madrid, 29 September 1985, p. 13

ALEIXANDRE, Vicente, 'Federico', *OC*, II, pp. ix–xi

– ' "Héroe" ', introduction to the facsimile of the magazine *Héroe*, Vaduz, Liechtenstein, Topos Verlag, 1977, pp. vii–xii

– *Epistolario*, selección, prólogo y notas de José Luis Cano, Madrid, Alianza, 1986

Almanaque Bailly-Baillière, o sea Pequeña enciclopedia popular de la vida práctica, Madrid, Bailly-Baillière, 1936

ALONSO, Dámaso, 'Federico García Lorca y la expresión de lo español' [1937], in *Poetas españoles contemporáneos*, Madrid, Gredos, 3rd ed., 1978, pp. 257–65

– 'Una generación poética (1920–1936)' [1948], ibid., pp. 155–77

– *La poesía de San Juan de la Cruz (desde esta ladera)*, Madrid, Aguilar, 4th ed., 1966

– 'Federico en mi recuerdo', in García Lorca, *Llanto por Ignacio Sánchez Mejías*, facsimile edition of the original manuscript, Institución Cultural de Cantabria/Diputación Regional de Cantabria, 1982, pp. 7–13

ALTOLAGUIRRE, Manuel, 'Nuestro teatro', *Hora de España*, Valencia, no. IX (September 1937), pp. 27–37

– *Obras completas*, critical edition by James Warrender, Madrid, Ediciones Istmo, 1986

ALVAREZ CIENFUEGOS, Alberto, 'El *Romancero gitano* de Federico García Lorca', *El Defensor de Granada*, 8, 11, 15 September 1928

ALVAREZ DE MIRANDA, Angel, *La metáfora y el mito*, Madrid, Taurus ('Cuadernos Taurus'), 1963

ANDERSON, Andrew, 'García Lorca en Montevideo: un testimonio desconocido y más evidencia sobre la evolución de "Poeta en Nueva York" ', *Bulletin Hispanique*, Bordeaux, lxxxiii (1981), pp. 145–61

– 'García Lorca at Vassar College. Two Unpublished Letters', *García Lorca Review*, New York, xi (1983), pp. 100–109

– 'Una amistad inglesa de García Lorca', *Insula*, Madrid, no. 462 (1985), pp. 3–4

– 'García Lorca en Montevideo: una cronología provisional', *Bulletin Hispanique*, Bordeaux, lxxxvii (1985), pp. 167–79

[Anonymous], ' "La Barraca" en Burgo de Osma. El teatro universitario que creara D. Fernando de los Ríos', *Luz*, Madrid, 12 July 1932

[Anonymous], 'El ensayo de "La Barraca" estudiantil. En busca del teatro español', *Luz*, Madrid, 25 July 1932, p. 9

[Anonymous], *Extracto de la memoria del Teatro Universitario 'La Barraca'*, pamphlet published by the Unión Federal de Estudiantes Hispanos in 1933, facsimile reproduction in SÁENZ DE LA CALZADA, between pp. 42 and 43

[Anonymous], *El poeta en La Habana. Federico García Lorca, 1898–1936, see* QUEVEDO

APPERLEY, G. O. W., *G. O. W. Apperley (1884–1960). Oleos y acuarelas*, Madrid, Galería Heller, 1984

ARAGON, Louis, 'Fragments d'une conférence', *La Révolution surréaliste*, Paris, 15 July 1929, pp. 23–5

ARANDA, J. F., *Luis Buñuel. Biografía crítica*, Barcelona, Lumen, 2nd ed., 1975

ARCINIEGAS, Germán, 'Federico García Lorca', *Diario de la Marina*, Havana, 1 April 1979, p. 16

ARCONADA, César M., 'En la Residencia de Estudiantes. Mujeres, árboles y poetas', *La Gaceta Literaria*, Madrid, 15 August 1928, p. 2

ARRARÁS, Joaquín, *Historia de la Segunda República Española*, 4 vols., Madrid, Editora Nacional, 5th ed., 1968–70

AUB, Max, *Conversaciones con Buñuel, seguidas de 45 entrevistas con familiares, amigos y colaboradores del cineasta aragonés*, Madrid, Aguilar, 1985

AUCLAIR, Marcelle, *Enfances et mort de Garcia Lorca*, Paris, Seuil, 1968

AZCOAGA, Enrique, ' "La Barraca" de Federico García Lorca', *Tiempo de historia*, Madrid, I, no. 5 (April 1975), pp. 56–69

BAEDEKER, Karl, *Spain and Portugal. Handbook for Travellers*, Leipzig, Karl Baedeker, 2nd ed., 1901

BAEZA, Ricardo, 'Marginalia. De una generación y su poeta', *El Sol*, Madrid, 21 August 1927, p. 1

– 'Marginalia. Los *Romances gitanos* de Federico García Lorca', *El Sol*, Madrid, 29 July 1928, p. 2

– 'Marginalia. Poesía y gitanismo', *El Sol*, Madrid, 3 August 1928, p. 1

BAL Y GAY, Jesús, 'Tambor y pregón de "La Barraca" ', *El Pueblo Gallego*, Vigo, 26 August 1932, p. 12

– 'La música en la Residencia', *Residencia*, Mexico, commemorative issue, December 1963, pp. 77–80

BELAMICH, André, introduction ('Envergure de Lorca') and notes to FGL, *Oeuvres complètes*, Paris, Gallimard (Bibliothèque de la Pléiade), 1981

– *Lorca*, Paris, Gallimard, 1983

BENITO ARGÜELLES, Juan, 'Itinerario asturiano de "La Barraca" ', *Los Cuadernos de Asturias*, Oviedo, III, no. 15 (1982), pp. 88–91

BENTLEY, Eric, 'El poeta en Dublín (García Lorca)', *Asomante*, Puerto Rico, 1953, pp. 44–58

BERGAMÍN, José, 'Muerte perezosa y larga', in *La música callada del toreo*, Madrid, Ediciones Turner, 1981, pp. 71–81

BEURDSLEY, Cecile, *L'Amour Bleu*, translated by Michael Taylor, New York, Rizzoli, 1978

BIANCHI ROSS, Ciro, 'Federico en Cuba', *Cuba Internacional*, Havana, no. 9 (1980), pp. 24–31

– 'Federico García Lorca. Su último día en La Habana', *Cuba Internacional*, Havana, no. 200 (July 1986), pp. 58–61

BINDING, Paul, *Lorca. The Gay Imagination*, London, GMP Publishers, 1985

BLANCO-AMOR, Eduardo, 'Guía para un estudio integral del renacimiento gallego', lecture given in Montevideo on 17 March 1928 and published as a pamphlet by the city's Centro Gallego

– *Romances galegos*, Buenos Aires, Editorial Céltiga, 1928

– 'Cateo y denuncia de un posible arte gallego', lecture given on 30 November 1929 to the Centro Gallego of Montevideo; Montevideo, Centro Gallego, 1930

– 'Apostillas a una barbaridad', *El Defensor de Granada*, 7 July 1935, p. 1

– 'Nueva obra teatral de García Lorca', *La Nación*, Buenos Aires, 24 November 1935, p. 3

– prologue to FGL, *Seis poemas galegos*, Santiago de Compostela, Editorial 'Nós', 1935

– 'Los poemas gallegos de Federico García Lorca', *Insula*, Madrid, nos. 151–3 (1959), p. 9

[–] Carlos Casares, 'Leria con Eduardo Blanco-Amor', *Grial*, Vigo, no. 4 (1973), pp. 337–44

[–] Moisés Pérez Coterillo, 'En Galicia con E. Blanco-Amor y al fondo . . . Lorca', *Reseña*, Madrid, no. 73 (1974), pp. 14–18

– 'Federico, otra vez; la misma vez', *El País*, Madrid, 'Arte y Pensamiento', II, no. 5 (1 October 1978), pp. i, vi–vii

– *Romances galegos*, Galaxia, 'Colección Dombate', Vigo, 1980 (comprises *Romances galegos, Poema en catro temps, Cancioneiro*)

– X. G. [Xoel Gómez], 'La última entrevista con Eduardo Blanco Amor', *Galicia-80*, Orense, no. 1 (1980), pp. 13–16

– 'Apuntes sobre el teatro de Federico García Lorca', programme notes for the première of *Así que pasen cinco anos*, Madrid, 1978

BORRÁS, Tomás, [no title; on the theatre of Martínez Sierra], in Martínez Sierra (1925), pp. 9–14

BORROW, George, *Los Zincali (Los gitanos de España)*, traducción de Manuel Azaña, Madrid, Ediciones Turner, 1979

BOSQUET, Alain, *Entretiens avec Salvador Dalí*, Paris, Pierre Belfond, 1966

BRAVO, Francisco, *José Antonio. El hombre, el jefe, el camarada*, Madrid, Ediciones de la Vicesecretaría de Educación Popular, Madrid, 1941

BRENAN, Gerald, *The Face of Spain*, London, The Turnstile Press, 1950

– *South from Granada*, London, Hamish Hamilton, 1957

– *The Spanish Labyrinth*, Cambridge University Press, 1960

BRICKELL, Herschel, 'Six Poems of García Lorca done into English Bring Home Anew his Murder by Fascists' (a review of García Lorca, *Lament for the Death of a Bullfighter and Other Poems*, translated by A. L. Lloyd, Oxford, 1937), *New York Evening Post*, 22 September 1937, p. 19

– 'A Spanish Poet in New York', *The Virginia Quarterly Review*, XXI (1945), pp. 386–98

BUÑUEL, Luis, *Mon dernier soupir*, Paris, Robert Laffont, 1982

– *Obra literaria*, introducción y notas de Agustín Sañchez Vidal, Saragossa, Ediciones de Heraldo de Aragón, 1982

BURGIN, Richard, *Conversaciones con Jorge Luis Borges*, Madrid, Taurus, 1974

BUSSELL THOMPSON, B., and J. K. WALSH, 'Un encuentro de Lorca y Hart Crane en Nueva York', *Insula*, Madrid, no. 479 (October 1986), pp. 1, 12

BYRD, Suzanne W., *García Lorca: 'La Barraca' and the Spanish National Theater*, New York, Ediciones Abra, 1975

– *La 'Fuente Ovejuna' de Federico García Lorca*, Madrid, Editorial Pliegos, 1984

CABALLERO, José, *El taller de José Caballero. 1931–1977*, Madrid, Galería Multitud, 1977

– 'Con Federico en los ensayos de "Yerma" ', *ABC*, Madrid, 'Sábado Cultural', 29 December 1984, p. i

CABANELLAS, Guillermo, *La guerra de los mil días. Nacimiento, vida y muerte de la II República Española*, 2 vols., Buenos Aires, Editorial Heliasta, 1975

CABRERA INFANTE, Guillermo, 'Lorca hace llover en la Habana', *Cuadernos hispanoamericanos*, Madrid, nos. 433–43 (1986), pp. 241–8

CABROLIÉ, Martine, 'Enquête sur le milieu socio-économique de la famille de Federico García Lorca', unpublished university thesis, Université de Toulouse-Le Mirail, 1975

CAFFARENA, Angel, 'Federico García Lorca y las distintas ediciones del *Romancero gitano*', *La Estafeta Literaria*, Madrid, no. 362 (28 January 1967), pp. 8–9

CAMBOURS OCAMPO, Arturo, *Teoría y técnica de la creación literaria. (Materiales para una estética del escritor)*, Buenos Aires, Editorial Pena Lillo, 1966

CAMPOAMOR GONZÁLEZ, Antonio, '*La Barraca* y su primera salida por los caminos de España', *Cuadernos hispanoamericanos*, Madrid, nos. 435–6 (1986), pp. 778–90

CAMPODÓNICO, Luis, *Falla*, Paris, Seuil, 1959

CANO, José Luis, 'Ultimos meses de García Lorca', *Asomante*, Puerto Rico, xviii (1962), pp. 88–93

- *García Lorca. Biografía ilustrada*, Barcelona, Ediciones Destino, 1962
- *Los cuadernos de Velintonia*, Barcelona, Seix Barral, 1986
CARDOZA Y ARAGÓN, Luis, 'Federico García Lorca', *El Nacional*, Mexico, 30 September 1936
- interview by F. Gaudry and J. M. Oliveras, 'Artaud en México. El grito y la decepción. Entrevista con Luis Cardoza y Aragón', *Quimera*, Barcelona, nos. 54–5 (1986), pp. 59–61
- *El río. Novelas de caballería*, Mexico, Fondo de Cultura Económica, 1986
CARMONA, Darío, 'Anecdotario', introduction to the facsimile edition of *Litoral*, Frankfurt, Detlev Avvermann, and Madrid, Ediciones Turner, 1975
CARO BAROJA, Julio, *Los moriscos del reino de Granada. Ensayo de historia social*, Madrid, Ediciones Istmo, 2nd ed., 1976
CASARES, Carlos, 'Leria con Eduardo Blanco-Amor', *Grial*, Vigo, no. 41 (1973), pp. 337–44
CASSOU, Jean, 'Lettres espagnoles', *Mercure de France*, Paris, clxxxix, no. 673 (1 July 1926), p. 235
CASTRO, Américo, 'Homenaje a una sombra ilustre', in [Various], *Homenaje a Alberto Jiménez Fraud*, pp. 15–17
CASTRO, Eduardo, 'Leyenda y literatura de "la romería de Yerma" ', *Diario de Granada*, 6 October 1982, p. 7
CERNUDA, Luis, 'Notas eludidas. Federico García Lorca', *Heraldo de Madrid*, 26 November 1931, p. 12; reproduced in *Prosa completa* (1975), pp. 1237–41
- 'Federico García Lorca (Recuerdo)', *Hora de España*, Barcelona, no. 18 (June 1938), pp. 13–20; reproduced in *Prosa completa* (1975), pp. 1334–41
- *Poesía completa*, edited by Derek Harris and Luis Maristany, Barcelona, Barral Editores, 1973
- *Prosa completa*, edited by Derek Harris and Luis Maristany, Barcelona, Barral Editores, 1975
- *Epistolario inédito*, compiled by Fernando Ortiz, Seville, Compás, 1981
CHACÓN Y CALVO, José María, 'Lorca, poeta tradicional', *1930. Revista Avance*, Havana, 15 April 1930, pp. 101–2
CHESTERTON, Gilbert, *Charles Dickens*, London, Methuen, 8th ed., 1913
CHICA SALAS, Susana, 'Synge y García Lorca: aproximación de dos mundos poéticos', *Revista Hispánica Moderna*, New York, April 1961, 128–37
CIERVA, Ricardo de la, *Historia de la guerra civil española. Perspectivas y antecedentes*, Madrid, Librería Editorial San Martín, 1969
COBB, Christopher H., *La cultura y el pueblo. España 1930–1939*, Barcelona, Editorial Laia, 1980
COCTEAU, Jean, *Orphée. Théâtre et cinéma*, edited by Jacques Brosse, Paris, Bordas, 1973
COMINCIOLI, Jacques, *Federico García Lorca. Textes inédits et documents critiques de Jacques Comincioli*, Lausanne, Rencontre, 1970
CORREAS, Horacio, 'Imagen de García Lorca en Rosario', *La Capital*, Rosario(?), 13 August 1961 (unidentified cutting)
COSSART, Michael de, *The Food of Love. Princesse Edmond de Polignac (1865–1943) and her Salon*, London, Hamish Hamilton, 1978
COSSÍO, José María de, 'Sánchez Mejías', in *Los toros. Tratado técnico e histórico*, Madrid, Espasa-Calpe, 8th ed., 1980, vol. III, pp. 875–81
- 'Breve semblanza de Ignacio Sánchez Mejías', in *Los toros. Tratado técnico e histórico*, Madrid, Espasa-Calpe, 2nd ed., 1967, vol. IV, pp. 973–7
COUFFON, Claude, *A Grenade, sur les pas de García Lorca*, Paris, Seghers, 1962
CRICHTON, Ronald, *Falla*, London, BBC Music Guides, 1982
CRISPIN, John, *Oxford y Cambridge en Madrid. La Residencia de Estudiantes, 1910–1936, y su entorno cultural*, Santander, La Isla de los Ratones, 1981
CROW, John A., *Federico García Lorca*, Los Angeles, University of California, 1945
CRUZ, Chas de, 'Han pasado dos poetas. El español Federico García Lorca y el chileno Pablo Neruda, viajeros del mundo, regaron con su lirismo las calles de nuestra ciudad', *El*

Suplemento. Primer Magazine Argentino, Buenos Aires, xv, no. 562, 25 April 1934; reproduced in *Cuadernos hispanoamericanos*, Madrid, nos. 433–4 (1986), pp. 33–6

CRUZ EBRO, María, *Memorias de una burgalesa, 1885–1931*, Burgos, Diputación Provincial, 1952

CUADRADO MOURE, Bernardo, 'Federico García Lorca, en Compostela', *Hoja de lunes*, La Coruña, 15 March 1982

CUMMINGS, Philip, introduction, dated 31 August 1929, to FGL, *Songs*, translated by Philip Cummings, with the Assistance of Federico García Lorca, edited by Daniel Eisenberg, Pittsburgh, Duquesne University Press, 1976, p. 23.

– 'August in Eden. An Hour of Youth', dated 15 September 1929, in FGL, *Songs*, Pittsburgh, Duquesne University Press, 1976, pp. 125–66

– 'A Glimpse of a Man', 'The Mind of Genius', 'The Poems', [1955?], in FGL, *Songs*, Pittsburgh, Duquesne University Press, 1976, pp. 167–84

– 'Corrected Chronology of my Relationship with Federico García Lorca', five typewritten sheets, 1986

'Curioso Parlanchín, El', see ROIG DE LEUCHSENRING, Emilio.

CUSTODIO, Alvaro, 'Recuerdo de "La Barraca". Santillana del Mar y "Así que pasen 40 años" ', *Primer Acto*, Madrid, October 1972, pp. 63–6

DALÍ, Ana María, *Salvador Dalí visto por su hermana*, Barcelona, Juventud, 2nd ed., 1953

DALÍ, Salvador, 'Sant Sebastià', in *L'Amic de les Arts*, Sitges, no. 16 (31 July 1927), pp. 52–4

– 'Federico García Lorca: Exposiciò de dibuixos colorits (Galeries Dalmau)', *La Nova Revista*, Barcelona, iii, no. 9 (September 1927), pp. 84–5

– 'Realidad y sobrerrealidad', *La Gaceta Literaria*, Madrid, 15 October 1929, p. 7

– *The Secret Life of Salvador Dalí* [1942], London, Vision Press, 1968

– *Hidden Faces* [1944], London, Picador, 1975

– 'Les Morts et moi', *La Parisienne*, Paris, May 1954, pp. 52–3

– *Journal d'un Génie*, Paris, Editions de la Table Ronde, 1964

– *Confesiones inconfesables*, with André Parinaud, Barcelona, Editorial Bruguera, 1975

– interview with Monica Zerbib, 'Salvador Dalí: "Soy demasiado inteligente para dedicarme solo a la pintura" ', *El País*, Madrid, 'Arte y pensamiento', II, no. 42, 30 July 1978, pp. i, vii

– interview with Lluís Permanyer, *Playboy*, Barcelona, no. 3, January 1979

[–] *La Vie publique de Salvador Dalí*, Paris, Centre Georges Pompidou, 1980

[–] *Salvador Dalí. Rétrospective 1920–1980*, Paris, Centre Georges Pompidou, 2nd ed., 1980

– *400 obras de Salvador Dalí, 1914–1983*, catalogue of the exhibition held in Madrid in 1983, 2 vols., Madrid–Barcelona, Ministerio de Cultura/Generalitat de Catalunya, 1983

– *Diario de un genio*, Barcelona, Tusquets Editores, 1983

– interview with Ian Gibson, 'Con Dalí y Lorca en Figueres', *El País*, Madrid, 'Domingo' (May 1987), pp. 10–11

– *Salvador Dalí escribe a Federico García Lorca [1925–1936]*, edited by Rafael Santos Torroella, *Poesía. Revista ilustrada de información poética*, Madrid, Ministerio de Cultura, nos. 27–8, 1987

DARÍO, Rubén, (pseud. Félix Rubén García Sarmiento), *Obras completas*, 5 vols., Madrid, Afrodisio Aguado, 1950–3

– *Poesías completas*, Madrid, Aguilar, 10th ed., 1967

DELGADO, Santiago, 'El encuentro (Federico y Miguel)', *Semanario Murciano y de Información General*, Murcia, 15 December 1935, pp. 4–6

DESCHARNES, Robert, *Dalí de Gala*, Lausanne, Denoël, 1962

– *Dalí. La obra y el hombre*, Barcelona, Tusquets, 1984

DEVOTO, Daniel, ' "Doña Rosita la soltera": estructura y fuentes', *Bulletin Hispanique*, Bordeaux, lxix (1967, pp. 407–35

– 'García Lorca y Darío', *Asomante*, Puerto Rico, xxiii (1967), pp. 22–31

Díaz-Plaja, Guillermo, 'Romanticismo y actualidad del teatro lorquiano', *Heraldo de Madrid*, 13 January 1931, p. 5
- 'Notas para una geografía lorquiana', *Revista de Occidente*, Madrid, xxxiii (1931), pp. 353–7
- 'García Lorca y su "Nueva York" ', *Luz*, Madrid, 28 December 1932, p. 3
- *Federico García Lorca. Su obra e influencia en la poesía española*, Madrid, Espasa-Calpe ('Austral'), 3rd ed., 1961
Diego, Gerardo (ed.), *Poesía española contemporánea. Antología 1915–1931*, Madrid, Editorial Signo, 1932
- 'El teatro musical de Federico García Lorca', *El Imparcial*, Madrid, 16 April 1933, p. 8
Diers, Richard, 'Introductory note' to FGL 'Trip to the Moon. A Filmscript', *New Directions*, Norfolk, Connecticut, vol. 18 (1964), pp. 33–5
Díez-Canedo, Enrique, 'Espectáculo de "El Caracol": *La zapatera prodigiosa*, de F. García Lorca; *El príncipe, la princesa y el destino*, diálogo de la China medieval', *El Sol*, Madrid, 26 December 1930, p. 4
Díez de Revenga, Francisco Javier, *Revistas murcianas relacionadas con la Generación del 27*, Murcia, Academia Alfonso X el Sabio, 1979
- *El teatro de Miguel Hernández*, University of Murcia, 1981
Dobos, Erzsebet, *Documentación del viaje de Federico García Lorca por Cuba en el año 1930*, doctoral thesis, Budapest, 1978
- 'Nuevos datos sobre el viaje de Federico García Lorca por Cuba en el año 1930', *Acta Litteraria Academiae Scientiarum Hungaricae*, Budapest, no. 22 (1980), pp. 392–405
Domínguez Berrueta, Martín, *La Universidad española*, Salamanca, 1910
- 'La cabeza de San Bruno', *La Esfera*, Madrid, 25 August 1917
Donato, Magda, 'En Madrid hay un club infantil', *Ahora*, Madrid, 16 January 1936, pp. [18–19], 23
Dos Passos, John, *Manhattan Transfer*, traducción y prólogo de José Robles, Madrid, Editorial Cenit, 1929
Durán Medina, Trinidad, *Federico García Lorca y Sevilla*, Excma. Diputación, Seville, 1974
Eisenberg, Daniel, 'A Chronology of Lorca's Visit to New York and Cuba', *Kentucky Romance Quarterly*, xxiv (1975), pp. 233–50
- editor's introduction to FGL, *Songs*, translated by Philip Cummings with the assistance of Federico García Lorca and edited by Daniel Eisenberg, Pittsburgh, Duquesne University Press, 1975, pp. 3–20
- 'Lorca en Nueva York', in Eisenberg, *Textos y documentos lorquianos* (1975), pp. 17–36
- *Textos y documentos lorquianos*, Tallahassee, Florida, private edition, 1975
- 'Cuatro pesquisas lorquianas', *Thesaurus. Boletín del Instituto Caro y Cuervo*, Bogotá, xxx (1975)
- 'Dos conferencias lorquianas (Nueva York y La Havana, 1930)', *Papeles de son armadans*, Madrid, Palma de Mallorca (November–December 1975), pp. 197–212
- *'Poeta en Nueva York': historia y problemas de un texto de Lorca*, Barcelona–Caracas–Mexico, Editorial Ariel, 1976
- 'Un texto lorquiano descubierto en Nueva York. La presentación de Sánchez Mejías', *Bulletin Hispanique*, Bordeaux, lxxx (1978), pp. 134–7
Esperabé de Arteaga, Enrique, *Diccionario enciclopédico ilustrado y crítico de los salmantinos ilustres y beneméritos*, Madrid, Gráficas Ibarra, 1952
Falla, Manuel de, *El 'Cante Jondo' (canto primitivo andaluz). Sus orígenes. Sus valores musicales. Su influencia en el arte musical español*, Granada, Editorial Urania, 1922
- *Escritos sobre música y músicos. Debussy, Wagner, el cante jondo*, introducción y notas de Federico Sopeña, Madrid, Espasa-Calpe ('Austral'), 3rd Aug. ed., 1972
Felipe, León, *Obras completas*, Buenos Aires, Losada, 1963
Fernández, Darío, 'Desde Argentina. El triunfo magnífico de Federico García Lorca', *El Defensor de Granada*, 9 March 1934, p. 1

FERNÁNDEZ ALMAGRO, Melchor, 'El mundo lírico de Federico García Lorca', *España*, Madrid, no. 391 (13 October 1923), pp. 7–8

– 'Primeros versos de García Lorca', *ABC*, Madrid, 15 October 1949, p. 3

– 'El primer estreno de Federico García Lorca', *ABC*, Madrid, 12 June 1952, p. 3

– *Viaje al siglo XX*, Madrid, Sociedad de Estudios y Publicaciones, 1962

FERNÁNDEZ-MONTESINOS GARCÍA, Manuel, 'Descripción de la biblioteca de Federico García Lorca (catálogo y estudio)', unpublished thesis, Universidad Complutense, Madrid, 1985

FERNÁNDEZ DEL RIEGO, Francisco, *Anxel Casal e o libro galego*, La Coruña, Ediciós do Castro, 1983

FORD, Richard, *A Hand-book for Travellers in Spain and Readers at Home*, 2 vols., London, John Murray, 1845

– *Granada. Escritos con dibujos inéditos del autor*, texto español e inglés, traducción y notas de Alfonso Gámir, Granada, Publicaciones del Patronato de la Alhambra, 1955

FORNÉS, Eduard (ed.), *Dalí y los libros*, Barcelona, Editorial Mediterrania, 1985

FRANCO GRANDE, José Luis (with José LANDEIRA YRAGO), 'Cronología gallega de Federico García Lorca y datos sincrónicos', *Grial*, Vigo, no. 45 (1974), pp. 1–29

FRANCO GRANDE, José Luis, 'Nin misterio nin segredos. O galego de García Lorca – Guerra da Cal', *Faro de Vigo*, 8 November 1985, p. 52

GALLEGO BURÍN, Antonio, *Guía de Granada*, Granada, 1946

GALLEGO MORELL, Antonio, 'Treinta partidas de bautismo de escritores granadinos', *Boletín de la Real Academia Española*, Madrid, January–April, 1954

– *Antonio Gallego Burín (1895–1961)*, Madrid, Moneda y Crédito, 1968

GANIVET, Angel, *Obras completas*, 2 vols., Madrid, Aguilar, 1961–2

GARCÍA BUÑUEL, Pedro Christian, *Recordando a Luis Buñuel*, Excma. Diputación Provincial de Zaragoza/Excmo. Ayuntamiento de Zaragoza, 1965

GARCÍA ESCUDERO, José María, *El pensamiento de 'El Debate'*, Madrid, Biblioteca de Autores Cristianos, 1983

GARCÍA GÓMEZ, Emilio, *Silla del moro y nuevas escenas andaluzas,* Madrid, Revista de Occidente, 1948

GARCÍA HIDALGO, J., 'Pintoresco relato de una vida extraordinaria. A los setenta y dos años, campeón del "cante jondo" ' (interview with Diego Bermúdez Calas, 'el Tenazas'), *Heraldo de Madrid*, 15 October 1928, pp. 8–9

GARCÍA LASGOITY, María del Carmen, 'Yo estuve con García Lorca en la Barraca', interview with Valentín de Pedro, *¡Aquí Está!*, Buenos Aires, no. 938 (14 May 1945), pp. 2–4; no. 939 (17 May 1945), pp. 20–2, 25; no. 940 (21 May 1945), pp. 2–4

– 'Recuerdos de "La Barraca" ', in SÁENZ DE LA CALZADA, pp. 168–71

GARCÍA LORCA, Francisco, *Federico y su mundo*, edición y prólogo de Mario Hernández, Madrid, Alianza, 2nd ed., 1981

GARCÍA MAROTO, Gabriel, *La nueva España 1930. Resumen de la vida artística española desde el año 1927 hasta hoy*, Madrid, Ediciones Biblos, 1930 (recte, 1927)

GARCÍA MATOS, M., 'Folklore en Falla', *Música. Revista trimestral de los conservatorios españoles y de la sección de Musicología del CSIC*, Madrid, nos. 3–4 (January–February 1953), pp. 41–68, and no. 6 (November–December 1953), pp. 33–52

GARCÍA PINTADO, Angel, '19 razones para amar lo imposible', *Cuadernos El Público*, Madrid, no. 20 (1987), pp. 7–11

GARCÍA–POSADA, Miguel, 'Un documento lorquiano: El pasaporte que utilizó Federico García Lorca en su viaje a Estados Unidos y Cuba', *Insula*, Madrid, nos. 368–9 (1977), p. 25

– *Lorca: interpretación de 'Poeta en Nueva York'*, Madrid, Akal, 1981

– 'García Lorca en Uruguay', *Triunfo*, Madrid, 6th series, nos. 21–2 (July–August 1982), pp. 82–8

– 'Realidad y transfiguración artística en *La casa de Bernarda Alba*', in Ricardo Domenech (ed.), *'La casa de Bernarda Alba' y el teatro de García Lorca*, Madrid, Cátedra/Teatro Español, 1985, pp. 149–170

GARCÍA DE VALDEAVELLANO, Luis, 'Un educador humanista: Alberto Jiménez Fraud y la Residencia de Estudiantes', introduction to Alberto Jiménez Fraud, *La Residencia de Estudiantes. Visita a Maquiavelo*, Barcelona, Ediciones Ariel, 1972

GARCÍA VENERO, Maximiano, *Madrid, julio 1936*, Madrid, Ediciones Tebas, 1973

GARRIGUES Y DÍAZ-CAÑABATE, Antonio, *Diálogos conmigo mismo*, Barcelona, Planeta, 1978

GARRIGUES Y DÍAZ-CAÑABATE, Emilio, 'Al teatro con Federico García Lorca', *Cuadernos hispanoamericanos*, Madrid, no. 340 (1978), pp. 99–117

GASCH, Sebastià, 'Mi Federico García Lorca', prologue to FGL, *Cartas a sus amigos*, edited by Sebastià Gasch, Barcelona, Ediciones Cobalto, 1950, pp. 7–14

GAUTIER, Théophile, *Voyage en Espagne*, Paris, Bibliothèque Charpentier, 1899

GEBSER, Jean, *Lorca. Poète–dessinateur*, Paris, GLM, 1949

GIBSON, Ian, 'Lorca's *Balada triste*: Children's Songs and the Theme of Sexual Disharmony in *Libro de poemas*', *Bulletin of Hispanic Studies*, Liverpool, xlvi (1969), pp. 21–38

– *En busca de José Antonio*, Barcelona, Editorial Planeta, 1980

– *Un irlandés en España*, Barcelona, Editorial Planeta, 1981

– *The Assassination of Federico García Lorca*, Harmondsworth, Penguin Books, 1983

– *El asesinato de García Lorca*, Barcelona, Plaza y Janés, 1985

– 'En torno al primer estreno de Lorca (*El maleficio de la mariposa*)', in Ricardo Domenech (ed.), '*La casa de Bernarda Alba*' y el teatro de García Lorca, Madrid, Cátedra/Teatro Español, 1985, pp. 57–75

– *Federico García Lorca. I. De Fuente Vaqueros a Nueva York (1898–1929)*, Barcelona, Editorial Grijalbo, 1985

– *Granada en 1936 y el asesinato de Federico García Lorca*, Barcelona, Editorial Crítica, 6th ed., 1986

– *Federico García Lorca. II. De Nueva York a Fuente Grande (1929–1936)*, Barcelona, Editorial Grijalbo, 1987

– 'Con Dalí y Lorca en Figueres', *El País*, Madrid, 'Domingo', 26 January 1986, p. 10

– *La noche en que mataron a Calvo Sotelo*, Barcelona, Plaza y Janés, 1986

– 'Los últimos días de Federico García Lorca', *Historia–16*, Madrid, no. 123 (July 1986), pp. 11–21

– *Queipo de Llano. Sevilla, verano de 1936 (con las charlas radiofónicas completas)*, Barcelona, Editorial Grijalbo, 1986

GIDE, André, *Corydon*, traducido por Julio Gómez de la Serna con un diálogo antisocrático del doctor Marañón, Madrid, Ediciones Oriente, [1929], 3rd ed., 1931

GIL-ALBERT, Juan, *Memorabilia (1934–1939)*, in *Obras completas en prosa*, Institución Alfonso el Magnánimo, Diputación Provincial de Valencia, vol. 2, 1982

GÓMEZ DE LIAÑO, Ignacio, *Dalí*, Barcelona, La Polígrafa, 1982

GÓMEZ MONTERO, Rafael, 'Federico García Lorca fue cofrade nativo de Santa María de la Alhambra', *Ideal*, Granada, 17 May 1973; *ABC*, Madrid, 18 May 1973

GÓMEZ-MORENO, Manuel, 'Monumentos arquitectónicos de la provincia de Granada', in *Misceláneas. Historia, arte, arqueología (dispersa, emendata, inédita)*, Madrid, Consejo Superior de Investigaciones Científicas, Instituto Diego Velázquez, 1949, pp. 347–90

GONZÁLEZ CARBALHO, José, *Vida, obra y muerte de Federico García Lorca (escrita para ser leída en un acto recordatorio)*, Santiago de Chile, Ediciones Ercilla, 2nd ed., 1941

GONZÁLEZ GUZMÁN, Pascual, 'Federico en Almería. Nuevos datos para la biografía de García Lorca', *Papeles de son armadans*, Madrid–Palma de Mallorca, no. civ (November 1964), pp. 203–20

GRANELL, Eugenio, preliminary study to his edition of *Así que pasen cinco años* and *Amor de Don Perlimplín con Belisa en su jardín*, Madrid, Taurus, 2nd ed., 1981, pp. 7–31

GUARDIA, Alfredo de la, 'La primera obra dramática de Federico García Lorca', *La Nación*, Buenos Aires, 17 November 1940, p. 4

– *García Lorca. Persona y creación*, Buenos Aires, Editorial Schapire, 4th ed., 1961

GUERRA DA CAL, Ernesto, 'Evocaçom e testemunho. Quem foi Serafim Ferro', *A Nosa Terra*, Vigo, 25 April 1985
- 'Federico García Lorca (1898–1936)', in *Rosalía de Castro. Antología poética. Cancioneiro rosaliano*, organização de Ernesto da Cal, Guimaraes Editores, Lisbon, 1985, pp. 193–9
GUILLÉN, Jorge, *Federico en persona. Semblanza y epistolario*, Buenos Aires, Emecé, 1959
- 'Federico en persona', in FGL, *Obras completas*, Madrid, Aguilar, 2 vols., 20th ed., 1978, I, pp. xvii–lxxxiv
HAMMICK, Horacio H., *The Duke of Wellington's Spanish Estate. A Personal Narrative*, London, Spottiswoode and Co., 1885
HERNÁNDEZ, Mario, 'Cronología y estreno de *Yerma, poema trágico*, de García Lorca', *Revista de Archivos, Bibliotecas y Museos*, Madrid, lxxxii (1979), pp. 289–315
- introduction to FGL, *La casa de Bernarda Alba*, Madrid, Alianza, 1981, pp. 9–46
- 'Francisco y Federico García Lorca', prologue to Francisco García Lorca, *Federico y su mundo*, Madrid, Alianza, 2nd ed., 1981, pp. i–xxxvii
- introduction to FGL, *Romancero gitano*, Madrid, Alianza, 1981, pp. 7–46
- introduction to FGL, *Poema del cante jondo*, Madrid, Alianza, 1982, pp. 11–53
- introduction to FGL, *La zapatera prodigiosa*, Madrid, Alianza, 1982, pp. 9–44
- introduction to FGL, *Canciones, 1921–1924*, Madrid, Alianza, 1982, pp. 11–25
- introduction to FGL, *Bodas de sangre*, Madrid, Alianza, 1984, pp. 9–64
- 'Un dibujo de Lorca: autorretrato en Nueva York', *Ideal*, Granada, 29 May 1986, p. 26
- 'Ronda de autorretratos con animal fabuloso y análisis de dos dibujos neoyorquinos', in FGL, *Dibujos*, Madrid, 1986, pp. 85–115
HERNÁNDEZ, Miguel, *Epistolario*, introducción y edición de Agustín Sánchez Vidal, prólogo de Josefina Manresa, Madrid, Alianza, 1986
HIGUERA ROJAS, Eulalia-Dolores de la, 'Habla el chófer de García Lorca', *Gentes*, Madrid, no. 37 (24 April 1979), pp. 30–33
- *Mujeres en la vida de García Lorca*, Editora Nacional/Excma. Diputación Provincial de Granada, 1980
HOMENAJE *al poeta García Lorca contra su muerte (Antonio Machado, José Moreno Villa, José Bergamín, Dámaso Alonso, Vicente Aleixandre, Emilio Prados, Pedro Garfias, Juan Gil Albert, Pablo Neruda, Rafael Alberti, Manuel Altolaguirre, Arturo Serrano Plaja, Miguel Hernández, Lorenzo Varela, Antonio Aparicio). Selección de sus obras (poemas, prosas, teatro, música, dibujos) por Emilio Prados*, Ediciones Españolas, Valencia–Barcelona, 1937; facsimile reprint, Granada, 1986
HUGO, Victor, *Oeuvres poétiques*, 2 vols., Paris, Gallimard (Bibliothèque de la Pléiade), 1967–8
IFACH, María de Gracia, 'Federico y Miguel', *Revista Nacional de Cultura*, Caracas, nos. 148–9 (1961), pp. 98–106
IGLESIAS CORRAL, Manuel, 'El arca de los recuerdos', *La Voz de Galicia*, La Coruña, 23 August 1983, p. 3
- 'Recuerdos históricos', *La Voz de Galicia*, La Coruña, 11 September 1983, p. 3
JACKSON, Gabriel, *The Spanish Republic and the Civil War. 1931–1939*, Princeton NJ, Princeton University Press, 1966
JAMES, Edward, *Swans Reflecting Elephants. My Early Years*, edited by George Melly, London, Weidenfeld and Nicolson, 1982
JASCALEVICH, Enrique, 'El amigo de Federico García Lorca. "Después de la fiesta, a las cinco de la mañana, escuchaba misa en San Carlos", nos dice Amada Villar', *El Hogar*, Buenos Aires (undated clipping)
JIMÉNEZ, Juan Ramón, 'Chopos', in *Residencia*, Madrid, I, no. 1 (1926), p. 26
- 'El romance, río de la lengua española', in *El trabajo gustoso (conferencias)*, Madrid, Aguilar, 1962, pp. 143–87
- *Olvidos de Granada*, introduction by Juan Gutiérrez Padial, Granada, Padre Suárez, 1969

- *Diario de un poeta reciencasado*, edición de A. Sánchez Barbudo, Madrid, Editorial Labor, 1970
- *Selección de cartas (1899–1958)*, Barcelona, Picazo, 1973
JIMÉNEZ FRAUD, Alberto, 'Lorca y otros poetas', *El Nacional*, Caracas, 13 September 1957
- *Historia de la universidad española*, Madrid, Alianza, 1971
- 'Cincuentenario de la Residencia', in *La Residencia de Estudiantes. Visita a Maquiavelo*, Barcelona, Ariel, 1972, pp. 62–85
JOSEPHS, Allen and Juan CABALLERO, introduction to FGL, *Bodas de sangre*, Madrid, Cátedra, 1985, pp. 9–90
LACASA, Luis, 'Recuerdo y trayectoria de Federico García Lorca', *Literatura Soviética*, Moscow, no. 9 (1946), pp. 38–46
LAFFRANQUE, Marie, 'Un Document biographique: l'extrait de naissance de Federico García Lorca', *Bulletin Hispanique*, Bordeaux, lix (1957), pp. 206–9
- *Federico García Lorca*, Paris, Seghers ('Théâtre de Tous les Temps'), 1966
- *Les Idées esthétiques de Federico García Lorca*, Paris, Centre de Recherches Hispaniques, 1967
- 'Pour l'étude de Federico García Lorca. Bases chronologiques', *Bulletin Hispanique*, Bordeaux, lxv (1963), pp. 333–77
- introduction to FGL, *Comedia sin título*, in FGL, *El público y Comedia sin título. Dos obras teatrales postumas*, introducción, transcripción y versión depurada de R. Martínez Nadal y Marie Laffranque, Barcelona, Seix Barral, 1978, pp. 275–316
- 'Equivocar el camino. Regards sur un scénario de Federico García Lorca', in VARIOUS, *Hommage à Federico García Lorca*, Université de Toulouse–Le Mirail, 1982, pp. 73–92
LANDEIRA YRAGO, José (with José Luis FRANCO GRANDE), 'Cronología gallega de Federico García Lorca y datos sincrónicos', *Grial*, Vigo, no. 45 (1974), pp. 1–29
LANDEIRA YRAGO, José, 'Con Federico García Lorca por Galicia. Viaxe da letra ao sangue', *Grial*, Vigo, no. 76 (1982), pp. 155–64
- 'Proceso a García Lorca', letter in *La Voz de Galicia*, La Coruña, 3 September 1983
- 'O encontro de Eduardo Blanco-Amor con García Lorca', *Grial*, Vigo, no. 83 (1984), pp. 82–92
- 'Galicia e o momento estelar de "La Barraca" ', *Grial*, Vigo, no. 87 (1985), pp. 76–88
- *Viaje al sueño del agua. El misterio de los poemas gallegos de García Lorca*, Vigo, Ediciós do Castro, 1986
- *Federico García Lorca y Galicia*, Vigo, Ediciós do Castro, 1986
LANZ, Hermenegildo, 'Misioneros del arte. "La Barraca" ', *El Defensor de Granada*, 5 October 1932, p. 1
LARGO CABALLERO, Francisco, *Mis recuerdos. Cartas a un amigo*, Mexico, Ediciones Unidas, 1976
LARREA, Juan, 'Asesinado por el cielo', *España peregrina*, Mexico, I (1940), pp. 251–6
LEGENDRE, Maurice, 'La Fête-Dieu à Grenade en 1922. Le "cante jondo" ', *Le Correspondant*, Paris, 10 July 1922, pp. 148–55
LEÓN, María Teresa, *Memoria de la melancolía*, Barcelona, Editorial Laia/Ediciones Picazo, 1977
LLANOS, Emilia, 'Suspiros del pasado', unpublished diary about her relationship with Lorca, in APP
LOXA, Juan de (ed.), *Federico del Sagrado Corazón de Jesús / Manuel María de los Dolores Falla Matheu*, Fuente Vaqueros, Granada, Comisión Organizadora del Hermanamiento Falla–Lorca, 1982
LOYNAZ, Flor, interview with Angel Rivero, 'Mis recuerdos de Lorca', *Revolución y cultura*, Havana, 1984
LUENGO, Ricardo G., 'Conversación de Federico García Lorca', *El Mercantil Valenciano*, Valencia, 15 November 1933
MACHADO, Antonio, *Obras. Poesía y prosa*, Buenos Aires, Losada, 1964

MADARIAGA, Salvador, 'Tres estampas de Federico García Lorca', in *De Galdós a Lorca*, Buenos Aires, Sudamericana, 1960, pp. 217–23

– *España. Ensayo de historia contemporánea*, Madrid, Espasa-Calpe, 12th ed., 1978

MADOZ, Pascual, *Diccionario geográfico–estadístico–histórico de España y sus posesiones de ultramar*, 16 vols., Madrid, Imprenta del Diccionario geográfico–estadístico–histórico de D. Pascual Madoz, 1847–9

MADRID, Francisco, 'Conversaciones a 1.000 metros de altura. Propósitos de Margarita Xirgu', *Heraldo de Madrid*, 9 September 1930, p. 7

MAESO, David Gonzalo, *Garnata Āl-Yahūd (Granada en la historia del judaísmo español)*, Universidad de Granada, 1963

MALEFAKIS, Edward, *Reforma agraria y revolución campesina en la España del siglo XX*, Barcelona, Ariel, 1971

MARCILLY, C., *Ronde et fable de la solitude à New York. Prélude à 'Poeta en Nueva York' de F. G. Lorca*, Paris, Ediciones Hispano–Americanas, 1962

MARINELLO, Juan, 'Las conferencias de García Lorca en la Hispano–Cubana de Cultura', *1930. Revista de Avance*, Havana, 15 April 1930, p. 127

– 'García Lorca, gracia y muerte', in *Momento español. Ensayos*, Havana, Imprenta 'La Verónica', 2nd ed., 1939, pp. 17–23

– *García Lorca en Cuba*, Havana, Ediciones Belic, 1965

– 'García Lorca en Cuba. El Poeta llegó a Santiago', *Bohemia*, Havana, 31 May 1968, pp. 23–27

MARRAST, Robert, 'La Dernière interview de García Lorca', *Les Lettres Françaises*, Paris, no. 1,003 (14–20 November 1953), pp. 1, 5

MARTÍN, Eutimio, 'Un testimonio olvidado sobre García Lorca en el libro *España levanta el puño*, de Pablo Suero', *Trece de Nieve*, Madrid, 2nd series, no. 3 (May 1977), pp. 74–88

– *Federico García Lorca, heterodoxo y mártir. Análisis y proyección de la obra juvenil inédita*, Madrid, Siglo XXI, 1986

MARTÍN DÍAZ, José, 'Postales de Barcelona. Los dos Federicos. Un triunfo de García Lorca', *El Defensor de Granada*, 24 December 1932, p. 1

MARTÍN MARTÍN, Jacinto, *Los años de aprendizaje de Federico García Lorca*, Excmo. Ayuntamiento de Granada, 1984

MARTÍN RECUERDA, José, *Análisis de 'Doña Rosita la soltera o El lenguaje de las flores' (de Federico García Lorca), tragedia sin sangre*, Universidad de Salamanca, 1979

MARTÍNEZ BARBEITO, Carlos, 'García Lorca, poeta gallego. Un viaje a Galicia del cantor de Andalucia', *El Español*, Madrid, 24 March 1945, p. 4; reprinted in *Grial*, Vigo, no. 43 (1974), pp. 90–98

MARTÍNEZ BARRIO, Diego, *Memorias*, Barcelona, Planeta, 1983

MARTÍNEZ LASECA, José María, 'El viaje premonitorio', chapter of his study 'En el cincuentenario de la República y de las Misiones Pedagogicas. Un sendero hacia el pueblo', published in *Memoria, Premios Numancia*, Soria, 1981

MARTÍNEZ NADAL, Rafael, introduction to FGL, *Poems*, English version by Stephen Spender and J. L. Gili, London, The Dolphin Book Company, 1942, pp. vii–xxviii

– 'El último día de Federico García Lorca en Madrid', in *Residencia. Revista de la Residencia de Estudiantes*, Mexico, commemorative issue, 1963, pp. 58–61

– 'Don Miguel de Unamuno. Dos viñetas', *Los sesenta*, Mexico, no. 4 (1965), pp. 39–51

– *'El Público'. Amor, teatro y caballos en la obra de Federico García Lorca*, Oxford, The Dolphin Book Company, 1970

– *Lorca's The Public. A Study of His Unfinished Play (El público) and of Love and Death in the Work of Federico García Lorca*, London, Calder and Boyars in association with Lyrebird Press, 1974

– 'Lorca's Last Day in Madrid', in *Lorca's The Public* (1974), pp. 11–17

– 'What I Know about *The Public*', in *Lorca's The Public* (1974), pp. 19–24

– *Cuatro lecciones sobre Federico García Lorca*, Madrid, Fundación Juan March/Cátedra, 1980

Martínez Sierra, Gregorio, *Granada. Guía emocional*, Paris, Garnier Hermanos, n.d. [1911]

– (ed.), *Un teatro de arte en España. 1917–1925*, Madrid, Ediciones de la Esfinge, 1925

Martínez Sierra, María, *Gregorio y yo. Medio siglo de colaboración*, Barcelona and Mexico, Grijalbo, 1953

Maurer, Christopher, 'Buenos Aires, 1933. Dos entrevistas olvidadas con Federico García Lorca', *Trece de Nieve*, Madrid, 2nd series, no. 3 (May 1977), pp. 64–73

– 'El teatro', in *FGLNY*, pp. 134–41

– 'Los negros', in *FGLNY*, pp. 140–51

– 'García Lorca y las formas de la música', in Andrés Soria Olmedo (ed.), *Lecciones sobre Federico García Lorca*, Granada, Comisión Nacional del Cincuentenario, 1986, pp. 273–50

– 'De la correspondencia de García Lorca: datos inéditos sobre la transmisión de su obra', *Boletín de la Fundación Federico García Lorca*, Madrid, I, no. 1 (1987), pp. 58–95

Menasché, Marcelo, 'El autor de *Bodas de sangre* es un buen amigo de los judíos', *Sulem. Revista social ilustrada para la colectividad israelita*, Buenos Aires, I, no. 2 (25 December 1933); interview reprinted by Hernández in his edition of FGL, *Romancero gitano*, Madrid, Alianza, 1981, pp. 153–6

Menéndez Pidal, Ramón (ed.), *Romancero hispánico (hispano-portugués, americano y sefardí)*, 2 vols., Madrid, Espasa-Calpe, 2nd ed., 1968

Milla, Fernando de la, 'Diálogos actuales. Eduardo Marquina, el teatro internacional de París y los autores nuevos, proyectos y sugestiones', *La Esfera*, Madrid, 31 July 1926, pp. 5–6

– 'Teatro. Retorno a la escena de Josefina Díaz de Artigas', *Crónica*, Madrid, 25 September 1932, pp. [9–10]

Millán, María Clementa, 'La verdad del amor y del teatro', *Cuadernos El Público*, Madrid, no. 20 (1987), pp. 19–27

Molina Fajardo, Eduardo, *Manuel de Falla y el 'cante jondo'*, Universidad de Granada, 1962

– 'Llegada de Falla a Granada', in Rafael Jofré García (ed.), *Manuel de Falla en Granada*, Granada, Centro Artístico, 1963, p. [25]

– *El flamenco en Granada. Teoría de sus orígenes e historia*, Granada, Miguel Sánchez, 1974

– *Los últimos días de García Lorca*, Barcelona, Plaza y Janés, 1983

Montanyà, Lluis, '*Canciones* de F. García Lorca', *L'Amic de les Arts*, Sitges, no. 16 (31 July 1927), pp. 55–6

Montes, Eugenio, ' "Un Chien Andalou" (Film de Luis Buñuel y Salvador Dalí, estrenado en "Le Studio des Ursulines", París)', *La Gaceta Literaria*, Madrid, III, no. 60 (15 June 1929), p. 1

Mora Guarnido, José, 'El primer libro de Federico García Lorca', *Noticiero Granadino*, 1 July 1921, p. 1

– *Federico García Lorca y su mundo. Testimonio para una biografía*, Buenos Aires, Losada, 1958

Morales, María Luz, 'La poesía popular de Federico García Lorca', *La Vanguardia*, Barcelona, 22 September 1935, p. 3

Morand, Paul, *Nueva York*, traducción de Julio Gómez de la Serna, Madrid, Ediciones Ulises, 1930

Moreiro, José María, 'Viaje a García Lorca. Reencuentro con sus personajes vivos', *Los domingos de ABC*, Madrid, 1 August 1971, pp. 18–25

Moreno Villa, José, 'Recuerdo a Federico García Lorca', in *Homenaje al poeta García Lorca contra su muerte*, pp. 23–4

– *Vida en claro. Autobiografía*, Mexico, Colegio de México, 1944

– *Los autores como actores y otros intereses literarios de acá y de allá*, Mexico, Fondo de Cultura Económica, 1976

Morla Lynch, Carlos, *En España con Federico García Lorca (Páginas de un diario íntimo, 1928–1936)*, Madrid, Aguilar, 1958

MORRIS, C. B., *This Loving Darkness. The Cinema and Spanish Writers, 1920–1936*, Oxford University Press, 1980

MURCIANO, José, 'En el Centro Artístico. Ismael. Federico García Lorca', *El Eco del Aula*, Granada, 27 March 1918, p. 5

NERUDA, Pablo, *Residencia en la Tierra*, 2 vols., Madrid, Cruz y Raya, 1935

– *Homenaje a Pablo Neruda*, Madrid, Plutarco, 1935. [The volume anticipates 'Tres poemas materiales', included shortly afterwards in *Residencia en la Tierra* (1935)]

– 'Federico García Lorca', *Hora de España*, Valencia, III (March 1937), pp. 65–78, lecture included in *Obras completas* (1957), pp. 1828–32

– *Obras completas*, Buenos Aires, Losada, 1957

– interview with André Camp and Ramón Luis Chao, 'Neruda por Neruda', *Triunfo*, Madrid, no. 476 (13 November 1971), pp. 17–23

– *Confieso que he vivido*, Barcelona, Seix Barral, 1974

NOVO, Salvador, *Continente vacío (viaje a Sudamérica)*, Madrid, Espasa-Calpe, 1935

O'CONNOR, Patricia Walker, *Gregorio and María Martínez Sierra*, New York, Twayne, 1979

O[LMEDILLA], J. G., 'En el Español, ayer tarde. Una función experimental del teatro "Caracol" ', *Heraldo de Madrid*, 25 December 1930, p. 7

ONÍS, Federico de, 'Lorca folklorista', in Río, *Federico García Lorca (1899–1936). Vida y obra* (1941), pp. 113–15; reproduced by Hernández in his edition of FGL, *Primeras canciones. Seis poemas galegos. Poemas sueltos. Canciones populares*, Madrid, Alianza, 1981, pp. 147–53

– *Antología de la poesía española e hispanoamericana (1882–1932)*, Madrid, Junta para Ampliación de Estudios e Investigaciones Científicas, Centro de Estudios Históricos, 1934

ONTAÑÓN, Santiago, 'Semblanza de García Lorca', in FGL, *Dibujos*, Madrid, 1986, pp. 19–25

OPPENHEIMER, Helen, *Lorca: The Drawings. Their Relation to the Poet's Life and Work*, London, The Herbert Press, 1986

OROZCO, Manuel, 'La Granada de los años veinte. En torno a unas fotos inéditas de Federico', *ABC*, Madrid, 6 November 1966

– *Falla*, Barcelona, Destino, 1968

– 'José María García Carrillo', *Ideal*, Granada, 23 August 1987, p. 4

ORTEGA Y GASSET, José, *La deshumanización del arte*, Madrid, Revista de Occidente, 1925

ORTIZ DE VILLAJOS, Cándido G., *Crónica de Granada en 1937. II Año Triunfal*, Granada, 1938

OTERO SECO, Antonio, 'Una conversación inédita con Federico García Lorca. Indice de las obras inéditas que ha dejado el gran poeta', *Mundo Gráfico*, Madrid, 24 February 1937; reproduced in *OC*, II, pp. 1088–90. See also MARRAST, Robert.

– 'Sobre la última "interview" de García Lorca', *La Torre. Revista general de la Universidad de Puerto Rico*, XII (1964), pp. 55–63

PAHISSA, Jaime, *Vida y obra de Manuel de Falla*, Buenos Aires, Ricordi Americana, 1956

PALACIO, Carlos, 'Una tarde con la viuda de Prokofiev', *Ritmo*, Madrid, no. 532 (April 1983), pp. 31–2

PAPINI, Giovanni, *El libro negro*, Barcelona, Luis de Caralt, 1960

PAREJA LÓPEZ, Luis, Francisco ORTEGA ALBA, et al., *Granada*, 4 vols., Granada, Excelente Diputación Provincial, 1982

PAYNE, Stanley G., *Falange. A History of Spanish Fascism*, Stanford and Oxford Universities, 1962

PEDEMONTE, Hugo Emilio, 'El primer monumento a Federico García Lorca', *Nueva Estafeta*, Madrid, no. 1 (December 1978), pp. 58–63

PEDREGOSA and FERRERAS, 'Moclín: El Cristo del Paño convocó a miles de romeros. Leyenda y literatura de "la romería de Yerma" ', *Diario de Granada*, 6 October 1982, p. 7

PEDRELL, Felipe, *Cancionero musical popular español*, 4 vols., Valls, Eduardo Castells, 1918–22

– 'Glinka en Granada', in *Cancionero musical popular español* (1918–22), II, pp. 75–8

PEDRO, Valentín de, 'El destino mágico de Margarita Xirgu', *¡Aquí Está!*, Buenos Aires, 28 April–30 May 1948

PENÓN, Agustín, draft of book on Lorca's death, with accompanying diaries and papers, confided to the author by William Layton for possible publication

PÉREZ COTERILLO, Moisés, 'Culto cubano a Federico García Lorca. El manuscrito de "Yerma" encontrado en La Habana', *Blanco y Negro*, Madrid, 6–12 February 1980, pp. 46–8

– 'La Habana: donde Lorca escribió "El público" ', *El Público*, Madrid, nos. 10–11 (July–August 1984), pp. 39–43

PÉREZ-DOMENECH, J., 'Hablan los jóvenes autores. Eduardo Ugarte dice que el teatro actual es de pura receta. La política y las tendencias en las obras de hoy. Hay que crear un teatro de ensayo', *El Imparcial*, Madrid, 2 May 1933, p. 4

PÉREZ FERRERO, Miguel, 'Voces de desembarque. Veinte minutos de paseo con Federico García Lorca', *Heraldo de Madrid*, 9 October 1930, p. 11

– 'Los españoles fuera de España. Federico García Lorca, el gran poeta del "Romancero gitano", ha sido durante seis meses embajador intelectual de nuestro país en la Argentina. Como Einstein, como Keyserling, como Ortega ... ¡170 representaciones de "Bodas de sangre"! Juego y teoría del duende. Desde antes de pisar tierra hasta el instante de abandonar Buenos Aires el poeta ha sido el hombre de moda que ha hecho mas eficaz propaganda de España que todos los congresos y misiones oficiales', *Heraldo de Madrid*, 14 April 1934, p. 4

PÉREZ GALÁN, Mariano, *La enseñanza en la Segunda República Española*, Madrid, Cuadernos para el Diálogo, 2nd ed., 1977

PÉREZ DE HITA, Ginés, *Guerras civiles de Granada*, Madrid, Atlas, Biblioteca de Autores Españoles, 1975, vol. III, pp. 33–694

PITTALUGA, Gustavo, *La romería de los cornudos*, Madrid, Unión Musical Española, n.d.

PIZARRO, Miguel, *Versos*, Malaga, Meridiano, 1961

POMÈS, Mathilde, 'Une Visite à Federico García Lorca', *Le Journal des Poètes*, Brussels, no. 5 (May 1950), pp. 1–2

– 'Españoles en París (XIV). Federico García Lorca', *ABC*, Madrid, 22 November 1967

PRADOS, Emilio, *Diario íntimo*, Malaga, El Guadalhorce, 1966

PREDMORE, Richard L., *Lorca's New York Poetry. Social Injustice, Dark Love, Lost Faith*, Duke University Press, Durham, NC, 1980

PRESTON, Paul, *La destrucción de la democracia en España. Reacción, reforma y revolución en la Segunda República*, Madrid, Ediciones Turner, 1978

PRIETO, Gregorio, *Lorca en color*, Madrid, Editora Nacional, 1969

PRIETO, Indalecio, *Convulsiones de España*, 3 vols., Mexico, Ediciones Oasis, 1967–9

– *Discursos fundamentales*, introducción y edición de Edward Malefakis, Madrid, Ediciones Turner, 1975

PRITCHETT, V. S., *Midnight Oil*, Harmondsworth, Penguin, 1974

[QUEVEDO, Antonio], *El poeta en La Habana. Federico García Lorca. 1898–1936*, La Habana, Consejo Nacional de Cultura, Ministerio de Educación, Havana, 1961

RAMOS ESPEJO, Antonio, 'En Valderrubio, Granada. La casa de Bernarda Alba', *Triunfo*, Madrid, 6th series, no. 4 (February 1981), pp. 58–63

– 'García Lorca se inspiró en un suceso periodístico. Los protagonistas de "Bodas de sangre" viven en el Campo de Níjar', *Triunfo*, Madrid, 25 August 1979, pp. 52–5

REYERO HERMOSILLA, Carlos, *Gregorio Martínez Sierra y su Teatro de Arte*, Madrid, Fundación Juan March, 1980

RÍO, Angel del, 'La literatura de hoy. El poeta Federico García Lorca', *Revista Hispánica Moderna*, New York and Buenos Aires, I (1935), pp. 174–84

– 'Federico García Lorca (1899–1936)', *Revista Hispánica Moderna*, New York and Buenos Aires, VI (1940), pp. 193–260

– *Federico García Lorca (1899–1936). Vida y obra*, New York, Hispanic Institute in the United States, 1941

- 'Poet in New York: Twenty-Five Years After', introduction to FGL, Poet in New York, translated by Ben Belitt, New York, Grove Press, 1955, pp. ix–xxxix
- 'Poeta en Nueva York: pasados veinticinco años', Madrid, Taurus, 1958

RÍOS, Fernando de los, Escritos sobre democracia y socialismo, edited by Virgilio Zapatero, Madrid, Taurus, 1975
- El sentido humanista del socialismo, edited with introduction and notes by Elías Díaz, Madrid, Castalia, 1976

RIUS, Luis, León Felipe, poeta de barro, Mexico, Colección Málaga, 1974

RIVAS CHERIF, Cipriano, [C.R.C.], 'Federico García Lorca. Libro de poemas', La Pluma, Madrid, no. 15 (August 1921), pp. 126–7
- 'La ascensión de "La Argentinita" ', El Sol, Madrid, 26 November 1932, p. 8
- 'Poesía y drama del gran Federico. La muerte y la pasión de García Lorca', Excelsior, 'Diorama de la Cultura', Mexico, 6 January 1957, pp. 1 and 4; 13 January 1957, pp. 1 and 4; 27 January 1957, p. 3

ROA, Paul, 'Federico García Lorca, poeta y soldado de la libertad', Revista de las Indias, Bogotá, no. 5 (March 1937), pp. 42–5

RODRIGO, Antonina, Mariana de Pineda, Alfaguara, Madrid, 1965
- Margarita Xirgu y su teatro, Barcelona, Planeta, 1974
- García Lorca en Cataluña, Barcelona, Planeta, 1975
- 'La auténtica "Doña Rosita la soltera" ', El País, Madrid, 'Miscelánea', 17 August 1980, pp. 4–5
- Lorca–Dalí. Una amistad traicionada, Barcelona, Planeta, 1981
- 'La historia del tesoro' según Lorca', El País, Madrid, 20 March 1983, p. 38
- Memoria de Granada. Manuel Angeles Ortiz y Federico García Lorca, Barcelona, Plaza y Janés, 1984
- García Lorca, el amigo de Cataluña, Barcelona, Edhasa, 1984
- 'Lorca y su compromiso con la mujer', Ideal, Granada, 19 August 1986, p. 2

RODRÍGUEZ ESPINOSA, Antonio, 'Souvenirs d'un vieil ami', from the memoirs of Lorca's teacher, translated by Marie Laffranque and included in her book Federico García Lorca, Paris, Seghers, 1966, pp. 107–10

R[ODRÍGUEZ] RAPÚN, Rafael, 'El teatro universitario. La Barraca', in Almanaque literario, 1935, published by Guillermo de Torre, Miguel Pérez Ferrero and E. Salazar Chapela, Madrid, Editorial Plutarco, 1935, pp. 275–7

RODRÍGUEZ SPITERI, Alvaro, 'Un recuerdo a Federico', Insula, Madrid, no. 155 (October 1959), p. 11

ROIG DE LEUCHSENRING, Emilio ['El Curioso Parlanchín'], 'Federico García Lorca, poeta ipotrocasmo', Cartelas, Havana, XV, no. 17 (27 April 1930), pp. 30, 46–7

ROMERO, Luis, Todo Dalí en un rostro, Barcelona, Blume, 1975

ROQUE BARREIRO, Amelia, 'Lorca en Cienfuegos', Revolución y cultura, Havana, 1985

ROS, Samuel, 'Ecos de sociedad. Marcha nupcial', Heraldo de Madrid, 9 June 1932, p. 7

RUIZ ALONSO, Ramón, Corporativismo, prologue by Gil Robles, Salamanca, Ediciones Ruiz Alonso, 1937

RUIZ CARNERO, Constantino, and José MORA GUARNIDO, El libro de Granada. Primera parte. Los hombres, Granada, Paulino V. Traveset, 1915

RUIZ-CASTILLO BASALA, José, Memorias de un editor, Madrid, Ediciones de la Revista de Occidente, 1972

RUIZ SILVA, Carlos, 'La figura y la obra de Eduardo Blanco-Amor', prologue to Eduardo Blanco-Amor, La parranda, Madrid, Ediciones Júcar, 1985, pp. 9–36

SABOURÍN, Jesús, 'Federico García Lorca en Santiago de Cuba', Revista de la Universidad de Oriente, Santiago de Cuba, March 1962, pp. 1–10

SÁENZ DE LA CALZADA, Luis, 'La Barraca'. Teatro Universitario, Madrid, Revista de Occidente, 1976

SAHUQUILLO, Angel, Federico García Lorca y la cultura de la homosexualidad. Lorca, Dalí,

Cernuda, Gil-Albert, Prados y la voz silenciada del amor homosexual, University of Stockholm, 1986

SAINERO SÁNCHEZ, Ramón, *Lorca y Synge, ¿un mundo maldito?*, Madrid, Universidad Complutense, 1983

SAINZ RODRÍGUEZ, Pedro, *Testimonio y recuerdos*, Barcelona, Planeta, 1978

SALADO, José Luis, 'En el ensayo general de "Yerma", la comedia de García Lorca, se congregaron, entre otros ilustres rostros rasurados, las tres barbas más insignes de España: las de Unamuno, Benavente y Valle Inclán', *La Voz*, Madrid, 29 December 1934, p. 3

SALAZAR, Adolfo, 'Un poeta nuevo. Federico G. Lorca', *El Sol*, Madrid, 30 July 1921, p. 1

– [Ad. S.], 'Notas críticas. *Manhattan Transfer* y sus perspectivas', *El Sol*, Madrid, 21 June 1929, p. 2

– [Ad. S.], 'La vida musical. Un crítico norteamericano en Europa', *El Sol*, Madrid, 21 June 1929, p. 8

– 'Discos. La Voz de su Amo. – Un cancionero viviente', *El Sol*, Madrid, 13 March 1931, p. 2

– 'Discos. Una colección de canciones españolas antiguas', *El Sol*, Madrid, 27 November 1931, p. 2

– 'In memoriam. Federico García Lorca en La Habana', *Carteles*, Havana, 23 January 1938, pp. 30–1

– 'In memoriam. El mito de Caimito', *Carteles*, Havana, 20 February 1938, p. 24

– '*La casa de Bernarda Alba*', *Carteles*, Havana, 10 April 1938, p. 30

SALAZAR, María José, 'Aproximación a la vida y a la obra de María Blanchard', in *María Blanchard (1881–1932)*, catalogue published by the Ministry of Culture, Madrid, 1982, pp. 14–24

SALINAS, Pedro, 'Nueve o diez poetas' (1945), in *Ensayos completos*, edited by Solita Salinas de Marichal, Madrid, Taurus, 1983, vol. III, pp. 308–21

– 'El romancismo y el siglo XX' (1951), ibid., pp. 219–47

SALOBREÑA GARCÍA, José, *Pequeña historia de un pueblo: Fuente Vaqueros, 'cuna de García Lorca'*, Granada, Gráficas Monachil, [1977]

– *Tierra natal de Federico García Lorca*, Granada, Excma. Diputación Provincial, 1982

SÁNCHEZ MEJÍAS, Ignacio, *Teatro*, edited with prologue and bibliography by Antonio Gallego Morell, Madrid, Ediciones del Centro, 1976

SÁNCHEZ VIDAL, Agustín, introduction to Luis Buñuel, *Obra literaria*, Saragossa, Ediciones de Heraldo de Aragón, 1982, pp. 13–79

– *Buñuel, Lorca, Dalí: el enigma sin fin*, Barcelona, Planeta, 1988

SANTA CECILIA, Carlos G., 'La insoportable levedad de Federico', *El País*, Madrid, supplement 'Lorca. La memoria viva (1936–1986)', 19 August 1986, pp. x–xi

SANTAINÉS, Antonio, *Domingo Ortega. 80 años de vida y toros*, prólogo de Luis Calvo, Madrid, Espasa-Calpe, 1986

SANTIAGO, Magda, 'García Lorca', *Excelsior*, Mexico, 6 January 1957

SANTOS TORROELLA, Rafael, *La miel es más dulce que la sangre. Las épocas lorquiana y freudiana de Salvador Dalí*, Barcelona, Seix Barral, 1984

– (ed.), *Salvador Dalí escribe a Federico García Lorca [1925–1936]*, Poesía. Revista ilustrada de información poética, Madrid, Minsterio de Cultura, nos. 27–8, 1987

SARABIA, Nydia, 'Cuando García Lorca estuvo en Santiago', *Bohemia*, Havana, 10 September 1965, pp. 58–61

SCHINDLER, Kurt, *Folk Music and Poetry of Spain and Portugal. Música y poesía popular de España y Portugal*, prologue by Federico de Onís, New York, Hispanic Institute in the United States, 1941

SCHONBERG, Jean-Louis [pseud. Louis Stinglhamber-Schonberg], *Federico García Lorca. L'Homme–L'Oeuvre*, préface de Jean Cassou, Paris, Plon, 1956

SCHWARTZ, Kessel, 'García Lorca and Vermont', *Hispania*, Appleton, Wisconsin, xlii (1959), pp. 50–5

SECO DE LUCENA [Y ESCALADA], Luis, *Mis memorias de Granada (1857–1933)*, Granada, Imp. Luis F.-Piñar, 1941

SECO DE LUCENA [PARADAS], Luis, *Topónimos árabes [de Granada] identificados*, Universidad de Granada, 1974

SERNA, José S., 'Federico, en tres momentos', *Barcarola*, Albacete, August 1982, pp. 183–5

SERRANO MORENTE, E., 'Desde Nueva York. Impresiones de un granadino. Lo grande en Norte América. Los "secos" y los "húmedos". Los contrabandistas de licores. Los hombres de "negocios". El folletín de los millones', *El Defensor de Granada*, 16 March 1929, p. 1

SIERRA SERRANO, Francisco, 'Apuntes para una lección olvidada: Lorca y Valderrubio', *Ideal*, Granada, 'Arte y Letras', 8 September 1986, p. 31; 15 September 1986, p. 31

SILVERMAN, Joseph H., 'José F. Montesinos', in José F. Montesinos, *Ensayos y estudios de literatura española*, edición, prólogo y bibliografía de Joseph H. Silverman, Madrid, Revista de Occidente, 1970, pp. 21–4

SOLANA, Daniel, 'Federico García Lorca', *Alhambra*, New York, I, no. 3 (August 1929), p. 24

SOPEÑA, Federico, *Atlántida. Introducción a Manuel de Falla*, Madrid, Taurus, 1962

– introduction to Manuel de Falla, *Escritos*, Madrid, Espasa-Calpe ('Austral'), 3rd ed., 1972

SORIA OLMEDO, Andrés, 'El poeta don Isidoro Capdepón', *Cuadernos hispanoamericanos*, Madrid, no. 402 (December 1983), pp. 149–52

SOTO DE ROJAS, Pedro, *Paraíso cerrado para muchos, jardines abiertos para pocos. Los fragmentos de Adonis*, edited by Aurora Egido, Madrid, Cátedra, 1981

SOUTHWORTH, Herbert Routledge, 'The Falange: An Analysis of Spain's Fascist Heritage', in Paul Preston (ed.), *Spain in Crisis. The Evolution and Decline of the Franco Regime*, Hassocks, Sussex, The Harvester Press, p. 1–22

STEFANO, Onofre di, and Darlene LORENZ, 'Conversations with Three Emeritus Professors from UCLA: John A. Crow, John E. Englekirk, Donald F. Fogelquist', *Mester*, University of California, viii, no. 1 (1979), pp. 29–42

SUERO, Pablo, 'Crónica de un día de barco con el autor de *Bodas de sangre*', *Noticias Gráficas*, Buenos Aires, 14 October 1933; reprinted in Christopher Maurer, 'Buenos Aires, 1933. Dos entrevistas olvidadas con Federico García Lorca', *Trece de Nieve*, Madrid, 2nd series, no. 3 (May 1977), pp. 66–8. Suero included the article in his *Figuras contemporáneas* (1943). It is reprinted in OC, II, pp. 974–88.

– 'Hablando de "La Barraca" con el poeta García Lorca', Buenos Aires, *Noticias Gráficas*, 15 October 1933; reprinted in Christopher Maurer, 'Buenos Aires, 1933. Dos entrevistas olvidadas con Federico García Lorca', Madrid, *Trece de Nieve*, 2nd series, no. 3 (May 1977), pp. 69–73, and in OC, II, 974–88

– *Figuras contemporáneas*, Buenos Aires, Sociedad Impresora Americana, 1943

– 'Los jóvenes poetas están con la España Nueva' and 'Los últimos días con Federico García Lorca. El hogar del poeta', in *España levanta el puño*, Noticias Gráficas, Buenos Aires, 1936. Chapters reproduced by Eutimio Martín in 'Un testimonio olvidado sobre García Lorca en el libro *España levanta el el puño*, de Pablo Suero', *Trece de Nieve*, Madrid, 2nd series, no. 3 (May 1977), pp. 79–88

– 'Los últimos días con Federico García Lorca. El hogar del poeta'; see 'Los jóvenes poetas están con la España Nueva' above.

SYNGE, J. M., *The Playboy of the Western World and Riders to the Sea*, London, Unwin Paperbacks, 1985

THOMAS, Hugh, *The Spanish Civil War*, Harmondsworth, Penguin Books, 10th impression, 1986

THOMPSON, B. Bussell and J. K. WALSH, 'Un encuentro de Lorca y Hart Crane en Nueva York', *Insula*, Madrid, no. 479 (1986), pp. 1, 12

TINNELL, Roger D., *Federico García Lorca. Catálogo–discografía de las 'Canciones españolas antiguas' y de música basada en textos lorquianos*, University of New Hampshire/Plymouth State College, 1986

TORRE, Elena de la, 'Notas neoyorquinas. Un gran poeta', *La Prensa*, New York, 3 March 1930, p. 18

TORRE, Guillermo de, '*Libro de poemas*, por F. García Lorca', Madrid, *Cosmópolis*, no. 35 (November 1921), pp. 528–9

– *Helios. Poemas (1918–1922)*, Madrid, Editorial Mundo Latino, 1923

– *Literaturas europeas de vanguardia*, Madrid, Rafael Caro Raggio, 1925

– 'Las ediciones Héroe. Poesía en alud', *El Sol*, Madrid, 1 April 1936, p. 2

– 'Federico García Lorca', in *Tríptico del sacrificio. Unamuno, García Lorca, Machado*, Buenos Aires, Losada, 2nd ed., 1960

TREND, J. B., *A Picture of Modern Spain, Men and Music*, London, Constable and Company, 1921

– 'A Poet of "Arabia" ', *Nation and the Athenaeum*, London, 14 January 1922, pp. 594–5

– 'A Festival in the South of Spain, *Nation and the Athenaeum*, London, 8 July 1922, p. 516

UCELAY, Margarita, '*Amor de don Perlimplín con Belisa en su jardín*, de Federico García Lorca. Notas para la historia de una obra: textos, ediciones, fragmentos inéditos', in *Essays on Hispanic Literature in Honour of Edmund L. King* (ed. Molloy and Cifuentes), London, Támesis Books, 1983, pp. 233–9

UNAMUNO, Miguel de, 'Hablemos de teatro', *Ahora*, Madrid, 19 September 1934, p. 5

'UNO AL SESGO', (pseud.), *Los ases del toreo. Estudio crítico de los principales diestros de la actualidad* [on Ignacio Sánchez Mejías], Madrid, Alfa, n.d. [1922]

VALBUENA MORÁN, Celia, *García Lorca y 'La Barraca' en Santander*, Santander, 1974

VALENTE, José Angel, 'Pez luna', *Trece de nieve*, Madrid, 2nd series, nos. 1–2 (1976), pp. 191–201

[VARIOUS], *Homenaje a Alberto Jiménez Fraud en el centenario de su nacimiento (1883–1983)*, Madrid, Ministerio de Cultura y Fundación del Banco Exterior de España, 1983

VÁZQUEZ OCAÑA, Fernando, *García Lorca. Vida, cántico y muerte*, Mexico, Grijalbo, 2nd ed., 1962

V. S., 'Estudiantes de la F.U.E. se echarán a los caminos con "La Barraca". Un carromato como el de Lope de Rueda. Teatro clásico gratuito por las plazas de los pueblos', *El Sol*, Madrid, 2 December 1931, p. 1

VEGA DÍAZ, Francisco, 'Una anécdota del poeta en la calle', *El País*, Madrid, 5 June 1980, p. 34

VELA, Fernando, 'El suprarrealismo', *Revista de Occidente*, Madrid, vi (December 1924), pp. 428–34

VIDARTE, Juan-Simeón, *Las Cortes Constituyentes de 1931–1933. Testimonio del Primer Secretario del Congreso de los Diputados*, Barcelona–Buenos Aires–Mexico, Grijalbo, 1976

VIDELA, Gloria, *El ultraísmo. Estudios sobre movimientos poéticos de vanguardia en España*, Madrid, Gredos, 1963

VILA-SAN-JUAN, José Luis, *García Lorca, asesinado: toda la verdad*, Barcelona, Planeta, 1975

VILLAESPESA, Francisco, *El alcázar de las perlas*, Madrid, Biblioteca Renacimiento, 1912

VILLAREJO, Pedro, *García Lorca en Buenos Aires. Una resurrección anterior a la muerte*, Buenos Aires, Libros de Hispanoamérica, [1986]

VILLEGAS, R., 'La romería de Moclín, deslucida por la lluvia', *El Día*, Granada, 5 October 1986

WATSON, J. N. P., 'In Honour of Salamanca. The Duke of Wellington's Andalusian Estate – I', *Country Life*, London, 4 September 1980, pp. 779–81

– 'Some "Near Run Things". The Duke of Wellington's Andulusian Estate – II', *Country Life*, London, 12 September 1980

WHITMAN, Walt, *Poemas*, versión de Armando Vasseur, Valencia, F. Sempere y Ca. Editores, n.d. [1912]

WILSON, E. M., 'John Brande Trend. 1887–1958', *Bulletin of Hispanic Studies*, Liverpool, xxv (1958), pp. 223–7

XIMÉNEZ DE SANDOVAL, Felipe, *José Antonio (biografía apasionada)*, Barcelona, Editorial Juventud, 1941

ZALAMEA, Jorge, 'Federico García Lorca, hombre de adivinación y vaticinio', *Boletín cultural y bibliográfico*, Bogotá, no. 9 (1966), pp. 1507–13

ZAMBRANO, María, 'El viaje: infancia y muerte', in *Trece de Nieve*, Madrid, 2nd series, nos. 1–2 (December 1976), pp. 181–90

ZAPATERO, Virgilio, introduction to Fernando de los Ríos, *El sentido humanista del socialismo* (see above)

Index

539

Permission Acknowledgments

Grateful acknowledgment is made to Herederos de Federico García Lorca and Fundación Federico García Lorca for permission to include various photographs and drawings, the Spanish texts, and Ian Gibson's English translations of the Spanish texts of material by Federico García Lorca. All rights reserved. For information regarding rights and permissions, please contact William Peter Kosmas, Esq., 25 Howitt Road, London NW3 4LT, England.

Grateful acknowledgment is made to the following for permission to reprint previously published material:
Constable Publishers: excerpt from *A Picture of Modern Spain* by J. B. Trend, published by Constable Publishers. Reprinted by permission.
Duquesne University Press: excerpt from "August in Eden" by Philip Cummings, included in Federico García Lorca's *Songs*, translated by Philip Cummings with Federico García Lorca, edited by Daniel Eisenberg. Pittsburgh, Duquesne University Press, 1976.
Excerpt from *The Secret Life of Salvador Dali* by Salvador Dali. Copyright © 1957. Originally published by Dial Press.

About the Author

Born in Dublin in 1939, Ian Gibson attended Trinity College there. He lectured in Spanish at the Queen's University, Belfast, and then became Reader in Modern Spanish Literature at London University. The Spanish-language version of his first book, *The Assassination of Federico García Lorca* (1971), published in Paris, was awarded the Prix International de la Presse and was immediately banned by the Franco regime; it has been translated into ten languages. The English version, *The Death of Lorca* was published to superb reviews in 1973: Cyril Connolly remarked that "Lovers of poetry, lovers of truth, lovers of Spain should all read this exemplary piece of literary research." In 1975 Ian Gibson left academic life to write full-time, and has since produced a number of books in both English and Spanish. In 1978 he moved to Madrid, where he now lives.